BIRTH TO FIVE: EARLY CHILDHOOD SPECIAL EDUCATION

Second Edition

Frank G. Bowe, Ph.D.
Hofstra University

Africa · Australia · Canada · Denmark · Japan · Mexico · New Zealand · Philippines
Puerto Rico · Singapore · Spain · United Kingdom · United States

NOTICE TO THE READER

Delmar Staff:

Business Unit Director: Susan Simpfenderfer
Executive Editor: Marlene McHugh Pratt
Acquisitions Editor: Erin O'Connor Traylor
Editorial Assistant: Alexis Ferraro

Executive Marketing Manager: Donna Lewis
Executive Production Manager: Wendy Troeger
Project Editor: Sandra Woods
Cover Design: Timothy J. Conners

COPYRIGHT © 2000
by Delmar Publishers Inc.
Delmar is a division of Thomson Learning. The Thompson Learning logo is a registered trademark used herein under license.

Printed in the United States of America
2 3 4 5 6 7 8 9 10 XXX 05 04 03 02 01 00 99

For more information, contact:
Delmar, 3 Columbia Circle, Box 15015, Albany, New York 12212-0515;
or find us on the World Wide Web at *http://www.delmar.com* or *http://www.EarlyChildEd.delmar.com*

For more information, contact:

Delmar Publishers
3 Columbia Circle, Box 15015
Albany, New York 12212-5015

International Thomson Publishing
Berkshire House
168-173 High Holborn
London, WC1V 7AA
England

Thomas Nelson Australia
102 Dodds Street
South Melbourne 3205
Victoria, Australia

Nelson Canada
1120 Birchmont Road
Scarborough, Ontario
M1K 5G4, Canada

International Thomson Editores
Campos Eliseos 385, Piso 7
Col Polonco
11660 Mexico D F Mexico

International Thomson Publishing GmbH
Konigswinterer Str. 418
53227 Bonn
Germany

International Thomson Publishing Asia
60 Albert Street
#15-01 Albert Complex
Singapore 189969

International Thomson Publishing Japan
Kyowa Building, 3F
2-2-1 Hirakawa-cho
Chiyoda-ku, Tokyo 102
Japan

International Thomson Publishing France
Tour Maine-Montparnasse
33 Avenue du Maine
75755 Paris Cedex 15, France

ITE Spain/Paraninsfo
Calle Magallanes, 25
28015-Madrid, Espana

Library of Congress Cataloging-in-Publication Data

Bowe, Frank G.
    Birth to five : early childhood special education / Frank G. Bowe. 2nd ed.
        p.   cm.
    Includes bibliographical references and index.
    ISBN 0-7668-0236-1
    1. Handicapped children—Education (Early Childhood)—United States. I. Title.
LC4019.3.B69   2000
371.9'047—dc21
                                                        98-36544
                                        CIP

Contents

PART IV

Preface

Early intervention for infants and toddlers from birth through age two, and preschool special education for three- to five-year-old children with disabilities, developmental delays, or deviations in development, are rapidly growing, still evolving fields. Parents and professionals alike are learning a great deal as they work with these young children, not only about the children but also about families, child development, education, and service coordination.

Early childhood special education (ECSE) today is the coming together of early intervention and preschool special education, as programs integrate to provide a "seamless system of services" for young children with disabilities and developmental delays. This book is about that fast-growing field.

The second edition of *Birth to Five: Early Childhood Special Education* is intended to serve personnel in this field—early interventionists, special educators, related services personnel, and similar workers—as well as teachers and interventionists in training. As was the case with the 1995 first edition, widely recognized as a comprehensive text (e.g., Thurman, 1999), the intent is to offer a thorough book that will help early intervention and preschool special education to come together into one seamless field.

This is a young field. While much has been accomplished, especially since 1986 when the federal government first set full-service mandates for early intervention and preschool special education services, much remains to be done. First, ECSE needs to reach out to *serve more eligible infants, toddlers, and preschoolers with disabilities.* The latest evidence (McNeil, 1997; U.S. Department of Education, 1998) suggests that early intervention programs are serving most, but not all, potentially eligible infants and toddlers. Some 40 percent of birth-to-two-inclusive young children with disabilities or developmental delays apparently are not being served under the public Part C program. More preschoolers with disabilities receive services under the public Part B program (an estimated 86 percent of those eligible), but a sizable number remain unserved.

Second, ECSE needs to *reach infants and toddlers at younger ages.* According to the U.S. Department of Education, almost 50 percent of the infants or toddlers served are in their final year of eligibility for Part C services (that is, twenty-four to thirty-six months of age). Similarly, the department suggested that the age at referral for infants and toddlers was frequently above one year of age (1997, pp. II-6–II-7). Both facts indicate that early intervention services often go unused during the first year of life, even when children are born with disabilities. As we begin a new century, we must work to lower the ages at which young children first receive early intervention services.

The field of ECSE is struggling to translate its ideals into reality in other ways as well. Although there is much consensus about what early intervention and preschool special education programs should be doing (e.g., DEC Task Force, 1993), all available evidence indicates that few local programs put these recommendations into practice on a daily basis (Odom, McLean, Johnson, & LaMontagne, 1995). Also, the field needs to *document evidence of its effectiveness.* Scientific proof that early intervention and preschool special education services are effective does exist, but far more data suggest that we are as yet unable to show that these services make a difference, especially for young children with severe disabilities. We need to know which specific strategies work best with which particular kinds of young children.

FEATURES OF THE BOOK

While that level of specificity is not yet possible, *Birth to Five: Early Childhood Special Education* explains what we do know. The book opens with an introductory Part I, which outlines theories and milestones of child development, offers a bird's-eye view of the field as a whole, and summarizes findings from the major research studies. In Part II, the book turns to the landmark laws that authorize and fund early intervention and preschool special education programs and services. Part III looks at practices—what interventionists and special educators do when they work with young children who have disabilities or developmental delays. Then, in Part IV, *Birth to Five* discusses the major disabilities or delays we see in young children. Part V concludes the book with an examination of controversies and a listing of resources that students and professionals alike may find helpful.

The principal change from the first edition (1995) of this book is a reorganization of content. Material on expected ("normal") child development now appears in Chapter 1, together with theories of child development. Chapter 3, which summarizes research in early childhood special education, has been brought forward (it was Chapter 18 in the first edition) in response to requests from teacher-training professionals. Professors told me they assigned the research chapter for students early in the semester because it prepares teachers-in-training to read professional literature by giving them the knowledge and skills to review research reports critically and intelligently; the chapter also offered, the professors noted, a brief, readable overview of the state of the art in research in this field.

The second edition features a color insert that offers concrete examples of how early childhood special educators can foster child development in all five domains. In addition, material on curriculum and teaching strategies has been added to the Part III "practice" chapters to give readers a better understanding of how the ideals and goals of early intervention and preschool special education can be translated into practice on a day-to-day basis. Each chapter throughout the book now concludes with Questions for Reflection, again in response to professor requests to give students "scaffolding" they can use in reviewing the material.

Information on designing buildings, rooms, and outdoor facilities to make them accessible to young children with disabilities, a strength of the first edition, has been expanded, reflecting the emergence of specific guidelines in these areas from the U.S. Architectural and Transportation Barriers Compliance Board, a small, independent federal agency. The board recently published specifications for "children's elements" and "play facilities," including outdoor playgrounds.

In other ways, though, the second edition of *Birth to Five* continues the emphases of the first edition. Clear and unambiguous explanations of what federal laws and regulations require are emphasized. Research with ECSE professionals consistently has shown that the number-one need these people articulate is for "knowledge of regulations related to IEPs/IFSPs" and "familiarity with current federal and state legislation and regulations" (Johnson, Kilgo, Cook, Hammitte, Beauchamp, & Finn, 1992, p. 143). *Birth to Five* responds to these expressed needs by providing detailed information about the Individuals with Disabilities Education Act (IDEA), as amended in 1997, and other key laws.

The federal government's final regulations for the IDEA, as amended in 1997, appeared in the *Federal Register* on March 12, 1999 (U.S. Department of Education, 1999). In addition, final rules interpreting the IDEA's Part C Early Intervention Program for Infants and Toddlers with Disabilities were published on April 14, 1998, and final regulations for the Preschool Program for Children with Disabilities appeared on June 1, 1998, also in the *Federal Register.* While this book explains the law and rules, readers should also consult the official regulations in the *Federal Register,* which is available at most public libraries.

The first edition's discussion of cultural diversity also continues with this edition because cultural competence by early childhood professionals is, if anything, more urgent today than it was in 1995. All available information suggests that the number of under-six children with disabilities who come from ethnic and racial minority group backgrounds is growing, while at the same time the number of interventionists, teachers, and related services personnel who come from those minority group backgrounds remains low. The most practical solution to the problems this disparity causes is to help paraprofessionals and professionals to become more culturally competent, that is, skilled in appreciating and working with minority cultures.

Finally, technology—both "low tech" and "high tech"—has a great deal to offer young children with disabilities, teachers and interventionists, and family members. *Birth to Five* continues in the second edition to try to offer readable explanations of these technologies and to convey their remarkable promise. It is the nature of technology to change, sometimes in breathtaking ways, so of course the second edition updates the information provided in the 1995 edition.

CONVENTIONS

This book adopts "people-first" language in describing children, youth, and adults with disabilities. Since 1988, all federal laws protecting the rights of or authorizing services for Americans with disabilities have used this kind of wording. It features nouns that define the person—infants, toddlers, preschoolers, students, university professors—followed by the word *disability* or variations thereof, or the name of the disability itself. Thus, you will find throughout this book terms such as "individuals with disabilities," "children with epilepsy," and "people with communication limitations." In each instance, the first words—and the emphasis—focus on what is human about people with disabilities. Only then are limiting or disabling conditions mentioned or identified.

The word *handicap* is avoided where possible. Originating from "hand-in-cap"—a phrase that connotes begging for charity—it is seldom used today. The term is used in this book in two cases. First, material quoted from pre-1988 sources, much of which used the words *handicap* and *handicapped,* necessarily retains these terms. Second, the word *handicapping* is at times used to describe the effects of environmental and other conditions on the daily lives of individuals with disabilities. Following Bowe (1978), the term *handicap* refers to barriers (architectural, transportation, communication, and attitudinal) that at times obstruct the paths of people with disabilities. Thus, an individual who is deaf is "handicapped" when a classroom teacher screens a film or video that is not captioned; similarly, a child who is blind is "handicapped" when overhead projectors, blackboards, or other visual media are used without accompanying audio description.

Relatively few abbreviations are used. Besides "ECSE" and "EC," the acronyms "IFSP" and "IEP" are often used, as is "IDEA." These abbreviations stand for, in turn, individualized family service plan, individualized education program, and Individuals with Disabilities

Education Act. The first time a frequently used term appears in any given chapter, the full term is given, followed by the abbreviation in parentheses; thereafter, in that chapter, the abbreviation is used. The author hopes that this approach strikes a balance between the Scylla of irritating the reader by using too many abbreviations and the Charybdis of causing equal irritation by repeating lengthy phrases too often. The list of acronyms that follows may also help. Similarly, in an effort to avoid innumerable uses of the awkward phrases "he or she" and "him or her," this book adopts the convention of alternating "he/him" in even-numbered chapters with "she/her" in odd-numbered chapters.

ACKNOWLEDGMENTS

As she did with the first edition, Delmar Acquisitions Editor Erin O'Connor Traylor guided the development of the book. I appreciate her assistance. Ann Matera and the staff at Stratford Publishing in Albany, NY, did a wonderful job of copyediting. I also thank the reviewers who offered helpful comments during the preparation of the second edition:

Elaine Boski
Collin County Community College
Plano, TX

Craig Boswell, Ph.D.
University of Central Oklahoma
Edmond, OK

Cheryl Geisen
College of the Canyons
Santa Clarita, CA

Donna Raschke, Ph.D.
University of Northern Iowa
Cedar Falls, IA

Carol L. Russell, Ed.D.
Emporia State University
Emporia, KS

Eugene Scholten, Ph.D.
Grand Valley State University
Allendale, MI

Vicki D. Stayton, Ph.D.
Western Kentucky University
Bowling Green, KY

Terry L. Weaver, Ph.D.
Union University
Jackson, TN

Margie Zeskind
Miami Dade Community College
Miami, FL

I also thank my assistant Kathleen Pelligrini, at Hofstra, and my undergraduate student assistant, Joshua Liebman, for their help copyediting and otherwise reviewing the manuscript for accuracy and comprehensiveness.

ACRONYMS

Birth to Five: Early Childhood Special Education contains relatively few acronyms. The book spells out, in full, terms that are used in any given chapter, then introduces the acronym. That pattern repeats in the succeeding chapters. Despite this, some readers may benefit from having the acronyms collected and explained here. Readers may also consult the glossary at the book's end for definitions of the terms given here.

ADA	Americans with Disabilities Act
ADD	Attention Deficit Disorder
ADHD	Attention Deficit Hyperactivity Disorder
AIDS	Acquired Immune Deficiency Syndrome
ASL	American Sign Language
CDA	Child Development Associate
CDC	Centers for Disease Control and Prevention
CEC	Council for Exceptional Children
CMV	Cytomegalovirus Infection
CP	Cerebral Palsy
CPS	Current Population Survey
DAP	Developmentally Appropriate Practice
DEC	Division for Early Childhood
EC	Early Childhood
ECSE	Early Childhood Special Education
ED	Emotional Disturbance
EEPCD	Early Education Program for Children with Disabilities
FAE	Fetal Alcohol Effect
FAS	Fetal Alcohol Syndrome
HCEEP	Handicapped Children's Early Education Program
HHS	Health and Human Services, U.S. Department of
HIV	Human Immunodeficiency Virus
ICC	Interagency Coordinating Council
ICU	Intensive Care Unit
IDEA	Individuals with Disabilities Education Act
IEP	Individualized Education Program
IFSP	Individualized Family Service Plan
IHDP	Infant Health and Development Program
LBW	Low Birth Weight
LD	Learning Disabilities
LRE	Least Restrictive Environment
MD	Muscular Dystrophy
NAEYC	National Association for the Education of Young Children
NE	Natural Environment
NICU	Neonatal Intensive Care Unit
NLTS	National Longitudinal Transition Study
ROP	Retinopathy of Prematurity
SCI	Spinal Cord Injury
SES	Socioeconomic Status
SIPP	Survey of Income and Program Participation
SSI	Supplemental Security Income
TBI	Traumatic Brain Injury
VCS	Vulnerable Child Syndrome

For Phyllis, Doran, and Whitney

PART

I

Introduction

INTRODUCTION

Early childhood special education (ECSE) is a way of thinking, one that is outlined in the Individuals with Disabilities Education Act (IDEA), the nation's bedrock special education law. It is also a way of behaving, as is implied by the enabling federal legislation. One core concept behind these ways of thinking and behaving is described by the term "entitlement": Infants and toddlers are entitled to early intervention services if they satisfy state criteria. Similarly, three- to five-year-old children are entitled to free preschool services to meet their special needs if they satisfy federal and/or state eligibility standards. Another such concept is "family-focused": ECSE programs are to be planned by, and conducted with, parents, guardians, and other family members. A third is "coordinated": ECSE services are to be organized so as to be seamless, with no unnecessary gaps or duplications in service.

Such services are provided to children and families in a wide variety of settings. Many Head Start centers, for example, serve preschool-age children with disabilities. So do many day-care centers, nursery schools, university-affiliated child-care centers, and speech-and-hearing clinics. The University of Wisconsin, for example, sponsors an Ausubelian preschool classroom that applies the teachings of David Ausubel, Jean Piaget, and Jerome Bruner (Fowell & Lawton, 1992). Similarly, the University of North Carolina has a Frank Porter Graham Center serving young children with and without disabilities. The Westwood Learning Center in Woodstock, Illinois, serves children with disabilities as one component of a comprehensive, districtwide program for three- to five-year-old children (Heckman & Rike, 1994). Of course, programs specializing in services for young children with different kinds of disabilities or delays also exist in every state. The Lexington Center in New York City, for example, provides early intervention and preschool special education services to young children as an extension of its K–12 program for children who are deaf. The Variety Preschoolers Workshop, in Syosset, New York, is a self-contained facility for young children with disabilities, most of whom have emotional/behavior disorders.

Part I offers an overview of ECSE: what it is, who it serves, how it is governed by federal and state statutes, and what roles program workers (professionals, paraprofessionals, and volunteers) and parents play in service delivery.

One of the themes introduced in Part I—a theme that pervades *Birth to Five: Early Childhood Special Education*—is the dramatic potential of individuals with disabilities to lead rewarding, meaningful, and self-sufficient lives. Just fifty years ago, many people with disabilities were placed in institutions almost routinely, because professionals and parents alike assumed that they could not function in the community. Today, such routine institutionalization is almost unthinkable. Just forty years ago, many children and youth with disabilities were refused entry into local public schools; parents had to pay tens of thousands of dollars each year to send these children to private schools. Today, such discrimination by public schools is illegal—and free education through high school is guaranteed.

Just thirty years ago, cities and towns throughout the nation were filled with innumerable architectural, transportation, and communication barriers. Finding a curb that had a "curb-cut"—a leveled area across which a wheelchair could travel from street to curb—was almost impossible in many municipalities. Getting a bus that had a wheelchair lift was nearly as difficult. For someone who was deaf, making a simple telephone call to order a pizza or talk with a friend was out of the question. For someone who was blind, working as a newspaper reporter or a teacher was unfathomable, because making printed materials accessible to people who could not see was too expensive and too time-consuming to be practical. Today, tens of thousands of municipalities have installed curbcuts, ordered lift-equipped buses, and taken many other steps to remove architectural and transportation barriers. Individuals who are deaf routinely make and receive phone calls, to and from anyone, anywhere; and people who are blind quickly and easily convert information from print to voice, large print, or Braille.

These developments have opened up daily life for individuals with disabilities to an extent few could have predicted just a few years ago. In a nutshell, disability matters much less today than it did in the past. That is exciting. But it brings to the forefront another question: Does an individual with a disability have the education, the training, and the skills required for self-care, for employment, and for other aspects of daily life? Because artificial barriers increasingly are falling, the focus is shifting from what people with disabilities lack to what they have. Stated differently, never has it been more important for individuals with disabilities to have knowledge, skills, and experience in all aspects of daily life.

ECSE is where it all begins—where infants, toddlers, and preschoolers with disabilities take their first steps toward rewarding, independent, and self-supporting lives. By intervening quickly and effectively, ECSE workers and families can give young children with disabilities or developmental delays a firm foundation for life. Examples are children with fragile X syndrome (Freund, 1994) or fetal alcohol syndrome (FAS) (Olson, 1994). Early intervention is facilitated when practitioners can identify the disability very soon after birth. The new hearing tests for newborns (Clarkson, Vohr, Blackwell, & White, 1994; White & Behrens, 1993) are therefore very exciting. Impairment of hearing may now be identified even before an infant leaves the hospital for the first time. Similarly, children who are medically fragile, many of whom are technology-dependent, can now benefit from early, targeted assistance (Beck, Hammond-Cordero, & Poole, 1994; Baroni, Tuthill, Feenan, & Schroeder, 1994; Krajicek & Tompkins, 1993).

Part I lays the groundwork for *Birth to Five: Early Childhood Special Education*'s consideration of ECSE today. Chapter 1 traces the theoretical and philosophical foundations for the field and defines key terms. The theoretical bases for ECSE, notably the belief in developmental plasticity, the acceptance of direct instruction and of the teachings of applied behavior analysis, and the conception of the child as "a little scientist" (to adopt Piaget's term) are explored. The beliefs ECSE shares with the broader field of early childhood (EC) are outlined, after which divergences of opinion are discussed. These similarities and differences were thrown into sharp relief as first the National Association for the Education of Young Children (NAEYC), a major advocate for EC programs, and then the Division for Early Childhood (DEC) of the Council for Exceptional Children (CEC), a national advocate for ECSE programs, published guidelines with suggested practices. Chapter 2 explains why ECSE programs are publicly funded. This federal and state financing brings with it a number of specific requirements. Among them are rules about eligibility, personnel qualifications, service quality, and many other aspects of operating programs for young children. The planning documents used in ECSE—the individualized family service plan (IFSP) and the individualized education program (IEP)—are introduced in this chapter. Eligibility requirements are outlined, and national data on the children being served are offered.

Chapter 2 addresses cultural diversity issues with respect to the children served and also with regard to ECSE professionals, paraprofessionals, and volunteers. Because so many young children participating in early intervention and preschool special education programs come from families that are members of ethnic and/or racial minority groups, it is important that ECSE workers appreciate the unique characteristics of minority cultures and become knowledgeable about how to show sensitivity to members of these cultural groups. Though this chapter offers guidelines, the overriding principle is one of individualization: ECSE workers must remind themselves that each person and each family is unique. Not all, or even most, families that are members of a given minority group will hold the values or display the behavior that these guidelines offer. Their intent is to help ECSE workers look for possibilities and be sensitive to tendencies. Let the families and children themselves tell you which of these possibilities are actualities for them. The chapter concludes with a discussion of the different roles played by federal and state governments, as well as by local service providers and by families.

Chapter 3, which concludes Part I, reviews research in ECSE. First the chapter introduces the broad concept of research and defines key terms. It then raises and answers ten important questions about how the ECSE field is doing. This chapter should help students derive far more benefit from their reading of professional journals and research reports.

Theory, Development, and Philosophy

Early intervention by its nature is an intimate service that touches a family's life at a time of double vulnerability. (Healy, Keesee, & Smith, 1989, p. 3) It is this synergistic double jeopardy of increased exposure to and greater sequelae from health and environmental risks that predisposes children living in poverty to adverse developmental outcomes. (Kaplan-Sanoff, Parker, & Zuckerman, 1991, p. 68)

OVERVIEW

Early childhood special education (ECSE) works with very young children, those who are under the age of six. It is appropriate for *Birth to Five* to begin with the children being served, thus the chapter opens with an overview of development theory. What are the major psychological and learning theories that inform our understanding of child development? For some readers, this material will be review; for others, it is essential background information. In fact, students who come to *Birth to Five* without any prior training in psychology may do well to read up on the major theories described in this section.

The chapter then turns to consider domains of development in young children. How do maturation and learning occur in children during the birth-to-five period? ECSE describes their development in terms of five areas, known as domains of development: physical, cognitive, adaptive, communication, and social or emotional. Each domain is introduced and briefly described in this chapter.

From development, we move to the philosophy of ECSE as a field. That philosophy derives from our understanding of child development; that is, our philosophy is a statement of what we as educators should do given what we know about development in young children. What are the broad and underlying beliefs that characterize early childhood special educators as a group? This section introduces the philosophy of ECSE as it relates to the philosophy of the broader field of early childhood (EC) education. As we will see, those philosophies have much in common, but they do differ on some key points. In general, the ideals of EC education, as expressed in Bredekamp and Copple (1997), envision the teacher as a guide and facilitator who helps children learn for themselves, while ECSE, as described by the Division for Early Childhood (DEC) Task Force on Recommended Practices (DEC Task Force, 1993), sees the teacher in a much more active and directive role.

THEORETICAL BASES

Families are inherently vulnerable at the time of the birth of a child. When that child has or appears to have a disability, the family is often even more susceptible to being hurt or divided by the experience. These vulnerabilities may lead families of young children with disabilities to seek ECSE services. At other times, disability is not evident at birth but becomes apparent during a child's first few years of life. That is particularly the case with low-socioeconomic status (SES) families. Craig Ramey and his associates launched what they called "The Abecedarian Project" for exactly this reason: Such factors as low-SES, low parental education attainment levels, and single-parent households are associated, to unusual degrees, with at-risk status in young children, especially for mild to moderate mental retardation (Martin, Ramey, & Ramey, 1990). The Abecedarian Project offered early and intensive support for parents on infant stimulation, preacademic training, and other steps family members could take to accelerate cognitive development in young children. Absent such interventions, Kaplan-Sanoff et al. (1991) agreed, children in low-SES families are at considerable risk of delays in development. The **double jeopardy**[*] they referred to arises because the children tend not only to have more accidents and illnesses than do children in higher-

double jeopardy is a term used by some researchers to help explain risks children face due to *both* biological and environmental risk factors, acting together. Children from families of low socioeconomic status tend to have more illnesses and accidents, *and* to suffer more long-lasting consequences from these, than do children from families of high socioeconomic status.

[*]**Note**: Terms appearing in boldface are defined in page margins. The terms and their definitions also are listed in alphabetical order in the glossary at the end of this text.

SES families but also to suffer more than other children, and for longer periods of time, from those illnesses or accidents that do occur.

The philosophy and theory behind such efforts as the Abecedarian Project stress the importance of early, effective intervention. Project Head Start began in 1964 because of a similar driving philosophy: Preschool services would give young children, especially children from lower-SES homes, a "head start" toward success in kindergarten and first grade. Early intervention and preschool programming both were founded on beliefs about **developmental plasticity**: Young children, to an extent not found in adolescents and adults, can change course if provided with timely, directed assistance.

ECSE draws on a rich theoretical framework that undergirds early intervention and preschool services. Much of this theoretical work has been carried out in fields such as educational and developmental psychology (Kohlberg et al., 1987; Kohlberg & Mayer, 1972). Increasingly, however, the field is generating its own body of knowledge, its own theories, and its own philosophies. Three approaches are found in ECSE today: developmental, behavioral, and other, including work by Abraham Maslow and by Elizabeth Kubler-Ross.

Developmental Approaches

The American psychologist Arnold Gesell, working in the 1920s and 1930s, described children's behavior at different stages of development. He suggested that development, both physical and cognitive, progressed very rapidly through a series of stages, leveling off by about age six (Gesell, 1925). Nearly forty years later, the Swiss psychologist Jean Piaget described the **sensorimotor** and **preoperational stages** through which birth-to-thirty-six-month-olds typically pass. Sensorimotor-stage tasks include performing goal-directed actions and acquiring the idea of object permanence. Preoperational-stage tasks include pretend play and use of such symbols as words (Piaget, 1962). All these tasks are facilitated by intact senses, particularly vision and hearing.

Piaget's findings created a view of infants, toddlers, and preschool-age children as *active* agents. Young children, Piaget said, are little scientists, performing trial-and-error experiments on the world around them. Child-care workers can help them to develop skills for which they are developmentally ready. Piaget's work set the stage for EC approaches in which program staff guide and facilitate young children in child-initiated and child-directed activities (Bredekamp, 1987). These are aspects of a **developmentally appropriate** approach to EC services. Piaget did not believe that parents or professionals should attempt to teach young children abilities that are characteristic of later stages. Young children can, however, be guided in performing stage-appropriate activities (Piaget, 1962; Piaget & Inhelder, 1969).

The challenge in ECSE is to find ways to help children with special needs to do the work Piaget believed to be appropriate for their stages. How, for example, can child-care workers help toddlers who are deaf learn language despite their inability to hear what is said around them? Piaget's theoretical framework helps us to understand the task as being one of assisting children who are deaf to learn language as active participants in the task. That approach runs counter to traditional attempts to *teach* these children words and syntax, efforts that do not give the children as active a role to play. Psycholinguists have shown that language is best acquired when it is constructed anew, when children take in many thousands of discrete utterances and use them to generate rules (Chomsky, 1957, 1968).

Similar suggestions have been made by Jerome Bruner, who advanced the notion of **discovery learning**. Bruner, a cognitive psychologist, stated, for example: "We teach a subject . . . to get a student to think . . . for himself, to consider matters as an historian does, to take

developmental plasticity is the belief that young children in particular can develop rapidly, changing their behavior—and indeed their lives—if services are provided early in life.

sensorimotor stage is the Piagetian period in which young children perform goal-directed actions and acquire the idea of object permanence.

preoperational stage, for Piaget, is the stage in child development just before children acquire the ability to engage in symbolic mental actions. A preoperational child, for example, cannot grasp the concept of reversibility.

developmentally appropriate services are designed to be suitable for children at particular stages of development. Thus, very short individual activities are developmentally appropriate for infants and toddlers, while lengthy large-group activities are not.

discovery learning (Jerome Bruner) is an approach in which children learn things themselves as teachers structure the environment to facilitate children's discovery.

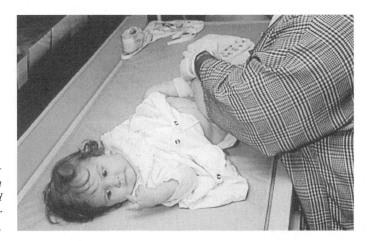

Very young children characteristically show fascination with their own bodies and enjoy watching their fingers move.

part in the process of knowledge-getting. Knowing is a process, not a product" (Bruner, 1966, p. 72).

The late Harvard professor Eric Erikson added a psychosocial perspective to our understanding of early childhood. Erikson proposed that each of us must pass through, and successfully resolve, "developmental crises" throughout life. Infants and toddlers, he suggested, must master the **trust versus mistrust** crisis, in which infants learn to trust their caregivers, particularly parents. Toddlers then confront the **autonomy versus shame and doubt** stage, during which they learn to assume some responsibilities for themselves, including self-feeding and toileting. They also gain confidence by exploring their environments, without being dissuaded by parental limits or punishment. Erikson insisted that infants and toddlers who do not successfully resolve these crises are harmed for life, or at least until later resolution. The next stage, Erikson said, is that of **initiative versus guilt**. At this level, children learn to have confidence in their own explorations and inventions, that is, in taking the initiative. If they are thwarted at this stage, Erikson believed, they may become hesitant and lacking in self-confidence. Their curiosity and desire to strike out on their own may be suppressed and even replaced by a sense of guilt about "going too far" or "stepping outside the boundaries of approved behavior."

Those insights are particularly helpful for EC specialists and for parents, because they warn against parental overprotection, which is a major concern of EC educators. Erikson taught us the importance of allowing young children to pass unhindered through these developmental stages and to resolve for themselves the crises they present. With respect to the "autonomy versus shame and doubt" stage, this approach means permitting children to explore their environments, to learn to trust themselves, and to take pride in their accomplishments. Erikson's insights are particularly valuable in warning parents and professionals about the dangers of **experiential deprivation**. When young children are not allowed to confront strange, even dangerous, situations—as when parents protect them unnecessarily—the children do not resolve Erikson's autonomy stage successfully. They enter school still unsure of themselves, having internalized parental fears (Erikson, 1963).

Urie Bronfenbrenner (1979, 1989) and Lev Vygotsky (1978) encouraged us to look at *context*. According to Bronfenbrenner, the child develops within the context of the family while the family, in turn, evolves within the context of the community. He called this "ecology." Thus, in assessing the child's development, Bronfenbrenner urges us to examine the familial and community contexts as well as the child herself (e.g., contextual or ecological

trust versus mistrust is the Eriksonian stage in which infants learn to trust their caregivers, particularly parents.

autonomy versus shame and doubt is the Eriksonian stage in which toddlers learn to assume self-responsibility, including feeding and toileting activities.

initiative versus guilt is the Eriksonian stage in which preschool-age children struggle between exploring for its own sake and feeling guilty for doing so.

experiential deprivation occurs when young children are not allowed to confront strange, even dangerous, situations—as when parents overprotect them. According to Erikson, overprotected children may enter school still unsure of themselves, having internalized parental fears.

assessment). Similarly, in deciding how to enhance a child's development, Bronfenbrenner would have us use familial and community resources.

Vygotsky also focuses attention on the social context. His sociohistorical theory urges us to develop strong support networks around the child and around the family. Vygotsky's main claim to fame, however, is his concept of the **zone of proximal development**. Oversimplified, this idea tells us that a child is ready, at any given moment, to learn some things but not others. Vygotsky urges us to identify exactly what the child is about ready to learn and to teach it at that time. One good clue: If the child can do something in the presence of (and with a little help from) a teacher, but is not able to do the same task independently, that task probably is within Vygotsky's zone. Tasks that are more challenging cognitively should not be introduced until the child has developed further. The teacher's support at the "zone" serves much the same purposes as it does in Bruner's theory of discovery learning—it provides "scaffolding," which structures the child's explorations.

Other work that is helpful in ECSE was carried out by Lawrence Kohlberg, who was a psychology professor at Harvard University. Kohlberg believed that children progress through stages of moral development. According to his theory, children begin with a "law of the jungle" mentality in which the operative questions are, "Will I be punished or rewarded for doing this?" and "Can I manipulate my parents (caregiver) and get away with this?" He saw these as low-level stages of moral reasoning. Only later in childhood and in adolescence do people begin to recognize that rules are created by people for reasons, and that a mature human being makes her own decisions, based on personal value systems—then faces the consequences (Kohlberg, 1984).

Kohlberg's work has attracted surprisingly little attention in disability-related fields of study. Gliedman and Roth, writing in *The Unexpected Minority* (1980), offered a brief but trenchant analysis of how Kohlberg's theory applies to children with disabilities, criticizing his theory of stages because they saw it as applying only where children are confident that their worlds make sense. For many children with disabilities, particularly those with cognitive or sensory impairments, the world around them may not in fact be one inspiring a sense of justice and morality. Gliedman and Roth added that many caregivers may not permit young children with disabilities to make their own moral decisions and to act upon those, thus interfering with the process through which Kohlberg believed children must progress to reach the higher levels of moral reasoning.

Behavioral Approaches

A very different stream of work in psychology gave us the principles of applied behavior analysis. B. F. Skinner's approach of **operant conditioning** related behavior to its consequences, specifically to reinforcements. As people "operate" on the environment, things happen. Actions that are followed by pleasant events tend to be repeated; Skinner called this process **positive reinforcement**. Actions that remove us from unpleasant circumstances likewise tend to be repeated; Skinner called this process **negative reinforcement**. Skinner and the legions of behaviorists who followed him demonstrated that consequences shape behavior. **Applied behavior analysis** works as long as the consequences immediately and consistently follow behavior. In contrast, by removing reinforcement altogether, it is possible to eliminate some behaviors. **Extinction** can help parents and professionals remove undesirable habits and behavior patterns in young children. **Punishment**, to Skinner, makes behaviors less likely; they may, however, reappear in other contexts (displacement), for which reason Skinner preferred reinforcement to punishment.

---

zone of proximal development (Lev Vygotsky) is the edge to which children's development has brought them, that is, what they can learn, if helped. Teachers should not attempt to introduce more cognitively challenging material, however, until children progress to higher levels of development.

operant conditioning is a process through which behavior is altered by manipulating its consequences.

positive reinforcement is the presentation of a consequence that increases the frequency of the behavior it follows. Also called "presentation reinforcement," it contrasts with negative reinforcement, in which a consequence is removed.

negative reinforcement increases the frequency of the behavior it follows by removing an undesired consequence. Also called "removal reinforcement." An example is when children are released from doing daily assigned household chores when they behave appropriately during dinner.

applied behavior analysis (behavior modification) uses control of consequences to influence behavior.

extinction occurs when reinforcement is removed altogether so that behavior decreases and then ceases.

punishment is any consequence that decreases the frequency of the behavior it follows. One possible outcome, however, is displacement, in which some other behavior increases in frequency.

One of the most important ideas Skinner gave us is that of shaping. Skinner was able to teach pigeons to play a toy piano by first reinforcing any movement by the pigeon toward the piano, then only those further movements bringing the pigeon even closer to the piano, and finally only direct pecks on piano keys. Also called the method of *successive approximations,* shaping is a key tool parents and early intervention specialists can use to help an infant or toddler learn new behaviors. This method is useful because young children with disabilities or developmental delays frequently are not able to do things just right the first time. Shaping is particularly useful in physical and occupational therapy, speech and language pathology, and other interventions requiring young children to develop new habits. Through successive approximations, parents and professionals can produce increasingly acceptable behavior (Skinner, 1953). A great deal of experimental evidence demonstrates that applied behavior analysis helps children with disabilities (Wolery, Bailey, & Sugai, 1988), but its methods nonetheless remain controversial.

Other Approaches

The psychologist Abraham Maslow, in his influential *Motivation and Personality* (1954), posited five levels of needs. The lowest two are for survival (shelter, food, sleep) and safety (physical and psychological). Until those needs are met, Maslow said, they dominate a person's interactions with the environment. Once they have been met, however, they are satiated, and no longer drive behavior. Middle-level needs are for love and esteem, neither of which is ever completely satisfied. The highest-level needs, according to Maslow, are what he called self-actualization needs. These needs are, to quote a U.S. Army slogan, to "be all you can be"—to fulfill your potential. Maslow believed that self-actualization needs could never be satisfied; the more they were fulfilled, the more an individual intensified the search for more ways to "self-actualize."

Maslow's work helps us to understand both young children with disabilities and their families. For the families in particular, the birth of a child with a disability, especially a severe one, threatens safety and survival; the parents are driven to find safe havens, in the form of competent and caring professionals who can cure, or at least ameliorate, the child's condition. Some parents persist in what an objective observer might regard as an unrealistic and unremitting pursuit of a cure, putting aside virtually everything else, including their own needs and the needs of other family members. Maslow's work helps us to understand why these parents act as they do.

Elizabeth Kubler-Ross, in her powerful book *On Death and Dying* (1969), suggested that families will cope with death (and, by extension, with the disability of a family member) first by denying the reality. Any early intervention or preschool special education program staff member who has worked with parents of newly diagnosed children knows that denial is a powerful impulse in these parents. Later, anger emerges, as they eventually face the reality. Parents may move to Kubler-Ross's third stage, that of bargaining with God: "If you cure my child, I promise to. . . ." Depression and, ultimately, acceptance complete the process. Children with disabilities may themselves move through these five stages. However, experience suggests that children who are born with disabilities or who become disabled very early in life have no sense of a prior (nondisabled) self and therefore may not experience the kind of loss that is a premise of Kubler-Ross's theory. Rather, as Gliedman and Roth (1980) demonstrated, what anger these individuals feel tends to come from their perception (usually quite accurate) that the world into which they were born is not one they experience as being fair and just.

Abraham Maslow's theory of development helps us to understand how critical survival and safety needs are in enabling children to feel free to satisfy higher-level needs.

DEVELOPMENT

Development in young children is remarkable for its *diversity*. Although charts showing average developmental milestones are readily available, both in professional and lay literature, the cautioning of experts that divergence from these averages is normal and to be expected is often overlooked. That is why the major issue in early childhood development is not so much the age at which a child does something but rather the *sequence* the child follows. Gross motor skills are usually displayed before fine motor skills appear. Babbling most often precedes articulate speech. Children generally sit before they stand. It is these patterns, or sequences, that signal "normal" development. Some young children proceed through one developmental phase faster than others do. By the time they enter kindergarten or first grade, however, most children have caught up with their peers in all major areas of development.

The age at which a young child first speaks, for example, is widely reported to be one year of age. But some children speak as early as eight months, some as late as eighteen months. Some children walk as early as seven months, some as late as two years. There is a range of normal ages at which children reach developmental milestones. Walking, to continue with this example, usually occurs between eleven and fifteen months of age; anything within that range is normal. In fact, first walking at twenty months is within a normal range, although somewhat late. A child who first walks at two years, however, is delayed.

The concept that the sequence matters more than the actual time periods is central in the field of child development. When young children proceed as expected from one level to another, even if some of those stages occur later than anticipated, development will appear to be normal. The sequence is so critical that experts allow considerable leeway for achievement of milestones in development. To illustrate with a common measure, children's weight by thirty-six months is typically reported to average thirty pounds. However, weights as high as thirty-five pounds and as low as twenty-eight pounds are still within a normal range. More important for a child's physical development is that a rapid weight increase during the first twelve months be followed by a somewhat slower, but also steadier, increase during the next two years. That sequence—very rapid growth followed by slower but smoother growth—matters much more than the specific weight attained at any given age.

Developmental delays and disabilities are most likely to occur when a child is exposed to *multiple risk factors.* Risk factors may be *biological, environmental,* or both. Biological risks include exposure to illegal drugs such as cocaine in utero. One effect of maternal use of cocaine during pregnancy is oxygen deprivation, as the supply of oxygen passing through the placenta is limited by vasoconstriction (Schneider & Chasnoff, 1987; Williams & Howard, 1993). The evidence at present seems to show that unless further problems emerge, many fetuses and infants can survive such oxygen debts with little or no developmental consequences. However, if environmental factors are added—as when a cocaine-abusing mother neglects her infant—delays may result. The point is that delays are often due not to one, or even two, risk factors but rather to multiple pre-, peri-, and postnatal stress factors *and* low family stability, often indicated by poverty and peripatetic lifestyles.

Development proceeds in spurts. Children may begin speaking, for example, and then seem to plateau at one- or two-word utterances while they master motor development—walking and balancing while walking, in particular—after which speech and language development seem to accelerate again. Other children do not show this pattern. Such alternations in development are yet another reason ECSE workers and parents alike should exercise caution when assessing whether apparent delays in development are serious enough to warrant extensive intervention.

Five Domains of Development

domains are areas of development. Part C of the Individuals with Disabilities Education Act recognizes five such domains: adaptive, cognitive, communication, physical, and social or emotional.

The Individuals with Disabilities Education Act (IDEA) recognizes five developmental **domains**: adaptive, cognitive, communication, physical, and social or emotional (Figure 1.1). Although this book considers each developmental domain in turn, it should be understood from the outset that such segmentation of development is artificial. Development in any one domain is affected by development in other domains. To illustrate, consider that the reported average age for a child's ability to stand alone is thirteen months, compared to twelve months for the first word. Many parents begin to worry if the child does not walk or speak "on time." However, the two domains interact in predictable ways. Young children typically reach the one-word milestone on time and then seem to plateau for about a year. That second year of life appears to be devoted to mastering physical mobility. The need to move is characteristic of the toddler period. This imperative sweeps all before it: The child *must* move. Not until walking, balancing while standing, and related physical activities are mastered does the child return to discernible progress in verbal communication. At two years of age, the toddler says two or three words in sequence. Some children begin walking earlier than thirteen months, and they may delay speaking first words until after they master physical mobility; others may begin speaking earlier and walking later. Such divergences in development are very normal.

The domains are interrelated in other ways as well. To continue with the example of mobility and communication, a child typically will begin using the pronoun "I" only after achieving independence in physical mobility. That is, the toddler's ability to move away from the caregiver appears to promote the cognitive development task of establishing a separate identity. The whole concept that the toddler is a different person from the primary caregiver is one that develops from experience. And that experience is frequently physical in nature. A young child with a severe physical disability who does not move about independently by the expected ages may also be delayed in use of the word "I"—and all that that implies. Such interconnections are natural given the relationships between physical and communication development.

Cognitive development refers to the growing capability of the infant, toddler, or preschooler to perform intellectual tasks. Piaget demonstrated that the child's mind is able at a certain point to do things not previously possible: To illustrate this, he hid an object and distracted the child's attention. At a very young age, the child promptly forgot the hidden object; at a later age, the child refused to allow Piaget to distract her and persistently sought out the hidden object. Similarly, children become able to understand that they are distinct human beings, with their own experiences, only after long periods of time in which they believe that what their mothers or other caregivers see, hear, and feel is identical to what they themselves see, hear, and feel.

Social or emotional development has to do with affective growth. Erikson was concerned with the infant's attachment to the caregiver, and the development as a result of that relationship of a sense of trust enabling the young child to venture out into the immediate environment to explore and learn. The preschool-age child, he believed, confronts societal rules and expectations during such explorations, and from those confrontations learns to balance personal desires against social constraints. **Adaptive development**, a related concept, looks more toward self-help capabilities. As young children grow, expectations rise that they will take care of themselves, with ever-dwindling needs for adult supervision. However, to the extent that exploration and other kinds of play are limited by worried adults, young children with disabilities may not acquire the self-reliance that developmental theories assume will emerge.

Physical development affects both social or emotional and adaptive development, as progress in these areas may depend on a child's physical ability to do such things as play, eat, dress, use the bathroom, and so on, independently. *Gross* motor development (large-scale muscle use) typically occurs prior to *fine* motor development (more precise muscle use, as in manipulation of small objects). **Communication development** is much more than simply speaking and listening. Children communicate needs, emotions, and other things nonverbally as well as verbally. According to the U.S. House of Representatives Committee on Education and Labor, communication development is a multifaceted process:

> [T]he term communication development is intended to include language, speech, and hearing. Communication development includes acquisition of communication skills, during preverbal and verbal phases of development, receptive and expressive language, including spoken, non-spoken, and sign language means of expression, the use of augmentative communication devices, and speech production and perception. Communication development also includes oral-motor development, specifically those neuromuscular and structural conditions affecting pre-speech oral-motor development, speech sound production, and feeding and swallowing processes. Related to hearing, communication development includes development of auditory awareness, auditory, visual, tactile and kinesthetic skills, and auditory processing for speech or language development. (House Report 102-198, 1991, p. 12)

cognitive development refers to age-appropriate mental functions, especially in perceiving, understanding, and knowing, that is, becoming capable of doing intellectual tasks.

social or emotional development (sometimes called psychosocial or affective development) refers to young children's age-appropriate ability to understand their own feelings, and those of others, and to respond to both with behavior that is socially acceptable for children of that age. It also includes behavior children exhibit in play.

adaptive development (sometimes referred to as "self-help" development) refers to a child's ability to display age-appropriate self-care and other behaviors in such a way as to adapt meaningfully to different circumstances.

physical development (sometimes called motor or coordination development) is the display of age-appropriate fine motor control and gross motor control abilities.

communication development (sometimes referred to as speech and language development) refers to a young child's ability to express thoughts and feelings and to understand vocal, nonverbal, signed, or other communication by others.

Although the five developmental domains are important, ECSE workers must not lose sight of the need to attend, first and foremost, to the whole child. Children have developmental needs in *all five* areas, not just those in which they have disabilities or delays. In addition, most young children with disabilities will have unique needs or express delays in more than one developmental domain. Take, for example, a preschooler with cerebral palsy. Are the primary needs in the domain of physical development (in which case physical and occupational therapy, braces and other mobility aids, and so on, are indicated); or is the major issue the child's difficulty in expressive communication (in which case augmentative communication technologies and speech pathology might be more helpful)? Similarly, are the needs of a child who has autism best understood in terms of her social or emotional development or her physical development? Frith (1993) proposed that autism is probably caused by a physical (organic) problem in the brain that has yet to be identified. Autism does not respond to psychological intervention services in the same ways as for example, emotional disturbance does. Are the needs of the children best approached as intellectual, communication-related, social and emotional, or adaptive? Experts have yet to agree.

Development: Birth to Five

In this section, development is traced in each of the five domains. The emphasis here is on expected ("normal") development. Much more information on developmental delays and deviations is offered in Part IV.

Adaptive Development

Infants first establish a rhythm with the primary caregiver, usually the mother. They respond differently to a responsive, low-activity-oriented parent than to a task-oriented, high-activity-level parent, for example (Allen & Marotz, 1989). As a parent who likes physical play approaches, the child visibly readies herself for physical activity; at the approach of a parent who likes to discern the infant's mood and respond accordingly, however, the child relaxes physically and smiles. These are early illustrations of adaptive behavior—the infant is adapting to different situations.

Adaptive—development of age-appropriate self-care and other behaviors so as to adapt successfully to different circumstances

Cognitive—development of age-appropriate mental functions, especially those of perceiving, understanding, and knowing

Communication—development of abilities to express thoughts and feelings and to understand others' vocal, nonverbal, signed, gestural, and written expressions

Physical—development of age-appropriate abilities by controlling and coordinating gross motor and fine motor movements

Social or emotional—development of age- and situation-appropriate abilities to understand one's own feelings and those of others, and to respond to both with behavior that is socially acceptable

---

FIGURE 1.1 The five developmental domains

Self-Help Behaviors. While infants can do few things for themselves, toddlers can do much independently—and indeed often insist on doing so. During the second year of life (twelve to twenty-four months), toddlers indicate the need to use restroom facilities, demonstrate an ability to feed themselves with their fingers and to hold a cup for drinking, and remove clothing that has been unfastened. By the end of the third year, many young children can use bathrooms with little or no assistance, can feed themselves, and can both put on and take off many items of clothing. They can also put things away and assist others in cleaning a room.

Young children with disabilities or developmental delays increasingly are learning self-help skills at day-care, nursery, or other ECSE programs, in addition to or rather than at home. This experience contrasts with that of many nondisabled young children. ECSE personnel teach self-help skills for several reasons. First, parents may tend to neglect these behaviors, excusing the child on the grounds that the child does, after all, have a disability. Second, parents may be unsure how to teach children with special needs, in particular how hard to push for developmentally appropriate achievements. Third, other developmental needs, including learning how to use adaptive equipment and how to cope with their limitations, often mean that many hours each week may be spent with ECSE personnel; being young children, they will have self-help needs during these times and will need assistance from ECSE personnel in meeting those needs.

Social Behaviors. Children with disabilities learn to enter, gain status in, and remain members of groups in day-care, nursery, and other EC and ECSE programs. The strategies these children use vary by age and situation. Children who are able to gain entry into pre-existing groups rely not only on their personalities but also on their ability to read the group, its members, and its dynamics. These skills are rarely taught. Rather, children seem to learn them through trial and error. Children who are successful in entering infant and toddler, preschool, and kindergarten groups are those able to match their behavior to that of other group members (Ross, 1985). That is, they first observe what group members are doing. They display cooperative behaviors, seeking not to dictate or control activity but rather to join ongoing activities. Often, they bring to the group an interesting object and offer to share it. Success in using the object as an entry strategy appears to depend in part on the child's knowledge of the object and how it might be used (Kantor, Elgas, & Fernie, 1993).

Status in early childhood groups appears to depend in large part on the social history of a child within a particular group. While physical factors (height, weight, facial attractiveness) and personality variables (outgoing versus withdrawn, adaptable versus rigid, accommodating versus aggressive) are important, social history (the group members' collective experiences with a child and the patterns of interaction group members have used with that child) matter as well (Kantor et al., 1993).

Maintaining membership in a group requires the ability to keep one's behavior, both physical and verbal, in tune with that of other group members. One study conducted in the mid-1970s suggested that children who introduce and elaborate upon play themes (things to do), who take roles in play activities already in progress, and who consistently display situation-appropriate verbal and nonverbal behaviors will be most successful (McDermott & Church, 1976). By contrast, "rejects" or "loners" appear to offer poorly timed comments or actions and to depend exclusively upon a limited number of strategies, even when those approaches are not accepted by a group (Corsaro, 1985; Ross, 1985). Young children need to master pragmatics, the socially appropriate use of language. There are things one says while engaged in free play, other things that are said in story time or other more supervised activities. There are things one says to other children but not to teachers or other ECSE personnel. Failure to master pragmatics may, by itself, limit a child's success in integrating with nondisabled children.

Although inappropriate behaviors—insisting on a new activity before the group completes the current one, saying things that are out of place, being physically aggressive—may lead to rejection or even make a child a social outcast, it is important for ECSE workers to remember that children *can* change their behaviors and gain or regain acceptance from peers. One doctoral dissertation focused on how a child who was rejected one year was able to gain acceptance the following year with a different group after learning more appropriate play behaviors (Massoulos, 1988).

Cognitive Development

The infant's brain appears to develop in phases (Volpe, 1987). Neurologic imaging techniques, particularly magnetic resonance imaging (MRI) and computed tomography (CT), are helping us to understand how that happens. The first phase, that of tissue differentiation and neural tube closure, occurs within the first few weeks of gestation. The second phase, which lasts from the fourth week to the middle of the third month of gestation, leads to formation of the face and head. Overlapping that phase, and continuing until the fourth month of gestation, the third phase features neuronal migration to nearby brain areas. The fourth phase of mental development is characterized by neuronal migration to the farther reaches of the brain. Nickel (1992) called the third and fourth phases "organization" and "myelination," and reported that both continue after birth; indeed, myelination lasts well into adulthood.

Infant cognitive development is heavily influenced by the environment. A debate has raged for years on the relative contributions to cognitive development of nature (heredity) versus nurture (environment). In fact, both appear to be essential. A stimulating play area with aural, visual, and tactile sensations is important. Just as critical is parental permissiveness, the need for primary caregivers to grant the infant unrestricted opportunities to explore. The infant further prods her own cognitive growth by completing the developmental imperative to walk. By freeing the hands, walking accelerates exploration of the environment—and with it, cognitive development.

A critical aspect of cognitive development, especially during the first two years of life, is the creation in the brain of structures or connections to handle language. During those years, neural connections, or synapses, are formed that prime the brain to learn the native language. After the age of two, synapses specialized in language that have not been tapped to perform those functions begin to be suppressed or even eliminated in the brain, a process that continues into adolescence. The key is for language as such—*any* language—to be laid down during the first two years. Thereafter, the brain's ability to acquire a first language gradually dissipates. By age fifteen it disappears altogether. In 1973, the scientist Jacob Bronowski wrote in *The Ascent of Man* that he could speak English not so much because he learned Polish as a child as because he learned *language* at that time. The fact that language is best learned in early childhood has long been known. What is new is the understanding of how the brain does its work. The most recent theories suggest that language makes liberal use of many sections of the brain, with names of objects stored in one location and their attributes in others. While speech is centered in Broca's area in most people, and language usually in Wernicke's, that is not always the case. Language is so central to brain function that the brain finds room for it virtually anywhere.

Drs. Antonio and Hannah Damasio (1989) of the University of Iowa have developed a well-received theory of cognition and language that helps to explain the role language plays in cognition. Antonio Damasio illustrated the theory:

> *When I ask you to think about a styrofoam cup you do not go into a filing cabinet in your brain, and come up with a ready-made picture of a cup. Instead, you compose an internal image of a cup drawn from its features. The cup is part of a cone, white, crushable, three inches high, and can be manipulated. In reactivating the concept of this cup, you draw on distant clusters of neurons that separately store knowledge of cones, the color white, crushable objects and manipulated objects.* (quoted in Blakeslee, 1991a, p. C10)

Ojemann (1983) concurred that the brain is organized for language acquisition and language use. This neuropsychological view of cognition is one in which the brain is active in generating syntheses or knowledge from information, and in which language serves as an organizing mechanism that assists in this creative process. Cognition, then, is not so much a function of factual memory as it is of creation. The theory, advanced most forcefully by the Damasios, has consequences familiar to us all. Among many other things, it helps to explain why eyewitnesses at crime scenes will report such different versions of what happened, and why people remember childhood experiences in ways that differ sharply from how others recall these same events. People do not store events or complex images as such; rather, they re-create them mentally.

Cognition is, of course, far broader than language use. The primary work of young children in the cognitive domain is to learn about themselves, their environments, and the basic laws of nature (gravity, cause and effect, and so on) that are essential to safety. They must also master preacademics, including readiness to read and basic computational skills. Children must also learn adaptive behavior as they enter into and become skilled at responding to new and different situations. For children with disabilities, delays, or deviations in development in *any* domain, cognitive development is urgently important.

To learn, children must first *attend* to information (Figure 1.2). In the early childhood years, much of that input is auditory and visual. Especially during play, children learn a great deal about the size, texture, and other properties of objects. When guided by a caregiver, they will acquire words to describe what they are learning. When a building block falls off a tower, for example, the caregiver could introduce the word "gravity" and use this concept to explain why the block fell. Simpler words such as "big" and "small" or "hard" and "soft" may be taught in much the same manner. In each instance, the early childhood educator or other caregiver, such as a parent, is calling the child's **attention** to a property of physical objects. The child then attends to that aspect of the play experience.

However, much information that young children attend to makes no sense to them. This is especially true of things they hear, as when two adults converse about inflation or about politics. While the children may attend to these conversations, they are not able to *perceive* the information because it holds no meaning for them. Another illustration of the **perception** phenomenon is when two people at a bus stop converse in Portuguese. A child may pay attention, perhaps out of curiosity, but the words being spoken are not perceived in the brain because the child cannot relate them to her experience.

A third concept important in cognitive development is that of information **processing**. Piaget believed that young children **assimilate** information by fitting new facts into existing mental structures or accommodate information by altering those structures. Upon seeing a duck, for example, a child may assume that because it is a nonhuman that walks, it must be

attention is the process through which a child acquires information through the senses. Learning cannot occur absent attention.

perception is a process in which information entering the sensory register takes on meaning, for example, is interpreted.

processing occurs when information that has been perceived is analyzed and used by an individual.

assimilation, for Piaget, occurs when new information is added to existing knowledge but does not change a child's view of the world.

an animal. The whole concept that it might be a bird is a new one, requiring that the child **accommodate** by changing her idea of what constitutes "birdness." Once that accommodation is made, the child may, much later, use **memory** to retrieve the notion that ducks are birds.

What exactly, then, is learning? Behavioral theorists such as B.F. Skinner suggested that learning is a change in behavior. That is, we know a child has learned something when her behavior alters. Similarly, if she does not behave differently, we can safely conclude that she has not learned. Others, such as Albert Bandura, asserted that learning may in fact occur without being displayed in behavior. Such cognitive behaviorists believe that learning is a change in the *capacity* to behave, but not necessarily in behavior itself. These theories underlie two approaches to instruction that will be considered in later chapters. Applied behavior analysis, which grew out of Skinner's work, holds that behavior itself must change for learning to occur. Cognitive behavior modification, which has its roots in Bandura's work, contends that learning may occur, and in fact be shown to have occurred, without a change in behavior.

Communication Development

Communication development relates to hearing, vision, speech, and language in particular. This section examines each, in turn. The reader is urged to attend to how speech differs from language. The key terms are defined in Figure 1.3.

The infant's communication development includes several abilities that typically emerge during the first year of life. One is the ability to use *multimodal* channels for communication. Infants learn to look at, as well as listen to, people and things that make sounds; they

---

Attention Children must attend in order to learn. A common problem in autism, for example, is apparent overselection of what to attend to; the child may attend to some sensory variables, ignoring others. Children with Down syndrome may have hearing losses such that they cannot attend to unstressed parts of speech such as conjunctions and prepositions, nor to high-pitched sounds such as consonants. In each instance, ECSE help is needed to facilitate attention to the entire stimulus, or learning will not occur. In attention, relevant information is found, while irrelevant information is ignored.

Perception Information must not merely enter the brain's sensory register but must also be perceived. Perception is interpretation: Sensory information (sounds, smells, colors, and so on) takes on meaning to the child. Young children hear much dinner-table conversation but fail to perceive it because it holds no meaning for them. A child with a learning disability may hear the word "bat" but perceive it to have been "tab."

Processing Information that has been attended to and perceived is then analyzed and used; this stage is called information processing. In **assimilation**, Piaget said, new information is added to existing knowledge; in **accommodation**, new data alter existing knowledge, changing the child's view of reality.

Memory Information is retrieved from memory and used as needed. Many theorists hypothesize that data are reassembled, or re-created; in this view, retrieval is not just pulling information from memory but rather is an active process of reproducing knowledge.

FIGURE 1.2 Cognitive development: key terms

---

accommodation, for Piaget, is a process in which new information alters a child's understanding of reality.

memory is retrieval of information. Recent studies suggest that data actually are re-created, not merely retrieved from storage.

Speech is the oral expression of meaning, usually, but not always, with symbols (words).

Language is a formal symbol system in which words are ordered according to rules to express meaning. It may be spoken, written, or signed. It may be expressive or receptive. Most people have far larger receptive than expressive capabilities.

Communication is the expression and reception of meaning. It may occur through speech/hearing, reading/writing, signing/seeing, or gestures.

Phonemes are units of sound that cannot further be divided. An example is "ph" in "phoneme," expressed as /f/. The study of phonemes and the role they play in speech is phonology.

Morphemes are the smallest units of words that carry meaning. "Morphemes," for example, has three such units: "morph," "eme," and "s," meaning, in order, "form/substance," "part," and "plural."

Syntax is a rule system for language governing the order of words or parts of sentences.

Pragmatics is the social use of language. People use different ways of communicating with a boss, for example, than with a spouse.

FIGURE 1.3 Communication-related terms: definitions

touch, smell, and even taste objects; and they find comfort in the caregiver's voice, touch, and smell. Infants and toddlers also learn to express their desires in not just one but rather several ways all at the same time, as when they grab the mother's dress while crying. A second, related skill is to use *sensory integration*—to bring together what is seen, heard, and felt so as to make sense of all available information. And a third is *habituation*. Infants and toddlers are exposed, as are all of us, to much more sensory information than is needed to comprehend what is happening. While very young infants attend to virtually every new sound and sight, they quickly learn, in effect, to ignore "old" sights and sounds and to attend to what is different, and new, in the environment. Habituation helps to prevent sensory overload and to expedite our response to changes in the environment.

Hearing. Infants are born with normal or near-normal hearing. They can hear virtually as well at birth as they can as adults, although the ability to hear quiet sounds appears still to be developing during infancy. Even neonates, however, can tell the difference between sounds; they demonstrate this by calming to sounds they like and responding to unexpected sounds by blinking, crying, stopping a movement, or making a startle response. By one or two months of age, infants have integrated their hearing to the point of being able to use it for directionality; they turn their heads correctly to the source of a sound.

From that point forward, the sense of hearing is used for two principal functions. First, it is the major means by which children acquire **language**; language, in turn, is the principal way children learn information from parents, caregivers, peers, and teachers. Second, hearing serves as a means of connection with the environment. Hearing has the characteristics of always being on, of functioning both at a distance and at close range, of being multidirectional, and of working around corners. Because of these features, hearing is an early warning system far superior to vision or touch. Vision, by contrast, is on only when the eyes are open, is unidirectional, and does not work around corners—eyes take in light only from straight

language is a formal symbol system in which words are ordered according to rules to express meaning. It may be spoken, written, or signed, and may be expressive or receptive.

lines. It is the language acquisition function of hearing that is of most concern to ECSE professionals.

Language. By five to eight months, most infants demonstrate understanding of simple words and phrases ("bye-bye," "da-da," and so on). Language development is very rapid during the first year of life, even though the child often does not demonstrate her knowledge. By the time the first words are spoken, infants understand far more than they can produce in speech.

Bruner (1981) suggested that infants perform purposive communication even before they say their first words. He offered three categories of such purposive prelinguistic communication. One is to obtain others' assistance, a second is to get people's attention, and a third is to share attention with others. Research suggests that children use a wide variety of gestures and vocalizations to accomplish these three purposes (Carpenter, Mastergeorge, & Collins, 1983; Dore, 1974; Wetherby, Cain, Yonclas, & Walker, 1988).

Language is acquired by very young children almost as if by osmosis; children take in many thousands of utterances and from them learn what words mean, how they are formed, and how they work together. It is much more than that, of course. Children's minds are active in the language acquisition process, integrating discrete statements to extract the underlying rules, or structure, that produced them. Thus, each child "invents" anew the language of her community. This is why young children produce sentences no one around them ever said, and why they make characteristic errors of grammar and **syntax**. Children will say "go-ed" before they say "went," "outen" before "turn out," and "drived" before "drove." They will say "mans," "foots," and "womans"—all instances of correctly applying grammatical rules, and all examples of how English sometimes disobeys its own rules.

Development continues during the second and subsequent years, and the relative superiority of receptive to expressive language persists as well. During the second year, the child is putting together actual sentences—including subjects, verbs, and objects—and doing so quite successfully. This shows that the toddler has acquired an understanding of different parts of speech and has generated some rules for putting those together. From the age of three to five, young children demonstrate other syntactic structures as well, notably use of conjunctions to join two separate thoughts into one sentence. By the end of early childhood, most children can understand even compound-complex sentences, can differentiate declarative from interrogative questions, and can produce spoken language using these structures themselves. (The preceding sentence is an example of a compound-complex structure.) In addition, by age six most children know some 2,500 words (Wiig & Semel, 1984). Language development during early childhood, then, produces both mastery of the structure of language and knowledge of many hundreds of words.

Normal language development assumes intact hearing, normal or near-normal intelligence, and an environment rich in linguistic stimulation. These conditions are not always present. Children who are deaf will not hear the many thousands of sentences that children with normal hearing use as the raw materials with which to generate their own rules of language. Children with below-normal intelligence will usually develop acceptable language in time, but they may have difficulty expressing it and may have problems with complex structures and with abstract words. Children raised in homes where language is not used expansively and where few opportunities for development of sophisticated language patterns exist may be delayed in language development even if hearing, intelligence, and motor control are all normal.

syntax is a rule system for language governing the order of words or parts of sentences.

Speech. Vocal communication by the neonate is limited largely to crying. In the one-to-four-month period, however, infants will babble or coo when spoken to or smiled at, and may laugh out loud. The infant at this stage can make one-syllable sounds, and she delights in repeating them. Most communication, however, continues to be physical; the body itself, by being tense or relaxed, tells mothers and other caregivers how the infant feels and is a more useful yardstick at this stage than is vocalization for interpreting the infant's behavior. Infants typically begin babbling at three to six months of age. In babbling, simple sounds composed of two **phonemes**, a single consonant and a single vowel, are repeated again and again, sometimes combined with other one-syllable vocalizations.

phonemes are units of sound that cannot further be divided. An example is "ph" in "phoneme," expressed as /f/. The study of phonemes and the role they play in speech is called phonology.

morphemes are the smallest units of words that carry meaning.

The much-awaited first word usually occurs between about nine and fifteen months of age. Parents can understand the infant's speech, but outsiders frequently cannot. Indeed, often it can be argued whether an actual word was or was not produced. Typically, these are repeated syllable sounds such as "da-da" or "ma-ma," and as such differ little from babbling. It is not clear that they are composed of **morphemes**, or units of meaning. A better indicator for "first word" would be something like "car" or "bottle," or some other word that is not composed of two identical sounds. Two- and three-word utterances typically appear just before the second year (eighteen to twenty-four months); however, children who continue to be very active physically may not speak several words in a string until later. The clarity of children's speech improves dramatically once they enter formal programs with other children. By necessity, they must articulate much better to make themselves understood.

All of this development assumes intact hearing in particular, as well as average or near-average intelligence. It assumes, additionally, good fine motor control of voluntary muscles; cerebral palsy is an example of a condition that may delay speech production because the child has great difficulty controlling the many hundreds of small muscles used in speech.

Vision. Vision is still developing after birth. Neonates (infants from birth to twenty-eight days) are sensitive to light; this is why many families keep an infant's room dim. They can see objects and shapes but cannot yet focus on distant objects. The eyes may at times seem not to work together and may even appear crossed. At one month, the eyes begin moving in unison and no longer appear crossed. Glass (1993) reported that neonates should be able to see as far as 2.5 feet. They also should be able to track a bright object. By two months, infants should alternate gaze between objects and demonstrate a preference for a face over objects. Even at four months, though, infants often cannot tell the difference between the faces of the primary caregiver and others by vision alone, but must rely on sound, touch, and other supplementary sensory information (Allen & Marotz, 1989). By five to eight months, depth perception is present; the infant will show signs of being afraid of falling off a tabletop, for example. The infant also by that time can recognize familiar faces by sight alone. The infant's vision continues developing throughout infancy and reaches near-adult levels shortly after six months of age.

Physical Development

By the time a child reaches five years of age, her height is already half that of an adult. To double height again, that is, to conclude her growth, will take another ten years or so. The infant's weight triples during the first year of life, and body bulk increases 50 percent. These facts highlight the rapid physical development that characterizes the early childhood years.

Physical development usually proceeds from head to toe (cephalocaudal) and from the center out (proximodistal). The word "cephalocaudal" is from the Latin "cephalo," meaning "head" and "caudal," meaning "tail"; similarly, "proximodistal" joins "proximate," or near, to "distal," or remote from the center. Infants first lift, or rotate, the head, later, they also lift or move the shoulders, and yet later the trunk. The legs and feet are last, which developmentally has the important effect of making walking a task of the second year of life. Perhaps the most obvious illustration of center-out development is the sequence in which teeth appear: The infant's first teeth are in the center of the mouth; subsequent teeth appear on either side, moving from the center out. Or consider the infant's use of the arms. At first, arms are swung from the shoulder, and the entire arm is used to make gross, sweeping motions. Only later is the infant able to manipulate the arm independently of the shoulder; next the forearm by itself; and then the wrist, hand, and fingers. Thus, gross motor control precedes fine motor control.

The principles of cephalocaudal and proximodistal development provide guidelines for physical therapy and for early intervention. Infants lift the head before they voluntarily flex their legs. A neonate (newborn) will raise its head while prone (stomach down), stretching the legs out. Later, the infant will lie supine (stomach up) and pull its legs up against gravity. At about four months, the infant may position the legs in a diamond shape such that the feet touch while the knees are far apart. This results in enjoyable contact of one foot with the other. Similarly, infants will move the arms before manipulating fingers, the legs before wiggling toes; these center-out developments illustrate the proximodistal progression.

These patterns help therapists and teachers in two ways. First, they show what to look for; one anticipates emergence of movements by certain ages, and if they do not appear until long after they were expected, therapists and teachers are alerted to possible delays. Second, they provide *developmental guidelines* for intervention; the therapist knows what motions are essential precursors to other movements and can help the infant or toddler to master these prerequisites in order to succeed in later developmental tasks. To illustrate, consider the seemingly simple matter of watching something interesting. To do this, the infant needs to hold up her head and adjust her neck so that her eyes may focus on the interesting object; and she must maintain this posture over a continuous period of time, adjusting it as necessary to

Supports for young children now are commercially available. Photos of the Preston Tristander are reprinted from J. A. Preston, © BISSELL Healthcare Company.

keep the interesting object in view. Knowing this, physical therapists focus on developing those body-control capabilities as precursors to therapeutic and academic instruction (Kreutz, 1993). Similarly, as illustrated in the photographs on the previous page, occupational therapists may use special supports to enable a child with a severe physical disability to maintain visual vigilance over a period of time, in a variety of positions. Until recently, such equipment was custom-designed by rehabilitation engineers; today, however, it is commercially available. In addition, "adaptive toys" are available from a variety of libraries (Figure 1.4); again, until recently, such toys often had to be hand-made by rehabilitation engineers.

Both heredity and environment matter in physical development. In fact, development is affected not only by those two factors but also by the family's culture, SES, child-rearing practices, and other factors. The latter three may be grouped as *sociocultural influences*. They manifest themselves in physical development in the extent to which the infant, toddler, or preschooler is permitted to explore at will, free from artificial constraints, and in a safe environment. Generally, such permissiveness is associated with more rapid motor development, because the young child gains much more experience both with her body and with the surrounding environment. Overprotection, on the other hand, slows motor development. A physical disability may result in experiential deprivation similar in kind but more extreme in extent to that of an overprotected child: There is less exploration, less practice of physical activities and functions, and, often, less learning.

A great deal now is known about the physical development of the under-six child. Allen and Marotz (1989) and Malina (1982) are two excellent sources of information on developmental milestones in this domain. During the first twelve months of life, several important changes occur. The skeleton strengthens, cartilage yields to bone, and infants become able to

---

USA Toy Library Association
2530 Crawford Avenue, # 111
Evanston, IL 60201
http://www.ucpa.org/html/innovative/techtots/resource.html

National Lekotek Center
2100 Ridge Avenue
Evanston, IL 60201
http://collaboratory.nunet.net/ltc/lekotek/index.html

Alliance for Technology Access
2173 East Francisco Boulevard, # L
San Rafael, CA 94901
www.ataccess.org

Tech Tots Library Network
UCPA
1660 L Street NW #700
Washington, DC 20036
www.ucpa.org

FIGURE 1.4 Adaptive toys: resources

support their weight when standing. At or about one month of age, infants can move their heads from side to side, make crawling movements while in a prone (stomach down) position, and hold their heads erect for a few seconds while being held. Within the first three months, infants can grasp objects placed into their hands, but this is largely an involuntary response rather than a purposive one.

The first evidence of voluntary motor control appears when the infant is able to lift, or otherwise move, her head, at or about three months of age. As limbs strengthen, coordination improves, and at about six months the infant can roll over and sit up without support. By this time, the infant can use the opposing thumb and other fingers in a pincer motion to pick up objects, this time purposively. Often, these are shaken, in large arm/hand motions. She can transfer objects from hand to hand and, of course, into the mouth. Interestingly, at or about six months of age, the infant will reach for an object with the closer arm; prior to that, often the infant will reach across the body from the opposite side.

By nine months of age, she can reach a standing position, holding on to something. Between eight and twelve months, she stacks objects and can place a smaller one inside a larger one. The infant can pull the feet forward, putting one into the mouth, and can also pull herself up to a standing position. And at twelve to thirteen months, she can stand unaided and can walk while holding someone's hand; she might take a few steps unaided.

All of this does not just happen. The infant spends hour after hour practicing motor skills until they are mastered. Literally thousands of trials occur, as the infant practices the same skill over and over again. Once one skill is habitual, the infant focuses, with the same endless patience, on the next.

Something else happens that is important. As infants begin to move on their own, they become—and realize that they are—independent of the mother. They begin to grasp the

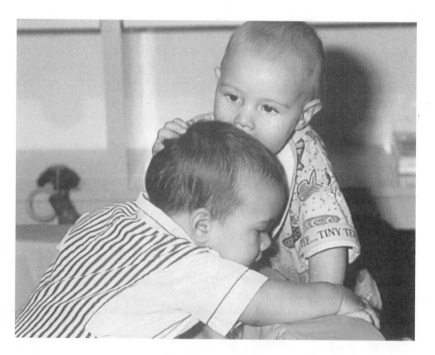

Infants use every sense to explore, including taste.

concept that they are discrete beings, not merely extensions of the mother; this is an intellectual breakthrough, and it is due in very large part to independent mobility.

This stage is related to a second important idea: The more the infant can move, the more she learns. Kermoian and Campos (1988) examined two groups of eight-month-olds on the Piagetian object-permanence test. In this test, the infant is shown an object, which is then hidden while she is being distracted. Infants who have attained object permanence know that the object still exists, and they look for it. Kermoian and Campos found that those who could move independently were much more likely to seek the hidden object than were those who could not.

By eighteen months, most toddlers can walk alone; at two, they can run. By the end of the second year, the toddler can build things with six or more blocks. Again, as in the first year, the toddler practices the same things over and over again. Even if a task takes days or weeks to accomplish—as might climbing onto countertops using chairs, stools, and so on—the toddler will persist, seemingly without limits to her patience.

Toddlers do something infants seldom do: They practice and refine fine motor control, not only gross motor control. Hand and finger movements are coordinated with more and more precision. During this time, the toddler learns to eat independently, using utensils. The point is a central one: By the end of the second year, or by about age 2.5, the toddler is using gross and fine motor skills not for the sake of the activity itself but to *accomplish* something, in this case, eating.

Independent walking has one huge effect: It frees the hands. With the hands free, the child can engage in other motor tasks. In fact, walking is the indicator that infancy has ended and the toddler period has begun. Zelazo (1984) pointed out that talking and functional use of objects (versus exploration of them) begin at about the same time that walking does: Walking, by marking the completion of a long, strenuous period of learning, may spur cognitive development because so much attention need no longer be given over to walking.

Movement appears to be central to self-awareness; for a child to differentiate herself from others, there must be a knowledge of the body and what it can do. Some children even learn better by moving and touching than they do by seeing. Motor behavior also integrates all the senses. As children move and pick things up, they taste them, smell them, touch them, and, if the things rattle, listen to them.

All of this assumes the coming together of maturational factors (neurological capabilities allowing the child to do something) with environmental facilitators (ways for the child to do those things, room to explore, permissive parents, the necessary equipment, and so on) (Halverson, 1971).

The critical time for motor skill development is eighteen to sixty months of age (Flinchum, 1975; Williams, 1983). If the child has not developed key gross and fine motor control functions by age five, she needs help. At some point during the third year, the child can dress herself quite completely, including socks and shoes. She can throw an object a few feet, underhanded, and can catch a large ball, using both arms and body.

By the fourth year, the child can bounce a ball and catch it after it bounces, using just the arms and hands. She can jump down from a chair to the floor, landing smoothly on both feet. The child can push a wagon, steering it successfully. Hopping and skipping now are skillfully done, often in games. During the fifth year, the child can skip with alternating feet while maintaining balance, even while skipping rope. She can roller-skate and, for short periods, ice-skate. The child can roll a ball precisely to hit an object and can kick the ball even if it is rolling at the time.

The mother-infant bonding process is essential for infant social and emotional development.

Social or Emotional Development

The domain of social or emotional development is one in which both definitions of delays or disorders and assessments must be comparative. Infants and toddlers are expected to display behavior in only a limited number of areas, notably sleeping, eating, basic motor activity, and social relations with primary caregivers. This restricted range of normal behavior, combined with the natural variation from child to child (as well as from parent to parent), means that early indications of delays or other problems in this domain are difficult to discern.

Considerable research has been done on infant/adult relationships, attachment, rhythm and reciprocity, and temperament. Generally, infants begin interaction when they develop the ability to prolong attention to selected stimuli, that is, to maintain focus. Smiling, vocalizing, and using facial muscles are all means of initiating and then maintaining interaction with a caregiver. During the third and fourth month of life, the infant tests this new ability to control interactions; that is, she looks to see how long she can keep an adult's attention, or to get the adult to do something. At around four to five months of age, the infant begins to display autonomy in interactions, moving attention at will from one adult to another, from an object to an adult and back to the object (Brazelton & Cramer, 1990). Aydlett (1993) suggested that infants between six and ten months of age will display increased intentional interaction with the mother or ECSE professionals. They will coordinate their actions to comport with behavior of the other person, and they will attempt to reinitiate play if that person disengages.

As the child begins speaking, she will indicate her needs and will express her feelings. By this time, she should display a range of emotions, from happiness to joy, discomfort to anger, and pride to shame. Especially during the second year of life, she will demonstrate a strong sense of self, a sense of possession of treasured toys and objects ("mine!"), and a sense of wanting to do things for herself. She plays best at this stage in pairs; "three's a crowd" is very true with toddlers. By three years of age, many young children display a rather full range of emotions—including the more subtle ones of envy, guilt, and pride—and do so appropriately. They can moderate their expression of these emotions: A three- or four-year-old should show gradations of, say, anger (from annoyance to rage) or happiness (from pleasure to joy). She should be able to recover quickly from emotional extremes. The child should display feelings of pride and accomplishment when she does things well, and regret when she does something wrong. By five to six years of age, she should regulate her behavior according to the situations in which she finds herself. For example, she will display much more affection to a loved one in the privacy of her home than she will in a preschool or kindergarten setting where other people can see her. Increasingly, as she prepares to enter kindergarten or first grade, she will demonstrate her ability to play not only by herself but also with other children in genuinely interactive and cooperative ways. She will show confidence in most age-appropriate behaviors and will demonstrate pride in her abilities.

During the infancy period, play is principally parent-initiated or -directed, as infants demonstrate fear of leaving primary caretakers. Toddlers establish more independence from the caregiver, and engage in practicing newly learned motor skills (walking, picking things up, throwing balls, and so on) and in exploration (especially in studying "interesting" objects or insects). Toddlers engage in parallel play when placed near other toddlers and exhibit a strong sense of property possession. By the time they are three years of age, many children play cooperatively with others (Allen & Marotz, 1989). When interactive play, as opposed to parallel play, becomes developmentally appropriate, social skills emerge as essential components of adaptive behavior. These skills do not lend themselves to being taught by adults as self-help skills do; rather, they must be learned with and from other children.

During the preschool years, what we consider to be "normal" behavior takes on more dimensions. Preschoolers are expected to engage in play with other children, to look to adults for clues on handling frustration, and to relate differently to familiar adults than to strangers. This increased variability has the effect of giving ECSE workers and parents more opportunities to discern what may be disabilities, delays, or deviations in behavior. However, unusual withdrawal or other displays of shyness on the one hand, and unusual aggression or other "acting out" behavior on the other, do not necessarily signal problems in social or emotional development. They may, instead, be among the first clues that something else is wrong. Children who are deaf, for example, may respond to their condition by avoiding social interactions with other children. They may seem to ignore adult instructions or warnings. The problem here is not that the child has social or emotional difficulties but that the inability to hear makes interpersonal communication very difficult for her. Mental retardation, autism, and even physical conditions may be confused during the preschool years with social or emotional conditions because the "symptoms" are so similar. The challenge for ECSE workers confronting apparent delays or deviations in social or emotional development is to be aware that these symptoms may suggest some other concern. That is why assessment in this domain should begin by first ruling out other possible causes for observed behavior.

For these and other reasons, it is important for ECSE workers not to "blame the victim." Social and emotional behavior usually responds to environmental conditions or antecedents. Behavior, that is, serves a function. Rather than looking only at the child and labeling behavior she dislikes as "difficult" or "inappropriate," the ECSE worker should attempt instead to comprehend the conditions giving rise to the behavior. She might ask, "What function does this behavior serve for this child in this context?" Some behavior serves to obtain sensory feedback, other behavior to secure reinforcement, and yet other behavior to escape or avoid stimuli (Wolery et al., 1988). Normal development includes many instances

Learning to play with another infant or toddler— and to share—are key steps in social or emotional development.

in which behavior plays communicative roles, that is, carries communication intent. Accordingly, the focus in ECSE is on the behavior itself rather than on the child. If we understand to what antecedents the child is reacting, we can change those, leading to more acceptable behavior. It is not necessary at any stage of that process to criticize or label the child for displaying "difficult behavior."

The point is a central one. Young children are limited in their ability to understand external stressors—and limited in how they can express their feelings about these events and incidents. The combination of not understanding what is happening and not being able to articulate her emotions may overwhelm a young child. Her behavior may be affected by changes other family members accept as necessary—the family moves to a new house or town, a new child-care arrangement is made—or by changes that upset other family members as well—a parent loses a job, mother and father are separated or divorced. That young children exhibit behavioral alterations after such external stressors is normal. It is not cause for diagnosing disability.

PHILOSOPHY

The philosophy guiding ECSE as a field draws from, and contributes to, the broader field of EC education. ECSE and EC education have more similarities than differences. Both are fields of direct service to young children and their families. There are, however, points of divergence between the guiding philosophies of the two fields. These differences become important when ECSE services are delivered in EC settings, as happens when young children with disabilities are integrated into preschool programs serving large numbers of children who have no disabilities. When a child with cerebral palsy is placed in a Head Start program, for example, the special educator and the general educator working with the child may approach the task of teaching that child very differently.

At the national level, two organizations have taken the lead in shaping the EC and ECSE philosophies. One is the National Association for the Education of Young Children (NAEYC), which issued "developmentally appropriate practice" (DAP) recommendations in 1987 (Bredekamp, 1987). This publication sparked intense interest in the general field of EC education, selling more than one-half million copies. It sparked more concern than interest, however, in the more specialized field of ECSE. Eventually, the Division for Early Childhood (DEC) of the Council for Exceptional Children (CEC) came out with its "recommended practices" (DEC Task Force, 1993). More recently, NAEYC has issued a revised version of its DAP recommendations (Bredekamp & Copple, 1997).

In each of these published guidelines, the use of the word "practice" is somewhat curious. Both the NAEYC and the DEC have acknowledged that their recommendations are not as yet widely used in programs serving young children (Bredekamp, 1993b; Odom, McLean, Johnson, & LaMontagne, 1995). In actuality, the "practices" are recommendations from leaders in the two fields. In other words, the practices are aspects of a philosophy. They tell us more about the ideal than they do about the real.

Nevertheless, as statements of philosophy, the NAEYC's DAP and the DEC's recommended practices are very important documents. They contain a wealth of information that practitioners and students alike will find germane. **Note**: The author strongly recommends that readers acquire their own copies from the publishers: NAEYC, 1509 16th Street NW, Washington, DC 20036; and DEC, c/o The Council for Exceptional Children, 1920 Association Drive, Reston, VA 22091.

Both sets of recommendations emphasize treating each child, and each family, as *unique*. Both express an aversion to *labels*, preferring to avoid terminology that might unnecessarily stigmatize a child. Both stress the need for *quality* in all aspects of programming. And both grant to *families* important roles in design and delivery of services.

The philosophical opposition to labeling extends to other kinds of invasion of the privacy of children and families. Thus, many ECSE programs will not identify which, if any, children attending the program have tested positive for the human immunodeficiency virus (HIV), for the hepatitis B virus (HBV), or for other communicable diseases. Rather, ECSE program administrators expect child-care workers, early childhood special educators, and other professionals and paraprofessionals to follow universal precautions to avoid contamination (Rathlev, 1994). The American Academy of Pediatrics recommends universal immunization against HBV for all infants; child-care workers should likewise be immunized as a routine precaution. No such preventive measure yet is available for HIV, the acquired immune deficiency syndrome (AIDS) virus. Because the virus is transmitted through bodily fluids, ECSE workers should wear gloves whenever blood may be spilled and should scrupulously avoid touching body fluids.

The increasing commonality in philosophy between EC and ECSE is a recent phenomenon. The 1987 version of NAEYC's DAP guidelines, for example, all but ignored children with disabilities. It included only one principle relating specifically to ECSE: "Modifications are made in the environment, when needed, for children with special needs" (Bredekamp, 1987, p. 11). In the years that followed, however, NAEYC recognized that EC programs throughout the nation served, and would continue to serve, many children with disabilities and delays in development. As Bredekamp (1993b) noted, much more specific information on serving children with disabilities was needed than appeared in the initial

age appropriateness is a philosophy in which activities are designed to match children's developmental stages. It is a key concept in NAEYC's Developmentally Appropriate Practice (DAP) guidelines. DEC's Recommended Practice task force suggested that programs be *chronologically* age-appropriate as well, because otherwise some young children with disabilities might wrongly be placed in settings designed for far younger children.

individual appropriateness is an approach in which services are customed-designed and -delivered to respond to a child's unique needs. Often, it is a concept more honored in theory than in practice, as childcare workers often find it difficult to individualize services as much as they would like.

developmentally appropriate practice (DAP) is professional work that emphasizes activities with young children that are both age-appropriate and child-focused. In DAP approaches, children are encouraged to be active learners, while professionals guide and facilitate their activities.

DAP guidelines. Taking one step in that direction, in an article for *Topics in Early Childhood Special Education,* she was at pains to emphasize that DAP builds upon two core ideas, both of which are treasured by ECSE professionals—**age appropriateness** and **individual appropriateness**:

> *Developmentally appropriate practice is, by definition, individually appropriate as well as age appropriate. A program cannot possibly achieve individual appropriateness without assessing and planning for children's individual needs and interests.* (Bredekamp, 1993b, 263)

ECSE today seeks, as much as does EC in general, to follow **developmentally appropriate practice** (DAP) guidelines. Early intervention personnel, preschool special education teachers, and support personnel—including therapists—attempt to "guide," "support," and "encourage" children—and to structure the environment so that children can explore, interact, and learn on their own. (The quoted words appear in the NAEYC guidelines, Bredekamp, 1987). Both fields are committed to ensuring that professionals follow the child, doing what the child wants to do and using those activities to facilitate development of age-appropriate behaviors (Salisbury, 1991; Wolery, 1991).

Another philosophy that ECSE shares with EC is that of valuing interdisciplinary approaches. As a whole, ECSE recognizes that many infants, toddlers, and preschoolers with disabilities have not one, or even a few, but rather many important needs. The expertise and ways of thinking of professionals from a wide variety of fields are needed to serve these children and their families effectively. Recent research bears this out. Looking at how family needs are assessed, for example, Garshelis and McConnell (1993) found that interdisciplinary teams of professionals identified family needs, including family priorities, more accurately than did the individual members of the same teams—even the best-trained and most experienced members. Such evidence, if confirmed by replication studies, reinforces the philosophy of interdisciplinary assessment and evaluation embodied in the IDEA. As states pursue seamless systems of delivery for preschool-age children with disabilities, interdisciplinary approaches are increasingly seen in preschool special education programs as well. Bredekamp (1993b) stated that NAEYC values this documentation from ECSE about interdisciplinary approaches, noting that EC has much to learn from ECSE's positive experiences with interdisciplinary service delivery.

Another area of increasing similarity between the two fields is that of the age ranges of children served. ECSE defines the word "early" to mean from birth, or from diagnosis of a disability or detection of a delay; EC, by contrast, tends to focus on serving a more traditional preschool-age population, that is, from three to five. Bredekamp (1993b) noted that EC is being pushed by ECSE toward services for younger children, and she welcomed that new emphasis: "The concept of intervention has the potential to play an important bridging role for the two fields, thus strengthening both" (p. 266).

Differences

While EC and ECSE are coming together philosophically, some differences remain. The most important difference between EC and ECSE may be one few observers mention. ECSE programs are by law free to families with young children who have disabilities or delays; programs may charge only under special circumstances, and then usually in early intervention (birth-to-two) more than in preschool (three-to-five) programs. EC, by contrast, is much more rarely free to families. Although Head Start and similar programs are free to qualifying (i.e., low-SES) families, most EC programs charge families for services. The difference becomes important when *choices must be made between cost and quality*. In ECSE much more than in EC programs, families and staff members alike press for higher standards, more options, and more family-friendly hours of service; in EC, Bredekamp (1993b) says, "parents are in larger numbers on the other side, advocating that higher standards will harm affordability" (p. 268).

A second area of difference is that ECSE measures and tracks development in children much more than is common in EC education. Bredekamp acknowledged as much: "Early childhood education has not emphasized outcomes to the degree that early childhood special education has and must. But goals (as early childhood educators call outcomes) *are* emphasized" (Bredekamp, 1993b, p. 262, emphasis added). She was clear that EC programs could learn from ECSE's experience about the importance of setting goals and tracking success in meeting goals. Similarly, the DEC's recommended practices include some subtle, and some not so subtle, divergences from DAP guidelines. A good example is NAEYC's emphasis on age appropriateness. The DEC task force was concerned that programs follow chronologically age-appropriate guidelines as well as developmentally appropriate principles, because task force members worried that a strict interpretation of DAP might lead to placement of children with disabilities in classes for much younger children, unless the need to balance developmental appropriateness and age appropriateness was recognized (DEC Task Force, 1993). Again, however, that is not a major divergence of approach.

A fourth difference mentioned briefly above is that ECSE, more than EC, features *applied behavior analysis*. Much of the research reported in special education literature as helping young children with disabilities used behavior modification techniques. Fowell and Lawton (1992) attacked DAP for neglecting learning theory in particular and for minimizing the importance of teacher-directed activities in early childhood. Johnson and Johnson (1992) claimed that NAEYC was anti-applied behavior analysis, contending that NAEYC "figuratively, if not literally, elbow[ed] behaviorists out of meeting rooms and committees when DAP was being drafted" (p. 441). The DAP orientation, they said, is one of Piagetian (constructivist) and Montessorian approaches, which feature child-initiated activities. While many ECSE programs also orient themselves according to what Piaget and Montessori taught, Johnson and Johnson commented, many apply research showing that behavioral techniques have much to offer. Other ECSE professionals pointed to the extensive research evidence that young children with disabilities require greater degrees of structure, more intensive teacher involvement, and more behavior modification techniques than DAP seemed to recommend. Bredekamp (1993b), in response, acknowledged that structured approaches, including applied behavior analysis, have their place in EC as well as in ECSE.

These differences are illustrated in Figures 1.5 and 1.6. The hypothetical mornings described show how ECSE and EC education philosophies "play out" in actual practice. The reader is encouraged to reflect on these scenarios. To what extent, for example, are the differences a function of the kinds of children being served in each setting?

However fervently desired by the leaders of two fields a coming together of EC's DAP and ECSE's applied behavior analysis orientation may be, finding and maintaining a middle course may prove difficult in actual practice. A recent book, *When Slow Is Fast Enough* (1992), by the University of Pennsylvania's Joan Goodman, vividly described how applied behavior analysis was implemented in the twenty ECSE programs Goodman visited in ten states. These programs served preschool-age children with mental retardation who needed intensive, frequently repeated instruction in preacademics. In response to those needs, the

As her children arrive at about 8:30 AM, Mrs. Madden and her aide, Terry, help them to take off their overcoats and then escort each, one at a time, to a nearby bathroom for toileting and washup. Each child must be attended to individually. Mrs. Madden and Terry take advantage of this one-to-one time to teach self-help skills such as unfastening pants, unzipping zippers, lowering underpants, using the toilets, re-dressing, and washing. The words associated with each of these activities are taught, as they have been for several months now.

The opening activity this morning is free play from 8:45 to 9:00. Each child selects and plays with a favorite toy or game. During this time, Mrs. Madden and Terry read the children's notebooks, most of which contain comments by the children's parents about what happened at home the previous evening and that morning. They have to read fast, however, because first one child then others require their attention. Two children with cerebral palsy need help picking up and holding toys. One child accidentally puts a jacket on backward and then screams in frustration; another tears a page in a favorite book and cries inconsolably; two others tug a toy between them, on the verge of a fight.

After free play, Mrs. Madden announces "circle time." This is a period when the children are asked to identify who came to school this morning, what the date is, which season it is, what the weather is, and so on. Even though it is three months into the school year, many of the children still do not know this information. Some lack the language to answer even simple questions, while others need constant prompting to be able to articulate their responses. Mrs. Madden has to adjust her questions to each child's level of functioning. She also has to interrupt the process repeatedly to regain one child's attention, to stop another child from turning away, and to prevent yet another from bothering a classmate. Mrs. Madden then surprises the children by opening a bag filled with colored objects. These allow her to teach, one by one, such concepts as "large," "yellow," "soft," "round," and "rough" and their opposites "small," "hard," "rectangular," and "smooth." The aide, Terry, reinforces the concepts with some of the children, reteaching the ideas and requesting appropriate responses. As with names and dates, these are things the children have worked on for several months. Mrs. Madden changes the objects frequently to keep the children's interest.

Art time follows from 9:30 to 10:00. The children need frequent one-to-one attention because they have difficulty handling the paper, the triangles, the paste, and the crayons. Mrs. Madden and Terry move from table to table offering help. At each table, they focus on a different objective. That is because each child's individualized education program (IEP) has its own goals; these goals tell Mrs. Madden and Terry what the priorities are with each child.

Snack time is next. As with the morning arrival routine, this offers Mrs. Madden and Terry opportunities to teach each child self-help skills, in this case self-feeding competencies, as well as language (here, words to identify foods, how each is eaten, and so on). The children with cerebral palsy need constant, one-to-one assistance with feeding; however, the other children frequently call out for help or otherwise demand attention, so Mrs. Madden and Terry have to shuttle between children, briefly leaving the children with cerebral palsy.

After snack time, work time begins at 10:15. This is a period for concentrated activity on IEP goals and objectives. Some children work on letter and word identification, others on counting, and yet others on reading out loud. Errors are ignored by Mrs. Madden and Terry, but correct answers bring both praise and tokens. The tokens later will be exchanged by the child for candy or extra time with a favorite toy.

Moving time (gross motor skills) follows. Here, Mrs. Madden and Terry focus on helping children to meet age-appropriate developmental milestones such as walking without assistance, carrying objects while walking, jumping over objects, and throwing and catching a ball. Again, the IEP tells Mrs. Madden and Terry which competencies to work on with each child.

Finally, it is almost time for the children to leave. While Terry helps the children, one at a time, with toileting and dressing, Mrs. Madden writes notes in each child's journal, which she places in the children's bags. Then they accompany the children, who walk down the corridor in a procession, to the buses, and help them onto the buses if necessary.

FIGURE 1.5 An ECSE preschool class

As her children arrive at about 8:30 AM, Miss Offerdahl and her aide, Judy, watch them take off their overcoats and go to the nearby bathroom. Miss Offerdahl and Judy assist the children only if asked or if something unexpected occurs. The children have long since mastered the basic self-help skills and want (indeed, insist!) on doing them independently.

Miss Offerdahl has arranged the room with different activity centers, each offering games or toys she thinks the children will find interesting. As they emerge from the bathroom, each child is allowed to go to whatever activity center appeals to her. Once the children have found their places, Miss Offerdahl and Judy walk unobtrusively from center to center, offering suggestions ("Why don't you try this?"), asking questions ("How many do you have?") and supervising the occasional disturbance ("Susie, please, move your scissors to your side of the table").

After this free-play period, Miss Offerdahl and Judy assemble the group. The children are asked to describe what they were doing. Occasionally, Miss Offerdahl offers a new word or asks for a fuller explanation. Once the descriptions are over, she tells them that they can begin a new activity together, one of creating their own play about Thanksgiving. She asks for volunteers to make the scenery, create the costumes, and write the script. The children are allowed to do whichever part they prefer. They then assemble into smaller groups to plan what each child will do. Miss Offerdahl and Judy move from group to group, telling them what supplies are available, what additional supplies can be obtained, and the like, while encouraging the children to include all essential parts of their activity ("Don't forget—someone has to bring gravy!"). Finally, Miss Offerdahl and Judy volunteer to write out the group plans and each child's assignments. The children each get a short note to take home.

Story time follows. During this period, Judy moves unobtrusively from child to child to offer more information or to settle disputes. Miss Offerdahl has chosen an engaging story that features opportunities for the children to count, so from time to time she stops the story to ask for a new count total. She also stops occasionally to pose questions ("Why do you suppose Sandy did that?") designed to encourage the children to think about what they are hearing.

During snack time, Miss Offerdahl and Judy stand nearby, ready to assist if asked. From time to time, they comment ("What a nice snack your mother gave you this morning!") or ask questions ("How many chocolate-chip cookies have you eaten this week?").

Play time gives the children a break from the sit-down routine of eating snacks. Miss Offerdahl and Judy encourage the children to engage in cooperative play, rather than just parallel (solitary) play. Scattered throughout the room are objects and activities that allow children to exercise both gross and fine motor muscles. Some of these are musical activities, while others are art or physical education activities.

After play time, Miss Offerdahl and Judy assemble the children again, this time to teach them several Thanksgiving-related songs. These songs, Miss Offerdahl explains, celebrate the holiday as a meaningful event in each of several different cultures. After they learn the songs, Miss Offerdahl asks them to comment on the cultural implications of each song ("What in this song talks about the importance of the spirit for Native Americans?").

Finally, it is almost time for the children to leave. Miss Offerdahl and Judy stand ready to help children with their overcoats if necessary, and remind each child to give his or her parents the note about the play and what the child is expected to do to prepare for it. Then they watch as the children leave for the day.

FIGURE 1.6 An EC preschool class

ECSE teachers Goodman observed used tight behavior management techniques that were very different from the child-initiated practices that NAEYC recommends for EC programs. Goodman concluded, after more than two years of observations, that less teacher control and more child autonomy would help the children: "[F]rom every standpoint—psychological, empirical, and moral—a corrective shift toward a freer, more child-centered (i.e., progressive) model is needed" (p. 250). Acknowledging the difficulty of making such a shift, she suggested that "[w]e need a different, not a lesser, vision. Rather than getting children prepared for the next environment, we need to prepare present environments that intrigue and appeal" (p. 254).

A fifth area of difference is in the relative emphasis each field places on working with families. ECSE values family participation very highly, to the extent that many programs are moving to grant broad decision-making authority to parents. Such a family-focused approach is not yet common in EC education. Bredekamp (1993b) conceded as much: "Partnerships with parents have long been a value of early childhood education, as reflected in the emphasis on parent involvement and decision making in Head Start. However, as children are perceived to be less 'at risk' and less vulnerable (i.e., older), the focus on families weakens" (p. 267).

A sixth and final area of difference is in transition planning. ECSE emphasizes the need to prepare young children with disabilities, delays, or deviations in development for success in the next environment. EC education, by contrast, tends to expect the next environment to conform to the needs of the child. Of course, because EC children typically have no disabilities, kindergarten and first-grade teachers and administrators can accomplish such steps much more readily than can their ECSE counterparts working with children who have severe needs. Goodman (1992) appeals to ECSE educators to make that effort, despite its difficulty.

As Goodman illustrated, the basic choice facing ECSE personnel is between preacademics and social development. Educators who believe that young children with special needs must receive intensive assistance in preacademics are almost compelled to use techniques from applied behavior analysis to ensure that such instruction takes place. However, ECSE workers who determine that social skills are more important than academics could easily slow down and give children far more freedom to choose activities. Goodman's preference in ECSE for young children having moderate mental retardation is for the latter. That

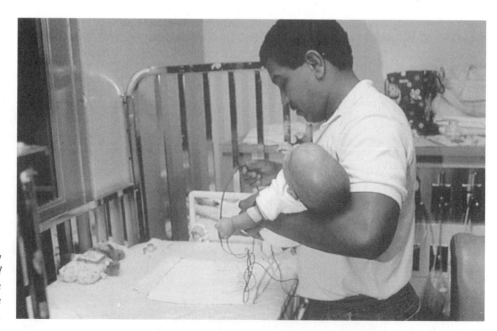

Premature infants usually develop with no lasting ill effects if early intervention services are provided on a timely basis.

is why she believes that "slow is fast enough." Other ECSE professionals may make different choices.

Much more must be done before most EC and ECSE programs nationwide reach the point where their activities reflect the highest levels envisioned in national guidelines. Bredekamp has repeatedly stated that the principal reason NAEYC issued its DAP guidelines is that many, perhaps most, EC programs nationwide were not yet practicing the approaches recommended in the principles (Bredekamp, 1987, 1993a, b). Similarly, the DEC Task Force (1993) and McLean and Odom (1993) noted that the DEC recommended practices continue to be more ideal than real in many ECSE programs throughout the nation.

Although national leaders are trying to bring ECSE and EC together, there remains a serious gap between the ideals expressed in the NAEYC and DEC guidelines on the one hand and the day-to-day reality of EC and ECSE programs on the other. At the local level, ECSE practitioners increasingly respect the need to offer developmentally appropriate programs and services, while EC professionals now recognize, to an extent seldom seen in the 1970s or 1980s, the importance of providing services to young children with disabilities or developmental delays within the same rooms, with the same materials, and at the same time as they serve children with no disabilities. There is much less automatic referral of problem children to special programs and the similarly automatic removal of children from integrated settings to special services that existed thirty or even twenty years ago. Having said that, it must be acknowledged that these welcome improvements are not yet uniform throughout the nation (Odom, McLean, Johnson, & LaMontagne, 1995). As Goodman (1992) predicted and as NAEYC and DEC both are discovering, it is easier to agree on philosophy than it is to implement "model practices" consistently in thousands of programs nationwide.

S U M M A R Y

The ways in which very young children develop during the birth-to-five period tell early childhood special educators how to work with them. A fundamental tenet of ECSE's philosophy is that of developmental plasticity: Research clearly shows that children can benefit significantly during the early childhood years when helpful therapies and instruction are offered to them and to their families. Similarly, ECSE workers believe that experiential deprivation is harmful to young children who have disabilities or delays in development. That is why these professionals seek to offer infants, toddlers, and young children with disabilities the full range of developmental and learning experiences that nondisabled young children get from birth to six years of age.

Child development in the birth-to-five period is best understood as a sequence of maturational and learning steps, or stages. The exact age at which a child reaches a particular milestone is much less important than the sequence through which the child passes to come to and master that developmental task. Similarly, child development occurs in all five domains of development. These domains are not mutually independent. Rather, they interact with each other. For example, communication development speeds up once the physical domain task of walking has been achieved.

The guiding philosophy of ECSE is one that reflects these beliefs about child development. In general, ECSE professionals tend to emphasize the importance for each child to acquire developmentally important competencies, so much so, in fact, that these professionals often rely on the techniques of applied behavior analysis to help children learn more rapidly. The broader field of EC education, not being faced as much with the challenges of disability or serious delays in development, tends to shy away from such techniques, preferring instead to play the more passive role of encouraging children to develop at their own pace. This difference between the ECSE and EC philosophies is entirely understandable given the different populations with which they work.

QUESTIONS FOR REFLECTION

1. How does the work of Erikson help us to understand development in the birth-to-five period?

2. What did Maslow teach us that helps us to understand why some parents persist, apparently beyond reason, in seeking "cures" for their children?

3. The text emphasizes that child development in any given domain interacts with development in other domains. In what ways does development in communication affect development in cognition? Vice versa?

4. What "tricks" could you teach a young child to help that child gain entry into a group of children who are playing together?

5. How does "experiential deprivation" affect development of young children whose limitations of hearing or vision or physical mobility might cause their parents to be overly protective of them?

6. How is physical mobility related to the achievement by a young child of a sense of independent identity?

7. Thinking about the developmentally important role that physical movement plays in early childhood, what concerns might you have as a teacher about a three-year-old who has cerebral palsy or some other physical limitation?

8. In your own words, what concepts guide NAEYC's developmentally appropriate practice?

9. Again in your own words, what different beliefs seem to shape DEC's recommended practices?

10. Reread Figures 1.5 and 1.6. What problems might arise if one of the children from the ECSE preschool class described in Figure 1.5 were to be placed in the EC preschool class described in Figure 1.6? If you were the EC preschool class teacher, how would you respond to those problems?

Prelude: Overview of Early Childhood Special Education

Nicole Anderson is a graduate of early intervention. Born two months early, Nicole was diagnosed with cerebral palsy at eight months. Shortly afterward, she received her first early intervention services. Through these services she began to learn speech and language skills, first using a photo album to point, then progressing to an electronic system, and finally moving to a verbal communications system. Today, at the age of six, she goes to school full-time—half day in regular education and half day in special education. She can speak in four- to six-word sentences with her peers and has developed friendships

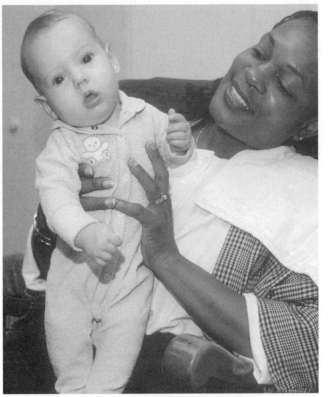

with her classmates. Her mother Maria says: "For Nicole [early intervention] skills have helped her to become as independent as she can be. And for me—I have learned about the team process and how to make it work for both of us. It has given us confidence for the future." (Durenberger, 1991, p. 19)

OVERVIEW

early childhood special education (ECSE) joins Part C and section 619 of Part B of the Individuals with Disabilities Education Act. ECSE is a unified system of services for infants, toddlers, and preschool-age children with disabilities from birth to five inclusive.

Early childhood special education (ECSE) provides services for children under six years of age and their families, in response to disabilities or developmental delays in the children. These services usually are free of charge to the families, because federal and state governments fund ECSE programs in the hope that early assistance will alleviate the impact of disabilities, reduce developmental delays, and lessen children's needs for later services.

Chapter 2 introduces the ECSE field, explains the rationale for public support, outlines the services offered, sketches the demographics of the population served, discusses the different professions active in ECSE, and explores important issues of cultural diversity. The chapter concludes with a discussion of the roles played by federal, state, and local units of government, as well as by families.

EARLY INTERVENTION AND PRESCHOOL SPECIAL EDUCATION

early intervention refers to services for infants and toddlers, and their families, to address the special needs of very young children who have disabilities, have developmental delays, or are at risk of developmental delays. The term is used in Part C of the Individuals with Disabilities Education Act.

infants and toddlers refers to children before they reach the age of three. Infancy begins at birth and ends with the achievement of independent walking, while toddlers are young children who have begun walking but have not yet reached the age of three. Another commonly used way to refer to this population is "birth to two inclusive," which more directly incorporates the first thirty-six months of life.

Part C is the state-operated program created in 1986 for infants and toddlers with disabilities and their families. It is an early intervention program for children under three years of age and (with family concurrence) their families.

Early intervention refers to services provided for **infants and toddlers** and their families to address the special needs of very young children who have disabilities, have developmental delays, or are at risk of developmental delays. All states are serving infants and toddlers in the birth-to-thirty-six-month age range together with their families, under a federal program created in 1986. This program is **Part C** of the **Individuals with Disabilities Education Act (IDEA)**. The IDEA is the nation's foundation law on special education. Although all states provide services for infants and toddlers, the scope and breadth of services offered vary greatly. **Preschool special education** is special education and related services for three- to five-year-old children with disabilities, and in some states, developmental delays. All fifty

The family is the center of early childhood special education.

Individuals with Disabilities Education Act (IDEA) The IDEA is the landmark special education law in the United States. Formerly called the Education of the Handicapped Act, it includes (as Part B) PL 94–142, the Education for All Handicapped Children Act of 1975.

preschool special education refers to special education and related services to meet unique needs of three- to five-year-olds with disabilities and, in some states, developmental delays.

preschool-age children are children aged three to five inclusive. Most EC programs focus on this population.

Part B is the part of the IDEA describing how children with disabilities aged three to eighteen shall receive a free appropriate public education.

diagnosed conditions (established conditions) are disabilities or other health conditions recognized by a state as limiting or very likely to limit activities young children can do. The term is used in Part C of the IDEA.

developmental delays are lags in child development in any one or more of the five domains (cognitive, communication, physical, adaptive, social or emotional). How much of a lag constitutes a "delay" is to be defined by each state. The term is used in both Part C and in Part B of the Individuals with Disabilities Education Act, for section 619.

at risk is a term used to refer to infants or toddlers who do not exhibit developmental delays but who for biological and/or environmental reasons are more likely than most to develop such delays. The concept is used only in Part C of the IDEA.

states serve **preschool-age children** under a mandate laid down in section 619 of **Part B** of the IDEA, also enacted in 1986.

The IDEA offered financial incentives encouraging the fifty states, the District of Columbia, Puerto Rico, and other jurisdictions to serve the birth-to-five population of young children with disabilities. They were to do so by late 1991 (Part B) or no later than September 1994 (Part C). Although participation in both Part C and section 619 Part B programs is voluntary for states and other jurisdictions, nearly all eligible jurisdictions accepted the challenge. As they moved toward compliance, they tended to fashion a seamless system of services all the way from birth to age five, in effect meshing Part C and section 619 Part B. This creative, single-system approach borrowed provisions of each section in the federal law. The term ECSE covers this unified system of services for infants, toddlers, and preschool children with disabilities, throughout the birth-five age range. (**NOTE**: What is now Part C—Infants and Toddlers with Disabilities was known as Part H until 1997. Readers may encounter the latter term in other readings; just remind yourself that it is now Part C.)

Part C: Early Intervention

Part C requires participating states to provide infants and toddlers who have **diagnosed conditions**—disabilities limiting or very likely to limit activities these young children can do—and their families with early intervention services. Such conditions as deafness (the inability to understand speech through the ear alone) are disabilities. The law also requires that infants and toddlers with **developmental delays** receive early intervention services as needed. Such children may include those who have not begun talking, walking, or reaching other milestones at expected developmental stages. Part C permits, but does not require, states to provide early intervention services for infants and toddlers who are **at risk** of developmental delays or disabilities but do not display any actual delays or activity limitations.

A large and growing number of young children have disabilities or developmental delays or are at risk for such delays. *Starting Points*, a report issued in April 1994 by the Carnegie Corporation of New York, summarized the facts contributing to this growth:

> *Of the twelve million children under the age of three in the United States today, a staggering number are affected by one or more risk factors that undermine healthy development. One in four lives in poverty. One in four lives in a single-parent family. One in three victims of physical abuse is a baby under the age of one . . . More than half of mothers of children under the age of three work outside the home.* (p. xiii)

The report added that about one birth in every four is to an unmarried woman; every year, one million adolescents become pregnant. More than five million children under age three are cared for during the day by persons other than their parents, often in facilities and programs of low quality (Carnegie Corporation of New York, 1994).

Figure 2.1 offers the statutory definition of infants and toddlers with disabilities. Part C uses the term "infants and toddlers with disabilities" in a way that grants the states considerable flexibility in deciding which young children with disabilities qualify for services. The states may define such key terms as "developmental delay," "diagnosed conditions," and "at risk." To point out that states enjoy much flexibility in deciding what kinds of children to serve is notably not to say that state, county, local, and private Part C service providers may be selective in deciding which young children to serve. Federal law mandates that *all* infants

infants and toddlers with disabilities refers to those from birth to age two inclusive who need early intervention services because they are experiencing developmental delays in adaptive, cognitive, communication, physical, and/or social or emotional development; or because they have a diagnosed condition that has a high probability of resulting in developmental delay. The term may also include, at a state's discretion, at-risk children.

entitlement means that infants and toddlers must receive early intervention services if they satisfy state criteria. Similarly, three- to five-year-old children must receive free preschool services to meet their unique needs if they satisfy federal and/or state eligibility standards. (The term "zero reject" expresses a similar idea, namely, that no child who meets eligibility criteria may be denied services.)

individualized family service plan (IFSP) is a written document outlining services for infants and toddlers, and (if the families concur) their families. IFSPs note the infant's or toddler's development in five domains, services the child (and family) will receive, and similar information, as well as the service coordinator's name.

(1) The term **"infant or toddler with a disability"** (A) means an individual under 3 years of age who needs early intervention services because the individual (i) is experiencing developmental delays, as measured by appropriate diagnostic instruments and procedures in one or more of the areas of cognitive development, physical development, communication development, social or emotional development, and adaptive development; or (ii) has a diagnosed physical or mental condition which has a high probability of resulting in developmental delay; and (B) may also include, at a State's discretion, at-risk infants and toddlers (section 632(5); 34 CFR 303.16).

FIGURE 2.1 Infants and toddlers with disabilities

and toddlers who meet state criteria must receive services: Part C is an **entitlement** program.

The age range covered, "under 3 years of age," means the first thirty-six months after birth. The definition emphasizes that *only* infants and toddlers "who need early intervention services" must be served. That qualification is not as self-evident as it may seem; infants and toddlers who have developmental delays or diagnosed conditions or are at risk may not require early intervention services. To take an obvious example, most at-risk infants, toddlers, and preschoolers will develop normally without formal intervention (Campbell, 1991; Shonkoff & Meisels, 1991). To take another example, a toddler may have epilepsy, but unless the condition has noticeable effects on the child's daily activities, there may be no discernible need for early intervention services.

Early intervention services are to be outlined in an **individualized family service plan (IFSP)**. Figure 2.2 shows the contents of an IFSP. The plan is a written document that identifies the type of service coordination the family desires, any other early intervention services approved by the family, the name of the service coordinator, and a plan for transition from Part C to preschool Part B or other services. The law requires, in the words of the U.S. House of Representatives Committee on Education and Labor, that the parent or guardian "must be an integral member of the multidisciplinary team charged with developing the IFSP" (*House Report 102-198*, 1991, p. 18). The IFSP identifies the infant's or toddler's special needs, notes family resources and concerns, outlines services available, explains any fees (including sliding fee scales), specifies the outcomes or results expected, and shows how the transition to preschool special education or to other programs and services will occur.

The plan is to be reviewed twice annually with the family and evaluated at least once each year. Its contents must, by law, be "fully explained to the parents," in their native language, if necessary. The family may decline any service and may refuse to participate in an assessment of family resources, priorities, and concerns without jeopardizing its right to other services for the child or for the family itself.

Families have the right to early intervention services that will meet an eligible infant's or toddler's unique needs in any of five areas of development: adaptive, cognitive, communication, physical, and social or emotional. Early intervention services feature assistance for both the infant or toddler and the family. Included by law are such direct services as special instruction for the infant or toddler; physical, occupational, or speech and language therapy; and psychological services, such as diagnosis, assessment, and mental health interventions. Services for the family include family counseling, training of family members in meeting the

(1) the infant or toddler's present levels of performance (e.g., needs) in five domains

(2) the family's resources, priorities, and concerns

(3) outcomes to be achieved

(4) early intervention services to be provided

(5) natural environment

(6) start date and duration of services

(7) service coordinator's name

(8) transition steps at about age three

FIGURE 2.2 Individualized family service plan (based on IDEA section 636)

needs of the infant or toddler, psychological services, social work services, and service coordination (case management) services.

Most early intervention services are not instructional but rather are similar to what special educators call "related services." In education—whether preschool, elementary, or secondary—the emphasis is on special education, with related services playing an important but supportive role. Those roles are reversed in early intervention. That is, the stress in early intervention is on **supports** designed to empower the family so that it functions more effectively on behalf of the infant or toddler. Supports are links to community resources, neighbors, and friends to whom the family may turn when in need.

supports are links to neighbors, friends, and community resources upon which the family may rely in times of need. Supports may empower the family so it functions more effectively on behalf of the infant or toddler.

Interdisciplinary service delivery is essential to successful early intervention and preschool special education.

These services for infants or toddlers and their families must meet state standards, including the licensing or certification of the early intervention specialists providing the services, as well as the licensing or other approval of caregiver facilities and programs. The services are usually free to the parents, although sliding-scale and other fee-for-services arrangements are allowed under Part C where authorized by other federal or state laws. Third-party insurance companies, for example, may pay for ECSE-related services. Parents enjoy the right to choose among state-approved options for early intervention. As noted, parents may decline any particular early intervention service; they may even decline all services. Some parents do exactly that, much to the consternation of early intervention professionals (Minke & Scott, 1993). The law also grants to parents specific due-process rights, including the right to appeal any adverse decision in case of disagreements between the family and the agency providing the services.

Early intervention services are specially designed to meet the unique needs of the infants and toddlers. Services not connected to the disability, delay, or at-risk status need not be provided. The House committee report accompanying what became the 1991 amendments to the IDEA noted, "[S]ervices that a family may need, but do not relate to the developmental needs of the infant or toddler with a disability, are not early intervention services" (*House Report 102-198*, 1991, p. 14). Such services may, however, be listed in the IFSP if doing so may help the family. An obvious example is routine medical care for the child and the family.

According to the *Twentieth Annual Report*, most states served about 1.65 percent of their birth-to-two-inclusive populations under Part C, with some states serving more than 2 percent (U.S. Department of Education, 1998). The most frequently provided services were, in order, special instruction, family training, counseling, and home visits. Other common services were speech therapy and social work. Much less frequent were respite care, nutrition services, and audiology (U.S. Department of Education, 1998, Table AH2, p. A229–231). The department's *Annual Reports* are a major source of information about special education in the United States. Each year, these reports provide statistical and other data about the field.

Section 619, Part B: Preschool Special Education

Another section of the IDEA authorizes **special education**—specially designed instruction—and **related services**—support services such as transportation, therapy, counseling, and the like—for **children with disabilities** who are in the three-to-five age range. A different definition is used for these preschoolers. As Figure 2.3 illustrates, Part B makes no provision for services for at-risk children. Notice that children, to be eligible, must "need special education and related services."

Special education and related services are to be provided by local education agencies (LEAs) free of charge to the family, although LEAs may impose incidental fees that are also charged to families of nondisabled children. The families enjoy due-process rights in any dispute with LEAs; these rights are very similar to those in Part C. Part B guarantees a free, appropriate public education regardless of the severity of a disability. In the classic case of *Timothy W. v. Rochester School District* (1989), a federal court of appeals affirmed the right of a young boy in New England to receive Part B services despite very severe and multiple disabilities that local education officials contended rendered him virtually uneducable. The IDEA is clear, the court ruled, in granting Timothy—and all other children with

special education is specially designed instruction to meet the unique needs of the child. The term is used in Part B of the IDEA.

related services are noninstructional support services such as transportation, therapy, and counseling. The term is used in Part B of the IDEA.

children with disabilities refers to children who meet the criteria in IDEA section 602(3), notably that they have a recognized disability and for that reason need special education and related services.

(A) "Child with a disability" means a child
   (i) with
      [1] mental retardation
      [2] hearing impairments, including deafness
      [3] speech or language impairments
      [4] visual impairments, including blindness
      [5] emotional disturbance
      [6] orthopedic impairments
      [7] autism
      [8] traumatic brain injury
      [9] other health impairments, or
    [10] specific learning disabilities; and
   (ii) who, by reason thereof needs special education and related services.

(B) The term 'child with a disability' for a child aged 3 through 9 may, at the discretion of the State and the local education agency, include a child
   (i) experiencing developmental delays, as defined by the State and as measured by appropriate diagnostic instruments and procedures, in one or more of the following areas: physical development, cognitive development, communication development, social or emotional development, or adaptive development; and
   (ii) who, by reason thereof, needs special education and related services (section 602[3]); 34 CFR 300.7).

FIGURE 2.3 Preschool-age children with disabilities

Preschool services include "special education" and "related services" designed to meet each child's unique needs.

disabilities—an unequivocal right to an education (*Timothy W. v. Rochester [NH] School District*, 875 F.2d 954 [1st Cir. 1989] cert. denied 110 S. Ct. 519).

The term "special education" is defined in the IDEA using words that distinguish it from early intervention:

> *602(25) "special education" means specially designed instruction, at no cost to parents or guardians, to meet the unique needs of a child with a disability, including—(A) instruction conducted in the classroom, in the home, in hospitals and institutions, and in other settings; and (B) instruction in physical education.*

Special education contrasts with general, or regular, education in that it is "specially designed" to "meet the unique needs of a child with a disability." To stretch the point, special education could be compared to custom-designed production, general education to mass-production manufacturing. Children with disabilities often receive general education along with children who have no disabilities in addition to special education.

The term "related services" is also defined in the IDEA. The term is used only with reference to Part B, not to Part C:

> *602(22) "related services" means transportation, and such developmental, corrective and other supportive services (including speech pathology and audiology services, psychological services, physical and occupational therapy, recreation, including therapeutic recreation and social work services, and medical and counseling services, including rehabilitation counseling, except that such medical services shall be for diagnostic and evaluation purposes only) as may be required to assist a child with a disability to benefit from special education, and includes the early identification and assessment of disabling conditions in children.*

That is, related services are supportive services that "may be required to assist a child with a disability to benefit from special education." Notable here is the word "benefit": Only those related services that are necessary for a child to benefit from special education need be provided. Related services that might help a child but are not necessary for the child to benefit from special education are not required. In addition, related services that might help a child to excel in school are not required under Part B. Some examples of related services are speech and language pathology services, physical and occupational therapy, transportation between the child's home and the building in which preschool services are provided, and counseling.

This definition requires, as does Part C, that programs "meet the standards of the state" agency with jurisdiction, in this case, the state education agency. States retain authority to set personnel and program standards.

Special education and related services for preschool children appear in an **individualized education program (IEP)**. The IEP is a written document that identifies the unique needs of the child, the special education and related services to meet those unique needs, annual goals and short-term objectives, the way in which the child's progress will be assessed, the date of initiation of services, and the projected duration of those services. The contents of an IEP are given in Figure 2.4.

Section 619 of Part B guarantees the preschool child with a disability the provision of **appropriate** services designed to meet his unique needs. The law considers "appropriate" to mean that the services satisfy state standards and meet the child's needs. The statutory language in section 602 is as follows:

> *"free appropriate public education" means special education and related services that—(A) have been provided at public expense, under public supervision and direction, and without*

individualized education program (IEP) is a written document that identifies the unique needs of the child, the special education and related services needed to meet those unique needs, annual goals and short-term objectives, how the child's progress will be assessed, the date of initiation of services and the projected duration of those services. The term is used in Part B of the IDEA.

section 619 of Part B of the IDEA authorizes preschool special education and related services for children from three to five inclusive.

appropriate is a term used both in Part C and in Part B of the IDEA, but it is not defined precisely in the statute. It appears to mean "meets the standards of the State" and "meets the unique needs of the child."

(1) the child's present levels of educational performance (e.g., needs), including how the child's disability affects participation in appropriate preschool activities

(2) annual goals for meeting all needs of the child

(3) services to be provided

(4) extent to which the child will participate with nondisabled children

(5) start date and duration of services; expected frequency and location of those services

(6) how the child's parents will be informed of progress

FIGURE 2.4 Individualized education program (based on IDEA section 602)

charge; (B) meet the standards of the State education agency; (C) include an appropriate preschool, elementary, or secondary school education in the State involved; and (D) are provided in conformity with the individualized education program required under section 614(d).

The term "appropriate" never has been statutorily defined, other than that an appropriate education meets state standards. A 1982 Supreme Court decision held that an "appropriate" education provides just enough to enable a child (in that case, Amy Rowley, a deaf student) to "benefit," that is, to achieve passing marks and be promoted from grade to grade (*Board of Education, Hendrick Hudson School District v. Rowley, 1982*).

The *Nineteenth Annual Report* indicated that all fifty states, plus the District of Columbia, had in place zero-reject, full-service mandates for preschool-age children with disabilities by the 1994–1995 school year. The report added that most preschool programs operated on an academic year calendar, whereas most early intervention programs run year-round. However, the report said, more and more states were adopting seamless systems in which services for three- to-five-year-old children were being designed more like services for birth-to-two-year-olds.

Rationale For ECSE

There are four bases for ECSE services, according to Dr. Lisbeth Vincent, who testified before the U.S. House of Representatives Committee on Education and Labor in 1986 as president of the Division for Early Childhood (DEC) of the Council for Exceptional Children (CEC) (Vincent, 1986, p. 341–361). These same considerations may also justify preschool special education. The first rationale, Vincent said, is the hope that by intervening early, parents and professionals may *ameliorate,* or *even eliminate, disabling conditions* in very young children. The children may have much brighter prospects for K–12 education and beyond when ECSE succeeds in its mission. The second basis is the hope that ECSE, while often expensive, may *reduce or eliminate the need for later, even costlier services.* Evidence on these two rationales is not yet conclusive (Guralnick, 1991). Some data suggest that the long-term effects of ECSE may be minimal, especially for infants and toddlers who have severe disabilities (White, 1990, 1993). Similarly, evidence that taxpayers will save money in the long run because of ECSE programs is not yet compelling.

The third rationale for ECSE is that *families receive needed support* and other services; in other words, services produce benefits not only for the child but also for the family. Finally, Vincent argued, *families function better* in their communities and make more positive contributions to community well-being when they are freed from the time-consuming and demanding task of taking care of a vulnerable child. They have more time for both work and leisure. Vincent concluded, "Families of these children report reduced stress and better community integration as a result of early intervention" (Vincent, 1986, p. 350).

Other rationales for ECSE are readily stated. The widely publicized study *Adult Literacy in America* (Kirsch, Jungeblut, Jenkins, & Kolstad, 1993), conducted for the U.S. Department of Education by the Educational Testing Service (ETS) of Princeton, New Jersey, found that illiteracy was twice as common among adults with disabilities as among nondisabled adults. Fully 26 percent of all adults performing at the lowest level on the ETS prose scale reported having physical, mental, or health conditions that prevented them from working or performing other daily activities (Kirsch et al., 1993, p. 17–18). Stated the report, "Without exception, adults with any type of disability, difficulty, or illness were more likely than those in the total population to perform in the lowest literacy levels" (p. 43). Addressing these problems requires that intervention begin early, and that it be intensive. This evidence argues for ECSE services to be widely available.

Similarly, the U.S. Department of Education, in its *Fifteenth Annual Report* (1993b), noted high dropout rates, low levels of employment, low wages, little postsecondary education, and low levels of independence in everyday living among youth with disabilities who were two years or more removed from school. The National Longitudinal Transition Survey (NLTS) findings discussed in the report were consistent with those in the two previous annual reports as well: There is a long-standing problem of underachievement among youth and young adults with disabilities. Again, to reduce dropout rates, increase rates of postsec-

Joint family-staff planning is a key element in the development of IFSPs and IEPs.

ondary program participation, raise employment levels and wages, and enhance individual independence in the community, it is essential for intervention to begin early and to be intensive.

WHAT IS ECSE?

seamless system is a term referring to a set of services that has no gaps or delays between Part C early intervention and Part B preschool services or other pre-kindergarten programs.

interdisciplinary services are services provided by specialists from different disciplines working together on a team (e.g., early childhood special educators and speech pathologists). The term contrasts with services that are provided by professionals representing only one discipline (*uni*disciplinary). The term *multi*disciplinary most often refers to a team (including family members) that plans and conducts assessments or evaluations. These terms are used most often in Part C of the IDEA. The term *trans*disciplinary refers to an approach in which the often artificial boundaries between disciplines or professions are transcended or ignored so as to deliver "holistic" services to a child and/or a family.

When states design seamless systems to serve the entire birth-to-five range of children with disabilities, they usually adopt a *developmental* approach emphasizing services that help infants, toddlers, and young children with disabilities to achieve developmental milestones at the earliest possible age. A **seamless system** has no gaps or delays between Part C early intervention and Part B preschool services or other prekindergarten programs. The developmental approach seeks to avoid labeling the infant, toddler, or young child. Rather, the child's strengths and needs are identified in the five developmental areas (cognitive, physical, communication, social or emotional, and adaptive). **Interdisciplinary services**—services offered by professionals from different disciplines working together on a team—are provided to meet the child's special needs and to promote the child's development. Other supports and services help families to respond more effectively to their young child's unique needs. Extensive parental input helps in designing all these services.

These characteristics of ECSE reflect what model programs serving infants, toddlers, and preschool-age children with disabilities have demonstrated. Since 1969, the federal government has sponsored dozens of model programs, experimenting with a variety of child and family services. The federal mandates now in effect emerged only after more than twenty-five years of experience with model programs showed that services for very young children with disabilities could help not only the infant, toddler, or preschooler in question but the family and society as well.

The IDEA allows states under certain circumstances to use elements of Part C to serve preschoolers and elements of Part B to serve infants and toddlers. These flexible statutory provisions have proven extremely helpful to states that wanted to create seamless systems of services. For example, as already noted, states may amend their definitions of the term "children with disabilities" to include three- to five-year-olds with developmental delays.

The 1991 IDEA amendments allow states to use IFSPs (rather than IEPs) to outline services for three- to five-year-olds. The major stipulation is that the IFSPs so used must contain all of the required elements of the IEP under Part B. As may be seen by examining Figures 2.2 and 2.4, the IEP refers to "educational" needs (the IFSP does not) and reporting about outcomes, while the IFSP includes the name of the service coordinator (the IEP does not).

The same amendments authorize states to do the obverse: They may use IEPs to serve two-year-olds who will turn three during an academic year. Again, any IEP so used must contain all the elements required of an IFSP. Notably, that includes services for families as well as for children, a statement (if authorized by the family) of family priorities and needs and a multidisciplinary assessment of the unique strengths and needs of the child being served.

Taken together, the effect of these statutory provisions is to authorize states to make Part C and section 619 Part B services more similar, and thus more seamless. That goal is clearly easiest to achieve in those states in which the state education agency (SEA) is also the Part C lead agency. Even states having other agencies as lead agencies for early intervention can use the law's flexibility to eliminate unnecessary barriers, gaps, and duplication of services.

WHO ARE THE CHILDREN BEING SERVED?

Although all fifty states serve infants, toddlers, and preschool-age children with disabilities under the IDEA, not all have comprehensive reporting mechanisms in place. The most recent figures show that 746,000 children from birth to age five received public services as of December 1995. Of that number, 187,000 were infants and toddlers from birth to age thirty-six months (1.65 percent of all infants and toddlers in the United States). By comparison, 559,000 three- to five-year-olds (4.6 percent of all children in that age range) received preschool special education services that year, a much higher proportion (U.S. Department of Education, 1998, Tables AA1 and AH1).

It is important to note that the U.S. Department of Education's annual reports explain very little about these children. No information is provided, for example, about what disabilities they had, nor about developmental delays. The *Nineteenth Annual Report* offered no clues about sex, race, ethnic group membership, family socioeconomic status (SES), urban or rural residence, or other characteristics of the children. It also contained no data on children not being served. Unless and until the states report such information to the department, we will not know much more about the birth-to-five population of children with disabilities or developmental delays than what has appeared in recent *Annual Reports*. The National Early Intervention Longitudinal Study (NEILS), a new study, being conducted by SRI International, may contribute important knowledge about the population. The final report of the project was not available at the time this book was being published. Readers may wish to log onto www.sri.com to view the latest reports on this important study.

Early Intervention

Three categories of infants and toddlers are recognized in Part C. The first is that of developmental delays. The law calls for these delays to be "measured by appropriate diagnostic instruments and procedures" and states that they may occur in one or more of five areas of development: cognitive, physical, communication, social or emotional, and adaptive.

All participating states serve infants and toddlers with developmental delays, and the IDEA requires each state to define what it means by a "developmental delay." As of late 1992, states continued to show a remarkable diversity of opinion on this matter (Shackelford, 1992). Some used a percentage formula, in which delay was expressed in terms of a difference between what a child is doing and what typical children usually do at the same age. A common formula called for demonstration of a 25 percent delay, as measured by some objective measure or test. Other states preferred to use standard deviation-based formulas, declaring as eligible infants and toddlers who scored two or more standard deviations below the mean in one or more areas of development. In statistics, the distance of a score from a group mean is expressed in terms of standard deviations; in a normal distribution, for example, about 2.5 percent of individuals taking a test would score two or more standard deviations below the mean. However, assessment of developmental delays in infants and toddlers is not as simple or straightforward as might appear from this brief discussion.

The second category of infants and toddlers recognized in Part C "have a diagnosed physical or mental condition which has a high probability of resulting in developmental delay." All states participating in Part C serve infants and toddlers with established (diagnosed) conditions. Established conditions are diagnoses known typically to result in developmental delay. While states differ as to which conditions they recognize as "established"

(Shackelford, 1992; Shonkoff & Meisels, 1991), most list Down syndrome, fragile X syndrome, and similar chromosomal disorders; sensory disorders such as deafness or blindness; and neuromuscular disorders such as cerebral palsy. By law, infants and toddlers are eligible for services if their condition appears in a state's plan, whether or not a delay is present, because these conditions typically result in delays.

Finally, the law allows, but does not require, a state to serve infants and toddlers who have no developmental delays and no diagnosed conditions but who are, nonetheless, at risk as defined by that state. During the early years of implementation of Part C, many states expressed enthusiasm about serving the at-risk population. When the Carolina Policy Studies Program analyzed state plans as of December 1989, for example, it found that more than half the thirty-nine state plans studied included provisions for serving at-risk infants and toddlers (Harbin, Gallagher, & Terry, 1991). Three years later, however, only thirteen states still planned to serve at-risk children (Shackelford, 1992). Many expressed concern about the cost of serving these children. By 1997, just six states served at-risk infants and toddlers (Eaton, 1997).

Preschool Special Education

The IDEA states that three- to five-year-old children are eligible for services if they have one of the following ten recognized disabilities: "mental retardation, hearing impairments including deafness, speech or language impairments, visual impairments including blindness, serious emotional disturbance, orthopedic impairments, autism, traumatic brain injury, other health impairments, and specific learning disabilities." Children having one or more of these conditions are eligible for preschool special education if they also "by reason thereof need special education and related services."

Children become eligible for section 619 preschool special education services "upon their third birthday" (Schrag, 1990c). Children who turn three during an academic year may, however, receive preschool special education services before their third birthday. Preschool programs usually serve children until they enter K–12 programs, or until about age six.

The IDEA allows states and other jurisdictions to amend their definitions for three- to five-year-olds to encompass children who need special education and related services because of developmental delays in one or more of the five areas of development listed under Part C. This flexibility allows states to continue serving developmentally disabled children

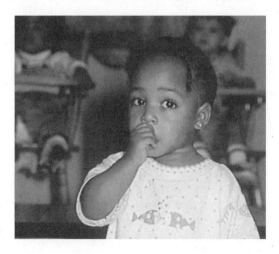

The critical question: "What is 'appropriate' for each individual child?"

Westwood Early Learning Center, in the Woodstock, Illinois, school district, serves three- to six-year-old children in sixteen kindergarten sections, six sections of ECSE, four sections for at-risk children, and one "developmental first grade." All children take part in all special activities, including puppet shows and visits from local firefighters. Young children with disabilities attend regular kindergarten for half the day and ECSE programs during the other half. According to Heckman and Rike (1994), such dual placement works because of continual communication between ECSE and kindergarten staff.

ECSE teachers offer tutoring, skill instruction, and confidence building to children with special needs who are dually placed. Heckman and Rike reported that all Westwood teachers have a better understanding of the knowledge and skills needed for successful mainstreaming after five years' experience integrating children with special needs. Teachers refer children for special education only when their needs demand a more intensive intervention than is provided in the integrated settings. The fact that sixteen kindergarten settings are available means that children with special needs may be distributed equally among all kindergarten classes. Materials and equipment are available to all staff on an equitable basis.

—Adapted from Heckman and Rike (1994)

FIGURE 2.5 One program's story

---

preschool child with a disability is a three- to six-year-old child who has one of the disabilities recognized under the IDEA. The term is used in some states to avoid the need to label a child prior to elementary school. (Preschool age begins at three and ends when the child enters kindergarten or first grade, usually at about age six.)

who remain in need of special services. Many states take advantage of this flexibility to create a catch-all category, **preschool child with a disability**, thus avoiding the need for labels with these young children. Children aged three to five who are at risk, however, are not eligible for services under section 619.

Cultural Diversity Among Children

As noted earlier, the U.S. Department of Education's annual reports have not offered data on the ethnic or racial minority group membership, socioeconomic status (SES), or other diversity indicators among children receiving early intervention or preschool special education. The U.S. Census Bureau's 1991–1992 study of families with children under six described in Chapter 11 did comment on these characteristics; however, that study did not report specifically on children being served under the IDEA.

The U.S. Department of Education has published some data on cultural diversity among older children with disabilities. The *Fourteenth Annual Report,* for example, included information from the NLTS on thirteen- to twenty-one-year-olds in special education. The NLTS found that 24 percent of youth in special education programs were African American, compared with 12 percent in general education. That is, the percentage of African American youth with disabilities was twice as high as the percentage of African Americans in the general population (*Fourteenth Annual Report,* 1992c, p. 15). Similarly, U.S. Census Bureau figures show that disability is 60 percent more common among African American adults than among white or Hispanic American adults; severe disability, meanwhile, is twice as common among African American adults as among white or Hispanic American adults (Bennefield & McNeil, 1989; Bowe, 1985a, b).

Other data suggest that infants, toddlers, and preschoolers from low-SES and minority families are more likely to be disabled or to show developmental delays than are children from higher-SES families. ECSE programs may serve populations that are between one-quarter and one-third minority even in geographical areas that are not ethnically diverse (Brinker, Frazier, & Baxter, 1992). Of course, in some localities, the percentages will be far higher; in a presentation to a 1989 conference of the National Alliance of Black School Educators, for example, Ruth Love reported an 85 percent rate of African American group membership in special education classes in Chicago (cited in National Council on Disability, 1993a, p. 20).

Our knowledge about what causes disability is limited. In many instances, we cannot identify any specific cause for birth defects or other congentital conditions. We do know that biology and ecology interact to produce disabilities and developmental delays. A landmark study in Norway (Lie, Wilcox, & Skjerven, 1994), for example, investigated the prevalence of birth defects among the second-born children of 371,933 women who had already given birth to a child with a disability. Women who moved between the births of their first and second children were far less likely to have second-born children with birth defects than were women who did not move. The findings strongly suggest that environment plays a role in producing birth defects.

But what environmental factors? Was there something about the neighborhoods in which they lived or about the areas where they worked? Did whatever environmental factors were involved act directly, or did they interact in some way with genetic factors? The research does not tell us. What we do know, from other studies, is that a family's SES, access to health care, and related characteristics are strongly correlated to disability and developmental delay in young children.

The connections between minority group status and disability in early childhood are many and complex. However strong they may appear on the surface, these relationships are better understood as relations between disability and family SES rather than between disability and ethnic or racial minority group status per se. In America today, minority group members are, on the whole, less well represented in higher-SES groups than are majority group members. Their overall lower standard of living compared with that of majority families is more directly linked to disability than is race itself (Bowe, 1985a, b).

Household incomes of families having members with disabilities are on average much lower than those of families with no disabled members. According to the NLTS, 57 percent of African American youth, 49 percent of Hispanic American youth, and 25 percent of white youth with disabilities live in families with household incomes below $15,000. In each case, the proportions reported were much higher than those for youth with no disabilities (*Fourteenth Annual Report,* 1992c, p. 15). U.S. Census Bureau data show that almost 50 percent of all African American adults with disabilities live in households with incomes below the poverty line (Bowe, 1985a). However, it is important not to over-state the case. Disability respects no economic nor social-class barriers. It can, and does, occur at all income and social levels.

Similar relationships between family income, racial, and ethnic minority status, and disability likely occur with respect to preschool-age children. When more complete national data on early intervention and preschool special education program participants become available, they will probably show above-average representation from minority and low-SES households. Disability is both a cause and effect of poverty. When a child has a disability, one adult member of the household often gives up, or sharply curtails, employment to provide care, thus lowering household income. Lower income in turn limits access to health care. Poorer families with sick children delay medical treatment longer than do wealthier families, both because medical care is expensive and because caregivers often are less accessible for poorer than for wealthier families. Delay in treatment may cause a condition to worsen into a disability (Bowe, 1985a).

Low-SES families are much more likely than middle- or upper-SES families to have children with serious pre-, peri-, or postnatal conditions. They are, in general, more susceptible to malnutrition, which exposes young children to viral and bacterial illness (Bowman, 1992). If these families, for reasons beyond their control, delay medical intervention, these viral, bacterial, and other insults are more likely to lead to permanent conditions (Bowe, 1985a, b). That is, low-SES families generally receive less adequate and less immediate medical care than middle-class families do; for these reasons, childhood illnesses and accidents that are treated without lasting effects in middle-class children often lead to more permanent conditions in children from lower-SES homes.

To illustrate, if a young upper- or middle-class child were to contract measles, the family would be likely to seek immediate medical intervention to bring down the child's temperature promptly. A lower-SES family in the same situation might not be able to afford such medical attention, or might not get to a doctor until days or weeks later. By that time, the high temperatures might have damaged critical nerves, leading, for example, to deafness. One report estimated that exposure to such viruses results in 2.7 times more incidents of school failure among children and youth from lower-SES families than among children from higher-SES families (Harnshaw et al., 1976).

Steven Parker, M.D., director of the Developmental Assessment Clinic at Boston University's School of Medicine, articulated a concept of "double jeopardy" that helps to explain these phenomena (Parker, Greer, & Zuckerman, 1988). His analysis emphasizes that *both* biological and environmental factors, acting together, place low-SES individuals, including many from minority groups, at greater risk for disability and developmental delay. Kaplan-Sanoff, Parker, and Zuckerman (1991, p. 68) summarized their views in these words:

> *Children living in poverty experience double jeopardy. First, they are more frequently exposed to risks for achieving optimal development such as medical illnesses, family stress, inadequate social support, and parental depression. Second, they experience more serious consequences from these risks than do children from higher socioeconomic status (SES).*

While few national figures on minority group members in ECSE programs are yet available, individual program data often are. These reports feature the expected higher prevalence of disability and developmental delay in low-SES, minority families. They also show that ECSE professionals must design outreach and recruitment programs with cultural diversity in mind. Ruth Rucker, director of the Edward C. Mazique Parent Child Center in Washington, D.C., told the U.S. Senate that recruitment of personnel from minority group backgrounds

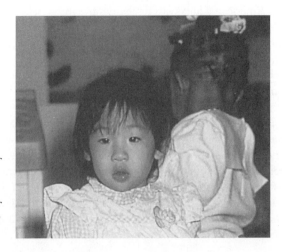

Many experts believe a disproportionate number of children in need of early childhood special education services are members of ethnic and/or racial minority groups.

was a top priority for programs like hers. She urged the Congress to "ensure meaningful involvement of traditionally underserved groups, including low-SES families and families of color, in planning and implementation of the Part H system, and to ensure that these families have access to culturally competent services within their local areas" (Rucker, 1991).

Emily Arcia, of Duke University, then at the Carolina Policy Studies Project, suggested that low-SES families are particularly likely to underutilize services such as those offered by ECSE programs (Arcia & Gallagher, 1993; Arcia, Keyes, Gallagher, & Herrick, 1992, 1993). The experience of the Institute for the Study of Developmental Disabilities at the University of Chicago illustrates Arcia's concerns. The Institute has run an Early Childhood Research and Intervention Program in downtown Chicago for more than twenty-five years. Yet until it mounted a sustained incentives program to attract minority families in the early 1990s, it served mostly white, middle-class suburban families who commuted from outlying areas. When the institute launched its incentive program, which included measures designed to meet the special needs of minority families, significantly more low-SES and minority families responded. Notably, the institute also began seeing infants and toddlers exposed prenatally to illegal drugs, a group it rarely had seen before because the mothers did not seek services for the infants (Brinker et al., 1992).

Cultural Competence

As it is practiced today, ECSE stresses close relations between professionals and parents. Those ties are most readily established and maintained when professionals are sensitive to cultural differences (Sontag & Schacht, 1994). Positioned on nearby pages are suggestions on cultural competence (Figures 2.6 to 2.10). These offer ideas about cultural competence in

General Principles

1. Program administrators, interventionists, teachers, and aides should reflect upon their own cultural heritages and upon their beliefs about people of other cultures. Such self-awareness is a critical first step toward becoming culturally competent.

2. Program staff should make a priority of assessing every aspect of the program for possible cultural insensitivity. For example, do IFSP and IEP meetings always start at the scheduled time, or is flexibility allowed in respect for cultural differences about time? Members of families might be asked to review all aspects of a program in order to suggest areas in need of improvement.

3. Programs should place emphasis upon recruiting and retaining a culturally diverse staff. The "feeling" families get about programs often has its roots in the kinds of people family members see when they visit the program. Similarly, a culturally diverse staff is more capable than is a culturally monotonous staff of keeping everyone aware of cultural sensitivities.

4. Programs serving children with disabilities should recognize that disability is perhaps *the* key cultural variable. Do all staff members use sensitive language in talking about disabilities? Does the agency take affirmative steps to employ and retain staff members who themselves have disabilities?

FIGURE 2.6 Cultural competence I

African Americans

1. Expressive communication for many African Americans is not exclusively verbal; rather, bodily movements convey considerable meaning. Many whites, by contrast, will "let the words speak for themselves."

   Professionals should be alert to nonverbal messages and respond appropriately to them.

2. Some African Americans consider time to begin when all expected people have arrived rather than on some preset schedule.

   Professionals in ECSE programs may show respect for this cultural tenet by beginning IFSP and IEP meetings when all invited individuals have assembled. At the same time, professionals might advise family members that agencies are under pressure from funding sources to adhere at times to a more strict sense of time (e.g., because staff members' time is billed by the hour).

3. In some African American families, government is seen as existing to serve citizens. Thus, there may be a readiness to refer children for services because the family feels entitled to them.

   If they believe underreferral is happening, as it often does (Arcia, Keyes, Gallagher, & Herrick, 1992), professionals should talk with family members to discover what is preventing referral. It may be that other pressures on the family (e.g., lack of available transportation, lack of available home child care, and so on) are causing the family not to refer a child for services.

FIGURE 2.7 Cultural competence II

cultural competence (cultural sensitivity) refers to the skill and knowledge of ECSE workers in relating to family members from different ethnic, racial, and cultural groups.

general and with respect to particular minority groups. Although these figures may be helpful, the overriding principle in cultural sensitivity is to recognize that people are *individuals:* Not all members of a racial or cultural minority will display all, or even many, of the beliefs or behaviors illustrated in these figures. Additional information is widely available (e.g., Appl, 1996; Chen, Brekken, & Chan, 1997; Garcia & McLaughlin, 1995; Little Soldier, 1992; Ross, 1995) and should be consulted. The issue of **cultural competence** or cultural sensitivity is particularly pressing with respect to African American, Hispanic American, Asian American, and Native American children and their families. Outreach to and recruitment of families are more likely to be effective when program staff are members of the same ethnic and racial minority groups as the families and thus understand implicitly their cultural values and accepted norms of behavior. When ECSE program staff are either themselves members of racial and ethnic minority groups or have been trained to exhibit culturally sensitive behavior, parents of minority children with disabilities are more likely to establish a rapport and cooperate with ECSE service programs over extended periods of time. Minority representation on program staff also provides the children with more suitable role models than otherwise would be the case. For all these reasons, recruitment and retention on program staff of professionals, paraprofessionals, support personnel, and clerical staff who are personally and/or professionally familiar with minority group dynamics are important (Brockenbrough, 1991; Ford, 1992; Sontag & Schacht, 1994).

Despite these benefits for programs, the reality is that the number of African American staff in the public school system, already low, is declining, which suggests serious ECSE

Latino and Hispanic Americans

1. Recognize that in many Latino and Hispanic American families, the family itself—not government agencies, nor social service agencies, nor "experts"—is the primary support system. Thus, Latino and Hispanic families may be reluctant to identify children for, and refer children to, agencies for services. This may help to account for the underrepresentation of disability among people of Hispanic origin that is so often reported (e.g., Bowe, 1985a; Bowe, 1994). The family may regard disability as a private, personal matter, one not suitable for outside intervention.

   Early interventionists and preschool special educators may respect this cultural tenet by empowering the family to better serve its own members. This may mean offering information and teaching therapeutic techniques. Similarly, a professional may respond to this belief by spending the time necessary to get to know—and be known by—the family, thus becoming trusted as someone who will help the family, rather than someone who seeks to take the problem from the family. In time, this may make the family more amenable to referring the child for services.

2. Some Latino and Hispanic American families place more emphasis upon interpersonal and intergroup cooperation than upon competition.

   Professionals working in ECSE settings can show that they understand and accept this cultural belief. Certainly, early intervention and preschool programs, too, seek to foster cooperation and only rarely feature competition.

3. In many Latino and Hispanic American families, time is considered to begin when all expected people have arrived for the event.

   Early intervention and preschool special education professionals should demonstrate that they understand and value this belief by, for example, not starting a team meeting until all invited family members are present. Professionals should also help family members understand that organizations often have a different view of time (due, for example, to the fact that fees are billed on an hourly basis).

4. Some Latino and Hispanic American individuals view people as being more important than the tasks those people perform. Thus, they would not favor even temporary sacrifices to someone's well-being for the sake of timely completion of a task.

   This is not a belief that contradicts philosophical tenets characteristic of ECSE programs. While many early intervention and preschool special education staff members keep long hours on occasion, they usually agree quite readily that this should not be the case except during emergencies.

Figure 2.8 Cultural competence III

shortages as well. Just 12.5 percent of public school teachers in 1980 were members of a minority group (American Association of Colleges of Teacher Education, 1988). Although one study found that fully 20 percent of special education majors were minority group members (twice as many as were majors in general education), even that proportion would not suffice to bring diversity to special education. That is because some one-third of all special education students are minority group members (American Association of Colleges of Teacher Education, 1988). Public school teachers are even less likely to be members of ethnic

Asian Americans

1. Aversion of eye gaze is a signal of respect for many Asian Americans. By keeping their eyes down, they convey modesty.

   The early interventionist or preschool special educator might say to the child: "Thank you for that indication of respect. I appreciate it. In my classroom, however, eye contact is important to me. It is not a sign of disrespect. Rather, it helps me by giving me clues as to how well you are understanding the lesson. So, while you are in my classroom, please do maintain eye contact with me."

2. In some Asian American families, especially those of Korean background, the family as a whole (which may well be an extended family) is the decision- making body.

   ECSE staff can show they respect this cultural value by not pressing parents for immediate decisions. Rather, accept as necessary a delay in decision making while the extended family is consulted.

3. Silence does not mean agreement for many Asian Americans. Rather, silence may indicate, "I understand your point, and at the appropriate time, I will respond to it."

   ECSE professionals need to avoid assuming that Asian American family members have consented to a course of action until an explicit statement to that effect is made by family members.

4. For some Asian American families, especially those of Japanese origin, stoic acceptance of fate may be important. Loss of face must be avoided whenever possible.

   For these reasons, some Asian American families may avoid referral of "problems" to agencies. ECSE workers should seek to convey an attitude of acceptance of disability (e.g., that no shame is associated with it).

FIGURE 2.9 Cultural competence IV

and racial minority groups today than in the past, according to a number of recent studies (Education Commission of the States, 1989; Gay, 1989; National Clearinghouse for Professions in Special Education, 1988). In part, these findings reflect greater career opportunities for minority-group members generally, as a result of which many pursue higher-paying, higher-status jobs than are offered by social service agencies, public schools, and family service organizations.

By the year 2000, as few as 5 percent of all public school teachers may come from minority groups—while minority enrollments in the schools continue to rise (Ford, 1992). Similar concerns may emerge in ECSE programs. As yet, the trend is uncertain because the U.S. Department of Education's reports have not indicated the racial and ethnic group membership of ECSE workers throughout the nation.

WHO ARE THE WORKERS IN THE FIELD?

According to the U.S. Department of Education's *Nineteenth Annual Report* (1997) substantial demand exists for ECSE workers, especially occupational therapists. The report found that there is also a great need for early intervention workers and preschool special education

Native Americans

1. Programs serving members of Native American (e.g., American Indian) populations need to recognize that disability occurs at very high rates on many reservations. Especially common are fetal alcohol syndrome (FAS) and fetal alcohol effect (FAE) due to heavy maternal drinking. This abuse of alcohol, in turn, may have its roots in the tendency of reservations to suppress native cultures and to devalue residents of reservations.

   If FAS or FAE is suspected, professionals need to recognize that one or both parents may also have FAS or FAE. One common characteristic of FAS (and to some extent of FAE as well) is an inability to comprehend cause-and-effect. Parents may need to be trained (rather than taught) in key areas of child rearing.

2. Many Native Americans value what other Americans might call "nontraditional" intervention techniques, including "natural medicine" and religious rituals. Professionals should not disparage these methods. Rather, ECSE staff should explain that federal and state laws require them to use more objective and "traditional" intervention techniques.

3. In some Native American families, cooperation is emphasized over competition. Children learn through observation and imitation.

   ECSE programs, too, teach children to play with each other and to cooperate in other ways. While the de-emphasis of competition in many Native American families may be a problem in K–12 settings, especially in high school, it is rarely a concern in early childhood.

4. Many Native Americans evince an unwillingness to criticize other people.

   Rather than assume that "absence implies consent," ECSE program staff should seek explicit expressions of consent before proceeding with interventions. Team members should also be alert to subtle signals that family members dislike or distrust a particular member of the team, rather than assuming that the family has no problems with any team member just because such concerns are not overtly voiced.

FIGURE 2.10 Cultural competence V

early childhood special educators are professionals trained in work with young children, methods of education, and other kinds of intervention for children with disabilities or developmental delays.

service coordinators (formerly called case managers) facilitate service delivery to families and represent the family in negotiations with public and private service providers.

teachers. In the area of preschool special education, to illustrate, for every six teachers employed, one position was left vacant or was filled by someone less than fully qualified.

Early childhood special educators. Trained in both work with young children and education methods as well as other kinds of intervention, early childhood special educators perform a broad range of functions. They serve as team members in developing IFSPs and IEPs, contributing particularly to goal setting and objective writing. They work with psychologists and other specialists on eligibility and evaluation, as well as on both child and family assessment. Frequently, the early childhood special educator is the principal professional working day to day with the young child with a disability, performing instruction and assessing progress toward goals. He may also be the key team member in regular contact with the family, keeping them informed of the child's progress and providing family support services, including suggestions for at-home supplemental activities to enhance the child's progress toward goals.

Service coordinators. These professionals emerged in Part C, and proved so important in facilitating service delivery to families that their use spread to all of ECSE. Early intervention is, by federal mandate, an individualized service program. Everything revolves around a particular infant or toddler and his family. The service coordinator represents the family and guides it. Formerly called the case manager, this person may be an early childhood special educator, a social worker, a primary health care provider, a therapist, or other individual able to help the family—even a parent. The service coordinator's job is a challenging one. He must advocate for the family to an entire phalanx of local, county, state, and private service providers, cutting through red tape and ensuring that services are delivered.

The name of the service coordinator appears in the IFSP. He is the family's contact with the entire social services system. In many states, the service coordinator also follows the child as the toddler moves to preschool special education, to ensure a seamless transition from Part C to Part B. The service coordinator may be a member of the team assembling the IEP for the preschool Part B program in those states. In other states, the service coordinator plays a less formal role in smoothing the transition to preschool special education.

Social workers. Early intervention is, and preschool special education is increasingly becoming, an interdisciplinary program of services. Social workers may help the family to qualify for and receive needed services for which the family and/or the infant or toddler are eligible. The profession of social work features knowledge and skills in negotiating the often confusing network of public and private service providers—and the myriad eligibility requirements. Social workers may also provide family, group, and individual counseling to help family members cope with their child's special needs.

The IFSP includes written statements on the family's "resources, priorities, and concerns." While IEPs need not contain such statements, they may—and increasingly do, as states move toward more seamless service delivery (Schrag, 1990c). Those statements may guide the social worker's counseling role. As mentioned earlier, social workers may also fulfill the function of the service coordinator. Part B also recognizes the contributions of social workers and includes their services among allowed "related services."

Therapists and other services personnel. Depending on the child's special needs, physical therapists, occupational therapists, speech and language therapists, psychotherapists, and others trained in providing specific services may work with the infant, toddler, or preschooler. Frequently, these specialists also train family members to perform therapeutic functions so as to reduce the number of formal therapy sessions required and thus contain costs.

Physical and occupational therapists help children with cerebral palsy and other physical disabilities learn to use orthotics and prostheses to feed and dress themselves and to get around independently at home, in school, and in the community. The principal difference between these two professions is that physical therapists work on developing the child's muscles and extremities and preventing atrophy, while occupational therapists concentrate on helping the children to perform daily tasks such as brushing teeth, holding a pen, and using an electronic device to "speak." A prosthesis is an artificial replacement, such as a mechanical arm; an orthosis is a device that enhances the function of a body part, such as a leg brace that helps a child to walk. *Speech and language pathologists* help young children both to learn language and to produce intelligible speech to the best of their abilities. They may also work with children on feeding problems. Therapists from each of these disciplines are recognized by the IDEA under both Part C and Part B.

Family therapists are a relatively new addition to the list of IDEA-approved ECSE professionals. Family therapy was added in 1991, in PL 102-119. The committee report accompanying these 1991 amendments explained that professionals with degrees in such fields as marriage and family therapy may be authorized service providers. The report added, however, that "services that a family may need, but do not relate to the developmental needs of the

social workers are trained human services professionals who help the family to qualify for, and receive, needed services for which the family and/or the infant or toddler is or are eligible. Social work services also are "related services" under Part B of the Individuals with Disabilities Education Act.

therapists and other services personnel include speech and language pathologists, occupational therapists, and other professionals delivering related services to preschool-age children or early intervention services to infants and toddlers with disabilities.

The IDEA allows, but does not require, states to serve "at risk" infants and toddlers.

infant or toddler with a disability, are not early intervention services under Part H" *(House Report 102–198,* 1991, p. 14). In other words, family therapists may provide IDEA-reimbursed services only to the extent that their assistance directly affects family care of the child. Services of family therapists may also be provided in preschool Part B programs, because the department allows family services as "related services" (U.S. Department of Education, 1992a, b).

Other services personnel. ECSE services may also be provided as needed by, among others, psychologists, orientation and mobility specialists, technology experts (who provide assistive technology devices and services), and medical specialists. Psychologists play a wide range of roles in ECSE; some act as service coordinators, while others concentrate on assessment. Orientation and mobility specialists help children who are blind or have low vision learn to get around independently, use canes or guide dogs, and navigate in unfamiliar territory. Brown and Rule (1993) offered additional information about ECSE professionals. Bailey (1989) provided a good overview of the specific roles played by a diverse group of professionals, including some not discussed here (for example, nutritionists).

Of growing importance in ECSE are the services of technology experts. Assistive technology devices and services can dramatically enhance the quality of life of many infants, toddlers, and preschoolers with disabilities. Chapter 10 explores these products in detail. Then-Vice President Al Gore highlighted the potential in a speech to the National Press Club, explaining that modern telecommunications can help young children with special needs:

> *We use it with Matthew Meredith, a six-year-old boy who recently underwent a bone marrow transplant. His doctors recommended that he shouldn't begin his classes at Randolph Elementary School in Topeka. So the school and local telephone company teamed up to bring first grade to him through two-way video services and a television camera.*
>
> *Matthew was able to take part in class. He used a fax to hand in class assignments. And the kids in his class got a glimpse of videoconferencing technology that will be common in a few years.*
>
> *In West Virginia, doctors are using the Mountaineer Doctor Television Project to link to specialists at West Virginia University. A while back, for example, two-month-old Zachary Buchanan had an irregular heartbeat. Using the network, his doctor sent an image of his heart to a pediatric cardiologist 100 miles away. His diagnosis: the condition wasn't serious—and he didn't have to travel halfway across the state for treatment.* (Gore, 1993, p. 4)

Professionals who understand the potential of such products and services; who keep up with the rapidly changing computer-related technologies; and who are expert at selecting, integrating, and customizing such products and services for young children with disabilities play an increasingly important role in ECSE. The impact of technology can be as diverse as the needs of the children. Children who are deaf, for example, may learn words and numbers by watching *Sesame Street;* the PBS series offers closed captions. Similarly, children with cerebral palsy may use laptop personal computers equipped with speech synthesizers to "talk," many for the first time in their lives. Technology specialists provide such devices and services.

early childhood educators are professionals trained in work with young children, usually children of preschool age, or three to five.

Early childhood educators are professionals trained in work with children under the age of six. Their training includes formal coursework in **early childhood** development and supervised practicum with young children. This preparation may occur at the BA level or at the MA level. Most are employed in early childhood (EC) settings that serve children in the three-to-five age range. Early childhood educators may have preservice (prior to employment) or inservice (while employed) training about disabilities, but not all EC educators have such knowledge and/or experience.

early childhood (EC) refers to programs for young children (usually three- to five-year-olds), such as Head Start. EC as a field is broader than is ECSE. However, many EC programs serve young children with disabilities.

Elementary educators. Preschool programs serving children with no disabilities that mainstream some young children with disabilities often are staffed by teachers trained in elementary education. In large part, this is because many EC programs find it difficult to recruit professionals trained specifically in EC- and ECSE-related disciplines. In a large national survey, Wolery, Martin, Schroeder, Huffman, Venn, Holcombe, Brookfield, and Fleming (1994) found that elementary educators were employed by half (52.3 percent) of the 461 mainstream EC programs they studied, about the same proportion (52.7 percent) that hired early childhood educators. Just 20.2 percent of the programs hired special educators.

elementary educators are professionals trained at the B.A. or M.A. level in teaching K–6 children. They usually are state-certified as meeting state-set minimum requirements.

Child development associate (CDA) paraprofessionals. In addition to the professional disciplines discussed above, paraprofessionals play important roles in ECSE. Prominent in Head Start programs and in some other EC settings are child development associate-credentialed paraprofessionals. Staff members with CDA degrees function as teacher aides in many mainstream programs serving children with and without disabilities. Wolery, Martin, et al. (1993) found that 25 percent of Head Start program staff were CDA-credentialed individuals. Head Start programs are required by federal law to have at least one CDA-degree staff member for every twenty children enrolled. Inservice training for these paraprofessionals appeared necessary, Wolery and his colleagues reported, because few were trained in ECSE-related disciplines.

Child development associate (CDA) paraprofessionals have a credential indicating postsecondary study in child development and child care. CDA-credentialed paraprofessionals often work in Head Start programs.

ROLES AND RESPONSIBILITIES

The actors in ECSE are the federal and state levels of government, the local service providers, and the parents. The IDEA outlines specific roles and responsibilities for each. The federal role is actually limited, despite the fact that federal laws and regulations govern the entire activity; the U.S. Department of Education's responsibility is to disseminate funds, offer technical assistance, and monitor state compliance. The state role features decisions on personnel and program requirements, as well as the monitoring of local service providers. Despite state and federal dictates and oversight, local service providers enjoy considerable discretion in making day-to-day program decisions. Parents and other family members play a powerful role, reflecting the historic contributions parents have made to the development of ECSE over the past forty years.

The Federal Role

The IDEA sets the requirements that programs receiving funds under the act must meet. Among these are the eligibility criteria states must meet to receive federal funds; the mandate that all appropriate services be provided free of charge to the family (unless, in early intervention, other federal or state laws permit charges, including sliding fee scales); the obligation that an IFSP or IEP be prepared for each child; the allowability of certain kinds of services (such as orientation and mobility and related vision services for blind or low-vision infants and toddlers) and disallowability of other types of services (such as surgery and other general medical interventions); and reporting requirements, including labels.

The U.S. secretary of education may approve state applications for funds and may conduct audits and other investigations to ensure that states comply with federal requirements. The secretary may also award personnel training, demonstration, and research grants to state agencies, universities, and service programs.

Because Part C in particular is an interagency program that envisions contributions from many discrete human services programs, the federal role also includes a heavy responsibility to remove as many barriers to interagency cooperation as possible consistent with other federal obligations. For example, the Developmentally Disabled Assistance and Bill of Rights Act (DD Act) of 1975 initially defined "developmental disabilities" in terms of four disabilities (autism, cerebral palsy, mental retardation, and epilepsy). The act authorized federal grants to states to coordinate education, health, welfare, and rehabilitation services—but *only* for children and adults with those four DD Act disabilities. Other gaps, duplications, contradictions, and barriers abounded. In recent years, many very significant changes have been made at the federal level, markedly easing long-standing strains in state and local cross-agency collaboration. To continue with the DD Act example, the federal definition of **developmental disabilities** now includes children with any condition of early onset requiring a multitude of services. Recently, the definition was again changed, after enactment of PL 99-457; the latest DD Act definition includes a clause (applying only to children under six) that comports with the Part C and preschool Part B definitions of infants, toddlers, and preschool-age children with disabilities. This change in definition makes interagency collaboration at the state and local levels much easier and ensures that young children will not fall between the cracks because of incompatible eligibility criteria.

Similarly, federal law now allows the Head Start program to use any recognized state definition of disability for the purpose of serving young children in Head Start programs; this change is very important, because states differ in their definitions of infants, toddlers, and children with disabilities. A third important change occurred in the Maternal and Child Health Services (MCH) block grant program: Federal law now specifically authorizes states to use these block grants for family-centered community programs.

In another important step, the secretaries of education and of health and human services (HHS) signed an interagency agreement on August 12, 1992, to "coordinate resources to identify, evaluate, and assess children with disabilities from birth through five to facilitate acquisition of appropriate available benefits and services." The agreement covered six HHS agencies (MCH; Administration on Developmental Disabilities; Health Care Financing

developmental disabilities are conditions of early onset (occurring well in advance of adulthood) that require a range of diverse services or interventions. The term formerly referred to four disabilities (autism, cerebral palsy, mental retardation, and epilepsy).

lead agency is the term used in Part C of the IDEA to refer to the state agency authorized to carry out the state Part C plan and to coordinate the work of other public and private agencies. In some states, the state education agency is the lead agency; in others, a health agency, social services agency, or child-care agency serves as the lead agency. Up-to-date addresses for state lead agencies are available at www. nectas.unc.edu, the Web site of the National Early Childhood Technical Assistance System, at the University of North Carolina. NEC*TAS may also be reached at 500 NationsBank Plaza, 137 E. Franklin Street, Chapel Hill, NC 27514.

child find is the term used in both Part C and Part B of the IDEA to refer to outreach and recruitment efforts by the state to identify, screen, and serve eligible children and families.

Interagency Coordinating Council (ICC) is an advisory body that gives the state Part C (infants and toddlers) lead agency information about, and support from, other key agencies in the state. With the ICC's help, the state lead agency creates a statewide system for implementation of Part C.

Early childhood special education (ECSE) practitioners include early childhood special educators, speech and language pathologists, occupational therapists, and other service personnel working together on an interdisciplinary team.

Administration; Administration on Children, Youth and Families; Social Security Administration; and National Institutes of Mental Health) and one U.S. Department of Education agency (Office of Special Education Programs). The agreement stressed delivery of individualized, community-based, integrated services *(Fifteenth Annual Report,* 1993b, p. 56).

The State Role

Part C requires that states participating in the early intervention program meet fourteen requirements. According to section 637, states must select a **lead agency** to carry out the state plan, coordinate the work of other public and private agencies, write policies for interagency contracts, and make other arrangements for service delivery throughout the state. By contrast, Part B permits little flexibility: The state education agency or a closely affiliated office must be the lead agency responsible for section 619 preschool special education services. Part C adds the responsibility of creating a comprehensive directory of services available statewide and a statewide database containing the numbers of infants and toddlers with disabilities or delays. In many other respects, however, the state role is similar under both Part C and Part B. In both cases, for example, the state sets personnel qualifications. Both Part C and Part B require states to mount **child find** efforts and public awareness programs to identify potentially eligible infants, toddlers, preschoolers, and their families. States must arrange to conduct evaluations, prepare IFSPs or IEPs, ensure procedural safeguards, and serve all such children identified and their families. In addition, states must implement personnel preparation programs to ensure an adequate supply of service providers. Finally, states must define the term "developmental delay" as they will use it in Part C and, if the state so elects, in section 619 Part B.

The IDEA describes the state role under Part C more extensively than it does the state role under Part B. Each state must not only designate a lead agency to assume primary responsibility for Part C programs but must also create a state **Interagency Coordinating Council** (ICC) to advise that lead agency. The lead agency, in turn, must negotiate interagency agreements with other state agencies (education, health, social services). These inter-

agency agreements form the basis for a statewide system of early intervention services. For example, personnel qualifications for family therapists, social workers, psychologists, and so on are set by the appropriate state agencies, but coordination may make it easier for professionals and programs alike to apply for certification or licensure. The lead agency, together with other participating state agencies, funds county and local agencies, as well as public and private service providers, reimbursing them for costs they incur. Finally, the lead agency is responsible to the U.S. Department of Education for ensuring that all providers funded under the IDEA comply with that act's mandates.

The law requires Part C and Part B lead agencies to work together, notably on outreach, transition, and other key tasks. It also assigns clear responsibility to the state lead agency for all in-state activities, including local service provider functions and local education agency programs. There are, for example, more than 15,000 local education agencies (school districts) throughout the United States. Rather than attempt to monitor and ensure compliance from each of those local programs, the U.S. Department of Education holds the fifty state education agencies and their counterparts in other jurisdictions completely and solely responsible for the actions of these local bodies.

The Local Role

While the federal and state actions are important, it is the local role that is paramount for infants, toddlers, and preschoolers with disabilities to receive services at the local level. The urgent need for family-focused services first emerged at the local level. Beginning in the late 1960s and continuing through the mid-1980s, preschool programs and early intervention centers had to contend with a dozen or more different sources of federal and state funding, few of which had been designed to work with the others (Swan & Morgan, 1993). Indeed, each had been created to respond to a specific need and to serve a particular population. To illustrate, PL 89–313 ("Chapter 1"), an important program that provided federal funds for services to young children with disabilities between 1965 and 1994, limited funding to state-operated or state-supported programs, usually residential schools and other institutions. Even where interagency service coordination was a goal, programs nonetheless excluded many individuals with disabilities.

A Rand Corporation study (Kakalik, Furry, Thomas, & Carney, 1981) highlighted the fact that those problems were not merely local but national in scope. The Rand report documented how both professionals and parents were frequently denied services—or were served only after a frustrating and lengthy journey through a maze of social service agencies. As a result of their experiences, professionals and advocates in many communities created local coordinating councils, which enabled representatives of different agencies to get together, identify barriers to services, and introduce (or recommend to their legislatures) changes that would make interagency coordination more effective. In time, these councils proved that services for families and young children with disabilities could be delivered faster and better, with far less frustration for parents and professionals alike. They became the model for the state Interagency Coordinating Councils established by the IDEA in 1986 (Swan & Morgan, 1993).

Such coordination is essential in ECSE. Programs caring for medically fragile or technology-dependent children in San Diego, California, for example, must pull together funding from many different sources. Federal and state Part C monies are used to coordinate and enhance services, but basic funding comes from DD Act, Medicaid, and other federal sources, as well as state and private sources. Such programs must also scramble for state licensing, because many states do not as yet have separate licensing categories for extended care facilities (Beck, Hammond-Cordero, & Poole, 1994).

Part C requires that services for infants, toddlers, and their families be provided, to the maximum extent appropriate, in **natural environments**. For very young children, that is usually the home. When services are given in other settings, the law prefers facilities that nondisabled young children also use. While the IDEA does not offer many more specifics, experience suggests that parental preference usually will be a good guide in selecting the natural environment. This and other aspects of the parental role are examined below. Part B has a similar **least restrictive environment**, requiring that preschool special education students (as well as older students with disabilities) are to be educated together with nondisabled students to the maximum extent appropriate (that is, without limiting the appropriateness of the education and related services they receive). Parents enjoy the right to offer input in this decision as well, but the local education agency retains the responsibility to make the selection in a way that complies with Part B requirements.

Inclusion is a lively issue in both Part C and Part B. DEC offered guidance in 1993 on how ECSE programs could adopt inclusive practices while remaining in compliance with the IDEA's requirements that both natural and least restrictive environments feature "appropriate" and "individualized" services (DEC Task Force, 1993).

The Parents' Role

Both Part C and Part B grant the parents of young children with disabilities extraordinary roles and rights. Parents may identify unique needs of their children and work with professionals to be sure that these needs appear in IFSPs or IEPs. They may see all records containing personally identifiable information about their children. They may also file complaints when they disagree with professional recommendations about services, placements, or other aspects of intervention and education. These remarkable parental powers come from a congressional determination that parents are in the best position of anyone to protect the rights of children with disabilities. Parents and, to a large degree, parents alone are responsible for the Part B and Part C mandates. In fact, what is now the IDEA was triggered by two federal district court cases in the early 1970s, *Pennsylvania Association for Retarded Children v. Commonwealth of Pennsylvania* (1972) and *Mills v. Board of Education of the District of Columbia* (1972). Both were brought by parents.

These powerful roles emerged first in PL 94-142's Part B in 1975. After a decade of experience with parental rights and roles in special education, Congress granted similar privileges and responsibilities to parents of infants and toddlers with disabilities in Part H (now Part C) in 1986. In many respects, the parental role under Part C is even larger than that under Part B. Under Part C, for example, parents may decline any service without jeopardizing their right to others; Part B contains no such explicit statement of parental prerogatives in refusing services. Family resources, priorities, and concerns appear in IFSPs only if the parents agree; similarly, a service agency may send information about an infant or toddler to another agency *only* with prior parental permission.

The family-related provisions of Part B and Part C are founded on the assumption that parents are both informed about their rights and active in asserting those rights. Many parents are. However, a Harris and Associates (1989) study of parental views on special education

natural environment is a philosophy emphasizing services for infants, toddlers, and their families in places that are typical or otherwise "natural." Early intervention services are to be delivered in such environments, to the extent that these are "appropriate" and meet the child's needs. The home is the usual such environment. The term is used in Part C of the IDEA.

least restrictive environment is a philosophy stressing the placement of children with disabilities in appropriate settings closest (when compared with other appropriate settings) to settings used by nondisabled children. The term is used in Part B of the IDEA.

inclusion is an approach in which children with disabilities (including those with severe disabilities) are placed in rooms with, and receive services side by side with, children who have no disabilities.

revealed disturbing trends. The Harris public opinion firm telephoned more than one thousand parents of children with disabilities. Only a few of the parents contacted were knowledgeable about their rights, more than ten years after Part B took effect. Three out of every five parents said they knew "little or nothing" about the IDEA. Similarly, few were aggressive in taking advantage of their rights; fewer than one in ten had filed a complaint on behalf of their children with disabilities (Harris & Associates, 1989). Despite many federal, state, local, and private efforts to inform parents about the IDEA and about other federal laws, the survey detected no evidence that parents' knowledge of their rights and responsibilities was increasing over time. These findings suggest that family education and empowerment remain urgently important, even after twenty-five years of special education requirements and one decade of widely available, federally supported early intervention services (Keeney, 1994). For parents to play the roles the IDEA envisions for them, they need to be aware of these rights and responsibilities.

SUMMARY

ECSE is the coming together of early intervention and preschool special education to form a seamless system for delivery of services to birth-to-five children with disabilities or developmental delays. This field provides direct services to young children and their families, under federal and state laws. These laws offer public financing for ECSE services and require states to serve all eligible young children. These laws also guarantee families with young children certain rights, including the right to be fully informed of the child's needs and of a program's intervention plans. Such plans are to be written in formal documents, called individualized family service plans (IFSPs) and individualized education programs (IEPs).

The IDEA and corresponding state statutes are remarkable laws filled with very specific prescriptions (dictates) and proscriptions (prohibitions). They are as detailed as they are at the insistence of parents for their own and their children's protection. The U.S. Congress concurred with these parental requests, largely in the belief that early intervention and preschool special education programs offering appropriate services for birth-to-five children with disabilities and delays would make important contributions to the national welfare. The rationale behind ECSE is that not only the children but that their families, neighborhoods, towns, and states, and indeed the nation as a whole, would benefit. Congress also believed that ECSE programs could save society substantial sums of money by helping people with disabilities to become self-sufficient, gainfully employed, taxpaying citizens in adulthood.

The IDEA envisions specific roles for the federal, state, and local levels of government, as well as for parents. The federal role is a limited one. The U.S. Department of Education provides financial assistance to states, offers technical assistance to state lead agencies and to individual programs, and monitors implementation of the law. States add substantial financial resources for ECSE, define eligible populations under Part C, determine personnel standards, license or otherwise approve local delivery programs, and decide how the state will carry out the federal mandate. The most important roles, however, are reserved for parents and local government. The IDEA grants parents extraordinary rights and responsibilities. The local programs, despite federal and state regulation, make the key decisions. They decide, along with the parents, which children will receive what services, from what disciplines, from which personnel, and in what settings.

As it stands today, ECSE is a field facing tremendous challenges. Despite more than thirty-five years of serving birth-to-five children with disabilities and developmental delays, the field continues to evolve rapidly. Perhaps the greatest current challenge is to meet the unique needs of children and families from lower-SES and racial and ethnic minority groups. How ECSE programs respond to this and other challenges is the subject of the next several chapters.

QUESTIONS FOR REFLECTION

1. What do the terms "entitlement" and "zero reject" mean as these are used in ECSE? How does the case of *Timothy W. v. Rochester* (1989) help us to understand these terms?

2. Compare "early intervention services" under Part C to "related services" under Part B. How are they similar—and different?

3. Compare the definitions for "infants and toddlers with disabilities" and "children with disabilities." How are they similar, and how are they different? Which unit of government defines the key terms in each case—federal or state? When might that matter to families?

4. In your own words, what are the major rationales for ECSE?

5. Differentiate "at risk" from "condition" and "delay." Why do few states recognize at-risk infants and toddlers as entitled to early intervention services? Are at-risk children aged three and over entitled to Part B services?

6. What is in an IFSP that is not in an IEP? Vice versa?

7. Why is it so important for ECSE workers to reflect upon the beliefs of their *own* cultural heritages before they focus upon becoming more sensitive to *other* cultures?

8. Which cultural minority groups feature eye-gaze aversion as an indication of respect? Which two tend to regard "time" as somewhat relative as compared to the more rigid view of time that characterizes the business world?

9. Why are disability prevalence rates more a function of socioeconomic status than of race or ethnic group membership?

10. What do service coordinators do? Why are they so important to many families that participate in early intervention?

How Are We Doing? Research In ECSE

When I ask myself the question, "Who uses research knowledge?" the answer that most rapidly comes into my head is "researchers." (Ronald G. Havelock, "Translating Theory into Practice," reprinted from *Rehabilitation Record*, November–December, 1969, p. 1)

OVERVIEW

Chapters 1 and 2 have introduced the field of early childhood special education (ECSE). In Chapter 1, we saw that ECSE draws upon our knowledge about human development to serve children under the age of six who have disabilities or delays in any one or more domains of development. The ways in which ECSE programs are supposed to deliver such services was outlined in Chapter 2. There we saw that services are to be individually selected and designed to respond to the unique needs of each child and family.

That is what *should* happen. In some respects, the information presented in Chapters 1 and 2 is more ideal than real. That is, the philosophy shaping ECSE and the custom-designed approaches of the field both feature rather lofty expectations. In this chapter, we explore what research is teaching us about what is actually happening in early childhood special education programs. Our intent is to understand how well the field is doing and thereby begin to understand how we as current and future interventionists and educators can improve the state of the art.

Over the years, the writer has come to appreciate that many students in personnel preparation programs in the areas of early intervention and preschool special education have not taken courses in research methodology. Understandably, then, a lot of them are apprehensive when professors like myself assign them readings in professional journals. To make matters worse, many researchers write those journal articles in a dense prose that intimidates more readers than it enlightens. Hence the chapter-opening quotation from Ronald Havelock: Research reports are most often read by other researchers, in part because only they can understand them!

That is why Chapter 3 is laid out the way it is. The chapter opens with an introduction to research and researchers. It then gives students or other readers who lack a background in research design and statistics some tools with which to read journal articles reporting on research projects. The chapter then explains the factors that make research in early childhood special education especially challenging. A "bird's-eye" summary of research in ECSE concludes the chapter.

Michael Wolery (1991), then of the Allegheny-Singer Research Institute in Pittsburgh, Pennsylvania, described current research in ECSE as "seeing through a glass darkly . . . knowing in part." That description seems about right. It does matter—and matters urgently—how early intervention and preschool programming begin for individual children with disabilities. Earlier would seem to be better. To date, however, research has had difficulty finding actual experimental evidence to support that intuition. The field of ECSE is young, in this as in many other ways, and the journey is one of both exploration and discovery. This chapter focuses on what we know and what we don't know, and in doing so helps to point the way to the future. Before ECSE as a field, and ECSE programs as individual entities, can advance, practitioners need to understand what they are doing and how well it is working.

The chapter opens with background information on the research enterprise, followed by suggestions for reading research reports in journals and books. Next, problems in ECSE-related research are examined. Studying young children and the methods used to help them is difficult, partly because of the tests and other measures that are available, partly because of research design problems (interventions tend to be brief, groups small), and partly because ECSE programs strive to reach so many diverse goals, all at the same time. The chapter then examines recent research in ECSE, focusing on ten questions and the answers research has produced. The chapter concludes with some observations on the role of research in the field, particularly what Guralnick (1993) called "second-generation" studies, that is, research that looks for interactions between child and family characteristics, program features, and goals or outcomes. Such information is urgently needed by ECSE practitioners nationwide.

RESEARCH AND RESEARCHERS

Why is research important in ECSE? The best way to answer this question is to consider what research does. First, in any field as new (relatively speaking) as ECSE, research helps administrators and practitioners to decide what we know and don't know. Much that appears to be obvious turns out, on closer inspection, to be not so self-evident. Second, research documents effectiveness and cost-efficiency, thus enabling ECSE workers to make the case that programs deserve increased financial support in a time of tight federal, state, county, and local budgets. Third, it offers information about disabling conditions and treatments for them that helps parents and professionals alike to set realistic outcomes for early intervention and preschool special education. Research provides essential information about which techniques work best with what kinds of children at which stages of their development. Such data are fundamental for program design and for individual planning.

As important as research is, it is not the only, or even dominant, factor in policy making in ECSE. Other considerations include the Constitution's equal-protection and due-process clauses, the availability of public financing, and the extent to which ECSE advocates are able to sustain political pressure for more services.

At times, research information may be used in controversial ways. Experimental data that support ECSE may be reported to policy makers selectively, while contrary evidence is suppressed or ignored. Karl White, of the Utah State University Early Intervention Research Institute (EIRI) and his colleagues (White, 1985/1986; White, Taylor, & Moss, 1992) complained that some overzealous ECSE advocates did exactly that in 1986 when Congress was nearing the pivotal decision to mandate services for children from birth to five with disabilities. They noted that Congress was given a great deal of data showing ECSE in its best light, but very little illustrating ECSE's problems. White added that a review of some of the earlier research cast doubt on ECSE's cost-effectiveness; had it been made available to Congress at the time, this information might have influenced the direction Congress eventually took in PL 99–457 (see "Is ECSE cost-effective? Cost-beneficial?" later in this chapter). Another way in which research is sometimes misused is as verification for already established policies. As one member of Congress put it to the author in an off-the-record conversation, "Policy research is any research that supports my policy." Here a decision precedes even looking at the research record, which is then sifted to extract studies that support that decision. Researchers cannot, of course, always control the uses to which their work is put. Nonetheless, some of these ways of using research information may be inappropriate, particularly for a young and growing field.

Other aspects of research are more within the researcher's control. Experimenter bias is one of these. The element of researcher bias can never be eliminated completely (Pedhazur & Schmelkin, 1991). Researchers in any field have their own beliefs and biases. Most are conscious of their own leanings, however, and try to remove bias from their experimental work. There are ways of doing that, among them double-blind designs in which those working with the experimental and control-group subjects know neither the study's hypothesis nor which subject is in each group. But designing a bias-free study is not always possible, nor is a bias-free review of other researchers' work. In ECSE, as in many other fields, beliefs are firmly held and emotions run strong, among researchers as among practitioners. To illustrate with work discussed later in this chapter, when Carl Dunst and Scott Snyder of the Western Carolina Center in Morganton, North Carolina, harshly criticized the Casto and Mastropieri (1986a) meta-analysis of research on ECSE, Casto and Mastropieri (1986b) suspected that bias might have been involved: "Interestingly enough, our review results conflict with Dunst, Snyder, and Mankinen (in press) in several important areas. This raises a question as to the degree of objectivity that Dunst and Snyder brought to the task of critiquing our efforts" (p. 279).

As a reader of research reports, you should be alert to possible bias. On such issues as "least restrictive environment" or "inclusion," for example, about which opinions are particularly strong, it makes sense to ask whether the writer of a study report has a record of advocacy on behalf of a particular point of view. This is not to say that researchers are unethical; it is simply to acknowledge that they are human—and that the research endeavor is therefore susceptible to bias. To continue with the above example, you should read both pro-inclusion and anti-inclusion articles with care, looking for any evidence of bias. Frequently, research is cited as supporting a point of advocacy; if you were to read those cited articles, however, you might find that they do not say what they were purported to say. There is evidence that some children may be harmed by placement in environments in which they are physically proximate with nondisabled children but are at the same time isolated from them in communication (as when the children are deaf) or in other ways. Frequently, such evidence is not included in literature reviews. There is other evidence that integration has differential effects on young children with mild versus those with severe disabilities; again, such qualifications are often not made. This is one aspect of intelligent consumption of research reports, a subject to which the chapter now turns.

Reading Research Reports

A quick glance at the References section of this book reveals that research reports are readily available to you. Such journals as *Exceptional Children, Infants and Young Children, Journal of Early Intervention, Journal of Special Education,* and others are available in public and university libraries; you may, of course, also subscribe to one or more of these. The question then becomes, "How can one read research reports so as to gain the most from them?" Taking an introductory research course is a good way to learn how to read these articles. Texts such as those by Pedhazur and Schmelkin (1991) or Kerlinger (1986) offer readable overviews of behavioral research. How to read and make good use of research is the subject of entire books. Here, the intent is to skim the surface, noting important issues for ECSE professionals, issues that do not require you to have advanced training in research methodology and statistics.

Research reports in professional journals have usually been peer reviewed, or critiqued by other professionals, including researchers, prior to publication. This process certainly lessens the burden on the lay reader. However, peer review does not guarantee that all articles published are free from bias, or even from error. Peer reviewers usually focus on research and design questions and on the relevance of the article to the journal's main readership. They do not even attempt to answer the lay reader's most important question, namely, "Is this study related to what I personally do every day?" Only you can answer that question.

Scientific inquiry is best described as the systematic pursuit of understanding how *variables* relate one to another (see Pedhazur & Schmelkin [1991] for an extended discussion).

A variable is anything that has at least two values, that is, that varies. People are male or female. Infants or toddlers with disabilities, under Part C, have established conditions or developmental delays, or are at risk for such delays. Children are delayed or not delayed in development. Disabilities are deafness, blindness, cerebral palsy, mental retardation, learning disabilities, autism, traumatic brain injury, and so on. All of these are variables. Researchers seek to understand how variables vary with respect to other variables. Are infant boys more likely to have established conditions than are infant girls? To have delays? Are children with cerebral palsy always delayed in development? And, of more direct interest here, what interventions, treatments, or educational techniques best help young children with disabilities?

There are two basic kinds of studies that you will read. The first is the experiment. In this case, a researcher manipulates one or more independent variables in order to observe the effect on a dependent variable. The controlled experiment is the best way to determine whether the independent variable(s) did in fact affect the dependent variable. This method is sometimes referred to as **quantitative research**, because it reports findings as numbers. However, due in part to frustration with results to date from controlled experiments (see Research Findings later in the chapter), you will probably see an increasing number of naturalistic observation reports. These **qualitative research** articles draw on techniques from anthropology and social psychology in an effort to report information so that the reader fully understands it. In this second kind of study, nothing is manipulated. Rather, the researcher attempts to describe, in as objective a manner as possible, what occurred and what it seems to mean. Let us consider first the controlled experiment, and then qualitative research.

Most experimental research seeks to disprove a *null hypothesis*. A null hypothesis says that there is no relation between variables. By proving the null hypothesis to be incorrect, the researcher shows that there is in fact some kind of relation. Of course, one could alternatively hypothesize that there is in fact such a relation—and even what direction that relation has (positive, negative) and how strong it is. Most studies you will read use the null hypothesis, however, because statistical tests are readily available for use with such hypotheses. Standard statistical tables are also readily available to help the researcher see whether a given

quantitative research usually manipulates one or more variables ("independent variables"), observing its or their effects on dependent variables. Such studies report findings as numbers, hence the name "quantitative."

qualitative research is an observational study and report in which nothing is manipulated or controlled.

Qualitative research features an observer who reports upon what happens but does not manipulate any variables.

finding is *statistically significant.* It is probably not going too far to say that the Holy Grail in behavioral research is a statistically significant finding. That being the case, it is important to understand that a statistically significant finding is one that is unlikely to have occurred purely by chance. Such findings are described using expressions such as "$p < .05$" or "$p < .01$." Those mean, respectively, that the finding was likely to have occurred strictly as a result of chance fewer than five times per hundred experiments like this one, or fewer than one time per hundred such experiments. Either level may be chosen to disprove the null hypothesis. Neither means that the result was not due to chance. No one can know that with absolute certainty. But a significant finding is one in which researcher and reader alike can have some confidence.

That a finding is statistically significant does not mean it is practically important. The difference is a central one. That a relation probably does exist does not mean that you should change your behavior because of it. Rather, the fact that a finding is statistically significant tells you that it probably is a real effect, and that you may proceed to ask the question, "What does this effect mean to me?" It may mean little or nothing. If you are a preschool teacher of children with severe retardation and you read a study showing a relation between multisensory approaches and achievement by children with mild retardation, the fact that a multisensory approach produced significantly more learning than did a unisensory approach with those students should cause you to ask some critical questions. One might be the extent to which the students studied were like the children you teach. Are there enough similarities to cause you to believe that the study has implications for how you teach those children? None of these questions has anything to do with the statistical significance of the study's findings. Rather, they have to do with what the findings mean to *you.*

Accordingly, the first question to ask of any research report probably is, "Are the families and children studied like the families and children with whom I work?" This is a question of *generalizability.* If, for example, you work with infants and toddlers, research on adolescents will probably be of little help. Perhaps not as obvious is the fact that much research draws upon programs that are geographically convenient to the researchers. It may be that families in rural South Carolina and their young children are reported upon in a study; if you work with inner-city families in Philadelphia, the generalizability of the study's findings to your

As you read reports on research, ask yourself, "Are the children studied like the children with whom I work?"

population may, in some respects, be problematic. The best advice is to read intelligently and critically. Ask questions as you read. Be especially alert to information that you can use.

As you read a research report, also be alert to evidence of subject *attrition*. Did the study begin with a substantially larger number of subjects than were still being tested at its end? That problem is particularly evident in longitudinal studies, but it can affect short-term studies as well. The issue of attrition presents fairly obvious challenges for researchers. Consider, for example, a commercial weight-loss or exercise program. People who do not receive benefits (or at least do not recognize any) tend to drop out; those who see benefits outweighing the inconvenience, cost, and so on of participation tend to remain in the program. To study only long-term participants and conclude from their results that an exercise or diet program is effective is to ignore the fact that dropouts differ from persistent participants. So it is in ECSE. At the very least, researchers should compare a sample of families that dropped out of the program with families that remained in it; if there are no significant differences on such measures as education, family income, severity of disability of the child, and so on, you would have more confidence in the generalizability of the research findings.

Good examples of generalizability problems exist in the literature on cocaine exposure in infants and young children. The initial reports suggested that high proportions of women giving birth had used cocaine during pregnancy. For example, Chasnoff (1989b) stated at a conference that thirty-six hospitals surveyed reported an average of 11 percent of new mothers studied admitted using some illegal drug while pregnant. Miller (1989) said at the same conference that hospitals testing the urine of newborns found evidence of cocaine in 10 to 15 percent of the infants. These proportions were disturbingly high. Do as many as one out of every seven, or even one out of every ten, women use cocaine during pregnancy? Only a careful reading of the data can answer that question. The hospitals that Chasnoff and Miller reported on may not have tested all, or even most, pregnant women and infants; rather, they may have tested only at-risk mothers and newborns, those whose behavior or backgrounds suggested possible use of illegal drugs. Examining the literature on cocaine and pregnancy, Williams and Howard (1993) concluded: "In most current research, only highly select samples of women have been studied; those who have been referred to a drug treatment program. Prevalence and patterns of cocaine use during pregnancy have seldom been ascertained for a sample of women seeking routine prenatal care, not to mention those seeking no prenatal care" (p. 66). This immediately cautions the reader to ask, "Eleven percent of *what?*" The classic example of this kind of generalizability problem is the apocryphal case in which a researcher tests everyone in a mental hospital. Finding that 40 percent of these people are mentally ill tells us nothing about the prevalence of mental illness in the outside community. The study has no generalizability.

If the study seems to be about the problems you deal with on an everyday basis, the next questions you should ask are about the study itself. What *exactly* was done in this experiment? With whom was it performed? Did everything actually occur as the researchers intended? One does not need a Ph.D. in behavioral research to realize that telling parents to spend twenty minutes daily doing physical therapy with their child does not mean that parents actually do that. To illustrate, White (1985/1986), discussing research findings from studies on parental involvement in programs for disadvantaged infants and toddlers, found that "very few of the effect sizes (less than 2 percent) came from studies in which the investigators *verified* that parents were actually involved to the degree intended" (pp. 410–411; emphasis in original). Effect sizes are discussed below. White, Taylor, and Moss (1992) echoed the point with respect to research on early intervention with children who have disabilities. Jack Shonkoff, of the University of Massachusetts Medical School, and Tufts University's Penny

Hauser-Cram (1987), reanalyzing many of the studies reviewed by White et al., complained that even among the best available articles on early intervention with young children with disabilities, "few studies reported sufficient information regarding the frequency of service delivery as either planned or implemented" (p. 653). Similarly, Guralnick (1991) concurred that researchers too often fail to explain fully what intervention was attempted: what was done, with whom, at what stage of development/age, how often, for how long a period of time each session, following what model or theory, and so on.

To continue with the parental involvement example, to say that parents were involved in a program is to beg the question: What was the nature of the involvement? Did they attend parent group meetings? Were they instructed by staff in treatment methods? Were they provided with information about the child's disability or needs? Were they included in meetings to develop the individualized family service plan? All of these—and many others—are aspects of what might be called parent involvement. Unless an article clearly explains what was done with parents, you as the reader do not know the relevance of, let alone how to apply, the findings.

It is equally important to find out *with whom* these things were done. Shonkoff and Hauser-Cram (1987), reviewing thirty-one high-quality studies on infants and toddlers with disabilities, commented: "Perhaps the most striking finding in this set of studies is the lack of information provided about families. Critical variables such as race, number of children in the home, and parents' education levels were specified in less than 30 percent of the cases" (p. 653). Guralnick (1991) expressed concern that many research reports do not adequately describe the subject population. This problem also occurs when reading reviews or analyses of prior research. One could read an entire article summarizing previous research on age at start, for example, without recognizing that most of the studies being reported upon were done with children who have one disability, retardation. Similarly, Goetze, Immel, Escobar, Gillette, Coury, and Hansen (1993) noted in reviewing research on infants with low birthweight (LBW) that most previous studies excluded LBW infants who had severe conditions, that is, who were most in need of early intervention services. Unless the reader knew this, she might erroneously conclude that study findings hold implications for treatment of LBW infants and toddlers who have severe disabilities.

Experimental research should feature *random* selection of subjects from the universe of such individuals and the random assignment of subjects to treatments. Only if both kinds of randomization are performed can researchers have confidence that findings related to the subjects would probably have been seen to the same extent had the entire universe of such people been tested. That is, randomization ensures generalizability. Unfortunately, as Guralnick (1991), Casto and Mastropieri (1986a), Dunst and Snyder (1986), and others pointed out, much research in ECSE features neither kind of randomization, let alone both.

Random numbers have some remarkable properties. One is that truly random assignment of subjects to treatments will wipe out many differences between groups. The variability of individuals is the bane of the behavioral researcher's professional life. For a controlled experiment to be useful, the two (or more) groups being compared need to be very similar. Randomization, fortunately, comes to the researcher's rescue. If subjects are chosen at random from the universe and assigned at random to treatments, both treatment groups will have about the same number of boys and girls as exist in the universe. Both will have about the same number of late developers, children with severe disabilities, or, for that matter, future Republicans. Randomization, thus, removes a great deal of variance between groups and helps to ensure that at the start of the experiment, the two groups are comparable on most measures. That, too, is an essential element. If two groups are comparable at the beginning of an experiment, but different after it, there is increased confidence that the independent variable(s) really did have an effect.

More difficult to ascertain (because it is less often reported) is another important question you should ask as you read research studies: *"Were benefits maintained over time?"* The fact that short-term benefits are observed does not mean that they will persist over time. Head Start is well known (see, for example, Zigler & Valentine, 1979) for producing effects that for some children are transitory, that is, that wash out within a few years. In addition, young children are notoriously variable in growth patterns. This is yet another bane of the ECSE researcher's professional life, particularly because effects may need to be assessed as late as three years following intervention. Goetze et al. (1993) and the Infant Health and Development Program (1990), to take two examples, found beneficial effects of intensive intervention on LBW children only at thirty-six- to forty-eight-month follow-up measures. The question of whether benefits occur, then, often has to be asked in longitudinal studies, which are much more costly to do than most other experiments.

As if these were not enough questions to ask about research studies, still others are important, for example, "Could any other factor(s) have accounted for the findings reported here?" This is a question of *validity*. When one speaks of a study's validity, what is meant is that the findings and implications of the project mean what they seem to mean. Stated differently, the study measures what its designers thought they were measuring. The IQ test, to illustrate, really does measure intelligence (and not the child's eyes, ears, or finger control). Perhaps most notable here is construct validity. What is an IQ? What is a delay? Those constructs must be understood before they can be measured in young children. Are the tests used valid with young children who have disabilities? That, as it turns out, is frequently a very serious problem. Many tests that are used in ECSE were never intended for use with children who have disabilities. Researchers, program administrators, and others use them (lacking anything better) but must always watch for evidence that they may not be valid in the ways in which they are being used.

Yet another good question is that of *reliability*. Generally, reliability is a question of error. The more error in the measurements, the less reliability. Error may come from many sources, but errors of measurement are perhaps most significant. Examples include test

Tests should be valid, measuring what they are supposed to measure and not something else (the child's vision, for example).

instructions that are not identical for each subject, variations in the time of test (morning, afternoon, and so on), or in other aspects of the test administration. Another way of expressing the idea of reliability is that if one gave a "perfect" test, and a "real" one, reliability is an expression of how close the real test scores come to the ideal ones. Because there are no perfect tests, one must turn to other methods to ascertain the reliability of a measure. One is to repeat the test to the same people over a period of time; in general, a reliable test will yield much the same scores each time. A second is to give two tests to a group of subjects, one known to be a reliable test and one about which there are questions. If the scores on both, or more precisely the rank order of the scores on both, are identical or close to it, the second test is probably also a reliable one. As a reader, you can look for such efforts. You can also ask if the findings reported in a study have been replicated by the same or other investigators.

Finally, bear in mind that the discussion section, or interpretation of a study's findings, is opinion. Here the researcher gives a uniquely personal view of what the study means. While the earlier parts of the article are objective by comparison, the implications section, by its very nature, is subjective. Both lay and professional readers may well have different points of view and alternative explanations for what the study findings say and mean.

If the report you are reading is one on qualitative research, your questions will be different ones. Qualitative research does not compare groups, nor does it use statistics to describe findings. Rather, in qualitative research a trained observer monitors what someone does and asks that person why he does those things. Coleman (1993) likened the observer's role to a special mirror in which both the professional being observed and the reader can "enter the mind" of the professional as seen by an outside observer (p. 22). He added that professionals frequently comment that this outside perspective helps "practitioners to reflect on their practice" (p. 23). In qualitative research, the researcher's job is to describe, in rich detail, what happens in an intervention program or in a classroom. "If we do a good job," Coleman said, "our descriptions will ring true to practitioners, will lead to improved interventions, and will make evident to nonprofessionals the non-trivial nature of effective early intervention practices" (p. 22).

There are important limitations to qualitative research. First, perhaps most seriously, it cannot explain variance. If one thing happens in one setting, and another in a second setting, all qualitative research can do is to describe what happened and perhaps add what participants in the two settings thought occurred. Quantitative research, by contrast, has the ability to explain, to a level of confidence, what happened, and to rule out alternative explanations, again to a level of confidence. Second, qualitative research is as subject to researcher bias as is quantitative research. If, as qualitative researchers like to say, there is no such thing as an objective reality but only a participant's view of reality, this holds true of the researcher as well the practitioner. A third concern is that the method, by its very nature, attempts to get into someone's mind and understand how and why people do things. That is a very ambitious goal, one few humans using any method are capable of achieving.

Qualitative research begins when the researcher attempts to enter the world of the practitioner. This process involves spending time in the classroom or program setting and asking questions about what is happening. It continues as the researcher attempts to understand the language of the practitioner—what words refer to which ideas and practices—so that the two can communicate. Much of what is done in qualitative research comprises participant observation, a technique that is widely used in anthropology and social psychology. The observer attempts to see the situation anew, with no preconceptions and no biases. She then tries to capture in words what is occurring, in what are called field notes. Later, the researcher reads through these notes and attempts to compress them into a manageable summary, which becomes the journal article.

How does the reader evaluate such an article? Coleman (1993) suggested that the reader must trust the researcher. He commented that the situations being described cannot be replicated, or revisited, so there is no independent way for the reader, or for another researcher, to find out whether what the article says happened really occurred: "The standard for establishing reliability is not replication of specific results; it is more general patterns of thought that are harmonious with the literature on the topic" (p. 27). Another technique readers may use is triangulation, that is, seeing whether information from different aspects of the research hangs together into a coherent whole. A third is to compare the report with other reports on other professionals in similar situations.

PROBLEMS IN ECSE RESEARCH

Research in ECSE is difficult, for many reasons. One is the basic fact that most intervention and preschool education is brief in duration. Experimental intervention may last just twenty minutes a day, one day a week, in the case of infants and toddlers under three, or three hours a day, perhaps three days a week, with preschoolers. Research means attempting to tease out what effects that assistance has, despite the fact that what goes on during the rest of the day has as much or more influence, and despite the fact that young children develop on their own, at very different rates, irrespective of intervention. This is particularly an issue in research on intensity (whether more intensive interventions are better than less intensive ones) because even the more intensive programs tend to offer modest levels of instruction, therapy, or other interventions. Establishing a difference between groups when both the more intensive and the less intensive treatments are rather mild can be problematic.

The core of experimental research, of course, is establishing differences between groups. When that is done, the null hypothesis may be rejected and a significant difference reported. What happens, though, when there is as much variation, if not more, within one or more of the groups than there is between them? *Within group differences* are, in experimental research, noise—unwanted variability. Yet the very nature of disability is that it varies tremendously. Even children who all have the same disability will differ one from another, in fact more than will children with no disabilities. Accordingly, there will be a great deal of noise in many experiments with children who have disabilities. That noise may drown out otherwise significant between-groups differences. This factor of variation within groups often makes ECSE research difficult to do.

To illustrate, suppose a study reports on a group of children aged three to five who have cerebral palsy. This begs the question: How severe was the cerebral palsy? The condition varies tremendously; some children are able to speak, others are not; some are able to manipulate small objects with excellent fine motor control, others cannot; some are retarded, others are not. That is, a group of children with cerebral palsy probably has within it much greater variation of individual performance than generally is found in a group of nondisabled children in the same age range. For this reason, variance within groups will be considerable—and may overwhelm variance between groups. Establishing a significant difference between groups is therefore a real challenge.

Bothersome differences within groups can be overcome in a number of ways. One is by restricting the differences within groups artificially by selecting only children with, in this case, mild cerebral palsy. That means that the children in each group are more like other children in the same group, thus reducing the "noise" within that group. While helpful to the researcher who wants to establish differences between groups, this strategy sharply limits the generalizability of the study. Any findings will be relevant only to the kinds of children studied, in this case, young children with mild cerebral palsy.

Researchers can also deal with differences within groups by using large numbers of subjects. The law of large numbers is such that a given difference between groups will be significant with a large number of subjects, even when it is not significant with smaller groups (Bernoulli, 1956, cited in Kerlinger, 1986). But finding large numbers of children with disabilities, in this case cerebral palsy, is difficult because most disabilities are low-incidence conditions. The researcher has little choice but to work with small numbers of subjects and hope that the treatment will be powerful enough to establish a difference between groups. Sometimes, the sampling problem is even more serious. The few children a researcher finds may already be in a preformed group. Suppose, for example, a preschool special education class contains three- to- five-year-olds who are mildly to moderately retarded. If these children are in that class because experts referred them there as an appropriate placement to meet their unique needs, clearly they will differ from children with retardation who are not in that class. Using preformed groups, as in this example, may be convenient for the researcher, but it is dangerous. It is an example of "selection error," and it represents yet another problem in ECSE research.

Sampling bias has another aspect. In ECSE, by law, all children who are eligible for services must be served. One cannot legally (or morally) deny services to eligible children in order to create a control group for an experiment. Researchers are often limited, therefore, to comparing different kinds of interventions or educational programs. One might think that there is a simple solution to this problem: to compare children, some of whom have been referred for services and some of whom have not. The problem here is that children who come in for services differ from children who do not. Most obviously, the families themselves differ. This issue will be explored in more detail later in this chapter, when research on age at start (the age of the child when services begin) is considered. For the present, suffice it to say that parental socioeconomic status (SES) influences age at start, meaning that family characteristics are confounded with age at start variables.

The interventions or education offered to young children with disabilities may have effects, but not the ones researchers anticipated. To illustrate, young children in a preschool class may be given a language development curriculum that is not given to another class. Afterward, language competence is measured. That no significant differences emerge is, of course, disappointing. But there may have been changes in social or emotional development, with the children in the experimental group acquiring greater social competence than did the children in the control group. Yet because this was not measured, no one knows. The overdependence on IQ tests is especially relevant here. Some studies, oddly enough, have used IQ tests to measure effects in an experiment on social development. As a reader, you need to be alert to such inappropriate measures.

RESEARCH FINDINGS

Research in ECSE tends to follow more than lead practice. Infants, toddlers, and preschoolers with disabilities are receiving services in thousands of programs coast to coast; parents and professionals alike in these programs are convinced that their efforts make a difference in the lives of the young children being served. An important task of the researcher is to document such effects. To date, however, researchers have had difficulty finding convincing evidence of such benefits. The work of White and his colleagues at Utah State University's

Early Intervention Research Institute (EIRI) in particular has been misunderstood. The EIRI researchers have been criticized for failing to see what everyone knows is obvious, that early intervention works. But White and his colleagues have not said that early intervention is not effective; rather, they have tried to point out that methodological difficulties—including sampling, measurement, and interpretation problems—so far have made defining effects, for the most part, an elusive task. Still, the fact that such basic questions as, "Are more services better than fewer?" and "Is ECSE cost-effective?" cannot yet be answered affirmatively without controversy angers many hardworking professionals in the field and makes the research itself controversial. However, Guralnick (1991, 1993), who is not associated with the Utah State program, concurred with White and his colleagues that research has shown less than often is assumed.

Three meta-analyses of large numbers of research studies in ECSE (Casto & Mastropieri, 1986a; Shonkoff & Hauser-Cram, 1987; Innocenti & White, 1993) concluded that early intervention has beneficial but modest effects on young children with disabilities. Reviewing seventy-four studies on the efficacy of early intervention, Glendon Casto and Margo Mastropieri (both with the Utah State EIRI) found few real effects in the ECSE age range (birth to five). Innocenti and White (1993), examining intensity in early intervention, found few indications that "more is better." White, Taylor, and Moss (1992); White and Casto (1985); and Casto and White (1985) conducted other meta-analyses in ECSE. Each was with the Utah State EIRI at the time. In addition, Shonkoff and Hauser-Cram (1987) analyzed thirty-one studies, but only with respect to children under three. They did find some differences.

A meta-analysis is an analysis of analyses; that is, it brings together many previous reviews of research and many individual studies and attempts to draw from this voluminous information some general conclusions. Casto and Mastropieri (1986a), Shonkoff and Hauser-Cram (1987), and White et al. (1992) used effect size to establish a common cross-study measure of findings. They expressed research findings in terms of standard deviations (S.D.s) by converting results of individual studies to standardized mean difference effect sizes (ES). In plainer English, ES is a Z-score, a score expressed in S.D. The general formula is: $M_1 - M_2/SD_2 = ES$, where M_1 is the mean for the experimental group, M_2 the mean for the control (contrast) group, SD_2 the S.D. of the control group, and ES the effect size. The advantage of ES is that it creates a single measure, which can be applied to compare studies that used different measures of outcomes. For example, differences in IQ in one study and in social competency in another can be discussed together after the findings from both have been converted to ES. A meta-analysis, then, is a "statistical analysis of a large collection of analysis results from individual studies for the purpose of integrating the findings" (Glass, 1976, p. 3; see also Glass, McGaw, & Smith, 1981).

While meta-analyses are helpful to students and professionals because they break down large bodies of information into smaller chunks of knowledge, they are controversial. (The *Journal of Consulting and Clinical Psychology*, 1983, vol. 51, p. 3–75 has a section on meta-analysis. See also *Educational Researcher*, 1984, vol. 13, no. 8, pp. 6–27.) Casto and Mastropieri's (1986a) study, for example, was immediately, and harshly, criticized by Dunst and Snyder (1986) and by Strain and Smith (1986). Of course, controversies in ECSE research go much further than the value of meta-analysis. The first studies on early intervention, in particular, produced glowing reports that helped to convince Congress to enact the Part H (now Part C) mandate to serve infants and toddlers. Only after PL 99-457 was signed into law did numerous reanalyses and further research call into question the earlier reports of success with very young children with disabilities. As the field of ECSE stands today, it is fair to say that there are more questions than answers. For that reason, a review of research is best approached by posing, and trying to answer in turn, a series of questions about ECSE.

Unanswered Questions and Unquestioned Answers

The questions facing ECSE appear on their face to be simple enough. An example: "Does the age at which services begin matter?" Most parents and professionals would agree that it does; that is the major rationale for early intervention and for preschool special education as well. Another: "Is more better than less?" Again, the commonsense response would be yes. As a young field, ECSE asks these kinds of questions. However, research to date suggests that questions in this form may not be answerable. Among other reasons, that is because different influences have diverse effects, with the effects on some children wiped out or canceled out by the lack of effects, or even by negative effects, on other children and parents.

Rather than ask such global questions, the evidence is that researchers should narrow their focus, asking instead such questions as, "Does age at start matter for infants and toddlers who are retarded?" and "Is more speech therapy better for children who are deaf?" Questions framed in this way—asking what helps which kinds of children—may be much more readily answered. Shonkoff and Hauser-Cram (1987) commented:

> In a field that emphasizes the importance of individual differences, and recognizes the limitations of a "one-size-fits-all" service model, there is a critical need for greater understanding of interactions among child, family, and service variables. . . . What we do not know is what specific program features work best, to what end, and for whom. (p. 656)

It is an indication of the growing maturity of the field that researchers are at least beginning to design studies addressing these important interactions.

The following section poses ten questions and attempts to answer them. It is worth noting that this discussion focuses only on research evidence. There may well be experiential or anecdotal evidence in support of some of the issues on which research to date has not been able to document effectiveness. Our focus here is not on such material, but rather on research itself.

1. "Is ECSE effective?" Research to date demonstrates that ECSE does in fact lead to real, measurable benefits for young children with disabilities (Guralnick, 1997). Casto and Mastropieri, reviewing seventy-four studies that included children from birth to age five inclusive (actually, birth to 5.6 years), stated: "The overall conclusion is that early intervention programs do result in moderately large immediate benefits for handicapped populations. These results are evident over a variety of outcome variables including IQ, motor, language, and academic achievement" (1986a, p. 420).

When they asked more specific questions, however, such as whether parental involvement mattered, Casto and Mastropieri had difficulty pinpointing sizable effects. They also commented, "It should be noted that the effect sizes when only good quality studies are considered are noticeably smaller" (p. 420). These and similar criticisms of ECSE research prompted other researchers—notably Dunst, Snyder, Smith (an ECSE expert in Pittsburgh), and Strain (of the University of Pittsburgh)—to attack their work. The exchange of views, in 1986 issues of the journal *Exceptional Children,* illustrates the passion researchers bring to their work—and disproves, yet again, the popular but erroneous image of the "objective scientist." Perhaps the best rebuttal to the attacks is an independent reanalysis of the studies. Fortunately, Shonkoff and Hauser-Cram undertook one soon after the *Exceptional Children* controversy arose. It is impossible to read Shonkoff and Hauser-Cram's contribution without appreciating anew Casto and Mastropieri's work.

Shonkoff and Hauser-Cram (1987), reexamining thirty-one of the EIRI-suggested research reports on infants and toddlers from birth to two, as compared with Casto and Mastropieri's analysis of studies of children from birth to five years of age, found moderate positive, or medium, effects. The thirty-one studies all dealt with infants and toddlers under three, and were, Shonkoff and Hauser-Cram said, "the best available data on the impact of early intervention services" (p. 651). Most studies looked at children with a range of disabilities, including physical, mental, and sensory. More than half of the outcomes reported were IQ or other developmental gains made by the children, although language measures were also taken. Shonkoff and Hauser-Cram expressed concern that only seven of the thirty-one studies even tried to measure parent-related outcomes, other than to ask about parental satisfaction.

Shonkoff and Hauser-Cram had difficulty, as did Casto and Mastropieri, finding clear evidence of program effectiveness for young children with severe disabilities. The relative lack of evidence of effectiveness for such children is a very important concern: It is these children who are most in need of ECSE. While effects with such children may take longer to emerge and may be more subtle than effects on children having mild to moderate impairments, the fact remains that ECSE's effectiveness cannot be proclaimed as proven until it is shown to help those most in need.

Support for overall efficacy of early intervention has been building for more than a decade. White, speaking at a National Institutes of Health (NIH) conference in late 1985, noted that most evidence on early intervention effectiveness available at the time was based on studies of disadvantaged (e.g., low-SES) children and families, not on children with disabilities. He was concerned about the low quality of much of the research on those children. Looking at the few high-quality studies on disability, he concluded, "However, the fact remains that there is evidence of a strong and replicable immediate effect for handicapped children based on studies of only good methodologic quality" (White, 1985/1986, p. 408). To summarize: Yes, ECSE is effective, most noticeably with young children who have mild to moderate needs.

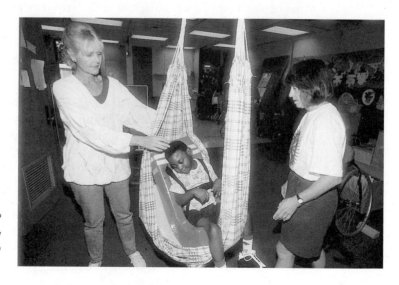

Does age at start matter? ECSE has had difficulty giving a clear answer to that question.

2. "Is earlier better?" The review continues with the commonsense statement that of course earlier intervention is better than later intervention—isn't it? This is a question of **age at start** (sometimes erroneously referred to as "age of start"; our interest, however, is not in how old the start is but in how old the children were when services began). It is not a question of duration of services. Given that the belief that earlier is in fact better is one of the most central in all of ECSE, the paucity of research on the issue is discouraging (Boyce, Smith, Immel, Casto, & Escobar, 1993). A number of studies have included age at start as one of many variables, but whatever effects are due to age at start are confounded with influences from other variables, notably duration. Another possible confounding factor is severity: Severe disabilities tend to be identified earlier, and treatment begun earlier, than is the case with mild disabilities. For this reason, children who begin services earlier may be more disabled than those who start later. A lesser problem in ECSE research, which is an important issue in other research, is the confounding of age at start with age at onset. **Age at onset** refers to the age of the child when the disability began. With some disabilities (deafness is a good example) the effect of the disability on the child's development varies strongly with age at onset; in deafness, to continue the example, children born deaf will experience speech, language, and academic difficulties that children who become deaf at, say, ten years of age will not have.

The Casto and Mastropieri (1986a) meta-analysis identified twenty-four reviews of prior studies that looked at age-at-start issues; of those, eighteen concluded that earlier was in fact better. Reanalyzing the reported studies, Casto and Mastropieri disagreed, finding that few research findings supported an early age at start for birth-to-five children with disabilities. Shonkoff and Hauser-Cram (1987), looking yet again at the studies, found two effects. First, with respect to infants and toddlers from birth to two (but not with three- to-five-year-olds), earlier starts are associated with better results. Specifically, Shonkoff and Hauser-Cram reported that children with mild disabilities who entered service programs prior to six months of age benefited most from early intervention services (p. 653).

Boyce et al. asked whether age at start matters, specifically with respect to medically fragile infants (those with chronic pulmonary disease, intraventricular hemorrhage, congenital neurologic anomalies, and so on). Many of these infants were born prematurely, so the age at start in this investigation was the corrected age (the age the infants would have been had they gone to term). Comparing three-month with eighteen-month start dates, Boyce et al. found no significant infant differences until thirty-six months after the interventions concluded—and no family differences even at that late date. Considering their findings, as well as those of earlier researchers, Boyce et al. concluded, "[W]e have some evidence that earlier might be better, but the effects are small and not consistent across all measures where they would be expected" (p. 303). White (1985/1986) agreed that evidence on age at start is minimal and inconclusive.

In part, these mixed results may be due to the crudeness of the available measures of impact (Neisworth & Bagnato, 1992). That is, effects may be there, but the tests used may not be able to find them. The problem may also be that effects, particularly with children having severe disabilities, may take some time to become evident. The Infant Health and Development Program (IHDP) (1990) and Boyce, Smith, et al. (1993) suggested that effects may not appear for as many as three or even four years. Finally, there may be noise within groups: Early onset may help with some kinds of young children, but not as much with others. Lovaas (1987), for example, found very notable effects of early onset with respect to children who are autistic.

There is another important factor here: Parental motivation is confounded with age at start. As mentioned above, certain kinds of parents seek, and get, earlier services for their infants and toddlers than do other kinds of parents. Thus, effects on young children may reflect parental influence as much as, if not more than, programmatic effects due strictly to early age at start. In general, middle- and upper-class families tend to be better educated than lower-class families and they may notice delays in development earlier. Such families may also be more in control of their daily lives, and have more time than lower-class families, especially large ones, to pursue diagnoses and treatment at earlier stages. Of course, middle- and upper-class families can also afford extensive medical care, including numerous referrals to specialists until a condition is accurately diagnosed. In addition to other pressing concerns that may cause them to delay treatment, lower-class families may not have those financial resources; not even Medicaid covers all poor families. All of this leads to a sobering fact: The age at start of services is *confounded* with socioeconomic factors; it is not the only difference between groups. The task of separating out those socioeconomic factors from the age at start issue in and of itself may not be possible.

Perhaps the best way to summarize the evidence here is to quote Farran (1990): "There is no strong evidence for 'the earlier the better' despite the common sense appeal of this homily" (p. 509).

3. *"Is more intensive better?"* This is another of those questions apparently "so obvious that one need not ask it." The question is not so self-evident, however. What is intensive? The question here is best understood as asking whether more frequent (thrice-weekly versus once-weekly sessions, for example) or same-frequency, more lengthy services (twice-weekly, sixty-minute versus twice-weekly, twenty-minute sessions) are superior. It is not quite that clear, however. If one is discussing home visits (a common method for serving infants and toddlers), is intensiveness best understood as how frequently, or for how long, a home visitor visits? What about parental use of techniques taught by the home visitor? Conceivably, less frequent home visits might be correlated with more intensive parental instruction of a child, making something of a mockery of measures of home-visit intensity. One also needs to ask, "Intensive in what?" As Innocenti and White (1993) pointed out, a full-day program does not provide twice the intervention of a half-day program because of lunchtime, nap, interruptions in instruction, and so on. One must also guard against confounding the issue of intensity with that of program duration. Were two children to participate in a preschool program, one for two years and the other for one, the first would clearly receive more services, but to say he got a more intensive intervention would be erroneous.

An important consideration in evaluating research on intensity is that even intensive intervention in most cases is fairly modest. Intensive may mean twenty minutes of physical therapy three times a week, for example, or a one-hour home visit by a professional once a week. Against this, one contrasts even less intensive activities. That research often fails to find significant effects of more intensive versus less intensive interventions should not be too surprising.

However complex the construct, it has attracted considerable research interest, largely because it is so important in ECSE. How frequent and how lengthy sessions should be are questions that emerge every time an individualized family service plan (IFSP) or individualized education program (IEP) is written. With personnel salaries comprising some 70 percent to as much as 90 percent of program costs in special education (see, for example, Graham & Bryant, 1993; Chaikind, Danielson, & Brauen, 1993), the issue of how much is enough obviously has major cost implications.

Parette, Hendricks, and Rock (1991) searched the literature (1960–1989) for studies on intensity of physical or occupational therapy with young children who have cerebral palsy.

They located just one such study, although twelve others reported upon therapy with children who had different conditions. The single study, Jenkins et al. (1982)—also reported in Jenkins and Sells (1984)—found that children with cerebral palsy who received therapy three times a week did no better than others who were treated just once a week. (After Parette et al.'s review, Law et al. (1991) reported findings very similar to those of Jenkins.) Parette et al. concluded that the literature fails to provide any guidance as to whether more intensive is better. In fact, they complained that the literature does not even explain what "intensive therapeutic intervention" means, and often does not measure intensity with any objectivity or specificity. Hanft and Royeen (1991), professionals in occupational therapy, responded to the Parette et al. review by insisting that intensity is not a proper subject for research because each therapist decides individually how intensive therapy should be for each particular client.

Warfield (1995) compared home visits to center-based group services, finding that the cost-effectiveness varied according to outcomes measured. With respect to reducing parental stress, home visits clearly were more effective and more cost-effective; on the other hand, in the area of teaching adaptive behavior to infants and toddlers, group services were more cost-effective. Given that home visits cost about 2.5 times as much as did group services, Warfield reported, programs should exercise care in choosing which services to deliver in the home.

Hanft and Feinberg (1997) made similar recommendations. Noting persistent shortages of occupational and physical therapists and acknowledging that "[r]esearch has been equivocal, and there has been little documentation that specific frequencies of intervention yield particular results" (p. 29), they sought to shift the debate from "How much is enough?" to "What exactly do the therapists do with their time?" Hanft and Feinberg suggested that professionals should respond to family-set outcomes (desired results) in making decisions about frequency and intensity of services. "Intensity and frequency of services, then, are not the most important variables" (p. 34). Far more important, they insisted, is "what professionals do with their time" (p. 34). What they should do is what is needed for a particular family and child to reach the goals they themselves have set.

Innocenti and White (1993) reviewed forty-two studies that reported data on intensity; most did not focus on intensity, but included it as one of several issues of interest. They concluded that little evidence exists for the proposition that more intensive is better. "In fact," they wrote, "if we examine only the high-quality studies, we observe an inverse relation between intensity and efficacy" (p. 37). They also analyzed twenty studies that manipulated intensity as an experimental variable. These, as well, offered little support for the intensity hypothesis. It should be noted, however, that most such studies used IQ as the outcome measure of choice, ignoring the possibility that effects may have occurred in other areas of development (i.e., social or emotional, adaptive). Very few studies examined effects on families, but those that did found no significant effects. Innocenti and White concluded, "We found almost no support for the intensity hypothesis for interventions with children with disabilities" (p. 45). They added an appeal for research that specifies more clearly "what is happening to the child during interventions" (p. 46) and what families do when a home visitor is not present.

Intensity was also addressed by Goetze et al. (1993). Looking at medically fragile infants, they compared a highly intensive intervention for infants and families, which included in-hospital and transition-to-community services, with the more common, less intensive hospital follow-up services. The highly intensive intervention took up to five times as many hours of professional and parent involvement with the infant and cost about three times as much as the less intensive treatment. However, few effects were noticed, even as late as twenty-four months following the intervention.

A very intensive early intervention program was mounted by the IHDP for LBW, premature infants. Those who participated most frequently finished with higher IQ scores and lower behavior problem scores, as compared to a group that participated less frequently in the intervention (Ramey, Bryant, Wasik, Sparling, Fendt, & LaVange, 1992). However, as suggested earlier, the IHDP excluded infants with serious health problems in addition to LBW and/or premature infants.

Intensity is a vital issue in ECSE. What is learned about the effects of more intensive versus less intensive programs affects program design, specifically how expensive programs need to be to provide appropriate services to young children. One of Goetze et al.'s most disturbing observations, in their review of previous research, was that very few studies have even addressed the issue of intensity for LBW infants with severe disabilities. Given that intensity of service is most likely to be an issue with children having severe, rather than mild, impairments, this lack of research is disconcerting.

Could it be that less intensive might actually be better? Suppose, for example, parents of children with severe disabilities benefit more by being given respite (a break from caring for the child) than they do by being taught how to develop their child's skills (White, 1985/1986). In this case, more intensive services (or more "parental involvement," as it may also be called) might actually be detrimental to parents. Conceivably, they might also harm

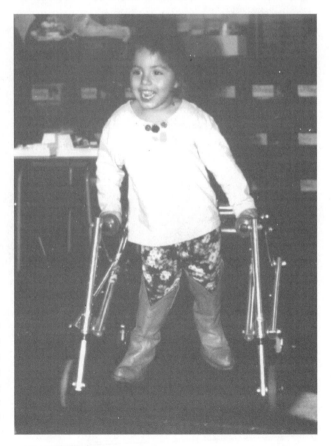

Is more intensive better? One would think so. But children with more severe needs tend to get more frequent services than children with more moderate needs, making research in this area difficult.

rather than help the child. Perhaps more obvious is the possibility that the beneficial effects of education or other intervention may be subject to the law of diminishing returns, namely, that some therapy helps a lot but subsequent therapy adds little to what the initial work contributed.

4. *"Does parental involvement help?"* The Individuals with Disabilities Education Act (IDEA), in Part C, requires that early intervention programs involve parents, notably in identifying family needs and priorities. Part B does not contain similar requirements but does encourage parents to become involved in preparing IEPs and in protecting their children's rights under the law. Parental involvement is a core concept of ECSE as it is practiced today. However, as is so often the case in this young field, what "parental involvement" means is not always clear. Parents may be involved in minor ways or in major ones. They may be consulted on program goals for their child and for the family as a whole, or they may just be given some printed materials about their child's disability and about community resources.

That parents should be involved in programs serving infants, toddlers, and preschoolers with disabilities is not in dispute. Parents are, after all, the most important people in these young children's lives. The law, particularly in Part C, is unequivocal in its insistence that parents be involved; and professional literature, too, has supported parental involvement. Casto and Mastropieri (1986a), for example, reported that twenty-six of twenty-seven previous reviews of the literature showed that more parental involvement is better than less. Despite all of this, Casto and Mastropieri, reanalyzing the studies, concluded that parental involvement can be linked to few outcomes and that "those intervention programs which utilize parents are not more effective than those which do not" (p. 421). That is a surprising statement—and a controversial one. Upon closer examination, the conclusion says something different from what it seems to be saying on the face of it. What Casto and Mastropieri said was linked to few effects on young children with disabilities was one specific kind of parental involvement. To illustrate, White, Taylor, and Moss (1992), reviewing 172 studies on early intervention, found that "using parents as intervenors was by far the most frequent way in which past early intervention research defined parent involvement" (p. 94).

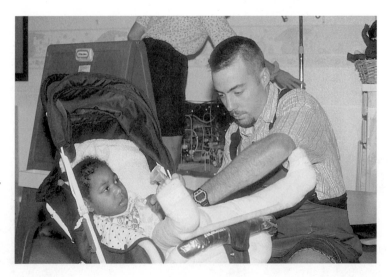

Whether the parental involvement helps depends in part on how parents are involved. If they are just trained to care for the child, benefits may be minimal.

This didactic approach is controversial in ECSE (Bailey, Palsha, & Simeonsson, 1991; Graham & Bryant, 1993). Many experts believe that empowering parents and helping families to function more effectively may be more helpful than training parents to perform quasi-professional functions in the home. Parental instruction is what the field is doing, however; practitioners say they spend more time teaching parents how to be intervenors than they do in any other aspect of their work with families (Mahoney & O'Sullivan, 1990). Accordingly, research has examined this approach. The findings, as Casto and Mastropieri (1986a) reported, are not encouraging.

Casto, Mastropieri, White, Taylor, and Moss were all associated with the Utah State University EIRI at the time these studies were published. For that reason, the Casto and Mastropieri (1986a) and White, Taylor, and Moss (1992) publications have been widely interpreted as EIRI attacks on parental involvement. A careful reading of their reports shows otherwise. Both reports, together with Boyce, White, and Kerr (1993), another EIRI publication, explicitly stated that the kinds of parental involvement being examined featured didactic instruction from professionals on how parents could assume some of their therapeutic roles in the home. To illustrate, take the words of Boyce, White, and Kerr: "We have selected the most frequent way parents have been involved in previously reported early intervention research" (p. 329). Notice that they did *not* choose that approach because they believed in it. Thus, the EIRI work does not attack parental involvement policies; rather, it points out that available research evidence does not support the premise that by teaching parents how to perform some quasi-professional roles, professionals are in fact helping young children.

White, Taylor, and Moss (1992) noted that parental involvement is confounded with so many other variables that teasing out the effects of parental involvement alone is extremely difficult. To illustrate, consider the kind of program the child is in. If it is a day-care program, featuring relatively little direct instruction, then parents-as-intervenors who teach the child at home to, say, speak more clearly, can be quite effective. The parental instruction is virtually the only teaching that is being done. However, if the child is in a center-based program with a strong direct-instruction component, parental teaching at home may add little, if anything, to what already is happening at the program. To illustrate, consider the study reported below.

Boyce, White, and Kerr (1993) compared a center-based program to a center-based program plus parental involvement focusing on fifty-one preschool children with moderate to severe disabilities. Children were assigned treatments randomly, with parental permission. Parents in the experimental group received fifteen weeks of instruction in parent-group meetings on how to intervene at home and on topics related to their children's needs. This kind of parental involvement was chosen, the researchers said, because it was the kind most frequently reported in the literature. Both child effects and family effects were measured. Although the parents did learn the material they were taught, no effects on the children's functioning were observed, even after a four-year follow-up; and no effects were found on parental functioning, either. The authors concluded, "[T]he results should cause us to reconsider and reevaluate the use of this type of parent instruction involvement" (p. 343).

Examining only studies on early intervention with infants and toddlers from birth to two, Shonkoff and Hauser-Cram (1987) did find effects of parental involvement. Cautioning that what is actually reported, even by these high-quality studies, was planned involvement as opposed to documented, actual involvement of parents, Shonkoff and Hauser-Cram concluded that "programs that planned extensive parent involvement showed significantly greater effects than those with little or no planned parent participation" (p. 653). Notably, the programs Shonkoff and Hauser-Cram examined reported plans for a diverse range of activities involving parents beyond the didactic approach found by the EIRI group to be of questionable value.

To summarize, research does not clearly support the parent-as-instructor approach to parental involvement, particularly where children are already receiving considerable professional instruction. This remains, however, the most popular approach to parental involvement in ECSE. It is important to explore other ways to involve parents, and to study the effects of those modes of involvement, until effective, and cost-effective, ways to do that are discovered. The question is not whether to involve parents; ECSE programs must do that by law. Rather, the question is how best to do it.

5. *"Is ECSE cost-effective? Cost-beneficial?"* Decision Resources Corporation (DRC) (Moore, Strang, Schwartz, & Braddock, 1988), in an *Expenditures Survey* report commissioned by the U.S. Department of Education, said that preschool special education for students with disabilities incurred 2.1 times the costs of teaching nondisabled preschool students. By "preschool programs" DRC meant early intervention (from birth to two) programs as well as preschool services for three- to five-year-olds. Both school- and home-based programs were included. The ratio they stated is quite close to the 2.3 factor they reported for K–12 special education (see also Chaikind, Danielson, & Brauen, 1993). Clearly, services for young children with disabilities can be expensive. The question now is, "Is the money well spent?"

cost-effective analyses look to whether one approach, or one program, provides more benefits per dollar than another.

That is a question of costs versus outcomes. When one asks if something is **cost-effective**, one is inquiring as to whether the costs incurred are less than costs for something else. If two programs are compared, both of which deliver the same services, yet the first does so at a lower cost than the second, it is possible to conclude that the first is cost-effective. Similarly, an evaluator might compare two programs, both costing about the same amount of money, but discover that one provides more services, greater benefits, and so on, and for that reason is more cost-effective. **Cost-benefit** analysis, by contrast, examines the benefits accrued by the child, assigns them a (frequently arbitrary) dollar value, and compares these benefits to costs. That is, the monetary value of the benefits may exceed that of the services. Cost-benefit can be estimated for a single program, even for a single child, whereas cost-effectiveness usually requires that at least two programs be compared.

cost-benefit analyses look at benefits, assigning values to them, and compare those values with the costs of providing the benefits.

In ECSE, it is often difficult to perform either kind of analysis. One problem is identifying all relevant costs; many studies neglect to include opportunity costs, where, for example, parents might give up income-generating opportunities in order to attend parent meetings. This chapter has suggested that more intensive services are not necessarily always better; for this reason, one cannot simply say that Program A offers twice the number of hours of speech therapy for the same price as Program B does and therefore conclude that Program A is more cost-effective. Quantifying costs and benefits of services is difficult. Cost studies may tilt the evidence in one way or another by, for example, not counting all relevant costs, or by using very liberal definitions of benefits or other outcomes. Recent cost studies have attempted to avoid these problems.

Looking only at early intervention programs serving medically fragile infants, Boyce, Smith, et al. (1993) calculated that "the cost per child for a child starting intervention at three months is almost three times as much as for a child entering intervention at 18 months" (p. 296). The cost per child was estimated at $5,434 for the early group (entered at three months, served for two years), while that for the late group was $1,845 (entered at eighteen months, served for one year). Both figures were expressed in 1990 dollars. These costs included not only salaries for professionals but also opportunity costs for parents, assigned a value of $9 per hour (p. 296). Only at the three-year follow-up did Boyce, Smith, et al. find noticeable child benefits associated with the additional costs of $3,600 per child. Those effects were small in regard to the children, and nonexistent in regard to the parents.

Goetze et al. (1993), studying intensive care unit (ICU) follow-up services, found that an intensive program of support for parents cost three times as much ($10,814 per child per year, in 1990 dollars) as more traditional hospital follow-up ($3,032/child/year). The additional expenditures, Goetze and her colleagues said, had few measurable impacts on either child or family as late as two years following intervention. Citing the IHDP finding of late-appearing effects, they reserved opinion pending three- and four-year follow-up studies.

Innocenti, Hollinger, Escobar, and White (1993) looked at the cost-effectiveness of parent involvement in early intervention. Adding a parental instruction component to a center-based program raised costs per child from $6,579 (center-based program only, in 1990 dollars) to $8,398 (program plus parent component), or $1,819 more. Looking at effects on both child and parent, Innocenti et al. concluded, "The parent involvement component was not immediately cost-effective, but may be in the long term" (p. 306). That is because the parent training component, which stressed parental instruction in child development and teaching processes, was associated with only limited impacts on child and family. Because some of the effects on the child may persist over a longer period of time, the possibility that the extra costs may result in longitudinal gains means that the parental involvement may in time produce benefits that outweigh the costs.

To summarize, early intervention and preschool special education are expensive, generally twice as costly as similar programs for children with no disabilities. Whether the programs are cost-effective, or even cost-beneficial, has not been established; it may not be possible to state definitively even for a single program and a particular child whether the expenditures were worth it.

6. "Does inclusion help children with disabilities?" Inclusion is a fairly new term. It refers not merely to integration of children with and without disabilities in the same programs or classrooms, but to the design of those settings and offerings, from the beginning, for children with and without disabilities (Salisbury, 1991). It further refers to program integration of children with both mild and severe disabilities (Biklen, 1992), going well beyond earlier interpretations of the Part B "least restrictive environment" (LRE) preference.

It is important to understand that LRE emerged not from research but from the courts as they interpreted the Fifth and Fourteenth amendments to the Constitution. The available research evidence for such a preference was, at the time, very limited. To illustrate, consider two frequently cited studies. Gottlieb and Davis (1973), in a qualitative (observational) study of elementary school children having mild or moderate retardation, found no evidence that physical proximity leads to social integration. The children who were retarded consistently (twenty-seven out of twenty-eight times) were rejected as game partners because, Gottlieb and Davis hypothesized, they were perceived by nondisabled children as less competent partners. Ray (1974), looking at toddlers with and without developmental delays, found little interaction between one group and the other even in this very young age range. The few other pre-1975 investigations of what later became known as, variously, mainstreaming, integration, LRE, and (much later) natural environment (NE) came to similar conclusions, or, to put it more precisely, no conclusions. As it turned out, Congress had little interest in research on the issue; rather, the lawmakers' concern was the interpretation of the Constitution, federal law, and court decisions.

What happened is that the LRE preference was enacted; later, research was carried out on the issue. By the time Congress enacted the NE preference in Part C in 1991, some evidence was available on the results of this approach. Even by this date, the research was by no means unequivocal. Much of it dealt not with infants, toddlers, and preschoolers but with school-age children; because young children differ from older children, and because ECSE settings and activities differ from those of elementary and secondary schools, research on LRE in K–12 should be interpreted cautiously for possible application to ECSE (see, for example, Brault, 1992).

To illustrate, consider best practice for ECSE (Vincent, Salisbury et al., 1980). Vincent and her colleagues suggested use of the "criterion of the next environment." That criterion, they wrote, means that "the definition of best educational practice must be that integrated programs are always the first choice" (Vincent, Brown, & Getz-Sheftel, 1981, p. 23). The discussion in Chapter 9 of DEC "recommended practices" suggests that the term best practice may imply (incorrectly) that such principles, and criteria, are based on hard research evidence. Such is not the case. Rather, best practice seems to be an amalgamation of theory, opinion, experience, and some research to which many professionals are deeply and emotionally committed (Peters & Heron, 1993). To illustrate, you will find articles advancing theses to the effect that there is extensive evidence that infants, toddlers, and preschool-age children with and without disabilities benefit under the Part B LRE preference and the newer Part C NE preference. Such statements may include citations to the literature. If you actually read the cited articles, however, you often find that such evidence remains elusive.

Consider, as an example, one recent paper by two researchers, Mimi Graham and Donna Bryant. Their article, "Developmentally Appropriate Environments for Children with Special Needs," published in a mid-1993 issue of the journal *Infants and Young Children,* was a wide-ranging, very informative review of curricula, indoor and outdoor learning environments, and personnel issues. It contained much valuable information and is cited as a source numerous times in this book. The weakness commented upon here pervades the literature and by no means distinguishes this report from hundreds of others.

These researchers flatly stated, "Nearly all studies of social interaction or play behaviors for preschoolers with and without disabilities in integrated settings report positive effects." They cited several such reports in support of this contention. One was Cavallaro and Porter's (1980) report on a qualitative (observational) study of how twenty at-risk and normally developing preschool children interacted in the classroom. Most children were about five years of age. "At risk" was defined as an IQ of one S.D. or more below the mean, or as developmentally delayed in language, motor, and/or other skills. Cavallaro and Porter recorded frequency and duration of behaviors, such as sitting near and playing with other children. They found that normally developing children tended to sit near and play with other normally developing children, at-risk children near and with other at-risk children. The authors suggested that the normally developing children were more comfortable with one another and that the at-risk children "suffer from inferior social status" (p. 363). Concluded Cavallaro and Porter:

> *The assumption underlying [mainstreaming] is that physical integration of at-risk and normally developing children will also result in social and programmatic integration in the at-risk child's classroom activities. [However] empirical evidence given by both sociometric and observational studies do not strongly support this assumption. . . . The present study provides evidence that physical mainstreaming alone does not result in complete social integration of delayed and normally developing children and that both classes of children make social discriminations on the basis of developmental status.* (p. 364)

It is difficult to understand how anyone, let alone two well-respected experts on research in ECSE, could consider Cavallaro and Porter's article an endorsement of integration in ECSE. Notice in the quoted passage that Cavallaro and Porter's own review of prior research (citations omitted above) had disclosed little evidence of benefits associated with integration.

Graham and Bryant then cited a 1980 study by Guralnick of four- to six- year-olds with and without disabilities. Guralnick began his report by reviewing the literature, which he found to be both equivocal and sparse. One study he discussed was Ray's (1974) report on educable mentally retarded (mildly to moderately retarded) children. That study, Guralnick reported, found only very limited interaction between children with and without disabilities. In his own research, Guralnick found that children with mild disabilities interacted with nondisabled children; however, he quickly noted that the children having mild disabilities were both one year older, on average, than the nondisabled children (a big advantage at that age) and exhibited social play skills very similar to those of nondisabled children. Among children in the study who had moderate or severe disabilities, Guralnick found limited interactions that "were typically brief and poorly organized" (p. 252).

Graham and Bryant offered few other articles in support of their contention that nearly all research supports their point of view; none that the author could locate (three cited sources were unpublished speeches) was any more convincing than the Cavallaro and Porter or Guralnick articles. The purpose here is to call attention to the fact that even experienced and respected experts in the ECSE field may sometimes read more into the research literature than is actually there. They may also overlook studies that do not conform to their interests or beliefs.

A good example is research on LRE and deafness, which was ignored by all the researchers whose work has been discussed here. Much of that research (for an excellent summary, see Moores, 1991) made two points that may be inconvenient for inclusion advocates. First, the kinds of children with hearing impairments who are integrated into regular classrooms are very different from those who are not; the most obvious differences are degree of hearing loss (mild is associated with integration, severe or profound is not) and age at onset (late is associated with integration, early is not). Second, physical proximity does not equal communication, or social or psychological closeness. For children who are deaf, being close physically to hearing children may mean being alone, ignored, and socially deprived.

To summarize, the research evidence for LRE, NE, and inclusion is equivocal. Most studies have focused on whether children with and without disabilities who are physically proximate actually communicate with each other. LRE, NE, and inclusion are values that many advocate for reasons unconnected with the elusive research evidence. The first two are also legislated parts of ECSE programs. The question, accordingly, is not whether to integrate children who have disabilities with nondisabled children, but rather which children with disabilities will benefit from such integration, under which conditions, and to what extent.

7. "Are we helping those most in need?" Research on early intervention and preschool special education consistently shows that children with mild disabilities benefit from ECSE services more than those with severe or profound disabilities do. As just discussed, children with mild disabilities may experience more than just physical proximity when placed into integrated settings, but children with severe or profound disabilities seem to be much less likely to secure the social, psychological, and other kinds of benefits potentially available in integrated programs. Early age at start, Shonkoff and Hauser-Cram (1987) reported, helps

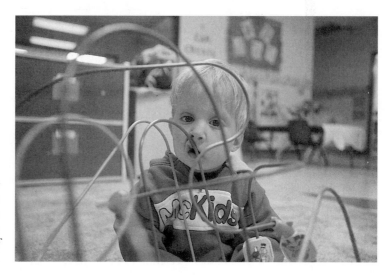

The evidence so far is that ECSE most helps children with mild or moderate needs. The field needs to redouble its efforts on behalf of those most in need.

children with mild disabilities; such benefits were much less evident for children with severe disabilities. Goetze et al. (1993) reported a disconcerting lack of research on the high-intensity versus low-intensity interventions for children with severe and profound disabilities. Guralnick (1980) found some benefits of integration for children with mild disabilities but not for those with severe disabilities. This relative lack of evidence that ECSE "works" with those children who are most in need—who have such severe or profound disabilities such that intervention at an early age, intensive and well-designed services, and so forth are needed if they are needed for anyone—is discouraging.

To summarize, ECSE as a field is not giving as much attention to children with severe disabilities as it is to children who have mild conditions, who have delays, or who are at risk. This is perhaps characteristic of relatively new fields. To illustrate, government-sponsored rehabilitation (of adults with disabilities) began in 1920 with a focus on mildly and moderately disabled clients. It took a specific mandate in the 1973 Rehabilitation Act—fifty-three years later—to force the field to give first priority to "the most severely disabled." As ECSE matures, hopefully lawmaking will not be required to provide at least as much attention for children with severe as for children with mild disabilities.

8. "Does teaming work?" As will be discussed in Chapter 7, Part C of the IDEA requires that multidisciplinary evaluations and assessments be done for each eligible infant or toddler and that IFSPs be written by multidisciplinary teams. As noted earlier, many preschool programs are adopting similar teaming approaches, although Part B does not explicitly require them. The research question is, "Are multidisciplinary teams effective?"

Perhaps the most interesting study on this issue is that of Garshelis and McConnell (1993). They examined how well individual practitioners identified family needs and priorities, compared with multidisciplinary teams. Their major finding was that teams were more accurate than individuals in such assessments. Even when the researchers examined the most perceptive professionals, they found that these experts did better as members of teams than they did individually. Evidently, different team members contribute bits and pieces of information about parent needs, concerns, and priorities—as well as about child strengths and weaknesses—that are, taken together, more comprehensive than those known to any one professional, even the most knowledgeable. If confirmed by further such studies, this investigation offers important support for the multidisciplinary team approach.

Minke and Scott (1993) used qualitative methods to study nine IFSP development meetings. They found parents playing an important, but not decisive, role as members of the multidisciplinary teams. They suggested that professionals sometimes have little appreciation of how much parents have to offer in identifying needs (particularly priorities) and in planning services. Some professional-parent tension was evident, as when staff withheld information or did not ask parents for their views. Bailey, McWilliam, and Winton (1992) suggested that these and other problems in parent-professional teaming may be due in part to the fact that many ECSE practitioners have not been trained in working with families; many, in fact, view themselves as experts on children rather than on family dynamics. Bailey et al. advanced a decision-making model that stresses decision making at the team level (involvement of all team members) and training for professionals about ways of optimizing parental participation.

To summarize, multidisciplinary teams do seem to be better than individuals at doing what the law calls for them to do, notably evaluations and assessments. Balanced against those moderate but noticeable advantages is the fact that a multidisciplinary approach is more costly than an individual practitioner approach.

9. "What should we teach?" The very important question of what should be done in ECSE programs needs to be addressed. In preschool special education, as Wolery (1991) reminded us, very little research has been done on what to teach in the classroom. Wolery noted that instruction could focus around skills needed in the most likely next placement, referencing work by Vincent and Salisbury. He commented that it might also evolve from family priorities and concerns. Early intervention curriculum issues, similarly, have been explored in the literature, particularly as these relate to the five developmental domains recognized by the IDEA (cognitive, physical, social or emotional, adaptive, and communication). Raab, Davis, and Trepanier (1993) argued against categorical services such as formal occupational therapy sessions and in favor of a resource-based program of truly individualized intervention that provides families with resources such as information and other kinds of support.

Graham and Bryant (1993) advocated a developmentally appropriate curriculum that de-emphasizes direct instruction; they urged ECSE programs to use the guidelines of the National Association for the Education of Young Children (NAEYC) (Bredekamp, 1987). Salisbury (1991) also recommended such an approach to an integrated and inclusive program (p. 153). The NAEYC guidelines were developed for use with young, nondisabled children, based on Piaget's work on discovery learning in children. They urged early childhood (EC) staff to facilitate and support, rather than direct and teach, children. Nonetheless, Graham and Bryant commented, "Research has, however, repeatedly shown the effectiveness of programs that are more structured and directive for children with severe disabilities" (p. 33). Children with developmental delays or established conditions may need specific, directive assistance to reach developmental goals. Alberto, Briggs, and Goldstein (1983), in a book chapter on helping young children with disabilities, recommended directive approaches for such infants, noting that these infants may not be able to use self-directed exploration as well as can infants with no disabilities. A good review of research on infant stimulation and teaching techniques is included in the chapter. In their recent research on directive instruction, Macfarland-Smith, Schuster, and Stevens (1993) described an approach to teaching preschool students with developmental delays based on behavior modification.

Casto and Mastropieri (1986a) noted that sixteen of seventeen previous reviewers of research studies addressing the question found that highly structured programs offering direct instruction were better than were loosely structured programs. Casto and Mastropieri cautioned, however, that most such studies dealt with disadvantaged young children, not young children with disabilities. They wrote that evidence on the degree of structure is "inconclusive" for ECSE (pp. 421–422).

To summarize, there is as yet little evidence on what to teach. Generally, more directive instruction appears both necessary for and helpful to young children with severe disabilities, and perhaps others as well. "Developmentally appropriate" or self-exploration strategies, in which program staff facilitate learning rather than deliver teaching, are becoming popular in ECSE programs. Research is needed to assess such approaches in relation to more traditional directive strategies.

10. *"Are we reaching the target population?"* Finally, we need to consider a question that helps us to gauge the progress of the field in responding to the need it is expected to meet. Are we serving most, or only a few, of the young children who are eligible for Part B preschool and Part C early intervention services? To do this, we examine two sets of numbers. First, we look at how many young children are being served. Our source for this information is the *Twentieth Annual Report to Congress on Implementation of the Individuals with Disabilities Education Act* (U.S. Department of Education, 1998). This report contains compilations of data collected and reported to the department by the fifty states and the District of Columbia. Second, we examine how many young children probably need and would benefit from early intervention and preschool special education services. Our source here is a study performed by the U.S. Bureau of the Census (McNeil, 1997). That study asked how many young children have developmental conditions for which they need intervention services.

According to the *Twentieth Annual Report,* a total of 187,000 infants and toddlers (birth to thirty-six months of age) received early intervention services as of December 1, 1996 (U.S. Department of Education, 1998, Table AH1, p. A-228). This is 1.65 percent of all young children in that age range in America. Our question is how to interpret those figures. Do they represent all eligible infants and toddlers? Most of them? Some of them?

For answers, we turn to the Census Bureau. In a Survey of Income and Program Participation (SIPP), the bureau asked a sample of Americans between October 1994 and January 1995 whether they had children under the age of three and, if so, whether those young children had a "developmental condition for which he/she has received therapy or diagnostic services." The proportion of American infants and toddlers reported by their families to have such conditions was 2.6 percent. The Census Bureau estimated that 313,000 infants and toddlers under three years of age had such conditions.

Thus, about 33 percent more young children were reported by their families to have conditions for which they received intervention or diagnostic services than were reported by state early intervention agencies, at about the same time, to have received early intervention services. Stated differently, about 313,000 − 187,000 = 126,000 young children, birth to thirty-six months of age apparently received therapy or diagnostic services, or both, from agencies *other than* early intervention agencies authorized under the IDEA's Part C.

Another way of looking at the same figures is to say that the IDEA's Part C successfully served about 60 percent of the target population in 1996, the most recent year for which data are available. One possible interpretation of these figures is that some families are unaware of the availability of free diagnostic and early intervention services under the IDEA. Another possible explanation is that some families prefer to use private services, possibly because they wish to preserve personal confidentiality. Whatever the reasoning, the fact remains that the IDEA's Part C has some distance to go before it can be said to have reached the target population.

What about preschool services? Here, the *Twentieth Annual Report* tells us that 559,000 young children aged three to five inclusive, or 4.5 percent of all American children in that age range, received preschool special education and related services during the 1996–1997 school year (Table AA1, p. A1). To interpret these numbers, we look again to the Census Bureau's study (McNeil, 1997). In that survey, the bureau asked a sample of Americans during the October 1994 to January 1995 time frame whether they had children over the age of three but under the age of six and, if so, whether those young children had a "developmental condition for which he/she has received therapy or diagnostic services." Families of young children aged three to five inclusive were also asked if the child had a "long-lasting condition that limits his/her ability to walk, run, or use stairs." The proportion of American preschool-age children reported by their families to have any of these conditions was 5.2 percent. Accordingly, the Census Bureau estimated that 652,000 young children aged thirty-six to seventy-two months had such conditions in 1995.

With respect to preschoolers with disabilities, the data suggest that the IDEA's Part B is reaching out to and serving a much higher proportion of its target population (86 percent) than is the IDEA's Part C (60 percent). Still, as of 1995–1996, an estimated 652,000−559,000 = 93,000 preschool-age children with serious health conditions did not receive special education and related services in publicly supported preschool programs.

One very important question that has attracted little research attention is "What should we teach?"

THE ROLE OF RESEARCH IN ECSE

The fact that only modest differences have been reported in many studies—and that no significant differences were found in many others—should not discourage us. ECSE does, after all, focus on individuals, who differ sharply one from another. The large variance within groups that is almost inevitable in this field may prevent differences between groups from rising above the noise of differences within groups. Then, too, the experimental and control groups examined may have been too small for results to attain statistical significance. Researchers may not yet know how to ask the most important (and interesting) questions. The tests and other instruments may not be sensitive enough to capture the differences our interventions make.

These problems, and others, have plagued ECSE research for years. They will remain with us, confounding new generations of researchers. What, then, is the role of research in ECSE? One very important role is to help us to keep a distance between our emotional ties to philosophies and value systems—such as LRE and inclusion, which we follow for reasons having to do with the Constitution, law, and regulation—from professional practices used because they have been shown, in controlled research studies, to work. The two should not be confused. Whether research eventually favors more directive instruction or more developmentally appropriate services for young children with disabilities matters. It may be that neither extreme will prevail. Possibly, one approach helps with some children, another with others.

The value of research is that it assists us to make those fine distinctions. It also provides us with documentation of effectiveness; such objective evidence is important for publicly supported programs. Finally, research helps to design individual service plans, telling us how much is enough to meet the unique needs of a child.

Guralnick has proposed that the role of research in early intervention (and by extension in preschool special education as well) has changed since the enactment of federal mandates in 1986. He suggested that research in early intervention now has entered a second genera-

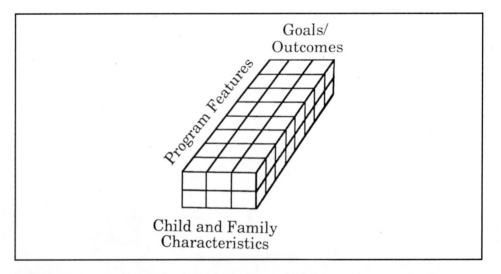

FIGURE 3.1 An organizational framework for designing and analyzing early intervention efficacy research. (From Guralnick, 1989; copyright 1989 by PRO-ED, Inc.; reprinted with author's permission.)

tion (Guralnick, 1993). White and his colleagues at Utah State's EIRI concurred (White, Boyce, Casto, Innocenti, Taylor, Goetze, & Behl, 1994). Shonkoff and Hauser-Cram (1987) made similar points.

In what Guralnick called the "second generation," research endeavors to answer questions about interactions between children and their families, interventions, and goals (outcomes). Guralnick's model for this kind of research is illustrated in a cubic box into which we may enter research findings as they emerge (See Figure 3.1).

SUMMARY

After just thirty-five–odd years of experience with formal services for preschool-age children, research has demonstrated that ECSE works: It does help infants, toddlers, and preschoolers with developmental delays and disabilities. We know that much. Does it help as much as it could? Probably not. We have much to learn, especially about intervention strategies, parental involvement, and intensity and duration of services.

Although many key questions remain unanswered, we as a nation have decided to move forward. Infants, toddlers, and preschool-age children with disabilities now enjoy the right to services that meet their unique needs. Federal law spells out, in quite specific detail, what is to be done. Intervention is to begin almost immediately after a disability is discovered (within thirty days for infants and toddlers, forty-five days for preschoolers). Parents are to be involved, heavily in early intervention, less centrally in preschool special education. The law, the regulations, and professional practice—all of these spell out how things are to be done, despite the fact that in many instances there is little or no research evidence that these are, in fact, the best ways to do those things. The alternative was to wait, to delay serving these young children. Congress rejected that option and instead decided to move forward, requiring programs under the IDEA to follow what experts, parents, and research testified to be the state of the art in ECSE. If subsequent research and practice show Congress that things should be done differently, it can—and no doubt will—change program requirements to conform to new knowledge.

QUESTIONS FOR REFLECTION

1. What, in your view, are the pros and cons of quantitative versus qualitative research methods?

2. How do "statistically significant" and "practically significant" findings differ?

3. Explain, in your own words, the concept of "generalizability."

4. In your own words, what is "validity" in research?

5. What different activities might a researcher be discussing when she uses the term "parental involvement"?

6. In what ways might "less intensive" professional intervention actually help young children more?

7. How might a journal author's personal beliefs about inclusion influence the research she reports upon and the meaning she attributes to her findings?

8. Why is research evidence about the efficacy of teams so important with respect to public funding for ECSE programs? How might a lack of such evidence affect funding?

9. Is curriculum an appropriate subject for research? If so, is "more directive" versus "less directive" instruction a good way to approach the subject? Would it help you as a teacher to have clear information on this topic?

10. Why does it matter whether the field of ECSE is or is not reaching most of its target population? What differences in policy, program, or funding decisions might result from data showing that the vast bulk of the need is being met?

While a free, appropriate public education for children from six to eighteen or twenty-one has been the law of the land for twenty-five years, wide availability of services for children under school age is much more recent. It was not until the early 1990s that most states, the District of Columbia, Puerto Rico, and other jurisdictions provided, under law, child and family services for the birth-to-five population of children with disabilities.

Services for infants and toddlers from birth to two inclusive and three-to-five-inclusive preschoolers with disabilities are highly regulated in the United States today. The way in which this came about is described in Chapter 14. That chapter details the history of federal legislation in the field of early childhood special education (ECSE), including both the pre-1986 discretionary (nonmandated) programs and the later imposition of what amounts to national mandates for infants, toddlers, and preschoolers with disabilities. Chapter 5 summarizes the rights of children and their families under the IDEA and other laws. Providing services to young children and their families requires going well beyond the IDEA. That is why Chapter 6 offers thumbnail sketches of other important federal laws, including programs for both families and young children.

In all three chapters, the emphasis is upon specificity of detail. ECSE program administrators, university teacher preparation personnel, researchers, parent advocates, and many others need specific details about the legislation. That is why Chapter 4 "peels the onion" to describe the history of ECSE. To take another example, service coordinators and program administrators need detailed guidance about finances. To meet that need, Chapter 6 offers much specific information on different funding sources. Consider the needs of a service coordinator who is attempting to qualify a toddler for the full range of services this young child needs. Federal and state Part C funding may support only some of the necessary services. To get other vital assistance, eligibility must also be established for services provided under the Developmental Disabilities and Bill of Rights Act (DD Act) and Medicaid. In addition, because the family is poor, the service coordinator is attempting to enroll the toddler in the federal-state Supplemental Security Income (SSI) program.

To do the work, the service coordinator must know very precise information. Exactly what services are authorized under Medicaid, for example? Which are required as components of the Early and Periodic Screening, Diagnosis, and Treatment (EPSDT) program that is affiliated with Medicaid? What does the DD Act add? And, of critical importance, how does each of these programs define the term "disability"? Does the toddler satisfy their eligibility requirements? In each instance, the service coordinator needs the level of detail provided in Chapter 6. In fact, even more information probably will be necessary to complete the process. Chapter 6 therefore concludes by listing some organizations that monitor developments in these many supplementary programs.

Training for ECSE workers, both future (preservice training) and current (inservice training), should include a review of the history and current status of the enabling legislation. An important survey of ECSE workers (Johnson, Kilgo, Cook, Hammitte, Beauchamp, & Finn, 1992) found that the highest-rated training needs of program administrators and service providers were "knowledge of regulations related to IEPs/IFSPs [individualized education programs/individualized family service plans] and familiarity with current federal and state legislation and regulations in ECSE" (p. 143). Workers in the field want more information about these programs. That is why Chapters 5 and 6 feature specific details on laws and regulations.

The IDEA

All persons born or naturalized in the United States, and subject to the jurisdiction thereof, are citizens of the United States and of the state wherein they reside. No state shall make or enforce any law which shall abridge the privileges or immunities of citizens of the United States; nor shall any state deprive any person of life, liberty, or property, without due process of law; nor deny to any person within its jurisdiction the equal protection of the laws. (Fourteenth Amendment to the Constitution)

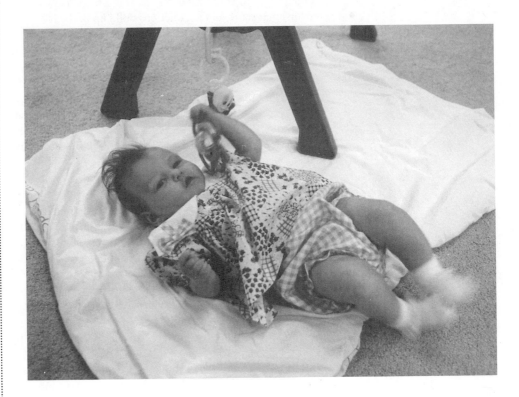

OVERVIEW

To understand early childhood special education (ECSE), it is important to know something about the federal legislation that supports early intervention and preschool special education programs. It is also important to comprehend where these laws came from, the ways of thinking they embody, and the kinds of language they use to authorize state and local services for young children with disabilities.

That is because the entire system of services for these young children has its foundations in these laws. In each state, the District of Columbia, Puerto Rico, and other jurisdictions subject to federal law, state law or jurisdictional statutes build upon federal legislation. These state and other jurisdictional laws mirror federal laws to a remarkable extent, so much so that if we know the federal requirements, we know the gist of virtually all of the state or jurisdictional dictates as well. For example, the kinds of children who are served, the sources of payment used to finance the services, the roles parents and professionals play in deciding what services shall be provided, when, and where—all of these decisions are based on federal laws. And, although states and other jurisdictions interpret them somewhat differently, add to them, and in some cases rely as well on their own supplementary legislation, the fact remains that states and jurisdictions build upon the federal statutes.

The federal legislation, in turn, has its roots in amendments to the U.S. Constitution. In particular, the Fifth and Fourteenth amendments are the sine qua non of Part B of the Individuals with Disabilities Education Act (IDEA). Until those amendments were interpreted to apply to children with disabilities, in two federal court decisions in 1971 and 1972, such children and their families enjoyed virtually no rights to elementary and secondary education. Some children did receive some services, in some states and localities. However, the key word in the preceding sentence is *some*. As late as 1975, the U.S. Congress determined that millions of children and youth with disabilities of all ages either were not being served at all or were receiving inadequate services.

In 1986, Congress mandated that all fifty states, the District of Columbia, Puerto Rico, and a few other special jurisdictions must provide "appropriate" services for all under-six children with disabilities by late 1991 in order to qualify for federal financial assistance. The deadline for serving infants and toddlers was later extended to 1993.

What the state and local governments must do is spelled out in considerable detail in the IDEA, the nation's premier law in early intervention and special education. The IDEA outlines a *way of thinking*. Its approach details how children with health needs are to be identified, evaluated, and determined eligible for services. It explains how professionals and parents are to work together to plan services for those children who are eligible. It carves out major roles for families, including parental participation in decision making, and establishes for families that due-process rights are exceptionally large by the standard of other American social service programs.

This very specific way of thinking has evolved over more than thirty-five years, especially over the past fifteen years. The IDEA features terminology that is equally specific. It uses *language* in a particular, at times even peculiar, way. Take the term "disabilities." Part B lists certain disabilities as included in preschool special education—and by doing that, excludes other disabilities. To make this use of language even more confusing, when Part C deals with early intervention services for children with disabilities under the age of three, it talks not about any disabilities as such but rather about diagnosed conditions, developmental delays, and even at-risk status.

Similarly, when the law speaks of "appropriate" early intervention services or preschool special education services, the term "appropriate" has a particular meaning quite different from the usual definition of that word. When it describes preschool services, the IDEA uses the terms "special education" and "related services" in very precise ways to detail just what kinds of services will be provided—and what kinds are not included. Similarly, when the law speaks of family assessment in early intervention being "family-directed," it has something quite specific in mind. In all these cases, it is necessary to know what meaning the terms carry. That understanding is best acquired by reading the statutory terms (the law itself), reviewing the federal rules interpreting the law (the regulations), and studying the history behind those terms and rules.

HISTORICAL FOUNDATIONS

Education for All Handicapped Children Act of 1975 (EAHCA) (PL 94–142) is the landmark 1975 federal law that first established the mandate that all school-age children with disabilities must receive a free appropriate public education.

The historical roots of ECSE trace back several centuries to work in Europe in the 1700s. This history may help to elucidate a central concept in ECSE. That idea is that the environment matters, and matters very much, in determining whether disabilities (conditions) are handicapping (limiting) for children, youth, and adults. A physical disability, for example—combined with the massive geographical, architectural, and transportation barriers of nineteenth-century America—could overwhelm an individual, while today getting around is no more than an inconvenience for an American with the same exact condition. This background is important, particularly because recent federal legislation requires the removal of environmental barriers, one after the other. That means today's infants, toddlers, and preschoolers with disabilities can enjoy a largely barrier-free America.

However, it was not until after the civil rights movement of the late 1950s and early 1960s that the idea arose that people with disabilities are minority group members, to whom society has some obligations beyond physical restoration of "normalcy." Parents went to court in the early 1970s, demanding that their children with disabilities have access to an education in the local public schools. That led to the **Education for All Handicapped Children Act of 1975 (EAHCA)**, PL 94–142. People with disabilities themselves testified before Congress in 1972, for the first time, arguing that they deserved some of the same rights Congress had recently granted to women and members of racial and ethnic minority groups. This movement led to title V of the Rehabilitation Act of 1973, PL 93–112, including section 504.

Suddenly, in the mid-1970s, Congress was deciding that the nation had an obligation to do something to the environment, to society itself, in order to accommodate people with disabilities. Now experts believe that disability by itself explains little. There is an interaction between a disability and the environment that produces a handicap. Society now is saying that it has an affirmative duty to remove that handicap by changing the environment. For example, an individual who is blind is handicapped while watching a silent film, perhaps one of the many Charlie Chaplin made, but not while listening to a symphony. The goal, idealistic as it may be, becomes making the characteristics of the symphony—the full aural accessibility of it—as widespread as possible in all aspects of the life of a person who is blind.

It is no accident that this new recognition was accompanied by a sharp change in language habits. Individuals who once were called "mental defects" and "morons" are now referred to as "developmentally disabled." Institutions have come to be known as "developmental centers." Today, people-first language is preferred; we say "individuals with disabilities" and "children with cerebral palsy." The term "handicapped" is out of favor; its use now is restricted to instances describing how the environment "handicaps" people with disabilities.

Constitutional Foundations

Under the U.S. Constitution, the states have jurisdiction over education and related services for individuals. The Tenth Amendment to the Constitution states, "The powers not delegated to the U.S. by the Constitution, nor prohibited by it to the states, are reserved to the states respectively, or to the people." The Constitution does authorize the federal government to pass any laws "necessary and proper" to carry out the responsibilities given to it by the Constitution, including the duty to "provide . . . for the general welfare of the United States." However, the Constitution contains no specific authority for the federal government in education or other fields such as early intervention. To act in those areas, the federal government must find a basis in "the general welfare" justifying such action.

Education, in particular, is a function of state and local governments. It is the states that require school attendance, usually between the ages of six and sixteen. For the federal government to become involved, some constitutional issue relating to "the general welfare of the U.S." must be invoked. In the early 1970s, that is exactly what happened. Two federal court cases, one in Philadelphia and the other in the District of Columbia, connected education for children with disabilities to two constitutional amendments. These court cases suggested that the general welfare of the United States was, and remained, at risk unless the federal government were to intervene. These cases galvanized Congress into acting to guarantee school-age children with disabilities an education (Duncan, 1993).

However, no state at the time required school attendance by children under the age of five. Thus, for the subject matter of this book, the constitutional foundations for congressional action on elementary and secondary education did not hold. While the Fourteenth Amendment to the Constitution guarantees equal treatment for all citizens under any state statute, if the state has no law regulating services for children under school age, there is no statute to be equally applied to all people in the state. Even today, only about half of all three- to five-year-old children attend public school programs; far fewer birth-to-two infants and toddlers participate in local programs or activities. How, then, could Congress

The IDEA promotes integration but only if appropriate early intervention services are provided in such integrated settings.

justify mandates for education and other services for children under school age with disabilities?

The answer, as it turns out, is that the federal government *encourages* states to serve birth-to-five children with disabilities by providing financial incentives. To qualify for federal funds under the IDEA, states must enact legislation ensuring all eligible infants, toddlers, and young children certain services. By accepting these federal funds, states obligate themselves to comply with the IDEA's requirements to make services available to all infants, toddlers, and preschool-age children with disabilities.

How this came about is our next subject. First, though, a brief detour is needed to explain a few things about federal laws and regulations.

LAWS AND REGULATIONS

In the United States, laws are given numbers indicating when they were enacted. Each number begins with the letters "PL," for Public Law. Because each Congress lasts two years (a representative's term of office), laws are numbered according to the Congress that enacts them. The 1995–1996 Congress, for example, was the 104th Congress. Its members of Congress were elected in the November 1994 election cycle and took office in January 1995. They served until the winners of the November 1996 election took office in January 1997. Thus, the period January 1995 to January 1997 was one Congress. Usually, however, a Congress adjourns prior to a congressional election, meaning that congressional terms most often run between January of an odd-numbered year and November of the following even-numbered year. All laws enacted between January 1995 and November 1996 were given PL numbers beginning with 104. Within each Congress, laws enacted are numbered consecutively, whether they are signed by the president, or passed over a presidential veto. The first to be enacted was PL 104–1, the second PL 104–2, and so forth. To illustrate with a famous special education law, what is now known as Part B of the IDEA was first enacted in PL 94–142. It was the 142nd law passed by the ninety-fourth Congress, which served between January 1975 and November 1976.

Once enacted, laws must be interpreted by the executive branch agency with jurisdiction. For legislation related to education, the U.S. Department of Education writes "regulations," or rules, which explain and interpret the laws. These regulations have the force of law. They are codified into a set of regulations, the *Code of Federal Regulations* (CFR). With respect to special education, the rules are embodied in title 34 of the CFR. The IDEA, for example, is found in 34 CFR 300, 301, and 303: elementary and secondary special education in 34 CFR 300; the section 619 Preschool Grants Program in 34 CFR 301; and the Part C early intervention program in 34 CFR 303. Copies may be found in many public libraries.

The Web site of the National Early Childhood Technical Assistance System (NEC*TAS) offers the latest amendments (reflecting changes made by the 1997 IDEA Amendments) to two key regulations: the April 14, 1998 final rule for Part C (*Federal Register, 63* [71], pp. 18289–18296) and the June 1, 1998 final rule for Part B, Section 619 (*Federal Register, 63* [104], pp. 29927–29932). These amendments changed the U.S. Department of Education's rules found at 34 CFR Parts 301 (Preschool Special Education) and 303 (Early Intervention). To view the changes, readers should point their browsers to www.nectas. unc.edu; to put these changes in context, read them side-by-side with the more complete rules published earlier in the *Federal Register* (U.S. Department of Education, 1992a, b; 1993a).

BEGINNINGS

Early intervention and preschool special education, as authorized by the IDEA, trace their beginnings back more than thirty-five years. During the early years, three laws in particular stand out as benchmarks in the development of what eventually became the mandate for services from birth to five. PL 89–313 is one; this 1965 amendment to the Elementary and Secondary Education Act (ESEA) offered federal funds the states could use on behalf of children with disabilities in the birth-to-five age range (as well as older children and youth); in 1994, it was merged into the IDEA, and it no longer exists as a separate law. In 1968, PL 90–538 launched what was then called the Handicapped Children's Early Education Program (HCEEP). HCEEP funded a network of demonstration projects serving young children with disabilities. And the ESEA amendments of 1970, PL 91–230, featured the Education of the Handicapped Act (EHA), which offered federal funds to the states for serving children with disabilities.

The 1965 ESEA, PL 89–10, broke new ground by offering federal funds to assist states to improve elementary and secondary education. Prior to that time, the entire burden of financing public education had been borne by state and local governments. Once PL 89–10 established the precedent for federal involvement in education, Congress wasted little time expanding the federal role. Throughout the balance of the decade, it amended the ESEA each year except 1969. Such rapid-fire amendments are highly unusual. In fact, just eight months after passing PL 89–10, Congress passed the ESEA amendments of 1965, PL 89–313, which provided federal grants designed to supplement state efforts on behalf of disadvantaged children in low-income areas. That law contained a program to help states pay for state-operated or state-supported programs for children and youth with disabilities. Also known as chapter 1 of the Education Consolidation and Improvement Act (ECIA), this program supplemented state efforts on behalf of students with disabilities from birth to age twenty-one inclusive, often in institutions (state schools for children who are blind, for example). The federal funds could be used to supplement a child's special education program, including instruction, physical education, mobility training, prevocational and vocational training, and purchase of equipment (PL 101–501, 20 USC 2791 et seq.).

It is difficult to overstate the role PL 89–313 played in the history of special education, despite the fact that this law did not require states to serve children and youth with disabilities. Although strictly a discretionary program that offered supplemental funding in support of whatever states wanted to do, the importance of PL 89–313 was manifold. First, it provided federal funds to expand and improve state-run programs serving children and youth with disabilities. Second, it authorized services for children in the birth-to-five age range; even the IDEA did not do that until many years later. Third, it offered funds for special education that were more generous, on a per capita basis, than those later appropriated pursuant to the IDEA. Congress justified the funding difference by pointing out that PL 89–313 monies were used at state residential and other separate schools, which have higher costs per student than do most local public schools. By the 1992–1993 school year, however, PL 89–313 provided just $9 more per child served than did the IDEA (McGivern, 1993).

PL 89–313 became increasingly controversial in the early 1990s. The program provided funds that states could use in state-operated or state-supported schools and other facilities, usually separate residential or day schools. Advocates of inclusion complained that PL 89–313 was in effect encouraging states to place children with disabilities into separate or segregated programs. Partly in response to these concerns, Congress in the 1980s and early

1990s permitted the states to use PL 89–313 monies to facilitate movement of children and youth with disabilities from state-operated or state-supported programs to local public school programs. Another, related source of controversy was the fact that distribution of PL 89–313 funds in the early 1990s was uneven. Some states were more aggressive than others in recognizing that PL 89–313 was one of only a few sources of funding for services to very young children with disabilities. In the early 1990s, five states secured almost half of the chapter 1 disability monies, using them predominantly for services to children under six with disabilities. This unequal distribution of PL 89–313 funds angered the other forty-five states (Davila, 1993). In fact, almost half of the federal funds appropriated under the PL 89–313 program for children with disabilities were being used for birth-to-five services (McGivern, 1993; Schroeder, 1993). That was not how Congress originally had envisioned the law. For these and related reasons, PL 89–313 was eventually folded into the IDEA, with provisions to hold harmless states that depended on PL 89–313 funds to help support schools for children who were deaf or blind.

HCEEP: PLANTING THE SEEDS

Early Education Program for Children with Disabilities (EEPCD) is the federal grant program providing discretionary support for "model" Early Childhood Special Education programs. EEPCD was formerly called the Handicapped Children's Early Education Program (HCEEP).

In 1968, the HCEEP, PL 90–538, funded experimental programs in preschool education and early intervention for children with disabilities. The act created the HCEEP, the first federal special education program designed *exclusively* for young children with disabilities. (PL 89–313 authorized services for children and youth with disabilities from birth to age twenty-one.) During 1969 and 1970, the federal government funded twenty-four HCEEP demonstration projects. Taken together with additional HCEEP projects funded over the next fifteen years, these "model" projects showcased innovative ways of serving birth-to-five year-old infants, toddlers, and young children with disabilities. Later known as **EEPCD (Early Education Program for Children with Disabilities)** projects, these efforts proved to be instrumental in leading to the eventual federal mandates to serve preschool-age children with disabilities.

Congress's intent with HCEEP may be illustrated by citing remarks made by members of Congress in 1968 to explain why they launched the program. Commented Congressman William Dent of Pennsylvania, "[T]he legislation will lay the foundation for any future programs meeting the needs of [preschool-aged] children [with disabilities] by providing demonstrations of successful approaches to the problem." Added Representative William Ayers of Ohio, "Our task now is to find how the knowledge gained from research can be put into practice" (cited in Weintraub, 1989, p. 19). Clearly, the congressional intent was to plant seeds—to support a variety of experimental, demonstration projects that would find ways to help young children with disabilities, disseminate the knowledge they gain in those projects, and train professionals in techniques that help young children.

Between 1968 and 1975, exciting work was done in several dozen HCEEP projects. The initial demonstration projects not only provided innovative services for very young children with disabilities but did so well enough to secure state, county, and local funding to continue their work after the federal funds ran out. In time, the HCEEP projects came to be known as the First Chance network. In 1973, state planning efforts were begun to supplement the local demonstration projects. More than twenty-five states participated in these early state planning efforts (Trohanis, 1989, pp. 54 and 59). By 1975, when Congress was considering what became PL 94–142, an impressive array of evidence had accumulated showing that large numbers of very young children with disabilities needed and benefited from early intervention and preschool special education services. The evidence was sufficient to convince the U.S. House of Representatives to include services for three- to five-year-olds as part of HR 7217 in 1975, before yielding to the Senate's preference to limit such services to those states that provided services for nondisabled preschoolers (Weintraub, 1986, p. 91). Thus, mandates for preschool services were left out of what became PL 94–142.

From 1976 to 1984, the HCEEP program continued to develop model projects serving very young children with disabilities. The projects also offered technical assistance to state and local education agencies interested in inaugurating preschool programs, as well as to local and private early intervention programs. State Implementation Grants (SIGs) were funded beginning in 1976 to build public awareness of, and support for, preschool services. By 1984, forty-six states and other jurisdictions (the District of Columbia, for example) had used SIGs. In 1983, building on this record of activity, PL 98–199 authorized early childhood state plan programs in HCEEP. The program began in 1984. Just two years later, PL 99–457 created the Part H early intervention program and expanded the section 619 preschool program into what were effectively national mandates to serve birth-to-five children with disabilities. The mandates emerged from the record—at that time eighteen years long—that HCEEP had created in discretionary grant programs (Trohanis, 1989, pp. 59–60; see also Hebbeler, Smith, & Black, 1991, for an excellent summary of the legislative and administrative history of the HCEEP). PL 105–17 changed Part H to Part C in 1997.

EDUCATION OF THE HANDICAPPED ACT

In 1970, the ESEA amendments of 1970, PL 91–230, included the EHA and HCEEP. Both focused on the special needs of children and youth with disabilities; and they were discretionary, not mandatory—encouraging, but not requiring, services for children with disabilities.

The EHA authorized grants to assist states "in the initiation, expansion, and improvement of programs and projects for the education of handicapped children at the preschool, elementary school, and secondary school level." Section 611 of the EHA was discretionary, as were all other programs in the law, but the authority to provide financial assistance for preschool education was noteworthy. The word "preschool" was interpreted broadly, allowing states to use section 611 funds to identify and serve infants and toddlers under age three with disabilities as well as children in the three-to-five age range.

The Education Act amendments of 1974, PL 93–380, included as title VI the EHA amendments of 1974. These EHA amendments for the first time *required* the states to pass state laws setting timetables during which they would move to a full services approach, under which all school-age children with disabilities would receive a public education. The states had to comply with these requirements in return for receiving greatly expanded federal grants in support of preschool, elementary, and secondary education for students with disabilities. State plans and timetables for eventually serving all children with disabilities were to be submitted to the federal government no later than August 21, 1974.

PL 93–380 is notable, as well, for the Family Education Rights and Privacy act (FERPA). Another title within the act, FERPA gave parents of school-age students the right to examine records kept in students' personal files. Parents and eligible students are entitled to review and copy educational records—and to have those records explained to them by school officials. Where records contain information parents and/or eligible students believe to be erroneous or misleading, the law grants parents and students the right to request that records be changed.

The lasting importance of PL 93–380 is that it signaled what was soon to come: the landmark PL 94–142.

EDUCATION FOR ALL HANDICAPPED CHILDREN ACT

On November 29, 1975, President Gerald Ford signed into law the Education for All Handicapped Children Act (EAHCA), PL 94–142. Only seven senators and seven representatives voted against the bill after a House-Senate conference committee presented it to them. PL 94–142 was recognized from the beginning as landmark legislation (see, for example, Abeson & Zettel, 1977; Ballard & Zettel, 1977). It represented, in Abeson and Zettel's words, "the end of the quiet revolution" in special education because it marked the shift from isolated and scattered local advocacy efforts to a nationwide commitment to full equality under the law for all school-age children and youth with disabilities. PL 94–142 contained, in Part B, a mandate to serve *all* school-age children and youth with disabilities, as of September 1, 1978. That mandate is now permanent (Harkin, 1989).

With respect to children with disabilities under age six, however, PL 94–142 holds a more modest place in history. Only states that provided public education for children aged three to five were required (as of September 1, 1980) to offer a free, appropriate public education to children with disabilities in that age range. The extension of PL 94–142's mandate to all children under school age in all states did not occur until eleven years later. So-called "birth-mandate states" (states that had state laws requiring the delivery of services to children with disabilities from birth) could and did use Part B funds to serve infants and toddlers. The U.S. Department of Education allowed such uses, but it forbade states from counting the infants and toddlers for purposes of the Part B child count (Bellamy, 1987).

From 1975 to 1986, states focused on complying with PL 94–142's mandate that all *school-age* children and youth with disabilities receive a free, appropriate public education. For the states, this was a massive undertaking. One unfortunate side effect was to relegate to lesser importance efforts to help infants, toddlers, and preschool-age children with disabilities. However, PL 94–142 did establish the principle of federal mandates in services for children with disabilities, a precedent that weighed heavily with Congress as it conducted oversight on and amended PL 94–142 in the years to come; it was only a matter of time before the mandate would be extended down to three and even to birth.

The 1975 act expanded Part B into a multibillion-dollar federal program assisting state and local education agencies to guarantee a free, appropriate public education for all school-age children and youth, no matter how severely disabled. Part B made it illegal for any public education agency to deny a free public education to any six- to eighteen-year-old child or youth with a disability as of September 1, 1978.

Children aged three to five (and youth aged eighteen to twenty-one) were not included under Part B unless states already provided public services for nondisabled children and youth in those age ranges, in which case they were to begin serving children aged three to five and youth aged eighteen to twenty-one with disabilities as of September 1, 1980. However, PL 94–142 did require states to *identify and evaluate* the needs of children with disabilities in the birth-to-five age range. In addition, Part C, one of the "discretionary" components of PL 94–142, created a Preschool Incentive Grant Program. This program offered states supplementary funding (in addition to the formula grants they received under Part B) to help reimburse them for serving three- to five-year-old children with disabilities. States had to be serving children in that age range in order to receive incentive grant awards. Congress authorized up to

$300 per child served; actual appropriations, however, were as little as $100 per child (Hebbeler et al., 1991). According to the U.S. Department of Education, states used these incentive grant funds to pay for development of interagency agreements, parent and professional training, and technical assistance to local providers, as well as for direct services to young children with disabilities (U.S. Department of Education, 1984; Hebbeler et al., 1991).

Because PL 94–142 demanded such revolutionary changes by state and local education agencies, Congress focused its energies over the next several years on oversight and monitoring rather than new lawmaking. By 1983, however, Congress was ready to amend the law.

The 1983 Amendments

Evidence had been accumulating since 1977 that states and communities throughout the nation were beginning to serve infants and toddlers with disabilities. As early as 1979, almost half of the nation's 16,000 school districts reported at least some services for at least some preschoolers with disabilities; three years later, in 1982, studies suggested that virtually all school districts had begun serving some young children with disabilities (Trohanis, Woodward, & Behr, 1981; and Wright, Cooperstein, Renneker, & Padilla, 1982; both cited in Hebbeler et al., 1991). It was a situation strikingly similar to that prevailing in the early 1970s with respect to school-age children: Some programs were serving some children—but not all children, and not always appropriately. The stage seemed set for Congress to take another step forward. On December 2, 1983, it did.

The 1983 amendments, PL 98–199, were a breakthrough for services to young children with disabilities. For the first time, Congress moved beyond supporting isolated, local programs and toward helping states to coordinate services on a statewide basis. The law offered grants to states for the purpose of planning services for children under six years of age with disabilities. These State Plan Grants were noncompetitive awards. That also was new; prior grants had been competitive, with only some of those states applying receiving awards. PL 98–199 used a broad brush in describing the purpose of the State Plan Grants: The program was for "planning, developing, and implementing a comprehensive service delivery system for the provision of special education and related services to handicapped children birth through five years of age" (IDEA, section 623[b]; Hebbeler et al., 1991). These amendments also provided significantly more funds than had been authorized in prior years for the Preschool Incentive Grant Program. For the first time, the law allowed federal funds for state grants to be used not only for three- to five-year-olds but also for children from birth to age three. (The 1986 amendments repealed this program, including the extension of services down to birth, and replaced it with a new Preschool Grants Program for children from three to five.) The message to states from PL 98–199's grants to develop service delivery systems for children under six was unmistakable: Congress was moving toward a mandate for the preschool-age population, and states should begin preparing to accept that coming mandate.

The HCEEP, now known as EEPCD, begun in 1968, continued under PL 98–199. This Part C program remained discretionary, but it was playing an increasingly important role. These model programs were demonstrating *how* preschool-age children with disabilities could be helped. The programs were providing an impressive body of evidence that early intervention and preschool special education could be effective—both for the children and their families. A rich variety of approaches was being demonstrated. Of twenty-one model programs examined by White, Mastropieri, and Casto (1984), for example, seven were home-based programs, in which staff visited families in their homes; eight were center-based programs, in which families came to centers specially equipped for young children with disabilities; and six used various combinations of home- and center-based approaches. Most involved parents in at least some decision making, and a few demonstrated a family-centered approach featuring strong parental decision making. Some provided services for one or two hours weekly, others for as many as fifteen hours weekly, for each child served. Despite these differences, the model programs themselves—and outside evaluators—insisted that the services were both effective and cost-effective (for an excellent review, see Hebbeler et al., 1991).

The 1986 Amendments

On October 8, 1986, Congress took the next step: *mandates* for both preschool special education and early intervention. One triggering event was the publication of the U.S. Department of Education's *Seventh Annual Report to Congress on the Implementation of the Education of the Handicapped Act.* Section 618 of the IDEA, in Part B, requires the department to issue this report each year. The *Seventh Annual Report* summarized work done by the HCEEP (now EEPCD) model projects and evaluations of their progress, as well as other research and demonstration projects in the area of services for preschool-age children. Robert Silverstein, who at the time was staff counsel for the House authorizing subcommittee, remembers one paragraph in particular that struck him, and others on Capitol Hill, as significant, because it suggested that the time had come to take yet more steps in early childhood services:

> *Studies of the effectiveness of preschool education for the handicapped have demonstrated beyond doubt the economic and educational benefits of programs for young handicapped children. In addition, the studies have shown that the earlier intervention is started, the greater is the ultimate dollar savings and the higher is the rate of educational attainment by these handicapped children.* (U.S. Department of Education, 1985; quoted in Silverstein, 1989, p. A2)

Silverstein remembers being surprised by the fact that this statement was made in an official report transmitted to Congress by the Reagan administration. He privately doubted that Reagan's team would overstate the benefits of federal social programming, since the Reagan administration was well known to oppose, on principle and with vigor, virtually any expansion of social service programs. In fact, the *Seventh Annual Report* exaggerated what had been learned, but only because the initial researchers did, too. Studies conducted since 1986 have helped us to understand that the early intervention and preschool special education work that had been done by 1986 had not in fact "demonstrated beyond doubt" that these programs produced both educational and economic benefits (see, for example, White, 1985/1986; Innocenti & White, 1993). But much truth remains, even today, in what the *Seventh Annual Report* observed, that is, that early intervention and preschool special education can in fact help many young children with disabilities and their families.

In 1986, Congress was also concerned that the Preschool Incentive Grants and the State Plan Grants had not yet produced a real change in services for children with disabilities in the birth-to-five age range. The number of children under six with disabilities being served seemed to have plateaued at about 100,000 below the estimated number of children who needed services (Silverstein, 1989, p. A3). In addition, Congress responded, as it often does, to its own internal imperatives. The Gramm-Rudman-Hollings deficit-reduction package was just beginning to take effect in 1986, and members of both the Senate and the House were conscious that they had a better chance to do something in ECSE for young children with disabilities if they acted in that year rather than a later year. In 1986 then Senator Lowell Weicker (R-Conn.), a powerful, vocal advocate for people with disabilities, was chairman of both the authorizing and the appropriations subcommittees with jurisdiction over special education. Weicker was thus in a position to move legislation, and he very much wanted to authorize greatly expanded early intervention and preschool special education services (Silverstein, 1989, p. A2).

By 1986, evidence was mounting that the HCEEP demonstration programs and the 1983 state grant awards were raising awareness throughout the nation about early intervention and preschool special education services for young children with disabilities. States were beginning to recognize the value of these services. To illustrate, Alicia Smith, representing the National Governors Association, testified before the House in 1986: "[I]f you do a quick check of the state-of-the-state addresses around the country this past year, you will find that there are only four governors who didn't mention the word 'prevention' and/or 'early intervention'" (Smith, 1986, p. 123).

Responding to these diverse developments, Congress created an entirely new early intervention program and greatly expanded the Part B (section 619) Preschool Grants Program. PL 99–457, the 1986 EHA amendments, gave the states a phase-in period, during which they could receive federal funds for planning services to infants and toddlers from birth to two and children from three to five with disabilities. (States could not use section 619 funds to *serve* infants and toddlers under age three, but they could use those monies to *plan* statewide systems for the under-six population, including infants and toddlers from birth to two.) By the end of the planning period, states were required, as a condition of receiving further federal financial support, to be providing universally available services for *all* children in those age ranges.

PL 99–457 was landmark legislation, second only to PL 94–142 in its impact on services for children with disabilities. It gave states five years to begin zero-reject early intervention and preschool special education programs. Funding for the section 619 preschool program for three- to five-year-old children with disabilities was vastly increased. From a 1986 level of $28 million, appropriations (actual dollars provided to states, not just authorization ceilings) leaped to $180 million (a sixfold increase) in 1987, to $201 million in 1988, and $247 million in 1989. In just three years, funding had grown by a factor of nine—an astonishing pace for those deficit-plagued years (Silverstein, 1989, p. A3).

Funding for the new Part H program on early intervention was much more modest. That was deliberate on the part of Congress. The intent in Part H was not to fully fund services but rather to provide "glue money" enabling states to pull together resources from many different sources. Explained Silverstein, "These are funds that will facilitate cooperation and coordination. Federal money was never intended to be the primary funding source for direct services to infants and toddlers" (Silverstein, 1989, p. A4). What was then Part H is now Part C.

The actual structure of PL 99–457 technically did not mandate services for preschool-age children with disabilities. Rather, Congress authorized (and appropriated) funds that states could elect to accept. If a state accepted those monies, the state would be obligated to comply with the legislative "strings" accompanying the funds. Those strings required zero-reject, appropriate services for all infants, toddlers, and preschool-age children with disabilities no later than a state's fifth year of participation in the programs. Because all states were already committed to obeying the requirements of Part B, their participation in the section 619 program was all but guaranteed (because that section is in Part B).

In section 619 the legislation stated that the secretary of education "shall make a grant to any State which" has a state policy guaranteeing a free, appropriate public education to all eligible children aged three to eighteen, has a state plan approved by the secretary, and provides special education and related services for preschool-age children with disabilities. Nothing in section 619 required zero-reject, full-service programs until 1991. The federal

forward funded refers to the fact that education programs authorized by federal laws are funded during any given federal fiscal year for the following fiscal year. The intent is to give states and schools notice of funds availability well in advance of the start of a school year.

fiscal year (FY) begins on October 1 and ends on September 30. Thus, FY 1991 concluded on September 30, 1991. In education, federal programs are **forward funded**, that is, they are available for use on July 1 of a fiscal year, rather than the following year; this system gives states and local school districts advance notice of exactly the amount they will have on hand when school begins in September. PL 99–457 authorized the secretary to make state grants in FY 1991 and in subsequent fiscal years *only* to a state that:

> *has a state plan approved under section 613 which includes policies and procedures that assure the availability under the state law and practice of such state of a free appropriate public education for all children with disabilities aged three to five, inclusive.* (section 619)

To qualify for the funds made available July 1, 1991, states had to have enacted zero-reject, free, appropriate preschool education laws. This structure—offering funds for four years without mandating zero-reject services, but requiring such universal service as a condition for receiving monies in the fifth and subsequent years—is the vehicle through which Congress mandated full services for preschool-age children with disabilities. The structure was necessary because the Fourteenth Amendment equal-protection clause did not apply in preschool education, which was not state-mandated for young children, whether disabled or nondisabled.

INDIVIDUALS WITH DISABILITIES EDUCATION ACT

In 1990, PL 101–476 renamed the foundation legislation, from the Education of the Handicapped Act (EHA) to the Individuals with Disabilities Education Act (IDEA). Throughout the act, signed into law on October 30, 1990, the term "handicapped children" was replaced by "children with disabilities." (The term "disability" had been adopted in the Technology-Related Assistance for Individuals with Disabilities Act (TRAIDA) PL 100–407, in 1988; all subsequent federal laws on disability have used the term "disability" rather than "handicapped.") The IDEA also features people-first language ("children with . . . " "youth having . . . ," and so on), in another effort to demonstrate greater sensitivity.

The House added language in section 610(j) emphasizing the need to pay more attention to the special needs of traditionally underserved populations. The new section opened with an indictment of the education system's treatment of members of minority groups, particularly overreferral to special education, mislabeling, and high dropout rates. The 1990 amendments included findings that African Americans comprised 28 percent of special education students, although they represented just 12 percent of all students in public schools. Dropout rates were reported to be 68 percent higher for members of minority groups than for whites. Looking at teachers and teachers-in-training, the legislation found that only 11 percent of special education undergraduate and graduate students were African Americans. For these reasons, the legislation directed the U.S. Department of Education to place more emphasis on recruitment of members of minority groups into special education careers.

PL 101–476 added two new categories to the statutory definition of children with disabilities: children with autism and children with traumatic brain injuries. The two new labels are now recognized as disabilities for the purposes of Part B, including preschool section 619 services. The law also expanded the scope of related services to encompass rehabilitation counseling and social work services. Finally, the 1990 amendments added descriptive video services (DVS). In DVS, spoken descriptions of on-screen actions are provided over the second of two audio channels in stereo television sets. This description helps blind and low-vision viewers follow television programs.

PL 102–52

Congress became concerned early in 1991 that many states were not on target to meet the fall 1991 deadline for providing full services to preschool-age children. The concern was magnified by Congress's realization that many state fiscal years begin in July; thus, action had to be taken prior to that. PL 102–52 was signed into law in June 1991. To help states that otherwise might have been forced to drop out of the Part H program, the law gave them one or, in some cases, two additional years to meet all "year five" requirements. The funding formula was designed to assist those states that were late without penalizing states that were on target. In no event, however, could the full-service mandate be postponed beyond the end of 1993. (Federal education programs are forward funded, so states could use that money until late 1994.) The law clearly stated that after a maximum of two years of extended participation, states are eligible for Part H funds only if they have in effect a statewide system of early intervention services for all eligible infants and toddlers.

1991 IDEA Amendments

In PL 102–119, Congress acted to provide a seamless transition between Part H and Part B. For the first time, states were expressly permitted to use Part H funds for toddlers past the age of three, if doing so would facilitate their transition either to preschool Part B programs or to other community service programs. In addition, states were, again for the first time, allowed to use Part B monies to serve toddlers under the age of three, whether or not those toddlers were in Part H (now Part C) programs. These statutory changes responded to state concerns about what to do when a child turned three. The U.S. Department of Education had told them (Schrag, 1990b) that children with disabilities become eligible for section 619 preschool Part B services upon their third birthday, but that states enjoyed broad discretion in deciding how to handle service provision, as long as no three-year-olds were denied services.

The legislation obligates states to plan the transitions occurring at or about age three, so as to effect a smooth transition, that is, a seamless one. Among other things, appropriate information may be sent by Part C service providers, with parental permission, to the local education agency and/or other community-based service providers, who will begin helping the child and the family. The law requires that both the sending and the receiving agency participate in the transition planning with the parents (Rosenkoetter, 1992).

The 1991 amendments further strengthened the roles of parents and families under Part C. The law now clearly states that parents may decline any Part C–related service without jeopardizing their rights to other services. Parents have the right to accede to or decline the transmission of personally identifiable information about their infant or toddler from one agency to another. The assessment of family resources, priorities, and concerns—which is part of the IFSP process—is to be family-directed. That is, families have the right to control what assessments are done, how the assessment data are used, and even whether a family assessment is done at all. The 1991 amendments added a preference that infants and toddlers be served in natural environments. Because parents know their infants or toddlers much better than do program personnel, this provision gives parents additional ammunition to ensure that their children are served in environments, including the home and community facilities, that the family finds comfortable and convenient.

PL 102–119 also gave states the right, at their discretion, to serve three- to five-year-old developmentally delayed children in preschool Part B programs. If states elect to do so, they

Personnel, including early childhood special educators as well as related services providers, must meet state standards for certification or licensing.

may use the same five categories of development (cognitive, physical, communication, adaptive, social or emotional) as are used under Part C. The House report makes clear that the Congress did not intend to expand the number of children eligible for section 619 services, nor to broaden eligibility criteria, but rather to grant states greater flexibility. Among other things, Congress recognized the potential danger of labeling very young children with stigmatizing names; adoption of the kinds of broad categories used in Part C might alleviate some of that stigma (*House Report 102–198*, 1991, p. 4).

The 1991 amendments also focused on the special needs of traditionally underserved populations. Section 671(a) of the IDEA added a new finding for what is now Part C:

> *[T]o enhance the capacity of state and local agencies and service providers to identify, evaluate, and meet the needs of historically underrepresented populations, particularly minority, low-income, inner-city, and rural populations.*

In section 678(b)(7), the 1991 amendments further required states to provide, beginning in FY 1992, satisfactory assurance that minority, rural, and low-income families have access to "culturally competent services within their local areas" and that such families will have "meaningful involvement" in the state's implementation of Part H. The House report added: "When implementing Part H of IDEA, particular attention must be given to the inclusion and participation of minority and low-income individuals in urban as well as rural areas across the country" (*House Report 102–198*, 1991, p. 11). Finally, PL 102–119 amended section 623, which authorizes the EEPCD to stimulate such demonstration programs to serve more low-income, minority, rural, and other underserved populations, and to serve at-risk children.

THE IDEA AMENDMENTS OF 1997

In PL 105–17, the IDEA Amendments of 1997, Congress rearranged some of the titles in the law. Parts A and B were unaffected. Part H, on early intervention, became Part C. The discretionary titles of the act—Parts C, D, E, F, and G—were combined into one discretionary title, which was named Part D.

The 1997 amendments allowed the states to continue using "developmentally delayed" in lieu of disability labels until a child turned ten years of age. Previously, a diagnostic label such as "mentally retarded" or "learning disabled" was required when a child turned six years of age. Also new in 1997 is the option of parents to use mediation services rather than litigation to resolve disputes with public agencies.

PL 105–17 also changed the funding formula for Part B, section 619 (preschool services). Previously, states received federal funds based strictly upon state population of children aged three to five inclusive. The new law continues to use that basis for funding, but only up to the amount allocated during FY 1997 (October 1, 1996 to September 30, 1997). Any additional funds will be awarded based upon state population (85 percent) and childhood poverty (15 percent). The intent of the change is to provide relatively more funding to states having large numbers of poor children, in recognition of the fact that childhood disability and poverty are closely linked.

The IDEA Today and Tomorrow

The IDEA guides all of us who work with young children with disabilities or delays in development. It provides very specific instructions that affect virtually everything early intervention and preschool programs serving children with disabilities do and how they do those things. For these reasons, a familiarity with the law is important for interventionists and special educators. Copies of PL 105–17, the IDEA Amendments of 1997, are available in most public libraries. Readers may also get copies by writing to their United States senators (Washington, DC 20510) or to their United States representative (Washington, DC 20515). Following is a road map to reading the IDEA.

The IDEA, as amended in 1997, opens with *Part A—General Provisions*. Contained here is a statement of findings, which offers a "general welfare" justification for federal action in education and child care. Generally, this statement indicts the states for not meeting the needs of these children. Also in Part A are the IDEA's four main purposes. These are as follows:

1. To guarantee a free, appropriate public education for children with disabilities; to provide funds to states so as to assist them in offering such an education; and to provide due-process rights for children with disabilities and their parents

2. To offer funds to states to implement Part C early intervention services

3. To support research, demonstration, and training programs to improve results in special education and early intervention

4. To monitor the states as they carry out their Part B (preschool) and Part C (early intervention) responsibilities under the law

Part A continues by offering definitions of key terms. Notable here are very specific definitions for "children with disabilities" (who is eligible for Part B services) and for "special education" and "related services" (what kind of help is authorized to be provided under Part B). The only disability that is defined here is "specific learning disability"; all other disabilities included in the definition of "children with disabilities" are defined in the regulations issued to carry out the IDEA by the U.S. Department of Education.

Part B—Assistance for Education of Children with Disabilities begins by outlining the formulas to be used in calculating how much financial assistance each state will get each year from the federal government. As noted earlier, this is a combination of state population and poverty. In section 612, Part B explains what the states must promise to receive these funds. Notable among those are (1) that the state will guarantee a free, appropriate public education to all eligible children with disabilities, "including children with disabilities who have been suspended or expelled from school"; (2) that the state will ensure that each child with a disability receives an individualized education program (IEP); (3) that state and local education agencies will place children with disabilities in settings that also serve children without disabilities, to the extent that such placements do not compromise the right of children with disabilities to receive an appropriate education that meets their unique needs; (4) that the state will act to protect the due-process rights of children with disabilities and their parents; (5) that the state will take whatever steps are necessary to ensure an adequate supply of special educators and related services personnel; and (6) that the state will set "performance goals and indicators" for improving special education, particularly in the areas of districtwide assessments of academic performance, and for reducing dropout rates.

Part B continues, in section 614, to explain how the federal government expects assessments of children with disabilities to be performed. Notable here is that if parents resist, or even refuse to permit an evaluation, the local education agency must contest this parental preference (through mediation or litigation) because the agency is obligated by the IDEA to provide special education and related services to all eligible children with disabilities. This section also describes, in great detail, what is to go into each IEP.

In the next section, section 615, the IDEA outlines the rights of children with disabilities and their parents, and explains how parents may assert those rights, either through mediation or through litigation. New for 1997 is a set of procedures to be followed if a child with a disability engages in violent acts or brings illegal drugs to school. If the actions might be attributable, in whole or in part, to the disability, then a "manifestation determination" must be made; in that process, a hearing officer decides whether the actions were "manifestations" of the disability. If so, the child cannot be punished for those actions. Rather, the local education agency must examine and if necessary revise its behavior intervention strategies. At any event, children with disabilities who are suspended or expelled from school continue to enjoy the IDEA's guarantee of a free, appropriate public education, even if that education must be provided in a juvenile facility or in a prison. Section 619 concludes Part B. It contains very little of substance, focusing almost exclusively upon funding formulas. However, because section 619 is in Part B, the other sections of Part B (state assurances, assessments, due process, and so on) apply to preschool programs.

Part C—Infants and Toddlers with Disabilities opens with its own statement of findings and policy in section 631. Notable here is the intent of the federal government to support state initiatives rather than dictate terms to the states. Definitions of key terms follow, including "infants and toddlers with disabilities" and "early intervention services." Section 636 outlines the contents of individualized family service plans (IFSPs) and explains who writes them. The rights of infants and toddlers and their parents are explained in section 639.

Part D—National Activities to Improve Education of Children with Disabilities contains many of the discretionary programs previously authorized by Parts C, D, E, and F of the IDEA as it existed prior to PL 105–17. Notable here are grant programs to assist states in enhancing services to children with disabilities, training programs for professionals and parents, research and demonstration programs, and information and referral programs. Part D differs from Part B and Part C in that nothing in Part D is mandatory; all programs authorized in Part D are discretionary—states, not-for-profit organizations, and individuals may elect to participate or not to participate.

Summary

This chapter has outlined the history and major provisions of the IDEA. It has been a long journey, spanning more than thirty-five years of legislation. Beginning with a network of local demonstration projects, the federal government demonstrated that early intervention and preschool special education for children with disabilities could make a difference in these young children's lives. By 1986, the evidence was strong enough for Congress to take the next step: creating mandates for universal service to under-six children with disabilities. The mandate for preschool special education took effect in 1991, on target with the original timetable, but some states needed one or two additional years to complete planning for services for infants and toddlers.

The IDEA provides vital rights to families and children. So do some other federal laws. We turn now to examine those rights.

QUESTIONS FOR REFLECTION

1. What provisions of the U.S. Constitution forced Congress to "encourage" more than "require" ECSE services for children under six who have disabilities?

2. What was the significance of PL 89–313 during its "lifetime" (1965–1994)?

3. How did the Handicapped Children's Early Education Program (HCEEP), later known as the Early Education Program for Children with Disabilities (EEPCD), build a foundation for the eventual enactment of Part C?

4. What of significance was in the 1985 *Seventh Annual Report to Congress?*

5. Why was PL 99–457 "landmark legislation, second only to PL 94–142 in its impact"?

6. What two disabilities were added to the definition of "children with disabilities" in 1990?

7. What change was made in the 1991 amendments about services for children just turning three years of age?

8. How do you explain the fact that Part C allows families of infants and toddlers to decline any and all Part C services, yet families of children age six and over with disabilities may have to fight local school districts to keep their children out of special education?

9. What advantages might accompany the decision to continue using "developmental delay" (instead of a disability label) as late as a child's ninth birthday? Can you think of any disadvantages?

10. Why does the IDEA guarantee a free, appropriate public education even for children with disabilities who have been suspended or expelled from school?

Rights of Children with Disabilities and their Families

"I sure wouldn't just sit there and let them tell me what they've done. I'd find out why did you do this, why is that, why do you want to do that? . . . Back then I let them tell me what they were going to do because I didn't even know I had rights. You know? Parents need to know *they have rights!* Speak up! . . . [Y]ou have a right to say what goes on in that child's life. Not them. They like to think they're the major authorities. They ain't. They can only tell you what they think would be best." (quoted in Minke & Scott, 1993, pp. 96-97; emphasis in original)

OVERVIEW

Children with disabilities and their parents enjoy extraordinary rights under the Individuals with Disabilities Education Act (IDEA). Among them are the procedural safeguards in Part C and Part B. They enjoy other important rights, however, beyond the IDEA. This chapter examines the Americans with Disabilities Act (ADA) of 1990, one of the most significant civil rights measures ever enacted by the U.S. Congress. The ADA contains some far-reaching provisions that help young children and their families enjoy the full benefits of all a community has to offer them. The act also offers some surprising benefits for parents, who may be subjected to discrimination on the job or in other activities of daily life because of their association with a child who is disabled. The chapter also explores section 504 of the 1973 Rehabilitation Act, a precursor to and supplement to the ADA.

As the chapter's opening quotation from Minke and Scott (1993) shows, many parents have grasped their new rights, understood them, and used them to their benefit and to the benefit of their children. Many have not, however. In a 1989 survey by Louis Harris and Associates, the polling firm found that only a minority of parents who have children with disabilities understood the rights they enjoy as parents and those that protect their children. Accordingly, it is important that early childhood special education (ECSE) workers acquaint parents with the full range of rights—and support them in securing those rights. The material in this chapter may assist in that vital endeavor.

SECTION 504

The IDEA provides rights, notably to early intervention, special education, and related services, for infants, toddlers, and young children with disabilities who are eligible under that law. Establishing eligibility for services under IDEA is a two-step process. First, children must qualify as disabled. Under Part C, that process may be done by reference to an established condition or documentation of a developmental delay. If a state opts to serve at-risk infants and toddlers, eligibility is determined by state rules defining who is considered to be at risk. Under Part B, eligibility is by reference to one of the conditions listed in section 602. States may, at their option, decide that preschool-age children who have developmental delays (as defined by the state) are also eligible for section 619 preschool special education and related services. However, not all infants, toddlers, preschoolers, and school-age children qualifying under these initial steps are eligible for services. The second step is to establish that children from birth to five with disabilities *need* early intervention services (Part C) or special education and related services (Part B).

This raises some questions. What about infants, toddlers, and young children with disabilities who do not require such services? And what about infants, toddlers, and preschoolers with disabilities who seek services not related to their disabilities? Recall that the IDEA authorizes special education and early intervention services involving instruction or therapy focusing on the disability. For many children, therefore, early intervention or preschool special education and related services will constitute only *some*, rather than all, of the services they need and desire (Ballard & Zettel, 1977).

Section 504 of the Rehabilitation Act of 1973 (PL 93-112, as amended by PL 102-456; 29 USC 701) protects children who have disabilities but who may not qualify as children with disabilities under the IDEA. To illustrate, a court recently found that a child with attention deficit hyperactivity disorder (ADHD) was in fact a person with a disability under

section 504 is a civil rights provision in the federal Rehabilitation Act. It prohibits any program receiving or benefiting from federal financial assistance from discriminating on the basis of disability. Section 504 predated, but remains in effect concurrent with, the Americans with Disabilities Act.

section 504, even though the condition was not recognized at the time under the IDEA (*Brittan [CA] Elementary School District,* 16 EHLR 1226, 1990; see also, "New OCR Rulings," 17 IDELR 104-106, 1991). Section 504 is a civil rights statute comparable to title VI of the Civil Rights Act of 1964 (minority groups) and to title IX of the Education Amendments of 1972 (women). The basic statutory language is brief:

> *No otherwise qualified individual with a disability in the United States shall, solely by reason of the disability, be excluded from the participation in, be denied the benefits of, or be subjected to discrimination under any program or activity receiving federal financial assistance.* (29 USC 794)

Section 504 applies to individuals with disabilities regardless of age; it protects young children, school-age children, youths, and adults. Because section 504 is a civil rights statute, it adopts a three-part definition of disability. The first prong of this definition protects people who have a physical or mental impairment that substantially limits one or more of the major life activities of such individual. The second protects people who once had such a condition and have recovered; they are protected against unjust discrimination on the basis of any records of the previous condition. The final prong protects people regarded as having such an impairment, usually falsely.

The statute applies to schools, libraries, hospitals, social service agencies, nonprofit organizations, and government agencies (including federal agencies such as the U.S. Department of Education) that receive federal financial assistance. Receipt of such grants obligates these organizations and agencies to practice nondiscrimination in all of their programs and activities. The statute requires provision of auxiliary aids such as interpreters for deaf people and appropriate media for blind people, as well as other assistance necessary so that people may benefit from programs and activities. These requirements remain in effect. Although the ADA later imposed similar requirements, that act does not repeal section 504.

With respect to public education that is supported, directly or indirectly, through federal grants, including day-care and other programs for infants or toddlers and preschool programs, section 504 says that the services offered to children with disabilities must meet their needs "as adequately as the needs of non-disabled persons are met." In other words, the federal requirement is for access to services. Section 504 says that an individualized education program (IEP) is one means by which such access may be provided. For children who do not have an IEP (because they do not require modified instruction) or individualized family service plan (IFSP) (because they do not require early intervention services), the standard section 504 sets is one of nondiscrimination: The services are to be as effective as are those provided by the public agency for people with no disabilities.

Regulations implementing section 504 preceded those for what is now the IDEA's mandate to serve children with disabilities. The section 504 rules appeared in April 1977, the PL 94-142 regulations in August of that year. The two sets of rules contained similar requirements with respect to elementary and secondary education, thus reinforcing each other. Section 504 differs from the IDEA in that it provides no funding, being, rather, a civil rights statute; the IDEA, on the other hand, is a federal funding program that sets rules for participation and for receipt of federal funds. In the late 1970s, section 504 played an important role: It protected children in any state that declined to participate in PL 94-142, that is, rejected federal special education funds. No state now does this, though in the past, some did. To the extent that any state declines to participate in Part C, section 504 could again play such a role.

Section 504 interprets nondiscrimination to mean equal access to admissions, fair eligibility requirements, and program accessibility that provides equal benefit from programs and activities. Program accessibility was a new concept when the initial section 504 regulation was signed on April 28, 1977 (Bowe, 1978). It is best understood in contrast to barrier-free buildings: All rooms in a building need not be accessible if classes may be relocated to an accessible room. To take another example, were a public library to have some books shelved on the second floor of a two-story building with no elevator, the library staff would need to provide some mechanism, including personal assistance from a librarian or staff assistant, so that an individual who could not personally retrieve the book could nonetheless get it. The program is accessible, even if the building is not.

Section 504 states that it is not discrimination for a program to declare ineligible for services an individual who has unique needs that the program is not staffed or equipped to meet. A school for blind children, for example, may decline to admit a deaf-blind child on the grounds that neither the staff nor the educational programs, including the materials used, are prepared to meet the special needs of a child who is both deaf and blind. Programs may set eligibility criteria that reflect their service offerings without fear of discrimination charges from people who have different service needs.

Under section 504, an individual with a disability may file charges alleging discrimination with the federal agency that directly or indirectly funds the offending agency's program. With respect to social service programs, that is usually the U.S. Department of Health and Human Services. With respect to schools (elementary, secondary, vocational, trade, two-year and four-year college, graduate), it is usually the U.S. Department of Education. Relief is generally limited to admission, reinstatement as a participant in a program, or provision of needed **reasonable accommodations** such as sign-language interpreting for deaf people. In addition, section 504 recognizes the due-process procedural safeguards in Part B (see "Procedural Safeguards" section of this chapter) as "one means" under which individuals with disabilities may enforce their rights in public education.

reasonable accommodation in the ADA and section 504, refers to an adjustment enabling a qualified individual with a disability to perform a task.

AMERICANS WITH DISABILITIES ACT

Americans with Disabilities Act (ADA), PL 101-336, is the landmark 1990 federal civil rights law for individuals with disabilities. The law bans discrimination in employment, local government services, transportation, places of public accommodation, and telecommunications.

places of public accommodation are restaurants, hotels, motion picture and other theaters, sporting facilities, stores and shopping malls, and doctors' and lawyers' offices. Under the ADA, title III, these must be accessible to people with disabilities and offer these people equal enjoyment to that accorded to people with no disabilities.

The 1990 **Americans with Disabilities Act** (ADA; PL 101-336; 42 USC 12101 et seq.) protects individuals with disabilities, regardless of age, from discrimination. The act is enormously important for young children with disabilities and their families. Title I of the act proscribes discrimination on the basis of disability in employment at virtually all of the nation's private companies with fifteen or more workers. Title II bans discrimination on the basis of disability at any state, county, or local government agency; it specifically proscribes less-than-equal access to public transportation. Title III of the ADA prohibits discrimination in community stores and other **places of public accommodation**. And title IV ensures users of telecommunications devices for the deaf (TDDs) equal access to local, long-distance, and international telephone networks.

The act adopts, as does section 504, a three-part definition of "individuals with a disability." Under the first prong of the definition, a person (of any age) who has a permanent medical condition that significantly limits one or more major life activities (going to school is a major life activity) is considered to be an individual with a disability. The other two prongs are the same as those in section 504 outlined previously.

The ADA has a significant feature that may surprise many parents. It protects *associates* of persons with disabilities. These include family members, who are protected against discrimination on the basis of their association with individuals with disabilities. Thus, a parent may not be denied access to services because a child is disabled. This protection is particularly important for parents with respect to their own employment and employer-provided insurance coverage. It is illegal, for example, for a company to refuse to hire someone just because that person's child has a disability. It is similarly illegal for the employer to offer that person an insurance package that is less comprehensive than that provided to other workers, again because the individual is associated with (related to) a child with a disability.

While not directly affecting infants, toddlers, and preschool-age children with disabilities for a number of years to come—until they enter the labor market—title I is nonetheless hugely important because it assures families that if their children with disabilities secure an education, they will have an equal opportunity to work—and support themselves—upon reaching adulthood. This guarantee of nondiscrimination in employment applies to more than one million American companies—virtually all employers having fifteen or more workers. The knowledge that a fair chance at self-support awaits them at the conclusion of their schooling is a very significant motivating factor for children with disabilities and their parents, teachers, therapists, and counselors.

Title II of the ADA requires that state, county, and local government agencies provide nondiscriminatory treatment for people with disabilities in all programs and activities that serve members of the general public. Section 504 of the Rehabilitation Act requires such actions by recipients of federal financial assistance; all states, and most county and local governments as well, are beneficiaries of federal funds, and thus covered by section 504. Title II erases whatever doubts might have existed about that. It also moves a major step beyond section 504 with respect to transportation. At the time the ADA was enacted (July 26, 1990), the section 504 standard on public transportation was a vague special efforts mandate. Title II establishes specific, hard-hitting obligations on county and local public transit agencies. For example, beginning August 1990, all new mass-transit buses were required to be lift-equipped. Similarly, all new rail cars on commuter rail, rapid rail, and other local train service trains had to be equipped to accept wheelchairs.

These title II requirements are important to families with young children who have disabilities. Title II requires state, county, and local government agencies to provide services to people with disabilities as effective as those offered to nondisabled individuals. Title II forbids discrimination on the basis of disability by any state, county, or local government agency. The title became effective January 26, 1992. Title II defines a qualified individual with a disability as follows:

> . . . [A]n individual with a disability who, with or without reasonable modifications to rules, policies, practices, the removal of architectural, communications, or transportation barriers, or the provision of auxiliary aids and services, meets the essential eligibility requirements for the receipt of services or the participation in programs or activities provided by a public entity. (section 201[2])

Title III explicitly recognizes that infants, toddlers, and young children are not only people with disabilities but also citizens of their local communities. They and their families lead lives not related to their disabilities. They patronize restaurants, entertainment centers, and other public and private sources of human, medical, and other services. In the past, families of children with disabilities frequently met with discrimination from community service providers, both public and private. On May 23, 1988, Lisa Carl, who uses a wheelchair because of cerebral palsy, was denied admission to a movie theater in Tacoma, Washington. The theater manager told an advocate who called the theater to protest, "I don't want her here and I don't have to let her in." In Denver, Colorado, on June 16, 1989, six young people using wheelchairs were told by the manager of a restaurant that they "[took] up too much space." Unless they could get out of and fold up their wheelchairs, he said, they would not be served. When they declined to do so, the manager called the local police, who took the six to jail (Bowe, 1992a; *From ADA to Empowerment*, 1991).

Such actions—denial of service at a movie theater or at a restaurant—are now outlawed by title III, which bans discriminatory treatment by places of public accommodation. The law includes a list of such places; among them are preschool, elementary, secondary, and private schools; day care-centers; social service agencies; stores; shopping malls; restaurants; hotels; movie theaters and other theaters; sports complexes and other entertainment centers; and private offices of doctors, dentists, lawyers, and other professionals serving members of the general public. Such places of public accommodation must make their facilities physically accessible to people with disabilities, unless doing so is not readily achievable. They must provide equal enjoyment for customers with disabilities unless doing so would impose an undue hardship on the business. The law defines such terms as readily achievable and undue hardship; implementing regulations issued by the U.S. Department of Justice (*Federal Register*, July 26, 1991) explain further what is meant by these and other key terms in title III.

Among other things, if a service program or establishment such as a hotel sponsors its own client- or participant-transportation program (as a day-care center or school might), the vehicles used and other aspects of the transportation program must be available equally to nondisabled clients and participants with disabilities alike. Services that are less than equal to those offered to nondisabled persons are outlawed as are opportunities that are less effective than those accorded to persons without disabilities. Any eligibility criteria that have the effect of screening out individuals with disabilities are banned. Reasonable accommodations and

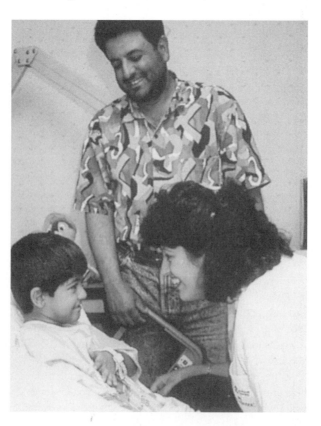

The law provides due process and other rights not only for the child but for the family as well.

other assistance are required to be provided (i.e., interpreters for deaf parents) unless doing so would fundamentally alter the nature of the goods, services, or facilities being provided by the place of public accommodation. Title III took effect on January 26, 1992.

Under title IV, all users of TTYs are entitled to free use of relay services to make and receive local and long-distance telephone calls. Since July 26, 1993, all 1,600 local and long-distance telephone companies in the United States have provided round-the-clock access to relay services, which allow individuals who are deaf, hard-of-hearing, and/or speech-impaired to call and be called by some 100 million residential and business telephone numbers. For those who need relay services, title IV makes a very big difference. Whether they need access to telephone service for personal or business reasons, TTY users are no longer limited in the amount or kind of calls they may make or receive.

Individuals with disabilities who win complaints under the ADA are entitled to remedies that vary from title to title. They may be awarded reinstatement of employment under title I and reinstitution of services under titles II, III, or IV. They may also be eligible for monetary rewards, including compensatory damages in the event of intentional discrimination, as in employment under title I (Bowe, 1992a).

PROCEDURAL SAFEGUARDS

procedural safeguards
(due-process rights) are granted to families in both Part C and Part B. An example is the right to see all relevant records pertaining to the child.

Procedural safeguards for families were enacted as the Family Educational Rights and Privacy Act (PL 93-380; 34 CFR Part 99), were expanded in the Education for All Handicapped Children Act (EAHA) (PL 94-142), and were applied to families with infants or toddlers in PL 99-457 and PL 102-119. These statutes are powerful; and the Part B case law (collected cases and decisions) is extensive. The court decisions led to many regulatory or even statutory changes, as courts interpreted the IDEA and its meaning. Equally significant, the very existence of these due-process rights may spur program-parent negotiations, as programs seek to make it unnecessary for parents to assert these rights. This may help to explain why only a small minority (about 10 percent) of parents filed even one due-process complaint against a local education agency during Part B's first ten years (Harris & Associates, 1989).

IDEA Part B

Section 615 (Procedural Safeguards) of the IDEA requires state and local education agencies to provide complaint mechanisms for families and for children and youth with disabilities. Parents (the term parents in this context refers throughout to parents or guardians) are to have the opportunity to examine all relevant records an education agency holds about their child. These may be extensive: information on the child's health, intelligence, and academic achievement; copies of IEPs and supporting documentation; teacher assessments; and many other checklists, charts, and so on. While necessary for instructional purposes, the collection and maintenance of such comprehensive records conflicts with a family's desire for privacy (Hartshorne & Boomer, 1993). That is why the IDEA ensures the parents the right to inspect such records at any time. Parents may also secure, often at public expense, a second, independent evaluation of their child if they disagree with the school district's evaluation. Regardless of who pays for the independent evaluation, the school district is required to take into consideration the findings and recommendations of the outside evaluator.

If a child's parents are unknown or cannot be found, the education agency must appoint a surrogate to represent the child. Parents or (where appropriate) surrogates are to be given written prior notice of any school plans to evaluate, assess, place, or change services for a child with a disability. Such notices are to be given in the parents' native language unless it is clearly infeasible to do so. Prior notice allows the parents to forestall actions they believe are detrimental to the child.

If parents disagree with the IEP team about any aspect of their child's education, the IDEA urges the parents to turn first to mediation. In binding mediation, both sides agree to accept the mediator's decision. Disputes that are mediated usually are resolved much faster, and at much lower costs, than are litigated disputes. However, parents still retain the right to go to court instead of to a mediator. If they do, parents may begin by presenting complaints against an education agency to an impartial due-process hearing officer, who must make a decision within forty-five days. The law and the U.S. Department of Education's implementing regulations govern how the hearings are to be held. Both sides must be permitted to introduce evidence. The parents may bring an attorney or other advocate to assist them. School districts are required to inform parents about free or low-cost legal assistance that may be available (Charmatz, 1993; Turnbull & Turnbull, 1991). The losing party (the parents or the school district) may appeal an adverse decision to a state review officer. Following exhaustion of these administrative remedies, either party may proceed to state or federal district court for relief. If the case reaches the U.S. Supreme Court, its decision is final.

In the event that the parents are successful, a federal court may award them reasonable attorney's fees, in compliance with the Handicapped Children's Protection Act of 1986, PL 94-372. However, the burden of proof in section 615 procedural disputes is on the party seeking relief—in most cases the parents (Turnbull, 1990). In general, parents are not as familiar as education agencies with the intricacies of Part B. These factors—the parental burden of proof and parents' relative lack of expertise—suggest that school districts, on the whole, will enter disputes with a stronger hand (Turnbull & Turnbull, 1991).

Section 615 requires that while a dispute is pending, the child with a disability is to continue receiving a free, appropriate public education and is to remain in the current placement. This requirement is very important, because prior to the enactment of what is now the IDEA, schools sometimes suspended or expelled students with disabilities and refused to readmit them until forced to do so by a higher authority. Such actions are no longer permissible.

Parents are explicitly permitted under section 615 to use the protections offered by section 504 as well. However, the IDEA administrative remedies must first be exhausted before actions under section 504 may begin.

The relevant provisions of the Part B procedural safeguards appear in Figure 5.1. Notice especially the requirements for written prior notice, the rights at hearings, the right to go to court, and the stay-put provisions governing the pendency of any dispute. The 1997 amendments offered parents the right to use mediation, as provided for in section 615.

IDEA Part C

Section 639 of the IDEA's Part C requires states to create a system ensuring timely resolution of complaints. The U.S. Department of Education's implementing regulations give states two options: First, they may adopt the IDEA Part B procedures (see earlier), applying them to Part C complaints. Second, states may set up separate procedures to comply with

Section 615.(a) Any State educational agency, State agency, or local educational agency that receives assistance under this part shall establish and maintain procedures in accordance with this section to ensure that children with disabilities and their parents are guaranteed procedural safeguards with respect to the provision of free appropriate public education by such agencies.

(b) The procedures required by this section shall include—
    (1) an opportunity for the parents of a child with a disability to examine all records relating to such child and to participate in meetings with respect to the identification, evaluation, and educational placement of the child, and the provision of a free appropriate public education to such child, and to obtain an independent educational evaluation of the child;
    (2) procedures to protect the rights of the child whenever the parents of the child are not known . . . ;
    (3) written prior notice to the parents of the child whenever such agency—(A) proposes to initiate or change; or (B) refuses to initiate or change the identification, evaluation, or educational placement of the child . . . or the provision of a free appropriate public education to such child; (4) procedures designed to ensure that the notice required by paragraph (3) is in the native language of the parents, unless it clearly is not feasible to do so; (5) an opportunity for mediation in accordance with subsection (e); (6) an opportunity to present complaints . . . ;
(d) Procedural Safeguards Notice.—(1) In general, a copy of the procedural safeguards available to the parents of a child with a disability shall be given to the parents, at a minimum—(A) upon initial referral for evaluation; (B) upon each notification of an individualized education program meeting and upon reevaluation of the child; and (C) upon registration of a complaint [from the parents]. . . .
(e) Mediation.—(1) In general.—Any State educational agency or local educational agency that receives assistance under this part shall ensure that procedures are established and implemented to allow parties to disputes involving any matter described in subsection (b)(6) to resolve such disputes through a mediation process which, at a minimum, shall be available whenever a hearing is requested under subsection (f) or (k).
    (2) Requirements.—Such procedures shall meet the following requirements: (A) The procedures shall ensure that the mediation process—(i) is voluntary on the part of the parties; (ii) is not used to delay a parent's right to a due process hearing under subsection (f), or to deny any other rights afforded under this part; and (iii) is conducted by a qualified and impartial mediator who is trained in effective mediation techniques. . . .
(f) Impartial Due Process Hearing.—(A) In general.—Whenever a complaint has been received under subsection (b)(6) or (k) of this section, the parents involved in such complaint shall have an opportunity for an impartial due process hearing. . . . [Either party may appeal the decision to the state education agency and then to federal courts. If parents are the prevailing party at court, the court may award them attorneys' fees.]. . . .
(h) Safeguards.—Any party to a hearing conducted pursuant to subsection (f) or (k), or an appeal conducted pursuant to subsection (g), shall be accorded—(1) the right to be accompanied and advised by counsel and by individuals with specialized knowledge or training with respect to the problems of children with disabilities; (2) the right to present evidence and confront, cross-examine, and compel the attendance of witnesses; (3) the right to a written, or at the option of the parents, electronic verbatim record of such hearing; and (4) the right to written, or at the option of the parents, electronic findings of fact and decisions. . . .
(i) Maintenance of current educational placement.—Except as provided in subsection (k)(7), during the pendency of any proceedings conducted pursuant to this section, unless the

(continued)

> State or local educational agency and the parents otherwise agree, the child shall remain in the then-current educational placement of such child, or, if applying for initial admission to a public school, shall, with the consent of the parents, be placed in the public school program until all such proceedings have been completed.
> (k) Placement in alternative educational setting.—
>   (1) Authority of school personnel.—(A) School personnel under this section may order a change in placement of a child with a disability—(i) to an appropriate interim alternative educational setting, another setting, or suspension, for not more than 10 school days. . . . and (ii) to an appropriate interim alternative educational setting for the same amount of time that a child without a disability would be subject to discipline, but for not more than 45 days if—(I) the child carries a weapon to school . . . or (II) the child knowingly possesses or uses illegal drugs or solicits the sale of a controlled substance while at school. . . .

FIGURE 5.1   Procedural Safeguards: Part B (excerpts)

the requirements of section 639. The use of the Part B procedures is simplified by the fact that the Part C requirements mirror those of Part B. For example, the term parent is defined in the same way in Parts B and C, and in the department's 34 CFR 300 and 34 CFR 303 rules. Sections IDEA 615 and 639 both call for prior written notice in the parents' native language. And both adopt the PL 93-380 Family Educational Rights and Privacy Act (FERPA) requirements.

As with Part B, the burden of proof in section 639 procedural disputes is on the party seeking relief, in most cases the parents (Turnbull, 1990). Similarly, because Part C agencies generally have greater expertise than parents about the federal and state laws, they would appear, on the whole, to be better positioned to prevail over many challenges from parents (Turnbull & Turnbull, 1991).

There are, however, differences between the procedural safeguards under Parts B and C. First, attorney's fee awards are not available under Part C. As a result, attorneys may be less willing to represent families in section 639 procedures. Second, Part C has no explicit provision for independent evaluations (Turnbull & Turnbull, 1991). Third, complaints must be resolved within thirty days under Part C (versus forty-five days under Part B). Despite these differences, the similarities dominate, especially because states may reduce or even eliminate these differences. There is nothing in the law preventing a state from providing for attorney's fee awards to the prevailing party. Similarly, a state may allow parents to introduce private, outside evaluations by physicians or other specialists during due-process hearings. And states may adopt the Part B procedural safeguards, in which the thirty-day time limit is eliminated in favor of the forty-five-day timetable.

However, another difference between Part B and Part C procedures may not be able to be resolved by state action. Unlike Part B, Part C does not specify that parents may use section 504 as an alternative legal basis for action. Part C's apparently exclusive reliance upon the IDEA safeguard routes may preclude states, and even courts, from providing alternative routes for complaint resolution (Turnbull & Turnbull, 1991).

Relevant components of the Part C procedural safeguards follow, in Figure 5.2. Added in 1991 were the requirement for prior written consent by the family to any interagency transfer of personally identifiable information and the right of a family to decline service.

Section 639. The procedural safeguards required to be included in a statewide system under section 635(a)(13) shall provide, at a minimum, the following:

(1) The timely administrative resolution of complaints by parents. Any party aggrieved by the findings and decision regarding an administrative complaint shall have the right to bring a civil action with respect to the complaint, which action may be brought in any State court of competent jurisdiction or in a district court of the United States without regard to the amount of controversy. In any action brought under this paragraph, the court shall receive the records of the administrative proceedings, shall hear additional evidence at the request of a party, and, basing its decision on the preponderance of the evidence, shall grant such relief as the court determines is appropriate.

(2) The right to confidentiality of personally identifiable information, including the right of parents to written notice of and written consent to the exchange of such information among agencies consistent with Federal and State law.

(3) The right of the parents to determine whether they, their infant or toddler, or other family members will accept or decline any early intervention service under this part in accordance with State law without jeopardizing other early intervention services under this part.

(4) The opportunity for parents to examine records relating to assessment, screening, eligibility determinations, and the development and implementation of the individualized family service plan.

(5) Procedures to protect the rights of the infant or toddler with a disability whenever the parents of the child are not known or unavailable or the child is a ward of the State, including the assignment of an individual (who shall not be an employee of the State lead agency or other state agency, and who shall not be any person, or any employee of a person, providing early intervention services to the infant or toddler or any family member of the infant or toddler) to act as a surrogate for the parents.

(6) Written prior notice to the parents of the infant or toddler with a disability whenever the state agency or service provider proposes to initiate or change or refuses to initiate or change the identification, evaluation, placement, or the provision of appropriate early intervention services to the infant or toddler.

(7) Procedures designed to assure that the notice required by paragraph (6) fully informs the parents, in the parents' native language, unless it clearly is not feasible to do so, of all procedures available pursuant to this section.

(8) The right of any parents to use mediation in accordance with section 615(e); except that. . . . (b) During the pendency of any proceeding or action involving a complaint, unless the State agency and the parents otherwise agree, the child shall continue to receive the appropriate early intervention services currently being provided or, if applying for initial services, shall receive the services not in dispute.

FIGURE 5.2 Procedural safeguards Part C

Discussion

Part C offers powerful due-process safeguards for families, which mirror those provided under Part B. Section 639 of Part C requires states to create procedures to protect the rights of parents, guardians, infants, and toddlers. The state's lead agency must investigate any complaints, whether about an individual child and family or about systemic violations of law. The lead agency must correct any individual or systemic violations it identifies.

Recall that states may adopt the Part B section 615 due process safeguards in lieu of creating new procedures under Part C's section 639. The Part B safeguards, found in section 615 of the IDEA, have been in place in all states for many years. They may not be familiar to officials at state health, social services, or other agencies, however. The procedures ensure that families and children with disabilities are not at the mercy of program officials. Families may challenge virtually any agency decision, from initial labeling through placement and service delivery. Parents may even challenge the qualifications of special education and related services personnel as not meeting state standards. These procedural safeguards may be invoked by parents at any time. In most states, the Part B impartial hearing officer is a school official from a neighboring school district, a private expert, or an attorney (Charmatz, 1993). The IDEA provides extensive rules governing the way in which impartial hearing officers reach decisions. Either party (parents or school district) may appeal an unfavorable decision, usually to a state review officer. Either then may proceed further, to state or federal district court. Part C contains very similar rules. Accordingly, courts probably will draw on the case law concerning Part B procedural safeguards in deciding Part C cases (Turnbull & Turnbull, 1991).

The federal regulations implementing Part C (34 CFR 303) added: "It is important that the administrative procedures developed by a state be designed to result in speedy resolution of complaints. An infant's or toddler's development is so rapid that undue delay could be potentially harmful." For that reason, section 303 insists that complaints be resolved and a written decision issued within thirty days of the date of complaint. The only exception permitted is where a state adopts Part B procedures, in which case resolution is required within forty-five days.

States must also allow parents to take their complaints to state or federal courts. Part C is silent on whether parents of infants or toddlers must first exhaust administrative remedies, that is, file a complaint first with the lead agency and await its decision before proceeding to court.

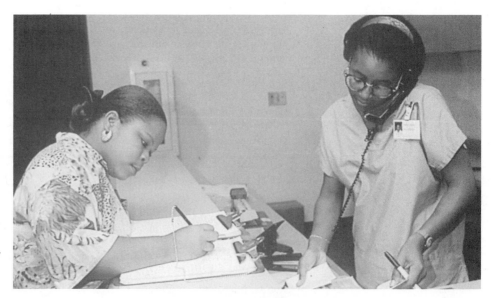

Virtually all records about a child must be open to and available for family members to inspect. They may, if they wish, append comments to such records.

The statutory language of section 639 implies that administrative complaints will usually be heard first. However, in states where the thirty-day (or forty-five–day) time-table is routinely flouted, parents may win the right to proceed directly to court (Turnbull & Turnbull, 1991).

States also must maintain strict confidentiality of all personally identifiable information, that is, any record containing or implying the name or identity of an infant, toddler, or parent. Protection of personally identifiable information is a widespread practice in human services agencies today. The 1991 amendments to the IDEA added a requirement that parents be given written notice of, and an opportunity to provide written consent to, any reporting of personally identifiable information from one agency to another.

As in Part B, parents have the right to written prior notice of any significant proposal for change or other decision by an authorized Part C agency. This notice is to be provided in the parents' native language, if at all feasible. Native language may include American Sign Language (ASL) in the case of parents who are deaf. For parents who are blind, the notice may be provided in Braille or may be read aloud. And, again as in Part B, Part C contains a stay-put provision ensuring that the child and family will continue receiving services throughout the duration of any complaint or other dispute.

IN BRIEF

Other laws provide additional rights for infants, toddlers, and preschoolers with disabilities and their families. Among the more important are the following pieces of legislation.

Fair Housing Amendments Act (FHAA)

PL 100-430 protects children with disabilities and their families from unjust discrimination if they are or wish to be tenants in private housing. The bill was signed on September 13, 1988, and took full effect on March 13, 1991. In condominiums and apartment buildings having four or more units, families with members who are disabled may not be denied the chance to rent or buy units. They are also allowed to make renovations or other alterations, at their own expense.

Private one- and two-family homes continue to be exempt from federal (and, usually, state) regulation on accessibility for people with disabilities. Until the FHAA took effect, accessibility features in apartment buildings and condominiums, as well as multiunit townhouses, were required in only a few states. As a result, finding accessible housing was a major problem for families with members who had physical disabilities; it was also a concern, though a lesser one, for families with children who had other kinds of disabilities. Even with the FHAA, most estimates suggest that fewer than 2 percent of all homes and other units of housing today are accessible to people with physical disabilities (Bowe, 1992a). In time, new construction will result in ever more accessible housing.

The law establishes standards of accessibility and **adaptability** for new multifamily housing; apartment and condominium buildings built for first occupancy after March 13, 1991, are much more accessible and much easier to adapt than are older units. In addition, real estate agencies are now prohibited from discriminating against people with disabilities who are seeking private homes or apartments. Real estate agents who steered families with members who have disabilities away from some housing complexes were an important problem.

The law also strengthens the rights of individuals with disabilities to live in group homes. Until the FHAA was passed, only New York, Michigan, and a handful of other states that had strong laws in favor of group homes were effective in overcoming local opposition to

adaptability refers to the requirement in the Fair Housing Amendments Act of 1988, PL 100-430, that new, four-unit or larger multifamily housing structures be adaptable or readily changeable to meet the special needs of individuals with severe disabilities. An example is cabinets or light switches that may be easily lowered.

group homes. Group homes are an important housing option for older adolescents and adults with severe disabilities. Waiting lists remain long in many states; parents are well advised to request placement eight or more years prior to the time the child is expected to need a place to live (42 USC 3601 et seq.).

Air Carriers Access Act

Although section 504 has required since 1978 that airports be accessible, individual air carriers considered themselves not to be recipients of federal financial assistance, and therefore believed that they were exempt from the section 504 nondiscrimination mandates. PL 99-435 made it clear that commercial airlines must comply with section 504, on the grounds that they "benefit from" publicly supported airports and traffic control centers. The 1986 law requires carriers using U.S. airports to provide nondiscriminatory treatment for passengers with disabilities (49 USC 1301).

Television Decoder Circuitry Act

Enacted on October 16, 1990, PL 101-431 requires all new television sets measuring thirteen inches or more diagonally that are made or sold in the United States after July 1, 1993, to have built-in caption decoder chips. Such chips enable the set to receive and display captions (subtitles). In effect, PL 101-431 grants deaf and hard-of-hearing people, as well as others needing captions (illiterate Americans, immigrants trying to learn English, and so on), the right to understand television programming. The law does not require that programs be captioned. However, the fact that tens of millions of television sets have been sold since the law took effect means that the number of households with caption-equipped sets is now very substantial, a fact that encourages program producers to caption their offerings (47 USC 609, 47 USC 303).

Telecommunications Act

The Telecommunications Act of 1996 (PL 104-104) requires that all new telecommunications equipment and services be accessible to and usable by people with disabilities, unless it is not feasible to do so. Included are customer premises equipment (including telephones, Caller ID units, and so on) and services that are provided by local and long-distance telephone companies. The act also requires that all new video programming be captioned. (Recall that the Television Decoder Circuitry Act, discussed previously, does not require that programs be captioned.) Captioning of broadcast and cable television offerings will be phased in under the Telecommunications Act, with most entertainment programs, movies, and news programs being captioned no later than the year 2003.

S U M M A R Y

After reading summaries of these federally established rights, one after the other, some people may ask, "Was it really necessary to enact legislation to secure these rights?" The answer, unfortunately, is yes. Individuals with disabilities used to be routinely excluded from even the few housing units that were accessible, as landlords acted out of ignorance and fear.

Similarly, people with disabilities were denied permission to board aircraft unless they first showed a certificate, or letter, from a doctor stating that they could travel safely.

These rights make a big difference in the quality of life that families with children who have disabilities may enjoy. Their full effect is reached only when parents, siblings, and children with disabilities themselves become aware of these rights and insist on them. ECSE personnel and other advocates need to become familiar with these rights—and to convey information about them to parents.

QUESTIONS FOR REFLECTION

1. Why is section 504 of the Rehabilitation Act still important for children who have attention deficit disorders?

2. Some children who have disabilities may not require early intervention services, nor special education and related services. What rights do those children enjoy with respect to services they *do* need?

3. If a state were to decide to drop out of the Part C program, what civil-rights statute would the state still have to obey?

4. Suppose a parent who has a child with high-cost medical needs were to seek employment. What help does the Americans with Disabilities Act offer? Why could such help be important to this parent?

5. On an everyday basis in the community, how does title III of the Americans with Disabilities Act help families having children with disabilities?

6. Why do you think the 1997 amendments to the IDEA encouraged parents to use mediation rather than litigation?

7. Why is "stay put" ("maintenance of current educational placement") an important right for families?

8. What importance does "written prior notice" hold for parents of infants, toddlers, or children with disabilities?

9. Why is the prohibition against discrimination on the basis of disability by landlords and real estate brokers under the Fair Housing Amendments Act so important for many families?

10. What kinds of young children, other than those who are deaf, might benefit from the requirement, contained in the 1996 Telecommunications Act, that most video programming be captioned?

Other Laws for Service Coordination

A child who clearly qualified for early intervention moved into a county in Minnesota. The parents were interested in providing their child some time in a typical setting with other children his age (twenty months) as he had no siblings. The county defined this setting as educational, the school district defined it as respite, and both agencies refused to provide the service. (Behr, 1991, p. 33)

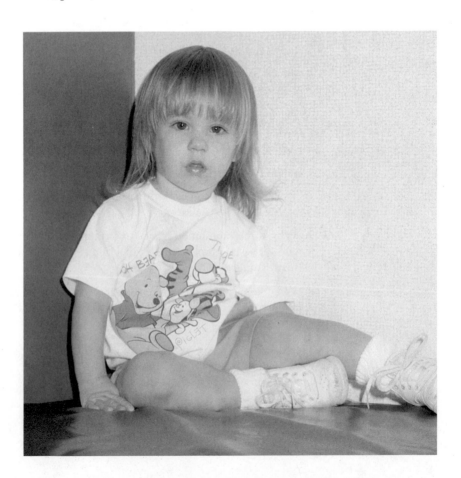

OVERVIEW

Federal Part C funds are intended to be "glue money." As a result, other funding sources for early intervention are very important. Some services for preschool-age children with disabilities may also be funded by sources other than education agencies. This chapter discusses the important sources of supplementary funding for services to the birth-to-five population.

The service coordinator plays a critical role in helping the family to learn about and tap into sources of support and assistance beyond those offered by early intervention programs themselves. Figure 6.1 illustrates some of the linkages a service coordinator might establish on behalf of a family. Of highest priority for the service coordinator is ascertaining the family's views on its own priorities and resources. Once the service coordinator understands that family's capabilities and needs, the next step is to work with the family to establish eligibility for and receive assistance from appropriate programs. Information on many of these supplementary programs is offered in this chapter. It is important, however, that the reader understand

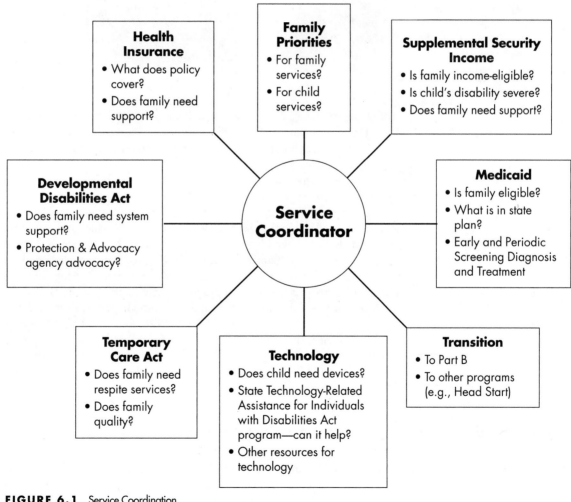

FIGURE 6.1   Service Coordination

Family members need to know about rights and services in oher programs, not only in early childhood settings. An important role of the early childhood special educator and of the service coordinator is to advise the family about other community services and programs.

that eligibility standards, services offered, and benefits available vary sharply from state to state. That is why the service coordinator must get current information about how each program is implemented in the state. The resources listed at the end of the chapter can help in that important work.

There are strings attached to each source of funding. However, a large part of the federal role since the enactment of PL 99-457 has been to remove some of the more contradictory program requirements. States, too, have streamlined requirements. The need for such alterations is exemplified in the chapter's opening quotation, which is drawn from the testimony of Jeanette Behr of Lake Elmo, Minnesota, before the U.S. Senate, as she was describing the frustrations of another family. While changes in program rules since that time have helped considerably, trade-offs still have to be made: Tapping Developmental Disabilities Act funds for birth-to-five children, for example, may mean fewer dollars available to meet the needs of children and youth aged six and above who have developmental disabilities.

Partly because of these strings, Clifford (1991) found that only two of the six states he studied used more than two of the funding sources discussed in the chapter. Were he to contact the same states today, he would certainly discover greater use of multiple sources of funding. It would be an unusual state, however, that taps all of the following sources for ECSE-related services.

SUPPLEMENTAL SECURITY INCOME

Supplemental Security Income (SSI) is a federal-state program to guarantee a minimum income for people who are poor, disabled, or elderly. Beneficiaries are ensured a minimum income to supplement family-earned and unearned incomes; the guaranteed amount has

Supplemental Security Income (SSI) is a federal-state guaranteed minimum income program for individuals who are poor and have disabilities. Most SSI beneficiaries also receive Medicaid.

been below the poverty level for the past several years, however. SSI was created in 1974, bringing together many diverse state programs. Since that time, the term disability has been defined under SSI rules principally in two ways. First, the Social Security Administration (SSA) uses a list of definitions; individuals must then demonstrate that they have a listed impairment, or one that is similar in severity to a listed condition. Second, individuals must show that they are unable to engage in substantial gainful activity (SGA). SGA is, in effect, the ability to work for minimum wage. Until 1990, children were held to a similar standard: They had to present evidence that they had impairments on the list, or of comparable severity.

It is important to note that the definitions used in SSI are different from those used in the Individuals with Disabilities Education Act (IDEA). Some parents mistakenly seek IDEA eligibility for their children, thinking that will qualify their children for SSI as well. It won't.

On February 20, 1990, the Supreme Court ruled in *Sullivan v. Zebley* that a listings-only approach failed to grant eligibility to some children for whom Congress had intended SSI to be made available. The Court ordered the SSA to develop a new definition for disability that could be used with children. Almost one year later, on February 11, 1991, the SSA published a regulation in the *Federal Register* that uses a multidisciplinary approach to defining disability among children. The new rules were less stringent for younger children, because the SSA discovered during consultations with experts on childhood disability that "the younger the child is, the greater the impact of the impairment on the child's ability to develop and function" (Parker, 1991, p. 82; Social Security Administration, 1991).

The SSA and its state-based Disability Determination Services (DDS) now recognize three groups of young children: newborn and young infant (birth to age one); older infant and toddler (age one to three); and children (from three to eighteen). The last category is further subdivided into preschool, school age, young adolescent, and older adolescent. The newborn and young infant category allows eligibility to be established quite easily, recognizing low birthweight alone, for example, as a qualifying condition: "[P]re-term infants with low birth weight meeting certain criteria and infants born with certain congenital abnormalities are given a defined period of disability, after which they will be scheduled for a review to determine if they are still disabled" (Parker, 1991, p. 82).

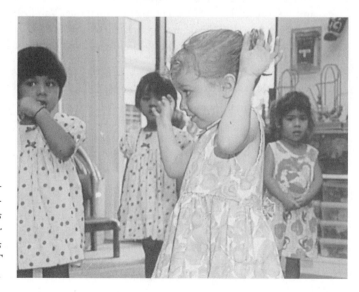

Early and Periodic Screening, Diagnosis, and Treatment (EPSDT) programs are required by law to offer treatment for conditions discovered during EPSDT screenings.

The welfare reform legislation of 1996 (the Personal Responsibility and Work Opportunity Reconciliation Act) continued the SSA's use of listings of qualifying disabilities. However, the act also stated, with respect to conditions that are not on the SSA's listing, that a child's impairment, or combination of impairments, is considered to be a "disability" if it or they cause "marked and severe functional limitations." Impairments not on the SSA's listing must produce (1) marked limitations in either of two broad areas of functioning, such as social functioning or motor functioning, or (2) extreme limitations in one such area, such as the inability to walk at all. Notably excluded under the Welfare Reform Act requirements are young children with milder behavior problems such as attention deficit disorder.

These new, tougher standards were designed to ensure that the SSI program provides support only for children with severe limitations. At the time the law was enacted in August 1997, nearly one million children under the age of eighteen had qualified for and were receiving SSI payments. The SSA estimated that about 135,000 children would be eliminated from the rolls of SSI recipients (Social Security Administration, 1997a, 1997b).

In all but a handful of states, children with disabilities who receive SSI cash payments also qualify for Medicaid, the medical assistance program for poor people.

MEDICAID

Medicaid is the federal-state medical insurance program for poor individuals. Many Supplemental Security Income Recipients receive Medicaid.

First enacted in 1965, title XIX of the Social Security Act authorizes a federal-state medical assistance program for low-income Americans. Generally known as a program of medical insurance for poor individuals and families, **Medicaid** has become a major payor of costs incurred in serving young children with disabilities. One study estimated that some 30 to 35 percent of children being served in programs specializing in developmental delays and disabilities are or would be eligible for Medicaid (Van Dyck, 1991). In part, that is because states must serve children in the birth-to-five age range whose families have incomes up to 133 percent of the poverty level (Fox et al., 1992; Omnibus Budget Reconciliation Act of 1989, PL 101-329; Swan & Morgan, 1993, p. 213). It is also because states must serve children whose medical conditions are discovered during Early and Periodic Screening, Diagnosis, and Treatment (EPSDT) screening examinations (Van Dyck, 1991; Swan & Morgan, 1993).

Medicaid is a federal-state program. The federal government requires that certain services be provided to all Medicaid-eligible individuals; these include the following categories of services:

- inpatient and outpatient hospitalization
- laboratory and X-ray
- rural health clinic services
- family planning
- physician
- EPSDT

Although all states must provide these services, federal legislation grants them considerable flexibility in deciding the frequency, scope, and duration of services they will reimburse. States may, for example, limit the number of physician visits they will cover annually.

States may supplement the federal requirements by offering more than thirty other kinds of services, including the following:

- case management services
- preventive and rehabilitative services
- home care or nursing care
- medical equipment and appliances
- home respiratory services

To be covered, such services must be included in the state's Medicaid plan. States pay some costs (calculated by a complex formula), so there is some incentive to limit services covered. It is important for service coordinators to monitor state rules to be sure services children need continue to be authorized.

Medicaid eligibility is important for infants and toddlers because many services called early intervention services in Part C are called health services in Medicaid (Brown & Brown, 1993). Similarly, Part B provides for medical and counseling services under the requirement to provide related services. These, too, may be considered health services under Medicaid rules. Prior to mid-1988, state education, health, and Medicaid agencies sometimes disagreed as to whether Medicaid-eligible children would receive Medicaid reimbursements for services listed in IFSPs and IEPs. The responsibility of Medicaid to pay for such services was clarified by PL 100-360, as discussed below.

The Social Security Act was amended by the Medicare Catastrophic Coverage Act of 1988, PL 100-360. A new subsection (c) was added to section 1903 of the act. This new subsection, which took effect on July 1, 1988, explained that Medicaid agencies must pay for services regardless of whether or not those services are included in a child's individualized family service plan (IFSP) or individualized education program (IEP). That is, a state Medicaid agency may not decline to reimburse families just because services are outlined in, and provided under, an IFSP or an IEP. (The catastrophic illness provisions of the act were soon repealed by PL 101-234, following public outcry over the higher social security taxes required to cover costs of catastrophic care. However, section 1903 remained in effect.) The subsection reads:

> (c) Nothing in this title shall be construed as prohibiting or restricting, or authorizing the Secretary[1] to prohibit or restrict, payment under subsection (a) for medical assistance for covered services furnished to a handicapped child because such services are included in the child's individualized education program established pursuant to part B of the Education of the Handicapped Act or furnished to a handicapped infant or toddler because such services are included in the child's individualized family service plan adopted pursuant to part H of such Act. (42 USC 1369b)

Using IEPs to illustrate, Conference Report 100-661 explained:

> Under the Education for All Handicapped Children Act of 1975, PL 94-142, children with handicaps are entitled to a free and appropriate public education with conformity with an individualized education program (IEP) which describes the educational and "related services" necessary to meet the child's unique needs. While the state education agencies are financially responsible for educational services, in the case of a Medicaid-eligible handicapped child, state Medicaid agencies remain responsible for the "related services" identified in the child's IEP if they are covered under the State's Medicaid plan, such as speech-language pathology and audiology, psychology services, physical and occupational therapy, and medical counseling and services for diagnostic and evaluation purposes (emphasis added). (pp. 268-269)

[1]Of the U.S. Department of Health and Human Services (HHS)

The effect of section 1903(c) was to override a federal administrative decision holding that services detailed in an IFSP or an IEP were not eligible for Medicaid reimbursement. The intent was to reinforce the IDEA's directive that state Part C agencies must arrange for IFSP services to be provided, and that state Medicaid agencies must reimburse providers for services covered in the state Medicaid plan (Fox et al., 1992).

The PL 100-360 changes are significant. It is not uncommon for children with complex conditions or lengthy medical histories to run up medical bills of $500,000 or more during the first year of life. Such expenses could bankrupt even middle-class families, let alone those less well off. Medicaid ruling 77-102 provides that children may be eligible based on their own financial resources (not their family's) after thirty days of hospitalization. Usually, the child-eligibility rules lapse once the child is released from the hospital; that is, continued eligibility once again rests upon family financial resources. (If Medicaid coverage for care at home is approved, the reversion to family eligibility does not occur.)

Early and Periodic Screening, Diagnosis, and Treatment (EPSDT)

The 1989 Omnibus Budget Reconciliation Act (PL 101-239) greatly expanded federal funding for the Medicaid EPSDT program. The 1967 Social Security Act created EPSDT, and it has been a required component of state Medicaid plans since 1972. The program is intended to ensure that all Medicaid-eligible children under age twenty-one receive important health services, including screening, examination, and treatment. The 1989 legislation facilitated state implementation of Part C, and also provided another source of funding for section 619 Part B preschool services: key services needed by many young children with disabilities or developmental delays. As noted above, the act requires state Medicaid programs to reimburse providers for all Medicaid-approved diagnostic and treatment services a child requires due to a condition or disease discovered in an EPSDT screening examination—*whether or not such services are included in the state Medicaid plan.* This is an important change, because in the past some states excluded some such services from their Medicaid plans (Social Security Act, 42 USC 1396s, sec. 1905[r][5]; Brown & Brown, 1993; Fox et al., 1992).

Under EPSDT, states must conduct outreach activities to inform all eligible children about EPSDT services. They must also connect those children with the services they need. Among other things, state Medicaid agencies must develop interagency agreements with state education agencies, state Part C lead agencies, and public health providers to ensure that children and their families learn about, and get, essential services. EPSDT-funded services include assessments of health, developmental, and nutritional status as well as vision, hearing, and dental services. States may offer additional services. However, because implementation of the EPSDT program varies so much from state to state, it is essential that professionals and parents alike find out what services their states offer. The state Medicaid office is a good source of such information.

Eligibility and Costs

Medicaid is a major source of funding for early intervention services. There are important limits, however, to the uses that may be made of it. First, only those children who meet Medicaid requirements (chiefly, family income must be very low) qualify regardless of type or severity of disability. Eligibility for Medicaid is based on financial need. While all states must cover under-six children in families with incomes below 133 percent of the poverty level, some states offer Medicaid eligibility to children under one year of age whose families have incomes as high as 185 percent of the poverty level (Brown & Brown, 1993). However, Medicaid remains a program for poor families, as defined by state and federal regulations. Second, only those services contained in the state Medicaid plan may be offered. While nothing prevents a state from adding new early intervention services to its Medicaid plan, state matching requirements effectively limit the number and scope of new services. Medicaid is already an explosively growing and very costly program; states often are reluctant to add to it (Safer & Hamilton, 1993, p. 14).

MATERNAL AND CHILD HEALTH SERVICES BLOCK GRANT

Created as part of the Omnibus Reconciliation Act of 1981, the Maternal and Child Health Services (MCH) block grant program replaced numerous smaller, more specific programs, some of which date back as far as the Social Security Act of 1935. The MCH block grant program (still often called title V in reference to its position in the Social Security Act) gives states relatively unrestricted federal funds. These are to be used to ensure access to maternal and child health services for people with low incomes, to reduce infant mortality and morbidity (serious illness), and to serve children in need of special health services. Each year, hundreds of thousands of pregnant women receive prenatal care services under the MCH block grant program. States may use MCH funds to increase the number of low-socioeconomic status (SES) children receiving health assessments, follow-up diagnostic services, and treatment services. They may also use these funds to prevent disabilities.

Since 1986, federal legislation on the MCH block grant program has stressed family-centered community programs on behalf of young children with disabilities. Case management services for such children are specifically authorized under the MCH program. These steps help to integrate MCH programs with IDEA Part B and Part C programs for children with disabilities. Beginning in 1991, states have been required to use at least 30 percent of their MCH block grant monies to provide preventive and primary-care services to children, and at least 30 percent for services to children with special health needs. In addition, the state agency that operates the MCH program must coordinate with the state's EPSDT program under Medicaid. Among the services MCH agencies may sponsor are home health care and respite services for families.

Federal law bans fees for low-SES women and children. However, sliding fee schedules and other charges are allowed if these reflect the income, resources, and family size of beneficiaries (PL 101-239, 42 U.S.C. 701).

DEVELOPMENTAL DISABILITIES ASSISTANCE AND BILL OF RIGHTS ACT (DD ACT)

This act provides formula grant funds to the states for planning and coordination of services for children, youth, and adults with developmental disabilities (defined as conditions beginning prior to age twenty-two that result in a multitude of needs that cross agency lines). To qualify for DD Act funds under the act's Part B, states must establish a state Developmental Disabilities Planning Council. The council members are representatives from state agencies that serve children with disabilities, notably the state education agency and the state Part C lead agency. The law requires each state to focus on system coordination among such agencies. That is, DD Act funds are intended to fill the gaps between other programs.

The definition used in the DD Act was amended after PL 99-457 was enacted in 1986, so as to coordinate DD services with early intervention and preschool activities. The act's definition of disabilities is lengthy; the first part of it is important to readers concerned with transition of five-year-olds, the second part to readers concerned with children from birth to five years of age:

> *[A] severe, chronic disability of a person 5 years of age or older which (a) is attributable to a mental or physical impairment or combination of mental or physical impairments; (b) is manifested before the person attains age twenty-two; (c) is likely to continue indefinitely; (d) results in substantial functional limitations in three or more of the following areas of major life activity: (1) self-care, (2) receptive and expressive language, (3) learning, (4) mobility, (5) self-direction, (6) capacity for independent living, and (7) economic sufficiency; and (e) reflects the person's need for a combination and sequence of special, interdisciplinary, or generic care, treatment, or other services which are of lifelong or extended duration and are individually planned and coordinated; except that such term when applied to infants and young children means individuals from birth to age 5, inclusive, who have substantial developmental delay or specific congenital or acquired conditions with a high probability of resulting in developmental disabilities if services are not provided.*

The part of this definition that follows the semicolon ("except that such term . . .") is much closer than earlier definitions of disability to what the IDEA uses under section 619 of Part B and under Part C. This congruity of definition clearly helps states to coordinate IDEA and DD Act services for young children with disabilities.

Part C of the act authorizes formula grants to the states to set up systems of protection and advocacy (P&A) to protect the rights of individuals with developmental disabilities. State P&A agencies may pursue administrative and legal remedies on behalf of individuals with developmental disabilities, including lawsuits, to ensure that these individuals receive the services to which they are entitled under federal or state law. The P&A agencies also have the authority to investigate allegations of mistreatment of persons with developmental disabilities at schools and residential facilities (PL 100-146, 42 U.S.C. 6000 *et seq.*).

HEAD START ACT

Head Start is the federally supported program of services for preschool children that was begun in 1965. Most children served are from disadvantaged families; at least 10 percent of the children served must be children with disabilities.

Begun in 1964, with the first funded programs appearing in 1965, **Head Start** is an important program serving young children with disabilities. Funded at nearly $3 billion in federal FY 1993-1994, Head Start annually serves some 70,000 three- to five-year-olds with disabilities, representing about 13 percent of all children in Head Start programs.

New rules on coordinating with IDEA Part C and section 619 Part B programs took effect on February 22, 1993; these require Head Start centers to write disability service plans showing how they will meet the unique needs of young children with disabilities. Outreach and recruitment activities, which are subject to detailed social service performance standards, are to locate young children with disabilities and bring them into Head Start centers. Head Start centers are not permitted to deny admission to any child on the basis of disability, nor on the grounds that the facility used by Head Start is not physically accessible to people using wheelchairs or having other mobility needs. As Zigler and Muenchow (1992) showed in their history of Head Start, physical accessibility was for many years a problem because Head Start programs often lease or rent space in older, inaccessible buildings. Other standards, specifying educational performance requirements, state that all children with disabilities being served in Head Start programs must have an IEP. Among other things, family goals are to be met and assistive technology products and services provided as needed. Developed over more than four years, these requirements may be found in the January 21, 1993, *Federal Register*.

Such high standards of service to children with disabilities were a long time coming. Head Start was first authorized in the Economic Opportunity Act of 1964, as part of President Johnson's war on poverty. Beginning in 1972, at least 10 percent of Head Start enrollees have been required to be children with disabilities, and special services have been mandated as necessary to meet their needs. The January 1975 reauthorization applied this 10 percent requirement to each state, not only to the nation as a whole. That year, Congress also appropriated $20 million to meet the excess costs of Head Start programs in serving children with disabilities; these funds could be used to purchase special education services, related services, and professional diagnosis.

Interagency coordination was a problem even in 1975. Almost a year before PL 94-142 was enacted, Congress ordered the federal Head Start agency to coordinate efforts with other federal and state agencies that had responsibility for serving children with disabilities, notably state education agencies with responsibilities under the EHA and other state agencies with responsibilities under the DD Act. Recognizing that additional costs might be incurred, the Senate committee report urged Head Start programs to seek funds from other state and local agencies with responsibility for helping children with disabilities (LaVor & Harvey, 1976). Although Head Start definitions are similar to those in the IDEA Part B, the federal Head Start law today allows the use of any state definition of disability that is recognized in the jurisdiction in which a Head Start program operates. That flexibility is essential to Head Start-Part C coordination because states differ in their definitions under Part C. For example, some recognize fragile X syndrome as an established condition, some do not; some accept 33 percent delays in development, while others insist on 50 percent delays; some serve at-risk children, others do not (Brown & Brown, 1993; PL 101-501, 42 U.S.C. 9831 *et seq.*).

PUBLIC HEALTH SERVICES ACT

The Centers for Disease Control and Prevention (CDC) administer a discretionary grant program on disabilities prevention under the Public Health Services Act, providing funds to about thirty states for coordination of local disability prevention projects (PL 101-538, 42 U.S.C. 301).

ALCOHOL, DRUG ABUSE, AND MENTAL HEALTH SERVICES BLOCK GRANT

Each state receives a Public Health Service Act Alcohol, Drug Abuse, and Mental Health Services (ADAMH) block grant based on state population and per capita income. Of the amount allocated for substance abuse, not less than 20 percent must be used for prevention and early intervention services (PL 101-538, 42 U.S.C. 300x).

THE CHILDREN WITH DISABILITIES TEMPORARY CARE ACT

The Temporary Child Care for Handicapped Children and Crisis Nurseries Act of 1986 (PL 100-403) authorizes grants to states to help support public or private agencies providing temporary, nonmedical care for children with disabilities. The services may be offered in or out of the home. The 1989 reauthorization of the act, PL 100-403, allows families to be charged on a sliding fee scale to help cover the costs of these services. One-half of the funds appropriated must be used for temporary care and the other half devoted to crisis nurseries (PL 101-127, 42 U.S.C. 5117 *et seq.*).

TECHNOLOGY-RELATED ASSISTANCE FOR INDIVIDUALS WITH DISABILITIES ACT (TRAIDA)

Signed on August 19, 1988, PL 100-407 provides funds (about $1.5 million per state) to state governments to disseminate information about assistive devices and services for people with disabilities, including children. Some TRAIDA funds may also be used to purchase technologies important to people with disabilities of all ages. In addition, TRAIDA also requires states to comply with section 508 of the Rehabilitation Act; section 508 calls for electronic equipment, such as computers, and electronic information, such as bulletin boards and databases, to be accessible to people with disabilities.

TRAIDA is important because it is the first federal law ever to focus entirely on technology for people with disabilities. It is also significant because state, county, and local government agencies must now take accessibility into consideration when they make arrangements to purchase, lease, or rent computers and information services. As technology becomes ever more important in education and other human services, the fact that the equipment and the services reached through it are to be usable by persons with disabilities will become increasingly important. PL 103-218, signed March 9, 1994, amended and extended the act (29 USC 2201).

SUMMARY

This chapter offered the reader information about federal programs and services that authorize supplementary funding for important services that many infants, toddlers, and preschoolers with disabilities need. States vary considerably in how they carry out these programs and in what services they provide. These variations are so numerous that it is not possible to detail all of them here. Information on provisions specific to a given state is available from organizations in the list that follows and in the Resources section.

For early intervention programs in particular, but often for preschool special education programs as well, coordinating all of these varied funding sources and meeting all of their variegated requirements is both challenging and time-consuming. Since 1986, however, many of the more glaring inconsistencies and more obvious gaps have been eliminated. Continued interagency coordination efforts at the federal, state, and local levels are required for additional streamlining to occur.

The state education agency, the state Part C lead agency, the DD Planning Council, and the state Medicaid agency are all sources of information about services available in a given state. The Social Security Administration may be contacted at the address below for information about disab ility programs:

Social Security Administration
Office of Disability
545 Altmeyer Building
6401 Security Boulevard
Baltimore, MD 21235

In addition, the following organizations are excellent sources of up-to-date summaries of the current status of these programs. While many of the federal and private organizations discussed in the Resources section may be helpful, the groups listed below have shown interest in, and expertise about, the programs outlined in this chapter. Tracking developments at the Social Security Administration, for example, and making those understandable for parents and ECSE workers, is a daunting task.

Children's Defense Fund
122 C Street NW
Washington, DC 20001

Georgetown University Child Development Center
2233 Wisconsin Avenue NW, Suite 215
Washington, DC 20007

Maternal and Child Health Resource Center
38th and R Streets NW
Washington, DC 20057

National Center for Clinical Infant Programs
2000 14th Street North, Suite 380
Arlington, VA 22201

National Early Childhood Technical Assistance System
NationsBank Plaza, Suite 500
137 E. Franklin Street
Chapel Hill, NC 27514

National Information Center on Children and Youth with Disabilities
P.O. Box 1492
Washington, DC 20013

Technical Assistance to Parents Project
Federation for Children with Special Needs
94 Berkeley Street, Suite 104
Boston, MA 02116

United Cerebral Palsy Associations, Inc.
1660 L Street NW, Suite 700
Washington, DC 20036

QUESTIONS FOR REFLECTION

1. What do service coordinators do for families that participate in Part C programs? Does the answer help you understand the importance of these laws to service coordinators as well as to parents?

2. Supplemental Security Income (SSI) has tightened its eligibility criteria. How do these changes affect families and young children?

3. What effects do you think the SSI changes are having on families that want to benefit from Medicaid?

4. Why are Early and Periodic Screening, Diagnosis, and Treatment (EPSDT) services so important for many young children with health needs?

5. How are Medicaid services financed? Of what relevance is this for a family contemplating a move from one state to another?

6. How might "system planning" and "system coordination" efforts by Protection and Advocacy (P&A) agencies help families having children with disabilities?

7. What act discussed in this chapter potentially offers respite services for families?

8. Which conditions or disabilities are included as "listed impairments" in your state's SSI rules?

9. Visit a local Head Start program. What kinds of disabilities are represented among the children it serves? How do you see Head Start complementing IDEA-funded programs?

10. Contact the organizations listed at the end of this chapter, asking for updates on the laws discussed here. Which groups appear to specialize in monitoring which of the laws?

Early childhood special education (ECSE) today is a field driven by idealism. The children are young, their potential seemingly unlimited. The field is new as well and filled with enthusiasm. The excitement is palpable everywhere in program after program, coast to coast, and border to border. More than anything else, ECSE is animated by its values: the belief that early intervention is the right thing to do, the certainty that preschool programs make a difference, and the conviction that family-focused, multidisciplinary approaches are optimal. It is this sense of doing good that motivates ECSE workers, volunteers, and parents alike.

The challenge for the field today is not only to do good but to do it well. Doing good well means individualizing services and supports so that all children—and all families—receive what they want and what they need in ways that help them. It means, at times, tempering enthusiasms for philosophically appealing ideas if following them is not in the best interests of a given child or family. Thus, if a child's needs are not being met in an integrated setting, doing good well means giving that child a more appropriate environment. Doing good well means, too, using limited resources judiciously, particularly in view of tight budgets at all levels of government. It means planning services and supports, and measuring outcomes. It means being accountable.

It is the challenge of doing good well that dominates Part III, which focuses on service delivery. In many respects, Part III is the heart of *Birth to Five: Early Childhood Special Education,* because this section builds upon the philosophy, history, and child development information presented earlier. Part III includes consideration both of ideals (individualization, appropriateness, integration, and parent empowerment, among others) and of practical realities (limitations of funding and time, restrictive regulatory requirements, and the like). Topics addressed include eligibility requirements, program models, delivery options, environments, and service individualization.

Not surprisingly, this part of the book includes some controversial issues. The problem of how and where to serve young children with disabilities continues to excite professionals and parents alike. One constant that arouses little controversy, however, is the notion that, although both the curriculum and the environment matter, the single most important factor in ECSE is the teacher. Nothing makes as large a difference as does the early childhood special educator's ability to recognize children's unique needs; to develop systematic plans to meet those needs; to offer stimulating activities to help children develop, grow, and learn; and to empower families to manage their children's needs better. The early childhood special educator guides the family and responds to its concerns, in the best interests of the child. Armed with support and guidance, the family is then empowered to do more for the child.

Part III addresses some of the challenges ECSE programs face. The federal statute mandates a radical change from past programs for young children. ECSE services traditionally have been child-centered; the Individuals with Disabilities Education Act (IDEA) envisions instead a family-focused approach. That approach is often difficult to implement, because administrators, teachers, and other professionals have usually been trained in child-centered methodologies, not in family-oriented services and supports. They may have problems yielding decision-making authority to lay parents. To take another example of how the federal mandate challenges ECSE professionals, special education and related services have been provided in past years by highly trained professionals, in many cases working alone; the IDEA calls for a multidisciplinary pattern integrating contributions from many professionals. Such an approach may prove to be problematic if turf battles divide program staff by discipline.

Helping ECSE professionals to deal with these and other conflicts is a sense of the relative importance of different values in ECSE. The IDEA promotes the values of individualization and appropriateness of services and supports as paramount considerations. Where competing beliefs lead in different directions, the anchoring values are those of services and supports that are both *individualized* and *appropriate*. The very heart of the IDEA is the planning and delivery of services and supports on an individualized basis. Services for children with disabilities must be custom-designed rather than mass-produced. An appropriate education is one that meets the child's unique needs through specially designed instruction combined with any necessary related services and supports.

The values of individualization and appropriateness require us to treat each child, and each family, as unique and entitled to whatever services and supports meet their special needs. Even as compelling a value as inclusion (placing children with disabilities alongside nondisabled children) must yield to individualization and appropriateness. If a child's and/or a family's needs cannot be met in an inclusive setting, ECSE professionals must abandon any philosophical adherence they may have to the ideal of inclusion; for the IDEA subordinates its placement preferences, both natural environment and least restrictive environment, to the higher requirement that services and supports be appropriate.

Chapter 7 discusses evaluation and assessment. Evaluation begins with screening and testing to establish eligibility for services. Assessment features ongoing monitoring and testing to identify specific interventions to respond to children's unique needs. State-of-the-art techniques of evaluation and assessment are evolving rapidly. More and better instruments and procedures are becoming available for use in ECSE programs. That is fortunate, because few IQ or other tests to date have had the validity, reliability, and other characteristics needed for accurate evaluation and assessment of children under six. While Chapter 7 presents a basic picture of assessment, fine-tuning often is required. In Part IV, therefore, additional material on assessment in each of the five developmental domains is offered. Chapters 12 to 16 offer suggestions on assessment of physical, communication, cognitive, social or emotional, and adaptive development.

Chapter 8 considers how services may be planned and delivered to meet the individual needs of young children and their families. While evaluation and assessment activities are both important and challenging, they do not stand alone. What matters in ECSE is using the information they provide to customize services to meet children's individual needs. This chapter also looks at service coordination across a wide range of disciplines and at the transition from early intervention to preschool programs to K-12 education.

Chapter 9, which examines service delivery, looks at natural and least restrictive environments and explores the many issues raised by the inclusion movement. It continues with an examination of architectural and other facility design considerations. The chapter concludes with a discussion of values and practical issues.

Part III concludes with Chapter 10, which discusses technology. Exciting new products and services provide ECSE programs with previously unimaginable capabilities, which can help children do things that their disabilities otherwise make impossible. These technologies raise interesting ethical and programmatic questions. Among them: If a child can "talk" by using an inexpensive, high-quality speech synthesizer, is it necessary, or even appropriate, for ECSE programs to continue to use speech therapy to attempt to teach the child to speak?

More fundamentally, however, today's technologies make possible, even routine, things that were unthinkable in years past. Today, even children with very severe disabilities can perform well in school, qualify for postsecondary education, and work to support themselves as adults. ECSE's challenge is to tap these technologies so that all children may begin to reach their potential.

Evaluation and Assessment

The psychologist experienced in testing school-aged children may expect a young child to exhibit appropriate "testing behavior"—sitting quietly at a desk, attending to the task at hand, and being motivated to complete the tasks presented. Such characteristic testing behavior is not present in this age group or, if present, is limited to a few brief moments. (Culbertson & Willis, 1993, p. 4)

OVERVIEW

evaluation is a formal process through which a child's initial and continuing eligibility for services under the IDEA is established. It is periodic, occurring at specific intervals. Evaluation may establish, for example, that a child qualifies for Part C services under the act as an at-risk toddler; similarly, it may establish that a child meets a state's developmental delay criteria.

assessment is the process of collecting data to use in determining how an individual child's development is proceeding in each of the five domains of development (cognitive, adaptive, physical, communication, social or emotional) or in academic areas. In family assessment, a family's resources, priorities, and concerns are identified.

informed clinical opinion supplements formal testing and is especially valuable where suitable tests are not available. The word "clinical" refers to assessments in which the expertise of the clinician comprises at least 50 percent of the procedure.

This chapter explores the often difficult processes of evaluation and assessment of young children, discussing the critical issues of screening, testing, and interpreting test data, as well as communicating with parents. The chapter concludes with observations on program evaluation.

The terms "evaluation" and "assessment" are often confused. To the layperson, they are synonyms; and indeed, specialists in assessment often use them interchangeably. Part C of the Individuals with Disabilities Education Act (IDEA), however, gives each term a specific meaning. One obvious difference between the two is that while evaluation is usually carried out only by qualified licensed and/or certified specialists who administer standardized tests, assessment is an ongoing process in which workers from many early childhood special education (ECSE) disciplines participate-early childhood special educators, speech and language pathologists, physical and occupational therapists, nurses, classroom aides, and others who work with children and families on a daily basis.

Evaluation, then, is a formal process through which a child's initial and continuing eligibility for services under the IDEA is established. It is periodic, occurring at specific intervals. Under Part C, evaluation documents the child's current performance or status in all five developmental domains. With respect to preschoolers, evaluation describes the child's current educational performance and need for special education and related services. In evaluation, federal and state criteria for eligibility are applied, setting against them the individual child's characteristics as determined through testing, observation, parent report, and other measures.

In **assessment**, children who have been evaluated as eligible are looked at again. This time, the concern is with specific strengths and weaknesses, because of the need to develop an individualized family service plan (IFSP) or an individualized education program (IEP). Assessment is a process that looks more deeply than does evaluation to understand the child's unique needs so that services may be designed or refined. Ongoing rather than periodic assessment helps to track how children respond over time to intervention, special education, and related services. Family resources and concerns may also be addressed, provided the family concurs. Assessment is often informal, carried out while services are being provided. As we work with children, we try something to see if it works—or to see if it tells us something new about particular children.

However precisely the words may be defined, the fact remains that evaluation and assessment in early childhood are both extremely challenging tasks. Few valid and reliable instruments are available for use with ECSE populations. Even those that are suitable for use in determining a child's current performance or status often cannot predict very well how the child will do in the later childhood years. Children under six change frequently, and often radically. They act differently when the parent is present than when she is absent, they act differently at home than they do at clinics or early childhood programs, and they act differently when they are alone than when they are with other young children. A few months can make a dramatic difference, particularly in communication and cognitive development. For all of these reasons, expert opinion is essential. Professionals who know the child must use their informed judgments to make decisions. That is why the IDEA emphasizes the importance of "**informed clinical opinion**." The word "clinical" refers to assessments in which the expertise of the clinician comprises at least 50 percent of the measure or test, as opposed to instruments with which the professional plays a much more secondary role (Culbertson & Willis, 1993; Neisworth & Bagnato, 1992). This chapter examines evaluation and

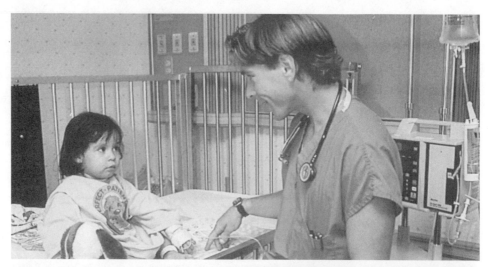

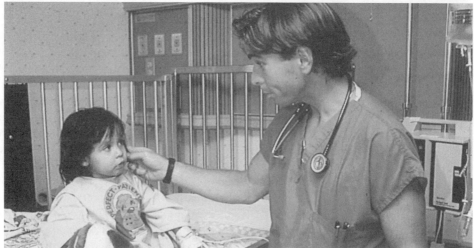

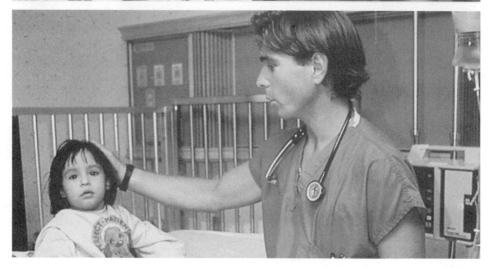

Evaluation and assessment with young children frequently require that the examiner take time to become known to, and trusted by, the child.

- Use multidisciplinary teams and approaches.

- Perform comprehensive measures, looking at both strengths and weaknesses.

- Use serial (repeated) measures, sampling at different times and in different settings.

- Respect parents and other family members as expert sources of information.

- Observe the child both at home and in the program.

- Consider cultural variables in testing and in test interpretation. Use bias-free instruments if available.

- Use informed clinical opinion to supplement formal instruments.

FIGURE 7.1 Principles in assessment and evaluation

assessment, looking not only at specific procedures and tests but also at how to make sound clinical decisions.

Seven general principles will serve ECSE personnel well in assessment and evaluation (Figure 7.1). First, a *multidisciplinary* approach is necessary. Even if it were not required by law, the fact that few valid and reliable tests are available for use makes such an approach essential. Second, evaluation in particular, but assessment as well, must be comprehensive. It must look at strengths as well as weaknesses, at resources as well as needs. Third, serial testing or observation is essential in early childhood, both because children change so fast and so often, and because tests and other procedures often leave so much to be desired. Fourth, parents should be regarded as experts on their own children. They should be consulted in any evaluation or assessment activity in the early childhood years.

Fifth, evaluation and assessment in early childhood should include observations both at home and in clinics, early intervention programs, or preschools. ECSE personnel may learn a great deal during a home visit that will inform their interpretation of test results and other evaluation or assessment procedures. Sixth, important cultural variables must be considered if a child comes from a racial or ethnic minority group. For example, behaviors such as avoidance of eye contact may be culturally defined and have little or no psychometric significance. Finally, as noted earlier, informed clinical opinion is inescapable. ECSE personnel bear the heavy burden of making decisions in the face of insufficient evidence, of presenting their recommendations to parents and to state agencies, and of defending these recommendations without the benefit of incontrovertible proof.

CHILD FIND

Under both Part C and Part B, states are responsible for identifying, locating, and evaluating children who have disabilities or are suspected of having disabilities or delays. The requirement to evaluate young children as part of a child-find program has been in place since 1980, although the mandate to serve all such young children who have disabilities or delays is, of course, much more recent. States are required to identify children from birth to age five inclusive and to evaluate their disabilities and needs. In 1980 only states providing services for nondisabled children under six needed to offer services to under-six children with disabilities.

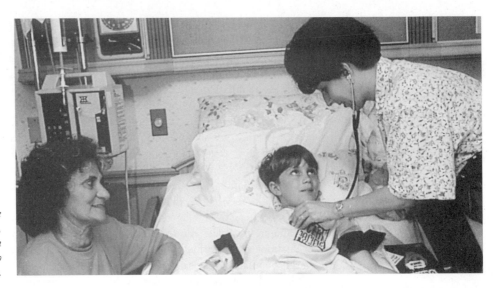

Routine screening may be performed at any time, including occasions when accidents bring children to medical facilities.

Those not providing such services for nondisabled children were required only to identify, locate, and evaluate children who had or were suspected of possibly having disabilities.

The Part B regulation (U.S. Department of Education, 1992a) mandates that states ensure that all children with disabilities are identified, located, and evaluated. *Early identification and assessment* is a related service under Part B. States must report to the department on those children being served. The child-find program is intended to locate not only children receiving no developmental services but also children in public and private service agencies and in institutions.

Although states must report to the department on children identified through child-find efforts, strict confidentiality rules govern how personally identifiable information may be released. Under Part C, not even the referral for early intervention services may be made without prior written parental permission.

The child-find program often uses screening instruments to identify children as potentially eligible for IDEA services. By their very nature, screening instruments are broad-brush measures. They should never be used for diagnostic purposes, nor should they be used to establish unique needs or to select interventions. Rather, screening procedures are used to identify children who should be evaluated further. Screening sometimes produces "false positives," instances in which a child is screened in for further testing although in fact there is no disability or delay. Screening also produces some "false negatives," cases in which children who do have disabilities or delays are wrongly screened out. The reality is that such errors are inevitable. Unlike evaluation and assessment, which by law are multidisciplinary, screening may be conducted by a single individual. Kenny and Culbertson (1993) noted that physicians and other primary-care providers are excellent choices to perform screening, because families routinely take children to doctors, well-child pediatric clinics, and hospitals. Because of their early contact with and comprehensive coverage of the birth-to-five population, pediatricians and other physicians are logical persons to conduct screening and to make referrals for more in-depth evaluation. It is disappointing, Kenny and Culbertson (1993) said, that few physicians screen more than a handful of their young patients.

Why do we screen? First, screening is much faster and much less costly than a full-scale evaluation. For example, excellent screening of infant hearing is now available for as little as $25; a follow-up test on infants "screened in" as possibly having a hearing loss costs at least four times that much. A formal evaluation of hearing impairment runs six to eight times as much as the initial screening cost, or $175 to $200. Time is also relevant. To continue with the example on hearing, the initial screening takes only a few minutes; the follow-up test takes quite a bit longer. The second reason for screening is to establish demographic parameters (Kenny & Culbertson, 1993). No one knows the true prevalence of different disabilities in young children. To illustrate, the usual estimate is that some 2.5 percent of birth-to-six children are mentally retarded, but that is for statistical reasons. By definition, mental retardation is intelligence that falls at least two standard deviations below the mean. Statistical theory tells us that 2.27 percent of children are two or more standard deviations below the mean on intelligence. No one has actually counted the number of children under six who are mentally retarded. Until comprehensive screening and the necessary follow-up evaluations are performed, researchers will not discover how prevalent mental retardation is in this population. The same is true of other disabilities.

A number of instruments are available for use in screening. A notable example is the new neonatal hearing test mentioned earlier; an infant's vision, too, may now be screened at a very young age. The choice of which screening test to use involves many factors: what one is screening for (some tests tap all five developmental domains recognized by the IDEA, while others explore specific domain areas such as behavior or emotional development); who is administering the test (physicians use different measures than do speech and language pathologists, for example); how old the child is (some tests are suitable for use with infants, others are used with preschool-age children); and other factors. Several frequently used general-purpose screening instruments are described briefly below. For a much more comprehensive discussion of screening instruments, see Kenny and Culbertson (1993). McLean and McCormick (1993) and Campbell (1991) provide good reviews of screening procedures with infants and toddlers.

The Denver II (Frankenburg et al. 1990) screens for language skills, gross motor and fine motor control, and personal-social concerns, through 125 items. It may be used from birth to about six years of age. The norms are quite current, and data are available to indicate at what ages 25, 50, 75, and 100 percent of the norming sample succeeded on any given test item. Delays may be noted, and the screening test may be given repeatedly over a period of time—a very important consideration with ECSE populations. The instrument requires about twenty minutes to administer.

The Battelle Developmental Inventory (Newborg, Stock, Wnek, Guidubaldi, & Svinicki, 1984) has a screening version, suitable for use from birth to about eight years of age. This screening test taps into all five areas of development recognized by the IDEA: personal-social, adaptive, motor, cognitive, and communication. Both standard and age-equivalent scores may be obtained. The Battelle focuses on school-readiness skills more than on specific disabilities or conditions. The screening version takes about ten to twenty minutes to administer; the full version requires about an hour.

Ireton and Thwing have proposed four screening versions of the Minnesota Child Development Inventory (MCDI), a parent report instrument. Suitable for use in the birth-to-six age range, the MCDI (Ireton & Thwing, 1974b) has 320 questions organized into areas such as self-help, gross motor and fine motor development, and situation comprehension. The four screening versions are briefer, and are targeted to more restricted age ranges. The Minnesota Infant Development Inventory (Ireton & Thwing, 1974c) is intended for use from birth to about fifteen months. For children aged one to three years, the Minnesota Early Child Development Inventory (Ireton & Thwing, 1974a) offers sixty parent report items plus a problem report list. The Minnesota Preschool Inventory—Form 34 (Ireton & Thwing, 1974e) is intended for use with three- to six-year-olds; overlapping it is the Minnesota Pre-Kindergarten Inventory (Ireton & Thwing, 1974d), which focuses on 4.5- to 5.5-year-olds. Both assess school readiness.

Bricker and Squires (1989) suggested that parents are excellent sources of information about children who require testing; that is, parent reports may be used in place of or in addition to screening tests. According to Bricker, Squires, Kaminski, and Mounts (1988), mailing parents report forms every four months during an at-risk child's first two years of life is inexpensive (averaging about $2.50 per child) yet very accurate, yielding only moderate overscreening and underscreening rates (false positives or false negatives).

Screening instruments and parent reports should not be used for diagnostic purposes, nor for planning either interventions or preschool special education services. Rather, screening tests and parental symptom or problem reports should function as indicators pointing to the need for more thorough diagnostic and medical examinations.

TESTING

Testing infants, toddlers, and preschoolers is not an easy task even under the best of conditions. Difficulties arise because of legal requirements and because of variables in the children themselves, the examiners, and the tests and other procedures used.

Evaluation and assessment of infants are very different from the same activities with older children. Not surprisingly, prediction from infant tests to elementary tests is not good.

Legal Issues

Testing young children who have or are believed to have disabilities, delays, or deviations in development requires prior parental consent. The IDEA, Part B, section 615(b)(3)(B) requires that parents or guardians receive prior written notice of any proposal to test a child; section 639(a)(6) in Part C requires the same steps. In addition, communication of test results is limited by the IDEA's procedural safeguards. The law insists that no one test be used to make intervention, education, or placement decisions. Division for Early Childhood (DEC) guidelines (DEC Task Force, 1993) and National Association for the Education of Young Children (NAEYC) practices (Bredekamp, 1987) concur that important decisions should not be based on only one test or measure. The IDEA also requires a multidisciplinary approach that draws upon the particular expertise of specialists in different areas as well as that of caregivers and teachers who know the child well. Again, this is an approach that is widely recommended (Bredekamp, 1987; DEC Task Force, 1993). Part C proscribes communication of personally identifiable information about a child, including test results, from one agency to another without prior written parental permission. Both Part B and Part C expressly grant parents or guardians permission to examine relevant records, including test results. A child may not be denied services even if the parents withhold permission for testing. Once again, both DEC and NAEYC embrace these statutory principles.

The discussion now turns to variables affecting testing in ECSE.

Variables in Children

Infants in particular, but also toddlers and even preschoolers, require special treatment for testing to be effective. Infants have only a few hours each day in "alert status" when they are rested, fed, and attentive; the examiner must therefore work closely with the family and be ready to conduct testing at virtually any time during the day. Infants spend a great deal of the day sleeping. At other times, they may be irritable or drowsy. They cry a lot. They must virtually always be tested with the primary caregiver, usually the mother, present. From the age of eight months to one year in particular, the infant may be strongly attached to the primary caregiver, although stranger anxiety also occurs at later stages in early childhood.

Psychologists accustomed to testing school-age children will need to modify their approaches when testing younger children. Such children usually do not have a good under-

Assessment of hearing should be considered for all young children, especially those with Down syndrome, cerebral palsy, and other conditions known to be associated with secondary loss of hearing.

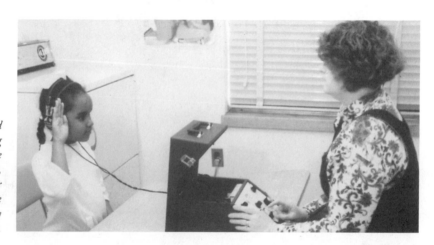

Testing children who are deaf challenges examiners both in test administration and in interpretation of results.

standing of the testing process. They do not arrive for testing primed to perform at their optimal level. Even after they have been told, "do your best, this is a test," most young children do not comprehend the importance of doing well in these situations. Children with severe disabilities may lack the background test writers assume children bring with them. Many children who are physically disabled, blind, deaf, or mentally retarded have been sheltered by their parents. Such experiential deprivation hurts the children in many ways. In this context, it limits their performance on tests, simply because they have not had the opportunities to learn about and practice certain skills. In addition, a child's performance in test situations may be affected by medication related to her disability. Children who are physically disabled may not have the endurance to persist with lengthy tasks.

Examiners must also contend with the more obvious child-related factors. Children with physical disabilities such as cerebral palsy may not be able to grasp and manipulate an object, as a test may require. Children who are deaf do not hear test instructions. The deafness interferes not only with speech comprehension but also with language development, meaning that even if the instructions are presented visually, the child may lack the linguistic competency to understand them. Children with other disabilities may not have the linguistic or even the cognitive capabilities to reflect upon their own thinking, as is required in many psychoeducational assessments that are used with school-age children and youth.

For all of these reasons, examiners should look not only at the child but also to the family. Tests should be supplemented with liberal amounts of parent and professional interviews as well as firsthand observation of the child in different settings.

Especially in infants and toddlers, development is very closely linked to family factors. For example, the degree of permissiveness parents show in allowing the child to explore play areas powerfully affects physical development. Parental insistence that children perform appropriately in different situations greatly influences adaptive development; conversely, parents who excuse children with disabilities from self-help and other kinds of adaptive behavior contribute mightily to delays or deviations in that domain.

Variables in Examiners

For these reasons, examiners must modify their own behavior when testing very young children. Frequently, they must also modify test instructions. The examiner may physically have to guide the hand of a child with mental retardation through a drawing task, rather than just verbally describe what is desired. In the event that stranger anxiety unnerves a young child, it may be necessary for the examiner to instruct a caregiver how to administer a test and observe the procedure from a distance. These kinds of divergences from established procedure are so often necessary that they have become common practice in ECSE. However, *all* such changes in procedure should be fully described in the test report and to the multidisciplinary team, because these modifications might alter, even if subtly, the meaning of test results.

The IDEA requires extensive testing of very young children with disabilities. The statute assumes that psychologists and others administering tests are experienced in working with this population. The fact is, however, that most school psychologists are not trained for work in early childhood. They are familiar with tests administered in elementary and secondary schools but not with instruments used with preschool-age children. Their test-giving patterns assume that most children being tested will exhibit good test-taking habits. The fact that relatively few psychometricians have experience with ECSE populations is a severe constraint. This is particularly true because testing young children with disabilities demands a thorough knowledge of the instrument being administered and a great deal of flexibility in deciding which subtests to give, in what order, and with what modifications. The same kinds of personnel shortages that plague ECSE in other areas permeate testing as well.

Variables in Instruments

Evaluation and assessment of young children are made even more difficult by the fact that few tests are available for use. Fuchs, Fuchs, Benowitz, and Barringer (1987) examined user manuals and other documentation for twenty-seven widely used aptitude and achievement

Selection of appropriate test instruments is very important in the birth-to-five age period because many instruments are not designed for use with young children having severe disabilities.

tests, finding "scant data on the appropriateness of their tests for use with handicapped children" (p. 263). Test authors typically report a range of validity and reliability data on their tests to help examiners understand how to use the instrument. *Usually, these figures are relevant to examiners* only *when used with the same kinds of children as were tested to generate those validity and reliability measures. But because children with disabilities often were not included in those original studies, the validity and reliability data have very limited meaning to examiners working with ECSE populations.*

In fact, some test authors specifically caution against using the instrument at all with children who have severe disabilities. For example, some tests require children to listen to instructions and then respond. But using such a test with a child who is deaf measures not the construct ostensibly being assessed but rather the child's hearing and linguistic competencies. Other tests require rapid manipulation of objects; cerebral palsy, by its very nature, slows and limits such activities. Shonkoff and Hauser-Cram (1987) added that use of cognitive tests "which are heavily reliant on motor performance in young children, presents a major validity problem for infants with functional motor deficits" (p. 654). Yet other tests use colors to differentiate objects; they are clearly not appropriate for use with children who are blind or have low vision (Fuchs, Featherstone, Garwick, & Fuchs, 1984; Fuchs, Fuchs, Garwick, & Featherstone, 1983; Neisworth & Bagnato, 1992).

A related problem has to do with what the scores mean. How does one interpret a score of 7 on a motor skills scale, for example? Norm-referenced tests handle this problem by reporting norms-data on the scores that children of different ages achieved on those scales. Again, however, in most cases these data are based on samples that excluded young children with disabilities. In addition, the norms hold only when tests are administered in the same way as they were to the norming sample. Instruments are often administered differently to children with disabilities than to children without disabilities.

The federal legislation requires, rather optimistically, that tests used with young children who have or are suspected to have delays, deviations, or disabilities meet a number of standards. The tests are to be valid and reliable for the purposes for which they are used. Few

Measuring vision in young children involves much more than just a Snellen chart or an Illiterate E chart. Assessing close vision as well as distant vision is essential.

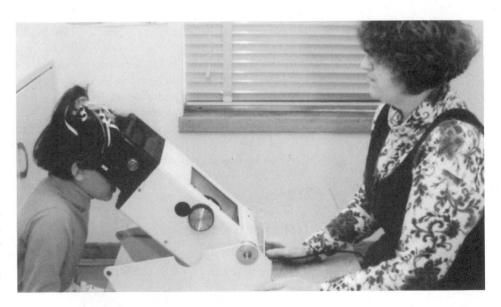

tests used in early childhood meet these psychometric criteria. Tests are to be administered in the child's native language or mode of communication; yet not all tests are available in Spanish, German, Japanese, or French. Few come in Braille, in large print, or on audio-cassettes for use with children who are blind. Meanwhile, few examiners are fluent in American Sign Language. The IDEA stipulates that tests are to be administered as test manuals say they should; but examiners often have to modify testing protocols. Strict adherence to the instructions in manuals may be worse than modifying them. Finally, the IDEA requires that tests measure what they are intended to measure, and not the child's disability (unless that is what is being tested). Yet again, inadvertently measuring the child's disability sometimes is unavoidable; adjustments in interpretation of test results may be both necessary and preferable to discarding the test altogether.

Fortunately, the enactment of PL 99-457 in 1986, PL 101-476 in 1990, and PL 102-119 in 1991 has generated considerable excitement in fields related to psychometrics with young children who have disabilities. Each year, hundreds of thousands of young children with disabilities, developmental delays, or deviations must be tested. There is a large market now, and test developers are responding to it. While state-of-the-art techniques for testing these children still leave a great deal to be desired, the good news is that many more—and better—tests are on the way. The late 1993 release of the Bayley II is a good example. It appears to be more useful in ECSE than was the original Bayley (1969), although that instrument certainly was a good one.

More generally, intelligence in infants, toddlers, and preschoolers is not the same as intelligence among school-age children. Especially in the domain of cognitive development, tests used in early childhood are different from tests for school-age children of what ostensibly are the same constructs. To adopt for the moment the terminology Piaget gave us: With infants and toddlers, intelligence tests tap sensorimotor skills, particularly physical and mobility capabilities; with school-age children, they tap operations. Not surprisingly, the power of intelligence tests administered to infants or toddlers to predict the results of intelligence tests administered to school-age children is modest at best; that is, a child's IQ at two is a poor predictor of the same child's IQ at eight. Early IQ test scores may account for only 16 to 26 percent of the variance in later IQ test scores—even for nondisabled young children. Correlation between IQ tests given to children with disabilities at seven months and tests given at eighteen months may be as low as .20 (McCall, 1976). The argument is sometimes made that higher predictive validity holds with children who are severely disabled. Fagan and Singer (1983), reviewing research on that question, concluded that predictive validity coefficients may be as low as .18 between tests given at one year of age and those administered to the same children aged four to six.

The norming problem is even more serious. Neisworth and Bagnato (1992) stated, "It is rare when any children with handicaps are included in the norm group for any of the major infant and preschool intelligence tests used by psychologists" (p. 9). What, for example, do scores on a physical development test mean when given to children with cerebral palsy, since such children were not part of the group used to establish the test's norms?

Test Interpretation

Professionals working with ECSE populations often need to use considerable judgment to interpret test results properly. Test interpretation in this field is rarely routine. One cannot simply turn to a norm table and use those figures to explain how a child compares to other children, because very few EC tests included children with disabilities in their norming samples. Even scoring subtasks requires judgment. In particular, the examiner should allow evidence of correct responses if the response is not completed for disability-related reasons. A child with cerebral palsy, for example, might look in the direction of a hidden object during an object permanence test, because he has been conditioned at home and in early intervention programs to expect others to read the glance and retrieve the object. It should not be a surprise if such habits appear in testing situations as well. The key to test interpretation in this case is to recognize that by looking steadily at where the object was last placed before being hidden, the child is in fact demonstrating awareness of object permanence. The glance is as convincing a demonstration as actual physical movement to search for the object would have been.

With children who are deaf, examiners need to recognize that a child's cognitive processing of information may be slowed by the child's need to focus attention on information acquisition. Serial information, in this case spoken test instructions, can be processed by normally hearing children "in background," so to speak, allowing them to think about information even as they are listening to it. However, when serial information is received visually, all of it must be acquired and understood before it may be processed. Children who are deaf may demonstrate a somewhat slower response than do children who can hear because they must wait until they capture and understand all the information before they can process it.

The predictive power of most tests used with young children who have disabilities is very limited. Examiners are best advised to use test results as a snapshot of a child's current performance—and not attempt to predict from a test how a child will do in later years. The suggestion made several times in this text that examiners use serial testing-periodic tests over several months—is relevant here. So many factors influence the test performance of a young child with a disability that no one test should be used for programmatic purposes, and certainly not for affixing a permanent label on a child.

The DEC recommended practices document includes assessment as well as other aspects of ECSE (DEC Task Force, 1993). The recommendations are particularly helpful when it comes to test interpretation. Whether one is interpreting evaluation or assessment results, findings should be expressed in specific developmental and behavioral terms that lend themselves directly to interventions; global labels that do not suggest treatments or other activities should be avoided. The guidelines also recommended that a broad base of information supplement a test. In particular, strengths as well as weaknesses should be tapped: DEC recognizes the legislative mandate to conduct assessment and evaluation in all five domains of development as an appropriate way to obtain a more complete picture of the child and the family (see Figure 7.2).

Clearly, considerable expertise is required to test ECSE populations. Examiners should be trained in working with young children and in how disability affects development. They also should be able to draw upon extensive experience in administering each test they use so that they may respond rapidly with test modifications when necessary. Experience may be the one of the only ways in which examiners can learn the answers to some questions. Suppose, for example, that test instructions are signed to a child who is deaf, rather than spoken as dictated by a test manual. This variation from standard testing protocol will clearly affect the interpretation of the test results. But how, and to what extent, is something examiners usually learn only after testing large numbers of children who are deaf.

- Assessment should be used to identify children's strengths, not just their weaknesses.

- Family assessments should be conducted only if the family requests them—and then family members should participate actively in all aspects.

- Assessment should have clear, concrete outcomes for the benefit of the child and the family. It should not be done only to satisfy funding or licensing agencies.

- Evaluating programs and interventions is a good use of assessment. Outcomes should be "fed back" to create program changes.

- Assessment and evaluation emphasize strengths as well as weaknesses, resources as much as needs.

- ECSE personnel should communicate evaluation and assessment findings to parents in ways that are understandable and useful to parents, avoiding both jargon and stigma.

- Assessment and evaluation procedures and tests should be culturally sensitive. Whenever feasible, ECSE program staff should use nonbiased instruments.

- Multiple "takes" are essential in assessing young children and their families. A wide variety of measures should be taken, notably including the views of family members. "Serial" testing, that is, sampling behavior on numerous occasions, is critical to obtaining accurate measures.

—adapted from Neisworth, in DEC Task Force (1993)

FIGURE 7.2 DEC recommended practices on assessment

CULTURAL DIVERSITY ISSUES

PL 102-119 placed increased emphasis on early childhood services for traditionally under-served children with disabilities. The law calls for ECSE workers, including test examiners, to have greater cultural awareness. Asian American children, for example, may avoid eye contact with the examiner. In almost all cases, this is indicative not of any psychopathology, certainly not of autism, but rather of cultural norms. Native American children are often taught that to look directly into an adult's eyes is a sign of disrespect. A white, middle-class examiner may think such children shy. African American and Native American mothers may use language less expansively at home, for which reason their children may also appear less verbal than white, middle-class children from homes where parents make liberal use of **elaboration** strategies to explain and reason with their children while disciplining them. Cultural competence in testing includes knowledge of these and related variables. Good practice requires that such aspects be incorporated not only into how tests are administered but also into how they are interpreted.

That point brings up a long-standing issue in special education. DEC's recommended practices on assessment include the following injunction: "Assessment approaches and instruments are culturally appropriate and nonbiased" (DEC Task Force, 1993, p. 17). As unobjectionable as this statement seems to be, it may also be unrealistic, given the state of the art in bias-free testing. For many years, IQ tests in particular have been used in such a way as to result in overreferral of ethnic and racial minority children, especially African Americans, into special education programs. The problem is widely recognized. Despite

elaboration occurs when an adult (parent or teacher) "talks out" the reasoning processes, that is, elaborates upon what steps were followed in reaching a decision.

more than two decades of concerted effort, however, psychometrics experts continue to differ on what is a "culturally fair" test and how to design one.

ECSE personnel need to be aware that almost any test or other instrument they use may be culturally biased in favor of white, middle-class, suburban children and against African American or Hispanic American, poor, rural, or inner-city children. The answer is not to use only culturally fair tests—few, if any, exist—but rather to select, administer, and interpret tests and other instruments with awareness of and sensitivity to cultural variables. African American and Hispanic American children in particular, and other ethnic and racial minority children as far as possible, should be tested by examiners who are members of the same minority group. When African American children are tested by white examiners (Epps, 1974) and when children from a linguistic minority are tested by English-speaking examiners not familiar with cultural and linguistic variables (Figueroa, 1990), the children's performances suffer. In addition, young children do worse in tests when the examiner is a stranger to them than when someone with whom they have had at least some informal contact performs the examination.

EVALUATION

Evaluation is a process of establishing an individual child's initial and continuing eligibility for services under the IDEA. It compares an individual child's characteristics, as determined by testing, observation, parent reports, and other measures (notably medical records and medical history) against federal and state criteria. Children must meet those criteria to qualify for services. Evaluation establishes eligibility. It is periodic, recurring at specific intervals.

Infants and toddlers are evaluated in all five developmental domains recognized under Part C; in each, established conditions or developmental delays, as defined by states, may be identified. Preschoolers are evaluated for one or more of the recognized disabilities and as needing special education and related services as a result; if a state elects to use delays with the three- to five-year-old population, evaluation establishes developmental delays in one or more of the same five domains.

Under Part C, evaluation is to be *comprehensive.* That is, it must incorporate all the measures discussed above (tests, observations, parent reports, medical evidence) and be applied in all five developmental domains. Part B, too, requires a comprehensive evaluation, in this case to determine the child's needs for special education and related services. Both parts of the IDEA also require that evaluation be *multidisciplinary,* conducted by a team whose members may also plan intervention, preschool special education, and related services (Campbell, 1991). Although ECSE personnel, including psychologists, do not perform medical tests, a medical history is an essential component of any evaluation. In particular, evidence of any pre-, peri-, or postnatal incidents; any early childhood illnesses or accidents; and any assessments of hearing, vision, and general motor coordination are critical to evaluation. The discussion turns now to an examination of those mandates.

The Federal Requirements

The statutory language, together with the U.S. Department of Education's implementing regulations, provides very specific guidance on what is to be done, how it must be done, and when it must be done. Both Part C and Part B recognize that informed judgments by expert personnel are necessary. Part C and Part B both proscribe the use of any single test or procedure. The Part B regulation, for example, requires that "[t]he evaluation is made by a multidisciplinary team or group of persons, including at least one teacher or other specialist with knowledge in the area of suspected disability" (section 300.532[e]).

Infants and Toddlers. The IDEA's definition of the term "evaluation" in Part C is shown in Figure 7.3, together with explanatory wording from the U.S. Department of Education's Part C regulation.

Part C requires the evaluation to be timely, that is, it must occur as soon as possible after the child has been identified, whether through a state child-find effort, an Early and Periodic Screening, Diagnosis, and Treatment (EPSDT) screening, referral from a primary-care provider such as a family physician, or some other means. The department's regulation for Part C defines "timely" as "within 45 days after . . . referral" (34 CFR 303.321[e], 303.322[e]). The words "comprehensive" and "multidisciplinary" mean that the infant or toddler is to be evaluated on a broad range of questions by a team including specialists on those various issues. Those questions are established by the statutory definition of "infants and toddlers with disabilities" as relating to all five areas of development: cognitive, physical, communication, social or emotional, and adaptive. If applicable, development is to be measured against state criteria for "delay" in each of those five areas.

Children with Disabilities. The IDEA does not contain a statutory definition of the term "evaluation" as used with preschool children with disabilities. However, the U.S. Department of Education's (1992a) rule offers considerable guidance. This material is presented in Figure 7.4.

Evaluation Instruments

The Bayley II Scales of Infant Development (Bayley, 1993) is a standardized, norm-referenced instrument suitable for use with infants and young children aged one month to 3.6 years.

The department's Part C regulation explains that evaluation is to:

(1) Be conducted by personnel trained to utilize appropriate methods and procedures
(2) Be based on informed clinical opinion; and
(3) Include the following:
    (i) A review of pertinent records related to the child's current health status and medical history
    (ii) An evaluation of the child's level of functioning in each of the following developmental areas:
        (A) Cognitive development
        (B) Physical development, including vision and hearing
        (C) Communication development
        (D) Social or emotional development
        (E) Adaptive development

(U.S. Department of Education, 1993a, section 303.322c)

FIGURE 7.3 Evaluation of infants and toddlers

The Part B regulation defines *evaluation* as follows:

procedures to determine whether a child has a disability and the nature and extent of special education and related services that the child needs. The term means procedures used selectively with an individual child and does not include basic tests administered to or procedures used with all children in a school, grade, or class (U.S. Department of Education, 1992a, section 300.500[b]). . . .

Tests and other evaluation materials:

(1) Are provided and administered in the child's native language or other mode of communication, unless it is clearly not feasible to do so;

(2) Have been validated for the specific purpose for which they are used; and

(3) Are administered by trained personnel in conformance with the instructions provided by their producer. . . .

    (c) Tests are selected and administered so as best to ensure that when a test is administered to a child with impaired sensory, manual, or speaking skills, the test results accurately reflect the child's aptitude or achievement level or whatever other factors the test purports to measure, rather than reflecting the child's impaired sensory, manual, or speaking skills (except where those skills are the factors that the test purports to measure).

    (d) No single procedure is used as the sole criterion for determining an appropriate educational program for a child.

    (e) The evaluation is made by a multidisciplinary team or group of persons, including at least one teacher or other specialist with knowledge in the area of suspected disability.

    (f) The child is assessed in all areas related to the suspected disability, including, if appropriate, health, vision, hearing, social and emotional status, general intelligence, academic performance, communicative status, and motor abilities . . . (section 300.532).

    (b) That an evaluation of the child . . . is conducted every three years, or more frequently if conditions warrant, or if the child's parent or teacher requests an evaluation (section 300.534).

FIGURE 7.4 Evaluation of children with disabilities (excerpts)

The second edition of this widely used instrument offers updated norms on mental, motor, and behavior domains of development in infants, toddlers, and young preschoolers. The mental scale assesses, among other things, sensory and perceptual skills, object permanence, language, and mathematical concept formation. The motor scale assesses gross body and motor coordination, fine motor skills, and movement. The behavior rating scale has thirty items on attention, orientation, and emotional regulation. Although the Bayley II appears to retain the features that made the original Bayley one of the most widely used and respected instruments in ECSE, very little independent evaluation of the scales' validity and reliability was available when this book was written.

Another widely used scale is the Battelle Developmental Inventory, which was mentioned earlier (see Child Find section). The Battelle, which may be used from birth to eight years of age, assesses development in all five domains recognized by the IDEA. McLean and McCormick (1993) identified several limitations of the Battelle. It can take almost an hour longer to administer than does the original Bayley. Because each item must be administered in the order specified, it is a more difficult test to use than the original Bayley, which gave examiners flexibility in this respect. Such flexibility is often necessary with very young children.

The Kaufman Assessment Battery for Children ([K-ABC] Kaufman & Kaufman, 1983) is a norm-referenced, standardized instrument for use with children between the ages of 2.5 and 12.5 years. It requires about one hour and fifteen minutes to administer. The K-ABC yields scores of cognitive, fine motor, verbal, and quantitative development. An advantage of the K-ABC is that it does not require a lot of verbal interaction between examiner and child; it is therefore useful with children who have language or hearing limitations.

The McCarthy Scales of Children's Abilities (McCarthy, 1972) is a similar instrument, requiring about the same amount of time to administer. Designed for use with children aged 2.5 to 8.5, the McCarthy has a gross motor component that the Kaufman lacks.

Toni Linder (1993) has promoted **transdisciplinary play-based assessment** (TPBA) as an approach that taps the natural desire of young children to play. In this technique, one professional (often aided by a parent) interacts with the child in a setting that features a variety of play materials. Linder suggests that the session begin with a free-play period, followed by a time during which the professional guides further play. These periods may be followed by child-child and child-parent interactive sessions and later by a snack session. The sessions are all videotaped. Afterward, the interdisciplinary team reviews the tapes, looking for evidence of developmental delays as well as capabilities.

Many other tests are available. The interested reader is referred to Culbertson and Willis (1993), an excellent reference on testing with ECSE populations for descriptions and comparisons of many different instruments. Rosetti (1986, 1990) discussed assessment of infants and toddlers specifically; McLean and McCormick (1993) offer a shorter discussion, also helpful, on many of the same issues.

> **Transdisciplinary play-based assessment** (TPBA; Linder, 1993) is a qualitative approach to testing in which young children interact with play materials, professionals, and other children.

ASSESSMENT

To write IFSPs or IEPs, one must know far more than simply that a child is eligible for ECSE services. Among children evaluated as being eligible, initial assessment is needed to determine what specific limitations the child has, so as to plan intervention, special education, and related services. Assessment thus probes more deeply than does evaluation; it looks to unique needs and how those change over time as services are provided. It is a continuing, rather than a periodic, procedure.

Part C calls for a family assessment, if the family concurs. Discussion on that topic follows. Part B requires assessment only of the child and her unique needs, although special educators are encouraged to consider family factors in assessing children with disabilities.

Infants and Toddlers

The Part C regulation (U.S. Department of Education, 1993a) calls for assessment in all five areas of development and outlines the process to be used. Figure 7.5 offers the regulatory wording.

To establish eligibility under Part C is only the first step. The second is to answer the question, "Eligibility for what?" There is no requirement in the federal law that all eligible infants, toddlers, and families receive the full range of possible services under Part C. Rather, the decision about services is made on a case-by-case basis. For some infants or toddlers,

---

An assessment of the unique needs of the child [shall be conducted] in terms of each of the developmental areas [cognitive, physical, communication, social or emotional, adaptive], including the identification of services appropriate to meet those needs (34 CFR 303.322[c][iii]).

Assessment means the ongoing procedures used by appropriate qualified personnel throughout the period of a child's eligibility under this part to identify

(i)   The child's unique strengths and needs and the services appropriate to meet those needs; and

(ii)   The resources, priorities, and concerns of the family and the supports and services necessary to enhance the family's capacity to meet the developmental needs of their infant or toddler with a disability.

(section 303.322[b][2])

FIGURE 7.5   Assessment of infants and toddlers

periodic observation, occasional testing, and parent information and referral services will suffice. For others, a comprehensive, multidisciplinary, multiagency effort requiring a great deal of coordination and costing considerable sums will be required. The point is that establishing eligibility under Part C does not qualify a child for any particular service, or group of services.

Assessment involves, to take an example, plotting a baseline of social or emotional behavior, using applied behavior analysis techniques, and tracking how the child's activities change under different reinforcement schedules. The ECSE worker tries something and sees how it works. When a teacher inaugurates a new language development curriculum for a child who is deaf, she monitors progress, always asking, "Is this working?" and "Should we try something else instead?" That, too, is assessment.

Families

One special kind of assessment is the "family-directed assessment of the resources, priorities, and concerns of the family and the identification of the supports and services necessary to enhance the family's capacity to meet the developmental needs of the infant or toddler" (IDEA section 636[a][2]). This assessment is important for several reasons. First, Part C, unlike Part B, specifically includes services for families. The plan that is developed following assessment is, after all, called an individualized family service plan (IFSP). Before services for the family can be identified and planned, ECSE professionals need to identify family needs. Second, infants and toddlers cannot be understood apart from their families. Tests and other evaluation and assessment processes are not as helpful with very young children as they are with older children. Bailey (1991) offered a definition of family assessment that helps to frame the issue: "The ongoing and interactive process by which professionals gather information in order to determine family priorities for goals and services" (p. 27).

The statute and the regulations are clear that family assessments are *voluntary* on the part of the family. The law specifically states that they are to be "family-directed," which means that the family decides whether and to what extent to participate. To make the meaning of "family-directed" clearer, Figure 7.6 shows the explanatory language from the House

Report accompanying what became the 1991 amendments (PL 102-119) and the department's additional explanations from its Part C regulation (1993a).

Bailey (1991) reported that in family assessments, families themselves tend to prefer informal rather than formal approaches and open-ended rather than forced-choice conversations. Interviews are a good example of both preferences. In an appendix to his article, he offered a family needs survey as a means of determining family priorities in advance of such interviews. Such a written instrument may be used only as an option, that is, as a means through which parents may voluntarily indicate priorities and interests. It cannot be presented to parents as a requirement for program participation. The form includes questions about the family's need for information, family and social support, financial support, child care, community services, professional support, and communication with others about their child.

Children with Disabilities

The department's Part B regulation does not define assessment with respect to preschool-age children with disabilities. It does note that "psychological services," which are related services, include assessment. The Part B rule also uses the term "identification and assessment" to refer to initial screening, as noted earlier (see Child Find section). Such activities are also considered "related services."

Neither the statute nor the department's Part B regulation provides for family-directed assessments of family priorities, resources, and concerns. However, programs striving to offer seamless services may provide such family assessments, at the family's request. "Social work services in schools," a related service under Part B, incorporates such assessment-related steps as "preparing a social or developmental history on a child with a disability," "group and individual counseling with the child and family," and "working with those problems in a child's living situation (home, school, and community) that affect the child's adjustment in school" (U.S. Department of Education, 1992a, section 300.16[12]).

[Part C] recognizes the central role played by families in designing and implementing effective early intervention services for their infants and toddlers with disabilities. Second, it states that the assessment must be family-directed and may, with the concurrence of the family, include an assessment of the family's resources, priorities, and concerns and identification of family preferences, supports, and services necessary to enhance the parents' and siblings' capacity to meet the developmental needs of their infant or toddler with a disability (House Report 102-198, 1991, p.18).

(1) Family assessments under this Part must be family-directed and designed to determine the resources, priorities, and concerns of the family related to enhancing the development of the child. (2) Any assessment that is conducted must be voluntary on the part of the family. (3) If an assessment of the family is carried out, the assessment must—
  (i)   Be conducted by personnel trained to utilize appropriate methods and procedures;
  (ii) Be based on information provided by the family through a personal interview; and
  (iii) Incorporate the family's description of its resources, priorities, and concerns related to enhancing the child's development.

(U.S. Department of Education, 1993a, 34 CFR 303.322[d])

FIGURE 7.6 Family-directed assessment

COMMUNICATING WITH PARENTS

Services to a child may not be withheld just because the family declines to participate or cooperate in a family assessment, which many families do. While evaluation and assessment of the child may strike them as both necessary and desirable, many parents resist the notion that they themselves be assessed by ECSE professionals. Such concerns are understandable. Assessment is by its very nature invasive, and some parents feel that family assessments may result in their being blamed for whatever problems a child has. ECSE personnel, who are sensitive to the potential privacy violations that worry many parents, can usually overcome such resistance.

ECSE personnel should open discussion of family assessment by acknowledging the central role of the family in early childhood. At no other stage in development is the family as crucial as it is during the birth-to-five period. For this reason, it is essential that early intervention and preschool special education personnel understand family dynamics and know how the child functions as a member of the family unit. A second point ECSE personnel may stress with the family is that the law, particularly Part C, expressly authorizes services for the family, not only the child. A family assessment assists in identifying such needs. If the family assessment is presented as an option, to be conducted at any time, families may be more receptive to the idea. Finally, ECSE personnel may address privacy concerns overtly by acknowledging that all data collected will be shared with the family and will not be released by the ECSE program staff to any other public or private agency without prior written parental consent. Indeed, the law requires family assessments to be family-directed, optional, and strictly confidential. Many families will respond positively to truthful and open communication from ECSE personnel.

Communication with families about other kinds of evaluation and assessment activities also requires honesty. Most parents do not have training in psychometrics; they may have unrealistic expectations of tests as somehow magically revealing hidden truths. It is essential for ECSE personnel to explain forthrightly that standardized and other tests and instruments used in this field are limited in what they can do. They should acknowledge the weaknesses of tests in validity, reliability, and norming. Such acknowledgment should, however, be paired with an assurance that the program will draw upon the varied skills of many professionals in a multidisciplinary evaluation and will combine test results with observations, interviews, and other sources so as to provide parents with information and recommendations that are useful and helpful. Another suggestion is to speak with parents of "samples" and of "sampling behavior." Given the reality of testing with very young children, it is more accurate to state that what is being done is sampling behavior more than actually testing the child.

Child and family assessments should begin with consultation with the family. Without going into details about the relative merits of various approaches, ECSE personnel should explain to the family the evaluation or assessment procedure they recommend, what it involves, what kinds of results might be expected, and why it is important. They should note family questions and promise to answer them as far as possible following the activity. Parents and other family members should be assured that all findings will be kept strictly confidential, as required by law.

The respective roles and responsibilities in assessment of professionals and families are subjects of lively controversies in ECSE. Traditional professional-family interactions in social service programs have featured professional-centered paradigms. Garshelis and McConnell (1993) summarized this type of thinking in these words: "For many years professionals have determined goals for families with children who have handicaps based solely on their own assessments of family needs" (p. 37). Advocates of family-centered approaches have reacted strongly against that approach, urging that families be equal partners as much in assessment as in other areas of ECSE programming (Bailey, Simeonsson, Yoder, & Huntington, 1990).

Trying to identify a middle ground between these two extremes, Joan Goodman (1994) argued that a "best interest of the client" standard should govern professional-family communication. ECSE professionals have responsibilities to the young child, Goodman contended, and must exercise those. They cannot, and should not, abdicate these in the name of empowering the family—even in family-directed family assessments. Goodman asserted that a best interest paradigm, properly implemented, respects the values and preferences as well as the ultimate decision-making authority of the family: "[W]e honor our clients more when, instead of deferring to their wishes, we put forth strongly our own considered judgments, leaving clients with the final decision-making authority" (p. x).

Accardo and Capute (1979) provided another framework for communicating with parents about results of evaluation and assessment procedures. They suggested that *cognitive* information—the nature of the activity, the findings, and what those mean—must be communicated clearly yet comprehensively, using as little jargon as possible. Key findings should be presented, as well, on an *operative* level. That is, parents should be given specific suggestions on how they may use the test results. Findings should be paired with recommendations, documented weaknesses matched with programs and curricula for intervention and treatment. Finally, *affective* aspects of communication with parents are crucial. Whether the results being presented are of child or family assessments, or of psychological or other evaluations, parents and other family members will have feelings about this information. These feelings should be acknowledged, particularly where evaluation indicates the need for long-term treatment.

Accardo and Capute added that if at all possible, both parents, as well as other adults identified by the family as responsible for a child's care, be invited to meetings at which test or other assessment results are presented. If only one parent attends and returns home to explain results to other family members, that parent shoulders an unfair burden. She may not be able to answer questions from other family members, for example, or may not be able to articulate findings and their implications. Families should be permitted to designate whoever they consider to be family. Each person should be offered an opportunity to question the evaluation team, and all such questions should be accepted and answered courteously. At the meeting's end, a statement should be made along the lines of, "We know you may have more questions, so feel free to call or visit at any time."

The most important part of communicating with families about evaluation and assessment is explaining what the findings mean for the child and for the family and recommending specific programs to the family. While evaluation and assessment activities are important, what is done with the information they generate is far more important. ECSE personnel should advise parents that they have a legal right to a second opinion. They should also assure parents that evaluation will be periodic, and that assessment is ongoing. Finally, ECSE workers should remind families that family services are an integral component of ECSE services, and that they should not hesitate to request support or other assistance they feel they need.

PROGRAM EVALUATION

ECSE administrators may schedule evaluations of the program itself. Program evaluation is the review, analysis, and reporting of what actually happened over a period of time, as distinct from program goals and other standards of performance. **Program evaluation**

program evaluation

attempts to answer the questions: Did a program do what it promised? Did it do these things efficiently and effectively?

formative evaluation looks to process issues such as how many families apply for services, how many are served, and how many of what kinds of services are provided. Formative evaluation may take place during an activity or program, while summative evaluation tends to occur afterward.

summative evaluation looks to outcomes, or results, to assess programs and activities, usually in comparison with other activities or programs. It is in contrast to formative evaluation, which focuses more on process than product.

attempts to answer the following questions: Did we do what we said we would do? Did we do it as efficiently as we could have, making good use of available resources? Were our approaches effective in meeting the needs of the children and families we serve?

In **formative evaluation**, the focus is on process issues. Planning and implementation in ECSE programs are reviewed with the aid of such methods as needs assessments (which inquire about the potential demand in the program's service area, and the extent to which the program offers the kinds of services that are needed) and program data analysis (which looks to determine how many children and families were served in a given period of time, with what kinds of services, and at what cost to the program). Such information may be used to assure funding agencies that the program is in compliance with federal, state, and other licensing or other requirements and is carrying out the plan of services that had been proposed. For example, formative evaluation may show that an ECSE program that promised to make at least two home visits monthly to each family being served actually averaged just 1.5 visits per month. These kinds of process evaluations examine the program's performance, as compared to its goals. Formative evaluation seldom compares two or more programs against one another.

In **summative evaluation**, the emphasis shifts to outcomes. It may be, for example, that family reports, child assessments, and other measures indicate that as much progress was made in those home visits as had been projected to occur under the full number of visits. Program evaluators may also find that center-based services are as effective as, but much more expensive than, home visits. These kinds of outcome data usually involve comparisons—in such cases, between outcomes as a function of more or fewer home visits and outcomes as a function of home versus center delivery (Escobar, Barnett, & Goetze, 1994).

Annual program evaluations can be very helpful in planning; they are also useful in communicating with funding and licensing agencies, because they provide independent evidence that the program does what it says it does. Murray (1992) suggested using program evaluation to answer critical questions about the program's impact on the people it serves. For example, are family-friendly approaches more effective in program-family relations than are more traditional child-focused or professional-centered relations? Are more intensive services more helpful to children than are less intensive services? Program evaluation may also help ECSE programs to monitor costs and to justify reimbursement claims. Murray noted, however, that few early intervention programs use computer database management. Cost allocation is far more easily managed with the assistance of computers than with calculators and paper records.

Program evaluation is most successful when an outside evaluator is contracted to perform the review. This evaluator should visit with the program staff early in a fiscal or academic year, propose and gain administrator acceptance of instruments and other measures to be used, and establish a means of maintaining ongoing communication throughout the year. At year-end, when all programmatic and fiscal data have been collected, the evaluator reviews these data and prepares a draft report. After the program staff consider the draft, and perhaps submit explanations for or elaborations upon the evaluator's findings, a final report is issued.

Large and mid-size accounting firms often perform pro bono audits and program evaluations. They can also recommend staff financial officers and independent evaluators. Pro bono accounting and program evaluation work by established accounting firms can be very helpful to program administrators who lack training and background in business and finance.

The involvement of ECSE personnel, including senior administrators, in program evaluation should not be minimized, even if an outside evaluator is retained. Critical decisions must be made before the evaluation can be conducted. Consider, for example, cost allocations. What kinds of costs will be included on the expenses side of the register? This question is particularly urgent when it comes to placing a value on presumed costs or intangibles. To take an obvious example, parent membership on planning and policy committees involves expenses, as does family member participation in support group sessions. Often, parents do not charge the program for their time. Should some dollar figure be assigned to that time to reflect more fully all actual and opportunity costs involved in running the program? If so, what dollar amount is fair and reasonable? Other examples involve results (outcomes). What kinds of measures should be sought? Parent evaluations? Student test scores? Placements of graduates in public school programs? Administrators and other workers in ECSE programs need to provide input to the outside evaluator on these and many other questions.

There is an unfortunate tendency in some human services fields to resist truly independent program evaluations. White (1988) pointed out that cost analysis is subject to bias. Where programs exist to meet human needs, and must be justified to policy makers on an annual basis in order to retain funding, some program "administrators cannot allow data to be collected that show that the program is not completely successful" (p. 441). This bias may show up in subtle ways. Administrators may not allow certain costs (notably opportunity costs) to be included, for example, thus making expenses appear lower than they otherwise would. Alternatively (or even additionally), administrators may use very liberal definitions of benefits or other outcomes as a way of inflating program results.

However costs and outcomes are defined, results may not be as clear-cut as one might wish. Program evaluation is difficult to carry out, for many reasons. Suppose it costs $10,000 per year to provide ECSE services to John Doe. How can one measure whether those costs are justified? In almost all cases, programs could do things in less expensive ways. Some cost-cutting measures make sense (and should be included in the outside evaluator's report). Others, however, would compromise program quality and might even subject the program to loss of its license for failing to meet state standards. And what about outcomes? It is possible to look at where John attends kindergarten and elementary school in subsequent years; if he is mainstreamed into a regular classroom, with few support services, one could say that the ECSE services succeeded with John—that the local community saved the extra dollars that separate classes, resource-room services, and so on, might have cost. Yet the matter is not so simple. How can anyone be sure that John would have needed such services absent ECSE? Perhaps, had no intervention and preschool special education been offered, John could have functioned well enough in a regular classroom to make it there. Even if one can establish that John could not have done these things without help, how does anyone know that it was the ECSE services that rendered separate instruction unnecessary? Perhaps it was parental assistance at home; perhaps it was a supportive, encouraging kindergarten teacher.

Murray (1992) pointed out that traditional program evaluation models are heavily quantitative in nature, that is, they look at numbers. In ECSE, such numbers unfortunately are often "soft." In particular, securing comparison data may be difficult or even impossible. There may be no other program serving the same kinds of children and families against which an ECSE program may be compared. Alternatively, a program may offer only center-based services, or home-based services, but not both, meaning that no comparisons across service placement may be made. In addition, using traditional pretest-posttest designs may not be feasible, because changes in children or families may be confounded with changes in the program itself, making it impossible to separate out what events contributed to what outcomes. Finally, as indicated throughout this chapter, instruments measuring child and family functioning that are both valid and reliable continue to be few and far between.

Whether the programs are effective, cost-effective, or cost-beneficial is often difficult to establish; it may not be possible to state definitively for even a single program or a particular child whether a program works and whether the expenditures were worth it. However, given continued budgetary pressures from all levels of government (federal, state, county, and local), ECSE programs will likely need to perform independent, outside evaluations so that program administrators, county officials, and state policy makers may obtain, as far as possible, objective evidence on what the program does and how well it does those things.

SUMMARY

Early screening and identification of children potentially eligible for ECSE services has been required in all states since 1980, yet it remains inconsistent. Pediatricians and other physicians are the logical professionals to conduct such screenings, but to date few test more than a handful of their patients. As awareness of the importance of early identification grows, screening should become more systematic.

Evaluation establishes initial and continuing eligibility for services. ECSE workers use assessment to identify specific interventions and to track progress of children as services are provided. Tests and other instruments for use in evaluation and assessment tend to have significant limitations. The state of the art in evaluation and assessment of young children who have disabilities, delays, or deviations in development, however, is evolving. The IDEA is stimulating vigorous growth in the field of ECSE instrumentation and procedures, and we can look forward to much-improved tests and other assessment activities in the years to come. Family assessments, which are more informal activities based on interviews and observation, may be used to supplement child assessments if the family concurs. Program evaluation in ECSE is often problematic, both because many programs do not have the computer technology necessary to track data and because information is frequently ambiguous, making it difficult to pinpoint what activities had what outcomes.

As important as evaluation and assessment activities are—and they are important—these procedures are but steps toward individualization of service delivery. Programs evaluate children and assess their progress because of a recognition that they differ between and within themselves. We know that children in this age range change rapidly. They also respond differently to intervention: What works with one child may not succeed with another. For all of these reasons, evaluation and assessment lead to individualized planning, the topic of the next chapter.

QUESTIONS FOR REFLECTION

1. Identify at least two differences between "evaluation" and "assessment."

2. Why are evaluation and assessment particularly challenging for professionals working with young children?

3. What is "informed clinical opinion" and why does it matter so much in early childhood special education?

4. Explain "false negatives" and "false positives" that may occur in screening.

5. How should psychologists who are experienced in testing K–12 children adjust their approaches when working with children under six years of age?

6. If a test is not normed on young children with delays in development or disabilities, how does that fact affect how test results are interpreted and used?

7. Identify an important difference between the meanings of the construct "intelligence" with respect to preschool-age children versus K–12 children.

8. How does parental "elaboration" help young children in cognitive and language development?

9. Why does the IDEA insist that assessments of family resources, priorities, and concerns be voluntary on the part of the family?

10. Explain Goodman's concept of the "best interest of the client" as it applies to program-family communication.

Individual Planning

Stated simply, the target population for early intervention must be thought of in terms of eligibility for assessment and ongoing formulation of an appropriate service plan—not in terms of eligibility for a fixed set of comprehensive services. (Shonkoff & Meisels, 1991, p. 24)

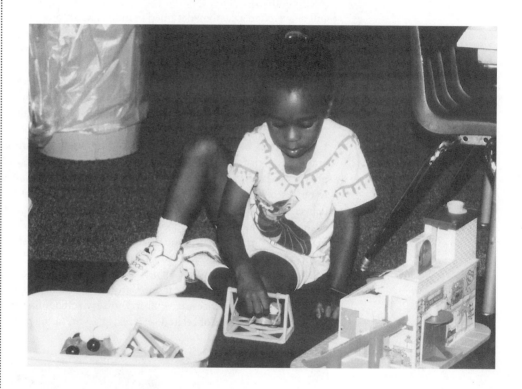

OVERVIEW

Early childhood special education (ECSE), as a profession, cherishes individualization of services. In fact, individualizing services for children and their families can fairly be said to be one cardinal principle of ECSE. The other is providing appropriate services. These twin values explain ECSE's overarching goal: to provide each child and family with what they need. The Individuals with Disabilities Education Act (IDEA) subsumes other values, however cherished, to those of individualization and appropriateness.

Early intervention services are "designed to meet the developmental needs of an infant or toddler with a disability" (section 632[4]). They are to be individually designed and delivered. They are also to be "appropriate," that is, to meet those needs. Similarly, special education is "specially designed instruction" to "meet the unique needs of a child with a disability" (section 602[3]). Here, too, the IDEA stresses that appropriate services are to be selected and delivered in a custom-designed manner. ECSE programs are told to evaluate and assess the needs of children and (if the family concurs) the family, and, using such information, to develop unique plans of service. Individualization and appropriateness are the core concepts that separate this field from other kinds of human services programs.

At the same time, individualization and appropriateness are concepts that link ECSE with the broader field of early childhood (EC). The National Association for the Education of Young Children (NAEYC) anchored its "developmentally appropriate practice" (DAP) recommendations to two core ideas: age appropriateness and individual appropriateness.

The values of individualization and appropriateness are implemented in ECSE programs through individualized family service plans (IFSPs) and individualized education programs (IEPs). These plans first identify the unique needs, priorities, concerns, and resources of particular children and their families and then outline how services will be delivered to meet these. Chapter 2 briefly described the contents of IFSPs and IEPs; this chapter elaborates in much more detail how such plans are to be prepared and what information they are to contain. The discussion meshes federal statutory and regulatory requirements to make clear how individualization is expressed in the plans.

In the opening quotation of this chapter, Shonkoff and Meisels (1991) suggested that individualization has another facet. Early intervention programs offer as many as thirteen different kinds of services, in addition to service coordination services. Special education authorizes eight kinds of related services, in addition to specially designed instruction. Not

Individualizing instruction is challenging for the early childhood educator, who must cope with widely varying needs.

all children need, nor should they be offered, all the services. Not all families need or want all, or even most, of the kinds of family services the law identifies either as early intervention services under Part C or as related services under Part B. The services individual children and their families are to receive must be determined through a customized, individualized process that identifies which services are "appropriate," that is, which services children and families need in order to benefit from the program.

One very important set of services under both Part C and Part B may be grouped together under the rubric of "transition services." Infants and toddlers and their families, being served under Part C, must be assisted in the transition from early intervention to programs that serve children aged three and above. In many cases, these will be Part B preschool services; in others, however, they may be community health, respite care, or other kinds of noneducational services. In addition, five-year-old children with disabilities and their families often need help to make the transition from preschool or other service programs to elementary school.

USING ASSESSMENT AND EVALUATION FINDINGS

Shonkoff and Meisels (1991) recommended tailoring services to the unique needs of individual children and their families. Early intervention and preschool special education both begin with assessments to identify those needs, followed by individualized planning of services to meet them. Neither adopts a mass-produced, all-for-all approach. Shonkoff and Meisels continued, "[The] definition of early intervention [emphasizes] a continuum of individualized services ranging from periodic assessment to the intensive mobilization of highly specialized therapeutic and educational resources" (p. 22). They recommended that a wide range of services be considered:

> *varying combinations of phone monitoring, information and referral, periodic reassessment, brief home visits, participation in activity centers, parent support groups, intensive home or*

Assessment and evaluation findings may be applied to selection of early intervention and preschool special education services.

center-based intervention, individual parent counseling, or specialized therapeutic interventions. (p. 23)

The approach Shonkoff and Meisels recommended draws on a considerable body of research over the past several years that suggests that what researchers call "aptitude-treatment interactions" are very important in ECSE programming, because young children with disabilities, delays, or deviations in development differ so much from one another in how they respond to different kinds of interventions and other offerings, including education. There are many other examples of aptitude-treatment interactions. For that reason, the results of evaluation and assessment activities must be considered in developing program recommendations for individual children.

Infants and toddlers are to be evaluated in all five areas of development: cognitive, physical, communication, social or emotional, and adaptive. If desired by the family, a measure of "the supports and services necessary to enhance the family's capacity to meet the developmental needs of the infant or toddler" (section 636[2]) may also be conducted by trained professionals. Part B requires an assessment that looks more narrowly at the child's needs for special education and related services. However, one related service is "parent counseling and training," another is "counseling services," and a third is "social work services in schools" (34 CFR 300.16). These potential offerings suggest that children's needs be described broadly rather than narrowly.

The sections that follow outline the provisions of IFSPs and of IEPs and offer suggestions for making these documents useful in providing services for birth-to-five children with special needs. Figure 8.1 highlights the statutory requirements for developing and using IFSPs; Figure 8.5 does the same for IEPs. The key provisions, including interpretations from committee reports and the U.S. Department of Education's regulations, are described.

INDIVIDUALIZED FAMILY SERVICE PLANS

The statutory language in section 636 is explicit in insisting that every infant or toddler receive an IFSP describing the child's strengths and needs in all five developmental areas and outlining proposed services. The legislative history reveals subtle implications of key

Developing IFSPs and IEPs can be time-consuming, but the plans may be short, tight-worded documents.

a) For each infant or toddler with a disability—
  (1) a multidisciplinary assessment of the unique strengths and needs of the infant or toddler and the identification of services appropriate to meet such needs;
  (2) a family-directed assessment of the resources, priorities, and concerns of the family and the identification of the supports and services necessary to enhance the family's capacity to meet the developmental needs of the infant or toddler; and
  (3) a written individualized family service plan developed by a multidisciplinary team, including the parent, as required by subsection (e).
(b) The individualized family service plan shall be evaluated once a year and the family shall be provided a review of the plan at 6-month intervals (or more often where appropriate based on infant or toddler and family needs).
(c) The individualized family service plan shall be developed within a reasonable time after the assessment required by subsection (a)(1) is completed. With the parents' consent, early intervention services may commence prior to the completion of such assessment.
(d) The individualized family service plan shall be in writing and contain—
  (1) a statement of the infant's or toddler's present levels of physical development, cognitive development, communication development, social or emotional development, and adaptive development, based on acceptable objective criteria;
  (2) a statement of the family's resources, priorities, and concerns relating to enhancing the development of the family's infant or toddler with a disability;
  (3) a statement of the major outcomes expected to be achieved for the infant or toddler and the family, and the criteria, procedures, and timelines used to determine the degree to which progress toward achieving the outcomes is being made and whether modifications or revisions of the outcomes or services are necessary;
  (4) a statement of specific early intervention services necessary to meet the unique needs of the infant or toddler and the family, including the frequency, intensity, and the method of delivering services;
  (5) a statement of the natural environments in which early intervention services shall appropriately be provided, including justification of the extent if any, to which the services will not be provided in a natural environment;
  (6) the projected dates for initiation of services and the anticipated duration of such services;
  (7) the name of the service coordinator from the profession most immediately relevant to the infant's or toddler's or family's needs (or who is otherwise qualified to carry out all applicable responsibilities under this part) who will be responsible for the implementation of the plan and coordination with other agencies and persons; and
  (8) the steps to be taken supporting the transition of the toddler with a disability to preschool or other appropriate services.
(e) The contents of the individualized family service plan shall be fully explained to the parents and informed written consent from the parents shall be obtained prior to the provision of early intervention services described in such plan. If such parents do not provide consent with respect to a particular early intervention service, then the early intervention services to which such consent is obtained shall be provided. (section 636)

FIGURE 8.1 Developing IFSPs

points. In addition, the U.S. Department of Education's (1993a) rules add a requirement that non–Part C services a child or family needs also be described in the IFSP. While the basic contents of the IFSP were given in Figure 2.2 in Chapter 2, it is helpful to "peel the onion" at this point by exploring subtle points in more detail. Figure 8.1 provides the statutory requirements for preparing IFSPs.

Assessment of Infant or Toddler

Part C opens its discussion of IFSPs by explaining that all eligible infants and toddlers and their families are to receive certain minimum services under Part C, including "(1) a multi-disciplinary assessment of the unique strengths and needs of the infant or toddler and the identification of services appropriate to meet such needs" (section 636). The term "assessment" is used here because the evaluation should already have been conducted and used to establish eligibility. The question now is, what are the child's immediate needs, and what services would meet those needs?

Family Assessment

Part C continues by calling for:

> (2) *a family-directed assessment of the resources, priorities, and concerns of the family and the identification of the supports and services necessary to enhance the family's capacity to meet the developmental needs of the infant or toddler* . . . (section 636[a][2])

The use of the term "family-directed" indicates that families have discretion about this family needs assessment. The literature suggests that many families that have no problems with an assessment of the infant's or toddler's needs are often uncomfortable being assessed themselves (Bailey, 1991; Garshelis & McConnell, 1993; Minke & Scott, 1993). Family members may decline such an assessment; if they agree to one, they determine what is assessed, how it is assessed, and what is done with the findings.

IFSP Team

Following child assessment and (if requested by the family) a family assessment, Part C requires "(3) a written individualized family service plan developed by a multidisciplinary team, including the parents, as required by subsection (e)." The parent clearly is a key member of the IFSP-writing team. *House Report 102-198* explains: "The parents or guardian must be an integral member of the multidisciplinary team charged with developing the IFSP" (p. 18). Part C calls for the IFSP to be "developed" by a multidisciplinary team, but not necessarily in a meeting. The U.S. Department of Education's regulations, however, speak of meetings to develop IFSPs (34 CFR 303.321[e][2][ii] and 303.342).

IFSP Review

Part C continues: (b) "The individualized family service plan shall be evaluated once a year and the family shall be provided a review of the plan at 6-month intervals (or more often where appropriate based on infant or toddler and family needs)" (section 636[b]). The IFSP needs to be reviewed every six months because infants and toddlers change so rapidly.

Timing of the IFSP

The law requires prompt action: (c) "The individualized family service plan shall be developed within a reasonable time after the assessment required by subsection (a)(1) is completed. With the parents' consent, early intervention services may commence prior to the completion of such assessment." The "reasonable time" requirement has been interpreted by the U.S. Department of Education to be forty-five days after referral (34 CFR 303.421[e][2]). In some instances, even that is an unacceptable delay, so the statute permits services to begin immediately after eligibility is established, without waiting for the IFSP.

IFSP Contents

Part C continues:

> *(d) The individualized family service plan shall be in writing and contain—*
> *(1) a statement of the infant's or toddler's present levels of physical development, cognitive development, communication development, social or emotional development, and adaptive development, based on objective criteria;*
> *(2) a statement of the family's resources, priorities, and concerns relating to enhancing the development of the family's infant or toddler with a disability;*
> *(3) a statement of the major outcomes expected to be achieved for the infant or toddler and the family, and the criteria, procedures, and timelines used to determine the degree to which progress toward achieving the outcomes is being made and whether modifications or revisions of the outcomes or services are necessary;*
> *(4) a statement of specific early intervention services necessary to meet the unique needs of the infant or toddler and the family, including the frequency, intensity, and the method of delivering services.* (section 636)

The U.S. Department of Education adds in its regulations that the "payment arrangements, if any" are to be included here (34 CFR 303.344). The statute allows parents to be charged for some services. If a given family will be charged, this fact should be noted in this part of the IFSP.

Social and emotional development is an important element in all IFSPs and IEPs, even when children have no special needs in that developmental domain.

(1) To the extent appropriate, the IFSP must include
   (i) Medical and other services that the child needs, but that are not required under this part; and
   (ii) The funding sources to be used in paying for those services.

(2) The requirement in paragraph (e)(1) of this section does not apply to routine medical services (e.g., immunizations and "well-baby" care), unless a child needs those services and the services are not otherwise available or being provided (34 CFR 303.344). . . .

The "other services" in paragraph (e) of this section are services that a child or family needs, but that are neither required nor covered under this part. While listing the nonrequired services in the IFSP does not mean that those services must be provided, their identification can be helpful to both the child's family and the service coordinator, for the following reasons. First, the IFSP would provide a comprehensive picture of the child's total service needs (including the need for medical and health services, as well as early intervention services). Second, it is appropriate for the service coordinator to assist the family in securing the non-required services (e.g., by (1) determining if there is a public agency that could provide financial assistance, if needed, (2) assisting in the preparation of eligibility claims or insurance claims, if needed, and (3) assisting the family in seeking out and arranging for the child to receive the needed medical-health services). (34 CFR 303.344, Note 3)

FIGURE 8.2 Other services in IFSPs

The statutory language at section 636(d)(4) refers to "specific" early intervention services. The U.S. Department of Education's regulations add that other services a family may need—but which are *not* early intervention services and therefore not reimbursable under Part C—may also be listed in the IFSP if doing so may assist the family in planning to meet its needs and those of the infant or toddler. This provision on "other services" is important, but it is widely misunderstood. For that reason, Figure 8.2 quotes the department's guidance on this issue.

The 1991 *House Report* provided congressional concurrence to the Department's regulations:

> *The definition in this section distinguishes between the health services that are required under this part, and the medical-health services that are not required. The IFSP requirements in subpart D provide that, to the extent appropriate, these other medical-health services are to be included in the IFSP, along with the funding sources to be used in paying for the services. Identifying these services in the IFSP does not impose an obligation to provide the services if they are otherwise not required to be provided under this part. (House Report 102-198, 1991, p. 14)*

To summarize: The IFSP may include non–Part C services if by adding such "other services" the plan becomes more practical and more useful to the family.

Natural Environment

The statute continues, in section 636(d)(5), as follows: "a statement of the natural environments in which early intervention services shall appropriately be provided, including justification of the extent, if any, to which the services will not be provided in a natural environment." Section 635(a)(16) adds: "to the maximum extent appropriate, [services] are provided in natural environments." The "natural environment" preference does not limit the obligation to provide appropriate services. Part C does not further explain what are considered to be appropriate services.

Start Date and Duration

The law continues, in section 636(d)(6), as follows: "the projected dates for initiation of services and the anticipated duration of such services." Many ECSE programs provide year-round services, as opposed to public schools' nine-month academic year. Because the IFSP covers a one-year period, the "anticipated duration" never exceeds twelve months.

Service Coordinator

Part C requires "(7) the name of the service coordinator from the profession most immediately relevant to the infant's or toddler's or family's needs (or who is otherwise qualified to carry out all applicable responsibilities under this part) who will be responsible for the implementation of the plan and coordination with other agencies and persons" (section 636). The committee report explained:

> [T]he bill also amends the provision in the Act that limited the service coordinator (formerly the case manager) to a person from the profession most immediately relevant to the infant's or toddler's or family's needs. Under the amendment, the service coordinator could also be a person who is otherwise qualified to carry out all applicable responsibilities under Part H. For example, social workers and others trained in areas of human behavior and human services may not be "from the profession most immediately relevant to the infant's or toddler's or family's needs" but they are trained to provide case management or service coordination services and therefore are clearly qualified to provide such services. In addition, a parent may become qualified to perform all of the service functions carried out by a service coordinator and provide the service coordination function for another family if the parent obtains appropriate training by qualified persons.
>
> (*House Report 102-198*, 1991, pp. 18–19)

Transition

Part C requires that IFSPs include "(8) the steps to be taken supporting the transition of the toddler with a disability to preschool or other appropriate services." Note that the statute again uses the term "appropriate" to describe the services required under Part C. The U.S. Department of Education (1993a) provided additional details about transition, as indicated in Figure 8.3.

Informed Consent

Section 636 concludes: "(e) The contents of the individualized family service plan shall be fully explained to the parents and informed written consent from the parents shall be obtained prior to the provision of early intervention services described in such plan. If such

Transition at age three.

(1) The IFSP must include the steps to be taken to support the transition of the child upon reaching age three, to
   (i) Preschool services under Part B of the Act, in accordance with section 303.148, to the extent that those services are considered appropriate; or
   (ii) Other services that may be available, if appropriate.

(2) The steps required in paragraph (h)(1) of this section include
   (i) Discussion with, and training of, parents regarding future placements and other matters related to the child's transition;
   (ii) Procedures to prepare the child for changes in service delivery, including steps to help the child adjust to, and function in, a new setting; and
   (iii) With parental consent, the transmission of information about the child to the local educational agency, to ensure continuity of services, including evaluation and assessment information required in section 303.322, and copies of IFSPs that have been developed and implemented in accordance with sections 303.340 through 303.346 (34 CFR 303.344[h]).

FIGURE 8.3 Transition for three-year-olds

parents do not provide consent with respect to a particular early intervention service, then the early intervention services to which such consent is obtained shall be provided." Section (e) was added in 1991. Notice that the first sentence of this section goes beyond Part B's IEP requirement that parents be given the option to sign or not sign the document; a more extensive informed written consent is mandated under Part C. The second sentence explicitly allows parents to decline services; again, that is more than is specifically stated in Part B.

The U.S. Department of Education emphasized that IFSPs need not be lengthy. An outline containing the required eight items would suffice, so long as the necessary documentation is appended (U.S. Department of Education, 1993a). The department explained:

Although the IFSP must include information about each of the items in paragraphs (b) through (h) of this section, this does not mean that the IFSP must be a detailed, lengthy document. It might be a brief outline, with appropriate attachments that address each of the points in the paragraphs under this section. It is important for the IFSP itself to be clear about (a) what services are to be provided, (b) the actions that are to be taken by the service coordinator in initiating those services, and (c) what actions will be taken by the parents. (34 CFR 303.344, Note 4)

INDIVIDUALIZED EDUCATION PROGRAMS

IEPs may be used for two-year-old children who will turn three during an academic year, as well as for three- to five-year-olds. Alternatively, ECSE programs may continue to use IFSPs as long as they include in those plans all of the elements that must be incorporated into IEPs (Schrag, 1990c; U.S. Department of Education, 1992a, p. 44840). Those elements are reviewed in this section. The "final rule" on Part B appeared in the September 29, 1992, *Federal Register* (U.S. Department of Education, 1992a). Some corrections were published about a month later, on October 27, 1992 (U.S. Department of Education, 1992b). These regulations, which contain far more detail than the statute, have the force of law. They should be consulted on any questions related to IEPs.

The statutory language in section 614(d) on preparing IEPs appears in Figure 8.5. Following, the process of preparing IEPs is reviewed, provision by provision.

IEP Meeting

The department's rule states that parents are to be full and equal participants in IEP meetings. The appendix interpreting the purposes of IEPs added:

> *The IEP meeting serves as a communication vehicle between parents and school personnel, and enables them, as equal participants, to jointly decide what the child's needs are, what services will be provided to meet those needs, and what the anticipated outcomes may be.* (U.S. Department of Education, 1992a, p. 44833)

One concern many parents have expressed is that they often feel overwhelmed by large numbers of school personnel at IEP meetings. This section requires that three, and sometimes four, people attend the IEP meeting: (1) parent(s) or guardian, (2) teacher(s) of the child, (3) a representative of the local education agency who is qualified to provide or supervise the provision of special education, and (4) the child, if appropriate. In instances in which related services are to be provided, it makes sense for a professional from that related service (for example, an occupational therapist) to attend. In addition, parents may wish to bring with them someone knowledgeable about the law and their child's unique needs (Ballard & Zettel, 1977).

The department was at pains to urge that IEP meetings be "small." The interpretation section of the September 1992 final rule stated:

> *Generally, the number of participants at IEP meetings should be small. Small meetings have several advantages over large ones. For example, they (1) allow for more open, active parent involvement, (2) are less costly, (3) are easier to arrange and conduct, and (4) are usually more productive.* (U.S. Department of Education, 1992a, p. 44835)

The same document added, "The legislative history of the Act makes it clear that attendance at IEP meetings should be limited to those who have an intense interest in the child" (p. 44836). The department's other guidance on family participation is summarized in Figure 8.4.

Educational Performance

An IEP contains "a written statement of the child's present levels of educational performance" (section 614[d]). Notable here is the requirement that only "educational performance" be described. Children's abilities and needs as these relate to special education and related services are to be outlined. The IFSP, by contrast, calls for statements of children's needs in all five developmental areas recognized under Part C. If the state adopts the developmental delay criteria for preschoolers, as it is permitted to do, it clearly would be appropriate here to describe the child's current performance and needs in those five areas of development and not to restrict the statement only to "educational performance."

The department's interpretation of IEP requirements explains:

> *The statement of present levels of educational performance . . . should accurately describe the effect of the child's disability on the child's performance in any area of education that is*

The parents of a child with a disability are expected to be equal participants along with school personnel, in developing, reviewing, and revising the child's IEP. This is an active role in which the parents

(1) participate in the discussion about the child's need for special education and related services, and

(2) join with the other participants in deciding what services the agency will provide to the child (U.S. Department of Education, 1992a, p. 44836).

(a) Each public agency shall take steps to assure that one or both of the parents of the child with a disability are present at each meeting or are afforded the opportunity to participate, including

   (1) Notifying parents of the meeting early enough to ensure that they will have an opportunity to attend; and

   (2) Scheduling the meeting at a mutually agreed upon time and place. . . .

      (e) The public agency shall take whatever action is necessary to ensure that the parent understands the proceedings at a meeting, including arranging for an interpreter for parents with deafness or whose native language is other than English.

      (f) The public agency shall give the parent, on request, a copy of the IEP (U.S. Department of Education, 1992a, p. 44815).

FIGURE 8.4 Family participation in IEPs

affected, including (1) academic areas (reading, math, communication, etc.), and (2) non-academic areas (daily life activities, mobility, etc.). (U.S. Department of Education, 1992a, p. 44837)

This language clearly implies that the needs of preschool-age children in the domains of physical, communication, adaptive, social or emotional, and cognitive development may be described as part of the statement on educational performance.

Goals and Objectives

The law says the IEPs should include "(b) a statement of measurable annual goals, including benchmarks or short-term objectives." This IEP requirement remains controversial long after most other components of the plan have become accepted practice in special education. Goodman and Bond (1993) argued that the words "short-term objectives" are widely misunderstood. Some IEPs, they reported, contain specific instructional objectives more suitable for monthly, weekly, or even daily lesson plans than for annual documents. Such an understanding is incorrect. Stated Goodman and Bond: "The IEP was never intended to specify what or how teachers should teach" (p. 408). They added:

> *The IEP assumes [under this interpretation] that instructors know in advance what a child should and can learn, and the speed at which he or she will learn. This is a difficult projection to make with nondisabled children of school age—for preschool children with cognitive, emotional and social disabilities, it is near impossible.*(p. 415)

The section 614(d) language properly is understood, Goodman and Bond argued, as requiring that the IEP contain sufficient information about goals and objectives to permit school

(i)   a written statement of the child's present level of educational performance, including—
    (I)   how the child's disability affects the child's involvement and progress in the general curriculum; or
    (II)   for preschool children, as appropriate, how the disability affects the child's participation in appropriate activities;

(ii)   a statement of measurable annual goals, including benchmarks or short-term objectives, related to—
    (I)   meeting the child's needs that result from the child's disability to enable the child to be involved in and progress in the general curriculum, and
    (II)   meeting each of the child's other educational needs that result from the child's disability

(iii) a statement of the special education and related services and supplementary aids and services to be provided to the child, or on behalf of the child, and a statement of the program modifications or supports for school personnel that will be provided for the child—
    (I)   to advance appropriately toward attaining the annual goals;
    (II)   to be involved and progress in the general curriculum in accordance with the clause (i) and to participate in extra-curricular and other nonacademic activities; and
    (III) to be educated and participate with other children with disabilities and non-disabled children in the activities described in this paragraph

(iv)   an explanation of the extent, if any, to which the child will not participate with nondisabled children in the regular class and in the activities described in clause (iii);

(v)   (I)   a statement of any individual modifications in the administration of state or district wide assessments of student achievement that are needed in order for the child to participate in such assessment; and
    (II)   if the IEP Team determines that the child will not participate in a particular state or district wide assessment of student achievement (or part of such an assessment), a statement of—(aa) why the assessment is not appropriate for the child; and (bb) how the child will be assessed;

(vi)   the projected date for the beginning of the services and modifications described in clause (iii), and the anticipated frequency, location, and duration of those services and modifications

(vii) (I)   beginning at age 14, and updated annually, a statement of the transition service needs of the child under the applicable components of the child's IEP that focuses on the child's courses of study (such as participation in advanced-placement courses or a vocational education program);
    (II)   beginning at age 16 (or younger, if determined appropriate by the IEP Team), a statement of needed transition services for the child, including, when appropriate, a statement of the interagency responsibilities or any needed linkages; and
    (III) beginning at least one year before the child reaches the age of majority under state law; a statement that the child has been informed of his or her rights under this title, if any, that will transfer to the child on reaching the age of majority under section 615 (m); and

(viii) a statement of—
    (I)   how the child's parents will be regularly informed (by such means as periodic report cards), at least as often as parents are informed of their nondisabled child's progress, of—
        (aa) their child's progress toward the annual goals described in clause (ii); and
        (bb) the extent to which that progress is sufficient to enable the child to achieve the goals by the end of the year.

FIGURE 8.5 Preparing IEPs

officials and parents to review progress. Thus, the IEP is an assessment tool, not an instructional planning one. The program should specify yearlong goals and intermediate objectives so that as the year proceeds, the child's progress may be tracked and needed adjustments made. Explained the U.S. Department of Education:

> *The statutory requirements for including annual goals and short term instructional objectives…provide a mechanism for determining (1) whether the anticipated outcomes for the child are being met (i.e., whether the child is progressing in the special education program) and (2) whether the placement and services are appropriate to the child's special learning needs. In effect, these requirements provide a way for the child's teacher(s) and parents to be able to track the child's progress in special education. However, the goals and objectives are not intended to be as specific as the goals and objectives that are normally found in daily, weekly, or monthly instructional plans.* (1992a, p. 48702)

Services

Part B continues by calling for "(c) a statement of the special education and related services and supplementary aids and services to be provided to the child" (section 614[d][1][A][iii]). This section also is to describe support services needed for integration in the general curriculum. This section of the IEP also is widely misunderstood. The program should specify the services that are to be provided in response to each of the child's unique needs. This may, for example, be "occupational therapy for thirty minutes three times weekly" for the purpose of meeting a child's need to acquire the upper-body strength to use a Braille writer. The regulations make clear that this section of the IEP should outline the services a child needs, regardless of whether or not the local education agency will provide them:

> *[T]he services must be listed in the IEP even if they are not directly available from the local agency, and must be provided by the agency through contract or other arrangements.* (U.S. Department of Education, 1992a, p. 44838)

The IEP must note not only the kinds of services but also their intensity:

> *The amount of services to be provided must be stated in the IEP, so that the level of the agency's commitment of resources will be clear to parents and other IEP team members.* (p. 44839)

Note that the statement is *not* required to identify the placement here. The federal regulations clearly indicate that the placement decision is to be made following development of the IEP, not beforehand or as it is being written:

> *An IEP must be in effect before special education and related services are provided to a child. The appropriate placement for a given child with a disability cannot be determined until after decisions have been made about what the child's needs are and what will be provided. Therefore, the IEP must be developed before placement.* (U.S. Department of Education, 1992a, p. 44834)

Districtwide Assessments

IEPs for preschool-age children need not contain these elements because such testing is not usually done with this population.

Transition

For all children about to turn three, the IFSP must contain a statement of the transition services needed as children move from early intervention to preschool or other programs. If the IEP is used instead of an IFSP for such children, the IEP may contain the necessary information about transition services. The IEP may also be used to describe transition services for five-year-olds moving from preschool programs to kindergarten or elementary schools.

Date and Duration

IEPs must also contain "the projected date for the beginning of the services and modifications . . . and the anticipated frequency, location, and duration of those services and modifications." The IEP is an annual statement, so the "duration" here will be under twelve months. Academic year schedules usually apply (nine months), but some children require extended school year services to prevent regression or to maintain skills. If year-round services are necessary to meet a particular child's unique needs, that should be specified here.

Progress Reports

Section 614(d) concludes by requiring that IEPs contain a statement of how parents will be apprised of progress. As noted earlier (and discussed in more depth in Goodman & Bond, 1993), the IEP is a planning and tracking document. The criteria and procedures are to be measures allowing school officials and parents both to agree that goals and intermediate objectives were or were not met. This system facilitates preparation of the following year's IEP.

"APPROPRIATE"

The term "appropriate" is used repeatedly throughout the IDEA. It is used several times in describing IEPs and IFSPs. However, the word itself is never defined in the IDEA. That it is an important term is abundantly clear. It surfaces, for example, at the very beginning of the IDEA, in section 601(c), where Congress explains why Part B was created:

> *to ensure that all children with disabilities have available to them a free appropriate public education that emphasizes special education and related services designed to meet their unique needs....*

The word "appropriate" also appears in section 602(8), where "free appropriate public education" is defined as "meet[ing] the standards of the State education agency" and "provided in conformity with" an IEP. Nowhere else does the IDEA explain what "appropriate" means.

That, as it turns out, was a very significant oversight. The law guarantees young children with disabilities "appropriate" early intervention services and "appropriate" education services—but what does this mean?

In 1982, the U.S. Supreme Court decided its first ever case on what is now the IDEA. At issue was whether Amy Rowley, an elementary school student who was deaf and whose parents also were deaf, was entitled to a sign-language interpreter in class. The decision, in *Board of Education, Hendrick Hudson School District v. Rowley*, turned on the court's interpretation of the meaning of the word "appropriate." The court's decision is excerpted in Figure 8.6. An

According to the definitions contained in the Act, a "free appropriate public education" consists of educational instruction specially designed to meet the unique needs of the handicapped child, supported by such services as are necessary to permit the child "to benefit" from the instruction. Almost as a checklist for adequacy under the Act, the definition also requires that such instruction and services be provided at public expense and under public supervision, meet the State's educational standards, approximate the grade levels used in the State's regular education, and comport with the child's IEP. Thus, if personalized instruction is being provided with sufficient supportive services to permit the child to benefit from the instruction, and the other items on the definitional checklist are satisfied, the child is receiving a 'free appropriate public education' as defined by the Act. (*Board of Education, Hendrick Hudson School District v. Rowley*, 1982, 102 S.Ct. 3034 [EHLR 553:656], pp. 188–189)

FIGURE 8.6 "Appropriate" in *Rowley*

"appropriate" education, the court decided, is one that *meets* the child's unique needs through specially designed instruction and any necessary related services.

The word "meets" sets a floor, but it also creates a ceiling. Services must "meet" individual children's needs; services that do not enable children to benefit are not sufficient. On the other hand, the word "meet" limits the amount or kind of services necessary. There is no requirement to provide more services, or more expensive ones, than are needed to "meet" the child's unique needs. Thus, if two hours a week of speech and language therapy meets the needs of a child, there is no requirement to provide four hours. Similarly, if therapy offered in small groups suffices to meet the need, there is no obligation in the IDEA to provide one-on-one services instead.

The requirement in Part C that early intervention services be appropriate and in Part B that education be appropriate is, accordingly, that these services benefit the child. This requirement outweighs the placement preferences in the statute (natural environment, least restrictive environment). That is, whatever placement is made, the services provided there must meet unique needs so that the child benefits from them. It is noteworthy that both the IEP and the IFSP specifications qualify their environmental preferences by insisting that placements and services be "appropriate." The IFSP, to illustrate, calls for a "statement of the natural environments in which early intervention services shall *appropriately* be provided" (section 636[d][5]; emphasis added). Similar language applies to IEPs in Part B.

The U.S. Department of Education recently issued a statement on "appropriate" that reaffirmed the primacy of appropriateness over placement. Suitably enough, since the Court ruled about the education of a deaf child, this statement discussed services for deaf children:

> *The Secretary is concerned that the least restrictive environment provisions of the IDEA and section 504 are being interpreted, incorrectly, to require the placement of some children who are deaf in programs that may not meet the individual student's educational needs. Meeting the unique communication and related needs of a student who is deaf is a fundamental part of providing a free appropriate public education to the child.*
> (U.S. Department of Education, 1992d, p. 49275)

To reinforce the point that the requirement to provide "free, appropriate public education" (FAPE) services is primary and the least restrictive environment (LRE) preference secondary, the department's statement continued:

The provision of FAPE is paramount, and the individual placement determination about LRE is to be considered within the context of FAPE. . . . Any setting, including a regular classroom, that prevents a child who is deaf from receiving an appropriate education that meets his or her needs, including communication needs, is not the LRE for that individual child. (U.S. Department of Education, 1992d, p. 49275)

Finally, family services may be provided, as appropriate, both under Part C and under Part B. Appropriate family services are those kinds of assistance a family needs to enhance the development of the child. Part C calls these early intervention services and specifies that they be recorded in IFSPs to the extent that the family approves, while Part B calls them related services and says they may be incorporated into IEPs. In fact, ECSE programs may continue to use IFSPs through a child's fifth year of life (Schrag, 1990c; U.S. Department of Education, 1992a). The important point is that services that a family needs so that the child will benefit are appropriate services and may be provided under Parts C and B.

WRITING THE PLANS

The IFSP and the IEP are written documents prepared after several preliminary steps are completed. First, eligibility must be established. Second, a multidisciplinary assessment of the infant, toddler, or child must be performed. The assessment should suggest services needed to meet the child's unique needs. The document must describe those services, together with ways in which progress will be monitored and evaluated. The IFSP includes a family-directed assessment of family resources, priorities, and concerns, to the extent that the family desires such a statement. Because Part B allows family counseling and other family assistance as "related services," an IEP may also contain such a review of family priorities and needs. In both cases, unfortunately, the actual preparation of these documents does not always comport with the ideals expressed in the IDEA.

The most important concern, as DeGangi, Royeen, and Wietlisbach (1992) noted, is that the process of creating the plan must feature mutual respect and information sharing between parents and professionals. So important is this sharing that it is fair to say that the process of developing the plan is more important than the plan itself. That is because parents and ECSE professionals may bring to the IFSP/IEP planning process different priorities, values, and goals. If the process features mutual respect and information sharing, both parties move toward a consensus position—to the child's benefit. If, however, the process is characterized by mutual distrust, hidden agendas, and lack of respect, the plan likely will ill-serve the child, the family, and the program itself.

To illustrate, in 1992, Minke and Scott (1993) studied three early intervention programs to see how actively parents actually participated in writing the IFSP. They found that parents usually made "basic decisions" (p. 92), for example, about interagency transfers of personally identifiable information, about applying for other services such as Medicaid, and about how active a role they wished to play in the ECSE program. Finally, parents usually decided overall goals for physical, cognitive, adaptive, communication, and social or emotional development for their children.

Minke and Scott found that service selection—which services would be provided in order to help reach each goal—was most often made jointly by parents and early intervention program staff. Programs varied in which services they had available. Typically, early intervention program staff would recommend certain of these services and would tell the parents about additional services available elsewhere. Parents were usually asked to decide which services they wanted delivered and which they did not; and generally they did so. However, Minke and Scott found that early intervention program staff at times steered the parents toward or away from certain services. They also found that program staff, directly or obliquely, determined the frequency with which such services would be provided more than parents did. One program staff member put it: "[The parent] was expected to listen to our suggestions. If she disagreed with anything, she could tell her reasoning behind why she didn't want certain things done. And we've had that happen on occasion. It's very rare" (p. 94).

Parental decision making was weakest, Minke and Scott found, in the later, detailed decisions, such as what strategies would be used to reach goals, which tactics would be adopted to pursue each strategy, and how progress would be measured. Said Minke and Scott: "Parents were not asked for input on strategies to achieve the selected goals in any of the nine [IFSP] meetings taped. Most (n=10) of the staff members interviewed indicated that they see this process as their own prerogative and that it is carried out without parent input" (p. 99). They added, "Staff members reported keeping a set of goals separate from the parents' goals and noted having 'unwritten' goals that guide their interventions" (p. 100).

An important, but often overlooked, right parents of infants and toddlers enjoy is to have a complete spectrum of services—including many non–Part C services—placed into the IFSP or IEP. ECSE program staff may have to do considerable research to identify the full range of services for which the family is eligible. Parents of preschoolers may receive similar support services; in fact, all IFSP services may be continued. As stated in *Senate Report 102-198* (1991):

> *The Committee urges State educational agencies, local educational agencies, and intermediate educational units to continue to provide the types of services set out in an IFSP to a preschooler where the family concurs that such services would be appropriate. In particular, because of the similarity between social work services (which are related services under Part B) and family training, counseling, home visits, and service coordination (which are early intervention services under Part H) the Committee urges the continuation of family training, counseling, home visits, and service coordination.* (pp. 7–8)

Surprisingly few families are aware of such rights. Research by Minke and Scott (1993) demonstrated that many ECSE workers assumed parents would not understand the more subtle, detailed aspects of IFSP service planning and therefore did not request family input into those decisions.

IEP development, too, sometimes departs from the ideal. Parents told one congressional commission, for example, that they were presented with a completely written IEP document and asked to sign it (Commission on Education of the Deaf, 1988). The U.S. Department of Education's final regulations expressly forbid such practices:

> *It is not permissible for an agency to present a completed IEP to parents for their approval before there has been a full discussion with the parents of (1) the child's need for special education and related services, and (2) what services the agency will provide to the child. . . . [T]he agency should make it clear to the parents at the outset of the meeting that the services proposed by the agency are only recommendations for review and discussion with the parents.* (U.S. Department of Education, 1992a, p. 44839)

The IDEA clearly and explicitly forbids ECSE programs from preparing complete plans in advance and just presenting them to parents for signature. Section 636(e), in Part C, for example, says:

The contents of the individualized family service plan shall be fully explained to the parents and informed written consent from the parents shall be obtained prior to the provision of early intervention services described in such plan.

Another aspect of the family-program interaction spelled out by the IDEA that is often overlooked is the fact that family members may themselves become service coordinators—for other families:

[A] parent may become qualified to perform all of the service functions carried out by a service coordinator and provide the service coordination function for another family if the parent obtains appropriate training by qualified persons.
(*House Report 102-198,* 1991, pp. 18–19)

TRANSITION

transition is movement from one stage or program to another. An important transition in early childhood special education is that from early intervention programs to preschool programs.

intensive care unit (ICU) is a hospital ward for premature, low-birthweight, and other infants needing comprehensive care. When used with infants under one month old, ICUs are called neonatal intensive care units (NICUs).

Transition must be addressed both in IFSPs and in IEPs. The principal concern in each case is with interagency coordination, that is, when a child and family are preparing to move from one agency and its services to another. The IFSP contains a statement of how the child's transition from Part C services to subsequent programs, whether preschool special education under Part B or some other service system, will proceed. The IEP, similarly, may outline the transition from preschool to kindergarten or elementary school and, for older children, from school to work, postsecondary education, or other postschool activities.

There are, however, other kinds of transitions. These, too, are important. Infants may move from hospital settings such as **intensive care units (ICUs)** to home- and/or center-based early intervention programs. Children of relocating families may move into new programs. And children may move from one preschool class to another. Each of these changes requires careful planning. They often cause stress for families, and for young children as well. In many instances, changes involve transfer of personally identifiable information from one agency or program to another. Such transfers are subject to due-process safeguards in the IDEA.

The legislation and the U.S. Department of Education's regulations address interagency transitions. Following, the key requirements are discussed for the most common of these interagency transitions.

Within Part C

The families of infants moving from hospital-based services, such as ICUs, to home- and center-based services need assistance in negotiating important shifts in priorities and services. While ICUs and other hospital-based programs focus on survival and health promotion, early intervention programs in the community—whether home- or center-based—tend to place priority on family-child interactions, developmental milestones, and family empowerment to facilitate parents' efforts to enhance the child's growth. Wolery (1989) suggested that despite the dramatic shift in focus from ICUs to community-based programs, "it is imperative that the needs and services that were given priority in the sending program not be ignored in the receiving program" (p. 3). In this instance, the infant's health should be monitored by the intervention program, even as parents are helped to move beyond immediate concerns about health to longer-term issues of their child's development.

From Part C to Part B

When what is now the IDEA was amended in 1986, resulting in the creation of Part H (now Part C) and expansion of Part B's preschool services, the need for smooth transitions between the two programs was a key concern of Congress. The 1990 and 1991 IDEA legislation continued to stress transition from Part H to Part B. The law now requires that a meeting between the sending agency, the receiving agency, and the parents take place to plan transition. The receiving agency, in this case a local education agency (LEA) or intermediate education unit, or other program offering appropriate services, must actually meet with the sending agency and with the family. The statute places the responsibility for initiating these transition meetings with the Part C agency, requiring the Part C state plan to include a

> *description of the policies and procedures to be used to ensure a smooth transition for toddlers receiving early intervention services under this part to preschool or other appropriate services, including a description of how the families will be included in the transition plans and how the lead agency will notify the appropriate local educational agency for the area in which the child resides that the child will shortly reach the age of eligibility for preschool services under Part B, as determined in accordance with State law; in the case of a child who may be eligible for such preschool services, with the approval of the family of the child, convene a conference among the lead agency, the family, and at least 90 days (and at the discretion of all such parties, up to 6 months) before the child is eligible for the preschool services, to discuss any such services that the child may receive; and . . . to review the child's program options for the period from the child's third birthday through the remainder of the school year; and to establish a transition plan.* (section 637)

The receiving agency, in this case a state education agency (SEA) and its LEAs, must cooperate. The law requires the Part B state plan to include procedures for transition from Part C to Part B at about the time of the third birthday.

The references in sections 637 and 612 to the child's third birthday should not be interpreted literally. Schrag (1960c) makes clear that plans and placements may occur at more convenient times, before or after the third birthday. Parents must give prior written permission for the sending agency to discuss or otherwise release with or to the receiving agency any personally identifiable information about the family and/or the child (IDEA section 639; U.S. Department of Education, 1993a, section 303.460). Families may reject or defer any early intervention services, presumably including referral to preschool programs (IDEA section 680; U.S. Department of Education, 1993a, section 303.405). The parental prerogative to decline or postpone any early intervention services, without jeopardizing any other such services, is absolute. It is not subject to service agency appeal through the Part C section 639 due-process procedures or any other such mechanism. Because state law generally does not require program attendance by under-six children, the state has no compelling interest in overriding parental desires.

From Part C to Other Service Programs

Similar requirements hold in other kinds of interagency transition planning. The IDEA places the major obligation for initiating such steps with the Part C lead agency and its service providers. Transition to community service, public health, or other services involves transmission of personally identifiable information—including assessment and evaluation data, copies of IFSPs, and similar material—from the sending agency to the receiving agency. The law is explicit in stating that such information may not be transmitted from the current service agency to any other agency without prior written parental permission. Referral of a child from an early intervention program to some other program constitutes a change in services. Section 639 in Part C requires written prior notice to parents whenever a service provider proposes to change placement or services.

These state plan requirements address the need for state, county, and local agency officials to prepare whatever interagency agreements or other procedures are necessary to ensure the transition of any individual toddler from a Part C program to a Part B preschool program or other program is smooth.

On a more individual level, each child's IFSP contains a statement of "the steps to be taken supporting the transition of the toddler with a disability to preschool or other appropriate services" (section 636[d][8]). If an IEP is used for a two-year-old about to turn three, the IEP must contain a similar statement (Schrag, 1990c). That is because IEPs may be used in place of IFSPs, and vice versa, only if all required elements appear in the document.

Parents and Transition from Part C

Guidance for parents in transition planning was offered by Fowler, Chandler, Johnson, and Stella (1988) and by Hanline and Knowlton (1988). The Fowler et al. process used two interviews, one during the fall and one during the spring preceding the transition to preschool. In the fall interview, parents identify priorities and concerns, which early intervention staff then use to plan transition. The spring interview is more specific (with exit to preschool just a few months away) and focuses on selecting one preschool program and making transition arrangements to it. The Hanline and Knowlton (1988) checklist helps parents assess their family's readiness for transition and provides a basis for family-professional discussions. The twelve-item checklist identifies those specific areas in which parents need additional information. Many preschools publish their own guides for use with parents during the preplacement transition period. Whatever materials are used, the critical element is providing families with information that not only allows them to choose a specific program but also to receive both factual and emotional reassurance that their child's needs will be met.

Noonan and Kilgo (1987) suggested that parents may wish to become transition coordinators themselves. They noted that learning how to negotiate transitions is an important step in parental empowerment, as parents assume responsibility for their own child. Parents-as-coordinators, then, are consistent with the family-focused philosophy of ECSE. Parents who are coordinators are also positioned to advocate for exactly those services in the receiving program that are most important to them. Finally, Noonan and Kilgo suggested, parents-as-coordinators may reduce family stress because they are more in control of the transition process. Wolery (1989), while agreeing with these ideals, cautioned that to qualify as coordinators, parents must be knowledgeable about available programs and services, sophisticated about their rights under the IDEA, and skilled at negotiating with public agencies.

The legislative history of the IDEA indicates that Congress supports offering parents this option to be their own coordinators:

Parents may want to assume certain responsibilities while retaining a service coordinator provided by the system to provide other aspects of the service. Parent training centers are encouraged to provide training to parents to better enable them to carry out their parental roles.

It is not the Committee's intent that this amendment be construed to require a State to pay a parent to serve as the service coordinator of his or her own child and family in those instances where the parents have rejected all or a portion of the service coordination services available under Part H. However, it is the Committee's intent that a State may, at its discretion, decide, as a matter of State policy or practice, to pay a parent to be his or her own service coordinator or reimburse a parent for carrying out certain tasks.

In addition, a parent may become qualified to perform all of the service functions carried out by a service coordinator and provide the service coordination service for another family if the parent obtains appropriate training by qualified persons. (House Report 102-198, 1991, p. 19)

From Preschool to Elementary School

Aside from the requirement that IEPs be in effect prior to the beginning of a school year, there is no statutory requirement covering movement from preschool Part B programs to K–12 programs under Part B. (The same is true for transitions from nonpreschool community programs to K–12 schools.) However, as Fowler, Schwartz, and Atwater (1991) pointed out, this transition is no less important than those addressed in the IDEA. In fact, it may be more important, because while few, if any, states require programming for under-six children, virtually all require that children at or about six years of age be placed in formal public or private educational programs. Moving from one program to another produces stress for the family and for the child, as new relationships must be formed and new rules of behavior learned. Wolery (1989) explained that such transitions are stressful because so many changes are involved:

[T]he sending and receiving programs may differ in terms of location of services, schedule, transportation systems, staff members involved, manner and frequency with which communication with families occurs, contact with social support such as other families, cost of services, expectations for family participation, and many others. Further, the receiving program may hold many unknowns for the family. (p. 3)

Fowler et al. (1991) noted that information about the receiving program and the behaviors necessary for success there can help to inform preschool curricula. "The logic of future environmental surveys," they said, "is straightforward: Look to the next environment to identify required skills, and use these skills to set goals and objectives for the current program" (p. 137). They cautioned, however, that while teaching such skills smoothes the transition, acquisition of these skills "must be viewed as optimal goals, not as behavioral prerequisites for placement in that setting" (p. 137). Figure 8.7 summarizes the key steps Fowler et al. (1991) recommended.

Particularly helpful to young children making the transition to kindergarten or first grade, Fowler et al. noted, are the ability to work independently and as a member of a small group, the ability to follow directions, and the ability to pay attention in class over sustained periods of time. Also helpful is action by preschool program staff to involve parents in planning the timing of exit from the preschool and in writing the next year's IEP if the child is eligible for continuing special education services. Ideally, both parents and sending program staff will visit the alternative placement options. Once a placement is decided, the receiving program staff should visit the current placement as well. These and other recommended practices are outlined in Repetto and Correa (1996).

1. Parents and program staff jointly decide what criteria will be used upon exit from preschool.

2. Program staff discuss with family members the family's role in transition, including consent for release of information.

3. Program staff alert the receiving agency (local education agency, kindergarten, or elementary school) about the need for planning meeting(s).

4. A multidisciplinary team does an assessment of the child to document current level of educational and related performance.

5. The receiving program staff establishes eligibility.

6. The IEP team develops the IEP in consultation with the family (it must be "in effect" prior to start of school year).

7. The team selects a placement from a continuum of appropriate placement options. This includes a visit to each by the family.

8. The sending program transfers records, with prior written parental permission, to the receiving program.

9. Child and family visit receiving program.

10. Sending program and family follow up with the receiving program to ensure "goodness of fit."

—adapted from Fowler et al. (1991), with author permission

FIGURE 8.7 Planning transition from preschool

Summary

Individualizing services for young children and their families is perhaps the greatest challenge facing ECSE programs. The IDEA prescribes that the process begin with evaluation and assessment, to identify the child's unique needs and strengths, after which a formal written document is prepared outlining the needs, services to be provided, and means of monitoring progress. Parents and ECSE staff should work as a team to develop these plans. The law offers sufficient flexibility so that families desiring to receive services from the program may do so throughout the birth-to-five period. It also provides that services be appropriate, that is, meet the individual needs of the child and, when suitable, the family's needs to enhance the child's development. These steps are statutorily required so that ECSE services are both individualized and appropriate, these being the two most important characteristics of ECSE services.

In most instances the early childhood years feature several critical transitions: Some young children move from hospital-based programs to home- and/or center-based early intervention programs; some move from early intervention to preschool programs; others move from early intervention to respite, community health, or other noneducational programs. At the age of five or six, all young children with disabilities move into kindergarten or first grade. These transitions must be planned well in advance and should feature strong family participation. Although such transitions may be made more smooth and effective by teaching skills and behaviors needed in the next environment, mastery of such skills should not be made a prerequisite for placement into the next setting.

Parents may reject or postpone any transition except the last. State laws in all fifty states require that children begin formal education at or about six years of age. Because similar laws are very unusual for children under six, the parental option of declining or delaying services for such children must be respected.

Although the field places great importance on the principle of individualization, ECSE as a profession—and individual programs from coast to coast—struggle to translate this ideal into an everyday reality, much as other EC programs do (Bredekamp, 1987). These and related program design issues are the topic of the next chapter.

QUESTIONS FOR REFLECTION

1. How does individualization of services draw from what we know about "aptitude-treatment interactions"?

2. What questions does the multidisciplinary assessment of infants and toddlers seek to answer?

3. Why are IFSPs to be reviewed twice yearly, while IEPs are to be reviewed annually?

4. Why could it help to include in an IFSP services that the IDEA will not cover?

5. Why is the early intervention program responsible for planning transition for children about to turn three years of age?

6. What are the IDEA requirements if a program elects to continue to use an IFSP after a child turns three years of age?

7. Who *must* be at an IEP meeting?

8. The U.S. Department of Education has adopted a broad interpretation of the meaning of "educational performance" as described in IEPs. What is included in this broad definition?

9. In your own words, what does "appropriate" mean?

10. Which kinds of "transition" are described in IEPs and IFSPs—and which kinds are *not*?

Service Delivery

[W]hat is most important is not a consensus about whether DAP [Developmentally Appropriate Practice] or ECSE offers more appropriate frameworks for the education of young children with disabilities, but rather, a consensus about the specific aspects of implementing high quality programs that are appropriate for all young children, regardless of developmental level or individual needs. These include programmatic issues such as how to

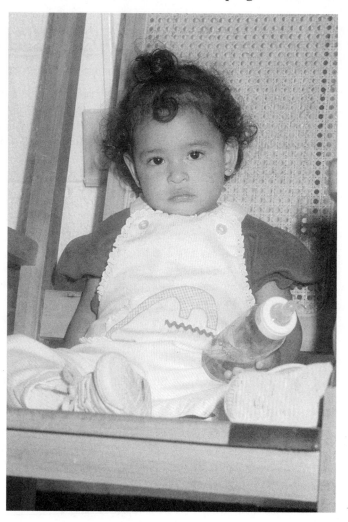

arrange environments, how teachers should interact, how programs should be monitored, and how data describing programs must be used to inform parents about their effectiveness in meeting children's needs. (Carta, Atwater, Schwartz, & McConnell, 1993, p. 243)

OVERVIEW

Early childhood special education (ECSE) is far more challenging today than anyone could have envisioned just a few years ago. The goals ECSE strives to reach are many, the needs of families and children diverse, and the resources to meet them limited. ECSE programs seek to empower families, to individualize services for both families and young children, to coordinate delivery of a broad range of services across many agencies, and, while doing all these things, to practice deeply held beliefs about what is right and good.

The family focus that most ECSE programs strive to implement broadens tremendously the scope and breadth of needs; different families bring program staff sharply contrasting resources, priorities, and concerns. Staff must also contend with the many unique needs of children with cognitive, physical, social or emotional, adaptive, and communication disabilities, delays, and deviations. The multidisciplinary approach ECSE programs value adds yet another dimension to this complexity, as professionals trained in unidisciplinary and child-centered techniques must adapt to cross-disciplinary, family-focused service delivery.

This chapter opens by reviewing child eligibility criteria. IDEA-funded services may *only* be provided to eligible children. The chapter then considers program curricula, both for infants and toddlers and for preschoolers. A wide variety of curriculum models is also available for adoption by ECSE programs.

A lively controversy in the field of ECSE concerns what we might call "the place of place." The statute expresses a congressional preference that early intervention services take place in what the law calls "natural environments" and that preschool special education services be provided in the "least restrictive environment." These statutory preferences are being interpreted by some to support full inclusion. Each ECSE program needs to examine its practices and determine to what extent movement toward inclusion is consistent with the best interests of the children and families it serves. The principle of inclusion suggests, too, that the entire question of how program services are structured—as separate systems or as integral components of larger systems—must be decided as well. It is these "place" issues that are discussed in this chapter.

More than occasionally, values that ECSE professionals hold dear conflict with one another. For example, families have the right under Part C to decline or postpone any services, both for the family itself and for the child. Such decisions may cause consternation among ECSE professionals who anticipate deleterious consequences if services are not provided immediately. In Part C, the family's desires prevail; the fact that a program offers, and wants to provide, certain services must yield to family opposition. Part B's dispute resolution process affords family and program personnel alike recourse to hearing officers and, if needed, judicial determinations. Other instances of value conflicts are discussed later in this chapter.

Ethical principles may also conflict with regulatory, administrative, and budgetary realities. Fully implemented programs based on individualization of services, family-centered approaches, and integrated service delivery may, at times, actually violate program rules or state guidelines, as when persons not certified to do so select test instruments. Similarly, time and other constraints may prevent services from being provided in a truly individualized manner. Most ECSE programs offer a specific kind of program and a particular range of services. Adding new services—let alone entire new programs—may not be feasible financially. ECSE workers must consider these real-world practical issues in deciding how to implement the legislative mandates to serve children under six with disabilities.

ELIGIBILITY

Let us now review the eligibility criteria outlined briefly in Chapter 2 as we prepare to discuss the subtleties of program operation in greater depth. Infants and toddlers are eligible for Part C services if they have a developmental delay or an established condition (disability). Children from birth to age two inclusive residing in states that recognize at-risk status may also be eligible for early intervention services if they are at risk according to the state definition. Preschoolers are eligible for Part B services if they satisfy the federal definition of "children with disabilities" (one of ten conditions requiring special education and related services) or, in states opting to use developmental delays, if they meet state criteria for delay. Some states use the term "preschool child with a disability" or some variation of that rather than disability labels. At-risk children are not eligible under Part B.

Part C

In all participating states, an infant or toddler with an "established condition" (disability) or a state-defined delay is automatically eligible for services. In addition, if a state elects to serve at-risk infants and toddlers, those children who meet the state's at-risk criteria also are eligible. The critical point is that *all* infants or toddlers in the birth-to-thirty-six-month age range with state-listed conditions or state-defined delays are eligible for services in participating states. Part C is an entitlement program, available on an equal basis to all infants and toddlers residing in participating states and meeting the criteria (Schrag, 1990a). If a state, for example, were to define "developmental delay" as performance two or more standard deviations (S.D.) below the age-appropriate means in one or more development areas, *any* infant or toddler scoring 2+ S.D. below the mean in physical, cognitive, communication, social or emotional, and/or adaptive development is eligible.

In this sense, early intervention programs performing work under contract to the state do *not* have discretion in determining eligibility; rather, state criteria in effect make that decision. That is not to say that individual programs may not decline to serve a given infant or toddler; they may do so if they do not have the facilities, personnel, or other resources to meet the infant or toddler's needs. It is to say that *the state* may not refuse to serve the infant or toddler. If a particular early intervention program cannot provide services, the state is obligated to find one that can and will.

Evaluating infants and toddlers to establish eligibility may involve verifying that they have established conditions as defined in the state's Part C plan. If so, they are presumptively eligible. Children with diagnosed conditions need not demonstrate actual delays; the diagnosis is sufficient to establish eligibility. For example, if Down syndrome is classified by the state as an established condition, medical records or other documentation by a physician that the infant or toddler has Down syndrome suffices to establish eligibility. Because established conditions are medical conditions known typically or even invariably to lead to developmental delays, there is no need also to document such a delay. Although states vary considerably in the conditions they recognize as "established" (Shackelford, 1992; Harbin, Gallagher, & Terry, 1991), some conditions are widely accepted. Shonkoff and Meisels (1991) listed some of the most common:

> [C]hromosomal disorders, such as Down syndrome or Fragile-X syndrome; inborn errors of metabolism, such as Tay-Sachs disease or Hurler syndrome; other genetic disorders, such as terous sclerosis; cerebral palsy and other neuromuscular disorders; disorders secondary to congenital

infections, such as symptomatic cytomegalovirus, toxoplasmosis, and human immunodeficiency virus; severe attachment disorders, such as autism; sensory disorders; and disorders secondary to exposure to toxic substances, such as intrauterine alcohol and cocaine. (p. 22)

If, however, there is no established condition, eligibility depends on documentation of a developmental delay, as defined in the state's Part C plan. States have broad discretion in deciding what kinds of delays to recognize. Tests, other procedures, and informed clinical opinion must document the existence of a delay in one or more of the five domains. Shonkoff and Meisels (1991) noted that tests and other procedures often used to establish such delays have "very questionable validity" (p. 23). They urged:

[R]ather than relying solely on standard deviations or percentage delays, a more appropriate approach would be a functional one that ascertains a child's and family's current abilities and resources and uses this additional information to interpret the clinical significance, not just the statistical significance, of test scores. (p. 23)

Serving at-risk children is up to the state. Shonkoff and Meisels (1991) cautioned that the at-risk designation should be applied only after considerable study. They noted that outcomes for children usually cannot be predicted from a single risk factor; at least two, and preferably three, risk factors should be present before a child is designated at risk of becoming disabled unless early intervention services are provided. In addition, risk categories and the screening instruments and other assessment procedures and tests used with infants and toddlers have, Shonkoff and Meisels noted, "relatively modest predictability" (p. 21). For that reason, they strongly recommended "serial screening" (see Chapter 7). Bowman (1992) discussed at-risk factors in a paper titled, "Who Is at Risk for What and Why." One possible combination of risk factors is parental undereducation, poverty, and ethnic or racial minority group status.

More states accept biological risk factors, such as low birthweight, chronic lung disease, or failure to thrive, than accept environmental risk factors, such as maternal mental retardation

Infants and toddlers with disabilities have state-defined "established conditions" or state-established "developmental delays." Some states also serve "at risk" infants and toddlers.

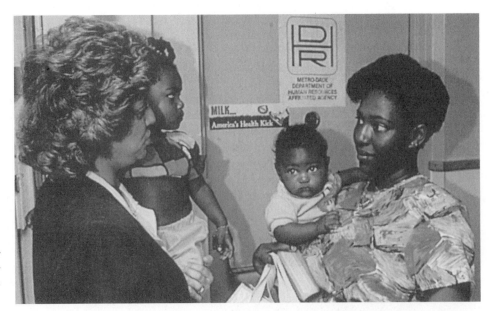

or mental illness, parental substance abuse, and extreme poverty. Arcia et al. (Arcia & Gallagher, 1993; Arcia, Keyes, Gallagher, & Herrick, 1992) have shown that such environmental factors are particularly prominent among members of racial and ethnic minority groups, who are among the "traditionally underserved" segments that the IDEA designates as priorities for service under Part C. Craig Ramey et al. (Martin, Ramey, & Ramey, 1990; Ramey & Ramey, 1992) documented the high incidence of mild retardation in particular among families with such environmental risk factors.

For these and other reasons, Congress encourages states to serve at-risk children (Silverstein, 1989). However, for budgetary reasons, most states are not currently planning to do so. Some states have to date declined to serve at-risk children because the evidence at hand is that most such children will develop normally. Shonkoff and Meisels (1991), for example, stated that "a significant proportion of children who meet the criteria for biological or environmental risk are likely to do well developmentally, with or without early intervention services" (p. 24). They went further, stating, "We now know that the majority of children who fall within many of the traditionally accepted categories of biological or environmental risk (e.g., those who were born prematurely or those who are raised by young, unmarried mothers with low incomes) will develop normally" (p. 22).

Part B

Any child aged three to five inclusive who has one or more of the disabilities that are recognized by the U.S. Department of Education—mental retardation, hearing impairments including deafness, speech or language impairments, visual impairments including blindness, serious emotional disturbance, orthopedic impairments, autism, traumatic brain injury, other health impairments, specific learning disabilities, deaf-blindness, or multiple disabilities—and who for that reason needs special education and related services is eligible for Part B services.

Two additional groups of young children may be served. Children who are two years of age but who will turn three during a school year may be served under Part B. In states that elect to use developmental delays in preschool services, children with documented, state-defined delays in any of the five domains are eligible. The state's Part B plan would indicate the kinds of delays considered to establish eligibility for services; through tests, other procedures, and informed clinical opinion, professionals document the existence of a delay in one or more of the five areas.

As is the case under Part C, the state may not deny services to any eligible preschool-age child with a disability. An individual program, however, may decline to provide services to such a child. This reflects the reality that some programs simply are not equipped to serve some children.

CURRICULUM

The word **curriculum**, understood broadly, refers to the following:

- *Who* to teach (the child? the family? both?)
- *What* to teach (content—facts and sequence)
- *How* to teach it (philosophy, methods)

curriculum is a planned sequence of activities, including both content and process, through which educators change children's behavior. Curriculum is a vehicle for reaching goals and objectives as identified in individualized family service plans and individualized education programs—an ordered arrangement of individually selected learning experiences that respond to children's particular needs.

- *Accommodations* to make for children's disabilities (devices, procedures, and so on, allowing children to "hear" despite deafness, "see" despite blindness, "move" despite physical disability, and so on)
- *Materials* to use (tangibles, paper, and so on)
- *Room layout* (activity centers and so on)

Understood in this way, a curriculum represents decisions about what is important for young children to learn: Should early childhood learning be about preacademics or should it be about play and social interaction? A curriculum also reflects decisions about how early childhood special educators should act in the classroom or play center: Should teachers and interventionists be active in instructing children or should they remain in the background as children teach themselves?

Thus, curriculum is a very big subject. It is the subject of entire texts. Rather than attempt to treat curriculum comprehensively here, an impossible task, this chapter focuses upon key issues facing ECSE. The reader is referred to booklength treatments for additional information. Among those recommended as resources for ECSE personnel are:

Wortham, S. (1998). *Early Childhood Curriculum.* Columbus, OH: Merrill. The second edition of this text offers specific suggestions for activities that are designed to stimulate development in the key domains (cognitive, social or emotional, physical, and so on). The book's strength is in nondirective strategies.

Bigge, J. (1988). *Curriculum-based Instruction for Special Education Students.* Mountain View, CA: Mayfield Publishing. This text is especially strong on direct instructional techniques for use with children who have severe disabilities or delays.

Goodman, J. (1992). *When Slow Is Fast Enough.* New York: Guilford Press. While not a curriculum textbook as such, this book is very enlightening as to actual practice in preschool special education programs serving children with moderate retardation and other disabilities. Goodman offers a memorable portrayal of what special educators do on a day-in and day-out basis with three- to five-year-olds who have special needs.

In very general terms, the basic choice facing early childhood special educators is between "direct instruction" and "developmentally appropriate practice" (DAP). Directive strategies feature a strong role for the educator or interventionist; the teacher decides what the content will be, individualizes both content and process to respond to the unique needs of each child, and delivers much of the instruction personally in an active manner. DAP, by contrast, has the educator in a facilitative role; the teacher decides upon content (by, for example, selecting the materials, placing them strategically throughout the room, and so on) but from that point forward allows the children to individualize the ways in which they experience that content in self-directed learning activities. These alternatives are not necessarily mutually exclusive (Bailey, 1997). Early childhood (EC) educators and ECSE personnel alike are finding ways to fashion a third, integrated approach that features the best aspects of each philosophy.

The state of the art at the turn of the century is one of ECSE personnel remaining dissatisfied by the commercial alternatives available to them (Bruder, 1997). Early interventionists and special educators alike find that they must pick and choose among competing packages. The balance of this chapter's section on curriculum considers the issues around which early childhood special educators are basing their choices.

Curriculum is a planned sequence of activities, including both content and process, through which educators aim to change children's behavior. Wolery and Sainato (1993), in their curriculum section of the DEC recommended practices document, suggested that curriculum includes content (behaviors and skills, whether academic, adaptive, or other), methods of delivering this content, and ways of individualizing it for particular children. Cole, Dale, and Mills (1991) emphasized the importance of matching different methods of instruction on the one hand to children's individual characteristics on the other. Examining learning by language-delayed children, they found no direct effect for type of instruction (direct versus interactive), but they did note an important interaction: Children with relatively lesser language delays seemed to learn more from direct instruction, while those with comparatively greater language delays appeared to learn more with interactive approaches. Those findings were opposite from what previous studies had suggested. The work of Wolery, Sainato, Cole, Dale, and Mills cautions us to individualize content according to what actually helps children to learn.

Curriculum is a vehicle for reaching goals and objectives as identified in individualized family service plans (IFSPs) and individualized education programs (IEPs): It is an ordered arrangement of individually selected learning experiences that responds to children's particular needs. Both NAEYC, in its DAP guidelines, and DEC, in its recommended practices, urged that curriculum decisions reflect the principles of individualization, family involvement, cultural competency and sensitivity, and fulfillment of the children's needs.

Carta et al. (1993) pointed out that assessment and curriculum must be integrated. When, for example, ECSE programs use such instruments as the Learning Accomplishments Profile (LAP) (Sanford & Zelman, 1987) or the HICOMP Preschool Curriculum and its companion Track Record (Willoughby-Herb & Neisworth, 1982), they will find direct indicators of what should be included in curricula for young children with disabilities. Johnson and Johnson (1993), however, cautioned that the LAP and HICOMP assessments look only at behaviors that result from intervention. They urged that ECSE programs study at least as carefully the processes behind those products, that is, "spontaneously occurring behaviors in naturalistic contexts" (p. 256).

Graham and Bryant (1993) emphasized that few curricula have been validated empirically and that no one curriculum has emerged as superior to others for use in ECSE programs. After studying more than one hundred ECSE programs throughout the nation, they advocated choosing curricula not to respond narrowly to a child's unique needs but rather to respond to the child holistically. In other words, although a child with cerebral palsy may need speech and language pathology services, curricular interventions must also meet this child's many other developmental needs. Graham and Bryant suggested that generalization be a key component of any curriculum. Many young children with disabilities have difficulty generalizing skills and behaviors to new settings (Lovaas [1987] was particularly concerned about this problem in his work with young children who have autism). Graham and Bryant therefore suggested finding ways for the curriculum to stimulate generalization.

Goodman and Bond (1993), examining the process of writing IEPs, made the same recommendation, but emphasized that the skills or behaviors selected, for generalization training or for other purposes, should be worthwhile activities. That is, the mere fact that assessment or evaluation shows that a child cannot perform a given developmental task does not make that skill important to teach. Goodman and Bond were particularly insistent on this point:

> *In a review of the literature and visits to 20 early intervention programs in 10 states, we repeatedly found IEP goals and objectives drawn from a similar set of developmental inventories. . . . Teachers, in writing their IEPs, tend to select the same areas as the developmental inventories and use the same items for objectives (e.g., recognition of colors, numbers, letters, shapes, simple dichotomous concepts like* big *and* little*). This is to be expected because, with the exception of the Batelle [Developmental Inventory], the authors of the inventories advocate using the same items for evaluation and curriculum objectives.* (p. 416)

They continued by asking, rhetorically, whether scissor cutting is developmentally important for anything other than more expert scissor cutting. The example may be simplistic, but the concept is not: The fact that a particular behavior has been identified in research as an indicator of development does not, in and of itself, mean that this behavior belongs in EC or ECSE curricula. And the fact that test developers included a task in an instrument does not, itself, mean that this particular behavior is important for young children to learn. Goodman and Bond (1993) emphasized that ECSE teachers should select curricula and specific instruction items for their relevance to children, rather than mindlessly "teaching to tests."

Curriculum and Individualization

However this integration of assessment and curriculum occurs, the aim is individualization of services. Graham and Bryant (1993) commented that individualization remained more a goal than a reality in most ECSE programs they visited. Wolery (1991) and Cole, Dale, Mills, and Jenkins (1993) concurred that individualization is a value prized by ECSE professionals but one that is often more notable by its absence than its presence in actual day-to-day practice. DAP, for example, recommended infant-to-caregiver ratios of 3-to-1 or 4-to-1 and group sizes under ten (Bredekamp, 1987). Certainly, when young children have disabilities or delays, even lower ratios are desirable so that the curriculum may be adjusted to each child's unique needs. One way of translating the ideal of individualized services into practice, Bredekamp (1987) suggested, is to use volunteers—foster grandparents, students and interns from local university programs, and parents—as teacher aides. The guidelines also recommended that peer arrangements, in which four- to five-year-olds work one-on-one with infants and toddlers, can help both older and younger children.

The severe budgetary pressures that many ECSE programs face render such unpaid assistance necessary if children are actually to receive the individualized programs promised them in theory. With staff salaries comprising as much as 70 percent to 90 percent of child-care program budgets (Graham & Bryant, 1993), there may be no other way to realize the small group sizes and child-teacher ratios recommended by NAEYC and DEC. Bredekamp (1993b) cautioned that state personnel regulations may limit the extent to which such arrangements may be pursued. Individual ECSE programs should check with state Part C lead agencies and state education agencies before making extensive use of unpaid volunteer assistance, to ensure that their licensing or other approval is not jeopardized.

EC Versus ECSE Curricula

There are, as has been suggested earlier, differences between EC and ECSE programs. ECSE programs tend to develop IFSPs and IEPs based on identified needs of children and their families. There is an orientation toward those needs and the services that meet them.

EC programs generally look less to children's individual needs and more to the developmental needs of all children in a given age range. McLean and Odom (1993) suggested that ECSE curricula in general place more emphasis upon performance of behaviors and skills, while EC curricula attend more to children's thinking processes. Graham and Bryant (1993) observed, "While similar themes are common to both orientations (e.g., independence, adaptation, contingent responsiveness, social competence, individualization), developmental and behavioral ideologies have often been translated into distinctly diverse approaches toward teaching and learning for the child with special needs" (p. 31). This diversity of approach has often been described as a contrast between informal, child-oriented, and permissive EC programs and formal, professional-oriented, and behavioral ECSE programs. Said Graham and Bryant:

> *Practices used in early childhood education often vary from those used in early childhood special education. Theoretically, early childhood practices tend to reflect the developmental principles of Piaget, Erikson, and Montessori; early childhood special education is grounded in the behavioral constructs of Skinner, Pavlov, and Watson.* (p. 31)

That was, of course, an overly generalized statement. Many EC programs use behavioral approaches, and many ECSE programs model themselves after Piaget. To illustrate the point, incidental teaching, or child-initiated approaches during which the teacher takes advantage of opportunities a child presents to help the child learn new things, is an approach more associated with EC than with ECSE. Yet, as Carta et al. (1993) pointed out, it was developed by two behaviorists working in ECSE-type settings (Hart & Risley, 1968). Nonetheless, there is much truth in Graham and Bryant's observations. Service delivery strategies and tactics that are effective in helping many young children with disabilities do tend to have a strong behavioral orientation. To take just one example among many, Lovaas (1987) showed that young children with autism can achieve far more in a highly structured environment than previously had been believed. This finding raises the question of structure in the curriculum.

Curriculum and Structure

Graham and Bryant (1993) stated that research "repeatedly [has] shown the effectiveness of programs that are more structured and directive for children with severe disabilities" (p. 33). Cole et al. (1993), however, raised questions about popular assumptions of how program structure interacts with severity of children's disabilities. Educators have assumed that children with more severe disabilities and those who function at a lower level benefit most from structured, direct instruction, while less severely disabled children and those who function at a higher level learn better from less structured, more interactive learning opportunities (Snow, 1989). But Jenkins, Cole, Dale, and Mills (1989) found the opposite effects in a preschool population. And further research with a more typical ECSE population by the same authors (Cole et al., 1993) produced the same results: Relatively higher-functioning children with disabilities did better in structured, direct-instruction (DI) programs, while relatively lower-functioning children learned more in an interactive approach. They concluded:

> *The conventional wisdom that slower children should receive DI, and relatively higher functioning children should be placed in more interactive, cognitively based programs, should be reconsidered.* (p. 26)

Cole et al. suggested that more structured, DI approaches require children to understand and follow specific instructions, while interactive approaches allow children who cannot participate effectively in such structured curricula nonetheless to benefit from spontaneously occurring incidents. Perhaps the best guidance for ECSE programs is not to assume that any given approach is the best practice for all children, and not to select curricula according to assumptions about their effectiveness with children functioning at different levels of disability. Rather, curricula designed and selected to respond to individual needs of children are likely to prove more successful. Such an approach may require more planning, but the evidence is that no single curriculum or type of curriculum has yet been shown to be more effective with ECSE populations than others.

Curriculum Choices

ECSE curricula include instruction in language, cognitive, social, and both fine motor and gross motor development. Some are targeted toward specific populations. These include the Early Partners curriculum for preterm, low-birthweight infants (Sparling, Lewis, & Neuwirth, 1993); the Learning Through Play curriculum for children with motor impairments (Fewell & Vadasy, 1983); and the SKI*HI curriculum for children with hearing impairments (Clark & Watkins, 1985).

Other curricula are suitable for more general ECSE populations such as the two examples already mentioned in this chapter: the LAP (Sanford & Zelman, 1987) and the HICOMP Preschool Curriculum (Willoughby-Herb & Neisworth, 1982). Others include the Carolina Curriculum (Johnson-Martin, Jens, & Attermeier, 1986); the Portage Guide to Early Education (Bluma, Shearer, Frohman, & Hillard, 1976); the Hawaii Early Learning Profile (HELP) (Furuno, O'Reilly, Hosaka, Inatsuka, Allman, & Ziesloft, 1985); and the cognitive-linguistic infant intervention of Dunst (Dunst, 1981).

Specific curricula may, of course, be adapted from general EC curricula such as the "partners for learning" and "learning games" publications by Sparling and Lewis (1979, 1985); the "active learning" program by Cryer, Harms, and Bourland (1987a, b); and Badger's (1981) "joy of learning" plan for infants and toddlers. Fewell has stressed play-based curricula (Fewell, 1991; Fewell & Glick, 1993).

DEC's recommended practices suggested that ECSE professionals select or design curricula that, in the words of curriculum section authors Wolery and Sainato (1993), "cause rapid learning and use of important skills" (p. 53). They added: "[O]nly strategies should be used that result in rapid learning. Such learning often provides feelings of success and mastery, and it saves time for other goals" (pp. 53–54). They suggested that a variety of behaviorist and naturalistic approaches have attracted research support and that such approaches—including response prompting, differential reinforcement, and response shaping, as well as adult responsiveness to child behavior and milieu or naturalistic teaching—may be recommended practices.

The concern Wolery and Sainato demonstrated for rapid learning reflected a decision commonly made in ECSE programs across the nation: The unique needs of young children with disabilities are such that educator control, including use of the principles of applied behavior analysis, is appropriate because it "saves time," to quote Wolery and Sainato. Carta et al. (1993), in the chapter's opening quotation, expressed a similar philosophy, saying that curriculum decisions come first. ECSE programs frequently determine that preacademics are critical for young children with disabilities. Following from that decision are others about how the day is structured, how the teacher behaves, and how materials are used. Stating it differently, ECSE programs do not reach abstract conclusions about the relative merits of child-initiated versus educator-initiated instruction. Rather, the pressing need for time to teach preacademics dictates the approach to be adopted.

Coming from a background in EC, Joan Goodman (1992) was struck by the ways in which this played out in the twenty ECSE programs she visited in ten states. These programs worked with preschool-age children with moderate mental retardation. Summarizing her observations, Goodman wrote:

> *Teachers are rarely sidetracked from their serious and earnest pursuit of the curriculum [selected largely from developmental checklists]. Despite their difficult charge and charges, they maintain a remarkably unflappable poise, mild-mannered but always in control of their children. . . . Teachers operate all day within this narrow, sedate, "professional" behavioral range and expect children to do likewise: sit, listen, respond when spoken to ("use your words"), stay "on tasks." . . .*
>
> *The problem is that moderately retarded children have difficulty meeting these expectations—both academic and behavioral. They do not catch on to preacademics, forget the right answers they may have given the day before, and are restless with the work demands. . . . Teachers, therefore, must work very hard to accomplish their goals. They cannot, Summerhill style, just put out the materials and let the children loose.* (pp. 89–90)

THE "PLACE" OF PLACE

The question of *where* services should be delivered is an emotional one in the field of ECSE. This long-running controversy began in elementary and secondary education, where it generated a heated debate that has yet to still. In a recent review of the issues in K–12 special education, James Kauffman (1993) used words like "clangorous" and "rancorous" to describe journal articles and convention speeches on the question of where. He suggested that the field has forgotten the "place" of place, its relative importance in service delivery:

> *Place has varied literal and metaphorical meanings, including location, perspective, status, and power. The issue of where students are taught has been at the center of efforts to restructure special education. Physical place has been the hub of controversy because it defines proximity to age peers with certain characteristics. A student's being in the same location as others has been assumed to be a necessary if not sufficient condition for receiving educational opportunity. Physical place can be measured easily, can be reduced to simple images, and has immediate and deep emotional overtones; thus it is fertile ground for fanaticism.* (p. 7)

Kauffman deplored that "fanaticism." He pointed out that the very core of the Individuals with Disabilities Education Act (IDEA) is that services be individualized for children. After all, the statute's statement of purpose ensures children with disabilities "a free appropriate public education which emphasizes special education and related services designed to meet their unique needs" (IDEA, section 601[c]). He added that while special education has many problems and needs improvement in many different areas, the location in which services occur is hardly the fulcrum for improvements. While many K–12 children with disabilities do feel stigmatized, this is not, Kauffman suggested, principally because of where they are served. The same comments could be made about ECSE. It is equally important in ECSE that each child be looked at as a unique individual and that services be specially designed to meet that child's needs. We can, and do, alleviate stigmatism in ECSE programs by reducing or even eliminating the use of labels, by looking to and talking about children's characteristics other than their disabilities, and by writing into IFSPs and IEPs the resources and strengths of children and families, as well as their needs. Location is not the only way in which we can be sensitive to these issues. Place is important, but it has its place.

Natural Environments

The words "natural environment" (NE) were added to Part C in 1991. The term appears in three places. First, the statute now defines the term "early intervention services" as including services that

> to the maximum extent appropriate, are provided in natural environments, including the home, and community settings in which children without disabilities participate. (section 632[4][G])

The second mention of "natural environment" occurs in section 635(a)(16), where states are told to ensure services are provided in nonnatural environments *only* when appropriate services may not be delivered in a natural environment. Finally, section 636(d)(5) states that IFSPs include "a statement of the natural environments in which early intervention services shall appropriately be provided." Notice that Congress took care in all three instances to subordinate the NE preference to the requirement that early intervention services be appropriate. The 1991 House Report explained:

> The term "natural environments" refers to settings that are natural or normal for age peers who have no apparent disability. The descriptor "to the maximum extent appropriate" is not meant to qualify the appropriateness of the natural environment as the primary setting for the child. Rather, it is intended to allow flexibility and individualized programming for the infant or toddler with a disability.
>
> For example, the primary natural environment for an infant or toddler is the home. Where group settings are utilized, the infant or toddler with a disability should be placed in groups with age peers without disabilities, such as play groups, day care centers, or whatever typical group setting exists for infants and toddlers without disabilities. (*House Report 102-198,* 1991)

Nothing in Part C precludes the family from deciding what is the natural environment for the infant or toddler; parental discretion would make sense, given that parents know their children far better than intervention personnel do. Parental determination of what is the natural environment also fits in well with the ECSE field's emphasis on family-focused programming (DEC Task Force, 1993).

Least Restrictive Environments

The words "least restrictive environment" (LRE) appear in section 612(a)(5), where state education agencies are told what assurances to provide in their triennial state plans so as to qualify for Part B funding. The state must assure the U.S. Department of Education that

> to the maximum extent appropriate, children with disabilities . . . are educated with children who are not disabled, and that special classes, separate schooling, or other removal of

children with disabilities from the regular educational environment occurs only when the nature or severity of the disability is such that education in regular classes with the use of supplementary aids and services cannot be achieved satisfactorily. (section 612[a][5])

This language is somewhat ambiguous. First, the preference for placement in the LRE is declared subordinate to the requirement for appropriate services. Thus, the LRE language is not an unqualified mandate. On the other hand, the subsequent language on removal does appear to suggest that children should be placed in regular settings, with necessary support services, unless appropriate education cannot be provided in such settings. This suggestion appears to be the principal basis for the "inclusion" movement, which is discussed in the next section.

The potential of integration in preschool settings has excited the attention of many researchers in ECSE. Among those examining LRE in preschools are McEvoy and Odom (1987), Odom and McEvoy (1990), and Strain (1990). McGinnis and Goldstein (1990) discussed "skill streaming" with preschool children, to prepare them for mainstreaming in kindergarten and elementary school. Despite all the attention preschool LRE has attracted, misconceptions about it and about what the law requires remain widespread.

A recent statement by the U.S. Department of Education makes clear that the intent is to ensure appropriate services. The October 30, 1992, "Notice of Policy Guidance" on the primacy of appropriateness over LRE is worth repeating here. The statement dealt with the meaning of "free appropriate public education" (FAPE) for children who are deaf, but the implications are far broader:

> *The provision of FAPE is paramount, and the individual placement determination about LRE is to be considered within the context of FAPE. . . . Any setting, including a regular classroom, that prevents a child who is deaf from receiving an appropriate education that meets his or her needs, including communication needs, is not the LRE for that individual child.* (U.S. Department of Education, 1992d, p. 49275)

With respect to removal of children from regular classes, which the statute restricts to instances in which services cannot be provided satisfactorily, the department added:

> *Just as placement in the regular educational setting is required when it is appropriate for the unique needs of a child who is deaf, so is removal from the regular classroom setting required when the child's needs cannot be met in that setting with the use of supplementary aids and services.* (U.S. Department of Education, 1992d, p. 49275)

What all of this means is that LRE is a *principle*, not a *place*. It is an idea that teaches ECSE workers to look first at a continuum of service or placement options and then to identify those that offer the services needed by a particular child and family. From among these "appropriate" placements, ECSE workers select the one that is most integrated. The principal test, then, is that of appropriate services; the IDEA ensures children an appropriate education, individually designed to meet their unique needs.

Inclusion

The principle of full inclusion is, in some respects, a logical extension of the ideals implicit in "natural environment" and "least restrictive environment." It arose in the late 1980s and early 1990s in response to the fact that children with severe disabilities were far less likely to be placed in integrated settings than were children with less severe disabilities (Biklen,

1985; Salisbury, 1991; Salisbury & Vincent, 1990). Its advocates insisted that children with severe disabilities have just as much right to integrated services as do children with mild or moderate disabilities (Manegold, 1994).

Inclusion is an ideal, a principle that builds upon the earlier "mainstreaming" (Guralnick, 1990; Klein, 1975) and "regular education initiative" (Will, 1986) movements. It differs from those approaches, however. Mainstreaming, particularly in the mid- to late 1970s and early 1980s, featured placement of children with disabilities in separate classrooms but integrated them in nonacademic activities such as recreation, lunch, gym, and so on. The regular education initiative advocated placing children with mild disabilities in regular classrooms and assigning responsibility for their instruction to regular classroom teachers; it did not, however, insist on such steps on behalf of children with severe disabilities. Inclusion, by contrast, recognizes no distinctions of severity and insists on placing all children in regular classrooms in neighborhood schools.

The inclusion approach has attracted considerable research interest. Ironically, however, the evidence seems to be that young children with mild, as opposed to severe, disabilities benefit more from inclusive settings than do children with severe disabilities. Cole et al. (1993) found cognitive and communication development gains in children with mild disabilities who were placed in inclusive settings. On the other hand, children with severe delays in development benefited more when placed in separate environments. Reviewing twenty-two papers on inclusion in ECSE settings, Buysse and Bailey (1993) reported that young children with disabilities appeared to make similar progress in either inclusive or noninclusive settings, in all but the social/emotional domain of development. That is, while the social development of young children with disabilities often accelerated when they were placed in settings with nondisabled children, their cognitive, communication, and motor development seemed to remain unaffected by type of placement. Practical realities often produce results very different from those envisioned by advocates of inclusion. In many instances, supportive services are provided only for the first few weeks; thereafter, child and teacher are left with little, if any, specialist support, producing anger and frustration in student and professional alike (Manegold, 1994).

Inclusion advocates are correct in stating that regardless of how severely disabled a child may be, she is entitled to services that do not compromise her liberty and that do not unduly stigmatize her. They are incorrect, however, in insisting that one placement or type of placement is appropriate for all children with disabilities. That view violates the IDEA's core principle of individualization of services. Inclusion advocates are also wrong in stating that children must be served in a particular place, regardless of unique need. That approach runs counter to the IDEA's cardinal principle of appropriateness.

However emotionally appealing, inclusion must be understood as a philosophy that goes beyond the IDEA. It is not something the law requires, or even promotes. Rather, the IDEA in its very essence is a law that looks at each child with a disability as being unique, with particular needs and strengths. The IDEA guarantees each eligible child the services that are appropriate. While movement of children with disabilities into regular settings is an admirable goal, it must be subsumed—as are all other values cherished by professionals and parents alike—to the IDEA's mandates of individualization and appropriateness. Children with disabilities should be served in integrated settings *only* when such placements benefit them.

Inclusion must also be understood as a misrepresentation of the ideals of the IDEA. Both NE and LRE support the act's overarching emphasis on individualization and appropriateness because both preferences are superseded by these higher-order mandates of individualization and appropriateness. Congress was at pains in PL 102-119, the 1991 amendments to the IDEA, to say that the NE preference is not intended to qualify appropriateness of services (*House Report 102-198,* 1992). Rather, NE guides services only to the extent that appropriateness is not compromised. LRE, similarly, is a principle, not a place, and it is subordinate to appropriateness (U.S. Department of Education, 1992d).

Inclusion, however, places the location of services above their appropriateness. Rather than suggesting, as does the IDEA, that ECSE professionals first evaluate children, identify needed services, and review a continuum of placement options to select the most integrated setting that is appropriate, the concept of inclusion suggests that children be placed in integrated settings irrespective of individual differences. It implies that children must first fail in such settings before other placement options will be considered.

Educators of deaf children have been particularly disturbed about inclusion. Donald F. Moores, editor of *American Annals of the Deaf,* wrote an editorial for a mid-1993 issue of that journal in which he pointed out that:

> *For many deaf children, the concept of total inclusion, as currently promulgated, could in reality be* exclusionary *in practice. Placing a deaf child in a classroom in physical contiguity to hearing children does not automatically provide equal access to education. In fact, it can be isolating, both academically and socially.* (Moores, 1993, p. 251; emphasis in original)

Chapman (1992) made much the same point with respect to another group of children: "For children with learning disabilities, whose needs have barely been met, inclusion in the mainstream seems like exclusion from remedial assistance" (p. 369).

Having said all of this, the concept of inclusion still has much merit. Provided that services in an integrated setting do meet all of the child's unique needs, inclusion of children with disabilities in regular classrooms offers social and other benefits. The keys, as always, are individualization and appropriateness.

Even so, practical realities often interfere. An obvious example is in the way EC programs are staffed. Wolery, Martin, Schroeder, Huffman, Venn, Holcombe, Brookfield, and Fleming (1994) surveyed 483 preschool programs across the United States. They found that very few settings serving children with and without disabilities employed *any* teachers with training in special education. Most had hired staff members with bachelor's degrees, not

The design and accessibility of outdoor environments are as important in ECSE programs as those of indoor facilities.

master's-trained professionals. Similarly, Bredekamp (1993b) was cautious about the extent to which this may be accomplished in the near future. She pointed out that as of 1993, only sixteen states required preservice training for child-care teachers "and even in those states, the amount of training required is embarrassingly minimal" (p. 268). She suggested that unless EC workers, on the whole, become much better trained, they will not be prepared to meet the special needs of children with disabilities.

Bredekamp also charged that "many states permit as many as seven or eight babies and eighteen to twenty preschoolers to be cared for by one untrained adult" (p. 268). Such ratios are not acceptable under many state Part C and Part B regulations. The IDEA insists that ECSE programs meet "the highest standards in the state" (section 635). Bredekamp's point that EC and ECSE must work together to improve state personnel standards in both areas is a good one. It is likely, however, that budgetary constraints will make the battle a challenging one in many states.

INDOOR AND OUTDOOR ENVIRONMENTS: ACCESSIBILITY

Graham and Bryant (1993) suggested that the way in which ECSE programs use space, materials, and activities to create environments suitable for learning by young children with disabilities is important. They noted that the Infant Toddler Environment Rating Scale (ITERS) (Harms, Cryer, & Clifford, 1989) and the Early Childhood Environment Rating Scale (ECERS) (Harms, Clifford, & Cryer, 1980) offer reliable and valid measures of children's settings. The ITERS and ECERS scales assess environments from the point of view of young children with no disabilities. Harms, Clifford, and Bailey (1986), however, offered additional ECERS items that look specifically at use of space and materials for children who have disabilities.

Remarkably little attention has been given in ECSE professional literature to the architectural design of program space. Young children with physical and sensory disabilities need accommodations that allow them to move about freely. Among the few efforts to provide ECSE programs with guidance on designing or retrofitting space are recommendations developed by a small federal agency, the U.S. **Architectural and Transportation Barriers Compliance Board (ATBCB)**, sometimes called the Access Board.

Architectural and Transportation Barriers Compliance Board (ATBCB) is a small independent federal agency charged with monitoring accessibility at many federal buildings. The agency sometimes is referred to as the Access Board.

Indoor Environments

In 1986, the ATBCB and the U.S. Department of Education (ATBCB/ED) worked together to prepare the board's *Recommendations for Accessibility to Serve Physically Handicapped Children in Elementary Schools.* This brief document was limited, as the title suggests, to design issues involved in helping elementary school students with physical disabilities. Six years later, North Carolina State University developed a set of *Recommendations for Accessibility Standards for Children's Environments* (Center for Accessible Housing, 1992). The ATBCB used these suggestions to prepare its own official guidelines for 1995. The 1992 Center for Accessible Housing and 1995 ATBCB specifications extended the 1986 ATBCB/ED recommendations to incorporate early childhood settings, that is, child-care centers, facilities serving young children, ECSE programs, and EC programs such as Head Start. The 1992 and 1995 guidelines also incorporated specifications for meeting the needs of children whose disabilities are not physical (i.e., children who are blind or deaf). These publications can help ECSE programs nationwide in selecting, designing, and retrofitting space. The board may be contacted at ATBCB, 1331 F Street NW, Suite 1000, Washington, DC 20004-1111.

The 1992 Center for Accessible Housing report (available from ATBCB) included a review of literature on architectural design for young children. One important finding from that review was that as of 1992, very few states had building, fire, or safety codes that included specifications for programs that include young children with disabilities among their target populations. Florida, with its *Building Standards for Educational Facilities for Handicapped Children* (Florida Department of Education, 1988) and North Carolina were the only states identified by the center as having such guidelines. The center noted that the voluntary national accessibility standards of the American National Standards Institute (ANSI), ANSI A117.1, did not contain standards for children's facilities. Neither did the three most important model codes—the Standard Building Code, the Building Officials and Code Administrators International Code, and the Uniform Building Code. Accordingly, most states do not require facilities that serve young children with disabilities to meet architectural standards ensuring their accessibility. The 1992 recommendations also discussed children's needs for access to technology, including augmentative communication devices and wheelchairs.

More recently, the ATBCB has issued guidelines for "children's elements" and for "play facilities" (ATBCB, 1997a, b). These are very important documents for ECSE programs to obtain and to use.

Among the most important design issues for ECSE program administrators to consider are the following:

- *Doors.* The 1992 Center for Accessible Housing report found that doors are often very difficult for young children, especially children with physical disabilities, to open, close, and hold open. Although door specifications are often set to comply with fire codes, the center's research team recommended consideration of doors that are easier for young children to use. Automatic doors are one option. Although costly, such doors help young children to move about in a facility much more independently; they also make it easier for them to get out fast in an emergency.

- *Ramps.* The center found that while ramps thirty-six inches wide (the width needed to accommodate a wheelchair) are acceptable, much wider ramps are better. Ramps eighty inches wide or more allow two wheelchairs to pass each other going in opposite directions, helping to avoid congestion and accidents in programs serving more than a few children with severe physical disabilities. The slope (steepness) of ramps was also a concern. The common 1:12 slope specification, while suitable for facilities serving adults, is too steep for young children to negotiate alone. A 1:12 slope rises one inch every twelve inches of distance. The center reported that many facilities serving young children with disabilities required teachers, volunteers, or parents to push children up or down 1:12 ramps, thus unnecessarily limiting the children's mobility and independence; 1:20 ramps are better.

- *Stairs.* The center's report noted that detectable warnings such as changes in flooring patterns are necessary to help children with visual impairments avoid accidents at the tops of stairs.

- *Elevators.* The center's evaluation of facilities serving young children identified the height of elevator control buttons as an important issue. These buttons (including call buttons located in lobbies and control buttons in cars) should be positioned no more than thirty-four to thirty-six inches above the floor. In addition, the report found that buttons three-quarters of an inch wide, or even an inch wide were too small for many young children with physical disabilities to use with accuracy.

- *Desk Height.* The center recommended that work surfaces, such as desks and tables, be provided in adjustable heights. Most of the facilities that center staff visited had work surfaces twenty-five inches or less from the floor. While these are suitable for many young children, the report suggested that some children, in some situations, will need higher or lower work surfaces. Fortunately, a wide variety of desks and tables with adjustable surface heights is available.

- *Storage Areas.* The report found that shelves and other storage surfaces thirty-six inches high sufficed to meet the need of young children (including children using wheelchairs) but that surfaces forty-three inches high were too high. Adjustable shelving was strongly recommended, because desirable shelf height is a function not only of body stature but also of body position and the child's forward-reach and side-reach capacities.

- *Toilets.* Toilet seats, the report suggested, should be about eleven or twelve inches high, and certainly lower than the fifteen- to seventeen-inch heights recommended for adult toilet seats. Toilet stalls should be more than thirty-six inches wide, to facilitate child transfers from wheelchairs to toilets.

These suggestions are most helpful when viewed from the perspective of their capacity to enhance children's independence. Especially in ECSE programs with severe staff limitations, architectural design features that alleviate pressure on staff to assist children physically throughout the building and throughout the day are highly desirable. An important consideration in serving children with physical and sensory limitations is giving them opportunities to develop and display suitable adaptive behaviors. When children are not only permitted but expected to do things for themselves, they are more likely to develop the skills necessary for functioning well in subsequent environments. By contrast, when poorly considered design specifications impede children's mobility, ECSE staff unnecessarily restrict the ability of young children with physical or sensory disabilities from learning the behaviors they will need for success in later schooling.

These considerations are related to other, broader concerns. A 1994 report by the U.S. Department of Health and Human Services (HHS) Office of the Inspector General, based

Early childhood personnel need to identify access features not only of program play areas but also of the community beyond the program grounds. Family members will appreciate suggestions on how to locate accessible shopping, banking, and other sites.

on inspections of 149 licensed day-care centers and Head Start programs in six states, found that the majority of such facilities had health or safety hazards that put children at risk (Audit Finds Day-Care Safety Flaws, 1994). The report stated that Head Start centers, which are subject to federal safety standards and receive federal funds, often failed to protect young children from chemicals placed under sinks, improperly filled fire extinguishers, sewage, and debris. Other day-care facilities are state-licensed and subject to state safety standards. The HHS report found that budget cutbacks in many states had limited auditors' ability to ensure that programs met such standards. Safety standards need to be upgraded in all programs.

Outdoor Environments

The ATBCB guidelines for children's environments addressed outdoor settings in such places as day-care centers, nurseries, preschool programs, and kindergartens. In addition, the Access Board recently offered recommendations for accessibility to recreation facilities. Work done by the National Park Service, the National Forest Service, and the National Accessibility Center at Bradford Woods, operated by Indiana University, paved the way for ATBCB recommendations on how to make playgrounds and other outdoor recreation areas more accessible for young children with disabilities. This issue was largely overlooked in the 1980s, but the ATBCB-led Recreation Task Force, formed in mid-1993, has now recommended specifications for access to swimming pools, amusement parks, winter recreation areas, and outdoor sports facilities.

The 1997 ATBCB report on play facilities offers two sets of specifications: one for young children aged two to five and another for children aged five to twelve. The ATBCB believes there is not yet enough information available with respect to children under the age of two. Regarding routes to and from play facilities, the ATBCB recommends that these be sixty inches wide and clear of protrusions at or below eighty inches above the surface. The slope of the routes should be 1:16 or less (i.e., rising one inch per sixteen inches of length). Any ramp in the play area should rise no more than twelve inches. No handrail should be more than twenty-eight inches above the ramp surface. These very specific suggestions should prove helpful to ECSE programs throughout the nation. For more information, contact the Access Board at www.access-board.gov or ATBCB, 1331 F Street NW, Washington, DC 20004.

VALUE CONFLICTS

The principle or value of individualization is central to ECSE in large part because it recognizes that young children with disabilities, delays, or deviations in development differ so much one from another that no one model of service delivery could meet all of their needs. At times, this value of individualization clashes with other concepts that are central to ECSE. To illustrate, consider the value of normalization, whether expressed in terms of natural environments, least restrictive environments, or inclusion. There is a general rule that ECSE professionals may follow in handling apparent conflicts between individualization and normalization. This rule holds that individualization is a superordinate requirement (Bricker & Veltman, 1990; Carta et al., 1993). As discussed earlier, the preference expressed in the IDEA for services to be provided in NEs or LREs is not an unqualified one. The law specifically limits that preference by subjecting it to the test of individualization. Both NEs and LREs are to be used only "to the maximum extent appropriate."

There are other examples of clashes between one cherished value and another. Family services may conflict with parental needs. A good illustration was offered by Affleck, Tennen, Rowe, Roscher, and Walker (1989). In their study, a team provided support, featuring weekly home visits, to mothers of low-birthweight children who were making the transition from hospital to home. Public health nurses offered information to the mothers, listened to their concerns, explained about normal and abnormal infant development, and demonstrated techniques of caring for the infant. At the follow-up evaluation stage, however, Affleck et al. found that some mothers who had participated in the study despite reservations about it actually regressed. These mothers felt less competent following the four-month intervention period than they had at its outset. They demonstrated this by being more hesitant with, and less giving to, their infants. (Other mothers in the study, who had entered it willingly and who felt they needed the public health nurse's assistance, learned and benefited from that support.) The findings of Affleck et al. are important because they suggest that if ECSE professionals impose services on families against parents' desires, they may harm the very people they are attempting to help.

Lisbeth Vincent (1992) described another way in which values may clash. An immigrant family in Los Angeles had so many needs—they lived in a one-room garage with no running water—that staff from a local ECSE program felt they had to address those family needs before they could adequately help the family's eighteen-month-old son, who had Down syndrome. The staff secured furniture, food, and clothing for the family, in the belief that doing so would free family members from distractions so that they could better provide the attention and special assistance the boy needed. While at first delighted to receive the assistance, the family later turned resentful. Only by accident, Vincent reported, did ECSE staff learn that the family's values led them to believe that the underlying message being delivered along with the furniture was, "You're not good enough to do these things yourself, so we are doing them for you." Here again, staff violated a cardinal principle of ECSE: Family assessments (in this case, the staff finding that the family lived in substandard housing) are to be done only with prior family consent.

PRACTICAL ISSUES

Individualization of services is an ideal. At times, practical realities prevent it from being realized. Examples of conflicts between ideal and real situations abound in ECSE. Most ECSE programs offer only a limited range of services. They may, for example, provide group activities for young children with disabilities but lack the facilities to offer integration into similar programs for nondisabled children. This problem is particularly evident in preschool services for three- to five-year-olds. There may be no such programs for nondisabled children in the community, and where such services do exist, they may be targeted toward disadvantaged children, who have pressing needs of their own. The *Fourteenth Annual Report to Congress on Implementation of the Individuals with Disabilities Education Act* (U.S. Department of Education, 1992c) noted that these problems are common in towns and cities across the nation. Alternatively, an ECSE program may offer integrated group programming but lack the capability to provide separate, specialized activities for children with severe disabilities. Families concerned that their children will not receive sufficient

Children using wheelchairs ideally should be able to play with all objects and ride all rides in early childhood play areas.

attention in large, integrated settings may be frustrated by the inability of such ECSE programs to respond to their requests for more individualized attention.

In the area of early intervention, according to Graham and Bryant (1993), the most frequent mode of service delivery is home visits. The most common model of service delivery in preschool programs—as in special education at the elementary and secondary levels—features a large-group activity area and pull-out (resource room) settings where such services as speech and language therapy, physical and occupational therapy, and the like, are delivered. Additional funding may be needed to add other capabilities—center-based services for infants and toddlers to supplement or even supplant home visits; or integrated settings in preschools, where specialized services are provided in the same room as other activities. Unfortunately, the reality of human service programming at the turn of the century in many areas is one of severe and increasing budgetary pressures. For these reasons, individualization may be possible only within a range of affordable options.

Another very common practical constraint on individualization of services is perhaps the most basic: time. Service coordinators, early childhood special educators, physical and occupational therapists, and the many other professionals working in ECSE programs may have large caseloads. Often they experience conflicts between their professional obligations to provide more time and attention to each child on the one hand, and severe time constraints on the other. Burnout is a frequent result of such conflicts. One survey of ECSE professionals found that they experienced so much conflict as a result of having too many cases and too little time that they would respond positively to job offers promising them more time for each child and family (Kontos & File, 1992). A variation on the time theme is the availability of services at times that are convenient for the family. The principle of individualization requires ECSE programs to make child and family services available when the family can take advantage of them. This may conflict, however, with the hours at which key professionals are available. Speech and language pathologists, physical and occupational therapists, and other such professionals are frequently freelance operators who split their time among several programs scattered over a wide geographical area. It may not be possible for them to schedule therapy sessions at a time or place that meets family needs.

These examples raise another basic issue: cost. Often, it is possible to arrange therapy at a time and place convenient for the family, but only at extra cost to the program. For example, professionals may be hired as salaried workers and assigned to the hours at which freelance therapists are not available. Overtime pay arrangements are another possibility, both with salaried and freelance professionals. Extra time and attention to individual children and their families may similarly be provided at additional cost to the program. Although these steps theoretically are possible, human services agencies, including EC programs, are under increasing budgetary constraints in many states and localities. The practical ability of programs to individualize services in these ways may be seriously limited by such budgetary pressures.

Summary

This chapter opened with a quotation from Carta et al. (1993), which stated that meeting children's needs is more important than the means by which this is done—whether with steps recommended by NAEYC in its "developmentally appropriate practice," by DEC in its "recommended practices," or, alternatively, with more traditional practices. The chapter went on to examine the "place" of place and the importance of individually designed, appropriately delivered services versus the comparatively lower importance of the location where they take place.

In the field of ECSE, dominated by strongly held convictions, polarization often results. In ECSE, the prevalence of such divisiveness has detracted attention from the children and their needs. While families are undeniably important in ECSE, programs should not promote parental involvement so far that they slight the valuable contributions of ECSE professionals, paraprofessionals, and support staff. A family-focused approach is thus a reasonable compromise between traditional dominance by professionals on the one hand and extreme family-centered approaches on the other. Similarly, while integration is valuable both as a means and an end, it must not overwhelm efforts to ensure that services are appropriate for children and their families.

Misunderstandings between EC and ECSE have been rampant in recent years. Although the two fields are coming together and alleviating some of these misconceptions, much more needs to be done. In particular, more careful use of language is imperative. Much controversy could have been avoided had NAEYC stated clearly in its 1987 DAP guidelines that its principles were not designed to criticize aspects of ECSE programs. The DEC "recommended practices" contributed equally to unnecessary controversies by using the term "family-centered" to describe practices that are better labeled "family-focused." This usage contributed needlessly to the widespread, but erroneous, belief that the IDEA requires family-centered practices in ECSE programs. Similarly, the DEC report's use of the term "normalization" may have resulted in more confusion than clarification. As the documents quoted in this chapter make clear, the DEC Task Force actually recommended that inclusion and other least restrictive placement practices be subsumed under the more important principle of appropriateness.

The early 1990s were characterized by excited debate among proponents of different methodologies, different ways of involving families, and different placements. As fevered as the discussions sometimes became, by the mid-1990s, fortunately, some semblance of reason took hold. DEC and NAEYC began working together to cool tempers and clarify positions. It is clear that, by law, ECSE holds two values above all others: individualization and appropriateness. Whatever ECSE workers do, they must ensure that services are designed and delivered to respond to children's unique needs and that the services provided actually do meet their needs. The way in which they meet their goals, in particular what curricula they use, is less crucial than that they do meet them. Similarly, where they do these things matters less than that they be done, and done well.

QUESTIONS FOR REFLECTION

1. Why may early intervention programs decline to serve a particular infant or toddler, despite Part C's "entitlement" nature?

2. Which level of government—federal, state, county, or local—decides what is and what is not a "delay"?

3. Explain, in your own words, what "direct instruction" means.

4. How does the teacher's role differ between "direct instruction" on the one hand and "developmentally appropriate practice" on the other?

5. What practical realities limit the extent to which ECSE programs can individualize services?

6. Why is "rapid learning" so important to ECSE professionals?

7. Explain the "fanaticism" that Kauffman deplored in the continuing debate about "place."

8. Why is LRE a principle and not a place?

9. What practical realities might limit inclusion of young children with disabilities into regular preschool programs?

10. How can facility design increase the independence of young children with disabilities?

Technology

Technology is a lot like freedom. . . . Once it's uncorked, there's no putting it back. Its fruits are there for everyone's enjoyment and benefit. It is often said that assistive technology is liberating, and that is certainly the case. But it is time to be clear that assistive technology is liberating not just for the individual with a disability but indeed for America as a whole. (Williams, 1991)

OVERVIEW

Technology holds great promise for young children with disabilities or developmental delays, for families, and for professionals in early childhood special education (ECSE). This chapter explores all these potential uses of technology.

Probably most immediately useful with young children are "low tech" products such as fasteners or no-slip surfaces; these are easy to use and low in cost. Generating great excitement today are speech-based high-technology products that "hear" and "talk"—products such as IBM's Via Voice, Lernout & Hauspie's Voice Xpress, and Dragon Systems's Naturally Speaking—because with these, even young children can use a personal computer (PC). They can "write" a story simply by speaking into the computer's microphone. They can "read" another story, just by listening to the synthesized speech coming from the computer's speakers. They can even read and compose electronic mail (E-mail) by themselves, something many young children take great delight in doing.

Technology can also enhance program-family communications. This certainly is a high priority for any ECSE program. With personal computers costing as little as $600 (complete with a modem), more and more families can afford to be on-line. This opens the door for ECSE programs to use "E-mail trees" (E-mail messages that automatically go to dozens of families simultaneously) and Web sites (World Wide Web home pages to which family members may "surf" to learn about the ECSE program's activities and plans).

Finally, technology can connect ECSE professionals to a vast array of information and support resources throughout the nation, and indeed the world. When an early interventionist first meets a young child who has a rare syndrome, for example, the professional can acquire much-needed information about that syndrome in minutes—by surfing the Web—and can exchange views about intervention strategies with other interventionists all over the world.

Technology is not without its challenges. Important issues of equity, particularly the unequal levels of computer ownership between wealthy and poor families but also the continuing uneven levels of computer use by boys and girls, must be addressed. This chapter discusses those concerns. It concludes with sources readers may contact for more information, as well as with Questions for Reflection.

"LOW-TECH"

Inexpensive, "low tech" products can make life much easier for children with physical disabilities and for their caregivers. A good example is Velcro. It is a great fastener and can be used in jackets, slacks, pants, skirts, shoes, and a wide range of other items. Velcro-equipped products are widely available in clothing and home furnishing stores. Another useful product is dycem. This is a no-slip surface. Placed on a table or on a wheelchair lapboard, it helps to prevent spilling of liquids and accidental dropping of objects. You can find dycem products at Home Depot or other home furnishing stores. As should be clear from these examples, low-technology products have no or few moving parts; they also tend not to be electronic.

Kitchen utensils, pencils and pens, and other items often found in ECSE settings now come equipped with wide, easily held grips. A good example is the Good Grip family of knives and other items sold in Williams-Sonoma stores. You can also find rocker knives, weighted cups, two-sided cup holders, and pizza cutters at Williams-Sonoma stores, as well as at Home Depot. Harder to find are plate guards, which are rims that fit around a plate; people with mobility limitations can use those in place of a second utensil to scoop up peas, applesauce, and so on. A good source for hard-to-locate items is the Maxi Aids catalog, (800) 522-6294; www.maxiaids.com.

As these examples illustrate, it is important not to overlook less sophisticated products. Indeed, a 1992 study of assistive technology devices owned and used by Americans with disabilities (LaPlante, Hendershot, & Moss, 1992) found that the overwhelming number of such products were not high technology but rather low technology. Such items as glasses, hearing aids, crutches, and wheelchairs were used by far greater numbers of people with disabilities than were any high-tech devices. As a general rule, low-technology products perform a single function, while high-technology devices handle several to many thousands of different tasks. A clock tells time; an IBM-compatible PC, by contrast, can run some 100,000 different programs, from word processing to financial management to filing to games.

Low-tech products that young children with disabilities in ECSE programs can use are both many and diverse. For children with vision impairments, there are talking clocks and calculators (and hundreds of other talking products), beeping balls, magnifiers of all descriptions, and raised-relief maps. For children with limited fine motor control, there are extra-large cards and other play products, wheelchairs of every imaginable size and function (including special "sport" chairs for recreation), extra-large utensils and double-handled cups for mealtimes, automatic seat lifters, sock and stocking dressing aids, and thousands of others. For PCs alone, there are key guards (plastic covers for keyboards that allow the user to rest a hand while the holes guide fingers or sticks to the correct keys), light pens, mouth sticks, and extra-large keyboards. For children who are deaf or severely hard-of-hearing, there are flashing lights to signal rings or other sounds, telephone amplifiers, and telecommunications devices for the deaf (TDDs).

ASSISTIVE TECHNOLOGY DEVICES

This chapter opened with a quotation from testimony presented to the U.S. House of Representatives by an individual with a physical disability, who commented on the revolutionary impact assistive technology could have. The National Council on Disability (NCD), a small federal agency, recently reported on a survey of adults with disabilities. Asked to assess its impact on their lives, using a scale of 1 to 10, with 10 being the highest, assistive technology users reported that such devices make a tremendous difference. Without such products, they said, they would rate the quality of their lives at 3, whereas with assistive technology, the ratings zoomed to 8.4 on average (NCD, 1993c, p. 2). Clearly, assistive technology is enormously important to individuals with disabilities who need it.

The council also surveyed 136 families with members who have disabilities, including some with infants and toddlers. These families reported that a majority of the infants and toddlers benefited from assistive technology. In addition to fewer health problems, families reported less need for child-care services and fewer hours of parental child care. Overall, as many as ten to fifteen hours weekly were freed for recreation and other family needs (National Council on Disability, 1993c, p. 51).

The Individuals with Disabilities Education Act (IDEA) defines the term **assistive technology devices** as follows:

assistive technology devices are any products that may be used by individuals with disabilities to do things they otherwise would have difficulty doing.

> *[A]ssistive technology devices means any item, piece of equipment, or product system, whether acquired commercially off the shelf, modified, or customized, that is used to increase, maintain, or improve functional capabilities of individuals with disabilities.* (section 602)

This definition is an expansive one, including commercial, general-purpose products that have potential uses for people with disabilities as well as specially designed or customized items. The operative aspect of the definition is that assistive technology devices are "used to increase, maintain, or improve functional capabilities of individuals with disabilities." The same definition is used in other federal laws, including the Technology-Related Assistance for Individuals with Disabilities Act (TRAIDA), the Americans with Disabilities Act (ADA), and the Rehabilitation Act.

As noted several times in this chapter, many adaptive products fit into or work with PCs. The first PCs, in the late 1970s and early 1980s, were similar to the first cars in that they were one-for-all models. The Ford Model T, for example, came in any color you wanted, as long as it was black. Similarly, the first PCs let you enter and retrieve information in any way you wanted as long as it was visual. The most important trend in PCs today for children with disabilities is the increasing ability of users to select the modalities through which they will interact with the machine. Today, one need not even touch a key to operate a PC. Children may speak commands to the machine using speech recognition. They may use joysticks, head wands, and other alternative or supplementary communication add-ons. Similarly, while most PC information is still presented visually, some software programs use music or even synthesized speech.

Speech recognition is an important alternative means of communication with PCs. Many of today's PCs feature "speaker-independent" speech recognition. Such systems can understand any speaker's voice. Earlier systems were "speaker dependent," that is, they had to be trained on one user's voice and could respond only to that individual's speech. Earlier PCs also required speakers to pause between words, speaking . . . like . . . this. Today's machines can often handle continuous speech at or near conversational speed. IBM, Lernout & Hauspie, and Dragon Systems offer inexpensive (about $100) software programs that recognize continous speech. Just a few years ago, such programs cost in the thousands of dollars.

To illustrate the potential of speech recognition, consider the problem of a speech and language pathologist who is trying to diagnose a four-year-old's problems with the English language. Ideally, the pathologist would like to see written samples of the child's language to analyze them for grammar, syntax, vocabulary, and other aspects of language use. Four-year-olds, however, seldom write long essays. A PC-based speech recognition system would allow the pathologist to tell the child to talk about favorite toys, life at home, or anything else. The PC automatically would produce a transcribed, printed version of the child's output. After the session, the speech pathologist could read the printout at his leisure, searching for the linguistic rules that must have been used to create that language.

Speech recognition also gives young children who do not yet know how to write access to **electronic mail (E-mail)**. Mueller (1992) described use of E-mail in a pediatric psychiatric unit classroom by children as young as eight. She reported that while the children began hesitantly with such sentences as "I am fine. How are you?" they gradually opened up in their communications, producing messages that conveyed real emotional content and provided emotional support to the children with whom they were communicating. During the same period, the E-mail messages gradually became longer, and grammar and spelling

speech recognition is computer comprehension of spoken words or sounds. Speaker-dependent speech recognition systems can understand one person's voice, while speaker-independent systems can comprehend the speech of many different individuals.

electronic mail (E-mail) involves exchange of written messages over telephone lines.

improved. The children became excited about E-mail, in part, she said, because of the rapid turnaround; messages sent to other cities, states, or even countries could be answered within hours or days versus weeks to months via air or surface mail. In addition, Mueller noted, the medium caused the children's disabilities to "disappear" because all messages, whether from disabled or nondisabled children, appeared identical on the screen. This "anonymous" feature of E-mail is vital in that it gives these young children some of their only chances to have others focus exclusively on the content of their messages, not on their disabilities or even their personalities. Gandell and Laufer (1993) offered a similarly encouraging report on E-mail use by children with disabilities. FrEdMail (Free Educational Electronic Mail) offers a low-cost telecommunications network for schools and other public agencies interested in K–12 education and related issues. It provides several learning projects in which children learn to communicate with others at a distance.

One commercial product that young children may use to speak to the PC is Dragon Systems's Naturally Speaking, a voice-activated PC program with a vocabulary of fifty thousand words. Unlike earlier systems, Naturally Speaking requires little user training; it can be used with a high degree of accuracy within minutes of unpacking. The system works well even for very young children who have never before used a computer; the child simply speaks into a microphone and sees his words appear instantly on the screen, free of misspellings and typographical errors. Very young children who know words but do not know how to spell them accurately can produce high-quality communications. An obvious application for Naturally Speaking is as an addition to a communications program to produce E-mail for transmission over telephone lines. Another exciting possibility is its use by children who have physical disabilities that make typing difficult or impossible.

Reaching the Potential?

As of 1990, just thirteen million of America's estimated forty-three million individuals with disabilities were using adaptive technologies (LaPlante, Hendershot, & Moss, 1992). About half who used assistive technology devices purchased them on their own, without third-party (i.e., insurance, government) assistance. More than 2.5 million Americans of all ages said they needed assistive devices but were unable to get them for reasons of cost. Among children and young adults, the most frequently used assistive technology devices were wheelchairs or crutches; braces (arm, leg, foot, back, neck); and hearing aids. Very few used high-tech, PC-based products. This report, based on the 1990 National Health Interview Survey on Assistive Devices, is troubling because it suggests that the vast majority of Americans with disabilities do not have access to today's high-tech devices.

According to the American Foundation for the Blind, no single product for blind people has helped even 10 percent of the population of blind and low-vision people. Similarly, fewer than half a million adults who are deaf own TDDs enabling them to make and receive phone calls—only about one in every five who could use the machines. While some of these distribution problems may be due to the stigma with which some individuals with disabilities associate special-needs products, there are other problems as well. Large numbers of people with disabilities, and their families, do not know what products are available. In other cases, cost is a factor.

Parette, Hourcade, and VanBiervliet (1993) offered suggestions for selecting technologies. The IDEA insists that assistive technology devices and assistive technology services be provided whenever they are (a) "appropriate" and (b) in the child's individualized family service plan (IFSP) or individualized education program (IEP). Appropriateness, in turn,

A well-equipped computer lab brings together keyboards, monitors, modems, printers, and alternative input and output devices for meeting special needs.

revolves around responsiveness to the child's unique needs: There must be an actual and specific need for such devices and/or services. By the same token, "appropriate" means that the devices/services must meet these needs; that is, there is no requirement to acquire more than the child needs. A balance between responsiveness to need on the one hand and cost-effectiveness on the other is not always readily achieved. ECSE professionals should work closely with both parents and experts on technology in identifying a range of possible devices and/or services before selecting the one—or those few—that both meet the need and are reasonable in price. The resources listed at the conclusion of this chapter can be very useful in these decision-making processes. Other considerations helping to guide the selection process, Parette et al. suggested, include the child's previous experience with similar kinds of products, the child's preferences (if known), the commercial availability of the product, ease of learning and ease of use, and availability of technical assistance and repair.

Accessible Computers

It is urgent in this knowledge age that computers be and remain accessible to and usable by people with disabilities. Gregg Vanderheiden of the University of Wisconsin at Madison is pioneering exciting new ways of making that happen. In an advanced technique he calls ShowSounds, Vanderheiden is trying to ensure that whatever a computer speaks to the user is also available on display so that an individual who is deaf can see and read it. Similar steps are needed, he believes, for people who are blind and for individuals with severe physical disabilities such as cerebral palsy or quadriplegia. In two working papers— "A Standard Approach for Full Visual Annotation of Auditorially Presented Information for Users, Including Those Who Are Deaf: ShowSounds" (Vanderheiden, 1992a) and "Making Software More Accessible for People with Disabilities: A White Paper on the Design of Software Application Programs to Increase Their Accessibility for People with Disabilities" (Vanderheiden, 1992b)—Dr. Vanderheiden suggested that commercial software developers ensure that any computer programs they write be fully accessible to Americans with disabilities.

Computers can be made accessible in other ways, as well. On Labor Day, 1991, tens of millions of Americans watched as Peter Bonavita "spoke" to his computer by blinking his eyes. Bonavita needed this adaptive capability because of amyotrophic lateral sclerosis (ALS), often called Lou Gehrig's disease. The computer translated the blinks letter by letter into words, then spoke them out. Although it could take five minutes to compose a sentence most people could speak in fifteen seconds, the machine is a breakthrough toward greater independence for the Vietnam veteran, who contracted ALS twenty-five years ago. This was a stunning example of how new input and output options are making communication possible even for people with very severe disabilities.

As noted earlier, many assistive technology devices work with PCs. When selecting PCs for ECSE program use, it is important to begin the search by specifying what kinds of adaptive technologies will be used. That is because not all assistive technology add-ons for PCs are compatible with all PC models. The first step, then, should be to decide what add-ons the children require. The next question is, "What model(s) are compatible with these add-ons?" The computer models of choice are obviously those that accept these essential add-ons (Lazarro, 1993; Lindsey, 1993).

speech synthesis is computer-generated speech.

Apple Macintosh.   Today's Macs come with built-in screen magnification programs that can enlarge letters and images on the screen. They also have built-in **speech synthesis** so that they can "talk" and keyboard modification programs allowing people with physical disabilities to customize keys to perform different functions. Built into the Mac is an Easy Access utility that includes Sticky Keys and Mouse Keys. With Sticky Keys, the user hits the shift bar five times to activate a capacity that allows function keys to be made to "stick" after being touched. Thus, people with cerebral palsy, quadriplegia, or other severe physical disabilities can implement multiple-key functions despite the fact that they cannot depress two- or three-key sequences simultaneously. With Mouse Keys, the numeric keypad can be used to perform functions usually done with the mouse. This modification is essential for many children with disabilities, because the Mac relies heavily on the mouse, and mice are not always easily used by people with physical or visual disabilities. Although one can bypass the mouse with Mouse Keys in this way, such circumventions are not always as readily accomplished as is direct use of the mouse. ECSE programs should take this consideration into account when reviewing possible purchase or lease of Macs. However, today's Macs can be used by most children with disabilities and the line is one that deserves serious consideration by ECSE professionals, especially the more powerful Macs that feature speaker-independent speech recognition.

Apple IIGS.   The Apple II series' most advanced model, the GS (for "Graphics/Sound"), has similar built-in screen magnification and keyboard modification programs. It can also accept adaptive technology add-ons, including CloseView enlargement programs, Braille printers, and others. The Apple II series, including the GS, was the single most popular brand in the public schools in the 1980s. However, it is a very old system. With its limitations becoming more apparent with each passing year, in 1993 Apple Computer discontinued the Apple II line. Although used models may still be acquired, ECSE programs are better advised to consider Mac or IBM-compatible systems, with their more modern designs ("architectures," in computer-speak). A good source of information about add-ons

5

for Apple II or Macintosh computers is the DLM publication, *Apple Computer Resources in Special Education* (Allen, TX). Retailing for about $20, it describes more than a thousand products that work with Apple computers.

IBM Compatibles. IBM machines and their clones work very differently from Macs and Apple II products. The most popular design in the business and academic worlds, the IBM-compatible architecture has not been adopted as widely in public school systems as have Apple II and Mac computers. However, IBM-compatible machines, notably the newer Pentium-based machines, are very capable and almost infinitely adaptable to meet special needs. Although most IBM-compatible machines lack built-in screen magnification and keyboard modification programs, both are readily available and often inexpensive as options. IBM itself offers a line of Independence Series products, including Screen Reader and other add-ons. IBM also sponsors a National Support Center for Persons with Disabilities in Atlanta, Georgia.

Other. Not all high-tech products connect to PCs. Some are stand-alone products. To illustrate, consider a class of products known as handheld organizers. Young children with cognitive disabilities may benefit from these speech-controlled devices. Voice Powered Technology, a California-based speech recognition company, offers a pocket-size (2.25" x 4"x 5/8") organizer that "hears" spoken queries ("Where am I supposed to go at 2:00 PM?"), searches its memory, and responds (via speech synthesis and/or on a liquid crystal diode [LCD] display), giving the child the specific information sought. It can hold one hundred phone numbers, appointments, and notes, all of which are retrievable via speech synthesis and/or LCD display.

Millions of Americans have seen singer Stevie Wonder "reading" his mail using a Kurzweil Personal Reader that translates print into a computerized voice. It works much as a photocopier does, but instead of printing a copy of a page, it reads the page aloud. Today, The Reading Edge, also from Xerox Imaging Systems, provides many of the same capabilities in a small, twenty-four-pound machine. "Talking" calculators and alarm clocks for blind people can be purchased for as little as $20 to $70. Controls for turning on or off electrical appliances, from room lights to television sets, just by clapping hands also are available. Figure 10.1 offers sources for information and products.

ASSISTIVE TECHNOLOGY SERVICES

assistive technology services include assessment, selection of devices, instruction in their use, and related services to support individuals with disabilities in use of technology.

Part C and Part B recognize **assistive technology services** as allowable early intervention and related services, respectively. These are services provided by professionals to assist ECSE programs, families, and children to identify what technologies are needed, to select suitable devices, to install or configure the machines so that they do what is needed, and to train children, family members, and ECSE workers how to use them. The term is defined in Part A:

> [A]ssistive technology services means any service that directly assists an individual with a disability in the selection, acquisition, or use of an assistive technology device. Such term includes
> (A) the evaluation of the needs of an individual with a disability, including a functional evaluation of the individual in the individual's customary environment;

AdaptAbility	Madenta Communications
Department 2292	9411A-20 Avenue
Colchester, CT 06415	Edmonton, AB Canada
Attainment Company	Maxi Aids
504 Commerce Parkway	P.O. Box 3209
Verona, WI 53593	Farmingdale, NY 11735
Flaghouse Inc.	Maddak Inc.
150 N. MacQuesten Parkway	6 Industrial Road
Mt. Vernon, NY 10550	Pequannock, NJ 07440
Hygeia Medical	Sammons/Preston
555 Westbury Avenue	P.O. Box 5071
Carle Place, NY 11514	Bolingbrook, IL 60440

Source: Kornreich Technology Center, National Center for Disability Services, Albertson, NY

FIGURE 10.1   Assistive technology catalogs

(B) *purchasing, leasing, or otherwise providing for the acquisition of assistive technology devices by individuals with disabilities;*

(C) *selecting, designing, fitting, customizing, adapting, applying, maintaining, repairing, or replacing of assistive technology devices;*

(D) *coordinating and using other therapies, interventions, or services with assistive technology devices, such as those associated with existing education and rehabilitation plans and programs;*

(E) *training or technical assistance for an individual with disabilities, or, where appropriate, the family of an individual with disabilities; and training or technical assistance for professionals (including individuals providing education and rehabilitation services), employers, or other individuals who provide services to, employ, or are otherwise substantially involved in the major life activities of individuals with disabilities.* (section 602)

Assistive technology services clearly are important for ECSE programs, ECSE workers, families, and children. Many thousands of technology devices are out there, and choosing among them is difficult. Fortunately, several sources can assist ECSE programs to identify experts who can help. The American Association for the Advancement of Science (AAAS) maintains a computer database with the names, addresses, telephone numbers, and areas of expertise of several thousand scientists and engineers with expertise in disability; many are themselves adults with disabilities. The AAAS Project on Science, Technology, and Disability can help professionals and families find experts in any given state, county, or even city. RESNA (formerly, Rehabilitation Engineering Society of North America), an association on technology and disability, is another excellent resource. The Trace Center at the University of Wisconsin maintains extensive databases both on devices and on assistive technology experts. The Job Accommodation Network (JAN), a service of the President's Committee on Employment of People with Disabilities (PCEPD) and the University of West Virginia, can help. Funded through a special congressional appropriation, JAN's sole purpose is to help people find out about, and select, technology devices and services. Addresses for AAAS, RESNA, the Trace Center, and JAN appear at the end of this chapter.

Rehabilitation engineering is a relatively new professional specialty. Emerging out of vocational rehabilitation in the late 1970s and early 1980s, it attracted people who combine knowledge about individuals with disabilities and expertise in engineering and technology. RESNA is the major professional organization representing rehabilitation engineers. The work of these professionals has changed over the years. In the early 1980s, they specialized in custom-designed solutions because few off-the-shelf devices were commercially available to meet the special needs of people with disabilities. Today, with many thousands of such products available, rehabilitation engineers spend less time creating new solutions and more time screening, selecting, installing, and configuring off-the-shelf products to meet individual needs.

One exciting kind of assistive technology service is the creation of an **environmental control system** in the child's home, discussed briefly earlier. Linking an inexpensive PC to lights, alarm systems, and other electrical appliances in the home allows a child with a physical disability to control many aspects of his environment from a remote location. Such systems can increase greatly the child's freedom and sense of personal responsibility. They may even prove lifesaving, because the child is able to set or release alarms, make "911" calls, and take other steps to protect himself in the home. Some products, such as NanoPac's CINTEX2, allow voice control of as many as 256 devices, through as many as one hundred commands (channel up/down, volume up/down, rewind/fast forward, play, record, on/off, and so on). In each of these instances, technology promotes adaptive development by enabling young children with disabilities to do important everyday tasks by themselves, reducing pressure on parents and other caregivers, while encouraging the children to become self-reliant.

Perhaps the easiest way to learn what is currently available to meet a particular child's needs is to consult JAN, described briefly earlier. Callers need only outline what the child is attempting to do and how the disability interferes with that activity. JAN's human factors engineers then search thousands of entries in a mainframe computer to identify a few devices or procedures likely to solve the problem. ABLEDATA, another information service, is also helpful.

environmental control system (ECS) enables people to operate electrical equipment via remote control, usually with the assistance of a small personal computer.

Multimedia programs give young children multiple modes of input and output, facilitating learning.

FINANCING OPTIONS

Third-party funding for assistive technology devices and assistive technology services is available from a large number of sources (Figure 10.2). However, persistence is necessary in many instances because financing is not automatic. A convincing case must be made that an individual's needs do in fact meet the criteria of a particular funding source.

The first source to which ECSE professionals should look is the IDEA itself. Part D offers discretionary funds for which school programs may apply in order to create advanced technology capabilities. The U.S. Department of Education's Office of Special Education Services (OSEP) annually announces grant competitions under Part D. For more information, contact OSEP at the U.S. Department of Education, 400 Maryland Avenue SW, Washington, DC 20202. The fact that federal funds are available to purchase and apply technologies, however, does not mean they will always be used to help children. To illustrate, Sawyer and Zantal-Wiener (1993), in an article about technology and special education, noted that computers and other high-technology products in schools are more often used for administrative purposes than for teaching. Even when PCs are reserved for instructional purposes, they are frequently applied to computer literacy, word processing, and drill-and-practice rather than for more creative applications. One purpose of Part D is to find new and better uses for technology.

Part C states that assistive technology devices and services may constitute early intervention services that may be financed with Part C monies. Similarly, Part B allows such devices and services to be paid for as related services. In both cases, reimbursement is available if the IFSP or IEP provides for devices and services that children require so as to benefit from the early intervention or preschool special education program. Devices and services that have purely personal uses—wheelchairs, braces, and the like—are not included. The test to apply is fairly simple: If a device and/or service is required for program participation and is used only at the program or school, it is eligible for Part C or Part B funding. If, however, the child uses it all day, seven days a week, in-program and out-of-program, then it is a personal device or service and is not reimbursable under Part C or Part B.

In some cases, this test is misleading: Parents may argue successfully that devices and/or services that are primarily program-related are also needed at home and during vacations for intervention or educational purposes. In such instances, their cost may be reimbursed under

---

IDEA, Part C (if in IFSP)

IDEA, Part B (if in IEP)

Medicaid (Mandated and Optional Services)

Medicaid EPSDT (Early and Periodic Screening, Diagnosis, and Treatment)

Supplemental Security Income

Developmental Disabilities Programs

Maternal and Child Health Block Grants—Title V

Technology-Related Assistance for Individuals with Disabilities Act

---

FIGURE 10.2 Selected financing options

Part C or Part B. As another illustration of exceptions to this test, OSEP recently issued a groundbreaking policy letter stating that, contrary to previous policy, hearing aids were to be acquired by schools and made available without cost to children with hearing impairments if the children's IEPs contained such devices (Hehir, 1993). The precedent appears to be such that other low-tech products may also be considered "assistive technology devices" and thus eligible for provision in IFSPs and IEPs.

Medicaid is a second, very important source of funding for assistive technology devices and services. Officially, Medicaid will reimburse costs for medically necessary equipment and services. However, the federal regulations governing Medicaid (42 CFR 440.10) state that physical therapy, occupational therapy, and speech and language pathology—all of which are allowable services—*include* "any necessary supplies and equipment." This phrase opens a wide door for all kinds of technologies. As Medicaid expert Allan Bergman, of the Brain Injury Association, put it in a recent interview: "For example, when an OT [occupational therapist] recommends assistive eating devices, Medicaid must pay for them. In the speech/language area hearing aids, alternative and augmentative communication devices, computers, and voice synthesizers are Medicaid reimbursable" (quoted in Kyes, 1994, p. 28). Bergman added that the same regulation allows reimbursement for vision aids.

In addition, state Medicaid programs are authorized by law to acquire "rehabilitation and other services to help. . . . families and individuals attain or retain capability for independence or self-care." This opens what may be an even wider door. The quoted passage was written into the Medicaid statute in 1965, yet a surprising number of federal and state Medicaid officials are unaware of it. Bergman commented that a request for reimbursement for these kinds of devices and services "is not welcomed by Medicaid, but it does happen when people push" (quoted in Kyes, 1994, p. 28).

Products and services identified during Early and Periodic Screening, Diagnosis, and Treatment (EPSDT) developmental screenings may be reimbursable even if not medically necessary. Again, families may need to persist in the face of stonewalling by Medicaid and EPSDT staff who are not familiar with these rules. When products and services are in fact medically necessary, securing reimbursement should be much easier (Brown, Perry, & Kurland, 1994). Chapter 6 offers much more information about Medicaid and EPSDT.

An important service for families is training for parents in use of PCs and software programs.

Supplemental security income (SSI) is a possible source of financing for assistive technology for children of families that qualify for this federal-state program. The most important role SSI plays with respect to technology is that becoming eligible for SSI automatically qualifies the family for Medicaid and EPSDT in all but a handful of states. In addition, the monthly SSI checks are largely unrestricted; they may be used, if needed, to rent, lease, or purchase devices. Developmental Disabilities and Bill of Rights Act (DD Act) funds also may be used for acquiring technology, as may Maternal and Child Health (MCH) block grants. Each of these programs is described in much more detail in Chapter 6. Also useful in learning about these programs are the Brown, Perry, and Kurland (1994) article and Kris Kyes's (1994) interview with Allan Bergman.

Other possibilities include state-run revolving fund and equipment distribution programs. Some states—California, Massachusetts, and Minnesota—offer free or low-cost telecommunications equipment, including TTDs for deaf individuals and Tele-Brailler machines for people who are both deaf and blind. The programs frequently feature flashing-light ring signalers, large-button dials, and other products useful in making telephones and related equipment more accessible for people with disabilities. In California, this equipment is available upon request at no charge; families must simply certify that a family member has a disability. In Minnesota and Massachusetts the equipment is free only to low-SES families; others pay part or all of the cost.

The National Cristina Foundation (591 West Putnam Avenue, Greenwich, CT 06830) distributes free PCs and adaptive devices. The foundation receives these as donations from companies and individuals. Additional sources include private, nonprofit organizations specializing in services for individuals with disabilities. Local chapters of the National Easter Seals Society (230 West Monroe Street, Chicago, IL 60606-4802) and United Cerebral Palsy Associations, Inc. (1660 L Street NW, Washington, DC 20036), for example, often provide financial assistance for purchase, rental, or lease of assistive technology devices and services. Other assistance may be available from local Lions, Kiwanis, or other civic organizations. One interesting resource is the Used Equipment Referral Service, an on-line information source for matching individuals who need equipment with those who have used products to sell.

DIVERSITY AND GENDER EQUITY ISSUES

The ways in which characteristics of young children with disabilities or developmental delays—notably sex, ethnic background, socioeconomic status (SES), and race—interact with technology use are important issues in ECSE. Research on these questions has just begun, however, and results as yet are not clear-cut.

A frequently raised concern about technology and young children with disabilities has to do with a presumed sex bias, that boys more than girls will accept and use technology. Williams and Ogletree (1992), surveying preschools, found no sex differences in young children's use of technology in preschool programs. In fact, they said, girls viewed the computer as female-oriented, while boys tended to think of the computer as male-oriented. Studies showing male advantages with computers have been conducted with school-age and college students. Williams and Ogletree suggested that such biases have not yet developed in young children, and that girls have as much to gain from using computers and other technologies in preschools as do boys. By contrast, Scott, Cole, and Engel (1992) reported that boys are more likely than girls, and white middle-class children more likely than minority or lower-SES children, to use computers, both at home and in community programs such as preschools. Perhaps the key is for teachers and other caregivers to introduce technology in an environment free of sex, ethnic, and racial bias.

Another troubling issue has to do with the extent to which SES relates to technology use. Sawyer and Zantal-Wiener (1993) argued that despite falling costs of technologies, equipment distribution, paradoxically, is becoming more unequal, not less. With fully equipped PCs now retailing for $1,000 or even less, some 40 percent of American households have at least one machine. The families taking advantage of falling prices to bring PCs into the home tend to be upper- and middle-class families. One would hope that lower prices (dramatically below those of just five years ago) would result in there being more PCs among lower-SES families; this does not yet appear to be happening, however. Students from upper- and middle-class families continue to be exposed to high technology much more frequently than are children from lower-SES families. It may even be that technology is widening the gap between "have" and "have-not" families, because children who use PCs, modem-based communications, and interactive learning tools have an advantage in school over children who do not have such capabilities at home. Sawyer and Zantal-Wiener noted that students with disabilities disproportionately come from working and lower-SES families.

On the other hand, Emihovich and Miller (1988) found that, contrary to popular expectation, African American young children learned more, not less, from Logo (see p. 249) sessions than did a control group of white children; the researchers speculated that the findings may relate to Logo's visual nature. Similarly, LaPlante, Hendershot, and Moss (1992), focusing more on low-tech than on high-tech products, commented that assistive technology devices actually may be more common in lower-SES families than in middle- or upper-SES families, because government assistance for purchasing such devices is much more readily available to low-SES families than to middle-SES families and is all but unavailable to upper-SES families. In addition, more low-SES families told Census Bureau interviewers that they had family members who needed such products. That is consistent with other

Today's speech recognition and other alternative input devices can help young children use E-mail and bulletin boards even before they learn to write or type.

national data: Disabilities, and thus needs for assistive technology devices, are more prevalent in lower-SES families.

One important aspect of realizing the potential technology has to offer for children with disabilities or developmental delays is for ECSE workers to adopt a firmly neutral position on gender, race, ethnic group, and SES, being careful to provide as many activities for girls as for boys, for poor children as for middle-class ones. If, as Williams and Ogletree suggest, early intervention use of PCs and related technologies may encourage girls to accept the machines as gender-appropriate—before cultural influences to the contrary alter their perceptions—and if, as Emihovich and Miller suggest, the highly visual nature of PC-based communications makes this medium culturally appropriate for African American children—it is important that ECSE personnel seize the opportunity. The United States is well into the "knowledge age" (sometimes called the "information age"), a period in which technologies that help people to gather, manipulate, and report data are growing in importance. As today's ECSE students move into K–12 and later educational programs, they will increasingly use such technologies. And when they eventually graduate and move into the world of work, familiarity and comfort with such technologies will prove to be of great importance to them. That is particularly true because adaptive products can help to alleviate the limitations these children have because of their disability.

COMMUNICATING WITH FAMILIES

telecommunications is the moving, storing, and manipulating of information by electronic means. It includes voice telephony as well as data telephony.

analog signals are continuous, rather than discrete. Thus, an analog clock is one whose hands move continuously.

digital signals are discrete. They are either "on" (e.g., 1) or "off" (e.g., 0). Thus, a digital clock shows 9:15 until it shifts abruptly to 9:16.

bit is the smallest unit of data in computing. It is expressed in 1s and 0s. Bits that together express a unit of meaning are a byte.

voice telephony is the traditional use of telephones to transmit voice-based information over telephone lines.

ECSE programs nationwide value frequent and meaningful communication with families. Translating this ideal into practice has always been problematic. Calling parents on the telephone during program hours, for example, can be very difficult; staffing the ECSE program in the evening hours for the purpose of calling and receiving calls from families at home is expensive. ECSE programs share this problem with the public schools. While 94 percent of American homes have telephones, just 2 percent to 4 percent of classrooms do. Even though schools have invested billions of dollars in instructional technology, it is still all but impossible for a parent to speak to a teacher on the telephone—to ask a question, to share information, even to say "hello." Fortunately, telecommunications technology has tremendous potential to enhance program-parent communications.

Telecommunications is the moving, storing, and manipulating of information by electronic means. It includes voice telephony as well as data telephony. The former refers to the familiar regular telephone service in which people talk and listen; the voices are transmitted over telephone wires or through the air, either in **analog** (continuous) or **digital** (**bits**, or "0" and "1" messages) form, or both. Digital information consists of data transported from one location to another, again either over phone lines or through the air. Data telephony includes electronic mail, facsimile transmission (frequently called "fax"), and computer bulletin board systems (often called "BBSs").

Voice Telephony

The major advantage of **voice telephony** (distance communication by voice) is that some 94 percent of American homes and apartments are equipped to make and receive voice telephone calls. A second advantage is that it works with family members who are not comfortable with

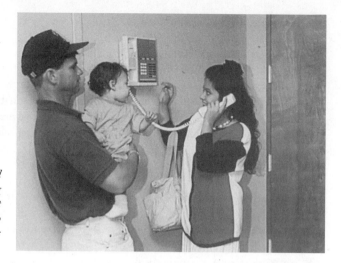

The telephone is a critical tool in ECSE, facilitating close program-family contact and helping families to juggle competing demands and often-hectic schedules.

reading and writing; in some programs, as many as 10 or even 20 percent of parents or other primary caregivers may not read or write well enough for writing to be an effective means of communication. However, voice telephony is time-consuming and often inconvenient. Both parties must be on the line at the same time. That can be hard to accomplish. If one or both parents works during the hours the ECSE program is open, the parents may not be reachable. Similarly, parents calling into the ECSE program may not be able to get the early childhood special educator, speech and language pathologist, or other professional on the line. The major advantage of data telephony is that it largely obviates these problems.

A low-tech, voice telephony solution to the problem of real-time communication between ECSE programs and families is to have an answering machine attached to an ECSE teacher's telephone line and have a recorded message played to each caller detailing the day's activities, plans for the next day, and so on. The cost is low (as little as $50 for the answering machine), and the time investment needed by the early childhood special educator or other ECSE worker is modest (a few minutes to record each day's message). Parents may also be given the option of leaving responses on the tape. Somewhat more sophisticated is voice-mail versions, which offer parents a menu of choices ("Press 1 for the day's schedule," "Press 2 for tomorrow's lesson plans," and so on). If used, voice mail should include the option of reaching a human being; few things are more frustrating than reaching a voice-mail system and not being able to get out.

As simple as voice telephony solutions may be, they are beyond the capability of many ECSE programs. Surveys of public school administrators, for example, show that only a small proportion of classrooms have a telephone jack, let alone a telephone and an answering machine. The Alliance for Public Technology estimates that only 7 percent of American schools have enough electrical outlets to plug anything new into classrooms and that just 4 percent have connections such as phone jacks in the classroom (*Technologies of Freedom,* 1993). It is probable that similarly low percentages occur at ECSE programs. Another disadvantage is that the approach is not truly interactive; the message(s) must be the same for all parents. Despite such problems, these are steps ECSE program administrators should consider because ECSE programs value parental communication so highly.

Data Telephony

Intermediate, more advanced, solutions include E-mail, fax, and computer BBSs. **Data tele-phony**, which uses these technologies, makes heavy use of "off-line" or "virtual time" tech-niques that circumvent the need for both parties to be on the line at the same time. In data telephony, a message is entered, usually by typing on a personal computer. The computer com-bines the bits into **bytes** (units computers understand). The message may be sent immediately, via a **modem** ("MOdulator DEModulator"), over existing telephone lines. One option is to send the message (called electronic mail [E-mail]) to the parents' mailbox in some **BBS**. This may be the ECSE program's own BBS, or it may be a commercial service such as AT&T Worldnet or America Online. In all cases, the ECSE member enters the E-mail message at his convenience; it is retrieved and read by family members at their convenience by dialing the BBS and looking into the family's mailbox. The communication cycle is completed when the ECSE worker retrieves the reply, again at his convenience. This is "virtual time."

Such solutions are inexpensive. All that an ECSE program needs to create a BBS is a PC, a modem, and a communications software program that has BBS capabilities. Such hardware/software combinations may be purchased for less than $1,000. However, the tele-phone line used for the BBS must be dedicated to that service; it cannot also be used for voice telephony, for example, or for faxes (unless the geographical region is wired with inte-grated services digital network [ISDN] lines, which are discussed later in the chapter). Another disadvantage of such E-mail or BBS communications is that only fifteen million American families both have modem-equipped PCs and know how to use them for com-munication via E-mail and similar communications technologies (*Technologies of Freedom*, 1993); that number represents about 40 percent of all computer-equipped homes. The num-ber is rising rapidly. Still, it will be some time before a majority of American families—including low-SES families, which traditionally lag high-SES families in getting and using technology—acquire PCs and communication hardware and software.

A **fax** machine breaks down words and images (including pictures) into bits and sends them via modem over telephone lines. Fax machines are ideal when pictures, drawings, or other images must be transmitted. Stand-alone fax machines accept paper input and receive faxes on paper as well. However, a fax/modem board may be placed into the PC. Such boards often come with communications software. The major advantage of fax/modem boards over stand-alone fax machines is that the fax/modem board can "broadcast" faxes to any number of preentered fax numbers. The ECSE worker creates a document, stores it in fax-ready form, and selects the "broadcast" option. In this way, the same fax message is auto-matically transmitted to every fax line in the fax/modem telephone directory, or to any num-ber of selected ones. Broadcast fax has the tremendous advantage of saving large amounts of time. With an investment of perhaps fifteen to thirty minutes, an ECSE worker can send a message to as many as a hundred or even more families, perhaps overnight, when phone rates are lowest. Another advantage is that no paper is required: The fax/modem board transmits directly from the PC and receives faxes into the PC. The disadvantage of fax com-munications is that fax machines must exist both at the ECSE program and at participants' homes. As this book was being written, only about 30 percent of American homes had fax machines. With internal fax/modem boards costing as little as $50 and external stand-alone fax machines some $100, they are within reach of many families.

Bell Atlantic, of White Plains, New York, has developed a technology that allows cus-tomers to dial telephone numbers just by saying a word or phrase. What distinguishes

VoiceDialing from telephones in customers' homes with similar capabilities is that the technology is embedded in the telephone network, not in the user's telephone. Bell Atlantic made the service available throughout its New York and New England service area in 1993 and 1994; other regional Bell telephone companies have licensed the technology to offer it in their regions. While VoiceDialing is a convenience for anyone, it is especially helpful for young children with disabilities. Children who are blind, learning disabled, or have physical or mental disabilities limiting their fine motor control are able to make telephone calls simply by speaking a word or phrase. Research performed by Bell Atlantic prior to the introduction of VoiceDialing in 1993 established that the system works even for people with poor voice quality. Thus, children with cerebral palsy or other disabilities affecting speech can use VoiceDialing just as effectively as can other children.

Near-Future Telephony

machine language translation is electronic translation of, for example, English-to-Spanish or French-to-English. Little or no human intervention is required. The hardware and software are in development, but it will be several years before the technology reaches general use.

High-end solutions include **machine language translation**, video telephony, and other innovations. These will greatly help to make program-parent communication effective. Machine language translation will soon be particularly important to ECSE programs that serve large numbers of minority-language families. Technology is moving rapidly toward systems in which an ECSE worker could speak in English and the telephone company's switching station would convert the message, in real time, to, say, Spanish, and vice versa. The same could be done with Japanese, French, Portuguese, Chinese, or any other major language. While some machine language translation capabilities exist today, it will be a few years before good ones become widely available.

video telephone service allows both parties to see each other while they talk. Video telephone service usually requires fiber-optic cables, which can carry voice, data, and video at the same time. Also required is a video camera and video receiver or monitor at both ends of the conversation.

Video telephone service allows both parties to see each other while they talk. This promotes understanding, especially of nuances. It can eliminate the need for some in-person

Alarm systems are among the "low tech" products that can really help families.

meetings, thus saving families considerable time in commuting between their homes and the ECSE program. Video telephone service requires fiber-optic cables, which can carry voice, data, and video at the same time. Also required is a video camera and video receiver or monitor at both ends of the conversation. Video telephones may be purchased today that may be used over copper telephone lines, but the image quality is jerky. With fiber-optic cables being installed in many parts of the United States, high-quality video telephone service should become widely available in the coming years. Already, the U.S. Department of Education and many state Part C and Part B lead agencies accept telecommuting and video telephone conferences as meeting the statutory requirements that IFSPs and IEPs be developed in meetings. The importance of telecommuting and other forms of video telephony can only grow in the years to come.

To illustrate the potential of coming information-age technologies, Francis Fisher offers a scenario of a mythical family circa 2002. This Hispanic family includes two young daughters, one of whom has asthma. The mother, Rosa, is using an advanced PC that is a hybrid PC and TV set:

> *Rosa particularly values the information she can get about asthma that helps her manage Crystal's disease. She can select the moving picture sequences which contrast children who have asthma with children suffering from more ordinary respiratory difficulties. Rosa can specify which of the demonstrated degrees of severity matches Crystal's symptoms and get guidance on medication. Now, she only goes to the clinic when the program tells her it is necessary. It helps that the explanations are available in both English and Spanish. . . .*
>
> *Increasingly Rosa is able to deal with government agencies through the TV. She used the terminal to apply for an apartment in the housing complex that would provide the family one more room. And now she can check over the network on how her application stands on the waiting list. Her entitlements for SSI and food stamps can also be verified when Rosa punches in the facts of her ever-changing family and economic situation.*
>
> *Rosa can also connect to Maria's school through a TV "number" and see teachers explaining for parents what is being taught in each class that week. The teachers describe the work that students are expected to do at home, with books, paper, and pencil or by interacting with the teaching program through the terminal. Using the voice mail utility, Rosa can leave messages for Maria's teachers and can check her own message box at the school for school events and for teacher comments about Maria.* (Fisher, 1992, pp. 2–3)

It will take some time for technologies with these kinds of options to become widely available. When they do, however, the impact will be very large. Rosa was able, for example, to secure videotapes on asthma at her convenience; the service is described as sophisticated enough to allow her to search through thousands of tapes, in this case by topic but she could search by program name or any of many other variables. Today, to see and tape such a program, Rosa would have to read weekly television guides for months, even years, before finding listings on asthma. Rosa also used this futuristic technology to apply for, and monitor her progress toward, government assistance; today, she must physically travel to a Social Security district office, spending hours each time waiting to see a clerk. It is clear that interactive technology would save Rosa enormous amounts of time, not only with SSI but also with such time-consuming tasks as renewing her driver's license. Rosa was also able, in this example, to secure timely information about Maria's school. The same terminal let Maria herself receive her homework assignments and transmit them to her teacher, all without the use of any paper.

ECSE PROFESSIONALS AND TECHNOLOGY

As exciting as these capabilities, both today's and tomorrow's, are, a thorough review of the literature reveals few articles or books about technology in ECSE. One exception, a report from Canada, describes how ECSE paraprofessionals used laptop computers during home visits to families with children who had developmental delays (Perry & Garber, 1993). Applying computerized versions of intake and assessment instruments, the paraprofessionals recorded observations and parent reports during their initial home visits, transmitting reports to the ECSE administrative office over telephone lines via modem. The laptops helped the paraprofessionals to guide parents through behavior checklists and to decide upon performance goals for their young children. The information was then compiled at the office, coded to protect privacy, and analyzed to produce statements of children's needs, service goals, and staffing requirements. Although Perry and Garber do not comment on cost savings, it is evident that this mode of data entry and storage saved considerable amounts of staff time and resources, as compared with traditional paper-and-pen processes.

In contrast to the paucity of articles about technology in ECSE, a large number of publications discuss technology in the public schools. A recent survey of 550 K–12 educators who use telecommunications on a regular basis (Honey & Henriquez, 1993) offers information that may be relevant to ECSE as well. The study found that personal interest in technology was most often behind early adopters' knowledge and familiarity with telecommunications. More than half, for example, had a PC with a modem at home and used these devices for both personal and professional purposes (Honey & Henriquez, 1993, p. 16). At their places of work, these relatively sophisticated educators used telecommunications for student activities as well as for their own professional work. Most learned telecommunications skills on their own, although some credited conferences they had gone to or other formal training. More than three in every four of these early adopters (76 percent) sent and received E-mail to and from professional colleagues; they frequently exchanged information on forums and bulletin boards. They also used telecommunications to access databases containing information relevant to their work.

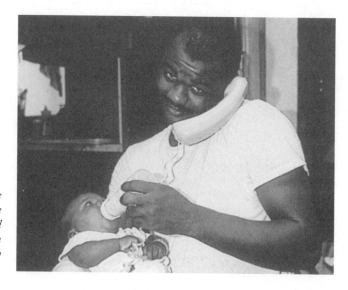

When ECSE programs take advantage of advanced voice telephone products and services, family members can get the information they need when they need it.

These early adopters said that telecommunications helped them to combat professional isolation, a big problem for many educators. The forums and bulletin boards let them post queries and exchange information rapidly and efficiently. They said that the opportunity to communicate with far-flung peers and the ability to receive information rapidly and easily were the two most motivating aspects of telecommunications use.

These educators reported using such popular electronic networks as America Online, as well as more specialized education networks. Almost half were on the Internet, the telecommunications infrastructure connecting many networks worldwide. Often called an "information highway," like a network of highways, it allows people to branch off into different networks for different reasons. The most common uses of the Internet are to exchange E-mail with colleagues, gain remote access to bulletin boards, and receive news and other information from databases. The Internet has more than one hundred million users worldwide who browse among millions of specialized databases called Web sites.

America Online offers an Assistive Technology Forum in which users swap information and suggestions about how to acquire, pay for, and use technology to meet special needs. It also has the Access ERIC database, through which educators can obtain data, articles, reports, and so on related to special education; users can post questions and can "download" (retrieve, into their own computers) files, including articles and even entire books. Prodigy has a Disabilities bulletin board, as well as more specific ones such as Arthritis, Hearing Loss, and Chronic Fatigue Syndrome, among many others. Finally, the Internet provides a vast array of resources, including ERIC; Internet users may browse through some 850 ERIC digests in the University of North Carolina at Chapel Hill's searchable ERIC full-text file.

In ECSE as in other human services fields, adoption of technology often lags that of the business world. A recent Bank Street College of Education survey of PC use by more than 500 K–12 educators working in elementary and secondary schools (Honey & Henriquez, 1993) found that 96 percent were self-taught. They became interested in PCs (91 percent had one at home) and other technologies, saw the potential for these products in education, and learned all they could, often on their own time and at their own expense. These leading-edge, or first-wave, adopters excited others at their schools and agitated from within for schoolwide adoption of technologies. An earlier Bank Street study, "Accomplished Teachers," found that PCs changed the ways teachers teach. They reported having more time for individual work with students and assigning more independent-study work to their students as a result of having PCs in the classroom. (For more information on these reports, contact Margaret Honey, Education Development Center, 610 West 112th Street, New York, NY 10025. The center is sponsored by the U.S. Department of Education to investigate the role of technology in children's lives and in education.)

Getting Started

Creating a telecommunications capacity for an ECSE program is not difficult. Local and long-distance telephone companies, such as the Bells or AT&T, have specialists working with educational and social service agencies and programs who can help. The first step is to assess the program's current telecommunications capabilities. As noted earlier, these probably are insufficient for more than routine office functions. Telephone lines should be added to activity rooms, classrooms, and media centers. Telephone companies can provide information about cost containment, including blocking of unauthorized calls.

A second step is to acquire the necessary "customer premises equipment" to use on these telephone lines. If the program's objective is to provide for E-mail and BBS access, all that is needed is an inexpensive PC, a modem, and communications software. An excellent way to choose these items is to ask a telecommunications enthusiast who may be a staff member, a volunteer, or a parent. In selecting this person, the critical skill to look for is an ability to communicate to laypeople in real English as well as an understanding of what the program wants to accomplish. The PC need not be a powerful one; an 8088 or 80386 version of the IBM-compatible machines or a 68000 or 68030 version of the Apple Macintosh is sufficient for most purposes. Although modems that transmit at speeds of up to 56,000 **baud** are available, 2400-baud modems are sufficient in most cases. If the ECSE program wants to create a BBS of its own, into which parents and staff alike may call, it is important to bear in mind that the machine must be dedicated to this function; if the PC is turned off, or being used for other things, users will be unable to connect to the BBS (unless, as mentioned, the lines are ISDN).

baud rate is the speed of data transmission, in bits per second (bps). The slowest (oldest) modems use 300 baud, the fastest use 56,000 baud or even higher rates.

The next step is to pick out communications and other software. Most word-processing software programs, such as WordPerfect, allow text to be saved as ASCII (American Standard Code for Information Interchange). This is a no-frills way to store data; there are no codes for bold, italic, underlining, and so on. ASCII often is used for E-mail and BBS communications. Communications programs often may be acquired free or at low cost from BBS services, as "shareware." More sophisticated software is needed if the ECSE program wants to create its own BBS or if it wants to use broadcast fax as a means of communicating with parents.

Training for staff, volunteers, and parents is important. Probably most helpful will be two levels of training—one for newcomers who have little or no prior experience with telecommunications, and a second, much briefer, training for experienced users. Some schools and universities provide communications software to their staff members for use from the home; ECSE programs may wish to consider such off-site access for staff and volunteers as a means of enhancing ongoing communications.

These steps may appear to be complicated, but they really are not. Electronic communication today is a relatively simple process in most cases. Most communications software is designed for easy use by beginners, as are most BBS services. (The Internet is still complex, though.) ECSE programs should encourage staff, volunteers, and parents to learn to use these capabilities because they do so much to facilitate communication. A useful article, "Getting on the Electronic Highway," in *Teaching Exceptional Children* (1994) explains how to use E-mail and BBS services, including the Internet, for education-related purposes.

TELEVISION

Television sets are among the most widely used low-tech products in the United States today, with virtually all households having at least one set. Many ECSE programs have television sets as well, and many also have videocassette recorders (VCRs). The ubiquity of television technology is potentially of tremendous importance in ECSE. That is especially true because television recently has become far more accessible to and usable by young children with disabilities.

Perhaps the most exciting television-related advance in recent years is the remarkable distribution of caption-ready television sets. All sets measuring thirteen inches or more diagonally that were manufactured in and/or sold in the United States after mid-1993 contain built-in "caption chips," which, when activated, display closed **captions**, or subtitles. Because fifteen to twenty million television sets are sold in the United States annually, some sixty million American households had caption-ready sets as of late 1997, and the number will grow with each passing year. The caption capability is offered at no additional cost; previously, caption users had to acquire and attach decoder boxes costing about $200 (Bowe, 1991b). Industry analysts estimate that by the year 2003, virtually every home in the United States will have caption-ready television sets.

Captions have obvious benefits for young children who are deaf. Indeed, without captions, most children who are deaf cannot follow TV programming at all. However, to consider captioning as a technology only for people who are deaf would be a serious mistake. Potential uses with other populations were so widely recognized when Congress considered what became the Television Decoder Circuitry Act of 1990 (PL 101-431) that more than a hundred organizations serving people with mental retardation, learning disabilities, and other special needs endorsed the legislation (Bowe, 1991b). Young children with mental retardation or learning disabilities benefit when the audio signal is supplemented by subtitles because they receive information in a multi-sensory mode, something we know helps them to learn more and better (Adler & Drew, 1988; Bos & Vaughn, 1988; Clements, Nastasi, & Swaminathan, 1993). Many ECSE programs may also find that captioning helps parents and other primary caregivers to learn English. Literacy organizations strongly endorsed the Decoder Circuitry Act because captions may dramatically increase literacy in the American population.

The technology will reach its potential only if it is used. ECSE staff should advise parents of young children with cognitive or communication limitations or delays to purchase caption-ready television sets and to activate the captions whenever captioned programming is being watched. Similarly early childhood special educators should consider activating the caption capability as a routine matter whenever educational programming is shown during program hours. Of course, where educational videotapes are available in captioned or uncaptioned versions, ECSE staff should order the captioned tape.

Activating captions is a simple matter. To display captions on a caption-ready set, the viewer touches a button on the remote control unit or on the TV itself, or activates an on-screen menu via the remote control unit (Bowe, 1991b; Hutchins, 1994). Captions appear if they have been prepared and transmitted by the broadcaster or video producer. Virtually all prime-time broadcast television programming now is captioned, as are most network newscasts. While many feature movies shown on cable channels are captioned, most other cable programs are not. Many educational television programs such as *Sesame Street, Mr. Rogers' Neighborhood,* and others are captioned.

Family and ECSE staff members purchasing new TV sets should evaluate the captioning capabilities as they do other television features such as color, sound, and so on. A few pointers may assist. First, only TV sets thirteen inches or larger (measured diagonally) are required by the Decoder Circuitry Act to be caption-capable. Second, some TV manufacturers place a "caption" key on the remote control device, making activation of captions easy. Other manufacturers placed the function within on-screen menus, which makes it harder and more time-consuming to activate captioning. Third, the size and font of captions vary from manufacturer to manufacturer. Some make captioned letters large (good for viewing at a distance) while others create smooth, well-formed letters with no visible dots. Examining these and other features of television captioning is easy; just ask the salesperson for the set's remote control, turn on the captioning function, and search from channel to channel until you locate a captioned program (Hutchins, 1994).

Two other recent developments related to television deserve mention. The first is "text mode." Although the Decoder Circuitry Act did not require TV makers to support this option, most do. In text mode, messages such as program listings or deaf community news are displayed as simple text on the screen. Local stations or cable companies could perhaps encode and transmit local information in text mode. This may be a simple and inexpensive way for ECSE programs and public schools to communicate with area families. The major benefit is that virtually all local households can receive such messages, at little or no cost, assuming their TV sets are 1993 or later models.

Descriptive video service (DVS) is another recent development. In DVS, spoken descriptions of on-screen action are inserted during natural pauses in program dialog. This narration articulates the visual image for the benefit of viewers who are blind. As of late 1999, few programs feature DVS. The technology is evolving, however, and families with young children who are blind may look forward to greatly increased video description in the coming years.

descriptive video service (DVS) transmits spoken descriptions of on-screen television action so that individuals who are blind may learn about actions they do not see.

DISTANCE LEARNING AND TELEMEDICINE

The once-separate media discussed thus far in this chapter, telephony and television, are coming together in the late 1990s. Fiber-optic cable, which can carry massive amounts of voice, video, and data over vast distances, promises very soon to make multimedia interactive communication at a distance far more convenient and effective than it is today. Video telephony is in use in many cities today. However, because participants must travel to specially-equipped locations and because costs remain high, the technology is not as widely used as once was projected. A few universities do offer **distance learning**, or instruction for off-site students, by means of satellite uplinks and downlinks. The experience of West Virginia University in training early intervention personnel is a good example (see Chapter 12).

distance learning links an instructor in one geographical location with students at other sites. Students see and hear the instructor, who in turn sees and hears them. The connections may be via satellite broadcast or, increasingly, via fiber-optic cable.

What fiber optics will do is to make both ends of distance learning far more convenient. When an area is wired with fiber, students may receive video, voice, and data transmissions at home or in their offices; faculty at universities similarly may teach in their regular classrooms rather than in specially equipped studios. The technology thus promises to bring real-time images of highly trained ECSE professionals to virtually any location, at almost any time, while simultaneously transporting the images of students to these professionals. The implications for preservice and inservice training are potentially tremendous. Nationally prominent experts would be able to "travel" to remote locations without having to actually make the often time-consuming trips.

The same technology could link the images of young children with rare disorders to faraway physicians or other care professionals, with real-time connections offering high-quality video, voice, and data. To illustrate this **telemedicine**, it would be possible for a cardiac surgeon such as Michael DeBakey in Houston to see moving images of the heart of a young child; while viewing the video, DeBakey could talk (at the same time, over the same fiber cable) with the child's local physician and even could exchange faxes with that physician, all without hanging up. Such applications bring special expertise in one location together with

telemedicine links medical specialists in one location with a patient in another, usually via fiber-optic cable, which can transmit high-quality video as well as voice and data.

rare or unusual conditions in another. Telemedicine not only could save, and improve the quality of, lives but could do so at far lower costs than are necessary at present. Transporting fragile children is very costly, as is compensating a specialist for travel time. In telemedicine, travel on both ends is obviated, with resultant savings not only of money but also of time.

Multimedia

multimedia personal computers can display video as well as words, sound, data, and still images.

CD-ROM stands for "Compact Disc—Read Only Memory." CD-ROM discs store information that computer users may read, scan, and search at high speed. The user may read the disk but not write to it.

Perhaps the newest buzzword in computers these days is **multimedia**, a shorthand term for PCs that can display video as well as words, data, and still images. Once much more costly than ordinary PCs, today's multimedia PCs sell for only about $150 more than their unadorned counterparts. For $1,500—even less with education discounts—ECSE programs get not only a Pentium-class PC, but also a CD-ROM player, a video-graphics-array color monitor, a sound card, speakers, and a microphone. Adding CD-ROM capabilities to a PC costs less than $100. (The term **CD-ROM** stands for "Compact Disc—Read Only Memory." As the term implies, the user may read the disc but not write to it.)

A major advantage of multimedia PCs for ECSE is the ability of these machines to provide information to children in a variety of media. Children who are deaf can see the information, children who are blind can listen to it, and children with mental retardation or dyslexia can use sound to reinforce video. The evidence is that such multiple-mode input helps, often considerably (Clements, Nastasi, & Swaminathan, 1993; Adler & Drew, 1988). Multimedia is one means of making computers "appropriate" for very young children, to adopt the National Association for the Education of Young Children's (NAEYC) term. That is because multimedia PCs offer young children individualized, customizable, and interactive opportunities for learning.

In one EC program, a child with cerebral palsy used a mouse to operate a CD-ROM program to create a story that featured motion picture cartoons, music, recorded narration, and sound effects. When the EC teacher asked each child to read a story to the group, this child participated as an equal member of the class. Despite her difficulties with speech, she was able to tell a story as engaging, if not more so, than her classmates (Oddone, 1993). This vignette illustrates how high-technology products can be used by even very young children to facilitate integration into regular EC settings. Paradoxically, as PCs become ever more powerful, they—and the software they run—become ever easier to use, even by young children. Just a few years ago, creating a presentation that mixed moving pictures, recorded narration, and music would have challenged even a Ph.D.-educated professional. Today, with the right hardware and software, even preschool children can do it.

Another interesting program is BEST's Colors & Shapes. The program both assesses preschool-age children's knowledge of colors and shapes and teaches them color and shape discrimination. Young children work through such concepts as object permanency and figure-ground discrimination. The software allows customization by input device, complexity of stimuli, response time allowed, and visual and/or auditory cueing. ECSE staff may use the program with young children having a wide variety of strengths and needs. The program automatically compiles performance statistics, allowing ECSE staff to track children's progress unobtrusively.

A word of caution: Programs using relatively old (pre-1992) PCs should be careful about adopting multimedia programs. That is because such PC hardware and the MS-DOS/PC-DOS/DR-DOS disk operating systems that control them were never intended for use with video. They may, in theory, be modified, but doing so requires the user to know the make and model of each component—including the video card, the audio card, and other internal parts—and spend hours adjusting the system. It is far better to acquire newer PCs with video capabilities built in.

LOGO

Seymour Papert, a professor of mathematics and education at Harvard University, argued that K–12 public schools have misapplied PCs (Papert, 1993). He noted that as of the end of the 1980s, the nation's fifty million elementary and secondary public school children were sharing just three million PCs, and that the uses to which these machines were put did not begin to tap the potential. Papert, who studied under Piaget for four years during the 1960s, argued that Logo and similar computer languages may be used by very young children to do innovative and educational things with PCs. Echoing his mentor to the effect that "play is a child's work," he contended that children learn best when they create, not when they merely perform rote, fill-in-the-blanks tasks. It is important that ECSE workers study the errors made in the 1980s in K–12 education so that they do not repeat them in the new century.

One reason the programming language Logo works so well with young children is that it allows them to, in effect, "teach the computer" and to do creative things with the Logo turtle (cursor). Research with young children (Hughes & Macleod, 1986; Clements, Nastasi, & Swaminathan, 1993) suggests that they can in fact work collaboratively, as when two preschoolers jointly decide how large to make a shape. The major advantage of Logo over crayon-and-paper drawings is that innumerable changes can be made as children experiment with different ideas; as a result, drawings made with Logo are typically far richer in complexity and detail than are paper drawings (Vaidya & McKeeby, 1984).

Although drill-and-practice routines do help young children with prereading and other academic skills, the evidence is that they can learn more, and more enjoyably, if multimedia, interactive, and open-ended programs are emphasized (Clements & Nastasi, 1992). Children are more likely to pose their own problems, play with alternative solutions, and generate creative ideas when using open-ended programs that call upon problem-solving skills than they are when using drill-and-practice routines; they are also more likely to evaluate their own work positively and to express a desire to return again and again to the computer (Clements et al., 1993).

It is important that ECSE workers provide scaffolding, or intellectual support, for very young children who are using computers, rather than leaving the children alone at the machines. When teachers pose questions ("What do you think will happen now?" "Why did that happen?"), children think about what they are doing and realize scholastic gains. A good example is the underlying mathematical and geometrical properties of Logo; unless ECSE workers point out these aspects, young children are not likely to associate what they are learning on the computer with those academic disciplines. It is the ECSE worker who draws connections between the children's actions to move the turtle and the ideas and concepts behind those actions (Clements et al., 1993).

VIRTUAL REALITY

The cutting edge of high technology in the 1990s is something called **virtual reality**. In computer-speak, something that is "virtual" does not exist; it just appears to do so. The previous section on data telephony used the term "virtual time" to refer to the fact that E-mail messages

virtual reality refers to something that does not exist, but appears as if it did; an artificial reality.

may be left at the sender's convenience and retrieved at the receiver's convenience. The receiver does not read the messages in real time (at the actual time when they are composed and sent). Similarly, virtual reality is a computer-generated artificial environment. High-resolution, interactive virtual-reality techniques have reached the point that they are convincingly real—and people respond to them as if they were. The technique has obvious applications for young children who have severe physical limitations, because it allows them to explore and interact with environments they cannot visit physically.

Indeed, Perelman (1992) argued passionately that education as we know it must inevitably yield to the power of such advanced technologies as virtual reality. People learn best in context, he insisted, which is why computer-generated environments into which one "wanders" by wearing wraparound goggles displaying nonexistent environments have so much power. What Perelman called "hyperlearning" taps the full power of interactive communications technologies to let people learn what they want, when they want. Perelman would have us discard education as we know it—instruction given by a teacher in a room to a class of students—and replace it to a large extent with virtual reality. We need not go that far. Without discarding all of traditional education, it is possible to bring similar benefits to children and families by taking advantage of virtual reality where we can.

Wasowicz (1993) illustrated the potential of virtual reality to allow people who are blind to read, individuals who are deaf to hear, persons who are mute to speak, and people who have physical disabilities to move about freely in once inaccessible environments. One virtual-reality program, she reported, allows people using wheelchairs to roll through the blueprints of an as-yet-unbuilt edifice, ascertaining where it is accessible and where it is not. Prairie Virtual Systems of Chicago markets the system, which links blueprints to virtual-reality computer software, thus enabling a person using a wheelchair to "walk through" the structure.

Such techniques could readily be adapted to let young children with severe physical disabilities "visit" a firehouse, "traverse" a shopping mall, or even "explore" the Grand Canyon. In fact, some ECSE programs already use such virtual-reality programs to motivate children in physical therapy sessions.

INFORMATION SOURCES

A wealth of information about technology and people with disabilities is readily available to ECSE programs. *Exceptional Parent* magazine publishes an "Annual Guide to Products and Services," which lists state-by-state agencies and organizations providing technical assistance on assistive technology and also provides toll-free numbers for products and services. *Closing the Gap* (P.O. Box 68, Henderson, MN 56044) is a tabloid-style newspaper published bimonthly that describes new assistive technology devices and products in an easy-to-read format. Special education uses are well covered in this publication. Somewhat more difficult to read is the professional *Journal of Special Education Technology*. Edited by Herbert Rieth of the Peabody College at Vanderbilt University (Box 328, Nashville, TN 37203), it is a publication of the Technology and Media Division of the Council for Exceptional Children. The book *Adaptive Technologies for Learning & Work Environments* (Lazarro, 1993) offers easy-to-read explanations of products for people with vision, hearing, mobility, and other disabilities (American Library Association, 50 E. Huron Street, Chicago, IL 60611). Also helpful is *Computers and Exceptional Individuals* (Lindsey, 1993).

An excellent way to keep abreast of low-tech devices is to write to mail-order catalog publishers requesting a copy of their latest catalog; doing so gets you on their mailing list, and they will send you catalogs at least annually. A number of companies serve as distributors of low-tech products for people with disabilities. Independent Living Aids (ILA, 27 East Mall, Plainview, NY 11803) offers hundreds of products in a sixty-four-page catalog. The Lighthouse, Inc. (111 East 59 Street, New York, NY 10022) annually describes more than three hundred classroom, play, and household products for people who are blind or have low vision in its *Product Catalog*. TeleConsumer Hotline (T-C Hotline, 1910 K Street NW, #610, Washington, DC 20006) annually publishes guides to products that people with hearing, vision, mobility, and other limitations can use with the telephone. Figure 10.1 gives additional sources of catalogs (see p. 232).

Below are some other sources of information.

Not for Profit

ABLEDATA
8455 Colesville Road #935
Silver Spring, MD 20910-3319
Offers a database describing 17,000+ products for people with disabilities, from more than 2,000 companies.

Alliance for Technology Access
2175 East Francisco Blvd., #L
San Rafael, CA 94901
www.ataccess.org
Through 45 community-based centers in 38 states, the Alliance provides information on devices.

American Association for the Advancement of Science Project on Science, Technology, and Disability
1333 H Street NW
Washington, DC 20005
Has an outstanding directory of scientists and engineers who are individuals with disabilities. Also has a wealth of technology-related publications, as well as a respected guide to accessible meetings and conferences.

Closing the Gap
P.O. Box 68
Henderson, MN 56044
A tabloid bimonthly newspaper, *Closing the Gap* includes many articles on special education uses of PCs.

ERIC Clearinghouse on Information & Technology
Center for Science/Technology
Syracuse University
Syracuse, NY 13244-4100
A good source of brief summaries on technology as applied to special education.

FrEdMail Network
FrEd ail Foundation
P.O. Box 243
Bonita, CA 91908
A low-cost, easy-to-use computer service, FrEdMail specializes in public education and related services for children.

Job Accommodation Network (JAN)
918 Chestnut Ridge Road
P.O. Box 6080
University of West Virginia
Morgantown, WV 26506
www.janweb.icdi.wva.edu
An outstanding source of information on products and people with
disabilities.

Project Enable
West Virginia R&T Center
806 Allen Hall
P.O. Box 6123
Morgantown, WV 26506-6123
Offers searchable files of the Americans with Disabilities Act and similar
laws as well as 60+ discussion groups on specific disabilities, devices, and special
education.

RESNA
1700 North Moore Street
Suite 1540
Arlington, VA 22209
www.resna.org
An organization of engineers and scientists who specialize in meeting the needs of
children and adults with disabilities.

Trace R&D Center
S-151 Waisman Center
1500 Highland Avenue
University of Wisconsin
Madison, WI 53705
www.trace.wisc.edu
Sponsors research on "cutting-edge" devices and services for people with
disabilities.

Used Equipment Referral Service
Assistive Technology Information Network
Division of Developmental Disabilities, University Hospital School
Iowa City, IA 52242
www.uiowa.edu/infotech/UERS.htm
An on-line service in which callers may browse among listings of used adaptive and
other equipment for sale.

World Institute on Disability
510 16th Street #100
Oakland, CA 94612
www.wid.org
Sponsors WIDNet, a bulletin board, as well as reports on such issues as access to
telecommunications.

For Profit

Apple Computer, Worldwide
Disability Solutions
20525 Mariani Avenue
Cupertino, CA 95014
Offers information and referral for products that work with the Apple
Macintosh.

AT&T Accessible Communication Products
745 Route 202/206
Bridgewater, NJ 08807
Sells telephone-related devices for people with hearing, speech,
and related needs.

BEST
63 Forest Street
Chestnut Hill, MA 02167
Offers "Colors & Shapes" and other instructional software for young children
with developmental needs.

Dragon Systems, Inc.
320 Nevada Street
Newton, MA 02160
Offers DragonDictate and other speech-recognition systems.

GTE Educational Services
5525 MacArthur Boulevard #320
Irving, TX 75038
(Includes SpecialNet)
Sponsors many education-related bulletin boards.

HITEC Group
8160 Madison
Burr Ridge, IL 60521
Distributes a wide range of fairly low-tech devices, some for young
children.

IBM International Center for Persons with Disabilities
P.O. Box 2150
Atlanta, GA 30055
Provides information on IBM products and IBM-compatible products and
services.

NanoPac, Inc.
4833 S. Sheridan Road #402
Tulsa, OK 74145-5718
Offers the CINTEX2 environmental control system that works with DragonDictate
or IBM VoiceType systems.

Xerox Imaging Systems
9 Centennial Drive
Peabody, MA 01960
Offers the Kurzweil Personal Reader, The Reading Edge, and other products.

SUMMARY

America is more than a decade into the knowledge age, an era in which the collection, analysis, and reporting of information is our nation's principal economic activity. The technologies driving this period of our history affect ECSE as they do other sectors of the economy. Perhaps most urgent is the need for ECSE workers and parents to learn how today's technologies can help young children with disabilities to do things they might not be able to do otherwise. In particular, the fact that PCs may be modified to meet unique needs of children with disabilities is tremendously important. With PCs and adaptive technology devices and services, children who are blind can "see," children who are deaf can "hear," children with mental limitations can "remember," and children who have mobility disabilities can "move" virtually without boundaries.

Also important, though, is the potential of today's technologies to alleviate isolation among ECSE workers. In many towns and cities across the nation, there is only one ECSE program. Experts who work with very young children with disabilities need to maintain close contact with others specializing in similar work, regardless of where those others are located geographically. Modern technology makes it possible for ECSE workers even in the most remote locations to maintain daily, even hourly, contact with experts from coast to coast.

The ability of today's telecommunications to enhance family-program communications promises to make a reality of one of the most cherished values in all of ECSE: family-focused programming. In the years to come, technology will provide real-time machine translation of languages, allowing ECSE programs to communicate instantly in whatever languages the families they serve speak at home.

QUESTIONS FOR REFLECTION

1. Explain, in your own words, the differences between "low" and "high" technologies.

2. Children with what kinds of special needs might benefit from speech-recognition programs such as Dragon Systems's Naturally Speaking?

3. What is the difference between "assistive technology devices" and "assistive technology services"?

4. Explain why old, slow, and outdated PCs might find new uses in environmental control systems.

5. Under what circumstances will Medicaid pay for assistive technology devices?

6. What about the IDEA? Under which circumstances does the IDEA authorize reimbursement of assistive technology costs incurred on children's behalf by ECSE programs?

7. How can "broadcast fax" and E-mail enable ECSE programs to quickly and inexpensively communicate with families?

8. How could VoiceDialing help young children with disabilities to make emergency phone calls?

9. How could an ECSE program use closed captioning to enhance cognitive and language development of *hearing* children?

10. How can the Alliance for Technology Access help ECSE programs and families to get helpful devices?

PART

IV

Children and Families

Birth to Five: Early Childhood Special Education now turns to an in-depth examination of the people early childhood special education (ECSE) programs serve: the children and their families. Chapter 11 offers demographic data, notably important new information from the U.S. Bureau of the Census about the potential size of the birth-to-five population of children with disabilities, as well as estimates on the number of children with different kinds of disabilities. The chapter also discusses the socioeconomic status (SES) of the children's families, including information on family income, race, and participation in public aid programs. The U.S. Department of Education has seldom reported such data concerning young children served under the Individuals with Disabilities Education Act (IDEA). The survey findings illuminate important characteristics of the population eligible for services, as well as the perceptions of family members about their needs and those of their children.

ECSE as a field emphasizes working with families, especially on multidisciplinary teams. Chapter 12 presents suggestions on effective program-parent relations. It also offers information on "teaming," much of it drawn from research at ECSE programs. The chapter concludes with implications of multidisciplinary teams and of family-focused approaches for training ECSE workers on both the preservice and inservice levels. Virtually every major survey of ECSE practitioners and programs has found that such training needs are massive—and urgent.

The next five chapters (13–17) provide extensive discussions of each of the five domains. For more than twenty years, elementary and secondary special education programs have featured what might be called a "deficit model," in which special education and related services are provided specifically in response to a child's disability. ECSE is trying something quite different: a "multidisciplinary team" approach in which ECSE programs treat children *holistically.* In this approach, assessment, early intervention, special education, and related services all focus not just on a child's primary need(s) but rather on all five domains of development. This way of thinking is important for the reader to bear in mind while reading Chapters 13 to 17. The domain of communication development, for example, is important not only for children with speech, hearing, vision, and other communication-related disabilities, delays, or deviations in development but rather for all children. Children with Down syndrome may have the greatest presenting needs in the domain of cognitive development, but they have needs in communication and physical development as well. Similarly, children with hearing impairments have important challenges to meet in the domain of social or emotional development as well as in communication development. The point is to attend to ways in which children may develop in all five domains, rather than thinking only of children's deficits.

Presented first, in Chapter 13, is the domain of physical development. According to the Survey of Income and Program Participation (SIPP) study discussed in Chapter 11, most common among birth-to-five children are limitations of *physical development.* Physical disabilities are much less common in elementary schools (about 15 percent of all children aged six to eleven). Among birth-to-five children, however, physical problems are more prevalent because they are more readily noticed by parents and professionals alike than are some other limitations.

Chapter 14 focuses on communication development. It includes discussion of hearing and vision as well as speech and language. Limitations in these areas, especially in making speech understood, are very common among young children, according to the Census Bureau. Sometimes referred to as "speech and language development," *communication development* has to do with a young child's ability to express thoughts and feelings and to understand others' vocal, nonverbal, signed, or other forms of communication. Speech in particular is very commonly mentioned by parents as a concern. Hearing and vision impairments are much less frequently reported in children from birth to age five. In this text, deafness and other severe hearing impairments, along with blindness and other serious visual impairments, are considered to be communication-related disabilities. The federal regulation for early intervention programs (U.S. Department of Education, 1993a) includes vision and hearing as aspects of physical development. However, if you think about their effects—deafness on hearing, speaking, and using language; blindness on reading, writing, and other aspects of social interaction—the important issues clearly are communicative in nature.

Chapter 15 examines *cognitive development*—age-appropriate mental functions, notably in perceiving, understanding, and knowing. That review considers learning disabilities and mental retardation as conditions related to cognitive development. It also explores how ECSE personnel may accelerate cognitive development in young children, including the use of modern technology.

Social or emotional development (sometimes called "affective" or "psychosocial") refers to a young child's age-appropriate ability to understand his or her own feelings, and those of others, and to respond to both with behavior that is socially acceptable for children of that age, in play and in other activities. This domain is discussed in Chapter 16. The challenge for ECSE personnel is in identifying children whose behavior significantly differs from that of young children without delays or disabilities. Chapter 16 includes discussion of serious emotional disturbance, conduct disorders, Attention Deficit Hyperactivity Disorder (ADHD), and related conditions.

Chapter 15, on cognitive development, and Chapter 16, on social or emotional development, feature extensive discussion of applied behavior analysis and cognitive behavior modification, respectively. These approaches have proven to be effective with many young children with disabilities, although they remain controversial with some early childhood (EC) specialists.

The five domain-specific chapters conclude with a discussion in Chapter 17 of *adaptive development* (sometimes referred to as "self-help"). This domain relates to a young child's ability to display age-appropriate self-care and other behaviors in such a way as to adapt meaningfully to different circumstances. Adaptive development in a sense comprises the other domains as well because it includes cognitive, communication, social or emotional, and physical development tasks and issues. Chapter 17 also discusses AIDS, autism, fetal alcohol syndrome, vulnerable child syndrome ("crack babies"), and epilepsy.

Each of the five domain-specific chapters features assessment. This material supplements that in Chapter 7, which considered assessment and evaluation from the broad perspective of infants, toddlers, and preschool-age children with all kinds of disabilities, delays, and deviations in development. Chapters 13 to 17 include sections on assessment as it relates specifically to each domain of development; that is, they consider, in turn, how hearing, vision, language, cognitive, adaptive, or physical limitations are measured.

The Children

This survey asked whether children under 6 years of age had a "developmental condition for which he/she has received therapy or diagnostic services," and asked whether children 3 to 6 years of age had a "long-lasting condition that limits his/her ability to walk, run, or use stairs." The proportion of children under 3 years of age identified as having a developmental condition was 2.6 percent. For children 3 to 5 years of age, 4.1 percent had a developmental condition, and 1.9 percent had difficulty walking, running, or using stairs (the proportion with either type of disability was 5.2 percent). (McNeil, 1997, p. 1)

OVERVIEW

The entire focus of early childhood special education (ECSE) is on the children being served and their families. Surprisingly little information has as yet emerged that helps us to understand what kinds of children these are and from what kinds of families they come. This chapter outlines findings from the U.S. Bureau of the Census, which conducted a national survey of families in 1991–1992 that included questions for families with children under six years of age. The Census Bureau repeated the effort in 1994–1995. This study, formally called the Survey of Income and Program Participation (SIPP), is one of the few independent sources of information about under-six children with disabilities and their families. That alone would make it an important study. It assumes even more importance because of the fact that the fifty states, the District of Columbia, and Puerto Rico report few data to the U.S. Department of Education about under-six children.

Perhaps the most important information offered in this chapter is evidence that nearly one million American children (965,000) under the age of six potentially qualify for services under the Individuals with Disabilities Education Act (IDEA). The U.S. Bureau of the Census (McNeil, 1997) estimated that, as of 1994–1995, about 313,000 infants and toddlers under three years of age, and another 652,000 children between three and six years of age, had disabilities. These proportions were 2.6 percent of all infants and toddlers and 5.2 percent of all preschool-age children in the United States.

These figures are substantially larger than our most current data on the number of children with disabilities or delays who are actually being served under the IDEA (see Chapter 2).

The Census Bureau also offers us provocative information about what kinds of disabilities under-six children have. The Census Bureau conducted a similar study in 1991–1992 (Bowe, 1994) that looked in depth at what conditions parents reported for their children. Speech impairments were the most-noted conditions. However, if one groups conditions according to one of the IDEA's five domains of development, the most-reported conditions were in the domain of physical development. The domain of communication development followed close behind. Far fewer children were reported to have conditions in the domains of cognitive, social or emotional, or adaptive development.

socioeconomic status (SES) refers to family income and other demographic characteristics. Disability is disproportionately common among low-SES families.

Finally, the Census Bureau's data shed important light on the **socioeconomic status (SES)** of families having young children with disabilities. The figures clearly show that such families are, on average, much poorer than are families that do not have such children. There is a strong, and positive, relationship between poverty and childhood disability.

This chapter opens by describing both data sources—the Census Bureau's studies and the department's *Annual Reports to Congress*. It then examines the SIPP study in detail, including the methods used to gather data, the ways data were analyzed, and the findings that emerged. The chapter concludes with a discussion of some of the implications of the SIPP study data, including the use of labels to describe children.

POPULATION ESTIMATES

How many infants and toddlers in the United States have disabilities or delays in development? How many are at risk? No one knows. How many children aged three to five have disabilities? How many have developmental delays? Again, no one knows. The U.S. Department of Education annually receives reports from the states, but these data have serious limitations.

Disability appears to be least common among children from white or Hispanic American families.

These numbers raise as many, if not more, questions than they answer. First, how many infants and toddlers had (a) disabilities, (b) delays, and (c) neither disabilities nor delays but were determined to be "at risk" for developmental delays if early intervention services were not delivered? The statistics available to us do not answer these questions.

State Reports

Although all states are serving at least some infants, toddlers, and preschool-age children with disabilities, very little is known about the children receiving services. There are other important data collection and reporting concerns. Although the law requires states to report child-count information about children under six who receive services, they have not had to report data on children they do not serve. And in regard to those served, only the numbers served must be reported; there is no requirement to divulge demographic information such as family SES, race or ethnicity, or even disability, delay, or at-risk status. While children and youth aged ten to twenty-one must be described by primary disability condition, the U.S. Department of Education demands no such information from states about children served under age six. For these reasons, the department's reports to date have contained few demographic details about under-six children.

The *Nineteenth Annual Report to Congress* (U.S. Department of Education, 1997) gives us some important information. A good example is what kinds of services are being delivered in early intervention programs. The *Report*'s Table AH2 compiles state reports of services delivered as of December 1994. Table 11.1 summarizes these data.

The numbers in Table 11.1 represent services delivered to infants and toddlers under Part C. Any given infant or toddler can receive more than one service; indeed, many get more than one. Nonetheless, the data are revealing. Notice that no one service accounted for even 20 percent of the total. Clearly, the needs of the nation's infants and toddlers are diverse indeed. These data also show substantial demand for services that respond to physical conditions—physical therapy, occupational therapy, special transportation, and so on. These

TABLE 11.1

Early Intervention Services (E.I.S.) Delivered to Infants and Toddlers

E.I.S.	Number	Proportion
All	488,196	100.0%
Special instruction	84,479	17.3
Family training/home visits	57,625	11.8
Speech-language pathology	54,827	11.2
Physical therapy	45,898	9.4
Occupational therapy	41,943	8.6
"Other"	29,316	6.0
Social work services	26,476	5.4
Transportation	23,946	4.9
Medical services	21,583	4.4
Health services	20,364	4.2
Nursing services	19,586	4.0
Nutrition services	13,424	2.7
Audiology services	13,288	2.7
Respite care services	11,310	2.3
Psychological services	9,196	1.9
Vision services	7,605	1.6
Assistive technology devices/services	7,330	1.5

Data from *Nineteenth Annual Report* (1997), Table AH2, as of December 1, 1994.

numbers suggest that physical disabilities and delays in physical development are common in the under-three age group. As we will shortly see, that is true. At the other end of the spectrum, delivery of assistive technology devices and services is low; this may indicate that early intervention personnel may not recognize the contributions such devices and services can make in the lives of infants and toddlers with disabilities and delays in development.

The *Nineteenth Annual Report* also contains information about where young children with disabilities or delays in development were being served. Tables 11.2 and 11.3 capture these data. Recall that early intervention services are to be provided in "natural environments," notably in the home or in child-care settings also used by children who have no disabilities. Preschool special education services are to be offered in the "least restrictive environment" consistent with delivery of appropriate services that meet individual needs.

Census Bureau Findings

An independent investigation was conducted by the U.S. Bureau of the Census (McNeil, 1993a). As a follow-up to the 1990 decennial census, the Census Bureau mounted its SIPP study with a subset of census respondents. The source of the data was a combined sample from the 1990 and 1991 panels, producing a total of 30,000 interviewed households from across the United States. The interviews were conducted between October 1991 and January 1992. Included were in-depth questions about family SES and family member participation

TABLE 11.2

Number of Infants and Toddlers Served in Different Early Intervention Settings

Setting	Number	Proportion
All	156,540	100.0%
Home	78,284	50.0
E.I. classroom	47,178	30.1
Outpatient facility	18,516	11.8
"Other" settings	4,865	3.1
Regular nursery school	4,299	2.7
Inpatient facility	2,398	1.5

Data from *Nineteenth Annual Report to Congress* (U.S. Department of Education, 1997), Table AH4. Data collected December 1, 1994.

in government programs, such as Supplemental Security Income (SSI) and Medicaid, as well as about disability (McNeil, 1993a). (The Census Bureau repeated the study three years later. However, this chapter focuses on the 1991–1992 survey because more data on under-six children are available [Bowe, 1994].)

The Census Bureau's study did more than just offer population estimates. It also described the children and their families in far greater detail than did the Department of Education's reports. To understand these additional data, it is necessary to describe the Census Bureau's data collection and analysis methods in some detail.

TABLE 11.3

Number of Preschoolers with Disabilities Served in Different Settings

Setting	Number	Proportion
All	479,884	100.0%
Regular class	243,266	50.7
Separate classroom	152,000	31.7
Resource room	44,657	9.3
Separate facility (public)	19,539	4.1
Home/hospital	12,474	2.6
Separate facility (private)	7,070	1.5
Residential schools	878	0.02

Data from *Nineteenth Annual Report to Congress* (U.S. Department of Education, 1997), Table AB7. Data from 1994–1995 school year. "Regular class" means the student spent less than 21 percent of the school day outside the regular classroom. "Resource room" means the student spent between 21 percent and 60 percent of the school day outside the regular classroom. "Separate class" means the student spent more than 60 percent of the school day outside the regular classroom. "Separate facility" (whether public or private) and "residential school" mean the student spent more than 50 percent of the school day outside regular school buildings.

THE SIPP STUDY

The 1991–1992 SIPP interviews included two questions asked specifically of families that had children under age six (McNeil, 1993a, b). These questions were 21 and 22 in Part D, Functional Limitations and Disabilities:

> *21a. Because of a physical, learning, or mental health condition, do any . . . children under 6 years of age have any limitations at all in the usual kind of activities done by most children their age?*

Follow-up question 21b asked which child(ren) had such limitations. Parents reporting one or more limitations were asked to choose from a list of conditions as the cause(s) of the children's limitations; they were permitted to report up to three conditions. The question about conditions was not asked with regard to children whose only reported limitation was with seeing, hearing, or having speech understood.

> *22a. Have any of . . . 's children under the age of 6 received therapy or diagnostic services designed to meet their developmental needs?*

Follow-up question 22b asked which child(ren) received services.

These questions elicited responses about both private and public diagnostic, treatment, and education services. That is an important point. A SIPP response indicating that a given child received services for developmental needs did not necessarily mean that a state served that child under the IDEA. Parents may have arranged for private services. Additionally, no distinction was drawn in the SIPP report between permanent conditions and temporary ones; some children may have had short-term medical conditions. These were family-reported disabilities; no attempt was made by the Census Bureau independently to evaluate the children, or to verify family reports of conditions. Such limitations aside, the SIPP had the important advantage of gathering information about family SES, race and ethnicity, beneficiary status, and other demographic variables that are necessary to understand the children and their needs. Combining these SES indicators with information on disability included in the SIPP database provides a glimpse not only of how many children have limitations and how many are being served but also what kinds of children these are and to what types of families they belong.

Data Analysis

Based on the 30,000 household interviews, the SIPP report (McNeil, 1993a) classified children as "disabled" if parents responded positively to question 21a and/or 21b. Children were said to have a "severe" disability if the parents chose autism, cerebral palsy, or mental retardation as a condition causing the child's limitation or disability. Family income from all sources (earned and unearned) was expressed in terms of a **low-income threshold**, similar to the poverty level but expressed in terms of monthly income because data were collected in October, November, and December 1991 and January 1992.

The low-income threshold at that time was approximately $14,000 per year. As used in the SIPP, the low-income threshold is similar to the poverty level standard, but for a given month, not a year as with the poverty level. The threshold depends on the consumer price index for that month and equals one-twelfth of the annual threshold. In the period between

low-income threshold is similar to the poverty level but is expressed in terms of monthly income. The term was used in the Survey of Income and Program Participation study.

October 1991 and January 1992, the average monthly low-income threshold for a family of four having two children was approximately $1,170, or about $14,000 a year.

After the interviews were conducted and the data analyzed, estimation procedures were used to inflate weighted sample results to obtain estimates for the civilian noninstitutionalized population of the United States. Standard errors for the estimates were calculated from a generalized model based on direct estimates of standard errors as calculated from 1984 SIPP data. A full report on data analysis techniques is offered in McNeil (1993a).

Family SES. The SIPP study reported important demographic information about birth-to-five children with disabilities. Fifty percent were from families with incomes under or near low-income thresholds. Using the Census Bureau's low-income threshold for a family of four with two children during the reference period (October 1991–January 1992), 35 percent of the birth-to-five children with disabilities were from families whose incomes were under the low-income threshold; and another 15 percent lived in families earning between 1.00 and 1.49 of that threshold, or up to $21,000 for a family of four. (The ratio 1.00 represented about $14,000; 1.49 was $21,000; 2.00 was $28,000, and so on) On the other hand, 11.8 percent of children with disabilities lived in families with incomes greater than three times that threshold (about $42,000 for a family of four with two children). These are young families, just starting their careers, so household incomes are lower than are those for more mature families at the peak of their earning years. On the other hand, the family incomes for these families were lower, on average, than those of families with under-six children who did not have disabilities. Table 11.4 and Figure 11.1 offer breakdowns by family income levels of families that have young children with disabilities. In examining the income figures, recall that the interviews took place between October 1991 and January 1992; accordingly, the figures are expressed in 1991 dollars.

In Figure 11.1, Level 1 refers to families with annual incomes falling below the low-income threshold at that time, approximately $14,000 per year. That translates into an average monthly income of about $1,170 for a family of four with two children, between

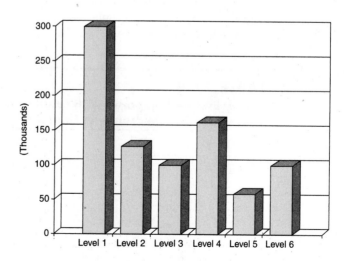

FIGURE 11.1 Family income

October 1991 and January 1992. Level 2 corresponds to the second income category in Table 11.4, that is, incomes between $14,000 and $21,000. Similarly, Level 3 includes families with incomes between $21,000 and $28,000, and so forth. The figure demonstrates much more clearly than the table does that a large plurality of families with under-six children who have disabilities are low-SES families, with annual incomes from all sources of under $14,000. That is an important finding. There is a direct correlation between family household income and disability status in children. Professionals and other staff members in ECSE programs know from firsthand experience that many young children with disabilities come from low-SES families. The SIPP figures give us what the department's annual reports have not: national numbers on family income of households having young children with disabilities.

Medicaid (see Chapter 6) is an important source of service funding for birth-to-five children with disabilities. The SIPP data showed that 38 percent of all birth-to-five children with disabilities lived in families that received Medicaid. Most, however (58 percent), lived in families that had private health insurance (494,000), while 10 percent lived in families having both private and public health insurance. An important conclusion is that virtually all of these families had health insurance of some kind, public or private (or both).

Families with young children who have disabilities were more likely than other families with young children to live in rental housing (52 versus 48 percent), to live in rural areas (29 versus 23 percent), and to receive government housing assistance (14 versus 8 percent). These numbers are another indication that many families with under-six children who have disabilities are relatively poorer than are families with children in this age range who have no disabilities.

Conditions.   The SIPP asked families to report the conditions that caused the child's limitations. Of the children with disabilities, 25 percent were said by their parents to have two or more conditions and 15 percent to have three or more conditions. Table 11.5 lists the most common conditions reported as first (primary) conditions. The proportions have standard errors of 2.6. The most frequently reported condition was speech impairment (20.8 percent). Second most frequently reported were learning disabilities (12.8 percent). To illustrate the standard error as it applies to these estimates, the 90 percent confidence interval for learning disabilities was 8.6 to 17 percent.

TABLE 11.4

Family Income Compared with Low-Income Threshold: Families with Under-Six Children with Limitations

Family Income Level	Number	Proportion
All levels	851,000	100.0%
Under $14,000	299,000	35.1
$14,001 to $21,000	127,000	14.9
$21,001 to $28,000	100,000	11.8
$28,001 to $35,000	164,000	19.3
$35,001 to $42,000	61,000	7.1
$42,000 and over	100,000	11.8

Sources: McNeil (1993a, b)

TABLE 11.5

First (Primary) Condition of Under-Six Children with Limitations

Condition	Number	Proportion
All conditions	851,000	100.0%*
Speech	177,000	20.8**
Learning disability	109,000	12.8
Asthma	82,000	9.6
Cerebral palsy	52,000	6.1
Back/side/foot/leg/arm/hand	49,000	5.8
Emotional problem/disorder	42,000	4.9
Missing legs/feet/toes/fingers	38,000	4.5
Mental retardation	36,000	4.2
Epilepsy, other seizure disorder	25,000	2.9
Deafness or serious hearing loss	19,000	2.2
Blindness or vision problems	19,000	2.2
Autism	18,000	2.1
Traumatic brain injury, spinal cord injury, other paralysis	14,000	1.6
All others	171,000	20.1

*Percentages total 99.8 percent due to rounding errors.
**Standard errors associated with specific condition percentages are 2.6 percentage points.
Sources: McNeil (1993a, b)

No other condition accounted for more than 10 percent of under-six children with any disability, although many parents chose "other" as their child's primary condition. (Other conditions included cancer, diabetes, drug or alcohol problem or disorder, hay fever, heart trouble, and tonsillitis. Each was relatively rare.)

Parents could choose up to three conditions as primary, secondary, and tertiary causes of limitations. The most common second condition reported by families also was speech impairment (22 percent of all birth-to-five children with two or more conditions). Mental illness or emotional conditions were next (13 percent). Learning disabilities accounted for 8 percent, as did physical conditions affecting the child's back, legs, or feet. Of the children reported by their families as having three or more conditions, speech (34 percent) and learning disabilities (22 percent) were the most common tertiary conditions listed.

The SIPP data on conditions are particularly interesting, given that the states need not report these to the U.S. Department of Education. Although grouping these conditions into one of the five domains recognized by the IDEA (cognitive development, physical development, adaptive development, communication development, and social or emotional development) is difficult without firsthand information about each child, one such classification scheme is offered in Table 11.6. The same numbers are illustrated in Figure 11.2. For the purposes of this table and that figure, asthma, cerebral palsy, traumatic brain injury (TBI), spinal cord injury (SCI), and back/leg/feet/arm/hand/finger impairments were classified as "physical." Speech, hearing, and vision limitations were classified as "communication." The "adaptive" category covers epilepsy and other seizure disorders, as well as autism. Mental retardation and learning disability were grouped together under "cognitive," while emotional problems/ disorders were classified as "social or emotional." According to this scheme, physical

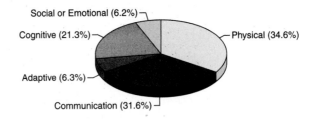

FIGURE 11.2   Domains in SIPP (birth to five)

development (34.6 percent) and communication development (31.6 percent) emerge as the largest groups, with cognitive development close behind (21.3 percent). Adaptive and social or emotional development were much less used in this scheme.

It is important to bear in mind that some conditions are far more likely to be identified in early childhood than are others. The suggestion here that 34.6 percent of birth-to-five children with limitations may have had conditions related to physical development is a good example. The department reported that a much lower (15 percent) proportion of six- to eleven-year-olds in special education had one of the physical conditions it recognizes: "**orthopedic impairments**," "multiple disabilities," "other health impairments," and "traumatic brain injury" (U.S. Department of Education, 1993b, Table AA6). Physical conditions are typically visible to parent and professional alike, for which reason early identification is common. Cognitive and social or emotional conditions, by contrast, are more easily dismissed by parent and professional alike as things children "will grow out of," for which reason early identification is less common.

That almost 13 percent of under-six children with any condition were reported as having learning disabilities was a surprise. Learning disabilities usually are understood as conditions affecting the acquisition of academic skills and knowledge, including reading, writing, and arithmetic (Ariel, 1992). Accordingly, one would not expect the condition to be particularly noticeable in the prekindergarten years. It is possible that some families are working

orthopedic impairments, including spinal cord injury and cerebral palsy, are recognized disabilities under the Individuals with Disabilities Education Act (IDEA).

TABLE 11.6
Developmental Domain of Under-Six Children with One of Twelve Limitations

Developmental Domain	Number	Proportion
All domains	680,000[a]	100.0%
Physical	235,000	34.6
Communication	215,000	31.6
Cognitive	145,000	21.3
Adaptive	43,000	6.3
Social or emotional	42,000	6.2

Sources: McNeil (1993a, b); see narrative for classification scheme.
[a]A total of 171,000 birth-to-five children of the 851,000 identified by families as having disabilities had a wide variety of conditions that were difficult to classify, so these "other conditions" are not included in this table.

with their young children on preacademic exercises, and that during those sessions some problems become evident. It is also possible that some parents of young children may prefer, as many parents of older children do, the label "learning disabled" to alternative labels such as mental retardation.

Race and Ethnic Status. The SIPP found that disability was reported among infants and toddlers from birth to two at a 2.15 percent rate among whites, a 2.48 percent rate among African Americans, and a 1.18 percent rate among people of Hispanic origin (who may be of any race). Looking at three- to five-year-olds, the rates were 5.45 percent (whites), 4.24 percent (African American), and 2.53 percent (Hispanic Americans). The relatively low rates among three- to five-year-old African Americans affected the overall under-six rates. Among whites, 3.78 percent of children, birth to five are disabled, somewhat more than the 3.38 percent of African Americans in that age range. The 1.85 percent rate among Hispanic Americans from birth-to- five is lower than either. Too few Asian Americans were identified for birth-to-two or three-to-five estimates to be made. The Census Bureau did report, however, that the rate of disability among Asian Americans under six years of age was 2.10 percent.

The population estimates by race and ethnic group status were as indicated in Table 11.7 and Figure 11.3. Some 701,000 under-six children were white, as compared to 125,000 who were African American and 17,000 who were Asian American. Another 52,000 were people of Hispanic origin (who may be of any race); because people of Hispanic origin are not members of a racial minority, they are not separated out in Figure 11.3. Rather, these children are included among other categories.

The data on race were generally consistent with previous data on the relationship between racial and ethnic minority status and disability. For purposes of comparison, other sources uniformly indicate that disability is reported much more frequently among African Americans than among whites, but less often among persons of Hispanic origin than among whites (Bowe, 1985a, b; Bennefield & McNeil, 1989). The SIPP data generally agreed with those earlier figures. The major exception is that disability was reported more frequently among white three- to five-year-olds than among African American three- to five-year-olds.

This apparent underreporting of limitations among African American preschool-age children is puzzling. It is possible that some African American children who had mild or moderate limitations were not identified as being disabled before entering school, perhaps because of inadequate parental information about developmental standards or perhaps because of relative difficulty in gaining access to medical care compared with whites. With respect to infants and toddlers, these reporting problems may be less severe due to the fact

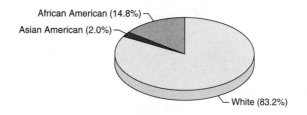

FIGURE 11.3 Race/ethnic status

TABLE 11.7
Distribution by Race and Ethnic Group Status: Children Under Six with Disabilities

Racial or Ethnic Group	Number	Proportion
All	843,000[a]	100.0%
White	701,000	83.2
African American	125,000	14.8
Asian American	17,000	2.0

Sources: McNeil (1993a,b)
[a]Data on race and ethnic group status was not available on all children.

that children from birth to two identified as having disabilities tend to be severely impaired. This is speculation, but it fits the data as well as any other possible explanation (McNeil, 1993a, b).

To illustrate, Arcia and Gallagher (1993), reporting on a survey of sixteen state Part H (now Part C) coordinators, found that rural residence, racial or ethnic minority status, and poverty appear to be associated with service underutilization. Similarly, Arcia, Keyes, Gallagher, and Herrick (1992), examining the March 1991 supplement of the U.S. Bureau of the Census Current Population Survey (CPS), reported that underutilization of services appears to be associated with several family SES characteristics. They found that approximately 11 percent of all children under five (and 20 percent of minority children under five)

In the Census Bureau study, disabilities were parent-identified; the census takers did not question parent reports of limitations or disabilities.

lived in families that have the SES characteristics—including poverty, maternal employment, ethnic or racial minority status, and parental undereducation—traditionally associated with service underutilization. That is, when children come from large families, live in poverty, have mothers who work, are members of ethnic or racial minority groups, or have undereducated mothers (or some combination of these characteristics), underutilization of available social services is highly likely.

Implications

All fifty states, the District of Columbia, and Puerto Rico began serving large numbers of children from birth to five with disabilities or developmental delays only recently. Reports from the department (1992c, 1993b) shed some light on the progress being made toward the IDEA's full-service mandates. However, a great deal remained to be learned, especially about the children being served and their families. The U.S. Bureau of the Census's interviews provided much useful new information about the target population—and raised new questions.

The SIPP data strongly suggested that outreach to ethnic and racial minority group families, especially lower-SES families, is urgently needed. As noted earlier, in Chicago the Early Childhood Research and Intervention Program did not get referrals from such families until it launched intensive outreach efforts designed to meet family needs (Brinker, Frazier, & Baxter, 1992). Also implicit in the SIPP data is the suggestion that primary-care providers do not always tell families about publicly supported early intervention and preschool special education services. Kenny and Culbertson (1993) argued that physicians and other primary-care providers are excellent choices to perform screening, because families routinely take children to doctors, well-child pediatric clinics, and hospitals; but they expressed concern that few pediatricians appear to perform such screening. The suggestion from the SIPP is that even when they do, pediatricians may not refer parents to government-supported services. This lack of referral may help to explain why many families received services outside the federal-state partnership under the IDEA.

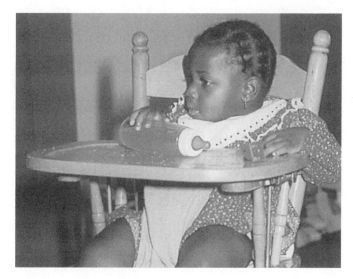

Disability is most frequently reported, according to the Census Bureau, in African American families.

The SIPP's figures on the numbers of children reported by their families as having different conditions should prove helpful to state Part C and preschool Part B lead agencies, as well as to early intervention and preschool programs. Until the SIPP report appeared, few estimates were available on the primary needs of children with disabilities in the birth-to-five age range. That physical disabilities are far more frequent among young children than among school-age students, for example, suggests that schools should place a renewed priority on physical accessibility of program facilities and play areas. Figure 11.2 illustrates the relative distribution among the five domains recognized by the IDEA of under-six children for whom such classification could be made (N = 680,000). As the pie chart makes clear, perhaps more than Table 11.6 does with the same numbers, *two-thirds of all under-six children with disabilities have primary needs in the domains of physical or communication development.* That kind of information can help ECSE programs plan to meet community needs, despite the fact that such proportions necessarily will vary from municipality to municipality.

Speech impairments are quite frequent among young children with disabilities who attend Head Start programs, and learning disabilities are present among children, as well. According to the U.S. Department of Health and Human Services' (HHS) *Eighteenth Annual Report* (1992) on services for young children with disabilities, some 70,000 children with disabilities were served in Head Start programs during the 1990–1991 program year. About two-thirds of these children had disabilities related to speech; other disabilities were much less common. About one in every ten had a health impairment, some 6 percent had learning disabilities, and about 4 percent had serious emotional disturbances. Fewer than 4 percent of children with disabilities in Head Start programs were diagnosed as physically disabled, mentally retarded, hearing-impaired, or visually impaired. These proportions bear striking similarity to those reported by the U.S. Census Bureau in its 1991–1992 study. They are particularly interesting in their confirmation of the relative prevalence of speech and learning disabilities in the under-six population.

The unexpectedly large number of birth-to-five children reported by parents as having learning disabilities (106,000) suggests both that early childhood (EC) programs attend to possible learning problems when assessing children referred for services and also that researchers study learning difficulties in the birth-to-five population so as to understand why so many parents reported learning disabilities in their young children. This raises the issue of "labels," an important issue that deserves discussion.

LABELS

For convenience, researchers, including census takers, use labels in communicating with parents. It is easier to ask a parent to report a single word (e.g., "blind") than it is to ask the parent to explain the child's special needs. However convenient labels may be for this purpose, they sometimes lead to problems. As the five domains are discussed in Chapters 13 to 17, labels will be used; the text will name and describe some of the more common physical, cognitive, emotional, and other conditions or disabilities that affect children's development. This means using labels. Hence, a few words about labeling are appropriate here.

For many years, professionals in education and related fields have been concerned about negative effects of labeling on children. Nicholas Hobbs (1975) and his colleagues explored the labeling issue at length in their landmark *Issues in the Classification of Children.* They examined sociological implications of labels, including how labels function as a means of social control. That same year, Congress enacted PL 94–142, now Part B of the IDEA. In the 1975 law, Congress explicitly required states to report the conditions (labels) of children being served. The confluence of cautions against labeling in Hobbs et al. and the congressional mandate to report conditions caused professional conflicts that have yet to subside.

Some parents and educators have suggested that a compromise is to "label the service, not the child." That is, rather than refer to a child as having cerebral palsy, one would report that the child needs—and is receiving—physical, occupational, and speech pathology services. Writing in the *Harvard Educational Review*, kindergarten teacher Anne Martin (1988) objected strongly to early labeling of young children:

> *Our entering children tended to be labeled and pigeonholed through screening and testing procedures. . . . I have been repeatedly dismayed and angered by their effects on the lives of children. . . . One of my brightest students was said to be possibly learning disabled, and my most skilled artist deficient in fine motor ability. My most cooperative learner was "oppositional" and displayed "negative attitudes." . . . The more I remonstrated and gave counterevidence (I was already starting to* know *these children, after all), the more I was met by grave, implacable insistence on the validity of the judgments.* (pp. 488–489; emphasis in original)

By 1986, when the mandate to serve children from birth-to-five was enacted, Congress was very sensitive to issues related to labeling. Part C explicitly proscribes labeling in favor of broader, less stigmatizing developmental domains such as physical development. The definition of "children with disabilities" in section 602 of the IDEA was changed in 1990 to allow states to serve three- to five-year-olds with developmental delays, and thus to avoid labeling children until they reached six years of age. The 1997 IDEA Amendments (PL 105–17) extended that until children reach ten years of age. One of the guiding philosophies of ECSE as a field is avoidance of labeling. This philosophy preceded the legislation; it followed it in even stronger form. The ECSE preference is clearly to eschew labels whenever possible.

Despite all of this, parents consulting physicians will often be told of a diagnostic condition, or disability. They may ask ECSE professionals about these labels. Referrals to Part C and to preschool Part B programs, similarly, are often accompanied by labels. Whether they like it or not, ECSE professionals must deal with labels. That is why this book discusses them.

The issue is not whether to use labels, but rather *how* to use them. Certainly, labels must not be used where they are not needed. Children should not be labeled in conversation they, or other children, hear. Labels should be used in reporting only when required by funding, licensing, and other agencies and authorities. Labels may also be used in professional literature, for example, when intervention strategies are described as having been administered with experimental groups and withheld from control groups. In both requisite reporting and professional literature, the intent of using labels is clarity and specificity. To write in a journal article, for example, that young children "have delays in communication development" is to obscure much important information; readers of the article deserve to be told in very concrete terms precisely what kinds of children participated in the experiment (Goodman, 1992). For exactly these reasons, readers of this text have the right to expect specific information, not just generalized observations.

Similarly, when parents mention a label and request clarification on what it means, they have a right to be told by ECSE professionals in specific terms what a given condition usually means and what kinds of interventions have been reported in the literature as effective with children having that condition.

The Census Bureau's study offers convincing evidence that ECSE programs need to prepare their personnel for dealing with families from diverse ethnic and racial minority groups.

Aside from those rather restricted exceptions, ECSE professionals are well advised to eschew use of stigmatizing labels. Their gratuitous use in casual conversation, especially when they are the only characteristics used to describe a child, can be damaging in many ways. Professionals may find themselves unable to get past the label. In spite of their best efforts, they may not be able to escape using the lens the label provides—and may see what they expect to see, based on the label, rather than what the child is actually doing. Parents may lower expectations based on labels. Children themselves may internalize these labels and define themselves by them. For all of these reasons, labels should be used judiciously, cautiously—and rarely.

The SIPP findings bring up something else: Why did so many parents use the label "learning disability" to describe their young children with disabilities? The Census Bureau's reports (McNeil, 1993a, b) do not answer that question. One line of research that appears promising is that of surveying a large number of parents of under-six children with disabilities to explore their understanding of disabling conditions, what they were told by pediatricians and other primary care providers, and what they understand different labels to mean.

SUMMARY

The SIPP studies offered important insights into the birth-to-five population of children with disabilities. Among other things, they showed that a substantial number of such children (965,000) potentially need services. Only about three out of every four were getting any developmental services for those disabilities, however; the SIPP estimated that 72 percent of infants and toddlers and 83 percent of three- to five-year-olds with disabilities were receiving such services. Even so, more young children were being served than was reported to be the case by the U.S. Department of Education, despite the fact that the department's

Working in All Five Domains

Make it a point to attend to, assess, and intervene to enhance development in *all* domains. By looking at the *whole* child, the interventionist or preschool special educator can help a child develop strengths—not just improve on areas of weakness.

1 The Adaptive Domain

■ Rather than concluding that a child is "stubborn" or "willful," consider that the child may not know the skills necessary for self-help. If the problem is a lack of knowledge, teach the behavior.

■ Use shaping (successive approximations) to develop behaviors. For example, reinforce the initial steps of unbuttoning a coat, then its partial removal, and finally its complete removal.

■ For some young children, being able to indicate that they have a need and want help is an achievement. Help them to monitor themselves and recognize when needs arise, and teach them how to ask for help.

■ Similarly, for some young children with severe physical or mental disabilities, genuine self-help or independence may be an unreachable goal. But they can learn to help others assist them. Such steps reduce their dependence on others.

■ Measure what you do and what happens afterwards. You may be surprised how often you do certain things. For example, most of us pay much more attention to undesired behavior than we think we do.

■ Seek to generalize desired behavior to other settings, and with other authority figures, especially parents. Young children spend more time at home than they do in early childhood programs, so behaviors are much more likely to become habits if they are used at home as well as in the classroom.

▼ Teach children alternative strategies/ tactics to use in place of unacceptable behavior. For example, teach them to count to ten silently rather than hit back.

▲ Get to know the children well—what they will work to get and what they will work to avoid.

■ Clearly articulate rules in objective, measurable terms. Keep them few in number.

■ Attend to behavior you want to encourage and ignore behavior you want to discourage. Perhaps the most basic concept of applied behavior analysis, it is also one of the hardest to carry out!

■ Alter the environment to make the classroom more suitable for learning— eliminate distractions, change assigned seats, give more but shorter breaks.

■ Do what you say, and say what you do (no hollow threats). Children with emotional or behavioral disorders tend to "test" teachers and interventionists. If you are consistent, they are more likely to respect and obey you.

numbers included not only young children with disabilities but also children with developmental delays and those at risk of such delays.

The SIPP finding that 34.6 percent of under-six children with a disability had a condition primarily related to the domain of physical development suggests that physical accessibility of indoor and outdoor facilities is an important consideration for ECSE program administrators. Also prevalent, according to the SIPP, are communication-related disabilities; these are discussed in Chapter 14. Considerations related to the remaining three domains—cognitive, social or emotional, and adaptive—are the subject of Chapters 15, 16, and 17, respectively.

The SIPP indicated that large numbers of families having young children with disabilities are lower-SES families. They are more likely than families with nondisabled children in this age range to live in rental units as opposed to owning single-family houses, more likely to receive Medicaid and other federal and state assistance, and more likely to live in rural areas or inner-city urban areas as opposed to suburbs. All of these data suggest that families with young children who have disabilities face a number of challenges apart from the child's special needs. It is to the subject of working with families, including families with multiple concerns, that the text now turns.

QUESTIONS FOR REFLECTION

1. Why is it important to know approximately how many young children are not being served by ECSE programs?

2. Why should ECSE professionals and researchers have information on sex, race, ethnic group membership, disability, delay, and so on, among under-six children?

3. Looking at Table 11.1, what kinds of disabilities or delays would you expect to find among under-six children?

4. What implications, if any, does the report that about 50 percent of families having under-six children with developmental conditions live at or near poverty levels have for you?

5. Why do you suspect many parents reported speech-related conditions among under-six children? What kinds of disabilities feature speech impairments or delays?

6. Recalling the Chapter 2 material on cultural diversity (if necessary, reread it), how would you explain the apparent underreporting of child disability by families of Hispanic origin?

7. Why might indiscriminate use of labels harm children?

8. Why might use of labels be acceptable in journal articles that report on large numbers of children, yet not be acceptable in ECSE programs when used to describe particular children?

9. What layperson's understanding of the term "learning disability" might explain the large number of parental reports of learning disabilities among under-six children?

10. Reflecting on the chapter as a whole, what kinds of needs, other than disabilities, could you expect to find among children served in ECSE programs?

Working with Children and Families

Michelle Marlow, a parent from Baltimore, Maryland, illustrated the importance of service coordination when she testified before Congress in 1991 about her efforts to raise her daughter. Tanika Marlow, then twelve years old, had been diagnosed as having mental retardation, cerebral palsy, and a seizure disorder:

> *As a family, you sometimes wonder with the service system where do I get on the merry-go-round. The merry-go-round is revolving around and around, and that is the service system. But where do I put my foot on in a way and at a place that is going to benefit me and enable me to help my child to live and learn and grow?* (Marlow, 1991, p. 22)

OVERVIEW

family-friendly programs involve parents and other family members (as defined by the family) and value their input.

family-focused programs see families as partners with professionals, while **family-centered** programs tend to be planned by, and conducted with, parents, guardians, and other family members, in a dominant role.

teaming is an approach in which individuals from different professions come together on multidisciplinary teams. Family members are integral parts of such teams.

Mrs. Marlow's concerns about how to make the "service system" work for her and her daughter reflect a growing recognition in the United States that programs for families and young children with special needs must begin with the family and the child. This **family-friendly** philosophy took hold in early intervention with infants and toddlers when Congress created Part H (now Part C) in 1986. It has since infused preschool special education as well.

This new family-friendly emphasis is revolutionary in human service delivery. Today, with early intervention and preschool services merging into a system of early childhood special education (ECSE) that forms a seamless continuum of services for children from birth to five with special needs, family-friendliness takes on even more importance. This chapter explores what is meant by two variations on family-friendly philosophies: **family-focused** and **family-centered.** It also discusses **teaming,** an approach in which individuals from different professions come together on multidisciplinary teams. Family members are integral parts of such teams.

An important point made by the recommended practices group of the Division for Early Childhood (DEC) is that families be self-defined (DEC Task Force, 1993). That is, the family itself decides who is considered to be "family." Many families of young children with disabilities consist of single mothers, adoptive parents, grandmothers, or other members of an extended family (Musick, 1994). The Survey of Income and Program Participation (SIPP) study reviewed in the previous chapter suggested that large numbers of families with children under six who have disabilities are lower-socioeconomic status (SES) units, with many other pressing needs. This chapter includes some ideas on helping families to secure needed literacy training, forge community and interest-group linkages, and become empowered to solve their own problems.

Another important issue relating to families is how ECSE programs can increase participation by fathers. Traditionally, the words "parent" and "family" referred, in practice, to mothers. However, some programs are demonstrating innovative thinking on how to get fathers more involved.

Program-family interactions should be informal, small-group sessions that do not intimidate or overwhelm family members.

The chapter concludes with a discussion of what family-friendly approaches mean for staff training. What are the implications for inservice training of ECSE workers and for preservice training of future workers?

FAMILY INVOLVEMENT

Early childhood (EC) programs, including ECSE programs, have long valued family involvement. The family-friendly beliefs espoused by ECSE practitioners, beginning in the late 1960s and early 1970s, consistently have included respect for family members, recognition that the family is the major constant in a child's life, and understanding that children's needs cannot fully be met unless the family joins with the program in meeting those needs. Family-friendly approaches involve a way of thinking in which professionals recognize their own natural tendencies to be directive, and even to turn parents into lay professionals by instructing them in the tools of their trades. A family-friendly philosophy teaches ECSE program staff to look to the family for identification of resources, needs, and especially priorities while writing individualized family service plans (IFSPs) and individualized education programs (IEPs). It also responds to the Individuals with Disabilities Education Act (IDEA) provisions granting parents the right to decline both early intervention services and family assessments. The philosophy now is permeating preschool special education as well, despite the fact that Part B is not as explicit on such parental prerogatives.

That families should be involved is a cardinal value defining ECSE as a field. To say that family involvement is important is not to say, however, that this philosophy translates in any uniform way to day-to-day practices in ECSE programs nationwide. Rather, the core value of "family involvement" is one on which many professionals in the field have strong differences of opinion. They agree that traditional approaches, in which professionals made most decisions unilaterally, are wrong for this field. They disagree, however, on the extent to which ECSE programs should be "family-focused" or "family-centered." Implementing family-friendly values in day-to-day program operations has been—and continues to be—a real problem in many ECSE programs.

Traditional Approaches

The traditional approach, in ECSE as in EC, features the professional in the central role, with support staff and family members revolving around that professional. Mahoney and O'Sullivan (1990) have shown that the most common way in which family members actually have been involved in ECSE programs is very limited: They have been trained by ECSE practitioners to serve as at-home instructors for their children. Casto and Mastropieri (1986a) and White, Taylor, and Moss (1992), reviewing large numbers of studies on family involvement in ECSE, concurred with Mahoney and O'Sullivan that home visits and other family-program interactions in ECSE have tended to be limited to training parents to offer therapy and other interventions in the home. Guralnick (1991) added that "family involvement typically meant parent participation in a series of informational and support meetings" (p. 178).

Donald Bailey of the University of North Carolina has done considerable work on family involvement in ECSE. In one article arising from that work, Bailey, McWilliam, and Winton (1992) suggested that traditional approaches continued to be standard practice as recently as

1992; that is probably still the case in many programs. They commented that "most programs currently are offering services that are primarily child focused" (p. 73). That should not be a surprise, because most ECSE personnel were trained in "child-focused" or "professional-focused" methods (Bailey, Simeonsson, Yoder, & Huntington, 1990; Bailey, Palsha, & Simeonsson, 1991). Another reason for the persistence of professional-focused approaches is the continuing existence of traditional state licensing and other requirements governing who may deliver services. A third is professional accountability: Professionals may feel that they cannot protect themselves against liability or other accountability claims unless they are permitted to make decisions with which they are comfortable.

Whatever the reasons, the evidence is that ECSE personnel do know they need training in family-friendly thinking. A survey of program administrators and service providers in six states (Johnson, Kilgo, Cook, Hammitte, Beauchamp, & Finn, 1992), for example, found that professionals recognized their needs for training in family-friendly approaches. Asked to rank-order a variety of training topics, administrators, supervisors, and service providers in programs for infants and toddlers all ranked highest the following training need: "The ability to communicate effectively in response to family concerns and needs" (p. 143). Staff in preschool programs ranked this item high but not as high as did early intervention personnel, perhaps because Part C places far more emphasis on family interactions than does Part B.

What exactly does a "family-friendly approach" mean—and how is it different from more traditional approaches? Figure 12.1 offers contrasts between family-friendly and more traditional service delivery approaches. The most striking difference may be that a family-friendly program brings the family into decision making, whereas traditional programs reserved most decision making for professionals.

It is important to emphasize that the family-friendly practices in Figure 12.1 remain ideal more than real in many ECSE programs. The extent to which local programs practice what they preach is a matter of some controversy in the ECSE field today. Among other things, economics plays a role. Providing services during family-friendly hours at locations

Interdisciplinary planning in advance and subsequent to IFSP or IEP development is essential so that families receive the supports and services they need.

Family-Friendly Approach	Traditional Approach
• ECSE programs see empowering families and offering supports as their highest goals.	• Diagnosis and treatment of the child are the top goals.
• Family priorities are respected. If family desires, "urgent" services are postponed.	• Professionals decide on priorities and inform families.
• Family members are key players on IFSP/IEP development teams.	• Professionals write the plan and give it to parents to sign.
• Services are offered at family-friendly hours, i.e., at the family's convenience, whenever feasible.	• Professionals and programs have set office hours, at their own convenience, with few exceptions.
• Services are delivered where convenient to the family.	• Services are delivered at the professional's office or clinic.
• Family members approve assessments in advance and receive full reports.	• Professionals decide on, select, administer, and interpret tests and other assessment instruments.
• Child care is offered during parent meetings or child therapy/class sessions.	• Parents are on their own with respect to child-care arrangements.
• Family communication is a key part of every staff member's job.	• Family communication is delegated to a low-ranking staff member.

FIGURE 12.1 Family-friendly versus traditional

preferred by the family can be expensive, for example. But there is no disputing the fact that the field is moving away from the kinds of practices identified as "traditional" in Figure 12.1 and toward those called "family-friendly." This widespread recognition of the urgency of learning new and better ways of working with families is part of a "reconceptualization" (Guralnick, 1991) of ECSE practices.

A "Reconceptualization"

During the late 1980s, what Guralnick (1991) called "a major reconceptualization" of the family's role in ECSE service delivery took place. Spurring this change was PL 99–457, the 1986 federal law that created the Part H program and greatly expanded the preschool Part B program. In hearings held in Washington, as well as in committee reports accompanying the law, a new view of family involvement began taking shape. Variously called "family-focused" or "family-centered," this approach emphasized family involvement not so much in assisting with service delivery as in determining priorities and in deciding what services would be delivered and how they would be provided. Families moved, in this reconceptualization, from positions of subservience to professionals into positions of decision makers and full partners in planning.

Today, there is broad consensus that parents should not be limited to surrogate provider roles. Similarly, there is wide agreement that families should participate in decision making on behalf of their children. The question today is how best to support families in these new roles. At issue is the relative centrality of the family in program design, planning, and operation. That is, disagreement remains as to the extent to which family members participate in (as equal partners) or actually control (as final decision makers) what is done in ECSE programs on behalf of the child and the family (Goodman, 1994). The words "family focused" and "family centered" are used to describe these two variations on current practice.

Family-Focused Programs

Family-focused programs seek to empower families, helping them to reach their own goals and to function more effectively (Dunst & Trivette, 1988). Traditional programs, by contrast, see their major role as diagnosing and treating a particular child's problem, regarding family issues as of secondary importance. Similarly, family-focused programs involve parents as peers in assessment and treatment, welcoming parental perspectives and concerns. More traditional programs, by contrast, regard assessment as a strictly professional responsibility, relegating family members' roles to those of passive recipients of professional summaries of outcomes and other results. Family-program communication is regarded as so important in family-focused programs that it is a critical job function for all staff members; in traditional programs, by contrast, a staff aide or even receptionist might be given the principal responsibility of communicating with parents.

Because families with very young children seldom know how to negotiate the maze of social services, family-focused programs appoint a service coordinator whose job is to cut through red tape and get services delivered. On the federal and state levels, such moves were supported as program after program—Medicaid, Supplemental Security Income (SSI), Developmental Disabilities, and others—changed their rules, altered their eligibility criteria, and rewrote definitions so as to comply with the needs of families for coordinated, seamless ECSE services. Those changes were reviewed in Chapter 6. At the county and local levels, service coordinators empower parents by making them aware of community resources. In some states, this function is performed by a direction center, which is the family's first stop after referral by a family physician or other primary-care provider. Such centers tell parents not only about local ECSE programs but also about other social service programs for which the family may be eligible. In yet other cases, where there are no county- or citywide direction centers, each ECSE program and each service coordinator must perform these vitally important roles.

Today, such practices are widely accepted in ECSE. The issue now is whether, and to what extent, programs should move even further away from traditional practices and embrace what is called the "family-centered" approach.

Family-Centered Programs

Much of the professional literature uses the term "family-centered approach" to describe what some experts believe ECSE programs should do. The titles of recent professional articles are revealing: "Family-Oriented Early Intervention Policies and Practices: Family-Centered or Not?" (Dunst, Johanson, Trivette, & Hamby, 1991); "Building Family-Centered Practices in Early Intervention: A Team-Based Model for Change" (Bailey, McWilliam, & Winton, 1992); and "Creating Family-Centered Services in Early Intervention: Perceptions of Professionals in Four States" (Bailey, Buysse, Edmondson, & Smith, 1992).

Figure 12.2 highlights some differences between a family-focused approach and a family-centered approach. These differences are best explained by noting what is *not* statutorily

Family-Focused Approach	**Family-Centered Approach**
• Family and ECSE program jointly decide upon priorities and services outlined in IFSP/IEP.	• Families decide upon IFSP/IEP contents, including priorities and services. They may veto staff ideas.
• Families make global decisions on goals; program staff make technical decisions.	• Families make both global and specific decisions, which ECSE program staff then implement.
• ECSE programs teach families how to help children at home.	• ECSE programs teach home-care skills only if the family requests that help.
• Family members serve as equal partners in child assessments, but the multidisciplinary team conducts them.	• Family members may, if they wish, decide all aspects of child assessments, even technical details.
• Family members set annual goals, but ECSE staff select curricula and materials.	• Family members may, if they wish, choose not only goals but also curricula and materials.
• Family members and ECSE staff work as a team to select placements and levels of integration.	• Family members may, if they wish, choose placements and/or levels of integration.

FIGURE 12.2 Family-focused versus family-centered approaches

required by the IDEA. A family-centered program, at least in theory, grants the family the decision-making authority on virtually every aspect of ECSE services. The process of assessment offers a good example of how the law does not place parents in quite that position. Bailey et al. (1992) characterized a family-centered assessment as one in which "parents may, if they choose, plan and coordinate child assessments" and in which "parents participate as equal partners in the assessment process" (p. 301). Looking at family-directed family assessments, Dunst et al. (1991) offered a set of six characteristics of a family-centered approach, together with twelve examples of these principles in action. A family-centered approach, according to Dunst and his colleagues, is one in which the assessment process is driven by family concerns and needs, while a family-focused one takes its cue from family needs as they relate to the family's ability to care for the child with a disability or a delay.

The IDEA, however, explicitly states that assessments are to be "multidisciplinary," that is, conducted by professionals who are trained in different aspects of assessment and evaluation. It provides that family members are to be integral members of such teams. That is not to say that the IDEA envisions families directing child assessments. Family assessments, however, by law must be family-directed. The parental role in child assessment principally is one of granting advance written permission to a program's request that child assessment occur. The actual conduct of assessment, whether child or family, must be multidisciplinary, involving professionals who have expertise in assessment as well as family members (Goodman, 1994). The IDEA, in sum, does not go quite as far as a family-centered approach might suggest.

The law also mandates that services be delivered by trained professionals who meet "the highest standards of the state" in their respective professions. While the family retains authority over broad goals and objectives, service delivery itself is assigned by the IDEA principally to professional staff. That is, service delivery, to be appropriate, must be conducted by staff members whose training and experience satisfy state standards. Selection and design of curricula, monthly/weekly/daily lesson plans, and other aspects of service provision are assumed by the IDEA to be the responsibility of such professionals. The family role, according to the statute, is rather one of identifying priority needs, choosing overall goals, and monitoring service delivery.

Similarly, a family-centered program would grant to parents veto power over anything that is written into the IFSP/IEP, while the IDEA appears to look for concurrence between program staff and family members as to what appears in the plan. The statute grants neither professional nor parent absolute authority over what appears in the plan. The family may decline any early intervention services without jeopardizing its rights to other services—or to the same services at a later time. That is not to say, however, that parents enjoy similar veto authority over what does go into the plan. Some programs, for example, simply do not have the resources, staff, or facilities to provide certain services. That is why the statute encourages cooperation between parents and programs, and why (to use the wording of the House Subcommittee on Select Education and Civil Rights) "the parents or guardian must be an integral member of the multidisciplinary team charged with developing the IFSP" (*House Report 102–198,* 1991, p. 18).

Another way of describing the difference is to say that under a family-centered approach, parents and professionals are not coequal partners. Rather, the parents exercise ultimate authority over what is done, how it is done, and who does it. Under a family-focused approach, however, professionals share power with parents on an equal basis, and consensus governs decision making. What family-focused programs do not do, but the family-centered approach implies should be done, is to give parents the ultimate decision-making authority, even over selection of curricula, materials, and methods. It is important to emphasize that the law authorizes family-focused approaches; it does not require family-centered techniques. ECSE programs that continue to be family-focused are not out of compliance with the law. The IDEA envisions partnerships in which parents make the broad decisions—whether their child needs help, what the goals should be—and professionals, in consultation with family members, make subsequent decisions and recommendations that draw upon their special knowledge (Goodman, 1994). Such an approach is what this book calls "family-focused."

Research by Dunst et al. (1991) and by Minke and Scott (1993) showed that ECSE programs tend to be family-focused rather than family-centered. Three other studies concurred: Bailey, Buysse, Edmondson, and Smith (1992); Mahoney and O'Sullivan (1990); and Mahoney, O'Sullivan, and Fors (1989). These reports focused on early intervention programs. That preschool programs also tend to be more family-focused than family-centered is not surprising, given the much greater level of attention to family orientation in Part C compared with Part B.

Dunst et al. (1991) surveyed state and local agency personnel and consumers (family members) in twenty-five states to collect information on the extent to which the programs administered by those agencies were family-centered or family-focused. Dunst and his colleagues recognized that the difference between these approaches is one of degree. They described "family-centered" programs as programs that empower families to solve their own problems, respect family values, and focus on promoting family and child strengths more than on treating family or child weaknesses or needs. Dunst et al. described "family-focused" programs, by contrast, as programs that teach families how to help their children, provide professional services to families and children, and focus more on addressing priority needs than on promoting strengths. Generally, then, family-centered programs tend to minimize professional expertise and services in favor of family expertise and resources, while family-focused programs tend to see families as needing professional advice and assistance.

Dunst et al. found that street-level practitioners and consumers viewed intervention programs as much more family-focused than family-centered. That is because many state programs, policies, and regulations retain characteristics of earlier, professional-centered philosophies—what Dunst et al. called "child-focused and deficit-oriented parenting programs of the 1960s and 1970s" (p. 124). Minke and Scott (1993), studying how IFSP documents are prepared in ECSE programs, found lingering effects of such thinking. They discovered that ECSE workers kept "unwritten" goals and objectives from parents, not requesting family input on some key questions. The workers told Minke and Scott that such decisions, including what interventions to use and what measures to adopt, were their prerogative to make as professionals.

It goes without saying that a family-centered philosophy should, in time, be implemented so as to produce family-centered approaches in actual practice. ECSE programs that are committed to family-centered values and beliefs should strive to move in the direction of ever-greater family-centeredness. To some degree, however, family-centeredness will always remain ideal, a worthwhile goal that few programs ever will reach in all aspects of their services. Given that federal and state money is involved, and that accountability for use of those funds rests with program officials, it is probably not practical for program staff to yield ultimate decision-making authority to families. The intent, however, is praiseworthy: to involve families as much as they themselves wish to become involved, to the extent possible, given practical realities and licensing and other requirements.

Shonkoff and Hauser-Cram (1987), reviewing studies on family involvement, added some suggestions on ways in which programs may effectively involve parents:

> *Criteria for extensive involvement in center-based programs were met when parents volunteered in the classroom, participated in planning and evaluating activities, and implemented carryover activities at home. In home-based programs, extensive involvement occurred when parents were required to assist in planning, developing, and implementing activities on a frequent (such as daily) basis. . . .Finally, some programs targeted their efforts on parents and infants together, linking the parents' role to the services given to the child. This latter type of program model appears to be significantly more successful than those that work with either parent or child in isolation. (pp. 653–654)*

Diversity

The DEC report (DEC Task Force, 1993) stressed the importance of cultural sensitivity and cultural competence in all aspects of ECSE program administration, service delivery, and relations with parents. In their introduction to the document, Odom and McLean (1993) stated:

> *[P]ractices must be able to be adapted for use with children or families who hold values or identify themselves as members of ethnic groups that differ from the mainstream in American society. Such a multicultural emphasis must acknowledge not only the individualized*

needs of children or families, but also the individual value system of the cultural group with whom they identify. (p. 4)

These recommendations are important for several reasons. First, as the SIPP data discussed in Chapter 11 illustrate, ECSE programs are likely to see large numbers of families from ethnic and racial minority groups. Second, as Chapter 7 showed, assessment—both family and child—requires comprehension of how value systems and cultural norms influence behavior. Third, day-to-day relations with families are smoothest when ECSE workers are sensitive to, and correctly interpret, behaviors that may differ from their own.

In a study of 536 families with infants or toddlers having developmental needs, Sontag and Schacht (1994) found that Native American and Hispanic American family members living in Southwest states were less likely than were white family members residing in the same states to participate in decision making about early intervention services provided to their children. They were also less likely than were white family members to provide information and support to other families; this finding may reflect cultural values such that disability is a private matter and unsolicited advice from outsiders is regarded as invasion of privacy. Despite these ethnic-group differences, Sontag and Schacht found that large majorities of family members, regardless of ethnic group status, reported strong needs for information about services and strong desires to participate actively in helping their own children.

EMPOWERING FAMILIES

empowerment is the process of helping people feel as if they are in control. It involves feelings as well as facts.

According to Dunst and Trivette (1988) and White, Taylor, and Moss (1992), **empowerment** involves feelings as well as facts. Empowered families feel as if they are in control; stated differently, empowerment is a shift from professional to parent of control over what happens in ECSE programs. Guralnick (1991) argued that early intervention (and, by extension, preschool special education as well) was most effective when it focused on empowering families. Affleck, McGrade, McQueeney, and Allen (1992) concurred: Supporting and enhancing "natural parent-child relationships" was far more important than training parents to be surrogate service providers. White et al. (1992) and Guralnick (1991) reviewed research showing that little long-term benefit for children or for families was associated with the traditional approach of parents-as-trainers, alone. The aim, Guralnick (1991) proposed, should not be only to train parents as caretakers capable of providing direct services to children but rather to empower families more broadly to function effectively.

The Variety Preschoolers Workshop in Long Island, New York, has learned from over thirty years of working with families that empowerment activities are not only desirable but indeed are necessary for programs to succeed in helping both family members and young children with disabilities. In addition to the steps they have found to be helpful (see Figure 12.3), ECSE personnel, including service coordinators, may arrange for parents of young children with disabilities to receive child development and literacy skills training at Head Start centers. The 1993–1994 federal appropriation for Head Start (which increased its overall budget to about $3 billion) included funds specifically for family training both in child-rearing techniques and in basic literacy. In addition, Head Start funded sixty-six family-service centers in the early 1990s to demonstrate new approaches in dealing with three problems experienced by many families whose children participate in Head Start: substance abuse, literacy, and employability.

The Variety Preschoolers Workshop in Syosset, New York, has demonstrated innovative ways of empowering families. The program, founded in the mid-1960s by Judith Bloch, involves family members in all aspects of service delivery. The Variety center specializes in work with young children having behavior and/or emotional disorders. The program uses what it calls "The Five Ps" (Parent/Professional Preschool Performance Profile) to obtain parent input on goals, needs, and objectives (Bloch & Seitz, 1989). The Variety Preschoolers Workshop social worker trains family members how to complete the instrument. Parents and program staff then independently rate the child's performance both at home and in the classroom. These ratings lead directly to intervention goals and objectives.

Bloch and Seitz (1989) reported that parents take part in four separate assessments over the two-year period in which children typically are enrolled at the program. These assessments look at self-help, motor skills, language, social and emotional development, cognitive activities, and classroom adjustment. Where parents indicate priority needs, the program staff accepts those: "the behavior items become the goals" (p. 227). Staff-parent divergences in ratings are rare; Bloch and Seitz reported that teacher-parent correlations were strong, suggesting that parental ability to judge behaviors was good (p. 240).

respite services are early intervention services offering breaks for family members from child care.

In addition, the Variety Preschoolers Workshop offers **respite services**, social and recreational activities, child care, and educational support to family members. Supports are emphasized, both by ECSE program staff and by other families. As Bloch and Seitz (1985) put it: "Parents become confidants, form mutual-aid networks, and often assume the role of a caring extended family" (p. 7). Two afternoons each week, and every Sunday, the building is open to families for respite care as well as social and recreational activities.

This comprehensive approach emerged over a period of years. Initially, Bloch and Seitz (1985) reported, families came to the center seeking help for the child but did not see themselves as potential program clients. In fact, some family members found it demeaning that program staff even brought up the possibility of family services. "Therefore, we chose to remain sensitive both to their needs and to their rights, to decide whether or not their family or they were clients" (p. 11).

FIGURE 12.3 How one program does it

The SIPP study of families with under-six children who have disabilities (Bowe, 1994) revealed that disproportionate numbers of such families were low SES and were undereducated. Fully half of all families with under-six children who have disabilities reported family incomes close to the low-income threshold (then about $14,000 per year). A major problem among these families was basic literacy. That has a large impact on children, because the influence of family literacy on child achievement is widely recognized as a large one. The "Adult Literacy Survey" (Kirsch et al., 1993) sponsored by the U.S. Department of Education reported that even adults who were high school graduates had low prose literacy if their parents had completed fewer than nine years of formal schooling. If their parents had attended at least some high school, the adults achieved prose literacy scores that were higher but still low. The highest scores among adults studied by the Educational Testing Service, which did the testing for the department, were achieved by those whose parents had high school diplomas and at least some college. Clearly, parental literacy matters.

The largest federal program assisting family members to acquire basic literacy is the Even Start Family Literacy Program, which is authorized by the Elementary and Secondary Education Act (ESEA). Another major federal program is the Adult Education Act, which provides federal funds for the education of adults. In this area, Ohio leads the nation with

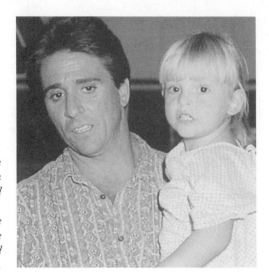

The role of the father in early childhood programs is just now being recognized after a long period of neglect. Some ECSE programs have found that fathers are excellent volunteers and recruiters of other fathers.

family support groups are loosely organized bodies of parents and other family members who come together, often at an ECSE center, to share information and offer each other assistance.

415 family literacy projects, while Tennessee has 107 and Hawaii 102; most states have fewer than 100 such projects (*A.L.L. Points Bulletin*, 1993, p. 2).

Many ECSE programs find that **family support groups** are a helpful mechanism for empowering families. Krauss, Upshur, Shonkoff, and Hauser-Cram (1993), investigating the impact of such groups on mothers of infants with disabilities, reported data that "support a strong endorsement of the efficacy of parent groups in enhancing both the size and the perceived helpfulness of the peer support available to mothers" (p. 17). That is, parent groups are an effective means of providing support to families; they make connections with other families, and they learn about community resources.

However, the Krauss et al. findings were not unequivocal. They reported that the effect of support groups varied depending on participant characteristics. Echoing Affleck, Tennen, Rowe, Roscher, and Walker (1989), Krauss et al. found that mothers who initially felt they did not need support from other mothers, but who attended group meetings anyway, actually seemed to regress after participation in the sessions. "[Their] natural adaptive mechanisms were disrupted rather than enhanced by professional intervention. Group experiences that compel mothers to listen to the complaints of others, or that make them feel obligated to share their feelings with other parents before they are willing to do so, are examples of such inappropriate interventions" (p. 18). On the other hand, mothers who believed they needed support from other parents, and who volunteered for participation in support groups, tended to respond favorably to the group sessions.

INVOLVING FATHERS

Since their beginnings, EC and ECSE programs alike have tended to accept without much questioning but also without much effort to change things, that "parent" and "family" translated, in almost all instances, to "mother" (Pearl, 1993). The family member most often accompanying the child to service appointments was the mother; she also was typically the only family member attending parent-program meetings. It was not until the late 1980s that child-care literature began to focus on the fact that fathers, too, had much to contribute in EC services—and to recommend that EC and ECSE programs actively bring fathers into programs serving their children.

Pearl (1993) commented that fathers may not participate as actively in the day-to-day care of young children as do mothers, but their acceptance of a child's disability or delay is essential to the entire family's response to the child's special needs. Few studies have looked at fathers' perceptions of ECSE programs and service needs. In one of only a handful of surveys that separated fathers' responses from those of mothers for purposes of data analysis, Bailey and Simeonsson (1988) found that fathers reported only half as many family needs as did mothers. Another study (Upshur, 1991) examined how fathers and mothers differentially rated early intervention services. She found, as did Vadasy, Fewell, Meyer, and Greenberg (1985), that fathers reported less stress as a result of group discussions. The Vadasy et al. study involved bimonthly meetings especially designed for fathers. After one year, fathers reported satisfaction. However, at a two-year follow-up, they were more likely than were mothers to report increased levels of pessimism about their child's prospects and about their own ability to make a difference on their child's behalf (Vadasy, Fewell, Greenberg, Dermond, & Meyer, 1986).

Levine, Murphy, and Wilson (1993), in a book called *Getting Men Involved: Strategies for Early Childhood Programs,* offered suggestions drawn from fourteen EC programs throughout the nation. In one such program, bus drivers (almost all male) assisted in program recruitment by reaching out to fathers. The bus drivers also doubled as classroom volunteers. Another program sponsored a peer group of fathers that met on a regular basis to discuss ideas and feelings. In yet another program, fathers made toys and painted classrooms.

According to the Association for the Care of Children's Health in its *Guidelines for Facilitating Father Support Groups* (1992), fathers are more likely to attend meetings if goals, times, and procedures are clearly specified in advance. Program staff should conduct needs assessments among fathers prior to a meeting, using priorities expressed in the survey to demonstrate to fathers, both in the invitation letter and follow-up phone calls, that the support group sessions will be specific and concrete, responding to issues they themselves have raised. Each session should begin—and end—with roundtable comments from all participating fathers. The session leader should target discussion toward feelings, avoiding abstract or intellectual discussions that are not on target. Program staff should follow up after group sessions by providing fathers with specific information on community resources and other solutions to problems identified during the group discussion.

Further work on involving fathers has been done at the Beach Center on Families and Disabilities at the University of Kansas. This center offers a video, "Including Fathers: Strategies for Service Providers" (1997), as well as article reprints on the topic. For more information, visit the center's Web site at www.lsi.ukans.edu/beach or write to 3111 Haworth Hall, University of Kansas, Lawrence, KS 66045.

SIBLINGS

The Variety Preschoolers Workshop's (see Figure 12.3) has shown that an important part of making a program family-friendly is providing support to families with respect to siblings who do not have disabilities or delays. Siblings are often overlooked, just as fathers are. However, both have important contributions to make. Brothers and sisters of children with disabilities may resent the seemingly excessive attention given to the child with special needs. Such anger may, in turn, produce acting out behavior as the nondisabled sibling seeks attention. These problems may be overcome in a number of ways. ECSE staff may suggest to parents that they set aside time for each sibling, perhaps a Saturday morning breakfast out each week. Other ideas include bringing the child with a disability to events such as plays, athletic contests, and concerts in which the nondisabled sibling is performing, to counter-balance those occasions on which he must go places and do things with his brother or sister who has a disability.

Other sibling-related problems include instances in which children and adolescents are—or feel they are—forced prematurely into adult roles. They may be surrogate care-givers, especially when parents or other primary caregivers need respite. When a child is deaf, hearing children sometimes become "interpreters," hearing what is spoken and trans-lating that into American Sign Language (ASL). While some children adjust well to such roles, others report feeling rushed into adulthood and denied their right to enjoy childhood and adolescence. ECSE workers may suggest to parents that they watch siblings closely for such reactions. Most parents know that siblings who have no disabilities do have needs, and that those needs are as important to these children as are the disability-related needs of other children. Parents may, however, benefit from occasional gentle reminders to give all of their children quality time and not allow a crisislike atmosphere in the home to overwhelm the day-to-day functioning of the family.

A good resource is the Siblings Support Project, a unit of the Children's Health Care System, in Seattle. It offers a well-received book by Meyer and Vadasy, *Living with a Brother or Sister with Special Needs: A Book for Sibs* (1996); sponsors a "SibKids" listserv for young brothers and sisters; and issues a newsletter, *Sib to Sib*. A "listserv" is an electronic service linking many E-mail users who share an interest in a specific subject. For information, point your Web browser to www.chmc.org/departmt/sibsupp or write to the Siblings Support Project, Children's Hospital and Medical Center, P.O. Box 5371, CL-09, Seattle, WA 98105-0371.

Especially useful may be efforts by parents to arrange for a child with a disability to have more opportunities to function as a "big sister" or "big brother" to younger siblings. Such chances are too often overlooked, yet they have tremendous potential for the entire family. A child with a disability takes as much pride in guiding younger sisters and brothers as do chil-dren without disabilities. He enjoys being assigned by parents as temporary surrogate care-giver ("You're responsible for Susie while we're away this afternoon. And, Susie, John's in charge. Do what he says."). Such assignments also help nondisabled siblings to see their sis-ter or brother as a whole person, not just someone with a disability.

TEAMING

The IDEA calls for family members to be integral members of the multidisciplinary team in ECSE. Two sets of issues arise concerning such teams. First are concerns about how effec-tively family members participate; second are turf battles and other instances of breakdowns in multidisciplinary cohesion.

Minke and Scott (1993), observing teams in action, were disturbed by failures they wit-nessed in collaboration and joint decision making. Specifically, Minke and Scott found instances of program staff withholding information from parents and other cases in which goals and objectives were entered into written plans without parental knowledge. They sug-gested some possible steps to avoid such problems, including the following:

1. Goals should be family-set, reflecting family priorities and concerns. They should not be staff-selected goals presented to parents for approval.

2. The final set of goals in the plan should be presented to the family prior to implementation. Program staff should regularly check back with families to ensure that their goals for the child and for themselves have not changed.

3. Family assessments, if conducted, should be fully and openly discussed in advance with family members. They should understand how the assessment would be conducted and how information would be used. Their statutorily defined right to direct this assessment must be made clear to them.

DeGangi, Royeen, and Wietlisbach (1992) offered a mechanism by which to examine whether these aspects of effective teamwork characterize the IFSP development process. Contending that the process of preparing the plan actually is more important than is the plan itself, DeGangi et al. urged program staff and family members to focus on differing priorities, values, and opinions about the effect of the disabling condition. That is, information sharing—about priorities, values, and opinions—is the single most important behavior both for program staff and for parents. DeGangi et al. concluded:

> *Among the traits identified as important qualities of professionals when effective collaboration occurs were flexibility, open-mindedness, respectfulness, and the capacity to maintain a nonjudgmental view toward families. The key qualities of parents who are effective at collaboration included flexibility and willingness to share concerns.* (p. 50)

Royeen, DeGangi, and Poisson (1992) offered an anchor guide to help parents and program staff members assess the extent to which such processes were followed in developing the IFSP. The guide includes eighteen questions program officials or family members may ask about the IFSP development process, for example: "Were the family's concerns in relation to

Parent education is often a popular family service at ECSE programs.

the child identified?" "Did the family members have the opportunity to describe their strengths promoting their child's development?"

Professionals may also differ in their opportunities to contribute to the process. Teaming ideally involves all team members and gives each a chance to offer information and to participate in decision making. When the process works as envisioned in the IDEA, it can be surprisingly effective; research by Garshelis and McConnell (1993) found that teams were more successful in identifying and understanding family concerns than was even the single most knowledgeable and experienced team member acting alone. Team members may, however, bring sharply contrasting views of the child's needs, of service priorities, and of desirable interventions. Understandably, professionals tend to see problems, and identify solutions, to which their training and experience make them sensitive. It takes time, in many instances, before people begin to understand the need for, and appreciate the value of, the potential contributions of other disciplines.

Other considerations are more practical. One may be anger on the part of lower-paid staff that more highly compensated members of the team receive far more money for attending a meeting than they do, despite the fact that all team members ostensibly are equally valued participants. A second may be archaic state reimbursement rules. Some states reimburse programs and personnel for direct service hours (time spent treating a child) but not for planning or meeting hours (time spent in teams). Such pay arrangements may discourage participation by some team members. Perhaps the most central concern about teaming in many ECSE programs is that of the amount of time required for teams to work. It is not just that effective teams do not come together overnight but require many months or even years to develop, as pointed out above; more practically, it is that each member of the team likely has a very large caseload and many other pressing obligations. Just getting the whole team together, in one place at one time, may be quite an accomplishment.

In focus groups, DeGangi et al. (1992) found that despite such pressures, teams can be effective. They identified the ability to listen as perhaps the most important characteristic of effective team members. Also critical were cultural competency and sensitivity, as when white team members reacted appropriately to behavior different from that they themselves would have exhibited. Highly valued were professional knowledge and competence, when staff members communicated their unique information in a warm and caring way. DeGangi and her colleagues identified problem solving and empowerment as areas of training from which professionals may emerge as better team members. Minke and Scott (1993) added that professional offering of information so that parents could make informed decisions was another critical element in successful teams.

OTHER PERSONNEL ISSUES

The *Nineteenth Annual Report* (U.S. Department of Education, 1997) reported that ECSE personnel shortages continued in 1995–1996. In early intervention, for example, one professional is needed for every seven that are employed.

One helpful development in addressing these shortages is the curriculum guide *Working with Families in Early Intervention: Interdisciplinary Perspectives*. Written by the Carolina Institute for Research on Infant Personnel Preparation at the University of North Carolina, the curriculum presents family-focused training for three disciplines: occupational therapy, physical therapy, and speech and language pathology. The institute also published a collection of case studies for use in a case method of instruction (CMI) (McWilliam & Bailey, 1992; McWilliam & Bailey, 1993).

Examining ten early intervention programs in the state of Indiana, Kontos and File (1992) found high levels of job satisfaction among seventy-three early interventionists, therapists, social service and family-service providers, administrators, and aides. Major sources of concern, however, were expressed in the areas of salary, promotion, and job advancement. These suggested that turnover rates as high as 20 percent annually among physical therapists to as high as 38 percent among speech and language pathologists may be due to the ready availability to these professionals of similar jobs elsewhere at higher rates of pay. Such opportunities allow ECSE personnel to continue to perform work they value highly, while also satisfying personal and economic needs. Kontos and File noted that many ECSE programs offer fewer fringe benefits than do public school programs. Most ECSE workers surveyed had health benefits, but usually only for themselves rather than for dependents as well. While a majority had life insurance benefits, relatively fewer had retirement benefits and other tax-shelter benefits. Similarly, most received annual cost-of-living adjustments, but relatively few had the opportunity to earn merit salary increases.

IMPLICATIONS FOR TRAINING

Bailey, McWilliam, and Winton (1992) suggested that ECSE program administrators recognize that "[c]hange is a gradual, long-term process that will require ongoing staff development" (p. 74). They recommended that professionals be trained in, and gain opportunities to practice, shared decision making, because it is probable that few, if any, received such instruction as part of their professional training: "[T]raining and decision making must occur at the team level so that all team members develop a shared perspective on change" (p. 74). Making decisions as team members does not come naturally to many professionals, who were trained much more for solitary and directive work with children. Sexton, Snyder, Wolfe, Lobman, Stricklin, and Akers (1996) suggested that active, hands-on, experiential training in teaming skills would be welcomed by early interventionists. They urged that demonstrations, exercises, and other ways of involving participants be used instead of passive tmethods.

The trend toward greater and more meaningful involvement of family members, particularly parents, suggests, too, that professionals, paraprofessionals, and volunteers know how to work effectively with families. Do they? Surveying early childhood special educators soon after PL 99–457 was enacted, Bricker and Slentz (1990) found that almost nine out of ten (89 percent) believed that professionals working with infants and toddlers required training, skills, and experience different in some important ways from those needed by professionals who work with preschool-age children. In particular, the ability to communicate effectively with families, and to work jointly with parents in decision making, were valued as skills that infant program personnel must have. Given that early intervention and preschool special education are coming together into a seamless ECSE, Bricker and Slentz's findings probably hold for preschool educators and related services personnel as well. An earlier study (McCollum, 1987) found similar patterns of expectations: Personnel working with families on a day-to-day basis on policies, programs, services, and assessments had a much greater need for training in techniques of working with families than did professionals employed in more traditional, child-centered programs.

Bailey, Buysse, and Palsha (1990) found that early intervention personnel rated themselves low in family-friendly ways of doing things, which may be a major barrier to implementation of family-friendly approaches. Dr. Bailey, working with other colleagues at the University of North Carolina (Bailey, Buysse, Edmondson, & Smith, 1992), added, "Most therapists and teachers . . . receive training that is almost exclusively child focused" (p. 299). The implication of these two studies is that many ECSE personnel may in fact not be prepared to work well with families. In a third article on professional competencies with families, Bailey, Simeonsson, Yoder, and Huntington (1990) reported that social workers received more preservice training on working with parents than did members of other ECSE-related professions. Commented Bailey in a fourth article on this subject (Bailey, Palsha, & Simeonsson, 1991), "[P]reservice programs in education and allied health care may need to identify strategies for teaching skills related to working with families and for helping students develop an identity that includes work with families as part of how they define themselves as professionals" (p. 162).

Bennett and Watson (1993) took these and many other suggestions as foundation points for a curriculum to offer preservice training for early intervention staff. Figure 12.4, adapted from a checklist they developed for monitoring student progress in such programs, highlights the skills child-care workers need to function well in family-friendly programs.

Johns and Harvey (1993) offered additional strategies. Their recommendations were designed for use in inservice training, but many of their suggestions also apply to preservice training. Noting that many professionals resist training in family relationships—claiming that they do not have the necessary time, or that they have no need for such training—Johns and Harvey suggested that advocates (including parents) who encounter staff resistance to training should first contact the program administrator. They recommended suggesting to the administrator that a series of workshops be scheduled over a twelve- to eighteen-month period, "because we know that integrating new principles into routine practices requires consistent training and support over time" (p. 56). In preservice settings, contacting graduate program coordinators or individual course instructors may serve the same purpose. Enlisting a practitioner as cotrainer, using an interactive style that fosters trust and allows all

---

1. Ability to observe objectively child and family behaviors relevant to ECSE programming
2. Flexibility to function well in inter-, multi-, and transdisciplinary settings and on teams
3. Good listening skills, including ability to reflect upon experience
4. Knowledge of and demonstration of skill in problem-solving behavior
5. Negotiation skills
6. Knowledge of, and ability to communicate to families about, community supports for families
7. Ability to act as consultant (facilitator) for family members, encouraging family members to be advocates and decision makers for their own child
8. Knowledge and skill in direct service delivery including therapy and other interventions

—adapted from Bennett and Watson (1993)

FIGURE 12.4 Skills essential for ECSE workers

participants opportunities to take part in the activities, and building the agenda around practitioner-suggested concrete (real) examples of problems and solutions are among the recommended steps. Johns and Harvey also advised including parents among participants at all sessions. Graduate and undergraduate students may particularly appreciate the opportunity such a plan offers for them to meet and work collaboratively with parents and professionals already at work in the field.

Patricia Brandt (1993) advanced training in problem-solving strategies. She suggested that professionals who adopt problem-solving approaches in collaboration with parents will find that family involvement actually advances their professional work, rather than interferes with it, as some had feared. By jointly focusing on concerns, goals, and solutions, professionals and parents can agree upon interventions. The principal outcome is an agreement between the family and the program on what the priority needs are, what interventions will be attempted, and what results are expected from those activities. Brandt indicated that four steps of successful problem solving must be followed: defining the problem, identifying alternative solutions, deciding upon one or more interventions, and planning how those activities will be undertaken. "Throughout problem solving," Brandt suggested, "the professional participates by guiding the family members through each phase with explanations and demonstrations as needed" (p. 79). She recommended that a written contract be prepared outlining the agreed-upon steps.

Bailey and his colleagues have shown that past training programs for professionals seldom included instruction in and experience with joint decision-making strategies. That is why preservice and inservice training in parent-professional collaboration on joint problem solving is so important. Bailey, McWilliam, and Winton (1992) offered a "decision-making model" for helping ECSE programs move from the reality of family-focused practice to the ideal of family-centered services. They described a weeklong series of workshops, in which parents and professionals jointly take part, during which program staff and consumers can identify aspects of the program that need to be changed, decide on feasible ways of making

Empowering family members includes offering them the information they need to make their own decisions.

these changes, and plan how they will be carried out. Bruder, Lippman, and Bologna (1994) described a similar model, one using five-day institutes.

The Bennett and Watson (1993) curriculum for preservice training of early intervention personnel suggests that coursework in child development and family dynamics, assessment (infant, preschoolers, families), infant intervention and family support strategies, and issues in service delivery form the core of preservice training. Following completion of such courses, Bennett and Watson recommended, students should meet internship and independent study requirements and then write a thesis.

Adopting a family-focused approach is far more difficult than merely espousing family-focused philosophies. Professionals participating in the Bailey et al. (1992) survey tended to perceive family members as requiring additional knowledge and skills before they could serve as effective team members. Others cited lack of administrative support; they pointed out that it is difficult for individual workers to engage in family-focused or family-centered practices if the organization as a whole remains child-focused or professional-focused. Difficulty in getting rooms for evening meetings with parents and freeing up funds for home visits are just two examples of how lack of administrative support could hamper even the best-intentioned efforts of a practitioner to involve families.

Ludlow (1994) proposed that distance learning be used to respond to another pressing problem in personnel training. Observing that many ECSE programs are located in communities far removed from university-based preservice training programs, she proposed that satellite broadcasts of coursework be used to leapfrog the physical distances between service programs and universities. Ludlow noted that distance learning—which involves use of television receivers, cameras or camcorders, and videocassette recorders at both ends—could help solve two important problems. First is that of inservice training: Personnel hired by ECSE programs often find that they cannot secure advanced or continuing training because they cannot take time off from work and leave their homes for extended periods of time. Second is that of preservice training: ECSE programs located in rural areas, such as Ludlow's West Virginia, are largely limited in personnel recruitment to a small, untrained pool of applicants.

Ludlow's program at West Virginia University has trained 120 distance-learning students in ECSE since 1991, even more than the number of on-campus students taking the same coursework. In distance learning, expert instructors (who may be located anywhere in the United States, or for that matter in the world) teach their courses in the usual fashion, but with a few minimal changes. A video camera focuses on them as they teach. Also located in the classroom are television receivers that display video and audio images of students who are connected to the classroom by means of telephone wires. The students may be at home or in a local classroom, yet they see and hear the instructor—and their voices and images are seen and heard by the instructor, as well.

Distance learning works best when the connections between the host site (the instructor's classroom) and the remote sites (the distance-learning students) are of fiber-optic cable, which can transport very high-quality voice, video, and data at the same time. Traditional twisted-pair copper wires cannot transport high-quality video images. However, distance learning may occur even in the absence of fiber networks, as at WVU. Ludlow's program broadcast from a university television studio in Morgantown to an uplink facility in Institute. The campus-based students attended class in the studio, while off-campus students traveled an average of thirty to forty-five miles to a nearby site equipped for downlink of broadcast signals. Ludlow's experience shows that such arrangements work. Fiber-optic cable, which has arrived in most parts of the United States, soon will make it possible to connect ordinary classrooms (not television studios) to student homes or offices (not special downlink facilities), making distance learning even more convenient for all involved.

SUMMARY

The family-friendly values of ECSE programs find expression in family-focused or in family-centered approaches. The two philosophies differ primarily in whether families are seen as equal partners (family-focused) or as final decision makers (family-centered). Both approaches diverge sharply from more traditional professional-focused or child-focused methods, in which families play much more peripheral roles. Research suggests that as of the early to mid-1990s, most ECSE programs retained at least some features of traditional philosophies but were moving rapidly toward family-focused and, in some instances, family-centered approaches.

In both family-focused and family-centered programs, parents and other family members are integral parts of multidisciplinary teams. ECSE programs have found that it takes considerable time for such teams to become fully effective, in part because staff members, consultants, and contractors frequently have been trained in child-focused and professional-centered methodologies. They need time to learn what other disciplines offer and time to learn how to make decisions as part of a team rather than as an individual practitioner. Program staff also need time to learn how to work effectively with family members. The ability to listen well, to share information, and to accept communal rather than personal responsibility appears to be critical to effective team action. Training in negotiation skills, problem-solving skills, and family interactions is needed both at the preservice and inservice levels.

Making ECSE programs family-friendly is an ongoing endeavor. Particular concerns of many programs are that staff members find ways to involve fathers as well as mothers and that they demonstrate sensitivity and competence in dealing with different cultural values,

Bulletin boards, whether physical ones or cyberspace-based computer ones, are effective means of disseminating information.

especially those held by families from ethnic or racial minority groups. Implementing steps to empower families is also an important concern in many ECSE programs.

QUESTIONS FOR REFLECTION

1. In your own words, what is a "family-friendly" approach? How does it differ from "traditional" approaches?

2. Differentiate in as many ways as you can "family-focused" from "family-centered" approaches.

3. The text argues that the law requires "family-focused" approaches and does *not* mandate "family-centered" approaches. What provisions in the IDEA relate to this issue?

4. What is the single most common way families have been involved in ECSE programs in years past?

5. What are some practical realities that might make it difficult for ECSE programs to become more family-friendly?

6. Give an example of an instance in which an ECSE program legitimately could decline to offer a service that a family wants.

7. In your own words, what does it mean to "empower" a family?

8. What kinds of parents might find support groups less than helpful?

9. Suggest two ways of involving fathers in ECSE programs.

10. How could ECSE programs help siblings of children with disabilities?

Physical Development

At eight months of age, the baby was not able to hold up his head, something normal children do within the first four months. A new pediatrician prescribed physical therapy. Private intervention sessions began that week, and within one month the child was not only holding up his head, he was sitting independently, something that normal babies do in that age. Following his therapy, motorically he became a normal child and sessions ceased. If he had not had such intervention, the child could have had motor problems for the rest of his life. (Verna Hart, 1986, p. 146)

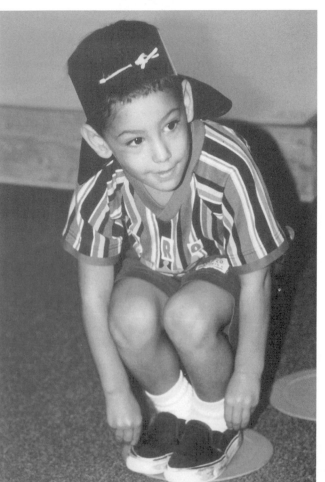

OVERVIEW

Virtually everything a young child does is affected if physical development is delayed or limited. The "work" of young children is to develop their abilities. They do that in large part by exploring their environments, finding things, and manipulating them. Infants, toddlers, and preschoolers play with physical objects, thereby learning size, color, and other characteristics of things such as their texture or firmness. Children use these objects to construct castles, to play house, to practice counting, to develop gross and fine motor control and eye-hand coordination, and to perform many other tasks of early childhood development.

Limitations or delays in physical development, accordingly, can have substantial and far-reaching effects. Consider, for example, how physical disability may affect cognition. Young children learn by *doing* things, especially in the toddler stage (one year to 2.5 or three years), when movement dominates their lives. A physical disability such as cerebral palsy interferes in two major ways. First, the condition makes movement itself difficult and slow. The infant or toddler explores less territory, manipulates objects less effectively, and for these reasons tends to learn less than does a young child with no disabilities. Second, overprotection by parents and other caregivers further constrains mobility (Gerales & Ritter, 1991). Both phenomena lead to experiential deprivation: The infant or toddler with cerebral palsy is deprived of developmentally necessary experiences.

Nor is that all of it. Cerebral palsy also affects performance on tests. Intelligence tests for young children typically involve the child using objects. By its very nature, cerebral palsy may sharply constrain how well, and how quickly, a child may manipulate objects or describe

Many buses today are accessible for children using wheelchairs. Drawing © Amy Ning. Reprinted with permission from the artist.

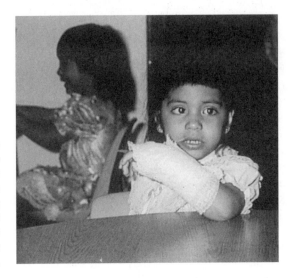

Accidents are common among young children who are physically active. Early childhood workers need to accommodate resulting limitations by finding ways the child may continue to participate in everyday activities.

them to an examiner. This may lead to an overestimation of the prevalence of mental retardation among children with cerebral palsy. The usual estimate is that 30 percent of children with cerebral palsy are also mentally retarded (Levine, 1986; Verhaaren & Connor, 1981). Given that tests may inappropriately measure physical skills while ostensibly measuring cognitive ones, that proportion may be too high. Or consider how physical development delays may affect adaptive behavior. Not only do many physical limitations constrain self-help behavior, but caregivers often do things for the child, frequently unnecessarily, thereby delaying the child's development in self-care.

Despite these many potential pitfalls, the fact remains that America as a society, and thousands of cities and towns as individual communities, are more accessible to people with physical disabilities today than ever before. Children using wheelchairs can now travel safely on public mass-transit buses, something that simply did not happen fifteen years ago. In many communities, too, playgrounds and movie theaters alike today have ramps, elevators, and automatic doors so that families with children who have physical disabilities can enjoy close to the same variety of recreation as can other families. Even wheelchairs themselves are different today than they were fifteen years ago. Sports chairs and other aids for physical mobility are now widely available, making it much more feasible for young children with physical disabilities to engage in an active, physically demanding childhood.

This chapter discusses normal physical development during the first six years of life. The information may help early childhood special education (ECSE) workers and parents to identify delays in development. Additional data on prevalence data on physical disabilities are offered to supplement those provided in Chapter 11. Information on developmental delays and disabilities is then given. Among the conditions discussed in this chapter are amputations, asthma, cerebral palsy, muscular dystrophy, spina bifida, spinal cord injury, and traumatic brain injury. Suggestions on working with medically fragile and technology-dependent children are also given. The detailed discussion of different disabilities may be particularly helpful in answering parents' questions about specific labels or conditions. The chapter continues with material on assessment and intervention. Some suggestions for working with parents are offered at the conclusion of the chapter.

A considerable number of rare disorders affect physical development in some young children. There are conditions such as dysautonomia, which limits a child's ability to self-regulate the body and to feel; it can have catastrophic effects on walking, which requires biofeedback, and even on eating and speaking, which also require the ability to feel. Another rare disorder is "-18Q syndrome," which also limits mobility and speech. A full discussion of these conditions is beyond the scope of this book because the disorders are so unusual. Interested readers are referred to the National Organization for Rare Disorders (NORD), 100 Route 37, P.O. Box 8923, New Fairfield, CT 06812. It is an outstanding voluntary organization concerned with identification, treatment, and cure of "orphan diseases."

PREVALENCE

prevalence is the number of cases in a population, as contrasted to incidence, the number of new cases.

incidence is the number of new cases annually, as contrasted with prevalence, which is the total number of such cases.

In demographics, the term **prevalence** refers to the number of instances of a given condition or characteristic in a population at any one time; the word **incidence** refers to the number of new instances or cases per year. This section presents prevalence data. The parallel sections in Chapters 14–17 do the same with respect to other domains of development.

Physical development limitations were reported as the first (primary) condition for an estimated 235,000 children from birth to five inclusive in the U.S. Bureau of the Census 1991-1992 Survey of Income and Program Participation (SIPP) study (Bowe, 1994). These children had family-reported conditions of asthma, cerebral palsy, traumatic brain injury (TBI), spinal cord injury (SCI), and other kinds of paralysis or muscle conditions; or they had physical conditions affecting the arms, hands, fingers, body, legs, and feet. Asthma is recognized as a disability under Part B by the U.S. Department of Education (1992a) to the extent that it interferes with the child's education and related activities.

Based on the SIPP findings, disabilities in the physical domain appear to be more common than are conditions in any of the four other developmental domains. The survey also found that physical development was the secondary concern for 40,000 (18 percent) of all birth-to-five children having two different kinds of limitations. All told, 275,000 children from birth to five had physical limitations, according to the SIPP.

As Table 13.1 illustrates, physical conditions are many and varied. Of the children in the SIPP study who had conditions related to physical development, 35 percent had asthma; 22 percent had cerebral palsy; 19 percent had impairments or deformities of the back, feet, legs, or side; 16 percent had amputated limbs; 6 percent had TBI or SCI; and 2 percent had impairments or deformities of arms, hands, or fingers.

ECSE programs are not required by the U.S. Department of Education to report the conditions, or even the developmental domains most of concern, for the under-six children whom they serve. Accordingly, these SIPP data are among the only figures suggesting the relative prevalence of physical conditions among young children with disabilities. It is immediately evident to anyone who has studied K–12 special education data that physical conditions appear to be much more common in the under-six age range than they are in the elementary and secondary school age ranges. Among six to eleven-year-olds, for example, the U.S. Department of Education reports that 15 percent have physical conditions such as "orthopedic impairments," "multiple disabilities," and "other health impairments" as their primary disabilities (*Fifteenth Annual Report*, 1993b, Table AA6). The much higher 34.6 percent figure derived from the SIPP study among under-six children may reflect the fact that physical conditions are very quickly noticed by parents, who seek assistance almost

TABLE 13.1
Types of Physical Limitations among Under-Six Children

Causes	Number	Proportion
All	235,000	100%
Asthma	82,000*	35
Cerebral palsy	52,000	22
Impairments of back, feet, legs, or side	44,000	19
Missing legs, feet, toes, arms, hands, fingers	38,000	16
Traumatic brain injury, spinal cord injury, or other paralysis	14,000	6
Impairments of arm, hand, fingers	5,000	2

* These estimates have standard errors associated with them. The 90 percent confidence interval for asthma, for example, is 32.4 percent to 37.6 percent, or 76,000 to 88,000 children.
Sources: McNeil, 1993a, b

immediately, while cognitive, social or emotional, and adaptive development delays may not cause parental concern until later. That is, the relative ease of identification of physical conditions may make this category more prominent than it otherwise would be; the actual proportion of children with physical as opposed to other kinds of developmental concerns may be lower than is suggested by the SIPP data. Consider that parents and professionals alike, including physicians, may see a cognitive or a communication delay and believe that "she will grow out of it." Such responses are less likely when parents and professionals are confronted with physical conditions.

DEVELOPMENTAL DELAYS

Within each domain, states define "developmental delays." These may be expressed in terms of first appearance of behavior as a function of expected date of appearance, for example, a twelve-month delay in walking alone. Delays may also be expressed in terms of standard deviations (S.D.s) from the mean; the most common usage is two S.D. below the mean in one domain. Most states accept 1.5 S.D. below the mean in two or more domains, as well. Many children with delays or disabilities in physical development are also limited in cognitive or adaptive behavior in particular.

Neonates who suffer respiratory problems often have delayed motor development. Neonates with low Apgar scores (well-baby ratings) are more likely to have delayed motor development than those with high scores. Low birthweight (LBW) and prematurity (which often go together) may lead to delays in motor development as well, with later ages of attaining sitting, standing, and walking. Malina (1982) showed that environment strongly affects age at attainment of motor development milestones. While heredity is important, whether or not a child has the opportunity to explore freely has a lot to do with how fast she reaches physical development milestones. There is a direct relationship between how much and how freely the infant/toddler can explore, for family or for disability reasons (e.g., "environment"), and how fast development proceeds.

ESTABLISHED CONDITIONS

Cerebral palsy, muscular dystrophy, traumatic brain injury, spinal cord injury, and other physical disabilities are recognized by many states as "established," that is, known to result in developmental delays. Under the Individuals with Disabilities Education Act (IDEA), it is not necessary to demonstrate a delay when such conditions are present. This section discusses the more common established conditions, including what ECSE professionals can expect with each and how treatment may help children with limitations of physical development. This material may also assist in answering questions from parents and other family members.

Asthma

asthma is a condition in which people have difficulty breathing because of obstructions in the airways of the lungs. It is a chronic respiratory disorder (sometimes called a chronic obstructive pulmonary disease). The U.S. Department of Education recognizes asthma as a disability when it affects a child's education.

The SIPP study estimated that 82,000 under-six children had asthma; it was the most common limitation of physical development reported by parents in the study, accounting for 35 percent of all children with physical limitations (Bowe, 1994). **Asthma** is a condition in which people have difficulty breathing because of obstructions in the airways of the lungs. It is a chronic respiratory disorder (sometimes called a chronic obstructive pulmonary disease) that often appears within the first year of life. However, because symptoms may be mistaken as something else (i.e., congenital heart disease), diagnosis may not occur until a child is in preschool. Asthma is quite common in children; in fact, some one-third of all Americans with asthma are school-age or younger. Among school-age children, asthma is one of the most frequent causes of absenteeism (Aaronson & Rosenberg, 1985). According to the Centers for Disease Control and Prevention, about ten million Americans of all ages have asthma, up from seven million in 1980; the recent increase is most notable among girls and women.

Symptoms include not only difficulty in breathing but also vomiting and a dry cough. The principal effect of asthma on children from birth to five is frequent absence from early intervention, preschool special education, or other programs. Hospitalization is often necessary; some families report taking an asthmatic child to the hospital several times during one night. Excessive absenteeism, in turn, constrains a child's progress in the program. It may also lead to social and emotional problems, because other children in the program learn not to rely on this child's being there; children like a friend who is reliably there and may not form close attachments to children on whose presence they cannot rely.

Attacks result in most cases from allergic reactions. These may be to pollens, molds, dusts, or animal hair. Infection of the respiratory system is another cause. Generally, the body produces excess antibodies in response to pollens or other antigens. This is an allergic reaction to the antigens. In someone with asthma, the antibodies are not effective in combating the antigens but rather trigger production or release of histamines, deleterious chemicals that in turn cause swelling in the airways. This swelling makes breathing difficult.

Sometimes, asthma develops following a respiratory infection that is not promptly and thoroughly treated. A viral infection in particular is a common precursor to asthma in young children.

There are psychological and genetic factors involved in asthma, as well. Children with emotional difficulties are more prone to asthma; the onset of asthma may in turn exacerbate those emotional conditions. Somewhat more than half of all children who develop asthma have relatives with the condition. However, the genetic basis, if one exists, for this inheritance is not yet well understood (Kuzemko, 1980).

An asthma attack can start suddenly, and the fear this causes may prolong the attack. Cold triggers asthma attacks, as can fatigue after exercise. What happens is that the bronchioles in the lungs become swollen and clogged with mucus, and the muscles surrounding them contract so that the air that should pass through is unable to do so. The body reacts to the lack of oxygen, and the child forces more and more air into the lungs. However, due to the blockages the child has difficulty exhaling that air; this leads to the wheezing noise characteristic of asthma. Most asthma attacks last a few hours, although some may persist only for a few minutes. Emotional stress can also trigger an asthma attack.

A somewhat similar condition is **cystic fibrosis**. Here, the body cannot make a protein called (after the condition) the cystic fibrosis transmembrane regulator (CFTR). This protein facilitates the transport of chloride (which, with sodium, makes up salt). Without CFTR, chloride cannot readily enter and leave cells. Thus, not surprisingly, one of the first indications of the condition is a salty-tasting sweat. More serious, the person's lungs become covered with a sticky mucus. This inflammation gradually destroys the lungs. Eventually, most people with the condition die from it, usually at about thirty years of age. According to the Cystic Fibrosis Foundation (1998), cystic fibrosis is the most common fatal genetic disease in America, at some 30,000 individuals (prevalence), with another 1,000 people added annually (incidence).

People with cystic fibrosis need antibiotics, enzyme supplements, and frequent hospitalization. Because of their reduced lung capacity, they typically expend more energy in any given activity than do other people. For this reason, they need frequent rest. Physical therapy, mostly "chest thumping" to loosen the mucus, is needed daily. Regular exercise, similarly, helps to maintain breathing and muscle strength.

Back, Leg, Side Impairments

"Impairments or deformities of back, feet, legs, or side" were reported in the 1991-1992 SIPP survey for 44,000 under-six children, or about 5 percent of children in the birth-to-five age range who had any disability and 19 percent of those with a physical disability (Bowe, 1994). **Congenital** conditions occur infrequently—about one in every 20,000 live births—and include shortened (truncated) limbs and shortened limb bones. **Adventitious** (acquired) limb impairments result from surgery or from accidents; these are somewhat less frequent than are congenital ones (Setoguchi & Rosenfelder, 1982). Some 200 neuromuscular diseases affect 500,000 Americans of all ages. Among them are myasthenia gravis, a hereditary condition affecting the myoneural junction; congenital and metabolic myopathies, also hereditary, which affect muscles; and spinal muscular atrophy, affecting the anterior horn cells. Two of the most common in children are muscular dystrophy and spinal bifida.

In **muscular dystrophy (MD)**, tiny leaks in the muscle membranes allow calcium to enter the muscle cells, activating enzymes that proceed to destroy the muscle. In time, the muscles of the legs, chest, and arms progressively weaken as fatty tissue replaces muscle tissue. Recent research has suggested that the absence of a protein, which the scientists identi-

cystic fibrosis is an inherited condition that causes mucus to build up in the lungs, compromising lung capacity and usually resulting in death by the age of thirty. Children with cystic fibrosis need to have physical therapy, get lots of exercise, and receive dietary supplements.

congenital conditions appear at or prior to birth; they are present at birth, as contrasted to acquired conditions.

adventitious (acquired) conditions appear after birth, usually as a result of illness or accident. They differ from congenital conditions, which are present at birth.

muscular dystrophy (MD) is a condition characterized by muscle weakness. There are several types of MD. Duchenne MD, the most serious form, is a progressive, usually fatal, condition. Other dystrophies are less serious and rarely fatal.

fying it called dystrophin, causes muscles to deteriorate. This was one of the first instances in which researchers found that an absence of a protein causes disease. About 20,000 boys and young men have MD, of whom 15,000 are children, according to the Muscular Dystrophy Association.

There are several dystrophies. The most common and severe is Duchenne MD, which usually leads to death by the early twenties. It affects about one in every 3,500 young boys. Duchenne MD has been linked to a gene located on the X sex chromosome; because females have two X chromosomes, the affected one is suppressed by the normal one, making the female a carrier of the disease. Males, however, have one X and one Y sex chromosome, which is much smaller. With no normal X chromosome to counter the affected one, boys develop the disease. Duchenne MD usually becomes evident in the toddler years, as the child is unable to walk or run as easily as before. The muscles that had been growing begin to atrophy between the ages of two and six. Usually, the individual needs a wheelchair by about age thirteen. In the late teens or early twenties, muscle atrophy has weakened the lung and heart muscles, leading to death.

In Becker MD, a less common and less severe version, muscles weaken, but not to the point of causing premature death. Several other, also less common, versions also occur. Congenital dystrophy is evident at birth when muscles appear small and weak; lifespan usually is short. Facio-scapulo-humeral dystrophy may appear in infancy but is more common in adolescence and adulthood. It begins in muscles of the face, shoulder, and upper arms, hence its name. Limb-girdle dystrophy begins in the lower trunk and legs; it may begin in the shoulders, in which case progression is slower. Life expectancy usually is normal with limb-girdle dystrophy. Myotonic dystrophy starts with the fingers, hands, feet, and lower legs; however, it rarely appears in children. Females as well as males can have some of these forms of MD.

Spina bifida is a condition in which the spinal cord does not completely close during the first month (twenty-eight days) of fetal development during pregnancy. In fact, the name refers to the spine being "divided into two" or "open spine." The condition may be caused by folic-acid insufficiencies in the diets of pregnant women, especially if these women also have a genetic-related inability to process folate (Centers for Disease Control and Prevention,

spina bifida is a condition in which the spinal cord does not close completely during fetal development.

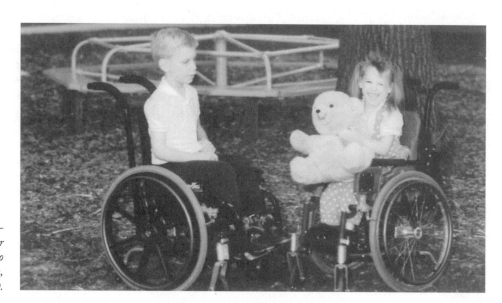

A wide variety of wheelchairs is now available for use by young children. Photo reprinted with permission, ROHO.

1992). According to the Spina Bifida Association of America (SBAA, 1997; see, also, Lary & Edmonds, 1996), spina bifida occurs about once every 1,000 pregnancies. The SBAA notes that more children have spina bifida than have muscular dystrophy, multiple sclerosis, and cystic fibrosis combined.

Spina bifida is the most common neural tube defect. Of the three main kinds of spina bifida, the most severe is myelomeningocele, where nerves of the spinal cord protrude through the back. Although surgery can and usually does help, the condition leads to significant, permanent limitations. An important side effect is hydrocephalus, a buildup of cerebrospinal fluid in the brain. This fluid cushions and protects the brain and spinal cord. In spina bifida, the spinal lesion prevents the brain from draining normally. Thus, the fluid collects in and around the brain, enlarging the head and leading to mental retardation. Other secondary conditions often found with spina bifida include some learning disabilities and attention deficits (with or without hyperactivity). Clearly, spina bifida can have consequences well beyond the domain of physical development.

The site of the lesion has much to do with these effects. As is the case with spinal cord injuries as well, spina bifida interferes with afferent (to the brain) and efferent (from the brain) messages. Thus, the child's ability to monitor bodily functions and pain (afferent) and to control voluntary muscle and other brain-directed patterns (efferent) is limited. The higher the lesion, the more pervasive these problems are. Regardless of the site of the lesion, pressure sores (decubitus ulcers) often occur, as they do with spinal cord injuries.

Cerebral Palsy

cerebral palsy (CP) is a condition in which oxygen deprivation in, or damage to, the brain limits voluntary control of muscles.

Cerebral palsy (CP) was reported as the first (primary) condition for 52,000 children from birth to five inclusive in the SIPP study, or about 6 percent of all children in this age range who had any disability and 22 percent of those who had a physical limitation (Bowe, 1994). As a condition that in virtually all cases occurs during the pre-, peri-, or postnatal period, and as one that affects gross as well as fine motor control, CP is almost immediately noticeable. Common estimates are that cerebral palsy occurs about three times in every 1,000 live births. This may be an underestimation, however, because much CP occurs in families with limited access to medical care, a population well known to be underrepresented in morbidity statistics. It is twenty-five to thirty times more common in infants weighing less than 1.5 kilograms at birth than among normal-weight infants (Gerales & Ritter, 1991).

Cerebral palsy is a condition that is perhaps best described as limiting voluntary control of muscles. If you think of it that way, you see that the principal issue is that of the brain's ability to control the body's muscles; the muscles themselves are of secondary concern. That is, the muscles are not the source of the child's problems; the brain's motor control centers are.

This suggests several things that are important. One is that CP is a physical condition affecting both movement and expressive communication. The movement limitations are urgently important in infants and toddlers, because they rely so much on motor activity to learn other things. As the children grow, the expressive communication limitation becomes, if anything, more important. That is why use of today's computer-based technologies to facilitate expressive communication is so urgent with children who have severe cases of cerebral palsy.

A second important implication of this way of viewing CP is that the muscles themselves, not being manipulated on a voluntary basis by the brain, may atrophy or weaken over time unless intervention is taken. But it goes beyond that: Speech is a motor control function, one in which many hundreds of small muscles are manipulated very precisely to produce intelligible sounds. In CP too, these muscles are not controlled as well or as easily by the individual. Speech and language services, accordingly, may be needed. Other aspects of expressive communication, including writing, are also limited. Indeed it is not going too far to say that the principal limitation in cerebral palsy is one of expressive communication.

Secondary conditions are quite common in children with CP. Hearing loss is frequent, visual impairments somewhat less so, and some degree of retardation exists in a minority of cases. Often the same cause triggered each of these problems. Cerebral palsy frequently occurs as a result of oxygen deprivation prior to, during, or just after birth. Other causes include maternal infections such as rubella (German measles), birth trauma, and chronic diseases, including fetal infections. The same conditions may affect hearing, vision, and intelligence as well.

For all these reasons, cerebral palsy is very likely to require multidisciplinary intervention. Children with CP frequently have problems related to learning, social and emotional growth, perception, vision, hearing, and intellectual functioning. Assistance from early childhood special educators, speech and language pathologists, physical and occupational therapists, and others will be required.

The late William Cruickshank (1976) showed that CP is not progressive; the condition does not worsen over time. This is not to say that muscles do not atrophy if not used; they do, and that is why physical and occupational therapy are so important. CP also is not contagious. And it is not remittent, coming and going. The condition varies from mild to very severe. In mild cases, children need a little more time to do things and may need assistive technology devices to hold and manipulate objects (Gerales & Ritter, 1991). In severe cases, by contrast, they literally cannot express themselves through speech, handwriting, or other conventional means, and must use assistive technology devices, such as "talking" personal computers. Such technologies help children with severe CP to dramatically reduce their dependence on others; before the advent of modern microprocessor-based assistive devices, such children depended on others for virtually every activity of daily life.

Words frequently used to describe the problems of children with CP include *spasticity* (stiffness, hypertonia, muscle contractions), *atonia* (lack of muscle tone; also hypotonia, less than normal muscle tone), *ataxia* (uncontrolled, jerky, irregular movements caused by fluctuating muscle tone, balance problems, overreaching for things), and *athetosis* (contortions, twisting motions). These words all suggest problems controlling voluntary muscles.

Hypotonia is a frequently reported condition in children who have Down syndrome (see Chapter 15). This illustrates a central theme in ECSE: Children should be assessed and helped in all five domains, regardless of whether their primary needs lie in one particular domain. In this instance, children with Down syndrome may have pressing needs for intervention in cognitive development, but they also need physical and other therapy for hypotonia. The point is to think of needs and respond to them, rather than thinking only of a child's primary deficits.

Physical therapy and occupational therapy aim to slow down the atrophying of muscles. They also assist the spastic and athetoid child in the morning to loosen muscles that became tight during the night. Maintaining good posture while standing or sitting is another goal of physical and occupational therapy, as severe atrophy may result from chronic abnormal posture.

Amputation

"Missing legs, feet, toes, arms, hands, and/or fingers" were reported for 38,000 under-six children, or 4.5 percent of all birth-to-five children in the SIPP study who had any disability and 16 percent of those with a physical limitation (Bowe, 1994). In some cases, limbs are missing at birth; in others, they are amputated for survival reasons, as when a bone is cancerous. Amputations are three or four times as likely to be congenital (occurring at or prior to birth) as adventitious (happening after birth) (Jones, 1988). Therapeutic amputations are more frequent among boys than girls, as boys tend to be more adventurous physically and have more accidents. Congenital conditions may result from drugs, as when a pregnant woman abuses controlled substances or when medicinal drugs are administered to the woman before she realizes she is pregnant. Maternal rubella in pregnancy may cause congenital conditions, as well.

Traumatic Brain Injury/Spinal Cord Injury

The 1991-1992 SIPP study reported that 14,000 children under the age of six, or 1.6 percent of all children in that age range who had any disability and 6 percent of those with a physical limitation, had a traumatic brain injury, a spinal cord injury, or some other kind of paralysis.

traumatic brain injury (TBI) was added to the Individuals with Disabilities Education Act (IDEA) as a recognized disability in 1990. Automobile, motorcycle, sports, and gun-related accidents resulting in sharp blows to (closed head injuries) or penetration of (open head injuries) the head cause TBIs.

Traumatic brain injury. Traumatic brain injury (TBI) was added to the definition of "children with disabilities" under Part B in 1990. The disability is relatively rare in young children but is quite common among adolescents and young adults. According to the New Medico Neurologic Rehabilitation System, every year 200,000 children sustain TBIs; one in every thirty Americans will have a significant brain injury before reaching driving age. While teenagers are the group at highest risk (due to motor vehicle and sporting accidents), preschool-age children are second. The absolute number of instances, however, is low. Boys are two to four times as likely to sustain TBI as are girls (Waaland, 1990). Nine out of every ten TBIs are caused by falls and by bicycle, motor vehicle, and sporting injuries (Allison, 1992). Others result from child abuse, gunshot wounds, and injuries from other projectiles (Humphreys, 1989).

Cognitive losses due to TBI frequently are temporary. A good example is short-term memory loss after damage to the temporal lobe; with therapy, good nutrition, and—perhaps most important—time, the ability to lay down new information returns. However, in some cases longer-term effects are hidden, not surfacing for months or even years after the accident. As the child reaches a new stage of development and is expected to do new things, long-hidden damage in the brain becomes apparent. The child does not progress intellectually or behaviorally as expected, and it is this delay or impairment that reveals the extent of the injury. Reported Mark Ylvisaker, of the College of St. Rose in Albany, New York:

> *A two-year-old may leave the emergency room walking and talking, and look like he's recovered. But years later, he may still be displaying the type of behavioral disregulation—inability to control impulses, inappropriate behavior in a social context, inability to plan, etc.—that is typical of a two- to four-year-old, but which is now drastically out of place in an older child.* (quoted in Allison, 1992, p. 4)

Particularly evident is damage to just-emerging capabilities. Infants and toddlers, who are acquiring receptive language skills, may demonstrate linguistic deficits if they sustain TBIs, while preschoolers may show deficits in interactive play with other children.

TBI is a common cause, as well, of epilepsy. Almost half of all head traumas result in some form of epilepsy.

Spinal cord injury. **Spinal cord injury (SCI)** occurs when the spinal column is damaged or ruptured. Many of the accidents that cause TBI can also cause SCI; the difference is that the spine, rather than the brain itself, is traumatized. As with TBI, accidents are the most common cause of SCI in childhood—automobile, bicycle, and sports accidents in particular. The spinal cord is the principal mode through which afferent (to the brain) and efferent (from the brain) messages are transported. Accordingly, when the cord is injured, both kinds of messages may stop. Children with SCI may injure or burn a toe, for example, and not feel any pain. They also are unable to "tell" the legs what to do.

The extent of the effects of SCI depends in large part not only on how severely the cord is damaged but also on the site of the lesion. The higher (closer to the head) the cord is traumatized, the more pervasive the effects. High-level SCI produces paralysis not only in the legs but in the arms and hands as well. That is called **quadriplegia**. Lower-level SCI, by contrast, principally affects the legs, in what is called **paraplegia**. Wheelchairs may be needed in both cases, although occasionally physical and occupational therapy can help a child avoid the need for a chair; some individuals even become "walking quads," overcoming quadriplegia to walk independently, perhaps with a cane or other means of support. Secondary problems from SCI include **pressure sores** (decubitus ulcers), which develop when the child does not shift weight on a wheelchair cushion or on a bed. ECSE professionals should become acquainted with techniques, some of which are illustrated in Figure 13.1, including special seating pads as well as rotation procedures, to prevent pressure sores. Urinary tract infections also may occur; again, as with pressure sores, the lack of afferent messages to the brain means that the child does not complain about urinary pain. ECSE professionals need to be alert to signs of such infections.

Young children often express keen interest in active recreation, for which everyday wheelchairs frequently are not suited. Fortunately, over the past five to ten years, a fast-growing market in "sport" chairs has developed in response to this interest. Sporty chairs are

spinal cord injury (SCI) occurs when the spinal cord is stretched, bruised, or even severed. It is one of many conditions categorized in the Individuals with Disabilities Education Act (IDEA) as orthopedic impairments.

quadriplegia occurs when all four limbs (arms and legs) are affected, usually by a spinal cord injury.

paraplegia occurs when the lower limbs (legs) are affected, usually by a spinal cord injury, but the upper limbs (arms) are not.

pressure sores (decubitus ulcers) develop when the child does not shift weight on a wheelchair cushion or on a bed.

Children having genetic conditions making them unusually small, as with the child in the center of this group, may have associated physical problems. Surgery is sometimes necessary to alleviate those problems.

1. Initiate seating as soon as possible following the acute stage.

2. Use rental and manufacturer-loaned chairs for evaluation.

3. Look for solid seat, contoured cushion, and pelvic support.

4. Involve physical and occupational therapists in evaluation and ongoing assessment.

5. Monitor child's posture, head position, visual field, skin condition, alertness, comfort, and ability to function independently.

6. Use a second, "sporty" chair for recreation purposes. Sports chairs are light, easily maneuvered, and have only essential seating and positioning features.

7. Reassess both regular and sports chairs every few months, because rapid physical growth in young children dramatically affects needs.

—adapted from Kreutz (1993) and Smith (1994)

FIGURE 13.1   Wheelchair seating and positioning

very different from everyday chairs: They are much lighter, more streamlined, with fewer parts. Some come with wheels that are angled outward for greater stability at high speed and for more maneuverability in wheelchair basketball, soccer, and other sports. Unfortunately, most insurance plans (including Medicaid and Medicare) reimburse costs only for one, primary wheelchair (Smith, 1994).

Arthritis, Other Fingers/Hands Impairments

juvenile rheumatoid arthritis is a condition in which joints become inflamed, and usually appears between the ages of eighteen months and four years; it generally has few if any lasting effects on children.

"Impairments or deformities of fingers, hands, and/or arms" were reported in the SIPP study by parents for 5,000 under-six children, or 2 percent of all such children who had a physical disability (Bowe, 1994). Such conditions are relatively rare. **Juvenile rheumatoid arthritis** usually appears between the ages of eighteen months and four years, often after a respiratory infection caused by bacteria or viruses (Schumacker, Klippel, & Robinson, 1988). Its principal effects are joint pain and swelling, especially after midafternoon. As often happens with asthma, children may miss parts or all of day programs or preschool if the condition becomes severe. Most children with juvenile rheumatoid arthritis recover within a few years, experiencing few, if any, permanent effects.

Juvenile diabetes (Type 1) is a disorder of metabolism in which the body is unable to retain sufficient energy from food. One important effect may be reduced finger sensation. Diabetes also can cause visual impairment, including blindness. The loss of finger sensation may make it all but impossible for the individual to read Braille or even raised letters and symbols in buildings.

Medically Fragile, Technology-Dependent Children

medically fragile, technology-dependent children require a range of intensive medical and other services as well as specialized equipment for ventilation and feeding.

Medically fragile, technology-dependent children require use of one or more pieces of equipment to prevent death or to forestall further disability. Formerly, such children usually died within hours or days of birth. Now, as reported by the now-defunct U.S. Congress

Office of Technology Assessment (OTA) in a 1987 report, medical and technological advances are giving thousands of such children an opportunity to live. They may need long-term hospitalization or other intensive care. More and more, however, they are being discharged to the home for care by the family (Beck, Hammond-Cordero, & Poole, 1994; Krajicek & Tompkins, 1993).

Technology-dependent children may need machines for ventilation or for feeding. Often, child-care workers and family members must monitor the infant, toddler, or preschooler virtually twenty-four hours a day. This creates tremendous needs on the family's part for respite care. The extensive support system required for monitoring may begin to fail over time, as the demands of employment, care for other children, and other deferred or delayed needs resurface (Beck et al., 1994).

Medically fragile, technology-dependent children include children who require vigilant monitoring and extensive technological support for ventilation, children who have had tracheostomies, and children using machines ("iron lungs") for ventilation. Often, very complex support arrangements must be made between the home, the hospital, a pediatric pulmonary center, and early intervention programs. Baroni, Tuthill, Feenan, and Schroeder (1994) offered a vivid case history describing how one young boy was helped through such teamwork. It is impossible to read their account without coming to appreciate the remarkable constellation of support services required to help children with severe pulmonary needs. Baroni et al. commented, for example: "Over the subsequent three years of his life, the array of services necessary to care for this one little boy expanded to include four hospitals, eight clinics, three financial agencies, five home care components (including therapies), and countless physicians, nurses, social workers, and therapists across services and settings spanning three states" (p. 74).

ASSESSMENT

The IDEA calls for a "multidisciplinary assessment" of all potentially eligible young children. It is important that ECSE professionals consider each child's status and needs in the domain of physical development, even if the child's primary needs appear to be in some other domain. In part, this holistic approach reflects recognition in the field that development in one domain may be affected by disabilities or delays in another domain. More broadly, however, it emerges from the focus inherent in ECSE as a field upon "the whole child."

The federal rules for early intervention programs outline the assessment functions of physical therapy, in section 303.12(9) as follows:

(i) Screening, evaluation, and assessment of infants and toddlers to identify movement dysfunction; [and]

(ii) Obtaining, interpreting, and integrating information appropriate to program planning to prevent, alleviate, or compensate for movement dysfunction and related functional problems. (U.S. Department of Education, 1993a)

The Bayley Scales of Infant Development (second edition) offer a psychomotor scale; this scale in the first edition of the Bayley was widely used for assessment of physical development. Another widely used set of scales is the Peabody Developmental Motor Scales (Folio & Fewell, 1983), which offer well-standardized gross and fine motor scales. Regardless of what scales or other measures are chosen, tests should be interpreted with care when a child has a physical disability, particularly CP, but also SCI, TBI, and other conditions such as MD. Assessors must remind themselves that these kinds of disabilities affect not only the child's daily activities but testing as well. Tests designed for use with infants and toddlers rely heavily on physical activity by the child; parental reports, developmental checklists, and other measures also look to what the child does motorically. Yet CP, SCI, MD, and many other physical disabilities by their very nature slow motoric response and limit fine motor control in all of these areas. The ECSE professional should interpret test results or reports with care, recognizing that test results and assessed activities may be skewed by the disability.

INTERVENTION

accessible refers to a standard such that at least one entrance, at least one path through a facility, at least one rest room, and so on, is usable by individuals with disabilities. This standard, which applies to existing facilities or buildings, is lower than the barrier-free standard.

barrier-free relates to buildings or facilities. All entrances, all rooms, and all levels or floors need to be accessible to people with disabilities. This standard applies to new construction and to newly renovated parts of existing facilities. The standard contrasts with "accessible," which is a lower standard.

The design of the built environment is a major consideration in serving children with physical disabilities. Whether services are delivered at the home, in a day-care center, or in a public school, the facility should at a minimum be **accessible** and optimally be **barrier-free**. An accessible environment offers at least one route into the facility; at least one way to reach any given room within the building; at least one rest room that has wide stalls, grab bars, and lowered sinks and mirrors; and at least one way to do the things other children do, including removable chairs, adjustable desktops, and the like. Programs and classes may be reassigned to ground-floor rooms if the building has no elevator. The "accessible" standard applies to existing buildings. The intent is to offer access that is "reasonable" and not excessively costly.

"Barrier-free," by contrast, applies to new construction and to newly renovated parts of existing facilities. The barrier-free requirement sets a much higher standard. In barrier-free buildings, each entrance is accessible, all rooms are reachable in a wheelchair or with the use of crutches, and all important switches and furnishings are usable by people with physical disabilities.

As mentioned in Chapter 9, the U.S. Architectural and Transportation Barriers Compliance Board, a small independent federal agency, offered guidelines for making facilities usable by people with physical disabilities. The guidelines, developed for use under the Americans with Disabilities Act (ADA), addressed the issues raised when young children use a facility. Particularly important are lowered switches and controls (for room lights, elevator call buttons, and so on); turnaround space in halls, rest rooms, and other common areas so that children using wheelchairs may reverse direction easily; and the height of workspaces such as tables and desks. Libraries should have lowered bookshelves and may have revolving book displays and revolving turntable stacks on tabletops so that children can easily reach any object on the table. Automatic doors and doors that open or close with relatively little pressure are other important aspects of design for young children with physical disabilities. Raschke, Dedrick, and Hanus (1991) offered illustrations of how playground and play equipment could be adapted for accessibility. See also Bowe (in press).

In addition, toys themselves may be adapted. Velcro, now a widely used convenience item, was originally developed for people who have fine motor control limitations. Virtually anything can be equipped with Velcro, heavy duct tape, or other fasteners. These may be used to secure toys to a surface, making it much easier for the child to play independently. Heavy cardboard may be added to the base of game pieces to give them greater stability. As Wershing (1994) reported, many such modifications are suggested by the children themselves as they play with toys. Game rules, too, may be changed; a good example of adapting games was given by Raschke, Dedrick, Heston, and Farris (1996). Wershing suggested that all such rule changes apply to all players, not only to the child with a physical disability.

Use of adaptive toys is but one part of what should be a broad-ranging program of ensuring that all children participating in an ECSE program have an equal opportunity to engage in active play. Every child needs to be able to play, because as Piaget said, "the child's work is play"—it is through play that cognitive and other kinds of development occur in young children. Children communicate with other children most often while they are playing, so communication development, as well, depends heavily on the child's ability to play freely. Adaptive development, too, is spurred when young children have a chance to respond creatively to new situations in play. Figure 13.2 offers addresses for catalogs of adapted toys and related products.

Much intervention in this domain involves **physical therapy**. The profession of physical therapy focuses on preventing or reducing muscle atrophy. The federal regulation for early intervention programs (U.S. Department of Education, 1993a) defined physical therapy in section 303.12.(9) as follows:

> [S]ervices to address the promotion of sensorimotor function through enhancement of musculoskeletal status, neurobehavioral organization, perceptual and motor development, cardiopulmonary status, and effective environmental adaptation. These services include. . . . (iii) Providing individual and group services or treatment to prevent, alleviate, or compensate for movement dysfunction and related functional problems. (U.S. Department of Education, 1993a)

The department's earlier definition had been considered by many in Congress to be too narrow. For example, *House Report 102-198* (1991) urged a broader view of the role of physical therapy:

physical therapy helps prevent and reduce muscle atrophy and promotes musculoskeletal development.

Switch Kids Inc.
8507 Rupp Farm Drive
West Chester, OH 45069

ChildCraft Education Corp.
2920 Old Tree Drive
Lancaster, PA 17603

Access to Recreation
2509 E. Thousand Oaks Boulevard
Thousand Oaks, CA 91362

Community Playthings
P.O. Box 901, Route 213
Rifton, NY 12471

Flaghouse Inc.
601 Flaghouse Drive
Hasbrouck Heights, NJ 07604

S & S
P.O. Box 513
Colchester, CT 06415

Constructive Playthings
1227 East 119th Street
Grandview, MO 64030

Abilitations
Select Service & Supply
One Sportime Way
Atlanta, GA 30340

Source: Kornreich Technology Center, National Center for Disability Services, Albertson, NY

FIGURE 13.2 Adapted toys catalogs

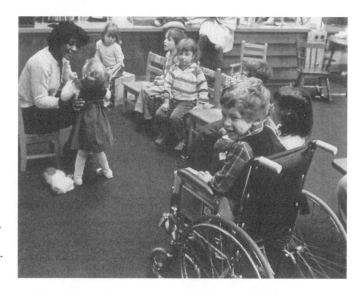

Children who use wheelchairs can participate in most early childhood activities and programs as long as facilities are accessible and modest accommodations are made. Courtesy of David Snyder.

The Committee is concerned that the existing definition of "physical therapy" in the regulations implementing Part H has not kept pace with advances in the field. The current definition lacks a clear scope of practice for physical therapists in the pediatric setting. The definition does not currently reflect the physical therapist's role in the promotion of sensorimotor function through enhancement of musculoskeletal status, neurobehavioral organization, perceptual and motor development, cardiopulmonary status, and effective environmental adaptation. Additionally, the current regulation is unclear with respect to individual and group treatment, as well as consultation services. (p. 12)

occupational therapy helps children learn to perform specific tasks (brush teeth, dress, maintain good posture, and so on) despite physical disabilities or other conditions such as Down syndrome.

While physical therapy focuses on prevention of atrophy in muscles, **occupational therapy** concentrates on helping children perform daily activities and self-care functions. In occupational therapy, the therapist teaches the child how to do something concrete and specific—how to dress, how to brush her teeth, and so on. The federal regulation for early intervention describes occupational therapy in section 303.12(8) as follows:

[S]ervices to address the functional needs of a child related to adaptive development, adaptive behavior and play, and sensory motor and postural development. These services are designed to improve the child's functional ability to perform tasks in home, school, and community settings, and include—
(i) Identification, assessment, and intervention;
(ii) Adaptation of the environment, and selection, design, and fabrication of assistive and orthotic devices to facilitate development and promote the acquisition of functional skills; and
(iii) Prevention or minimization of the impact of initial or future impairment, delay in development, or loss of functional ability. (U.S. Department of Education, 1993a)

Traumatic Brain Injury

Interagency coordination is particularly important for children with physical disabilities, because hospital, community health, and other agencies have important contributions to make. With TBI, the need for interagency cooperation is especially urgent due to the rapidly changing abilities of the child. Because TBI was added to the list of disabilities recognized under Part B only in 1990, many states do not yet have well-thought-out interagency networks to facilitate posthospital services. Among the few states with such systems in place prior to 1990 were Florida, Iowa, Maryland, and New York. Iowa's experience in particular suggests that individualized family service plan (IFSP) or individualized education program (IEP) meetings be held between ECSE program staff, parents, and medical professionals prior to discharge. Physical, cognitive, social, and other goals need to be set at this meeting. All such goals should be tentative, however; TBI challenges ECSE program staff to be unusually flexible. Psychological adjustment following TBI may be difficult because the recovery process is often prolonged (Figure 13.3). The greatest potential for improvement occurs during the first two years following discharge from the hospital; frequent reevaluations of the child during that time are essential because brain functions often return, increasing the child's ability to do things she could not perform earlier.

Heriza and Sweeney (1994, 1995) offered a two-part overview of pediatric physical therapy. Hanft and Striffler (1995) added that "individual hands-on therapy is not always the best way to assess every child" (p. 40), because consultation with educators can also be effective.

With children who have survived TBI, training is usually most effective, and most rapid, when applied behavior analysis techniques are used. Such approaches are discussed in Chapters 16 and 17. Other information is available from the National Head Injury Foundation in Washington, D.C., which reported in 1990 that more than 500 programs specializing in rehabilitation for people with TBI are now in existence. One cognitive rehabilitation program recommended by Page and Chew (1993) is the Reitan Evaluation of Hemispheric Abilities and Brain Improvement Training (REHABIT). The program includes instruction in expressive and receptive training, sequencing, manipulation, and cognitive skills. According to Brodsky, Brodsky, Lee, and Sever (1986), two evaluation studies showed that

1. Arrange for older child, adolescent, or adult who has gone through rehabilitation to spend time with the child. Such modeling and peer counseling can be very effective.

2. Expect variations from the Kubler-Ross (1969) stages; children with SCI or TBI often cycle through emotional states, rather than proceeding through each in sequence.

3. Early denial is good, as it shows hope. By the time equipment must be ordered, however, denial becomes harmful. Engage the assistance of a child mental health specialist as needed.

4. Focus on practical realities as soon as possible. By solving concrete, day-to-day problems, children gain confidence and move beyond initial worries.

5. The entire child-care team should offer support and encouragement.

6. Any behaviors that are self-destructive or otherwise harmful should be ignored so as to cause them to extinguish, and more adaptive behaviors taught in their place.

—adapted from Madden (1993) and Page & Chew (1993)

FIGURE 13.3 Psychological adjustment to SCI and TBI

REHABIT can be effective. The program may need modification for use with young children, however.

Spinal Cord Injury

Individuals with SCI learn to use new muscles to perform functions now limited by the injury. They also learn, from physical and occupational therapists, how to use **orthoses** and **prostheses**, and how to take advantage of any and all residual muscle strength. Assistive technology experts train people with SCI (and individuals with other disabilities as well) in the use of a wide range of assistive technology devices and services, including environmental control systems (ECS), discussed in Chapter 10.

Asthma

Intervention is primarily medical. A portable air compressor, which delivers antihistamine medication, may be used by a child, with assistance from ECSE professionals. In asthma, swelling in the lungs makes breathing difficult. Antihistamines are often is used to treat asthma, because they reduce the body's supply of histamines, thereby alleviating clogging in the lungs and easing the task of breathing. Other asthma medications include cromolyn sodium and steroids, which may be taken in pill form. The child should take medication prior to activities that in the past triggered attacks, such as exercise or test taking. In some cases, medication is injected by a nurse or physician.

ECSE personnel can take several other steps. First, unnecessary or prolonged physical activity should be avoided, because it may trigger an attack. Second, allergens such as pollen should be removed from the program environment if at all possible, or at least reduced via heating, ventilation, and air conditioning (HVAC) systems and filters. The recent increase in the reported incidence of asthma may be related to greater environmental allergens, which may flourish in carpets, in the air of tightly sealed rooms, and in furniture as dust mites. Third, events known to be stressful to the child should be minimized; if they are unavoidable, ECSE personnel should consider antihistamine medication in advance of the activity and should monitor the child during that activity. They should learn to recognize signs that an asthma attack is coming, or is under way. The characteristic patterns of labored breathing, dry coughing, and other indications of respiratory stress should alert ECSE personnel to the need to take action. Finally, ECSE personnel should watch for possible side effects of medication and know how to respond to those. Monitoring the condition is an important function for ECSE personnel.

Muscular Dystrophy

Some studies suggest that the steroid prednisone slows the muscle deterioration. Boys taking prednisone did not need wheelchairs until about three years after boys not taking it did. Steroids, however, have serious side effects—including high blood pressure, cataracts, diabetes, and significant weight gain, which can be a particular problem for boys with weakened muscles to carry. Researchers are now trying to identify the active ingredient in prednisone that slows MD, and isolate it, in the hope that they can offer help without the side effects.

orthosis is a device that enhances the function of a body part, as a leg brace helps a child to walk. It contrasts with a prosthesis, which replaces a body part.

prosthesis is an artificial replacement, such as a mechanical arm or knee, for a missing limb or body part.

They are also trying to design treatments that will replace dystrophin or compensate for its absence. This research was funded by the Muscular Dystrophy Association, the group for whom Jerry Lewis holds his Labor Day telethons.

Now that a gene associated with Duchenne MD has been identified, it is possible that at some time in the near future genetic interventions may alleviate, or even eliminate, the effects of the disease. Until that time, physical therapy to slow down muscle atrophy and occupational therapy to help the child cope with muscle weaknesses are the principal interventions. Assistive technology devices can enable the child to do things that he no longer can do alone, such as sitting in an upright position. Mobility can also be enhanced by braces, crutches, and wheelchairs; and fine motor control functions can be facilitated by pointing, switching, and similar devices.

Spina Bifida

The SBAA (1997) has estimated that the incidence of spina bifida might fall by as much as 75 percent if all women of childbearing age took appropriate amounts of folic acid.

Children with spina bifida often have allergies to latex (natural rubber), which is often found in catheters, diapers, elastic bandages, rubber bands, balloons, pacifiers, and many other products. Latex-free substitutes are readily available for most of these. The SBAA offers an extensive list of such substitutes at its Web site (www.sbaa.org). Bladder and/or bowel problems also are common with spina bifida. A *shunt*, or straw-shaped drain, can relieve the fluid buildup in hydrocephalus (Shaer, 1997). This shunt tubing empties the fluid into the abdominal cavity. Unfortunately, shunts sometimes become infected and may fail for other reasons as well (Shaer, 1997).

Most children with spina bifida do not require specially designed instruction because their learning needs are not affected by the condition (unless, of course, the children also have learning disabilities or attention deficits). However, assistive technology devices and services can help children with spina bifida to learn to walk, after surgery, using canes, crutches, and/or leg braces; others use manual or motorized wheelchairs (Shaer, 1997). For more information, see Lutkenhoff and Oppenheimer (1996) and Rowley-Kelly and Reigel (1993).

Cerebral Palsy

Computer speech synthesis can help children with CP much as it does children who are blind, deaf, retarded, or learning disabled. As with other children, speech synthesis systems offering a choice of voices (male, female, child, and so on) are important psychologically, because this will be the child's "voice." Because CP is a disability limiting expressive communication, children with CP need more than just a voice. Alternative means of input are often required, ranging from the simple (a "key guard" or plastic covering for the keyboard) to the complex (still experimental systems that translate brain patterns into words). Many alternatives to the keyboard are available. Any child with voluntary control over at least one muscle (even an eyebrow) can use alternative input mechanisms. Through microprocessor-based technologies, children with CP can express themselves, in precise and complete ways. Providing such children with such assistive technology devices and services is urgently important. As discussed in Chapter 10, both the IFSP under Part C and the IEP under Part

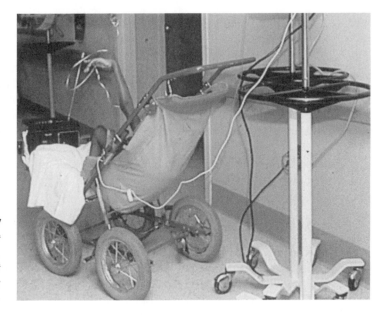

Medically fragile and technology-dependent children may have multiple, intensive needs that challenge child-care professionals.

B may provide for assistive technologies. With such aids, many young children with CP can function well in integrated settings. More controversial are such interventions as conductive education (Kozma & Balogh, 1995), for which little empirical evidence exists.

Amputation

As a general rule, children who never had (or who have no memory of) the missing limb adjust more readily to the condition than do children who lose the limb later in childhood. They more quickly accept braces, artificial limbs, and assistive technology devices and services. By contrast, children who vividly remember life before amputation may resist the introduction of artificial devices and aids.

Orthoses (products that help children do things the amputation might otherwise prevent) and prostheses (devices that replace a missing body part) play important roles in intervention with children who have amputation. Other assistive technology devices and services are also frequently helpful. Chapter 10 offers an in-depth discussion of such technologies.

Medically Fragile, Technology-Dependent Children

Lantos and Kohrman (1992) have suggested that newborns who are technology-dependent require much greater degrees of hospital-home coordination than most intensive care unit (ICU) programs offer. The needs of these infants for complex life-support devices—which must not only be selected, acquired, and operated but also maintained and, at times, repaired—brings technicians and computer experts into the family-hospital follow-up process. Renee Waissman (1993), of the Centre de Recherche Médecine in Paris, has commented that many parents who decide to accept responsibility to raise technology-dependent children, including children with chronic illnesses, "behave with conviction and a sense of responsibility when they decide to treat their child at home. However, they don't necessarily consider all possible consequences of their decision . . ." (p. 29). Helping parents to explore those possible outcomes is the responsibility of the professional. One aspect of that role is assisting parents to overcome what Waissman calls the "guilt of being healthy and being unable to transmit that health" (p. 30).

When medically fragile children begin early intervention or preschool programming, family relief may be short-lived. Public support for nursing or other monitoring during program hours may not be available under the IDEA, which does not authorize most medical care services. Unless the family is able to locate private health insurance or other coverage, the costs of having a nurse with the child throughout the day may soon bankrupt the family. Then, too, the fact that these children have one-on-one, constant adult monitoring limits their independence and may slow social and emotional growth. One solution to these problems is to place the child in a specialized setting, where child-care workers and early childhood special educators are trained in maintaining the equipment and caring for the child (Beck et al., 1994).

An excellent guide to the legal aspects of related services for children with severe physical and health-care needs is offered by Rapport (1996). She reviewed federal and state cases brought under the IDEA. Rapport noted that the U.S. Supreme Court's 1984 decision in *Irving Independent School District v. Tatro* (468 U.S. 883) continues to be the controlling case with respect to what are "medical services" (not covered by the IDEA) versus "educational services" (included in the IDEA). Under *Tatro,* services that can be performed by a nurse or other qualified person but that do not require a physician are the responsibility of educators if these services are necessary for the child to take part in the educational program.

WORKING WITH PARENTS

Perhaps the most important information ECSE professionals can share with parents of young children with physical disabilities is the existence of powerful federal accessibility laws. A physical disability in a child affects the family in many ways, every day. The family must think about accessibility when making restaurant or movie reservations, when visiting the library, and even when calling for a doctor's or dentist's appointment. That is why the ADA and other legislation reviewed in Chapter 6 are so important. Yet surveys show that most parents have only limited understanding of what the ADA says, what it means to them, and how to file complaints. With families whose children's physical limitations are both significant and permanent (that is, are disabilities), understanding these laws and how to make them work makes a tremendous difference in a family's ability to function every day in the community.

TBI can drain parents as can few conditions other than autism. That is because the condition does not stabilize for years following the accident. The ability to remember new information, for example, may disappear for months or even a year. This may make the child unable to learn anything new. In most cases, the ability returns; however, until it does, no one knows when it will. Educational and therapeutic interventions are based upon an intact ability to remember what is taught. This problem often traumatizes parents, who find it not only frustrating but frightening. Meanwhile, functions that children had learned may be lost, even if only temporarily; still, it is disconcerting for a parent to see a toilet-trained three-year-old return to diapers. In all of these cases, ECSE programs may work in close

1. Seek to empower the family to act as the child's primary caregiver and decision maker.

2. Eschew professional jargon in favor of clear, lay language.

3. Make sure the family understands that discharge does not mean the child is recovered; rather, it signals another in a long series of steps to rehabilitation.

4. Suggest that the family start a "recovery book" or journal into which they enter changes in the child's condition and abilities. Such a record can provide encouragement when needed, by showing how far the child has come since discharge.

5. Work with the family to assess home accessibility, dietary requirements, equipment and financing for equipment, and whether or not the child needs an attendant.

6. Support family members (including siblings) to prepare them for major changes in their routines as they provide long-term care for the recovering child. Offer respite care if available.

7. Offer the family a "map" of every important facility or building in the child's life (home, clinic, school, church/synagogue, neighbor homes, playgrounds, and so on), together with names and telephone numbers of professionals who can provide assistance as needed at each location. Encourage the family to seek recreation and other "fun times" both for themselves and for the child.

—adapted from Keeney (1994)

FIGURE 13.4 Helping parents of young children with TBI.

collaboration with hospital staff and the family to plan and carry out interventions while waiting for the condition to stabilize. Using lay language to explain needs and plans to parents is essential. Sarah Keeney (1994) offered suggestions on empowering parents of young children with TBI. These are summarized in Figure 13.4. Many of the suggestions also apply to children with other severe physical disabilities or conditions.

When children have delays in physical development, but not disabilities, the issues are different. Usually, physical access is not a major concern (the child is not using a wheelchair, braces, a cane, and so on). ECSE personnel need to focus instead on helping the family to understand how they may accelerate physical development by providing more opportunities to explore and play in safe locations. Meanwhile, developmental milestones in the domain of physical development are so well known to parents—the first step at one year comes to mind—that ECSE professionals may need to caution parents that very considerable variation occurs even among "normal" infants, toddlers, and preschoolers. Flexibility is necessary so that parents do not become unduly worried when children are late in reaching developmental targets.

S U M M A R Y

This chapter opened with a mother's report on how big a difference physical and occupational therapy made in her son's life. Such services are authorized under both Part C and Part B. The importance of physical and occupational therapy is difficult to overstate. Under-six children are naturally active physically—as indeed they must be, because so much of their cognitive, social or emotional, communication, and adaptive development emerges as they act physically on their environment. That is why physical therapy (to develop muscles and to prevent atrophy) and occupational therapy (to teach children how to perform everyday tasks despite physical limitations) are so essential in ECSE. Today's wide variety of seating and mobility devices help, too; especially useful for children needing wheelchairs are sports chairs with which they may take part in recreational activities.

As important as these interventions are, much more may also be done. The built environment is far more accessible today than in past years, and this fact alone greatly increases the ability of families with young children who have physical disabilities to get around in the community. ECSE program staff should ensure that early childhood program facilities are accessible to people with physical limitations, that buildings and other facilities such as play areas at programs to which ECSE staff often refer children and their families are also accessible, and that families of children with physical disabilities themselves make their homes accessible as well. Chapter 9 offered some suggestions on accessible design; Chapter 6 reviewed federal laws mandating access to buildings, transportation facilities, and vehicles. An important way in which ECSE staff may empower families is by making them aware of such laws and assisting them, where necessary, in filing complaints about violations with the appropriate authorities.

Some physical disabilities present special challenges both to families and to ECSE workers. Children who are medically fragile or technology-dependent, children recovering from TBI, and children with spina bifida often require ongoing medical, therapeutic, and other interventions over a period of years. Psychological adjustment can be challenging, because the children do not have the luxury of adjusting only once to a new level of functioning; rather, they often must readjust to what is almost a new disability as their condition alters.

QUESTIONS FOR REFLECTION

1. Explain in your own words what "experiential deprivation" means and illustrate it with a child who has a physical disability such as cerebral palsy.

2. Differentiate "prevalence" from "incidence."

3. Can you think of a good reason why physical conditions are proportionately more common among under-six children than among older children?

4. How might asthma affect a child's participation in an ECSE program? If you were an ECSE worker, how would you address those problems?

5. Which disability discussed in this chapter is closely associated with low birth weight?

6. Explain how brain damage as a result of a traumatic brain injury might not become apparent for several years after the accident.

7. What are "pressure sores" and how can they be avoided?

8. How might a physical disability affect a child's performance on an IQ test? (If necessary, review Chapter 7 on testing.)

9. Differentiate "accessible" from "barrier-free." Which standard applies in which cases?

10. In your own words, what are the differences between physical therapy and occupational therapy?

Communication Development

In the young child, motor involvement with corticospinal tract signs frequently is observed to be the most profound delay. Motor delays may initially manifest as hypotonia with increasing spasticity as the child ages. Delays or regression in social smile and cooing also has been reported. A mother of a 12-month-old in the Children's Hospital Oakland clinic recently reported the loss of her child's ability to vocalize to her. This infant over the course of her life exhibited progressive spasticity with a failure in her ability to sit independently and extreme difficulty in fluid reaching. To deflect questions and expressions of concern, this mother began telling strangers that her daughter was 6 months old instead of 12 months. (Johnson, 1993, p. 1)

OVERVIEW

Communication development is closely linked to other aspects of development in young children. This is evident in Johnson's story about an Oakland infant with human immunodeficiency virus (HIV). In the course of her short life, she exhibited delays in communication as a function of her other problems. For these and related reasons, the Individuals with Disabilities Education Act (IDEA) insists that assessment and intervention be "multidisciplinary." Had the Oakland infant lived, she should have been assessed in the domains of physical, cognitive, communication, social or emotional, and adaptive development. Her individualized family service plan (IFSP) and then her individualized education program (IEP) should have included interventions in not just one but several domains, to the extent that the program in which she was enrolled had the capabilities and to the extent that her parents concurred.

communication is the expression and reception of meaning. It may occur through speech/hearing, reading/writing, signing/seeing, gestures, or other means.

As infants, toddlers, and preschoolers develop cognitively, they improve in communication skills. Recognizing this interrelationship, Congress defined **communication** development broadly. In the U.S. House of Representatives committee report on the 1991 IDEA amendments, the Subcommittee on Select Education and Civil Rights stated:

> [T]he term "communication development" is intended to include language, speech, and hearing. Communication development includes acquisition of communication skills, during pre-verbal and verbal phases of development, receptive and expressive language, including spoken, non-spoken, and sign language means of expression, the use of augmentative communication devices, and speech production and perception. Communication development also includes oral-motor development, specifically those neuromuscular and structural conditions affecting pre-speech oral-motor development, speech sound production, and feeding and swallowing processes. Related to hearing, communication development includes development of auditory awareness, auditory, visual, tactile and kinesthetic skills, and auditory processing for speech or language development. (House Report 102-198, 1991, p. 12)

The definition focuses attention on language, speech, hearing, vision, and nonvocal means of communication such as American Sign Language (ASL). This chapter addresses normal and abnormal communication development. The disabilities of deafness and blindness, as well as stuttering, are considered, as are interventions to help young children.

PREVALENCE

Children with communication-related limitations comprise the second-largest category, after physical limitations, according to the 1991–1992 Survey of Income and Program Participation (SIPP) study. In fact, the single most common disabling condition reported by parents was speech impairment, at 20.8 percent of the children from birth to five inclusive with disabilities, or a remarkable one in every five. Deafness or other severe hearing problems were reported at a much lower rate (2 percent), as were blindness and other severe vision problems. Taking speech, hearing, and vision conditions together as limitations of communication development, such limitations account for a total of 25 percent of all birth-to-five inclusive children with disabilities. Children with speech, hearing, or vision impairments constitute about 1 percent of all children in this age range, according to the SIPP (Bowe, 1994). All told, including first, second, and third conditions, some 30 percent of under-six children with disabilities, or about 250,000, had limitations in communication development, according to the SIPP.

DEVELOPMENTAL DELAYS

State definitions of *delays* in communication tend to stress late-developing speech. This delay may be expressed in terms of first words occurring at twelve months following expected appearance, that is, at or after two years of age. Delays are also frequently expressed in terms of standard deviations (S.D.s) from the mean; the most frequent usage is two S.D. below the mean. As noted earlier, many states accept 1.5 S.D. below the mean in two or more domains, as well. That combination is common with communication delays, because physical and cognitive delays in particular often accompany delays in communication development—a good example is cerebral palsy. Finally, delays may be expressed in percentage terms, as a 25 percent delay in communication development. To illustrate, infants who are visually impaired are often delayed in head righting in the prone position (which usually occurs by three to four months of age); a 25 percent delay would mean this occurred at six months or later.

deviations are behaviors that are not normal at any age. Delays in development, by contrast, feature behavior that is normal, but for children of younger ages.

Developmental **deviations** are as much a matter of concern as delays, if not more so. Some children do not develop functional language; children born deaf, for example, will not master the native language without intensive and extensive intervention. They are not just delayed; the expected behavior is not late but absent or nearly so.

Professional judgment, or informed clinical opinion, is very important in communication assessment. That is because speech and language delays or deviations may signal some other problem, as in the case of deafness. It is also because measures of communication development in young children are not so much tests as they are documentation of behavior. Psychologists and other ECSE personnel should bear in mind that delays in speech and language may indicate other problems, notably mental retardation. Young children with delays in speech development should also be screened for possible hearing loss (see Assessment section).

Possible delays or deviations in communication development are listed in Figure 14.1. Generally, indicators are conservative (if any of the indicators holds true for a child, it is cause not for alarm but for a checkup with a specialist or clinic). Some suggest a hearing

For many children who are deaf, American Sign Language (ASL) is their first (native) language.

Neonates (Birth to twenty-eight days)
- Does not show a startle response to a loud noise
- Does not look eye-to-eye when being held

One to Four Months
- Does not exhibit the social smile
- Does not follow a moving object with eyes
- Does not turn head in direction of sound

Four to Eight Months
- Does not babble
- Does not laugh
- Does not search for hidden objects (or shows no awareness that an object has been hidden)
- Does not demonstrate interest in new, different sounds
- Does not calm to primary caregiver's voice

Eight to Twelve Months
- Does not obey "no" or other simple commands
- Does not blink eyes in defensive movement when objects rapidly approach head
- Does not play with sounds or make first word

Twelve to Eighteen Months
- Does not speak in variety of one-word utterances
- Does not answer questions with "yes" or "no" or other appropriate responses
- Does not appear to recognize self in mirror
- Is not delighted by new, different objects or pictures

Eighteen Months to Two Years
- Does not speak variety of two-word utterances, in speech that is intelligible to people familiar with the toddler's speech
- Does not obey simple spoken commands unless the request is also made in gestures or other visual mode
- Does not stop to explore objects on path while walking

Three Years
- Does not speak in variety of three- or four-word utterances
- Does not have speech that is at least occasionally intelligible to strangers
- Does not tell own name upon request

—adapted from Prizant and Wetherby (1993)

FIGURE 14.1 Indicators of possible delay: communication

loss, some a vision impairment, yet others a delay or disability in speech. Problems in communication should be identified prior to three years of age, because indicators of delays or deviations are readily observable by that time.

Other suggestions on indicators of possible delays were offered by Allen and Marotz (1989) and by Charlesworth (1992). Assessment of hearing and of vision will be discussed later in this chapter.

ESTABLISHED CONDITIONS

Most states recognize speech impairments, deafness or severe hearing loss, and blindness or serious visual impairment as established conditions known to result in developmental delays. Deafness, for example, is widely accepted by states as being an established condition; it usually results in severe speech and language delays if intervention is not accomplished quickly and effectively. Most states accept as established other conditions that result in communication delays as a secondary problem; such conditions include cerebral palsy, muscular dystrophy, and others. This section discusses the more common established conditions and outlines what ECSE professionals can expect with each.

Speech Impairments

The number-one limitation reported by parents in the 1991–1992 SIPP study was speech impairment. The Census Bureau estimated that some 177,000 children under age six had limitations in making themselves understood through speech. That was a remarkable 20.8 percent, or just over one in every five, of all under-six children with any disability. Nor was that all of it. The SIPP allowed parents to select up to three conditions as causes of their children's disabilities. Among children reported to have two conditions, 22 percent had speech impairments as their second-named condition. And of children having three or more conditions, 34 percent had speech impairments. Speech was not only the most common primary condition but also the most common secondary and the most common tertiary condition. Impairments of speech are also the most common disabilities in Head Start programs (U.S. Department of Health and Human Services, 1992).

speech is the oral expression of meaning, usually—but not always—with symbols (words).

Because the infant's first word and subsequent utterances attract so much family attention, delays or deviations in **speech** are among the first noticed and most reported of problems by parents. Impairments of speech are among the leading indicators of a wide range of disabilities. Hearing losses are first noticed by parents when infants and toddlers do not speak at expected ages; similarly, parents first bring children with autism to community clinics due to concerns about the child's speech. Only later do parents notice other indicators of these disabilities. Similarly, young children with cerebral palsy, Down syndrome, and learning disabilities, to name just three conditions, may display delays in speech development or speech impediments.

stuttering is dysfluent speech or disrupted oral communication.

Stuttering is a common concern in many young children. LaBlance, Steckol, and Smith (1994) suggested that stuttering is more common among boys than girls by a ratio of five to one, with most children who stutter beginning to do so in early childhood, between two and six years of age. They reported that stuttering is often preceded by delays in development of both speech and language. Van Riper (1993) explored the contributions of disturbed communication, disrupted feedback, and organicity in stuttering, and attempted to synthesize the many diverse theories advanced to explain why children stutter. The consensus: So far, no one theory successfully explains stuttering.

Deafness and Severe Hearing Impairment

Hearing loss is relatively uncommon in young children. The SIPP suggests that some 19,000 under-six children are deaf or severely hearing-impaired, or about 2 percent of all young children who have any disability. More than half of those with hearing losses have

deafness is the inability to hear and understand conversational speech through the ear alone.

congenital (present at birth) or early (first year) adventitious impairments (Riko, Hyde, & Alberti, 1985). Some children inherit **deafness** or another hearing impairment; however, well over 90 percent of all children who are deaf have two hearing parents (Brown, 1986).

The most common causes of hearing loss today are viruses or other agents triggering high body temperature. Notable among them is meningitis, for which vaccination for children under two is widely available. If, however, the fever persists for several days, the tiny hairs in the inner ear and the cells of the VIIIth nerve leading to the auditory cortex in the brain may be damaged. That produces a *sensorineural* hearing loss; the child becomes deaf or severely hard-of-hearing. A *conductive* loss is much less severe. Involving the outer and/or middle ear, it almost always yields to treatment with medication, and occasionally with surgery. Sensorineural loss, by contrast, is not now medically treatable. Conductive and sensorineural hearing losses are common as secondary conditions with cerebral palsy; they are also frequent in children with Down syndrome. Children with either of these conditions should routinely be screened for hearing loss.

Congenital cytomegalovirus infection (CMV) is a common cause of sensorineural hearing loss. The most frequent cause of congenital infections in humans, CMV affects up to 2.5 percent of all live births (Williamson & Demmler, 1992). It may also be acquired by young children. Although CMV is very common, most infants and children are asymptomatic. About half the infants and children who develop symptoms of some kind have sensorineural hearing loss. Visual impairment is less common. No CMV vaccine yet is available. Parents and child-care workers are advised to wash their hands after contact with children shedding CMV and to avoid sharing food or drink with them. Another viral infection, maternal rubella (German measles in pregnancy) was in the mid-1960s a major cause of both deafness and blindness. Since the development of the rubella vaccine, however, fewer than twenty cases in newborns have been reported annually by the Centers for Disease Control and Prevention.

The effects of deafness or other severe hearing impairment on young children are a function, in large part, of the *age at onset*. That is, a congenital loss of hearing will have a much greater, and much more broad-ranging, effect than will the same degree of loss occurring at age five. This is because children's development of language, speech, and much incidental knowledge occurs principally through the ears during early childhood. The trend in recent years has been for the average age at onset to decline; that is, today's children who are deaf are much more likely to have been born deaf or to become deaf during the first year of life. Prior to the 1970s, ages at onset of nine or even later were much more common.

About one out of every three children who are deaf has a secondary disability as well. Most common is cerebral palsy, although learning disabilities also are frequent. In many cases, the medical condition that caused the deafness also produced the other condition. Thus, oxygen deprivation prior to, during, or just after birth may lead to both cerebral palsy and deafness.

Blindness and Serious Vision Impairment

blindness is 20/200 vision, or tunnel vision where central vision subtends at an angle of 20 percent or less, as measured with corrective lenses.

low vision is 20/70 vision, or worse, to 20/200 vision, which is blindness.

Blindness and **low vision** are also relatively rare in young children, occurring in about one per 1,000 young children. The SIPP found 19,000 under-six children who were blind or had low vision, or 2 percent of all birth-to-five children with any disability. (Remarkably, Kay Ferrell of the University of Northern Colorado predicted this exact figure in her 1984 projections for 1990; see Ferrell, 1984; Deitz & Ferrell, 1993.) Visual impairments occur as secondary conditions with cerebral palsy, and less frequently with Down syndrome. The two most frequently used classifications for children with significant visual impairments are blindness and low vision; in each case, vision is measured with use of appropriate corrective lenses and is compared to that of unimpaired individuals. Blindness is 20/200 vision, or tunnel vision where central vision subtends at an angle of 20 percent or less, as measured with corrective lenses. Low vision is between 20/70 to 20/200 vision. Normal vision is expressed as 20/20, meaning that an individual standing 20 feet from an eye chart correctly identifies the letters/symbols it displays. In 20/200 vision, a child with normal (average) vision standing 20 feet from a chart could see the same letters or symbols that a child who is blind could see only if standing 2 feet from the same chart. A child with low vision can see a symbol at 20 feet that normally sighted children could see from 70+ feet.

The distinction between blindness and low vision is drawn for intervention and education purposes. Children who are blind usually do have residual vision (fewer than 20 percent are totally blind), but their vision is so poor that they learn best through other senses, chiefly hearing and touch. Children who have low vision, by contrast, have enough residual vision to be able to use it as a primary sense for learning and daily living purposes. Thus, with children who are blind the emphasis is upon auditory and tactile means of communication, but with children who have low vision it is upon visual means.

The cause of a child's blindness or other vision impairment frequently cannot be identified. The best-known and most common cause of blindness in infants continues to be **retinopathy of prematurity** (**ROP**; once known as retrolental fibroplasia). It is associated with prematurity, affecting about 4 percent of very low-birthweight (less than 1,000 g) infants (Glass, 1993). The condition once occurred when premature infants were placed into incubators and given excessive amounts of oxygen. With careful monitoring of oxygen levels, ROP all but disappeared in the late 1960s and 1970s. Now, however, Deitz and Ferrell (1993) reported, growing use of newborn life-support systems, including continuous bright light in the **neonatal intensive care unit (NICU)** twenty-four hours a day, has led to "a new epidemic" of ROP. Glass (1993) commented that ROP is now known to be associated with other predisposing factors, including not only prematurity but also hypoxia. (In hypoxia, body tissues lack sufficient oxygen, usually because of a reduction in the oxygen-carrying capacity of blood.) As more and more babies survive low birthweight and prematurity, many more potentially are at risk for ROP. Other important known causes of blindness are inheritance (as with retinoblastoma, a malignant tumor in the retina, or the "screen" in the rear of the eye, and congenital cataracts) and pre-, peri-, and postnatal illnesses and accidents that also may cause cerebral palsy, retardation, and other disabilities. Such illnesses and accidents tend to occur prior to age one, if they happen at all. Diabetes may also cause blindness, but rarely in early childhood.

Children who are blind or have low vision are affected by the condition to different degrees depending in large part on the age at onset. A congenital condition is likely to cause much greater developmental delays than a later-occurring loss. Young children who once had good vision have formed mental images of themselves, of their environments, and of nonverbal communication techniques, including body posture. Children who were born blind, by contrast, lack these firsthand mental images and must acquire substitute versions by other means.

As with deafness, blindness is congenital much more often today than in years past; that is, a child who is blind today is far more likely to have been born blind than were children in the 1950s and 1960s. And today's child who is blind is more likely than were such children in the past to have other disabilities. Cerebral palsy is a common accompanying condition. That is not surprising, since illnesses producing high fevers may damage the optic nerve and also damage motor control areas in the brain.

retinopathy of prematurity (ROP), once known as retrolental fibroplasia, is a limitation of vision occurring during the neonatal period.

neonatal intensive care units (NICUs) are hospital-based facilities for newborns in the first month of life.

Young children who are blind but who have no other major limitations will usually acquire communication competence by the time they enter school. During early childhood, however, many are delayed in communication development. Selma Fraiberg has contributed greatly to our understanding of blindness in young children. Her longitudinal studies of infants blind from birth (Fraiberg, 1968, 1970, 1975, 1977; Fraiberg & Freedman, 1964; Fraiberg, Smith, & Adelson, 1969) suggested that when early intervention and preschool instruction are not undertaken, children who are blind may demonstrate autistic-like behavior, have difficulty establishing and maintaining ties with other people, have echolalic speech, have poor definition of body boundaries, display motor stereotypes of the head and hands, and be delayed in achieving independent mobility. Examining the importance of sight in early childhood development, Fraiberg, Smith and Adelson (1969) commented:

> *The response smile to the configuration of the human face, the selective smile for the face of the mother, the father and siblings, the discrimination of mother and stranger, the entire sequence of recognition experience which leads to mental representation and evocative memory, are organized through visual experience. To a large extent, eye to eye contact is the matrix of a signal system which evolves between mother and child.* (p. 122)

Similarly, Fraiberg (1970) found that children with blindness tend to be delayed in use of the pronoun "I," in part because they are restricted by parents in exploration and mobility. With appropriate parental and early intervention assistance, such delays often are temporary. The delays occur because children who are blind or have low vision do not see objects to which words refer, thus learning their names later; do not see nonverbal communication cues that indicate expected behavior, including communication; and may not be invited to join in social activities with sighted peers.

Parents also may restrain the child who is blind from exploratory and independent play, fearing for the child's safety. Such *experiential deprivation* is a major factor in developmental delays among children who are blind. In an excellent overview of blindness and low vision, Warren (1984) urged parents and educators to provide young blind children with enriched linguistic stimulation, as well as extended opportunities to learn auditorially and tactually about their environments.

ASSESSMENT

pragmatics is the social use of language, or the knowledge of what expressions to use in which contexts.

Assessment in the domain of communication development is improving rapidly. The early 1990s witnessed dramatic advances in early detection of hearing and vision impairment, for example. Such progress is much-needed. Children with delays or disabilities in any of the five domains should be assessed in the area of communication. Young children with Down syndrome, for example, frequently have losses of hearing and sometimes of vision as well. Expressive communication is a well-recognized concern among children with cerebral palsy. Children with autism may not use situation-appropriate language; they may be delayed in **pragmatics**. The examples are legion, and the point is basic: The IDEA requires that children be looked upon holistically, that assessment be multidisciplinary, and that ECSE workers focus not only on children's deficits or delays but also on their strengths and resources.

Hearing

Recent research has given us very early identification of hearing loss. Procedures developed in late 1992 and early 1993 now permit screening of virtually all newborns even before they leave the hospital. These new tests have revolutionary implications. As recently as 1988, the U.S. Congress Commission on Education of the Deaf reported that the average age at which hearing loss was first identified in the United States was as late as three years of age (Commission on Education of the Deaf, 1988).

For a cost of just $25 per newborn, otoacoustic emission testing can screen infants for hearing loss even before they leave the hospital. Low-level, inaudible emissions are produced as the inner ear functions; otoacoustic emission testing measures those sounds. The full name of the procedure is "transient evoked otoacoustic emissions" (TEOAE). Otoacoustic emissions were first reported by David Kemp of the Middlesex School of Medicine in London in 1978 (Kemp, 1978). No physical response by the infant is required by the process, which was validated by the Rhode Island Hearing Assessment Project (RIHAP). For infants who test positive, follow-up auditory brainstem response (ABR) audiometry, which costs about $100, can be done. Again, no physical response by the infant is required. Electrodes attached to the head record electrical activity in the auditory nerve as the infant sleeps or rests quietly. Neither test is invasive, neither is time-consuming, and neither requires the infant's cooperation (White & Behrens, 1993).

In March 1993, a fifteen-member panel at the National Institutes of Health (NIH) endorsed these two tests. The NIH group was concerned that hearing loss is usually not identified until speech and language have already been delayed. The panel recommended that all infants (not just infants at risk) be tested during the first three months of life, preferably before discharge from the hospital (Squires, 1993). An entire issue of *Seminars in Hearing* (February 1993) was devoted to the new techniques. These approaches were recommended for national implementation in early 1998 by the National Institute on Deafness and Communication Disorders.

The U.S. Department of Education's regulations on early intervention services described the assessment function of "audiology" in section 303.12(2) as follows:

> *(i) Identification of children with auditory impairment, using at risk criteria and appropriate audiologic screening techniques;*
>
> *(ii) Determination of the range, nature, and degree of hearing loss and communication functions, by use of audiological evaluation procedures; [and]*
>
> *(iii) Referral for medical and other services necessary for the habilitation or rehabilitation of children with auditory impairment.* (U.S. Department of Education, 1993a)

Advances in assessment techniques have rendered some of these procedures outdated. Kramer and Williams (1993), in an overview of hearing assessment in early intervention, pointed out that testing only children meeting high-risk criteria—which include infectious diseases, parental concern about possible hearing loss, trauma, and neurodegenerative disease—limits the effectiveness of screening programs to perhaps 50 percent. That is because many children later found to have hearing losses do not meet such criteria, which also are referred to as "high risk register" criteria. The availability of low-cost, high-quality, noninvasive TEOAE techniques applicable even before hospital discharge makes it possible to test other children as well.

Audiological evaluation, the second step outlined in the federal regulations, may be used with children old enough to give voluntary responses to sounds. As with the screening tests, evaluation is performed on the unaided ear, in contrast to the way vision is tested. Pure-tone audiometry most often is used. In pure-tone audiometry, tones varying from very low in pitch to very high are presented to the subject at graduated levels of sound volume. The child raises his hand when he hears the sound. Results are expressed on an **audiogram**, which is a graphic display of hearing in terms of both pitch and volume. Pitch is displayed horizontally, ranging from 250 Hertz (Hz) to 8,000 Hz, or from very low to very high frequency. The vertical columns represent sound pressure. On audiograms, they descend from 0 decibels (dB) at the top (representing normal, or average, hearing) to 110 or 120 dB at the bottom. At the intersections of pitch and volume, a mark is made on the audiogram to indicate that this is the lowest volume to which the child made a response at that frequency. In the case of the right ear, an "o" is made; for the left ear, an "x" is entered. Marks are made when the child correctly responds at least 50 percent of the time at that particular frequency and volume combination.

Information about hearing loss in the "speech range" (500, 1000, and 2000 Hz), as measured in pure-tone audiometry, is important for educational and related purposes. In most people, hearing is best at those frequencies. A better-ear average (BEA) may be calculated by taking the dB levels of each of the three frequencies for the left ear and dividing by three, then doing the same for the right ear. The better (lower) average is the BEA. Generally, averages above 60 dB are of most concern, because hearing loss at or above that level is unusual in humans unless there is inner-ear damage. Lesser degrees of hearing loss are still important, however. Studies have shown that children with hearing impairment as mild as 20 dB are limited in speech comprehension. One report on screening with six- to eight-month-old infants found that they could discriminate the /ba/ sound from the /da/ sound with only 60 percent accuracy, that is, close to chance (Nazzo & Sabo, 1991). Fortunately, such losses can usually be corrected with medication, surgery, or amplification, as with hearing aids. However, correction for sensorineural hearing loss is not yet possible through surgery. Speech reception thresholds and speech comprehension levels may also be tested. These are particularly important when pure-tone audiometry reveals a hearing loss of 60 dB or greater in the better ear.

The third step in the federal regulation on audiology is referral for services. These services may include medication (as with otitis media and other ear-related illnesses), surgery (as with outer- and middle-ear problems), hearing-aid and other amplification selection, and speech and language services if appropriate.

Speech and Language

The U.S. Department of Education defined "speech-language pathology" in section 303.12(14) as including this assessment role:

> (i) *Identification of children with communicative or oropharyngeal disorders and delays in development of communication skills, including the diagnosis and appraisal of specific disorders and delays in those skills;*
> (ii) *Referral for medical or other professional services necessary for the habilitation or rehabilitation of children with communicative or oropharyngeal disorders and delays in development of communication skills.* (U.S. Department of Education, 1993a)

What is a "delay" in communication development? As Prizant and Wetherby (1993) pointed out, the answer to that question is not as obvious as it may seem. Children vary

audiograms are graphic displays of hearing loss along two dimensions; pitch (frequency) and intensity (volume).

greatly in the ages at which they speak their first words and in the ways in which they develop both receptive and expressive language. The speech and language pathologist needs to use observation with infants, toddlers, and preschoolers—preferably in natural environments. While a strict assessment protocol of stimulus and response can be very helpful, children this young do not perform all of the linguistic functions of which they are capable in such structured settings. It is essential to look for prespeech modes of communication, particularly gestures, as well as vocalizations. A variety of observations should be used, in different settings; indeed, communication assessment must be an ongoing process, not a one-time phenomenon. Prizant and Wetherby (1993), Roberts and Crais (1989), and Rosetti (1990) all offered checklists and suggestions for assessment with under-six children.

One instrument that may be used is the Communication and Symbolic Behavior Scales (CSBS), which is helpful in assessing both preverbal and verbal communication abilities in young children. Standardized on eight- to twenty-four-month-old infants and toddlers, the instrument analyzes and rates children on twenty-two scales. Composite scores may be obtained on gestures, speech, social-affective signaling, and other aspects of communication development. The Psychological Corporation's 1994 catalog, *Assessment and Intervention Products for Speech, Language, and Hearing*, features more than a hundred pages describing tests and other instruments. Wetherby and Prizant (1992), reviewing measures of communication in young children, caution that virtually all available instruments are limited, particularly in evaluating the full range of communication options young children use.

All assessments of language and communication should include efforts to identify any other condition, delay, or deviation that may be present (Prizant & Wetherby, 1993). Communication impairments frequently do not appear alone. Two reports suggest that as many as 60 percent of children with language disorders may also have emotional or behavioral limitations (Prizant, Audet, Burke, Hummel, Maher, & Theadore, 1990; Stevenson & Richman, 1976). Communication behavior tends to be obvious, attracting parental and professional attention. Other, perhaps more subtle problems should be explored whenever communication development is evaluated or assessed. Lockwood (1994) offered detailed guidelines for such testing.

Vision

The U.S. Department of Education's regulations for early intervention services described the assessment component of "vision services" in section 303.12(16) as follows:

(i) *Evaluation and assessment of visual functioning, including the diagnosis and appraisal of specific visual disorders, delays, and abilities;*

(ii) *Referral for medical or other professional services necessary for the habilitation or rehabilitation of visual functioning disorders, or both.* (U.S. Department of Education, 1993a)

Glass (1993) reported that a visually evoked response to a bright light may be obtained from fetuses at a gestation age of one or two months; the evoked response is eyelid tightening. She also alerted us to look for prolonged attention to unchanging stimuli, after birth, as an early indication of visual impairment, especially in preterm infants. Glass cited Sigman, Cohen, Beckwith, and Paremelee (1986), who found that such unusually long attention to nonvarying objects or other stimuli may also be an indicator of mental retardation.

Impairments of vision are uncommon among young children, and usually temporary as well.

Infants may also be checked for redness in the eyes, excessive tearing, oversensitivity to light, and a cornea that is larger than normal. Newborns' eyes may be examined to make sure they move. The next screening examination should be between six and twelve months; thereafter, vision should be assessed at three and five years, with the first formal examination occurring during that time. Parents should be especially alert to eye rubbing, squinting, and closing one eye. Less obvious signals of possible vision impairment include frequent daydreaming, avoidance of close work, and short attention span. Frequent headaches, nausea, and clumsiness are additional possible indicators (Teplin, 1995).

Diagnosis of a visual impairment should immediately trigger measurement of visual acuity by an eye specialist. Vision may be measured with young children by means of a Snellen Illiterate E chart; in this variation on the Snellen chart, all symbols are the letter E, and the child's response is to point in the direction of the letter's "legs." Of course, the Snellen Illiterate E chart (or the Snellen chart, for older children) measures vision at a distance, in this case, some twenty feet. Most schoolwork occurs at much closer range. For these reasons, X/20 measurements of visual acuity in young children are of limited utility. Fortunately, several tests of vision impairment with respect to the kinds of work children do in preschool and later are available. Tests of preferential viewing, for example, are fairly simple and may be done by an observer trained to watch the child's gaze shift (Barraga, 1983; Carter, 1983; Teller, McDonald, Preston, Sebris, & Dobson, 1987).

Deitz and Ferrell (1993) summarized evidence on developmental delays in children who are blind or have low vision that may assist ECSE professionals in the assessment process:

> *Although they exhibit rolling, independent sitting, independent standing, and stepping movements at the same general time as sighted infants, motor milestones that require projection of their bodies into space, such as elevating the upper torso by their own support, raising self to sitting, pulling to stand, crawling, or walking, have shown delays. Also, reaching for objects, searching for a lost object, and joining hands at midline seem to appear later in children with*

visual impairments than in their sighted peers. Delays in speaking two-word utterances and two-word sentences and in using self-referent pronouns have been reported. The clearest cognitive delay reported by Fraiberg [1977] was development of object concept and object permanence. (pp. 72–73)

Even more important than measurements of visual acuity are assessments of *functional* vision. Young children with blindness or low vision communicate with the world around them in three fundamental ways; each child will have his preference, and this should be respected. The first is use of residual vision; in this instance, the child taps whatever vision is left as his primary means of receptive communication. The second is audition; he prefers to listen to spoken instructions, taped materials, and computer speech synthesis. Finally, there is touch; he uses Braille and other raised symbols (Teplin 1995). How the child functions is an urgently important question in any assessment. While the child's preferred mode should be given considerable weight, ECSE workers may decide to focus on developing his abilities in other areas, as when he is helped to make better use of his vision. Such decisions should be reached in consultation with experts on adaptive technology. Such experts can recommend technology that will convert material from one mode to another; to illustrate, printed material such as this book may rapidly be converted to computer speech synthesis or to Braille. These and other steps are now discussed further.

INTERVENTION

Communication interventions should be planned by multidisciplinary teams with extensive parental involvement. Whether implemented at the early intervention or at the preschool programming level, services in all five domains of development should be included to the extent appropriate—first, because communication delays, deviations, and disabilities often have wide-ranging effects, and second, because communication-related problems frequently coexist with physical, mental, and emotional or behavior conditions or delays. For a child who is deaf, a certified teacher of the deaf should be on the multidisciplinary team; for a child who is blind, a certified teacher of the blind is appropriate.

The issue of environmental stimulation is urgently important in poorer, less well-educated families. There is a tendency in such families at times to use language more for purposes of controlling the child ("No!") than for purposes of developing communication competency in the child. ECSE workers suspecting communication impoverishment in the home may want to assist parents and other family members to learn how to expand upon, and explain, their communication with their children. When commands are not merely given but also explained, the child learns much more, much faster. Language development is most rapid when the child is surrounded daily with elaborations that offer new and different ways of expressing things. A parent who expands upon a command can at the same time teach the child synonyms, antonyms, and alternative sentence structures. Such expansion appears to be very important in adaptive development, as well.

Speech Impairments

One of the most common impairments of speech in young children, stuttering, is not easily eliminated (Figure 14.2). Telling a child to "slow down and take your time" seldom works. Rather, LaBlance et al. (1994) suggested that child-care workers and teachers should slow

- **Model Fluent Speech—and Dysfluencies.** Giving the child examples of good speech, at a moderated rate of speed, helps; by displaying some nonfluencies yourself (e.g., "uh," "that is," "you know," and so on), you set a relaxed tone that comforts the child.

- **Ignore Dysfluencies.** Children who stutter fear adverse reactions; this creates more tension, which in turn leads to more stuttering. By ignoring dysfluencies, you reduce pressure on the child. By attending to fluent moments, you reinforce (reward) such behavior.

- **One thing at a time.** Suggest that the child stop doing something else when talking. On your part, model such behavior. Often it is difficult for young children to speak clearly while also running, playing, or doing something else.

—adapted from LaBlance et al. (1994) and Van Riper (1993)

FIGURE 14.2 What works: stuttering

down their speech, because children who stutter tend to have more problems when conversing with fast speakers than with slow speakers. They also urged teachers to ignore much stuttering, attending to fluent speech instead. In this way, fluent speech is reinforced (rewarded), while stuttering is not. LaBlance et al. also suggested that child-care workers ask the child to cease another activity while speaking, because some young children find it difficult to do several things at once. They cautioned teachers not to expect miracles from these interventions; stuttering remains a much-misunderstood phenomenon despite several decades of research. In a text on stuttering, Van Riper (1993) concurred that although theories abound, interventions that cure stuttering, or even alleviate it significantly in a wide variety of children, remain to be found. Stuttering is, and likely will continue to be, an enigma.

The issue of "How much is enough?" arises in speech and language pathology. The field has not given us clear answers. Although IEPs and IFSPs differ greatly in describing children's needs, they vary much less when it comes to intervention, typically calling for two or three sessions per week. Hanft and Feinberg (1997) urged that interventions vary according to need and that they specify the outcomes desired (something they report is usually missing in IEPs and IFSPs).

Deafness and Severe Hearing Impairment

If a young child who is deaf is referred to you for early intervention and/or preschool special education, I urge you to consider very seriously recommending placement in a special program specifically designed for children who are deaf. That is because deafness is a catastrophically severe disability when it comes to education. If you think about it a moment, you will recognize that the overwhelming majority of teacher-child and child-child communication in early childhood special education is oral (speaking and listening) and the underlying vehicle used is language (words, syntax, grammar). Without hearing, language—the coin of the realm—does not develop, absent extraordinary measures. Thus, even if the interventionists or teachers sign, or if an interpreter is present, the child's ability to understand what goes on is severely compromised. Very intensive programming—mostly on language development—is required. That programming.is so qualitatively and quantitatively differ-ent from what usually occurs in early childhood special education that a separate placement may well be needed if the child is to have any chance of succeeding in an integrated place-ment in elementary school.

Language is learned by children during early childhood—if hearing is intact. This sug-gests immediately that the single most important task of ECSE professionals and of parents in working with a child who is deaf or severely hearing-impaired is to facilitate language development. Without immediate and effective early intervention and preschool special education instruction in language, children who are deaf or severely hearing-impaired will enter first grade knowing just a few words—and virtually no grammar, syntax, or other aspects of language. This is not an exaggeration; every year in every state, five- and six-year-olds who are deaf begin schooling knowing their names, a few object names, and virtually nothing else about the English language.

The urgency of the child's task—to learn *language,* any language—during early child-hood cannot be overemphasized. The developing brain creates connections for the purpose of using language. After the age of two, synapses specializing in language that have not been tapped to perform those functions apparently begin to be suppressed or even eliminated in the brain, a process that continues into adolescence. Thus, after the age of two, the brain's language-learning ability gradually dissipates. It is a slow process. Enough plasticity remains, fortunately, throughout the early childhood period and into the early elementary years, for language to be acquired later. The evidence from work with young children who are deaf is that the longer first-language acquisition is delayed, the harder it becomes for the child to demonstrate fluency. Children with deafness who learn some language, notably ASL, early in life are known to learn English much better and much more easily than do children who do not master any language before they begin their schooling (Commission on Education of the Deaf, 1988; Moores, 1982).

This is not to say that speech development is the top priority. Speech is not language. Speech is one mode, certainly the most frequently used mode, of expressing language; but language is a system of rules and symbols quite independent of speech. One can have lan-guage without speech: You are reading this text and understanding the language in it with-out either of us talking. Speech, by contrast, is largely a motor function, involving fine coordination of many hundreds of muscles. It is extremely hard to learn for many children born deaf and enormously frustrating for virtually all of them. To appreciate this, consider how even an accent or a minor speech impediment is immediately noticed by most people. Hope should not be held out to parents, or to the children themselves, that children born deaf will ever speak even that well.

Parents of young children who are deaf may not see it quite this way; to them, often, the most obvious need of the child is to speak. While *speech* delays are immediately noticed by parents of children who are deaf, *language* delays are less obvious, though in the long run much more important. That is because language is necessary, while speech really is not, for children to learn academic subjects in school and to perform gainful work as adults. Today's assistive technology devices can "talk" for children and adults, but no machine can yet gen-erate grammatical English—what computer experts refer to as "natural language process-ing." ECSE personnel must firmly explain to parents how speech and language differ and must try to educate the parents on why language acquisition is more urgent a task for the early childhood years than is speech. As important as speech is—and it undeniably is impor-tant—it pales in significance in comparison with language. Language—whether read and written, signed, or spoken—is the vehicle through which most learning—and virtually all academic learning—takes place in modern American society. Only if the child acquires a working knowledge of language will he later be able to learn mathematics, history, and biology.

The role of hearing in language acquisition is inescapable. The brain appears to be wired in such a way that it will generate the rules of language if, and only if, it is presented with the raw materials of spoken language and allowed to create, *de novo*, patterns and rules. To force the point: The brain is not wired to accept input about structure ("nouns are the names we give things and ideas," "verbs are action words," and so on), together with lists of many examples of such parts of speech. Given such input, the brain will record the information and store it as rote memory. The individual will attempt to apply these rules when requested to generate language but will usually fail.

This is exactly what has been done to generations of children who were deaf or severely hearing-impaired. They were *taught* language—not helped to learn it. The evidence on teaching language is in, and it is incontrovertible: The approach does not work. As the U.S. Congress Commission on Education of the Deaf reported in 1988, "The educational system has not been successful in assisting the majority of students who are deaf to achieve reading skills commensurate with those of their hearing peers"(p. 17). To illustrate, reading comprehension scores of students who are deaf or severely hearing-impaired, the commission reported, plateau at just third-grade levels, even after fifteen to eighteen years of schooling. Not surprisingly, the commission concluded, "The present status of education for persons who are deaf in the United States is unsatisfactory" (p. viii) (see also Moores, 1982, 1991).

That is why ECSE professionals need to set as their top goal giving young children who are deaf or severely hearing-impaired linguistic input—of the same kinds, varieties, and amounts as hearing children get—visually as well as auditorially. Most young children who are deaf or severely hearing-impaired do have residual hearing, but it is not sufficient to serve as a primary vehicle for language acquisition. At most, the hearing of these children is a supplement to visual input. Whether the words and structures of English are presented in signs, in finger spelling, and/or in reading and writing is much less important than that the input be as comprehensive and variegated as possible, and that it track the auditory input hearing children receive. That is, the input should consist of the same kinds of sentences, in all their tremendous range and scope, as hearing children hear. This task may appear daunting, but with today's technology, it is possible. Both television captioning and computer speech recognition can present these exact sentences in visual form to children who are deaf or severely hearing-impaired—allowing them to use vision to get the raw materials at the same ages, in the same sequences, and to something approximating the same extent as do hearing children through the auditory channel.

The IFSP or IEP should include an explicit statement of the child's communication needs, including personal and parental preferences. A range of communication modes is available. The choice of mode is a highly individualized one, and often an emotion-laden one as well. Hearing aids amplify, but also distort, speech; while very helpful for children with mild to moderate losses of hearing, careful fitting and daily checking of batteries are necessary for them to work as intended. In addition, children using hearing aids may need visual input to understand conversational speech. ECSE workers need to be sensitive to those needs, because early childhood (EC) programs rarely involve stationary seat work; with teachers, aides, and children constantly moving about in the room, the ability of a child to keep up may be seriously compromised unless all concerned are cognizant of the need to make communication visual. One helpful approach: ECSE workers should from time to time ask questions that cannot be answered with a "yes." This permits checking on the child's comprehension, yet avoids the ambiguity of "yes" responses (the child may nod, agree, or say yes to avoid embarrassment or confrontation; this is particularly a problem with children who have severe hearing impairments, including deafness).

Additional suggestions may be gleaned from the U.S. Department of Education's regulations on early intervention services, which defined the early intervention services component of audiology in section 303.12(2) as follows:

> *(iv) Provision of auditory training, aural rehabilitation, speech reading and listening device orientation and training, and other services;*
> *(v) Provision of services for prevention of hearing loss; and*
> *(vi) Determination of the child's need for individual amplification, including selecting, fitting, and dispensing appropriate listening and vibrotactile devices, and evaluating the effectiveness of those devices.* (U.S. Department of Education, 1993a)

The department further described "speech-language pathology" services in section 303.12(14) to include the following:

> *(iii) Provision of services for the habilitation, rehabilitation, or prevention of communicative or oropharyngeal disorders and delays in development of communication skills.* (U.S. Department of Education, 1993a)

cochlear implants are electronic devices that simulate "hearing" for children who are deaf.

Cochlear implants for children who are deaf have been widely publicized in recent years. Today's implants have as many as twenty-two channels for electronic transmission of sound, making them much better than the early, one-channel versions. However, even twenty-two-channel cochlear implants are limited in what they can do. They are most useful as an early warning safety system, helping children to hear environmental sounds, including approaching cars. They are less helpful in the area of speech comprehension; while some children with implants can understand some speech through the ear alone, many continue to need lipreading and other visual cues. Children must undergo regular training sessions for six months to a year following the surgery to learn how to interpret the sounds the implant sends to their auditory cortex. Accordingly, cochlear implants are not "magic bullets" to cure deafness, nor are they appropriate for all children who are deaf. Moreover, the implants are controversial in the deaf community. Leaders of the National Association of the Deaf, for example, are concerned that parents may opt for cochlear implants in a misguided attempt to turn their children into hearing children, thus dooming the children to years of frustration.

American Sign Language (ASL) is a language using manual signs and rules for combining them. ASL is a distinct language with its own rules, in contrast to Signed English.

Options for communicating with children who are deaf include "total communication," in which children use speech reading, residual hearing, finger spelling, and sign language—together with gestures and facial expressions—to communicate. Total communication generally adopts Signed English, because when speech and signs are used simultaneously it is necessary for the signs to track English word order. **American Sign Language (ASL),** a rich, expressive language, usually cannot be used in a total communication environment because it has its own grammar and syntax (Figure 14.3) very different from Signed English. ASL is highly valued by many deaf parents and a treasured part of deaf culture (Dolnick, 1993).

Most audiology, auditory training, speech reading, speech and language pathology, and related services are available in local hearing and speech clinics or other community centers. Such clinics and centers are used by children with no disabilities, thus allowing early intervention programs to observe Part C natural environment (NE) and Part B least restrictive environment (LRE) preferences.

In recent years, deaf culture advocates have sought to advance ASL as the first (native) language for use with young children who are deaf. This approach repositions English as a second language; it is taught using second-language techniques, and only after ASL has been mastered.

The approach responds to criticism of "total communication," an approach in which teachers and other caregivers spoke while also signing and using finger spelling. ASL advocates objected that the children were seeing neither English nor ASL, but rather some muddled amalgam vaguely resembling English. Was it any surprise, they asked, that children's expressive language was similarly muddled "deaf English"?

To understand how radical the change would be, consider that under this approach, teachers and other caregivers would neither speak nor move their lips. That is because ASL uses a different order than does English; one cannot simultaneously sign in ASL and speak in English. Similarly, because ASL has no written form, reading and writing in English would be postponed until perhaps third or fourth grade, after the children had mastered ASL.

The approach is probably best suited to the 10 percent of young children who are deaf whose parents also are deaf; in most such homes, ASL is in fact the native language.

For children who are deaf but whose parents are hearing, however, parental preferences should be carefully considered before this approach is adopted. For a discussion of the many controversies concerning the use of ASL as the primary language of instruction for children who are deaf, see Bowe (1992b) and Stuckless (1992).

FIGURE 14.3 Controversy in deafness

The Part B LRE preference is very controversial in deafness education. Research with children who are deaf suggests that the LRE mandate, as currently implemented, may actually be harming some children who are deaf (Moores, 1991). The Commission on Education of the Deaf (1988) expressed reservations about how LRE was being implemented by the U.S. Department of Education. In response to the commission's concerns, the department published a guidance in the October 30, 1992, *Federal Register* explaining that any placement (including a center-based program) that meets a child's unique needs may be the LRE for that child (Bowe, 1993b). The Part C NE preference is much less controversial in deafness. Very few studies have examined NE, despite the fact that it is now as new as LRE was in 1980. Recent research by Antia, Kreimeyer, and Eldredge (1994) suggested that social interaction can be stimulated between young children with hearing impairments and same-age children with no hearing losses, but that those beneficial effects that do occur fade rapidly after intervention to enhance such interactions is withdrawn. Consistent and persistent support both to children with no hearing impairment and to children with hearing losses is essential if interaction is to move beyond mere physical proximity to genuine interpersonal communication and joint play.

All of this requires that early intervention and preschool special education staff trained in techniques of working with children who are deaf or hard-of-hearing be made available to ECSE programs. Unfortunately, a national survey by Roush, Harrison, Palsha, and Davidson (1992) found that "fewer than half the programs currently preparing teachers of deaf students in the United States offer specializations in early intervention. Moreover, very few students are electing to specialize in early intervention even when such a specialization is available" (p. 428).

Blindness and Low Vision

Separate placements for young children who are blind or have low vision merit serious consideration by early interventionists and preschool special educators, as they do when young children are deaf. The reasons for recommending separate placements are different from those with deaf children, but almost as compelling. Children who are blind have very good prospects of succeeding in elementary school if, and only if, they have mastered use of the technology that makes such integration feasible. They have a lot to learn. They need to acquire good orientation and mobility skills, using canes and other navigation devices. They need to become accustomed to note-taking devices, such as Braille 'n Speak or Versa-braille—to say nothing about learning Braille itself! They need to learn how to operate scanners, special tape recorders, and other products. While it is true that all of these capabilities could be acquired during the elementary school years, it is also true that the child is likely to do far better if he enters first grade already possessing these vital skills.

Glass (1993) expressed concern about the high-intensity, continuous lighting found in most NICUs. Ambient light as intensive as 30 to 150 footcandles, or well in excess of adult office light, is common. In addition, preterm infants are often exposed to other lights, including heat lamps and the Mini Bili-Lite (which can produce 10,000 footcandles). All of this light may produce phototoxicity. Conceding that "the optimal level of NICU lighting has not been determined," she added nonetheless that "no study supports the safety of the bright light levels still common in many NICUs" (p. 17).

Glass also recommended the human face as the best stimulus for infant visual development. Her reasons were obvious ones: "The face is three dimensional. It contains some contrast at the edge of the hair or at the features; provides slow, contingent movement around the eyes and mouth; and it is situated at a variable distance from the infant" (p. 18).

For children diagnosed as blind or having low vision, perhaps the most urgent tasks of ECSE professionals, and of parents, are to facilitate the development of independent mobility and tactual exploration skills and to introduce the use of modern assistive technology.

Vision is measured with appropriate corrective lenses, in contrast to hearing, which is assessed without use of any assistive devices.

Children who are blind or have low vision have the same jobs as other children during the early childhood years. In addition, however, they must learn orientation and mobility skills so as to get around independently. Independent mobility is a sine qua non (literally, "without which not") of early childhood development. It is essential for the infant's, toddler's, and preschooler's learning. Getting around in the environment, including new and strange as well as familiar settings, is an added responsibility of early childhood for children who are blind or have low vision. It cannot be neglected; it should not be postponed.

The federal regulations on early intervention described "vision services" in section 303.12(16) as the following:

> (iii) *Communication skills training, orientation and mobility training for all environments, visual training, independent living skills training, and additional training necessary to activate visual motor abilities.*

orientation and mobility specialists help young children who are blind or have low vision learn to navigate around the home; the early intervention program; the neighborhood; and, later, the community as a whole.

These are to be provided by "qualified personnel" including **orientation and mobility specialists** (U.S. Department of Education, 1993a). The work of these specialists is outlined in Figure 14.4.

Another important task of early childhood for children who are blind or have low vision—and for ECSE workers and parents—is training in use of today's assistive technology devices and services. These are discussed in more detail later in the chapter, and in Chapter 10. The point to be made here is that thanks to this new technology, the lives of these children—now and throughout public education and into adulthood—are vastly richer and immeasurably easier today than they were even twenty years ago. As illustrated in Figure 14.5, the contributions these products and services can make are so substantial that they merit careful consideration by ECSE personnel.

Finally, it is very important that ECSE programming not be limited only to the needs and resources of the child with respect to vision. Children who are blind or have low vision are, despite their pressing vision-related needs, the same jumble of impossible contradictions that all children this age are. That needs to be borne in mind—and to be reflected in

Orientation and mobility specialists are trained professionals who are experts in helping children who are blind or have low vision to learn how to make maximum use of residual vision, hearing, and touch so as to navigate safely. They are also specialists in teaching children how to use public transportation in the community so as to get around independently. In addition to the prosaic skills of traveling, using the long cane, and so on, they develop in children who are blind or have low vision the confidence and feeling of independence so necessary for these children's development.

In most cases, orientation and mobility specialists work with families in the home, the immediate neighborhood, and the local day-care center or nursery or preschool. This enables ECSE programs to observe the NE preference in Part C and the LRE preference in Part B. However, if orientation and mobility training are only available in a center program, or if specialists in working with very young children are employed only there, such settings are natural or least restrictive because the necessary services are available nowhere else.

Young children who are blind or have low vision need to master independent orientation and mobility skills in addition to all the other capabilities children learn during the preschool years. That is why orientation and mobility training is a recognized related service under Part B and an authorized early intervention service under Part C.

FIGURE 14.4 Orientation and mobility

ECSE programming. Research reminds us that children who are blind or have low vision may be at greater risk for nonvision-related problems than are other children. Developmental delays may occur, absent early intervention and preschool programming, in adaptive (self-help), motor, social, cognitive, and language development (Scholl, 1986). Early intervention research with children who are blind or have low vision has been summarized by Olson (1987) and by White, Casto, Mott, Barnett, Pezzino, Lowitzer, Eiserman, Wingate-Corey, Immel, and Innocenti (1987). These studies suggested that such children benefit from early intervention services. However, as Behl, White, and Escobar (1993) pointed out, these studies had small subject populations, lacked comparison groups, and performed only short-term follow-up measures.

The importance of early intervention and preschool special education for children who are blind or have low vision is illustrated by findings reported in the U.S. Department of Education's *Fourteenth Annual Report* (U.S. Department of Education, 1992c). There, results from the National Longitudinal Transition Study (NLTS) of Special Education showed that the average IQ of blind students in special education programs was 87, or somewhat below average. The NLTS reported that parents had concerns about the functional skills of most (79 percent) of the children, and about the self-help skills of almost half (48 percent). Clearly, ECSE programs need to focus on assisting children who are blind or have low vision not only to prepare for academic work but also to achieve independence in mobility and adaptive behavior.

Ten infants blind from birth made up Fraiberg's longitudinal intervention study (Fraiberg, Smith & Adelson, 1969). Of these ten, five would have been considered at risk even if they had not been blind, due to factors such as extreme poverty, unemployment, and mental illness in their families. These ten infants received home intervention that began before one year of age. All reached the normal human-object relations expected at eighteen months of age. Their performance placed them in the upper half of children who are blind. All were found to have normal or near-normal intelligence.

One child's story illustrates how early intervention, preschool special education, and today's assistive technology can help a child who is blind to succeed in elementary school. Olivia, who was born prematurely, is blind from retinopathy of prematurity (ROP). The ophthalmologist told her family that Olivia was eligible for early intervention services.

These began when Olivia was 3.5 months of age. A social worker and parent-infant specialist visited her home, teaching her parents to touch and massage her, to tie bells to her wrists and ankles so she would learn where her hands and feet were, and to put things in her crib so that when she moved she would touch something.

Olivia entered a center-based preschool program specializing in services for children who are blind or have low vision when she was three. There she learned to become "tactually observant" and to interpret verbal descriptions of ideas. Meanwhile, her parents learned Braille.

Three years later, she entered first grade, the only student who was blind out of the 450 in her local elementary school. A vision teacher came to the school weekly to teach Olivia Braille, to translate her classbooks and materials into Braille, and to teach her how to use an abacus for math, to type, to use a computer, and to develop her auditory skills so that she could listen to texts on tape. In addition, a mobility specialist came to the school weekly to teach her to use a cane. Beginning in second grade, an occupational therapist also helped Olivia increase her upper body strength enough to use a Braillewriter.

In the classroom, Olivia's teachers spelled out loud whatever they wrote on the chalkboard and described any other visual materials. They touched Olivia frequently—and let her touch them—throughout the day, to "keep in touch."

—adapted from "Side by Side," by Debra Viadero, in *Teacher Magazine Reader*, undated

FIGURE 14.5 Olivia: one child's story

Technology

Technology is tremendously important for many young children with communication-related limitations, but particularly for children who are deaf or blind. The potential of technology for children with developmental delays or established conditions that limit their receptive or expressive communication is impressive with respect to two particular capabilities. One is computer speech recognition, or the ability of computer systems to "hear." The other is computer speech synthesis, the ability of computers to "talk."

The principal concern of young children with hearing loss is understanding what other people say. Speech comprehension is the basis for language development in early childhood: Children learn the language they hear. If they hear little or no language, they do not learn it. Today's personal computers may help children with severe or profound hearing loss dramatically, because they can hear—and print out as they're hearing it—what teachers, caregivers, and other children say.

Some of the newer personal computers feature "speaker-independent, continuous speech recognition." This capability represents an enormous breakthrough in technology for young children with communication-related limitations. Earlier computer speech recognition capabilities were limited in two important ways. First, they could not understand most voices, but rather were limited to the voice that trained them. One person "trained" the system by speaking many words and phrases, over and over again, so that the system could learn to match that person's voice with English words stored in its memory. This process is called "speaker-dependent speech recognition" because the computer's ability to recognize speech is dependent on one particular speaker. Second, earlier computers required speakers to pause . . . like . . . this . . . when . . . speaking . . . to . . . the . . . machine. That is, they could not handle continuous, or conversational, speech—today's machines can. They are not perfect, however. Commonly, computer speech recognition achieves 95 percent accuracy, that is, it correctly recognizes nineteen out of every twenty words it "hears." Background noise, unusual accents, and other factors can throw it off, bringing down the accuracy rate. To put the 95 percent rate into context, consider that if you achieved that rate, and no better, using a computer keyboard, you would toss it out and get a new one. But for children who need speech recognition, 95 percent accuracy is quite sufficient.

Offered by Dragon Systems, IBM, and Lernout & Hauspie, among others (see Chapter 10), continuous speech recognition capabilities are now remarkably affordable (about $100 for the software). These packages also offer speech synthesis (computer talk) as well. Today's speech synthesis has a natural-sounding rhythm, at least as compared to the earlier, flat-pitched voice that pronounced everything in the same machinelike monotone. The user can select from among several voices; typical choices include a man, a woman, a child, and a Spanish accent. For children who are deaf, the synthesized speech is their voice, so it should be one that they feel sounds right and reflects well on them. As with any voice, it is a very personal thing. But the fact that technology has reached this state of the art is wondrously liberating. Children who cannot speak intelligibly can prepare messages in advance and can program a laptop computer to "speak" those as needed. Of course, the computer also can provide real-time speech in response to words as those are typed on the keyboard.

Children who are blind can use the same speech synthesis capability with a scanner, a product that "reads" books, newspapers, and so on and sends those to the computer, which then speaks them aloud or translates them to Braille. Small, handheld Braille 'n Speak or Versabraille machines can be used to take notes and to read them later. The fact that these technologies are all computer-based means that translation from print to voice is as readily done as is print to Braille or Braille to voice. In years past, parents, friends, and volunteers had to read textbooks or other printed materials into a tape recorder or translate them by hand into Braille. The translations now can be performed in a matter of a few minutes, not the hours or weeks required in the past.

WORKING WITH PARENTS

Successful early intervention and preschool special education programs for young children who are deaf or severely hard-of-hearing work closely with parents. The single most important advice ECSE workers can give to parents is that they must establish in the home some means of reliable communication with their young child. Work performed at the Kendall Demonstration Elementary School, located on the Gallaudet University campus, at Lexington School for the Deaf in Queens, New York, and at other programs shows that parents who accept the child's deafness and learn ASL greatly reduce their own and their children's frustration levels. Other programs, such as those at the Clarke School for the Deaf in Massachusetts and the Central Institute for the Deaf in St. Louis, Missouri, as well as the correspondence program of the John Tracy Clinic in California, have shown results with oral approaches. Communication choice is a matter of parental preference. More important than how communication is effected is *that* it is established—and maintained—on a daily basis, between the child, his siblings, and his parents. As noted earlier, ECSE workers should

Stories told in American Sign Language . . .

. . . are easily understood . . .

. . . and illustrated!

call parents' attention to the urgent need for language development. This may be effected not only through closed captioning on television but also by parents reading with the child on at least a weekly, and preferably a daily, basis. Third, parents need to be cautioned against overprotection. Children only develop adaptive behaviors when parents give them ample opportunities to practice such behaviors. Experiential deprivation in the name of caution does not serve the best interests of the child.

It is imperative that young children who are blind establish independent mobility, not only to facilitate development of the self-concept but also for cognitive and adaptive development to proceed apace. Parents of school-age children who are blind express most concern about adaptive behavior and functional independence; knowing this, ECSE workers should help parents to take appropriate steps during the early childhood years to foster in the child a sense of independence and an ability to care for himself. ECSE workers should also introduce parents to modern adaptive technology, so they may understand how revolutionary is the impact of computer-based communications for children who are blind.

SUMMARY

This chapter included a look at children who have special needs in the area of expressive and receptive communication. Children who are blind principally face a limitation in receptive communication. Today's technology can translate inaccessible information from print into voice, Braille, or large print in a matter of minutes or even seconds. Equally important for young children who are blind are mobility skills, which allow them to achieve independence from parental and professional care. Such independence is vital for cognitive and adaptive development.

Children with severe hearing impairments are often limited in expressive communication. In fact, most children who are born deaf have great difficulty speaking intelligibly. Today's technology provides a "voice" for such children. It is a voice that can be very high in quality, affordable, and easy to learn to use. For young children who are deaf, the voice is a tremendous help, because its quality exceeds what most such children will achieve on their own even after many years of speech training. However, computer speech synthesis is of secondary importance with young children who are deaf or severely hearing-impaired. That is because their primary need is to acquire language. Deafness is only secondarily a limitation on expressive communication; it is primarily a restriction on receptive communication. The real task is to make spoken English comprehensible to children who are deaf. While computer speech recognition has advanced remarkably in recent years, to the point that it can now be used to translate from voice to text what parents, ECSE workers, and other children say, even this amazing capability does not solve the problem. Young children who are deaf must learn how to read before they can benefit from computer speech recognition. That is why parental and ECSE communication skills, as well as closed captioning on television, are so urgently important. It is through these means, especially the former—parents and professionals who sign, finger spell, gesture, and speak clearly so as to make it easy for the child to lip-read them—that young children who are deaf learn language.

With all of these kinds of communication limitations, ECSE's goal is to prepare children for success in school. Children who are blind can acquire the orientation, mobility, and adaptive equipment skills they will need to compete in integrated environments in the public schools. Achieving integration is far more challenging for children who are deaf, because the solutions are far more elusive. Deafness so disrupts the language acquisition process in early childhood that very intensive efforts are required for a period of many years before mastery of the language occurs—if it ever does.

There is much to learn about providing effective ECSE services to children with severe communication limitations. Both deafness and blindness are severe disabilities. The evidence to date is that ECSE programs tend to be much more successful with mild or moderate disabilities than with severe or profound ones. One of the field's greatest challenges in the years ahead is to help most those who need the most help.

QUESTIONS FOR REFLECTION

1. The text says most deaf children (90 percent) have two hearing parents. What implications can you draw from this statement?

2. Why might earlier identification of hearing loss make a big difference for young children?

3. Differentiate "blindness" from "low vision." What do the differences suggest for intervention strategies and techniques?

4. Explain the significance of age at onset with respect to vision impairment.

5. Name three senses through which young children who are visually impaired might acquire information.

6. What language-use patterns often are seen in poorer families and why are those of concern to ECSE workers?

7. Differentiate speech from language. Why is the difference an important one in ECSE?

8. What is wrong with "teaching language" to children who were born deaf, according to the text?

9. What is total communication?

10. What do orientation and mobility specialists do?

Cognitive Development

Between 40% and 50% of children with [Down syndrome] have congenital heart disease. . . . Sixty-eight percent of children with DS have a hearing loss. . . . Sixty percent of children with DS have ophthalmic disorders. . . . [m]ost frequent[ly] refractive disorders (near-sightedness or far-sightedness) 35% [and] strabismus (eyes turning in) 27%. (Roizen, 1997, pp. 36–37)

OVERVIEW

The young child's "work," Piaget said, is play: to do things, explore, touch/feel/smell/taste things in the environment, and practice new skills such as walking, running, skipping, and rolling a ball. Cognition proceeds directly from such "work." Cognitive development has to do with age-appropriate functions involving perception, understanding, and knowledge.

Young children learn by doing. By walking, the child frees the hands; that, in turn, speeds up the child's exploration of the environment, leading to more cognitive growth. Chapter 13 also showed that through movement the child physically distances herself from caregivers, which naturally leads to psychological distance. The child, in large part, displays her cognitive accomplishments in physical activity. The child is also tested that way: Tests and other procedures assess what she does physically. For these reasons, physical and cognitive development are closely linked. Adaptive development, as well, depends on both physical and cognitive growth.

When cognitive development does not occur as anticipated, it is often difficult to determine the cause, or causes. **Learning disabilities (LDs)** were the second most common disabilities reported by parents in the Survey of Income and Program Participation (SIPP) survey (Bowe, 1994). Recent research has raised questions about LD, including dyslexia, and has also offered some interesting ideas about possible new ways of assessing cognitive limitations. In work discussed later in this chapter, Sally Shaywitz at Yale found that some cognitive limitations in young children appear to be temporary. Craig Ramey and his colleagues have similarly demonstrated that early intervention can produce dramatic effects on children once thought to be, or at risk of becoming, mildly retarded. The U.S. Department of Education (1993b, pp. 11–14) reported frequent changes in labels in three states studying the issue: Maine, Maryland, and Michigan. Children aged six to eleven often were reclassified as LD from other categories. Tests of questionable validity and reliability with young children may lead to inappropriate labels. Clearly, the diagnosis and assignment of labels remain difficult. For these reasons, as Verna Hart told the U.S. House of Representatives, label changes can be frequent—and confusing.

learning disabilities (LDs) are conditions interfering with or limiting academic kinds of activities. They are believed to have neurological bases. Dyslexia is an example of an LD.

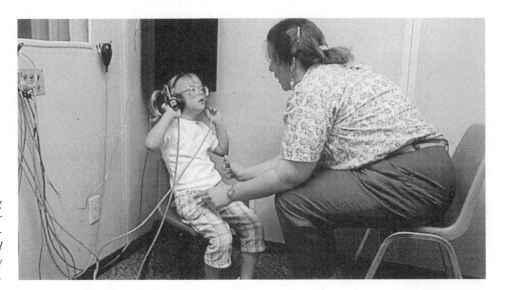

Routine testing of hearing acuity should be done for children with Down syndrome, cerebral palsy, and other conditions commonly associated with hearing loss.

Interventions that help to accelerate children's cognitive development include multimedia, computer-based programs, as mentioned in Chapter 10. Such approaches with young children who have Down syndrome are particularly exciting, because they seem to meet those children's special needs for input they can comprehend. This chapter discusses such interventions, together with other research on cognitive development. Important causes of mental retardation, including fragile X syndrome and Down syndrome, are described, as are prevention and treatment.

PREVALENCE

Conditions affecting cognitive development were cited in the 1991–1992 SIPP study as first (primary) conditions leading to limitations for 145,000 children aged birth to five inclusive, or 17 percent of such children. Notable was LD, reported as the first (primary) condition in 109,000 children under age six, or 13 percent of all birth-to-five children with a limiting condition. LD was reported as a second or third condition in 44,000 additional young children having multiple conditions. All told, 153,000 birth-to-five children were reported as having LD. It is possible that parents were reacting to such symptoms as physical clumsiness, language delays, and image-copying problems. However, many such symptoms were probably normal fluctuations of early childhood, mistakenly attributed to LD.

For another 36,000 children, mental retardation was reported as their primary condition, that is, 4 percent of all under-six children with disabilities. LD was reported as the second-most-common kind of condition, after speech impairment; mental retardation was the eighth most common. These are family-reported conditions.

DEVELOPMENTAL DELAYS

Most states define a "delay" in cognitive development as two standard deviations (S.D.s) below the mean, or about 70 to 75 IQ, or as 1.5 S.D. below the mean if there are other kinds of developmental delays as well. Some states look to adaptive behavior, such as with a twelve-month delay in expected cognitive accomplishments. In particular, infants, toddlers, and preschoolers who walk, feed themselves, and talk later than other children do may be classified as delayed in cognitive development; these, of course, are also indicators of possible delays in physical and communication development. Additionally, they may be considered to be delays in adaptive development. The boundary lines are not clear. Professional judgment (clinical opinion) is important in many state definitions of delay.

ESTABLISHED CONDITIONS

The federal regulations (U.S. Department of Education, 1993a) listed some suggested "established conditions" known to result, almost invariably, in delays. Chromosomal abnormalities such as Down syndrome are widely accepted by states as being established conditions. Meningomyelocele and cyanecephaly are two disorders of neural tube closure that may occur during the first few weeks of gestation (Anderson, 1989; Lozes, 1988). During the second phase of brain development (the second and third months of gestation), a number of chromosomal (trisomy 13) and other syndromes may appear, some of them due to teratogens (harmful agents). Fetal exposure to dilantin (an anticonvulsant the mother may take to control epilepsy), anticoagulants (which she may take to prevent blood clots), and other drugs may cause a range of perinatal disorders at this time (Nickel, 1992). This third phase, involving neuronal migration, has been associated with some LD (Livingstone, Rosen, Drislane, & Galaburda, 1991). Microcephaly and related syndromes, characterized by small heads and usually by mental retardation as well, are also associated with this third phase of brain development. Children born prematurely at this time (the end of the second to the end of the fifth month of gestation) may have impaired coordination, seizures, and visual perception problems. Nickel (1992) added that much less is known about developmental effects associated with later phases of brain development.

Learning Disabilities

That parents reported as many as 106,000 under-six children as having LD in the 1991–1992 SIPP was unexpected, given that most definitions of the term learning disabilities stress academic difficulties as a principal identifying characteristic. Since the definitions emphasize school-related tasks, finding LD as the number-two parent reported condition in children under six years of age (after speech impairments) was a surprise.

In early childhood, LD usually is not evidenced by reading and calculation difficulties so much as physical clumsiness, language development delays or disorders, and errors such as reversal in drawing and other vision-related play activities. However, these may also signal other disabilities. Distinguishing between LD and other sensory or processing disorders is not easy.

The term LD is defined in a number of ways. One widely used definition may be that of the 1988 National Joint Committee on Learning Disabilities (NJCLD). It begins: "Learning disabilities is a general term that refers to a heterogeneous group of disorders manifested by significant difficulties in the acquisition and use of listening, speaking, reading, writing, reasoning, or mathematical abilities" (p.1). This definition is not particularly helpful in early childhood. The federal definition is even less useful. It opens:

> *"Specific learning disability" means a disorder in one or more of the basic psychological processes involved in understanding or in using language, spoken or written, which may manifest itself in an imperfect ability to listen, think, speak, read, write, spell, or do mathematical calculations.* (U.S. Department of Health, Education, and Welfare, 1977, p. 65803)

The department's definition goes on to say that the manifestations must not be due to hearing, vision, intellectual, or other conditions. It is not clear how one is to identify "basic psychological processes" as causing problems children exhibit.

The definitions of LD today remain quite vague. Learning disabilities are understood to involve short- and long-term memory limitations, communication deficits, cognitive and organizational deficits (notably **metacognition**, or understanding one's own thinking processes and adjusting those so as to do better in school), perceptual motor difficulties, and problems in information processing.

Children with LD generally have input, processing, and/or output difficulties that cannot be explained by any other condition. Following the federal regulations, this is called the "exclusion" factor. When the child has problems understanding print, for example, it is not because of a vision limitation. Rather, the child may have difficulty separating "signal" from "field," or the words of interest from surrounding words, images, or pictures. (This is also called "figure-ground segregation.")

metacognition is awareness of one's own behavior and ways of thinking and learning.

Recently, Margaret Livingstone of Harvard University has found neurological bases for visual-processing lags, Ranjan Duara of Miami University has discovered brain-cell differences between dyslexic and nondyslexic individuals, and Paula Tallal at New Jersey's Rutgers University has documented auditory lags in young children with language impairments.

A study by three Harvard researchers and a brain expert in Boston (Livingstone, Rosen, Drislane, & Galaburda, 1991) suggested that dyslexia may be a function of the brain's inability to keep proper timing in visual information processing. **Dyslexia** is an important learning disability in which children display reading difficulties despite normal or near-normal intelligence and adequate opportunities to learn reading. Livingstone et al. reported that so-called "magno cells" (for magnocellular system cells), midbrain cells that handle low-contrast visual information, position, motion and shape, and figure-ground segregation, were found to be smaller in children with dyslexia than in nondyslexics. However, parvocellular system cells, believed to handle color vision, were not different in the two groups. Dr. Livingstone told a reporter that the data were based on only a few subjects "but we were so excited we decided to not delay publication" (Blakeslee, 1991b). The Harvard study performed anatomical observations in autopsy specimens and took physiological measures of visual information processing in five dyslexic and seven nondyslexic adults. Livingstone et al. suggested that magno cells help the brain maintain positional stability. Malfunctioning in the magnocellular system, then, could help explain why for some people with dyslexia, letters seem to float across—or even disappear from—a page.

According to related research, antibodies found in animals destroy a protein located only in magno cells (McGuire, Hockfield, & Goldman-Rakic, 1989, cited in Livingstone et al., 1991). If some humans have such antibodies, this may help to explain the Harvard findings of abnormalities in magno cells. Dyslexia, in this theory, would be an autoimmune disease acquired before or soon after birth. As the infant begins processing sensory information, the antibodies destroy the critical protein, making the child think she is seeing or hearing very odd things. Many people with dyslexia report that letters or words seem to slip off the page, become blurred, or ripple across the page. However, at present this theory remains speculative (Blakeslee, 1991b).

A 1991 report in the *Archives of Neurology* suggests that the rear portion of the brain's left hemisphere in dyslexics is smaller than the corresponding section in the right hemisphere. In nondyslexic individuals, both sections are approximately the same size. Ranjan Duara, the study's lead author, reported that MRI comparisons of twenty-one persons with dyslexia and twenty-four without also revealed that the corpus callosum, a band of nerve fibers connecting the two hemispheres, was much larger in dyslexics than in nondyslexics. He theorized that during the final phases of brain development just before birth, excess cells die in most people but apparently not in individuals who develop dyslexia. Duara posited that people with severe dyslexia seem to have the most excess brain cells (Duara et al., 1991; "Dyslexia," 1993).

Dr. Tallal's work with children who have language impairments is important, because auditory processing is so critical to cognitive development during early childhood, when little formal reading is done. Hearing requires discrimination between sounds at a very rapid pace. Dr. Tallal reported timing delays on audition among five- to eight-year-old children with language impairments. She found that these children need much longer intervals between sounds to tell them apart than do children with no language impairments. To illustrate with the phonemes /ba/ and /da/, the *b* and *d* sounds occur in the first 4 milliseconds, followed by a 40-millisecond transition to the "ah" sound. Tallal's research showed that children with no language impairments could distinguish the *b* and *d* sounds within a few milliseconds, but

dyslexia is a learning disability that interferes with reading and writing, because letters seem to float across a page, reverse, or otherwise become difficult to read. Children with dyslexia display reading difficulties despite normal or near-normal intelligence and adequate opportunities to learn to read.

that children with language impairments needed much longer, as much as 300 milliseconds, to process those initial sounds so as to distinguish /ba/ from /da/ (Tallal, Stark, & Mellits, 1985).

Tallal also found that young children with language impairments have processing problems associated with the sense of touch. In tests, young children were asked to put their hands under a table. The experimenter touched two fingers simultaneously or in very rapid sequence. Nondisabled children processed the sensory information as two touches, but children with language impairments reported only one touch (Tallal et al., 1985). This may explain why some young children with language impairments appear to be clumsy; they do not process tactual feedback information rapidly enough to guide subsequent motor activity.

The work of Livingstone and Tallal suggests that it is the *temporal* nature of information processing that is disturbed in their subjects. Tallal, for example, showed that young children with language impairments did well when auditory, visual, or tactual information was presented more slowly. However, she did not find that temporary variability of input information distinguished dyslexic from nondyslexic subjects. Livingstone's work suggested that for people with dyslexia, a major problem may be malfunctioning of one of the brain's two key visual information pathways. The magno system appears to have developed in humans, and in ancestor apes, to handle rapidly moving, low-contrast images and stereoscopic vision for depth perception; one can readily imagine early humans' need to discern the approach of a lion in the jungle underbrush, for example. The parvocellular system seems to have evolved to handle a very different need: identification of stationary objects and color, as when a man or ape searches for fruit. The suggestion in Livingstone's work is that the major sensory organs in humans have two quite separate pathways, and that it is in the area of processing rapidly changing images or sounds that people with dyslexia have difficulty.

In addition to the exclusion factor and presumed neurological problems, LD typically is defined in terms of discrepancies between expected and observed behavior. States vary in the amount or kind of discrepancy required to establish eligibility, but all point to irregularities in performance ("peaks," or areas of high performance, and "valleys," or areas of low performance). The concept of discrepancy is one that helps to differentiate LD from mental

Multimodal instruction helps many children with Down syndrome and other learning needs because visual, auditory, and tactile input may be integrated, leading to more complete learning.

retardation, which is a generalized lowered level of functioning. People with LD, according to most definitions, have peaks much higher than usually seen in children with mental retardation. However, the whole concept of discrepancy has come under severe attack in recent years (Aram, Morris, & Hall, 1992; Fletcher, 1992; Pennington, Gilger, Olson, & DeFries, 1992). It is particularly inappropriate for use during early childhood, due in large part to the inadequacy of both intelligence and other developmental testing instruments.

Sally Shaywitz, a pediatrician at Yale, offers yet another reason to distrust discrepancy formulas. She completed an important study in 1991 of children classified as "dyslexic" on the basis of discrepancy formulas, reporting that children move in and out of the classification. Some children diagnosed as LD in first grade no longer qualified for that label by third grade; meanwhile, a substantial number of children not previously diagnosed as LD appeared to have developed the condition. The nine-year study, which followed 414 children who began kindergarten in 1983, appeared in the January 16, 1992, issue of the *New England Journal of Medicine* (Shaywitz et al., 1992; Kolata, 1992b). One disturbing implication of Shaywitz's work, if confirmed by replication efforts, is that intervention program claims of "success" and longitudinal studies of different kinds of interventions with children who have dyslexia may need to be reevaluated, if not discarded altogether.

What could cause dyslexia and other learning disabilities? Alcohol consumption by the mother during pregnancy long has been a suspected factor. Exposure to lead is another well-known possible cause. Prematurity or low birthweight appears to be yet another possibility (Ariel, 1992; Benson & Lane, 1993). Two studies published during the last few months of 1994 provide exciting new evidence of anatomical causes.

Albert Galaburda and Glenn Rosen, who were members of the Livingstone team that discovered visual information processing problems in people having dyslexia, reported, with Matthew Menard, that people with dyslexia have more small neurons, and fewer large ones, in brain areas known to be specialized for auditory processing (Galaburda, Menard, & Rosen, 1994). Their findings suggest auditory processing difficulties that are strikingly similar in kind to the visual processing problems Livingstone et al. had reported three years earlier. In a separate study, Cardon, Smith, Fulker, Kimberling, Pennington, and DeFries, writing in the October 14, 1994 issue of *Science,* reported evidence for a genetic marker for dyslexia on chromosome 6.

Learning disabilities are difficult to identify. Often, it is necessary to "test for everything else" before settling on a diagnosis of learning disability, because no LD test is available. The new developments hold much promise for the eventual emergence of long-needed objective assessments. The suggestions from Livingstone, Gallaburda, Tallal, and their colleagues that much learning disability may be a function of visual and/or auditory processing indicate that it may be possible, in the near future, actually to test for some learning disabilities. Over the longer term, the reports of physiological abnormalities in the brain may help us yield even more definite indicators of learning disability.

Mental Retardation

While Down syndrome and fragile X syndrome are the most common known causes of mental retardation in children, they are far from the only possible causes. Most cases, in fact, have no known cause. Mild retardation is disproportionately represented in low-socioeconomic status (SES) families. Severe and profound retardation, however, are found in all social classes. One well-known cause of mild retardation is exposure to lead. Most automobile gasolines today are lead-free, as are most modern paints. However, older (pre-1978) homes and other buildings still have lead-based paint, which young children may ingest. Lead-based interior paint was banned in a 1978 federal law; lead-based paint still may be used in exterior walls and porches, however.

Children need not eat paint chips to get lead poisoning (Benson & Lane, 1993). Lead-based paint was used for many years on window sills, baseboards, radiators, and door jambs. Children may ingest lead dust by putting their hands on those surfaces and then putting their fingers in their mouths. One study in the late 1970s found that some 700,000 children under age six had elevated levels of lead in their blood (Rabin, 1989; Talan, 1990). In part due to such findings, federal rules require that as of October 1995 real estate transactions involving pre-1978 housing must disclose lead hazards (Rall, 1994). The Centers for Disease Control and Prevention in 1991 called for universal testing of all children beginning at about one year of age; two years later, the American Academy of Pediatrics endorsed routine testing (Rall, 1994).

A newer cause of mental retardation in children is pediatric acquired immune deficiency syndrome (AIDS) (children born with or acquiring AIDS in childhood). Another cause, an old but recently recognized one, is fetal alcohol syndrome (FAS) (maternal abuse of alcohol during pregnancy). Most retardation, however, is caused by unknown factors.

Mental retardation, from whatever cause, is defined along three variables. First, there are adaptive behavior deficits that are characteristic of much younger age ranges. Second, intellectual functioning is significantly lower than normal, with IQ test results at or below

mental retardation refers to a combination of adaptive behavior characteristic of younger age ranges, and intellectual functioning significantly lower than normal, when onset occurs prior to age eighteen. The current definition stresses that individuals with mental retardation need extensive systems of support.

Although they often have special learning needs, young children with mental retardation can be full participants in many early childhood activities.

70 to 75, or about two S.D. below the mean. Third, the disability arises during the developmental period, usually understood as the first eighteen years of life. The American Association on Mental Retardation (AAMR) put it somewhat more formally in its 1992 definition:

> *Mental retardation refers to substantial limitations in present functioning. It is characterized by significantly subaverage general intellectual functioning, existing concurrently with related limitations in two or more of the following applicable adaptive skill areas: communication, self-care, home living, social skills, community use, self-direction, health and safety, functional academics, leisure and work. Mental retardation manifests before age 18.* (p. 5)

The 1992 AAMR definition recognizes "systems of support" as important for individuals with retardation. One way in which children may demonstrate limitations in skill areas is by requiring support from others to perform those tasks of everyday living.

All three parts of the definition are important. The most important may be the second: It is the child's behavior, more than a score on a test, that signals mental retardation. Behavior that is acceptable in a one-year-old would be evidence of possible mental retardation if displayed by a three-year-old. Virtually all states recognize mental retardation as an established condition under Part C.

Down Syndrome

Down syndrome is the most common identifiable cause of mental retardation, accounting for perhaps one-third of all cases. In addition to mental retardation, characteristic facial features, hypotonia (floppiness in muscles), and hearing loss are common in Down syndrome.

First identified in 1866 by Dr. John Langdon Down, **Down syndrome** causes mild or moderate retardation. About 5,000 infants are born each year with Down syndrome; the majority are males. Down syndrome is the most common identifiable cause of mental retardation, accounting for perhaps one-third of all cases of retardation. Most other cases cannot be linked to a specific cause; they may have dietary, environmental, or other roots. Down syndrome includes characteristic facial features, hypotonia (floppiness in muscles), hearing loss, and numerous other physical problems (Msall, DiGaudio, & Malone, 1991). This condition is now known to be genetically caused in about 95 percent of cases, with unbalanced translocations of chromosome 21 accounting for most of the remainder. There are more than 1,000 genes on chromosome 21. The genetic basis for Down syndrome was first identified in 1959 by Dr. Jerome Lejeune (Cooley & Graham, 1991; Selikowitz, 1990). In what is called trisomy 21, cells have three rather than two 21st chromosomes.

Down syndrome occurs about one in every 800 live births (Roizen, 1997). The condition is, however, much more common than that proportion would indicate, not only because most fetuses with the syndrome are spontaneously aborted (through miscarriage), but also because readily available prenatal tests (including amniocentesis, chorionic villus sampling, and early amnio) can now identify the condition early in pregnancy; many prospective parents choose to abort rather than proceed to term.

Although mental retardation is the best-known effect of Down syndrome, the condition is far more complex than that, as the chapter-opening quote from Roizen (1997) suggests. Most children with Down syndrome have a measurable hearing loss, particularly in the high frequencies. Visual impairments are also common. Hypotonia is very common in Down syndrome. It can interfere with breast feeding (causing tongue protuberation that makes feeding a more laborious process than usual) and can also produce constipation due to hypotonic gut musculature. The syndrome includes cardiac conditions in about 44 percent of cases, including congenital heart disease (Cooley & Graham, 1991; Tingley, 1988). These cardiac conditions are a major cause of premature death and remain a concern throughout the early childhood years; indeed, most cardiac-related deaths in people with Down syndrome occur during the first five years of life. Other common causes of premature death include susceptibility to infection, immature digestive tracts (including duodenal atresia), and respiratory problems (Selikowitz, 1990). Absent these or other physical problems, people with Down syndrome typically live to fifty or fifty-five years of age, some longer.

During the first year of life, parents and professionals alike need to be alert to acquired loss of hearing and/or vision. In addition, tonic/clonic seizures (formerly called grand mal seizures) may occur in about 10 percent of cases. In the subsequent early childhood years, generalized delays will likely become evident. As should be evident by now, the syndrome affects physical, adaptive, and communication behavior, not just cognitive development. It is important for parent and early childhood special education (ECSE) professionals alike to bear in mind that Down syndrome infants, toddlers, and preschoolers have the same range and types of childhood problems as do other children; thus they should not focus their attention exclusively on syndrome-related concerns.

Fragile X Syndrome

fragile X syndrome is a condition resulting from damage to the X chromosome. Hyperactivity and mental retardation are common symptoms in males; females are usually only carriers.

Fragile X syndrome results from damage to the X chromosome (which is also implicated in Duchenne muscular dystrophy). Females have two X chromosomes, so if one is damaged but the other is not, symptoms usually do not appear; instead, females become carriers of the condition. In the few females who do have symptoms, these are mild, usually limited to learning difficulties; they rarely call for drugs or other treatment. Males, however, have only one X chromosome; the other sex chromosome, the Y chromosome, cannot overcome problems in the X chromosome. Fragile X syndrome is now recognized as the leading cause of mental impairment in males. Symptoms in males include mild to severe hyperactivity, mild to severe retardation, moderate LD, autism—or no symptoms at all. Fragile X syndrome is believed to occur in one in every one thousand male live births, one in every two thousand female live births. In only one-third of the women, however, do symptoms appear.

New tests are now available to screen family members in cases where inheritance of fragile X syndrome is a concern, costing as little as $250 (they previously were $700). Some states routinely screen public school children for the condition if family history suggests that it may occur. However, the disorder can appear with no prior family history.

ASSESSMENT

Assessment may identify delays or deviations. Delays are typical behaviors, but at later-than-expected ages. Babbling at three years of age, for example, constitutes a delay. Deviations, however, are very atypical behaviors. Copying drawings backward, for example, is unusual in children at any age. The Individuals with Disabilities Education Act (IDEA) insists that all potentially eligible young children be assessed by a multidisciplinary team. That team should examine cognitive development in each child, regardless of the fact that a given child may have primary needs in some other domain of development. The interconnections between domains are so dramatic that a multidisciplinary approach is essential.

Down syndrome is usually readily identified. Among common characteristics noticeable in infants are the lack of a Moro's reflex (the arms pull across the chest in an embracing manner), hypotonia, flat face (notably a low nasal bridge and a small nose), and eyes that slant upwards. Intelligence may also be assessed. Tests commonly used with young children include the Stanford-Binet Intelligence Scale and the Weschler Preschool and Primary Scale of Intelligence. The Stanford-Binet L-M version is widely used in ECSE programs. The fourth edition of the Stanford-Binet (Thorndike, Hagen, & Sattler, 1986), however, should *not* be used with young children who are or may be mentally retarded. The fourth edition's manual cautions against use with two-year-olds who fall in the lowest 10 to 15 percent on intelligence and with three-year-olds who are mentally retarded. Wilson (1992) argues that the fourth edition should not be used either with four- or five-year-olds who are or are suspected to be mentally retarded. He also urges that age-equivalent scores be interpreted carefully even with the more appropriate L-M edition.

Diagnosing LD during the early childhood years is very difficult, because the definition refers to academic work—notably reading, writing, and calculation—that may not be developmentally appropriate for the early childhood years. Yet some children do show the perceptual problems, seeming inability to do metacognition (examining one's own behavior and adjusting it to learn better), excessive distractibility, and/or poor coordination that are indicators of possible LD. Many of the parents in the SIPP study may have had such symptoms in mind when they said their children had LD. But actually diagnosing learning disabilities is problematic. Ariel (1992), for example, in a text on LD, stated:

> The early identification of learning disabilities is a complex process due to the following factors: (a) learning disabilities are viewed primarily as an academic handicap, making it difficult to predict academic difficulty before kindergarten or first grade; (b) learning disabilities are more difficult to detect early than are severe handicaps; (c) differential developmental patterns make it difficult to distinguish between the existence of learning disabilities and a developmental lag; (d) the impreciseness of the definition of learning disabilities makes it difficult to establish widely accepted eligibility criteria; and (e) the use of labels permeates the identification of any of the "mildly handicapping conditions." (p. 205)

The findings by Tallal and other researchers on processing problems in children may be used someday soon in ECSE assessment. Her technique of touching two fingers under a table in rapid succession, described earlier in this chapter, does not require elaborate laboratory settings. Dr. Tallal's work suggested that requiring children to perform rapid speech production may help in differentiating children who have LD from children whose problems are due to other factors. Giving children very rapid visual signals and then asking them to report what they saw may be a third method of assessment when one is testing for LD. That possible indicator draws on the work of Livingstone et al. (1991). In all three cases, the suggestion is that one key to diagnosing dyslexia and other learning disabilities in young children may be testing for ability to process information rapidly. Livingstone et al. suggested that auditory, tactual, and perhaps other brain processing functions may be impaired in ways similar to those they found in visual information processing among children with dyslexia.

The most practical approach in assessment of LD probably remains the one most commonly used in special education: Test the child for everything else, and if the problems are not due to other conditions, it may be a learning disability. Complete physical, psychological, and sensory examinations should be given together with a comprehensive family medical history.

Assessing children with fragile X syndrome can be challenging. Freund (1994) suggested that assessors look for behavioral indicators (extreme hyperactivity, autistic-like activities) believed to be associated with the condition, as well as for wide, protruding ears and a long face—both thought to be physical indicators of possible fragile X syndrome. Genetic factors are critical in this syndrome, so a thorough family history should be taken. As noted, screening tests may also be used.

INTERVENTION

Early intervention and preschool special education programs try to prevent mental retardation and cognitive development delays by providing infant stimulation and other enrichment programs. Two kinds of efforts may be distinguished. The first focuses more on prevention and tends to include at-risk children rather than children with moderate, severe, or profound retardation or other cognitive disabilities. The second looks more to curriculum to accelerate development among children already recognized as being mentally retarded or having other cognitive conditions.

Prevention

Considerable success in prevention among young children who are at risk has been reported in model programs. One early effort, dubbed the Abecedarian Project (Martin, Ramey, & Ramey, 1990), identified children prior to birth on the basis of risk factors such as single-parent

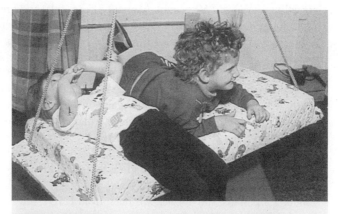

Children with needs in the domain of cognitive development have physical development needs as well. As is true with other children in this age range, they tend to learn most through physical activity. Such activity should be as unrestrained as possible so they may learn by doing.

household, mother's IQ, low parental education attainment levels, and poverty. The word "Abecedarian" means "one who learns the fundamentals of something" (Ramey & Ramey, 1992). Family participation began shortly after birth and continued until the children entered kindergarten. Half were assigned to an intervention program, half to a control group. The intervention program was intensive, running for a full day, five days a week, fifty weeks a year. It included social services and medical assistance for parents, as well as experiences for the children themselves designed to accelerate development in cognitive, communication, physical, and social or emotional domains of development. Results showed that intervention successfully prevented mental retardation in many cases. Tested at age three, 95 percent of the intervention program participants had IQs in the normal range (at least 85), with the average being over 100, while in the control group of infants and toddlers who did not benefit from the intervention, just 49 percent scored above 85 IQ. The nearly twenty-point IQ difference was impressive.

Project CARE (Wasik, Ramey, Bryant, & Sparling, 1990), a follow-up to the Abecedarian Project, compared early intervention combining child development center services with home visits with two control groups, one receiving home visits only and one receiving no intervention services. Infants were randomly assigned to one of the three groups and remained in the program until just before they entered kindergarten. Children participating in the intensive, center-based plus home-visit program averaged IQs over 100 when tested at age three. Children in the other two groups averaged IQs of 90 or below.

A much larger effort, the Infant Health and Development Program (IHDP) (1990) studied nearly a thousand children and their families in eight cities. Focusing on low-birth-weight (LBW) (<2,500 grams, or about 5.5 pounds) and premature (<37 weeks' gestational age) infants and toddlers, the IHDP aimed to prevent mental retardation in these at-risk populations. The program used a center-based approach supplemented by home visits. Children began in the program at twelve months of age and continued until the age of three. A control group of similar infants received routine medical follow-up services. Impressive results were obtained with the intensive experimental group, demonstrating that early intervention produced substantial gains. Stanford-Binet test scores at age three were much higher with experimental subjects than with control subjects. While many control infants had IQs of 85 or lower at age three, most experimental subjects tested at 95 or better.

The IHDP helped most with those LBW/premature infants and toddlers *least* in need of early intervention. The higher-weight infants (2001 to 2500 grams) did much better than did the lower-weight infants (<2000 grams). Infants with very low birthweight (<1000 grams or about 2.5 pounds) did not benefit much from IHDP intervention. The study's authors concluded that higher-weight LBW infants were healthier and thus more able to benefit from the intervention programming. The IHDP did not serve LBW or premature infants with serious health problems. Thus, even this intensive, high-quality model project does not tell us much about helping young children with severe cognitive delays or conditions.

Looking again at the IHDP data, Ramey and Ramey (1992) concluded that those LBW/premature infants whose families participated most frequently in the program gained most. Participation was measured by the number of home visits completed, the number of parent group meetings attended, and the number of sessions the infant attended at the eight program centers. Infants from high-participation families did much better, with just 2 percent testing as mentally retarded (IQ<70) at age three, compared with 4 percent of medium participants, 13 percent of low participants, and 17 percent of control subjects (nonparticipants) (Ramey & Ramey, 1992). The findings held even for very low birthweight and very premature infants. This is important, indicating that high-intensity programs with both center-based and home-based components can make a real difference for young children most in need of intervention *if* parents participate actively.

Summarizing the program implications from these three projects, Ramey and Ramey (1992) identified several interventions as most effective with under-six children. First, children should be encouraged to explore, both at home and in ECSE centers. Physical exploration of the environment, they said, is strongly related to cognitive development. Second, mentoring (assistance and modeling) of basic cognitive skills such as labeling and sequencing, and guided rehearsal in their use, are important. Gains should be celebrated, but errors should not result in punishment or disapproval. Finally, Ramey and Ramey (1992) suggested, parents and ECSE professionals should provide a rich linguistic environment, with much elaboration on requests and directions.

Stimulation

The issue of environmental stimulation is urgently important, especially in low-SES families where parents or other primary caregivers have attained low education levels (see Figure 15.1). It is vitally important for children with cognitive delays, deviations, or disabilities that parents and ECSE professionals alike make use of elaboration techniques: They should talk out what they are doing, why they are doing it, and not only what the child should do but why, and in what steps. ECSE workers suspecting communication impoverishment in the home may want to assist parents and other family members to learn how to expand upon, and explain, their communication with their children.

David Hodapp of Yale University stressed the need for teachers of children with severe disabilities, including mental retardation and fragile X syndrome, to match their spoken language to the child's communication abilities rather than to mental age or chronological age. Examining teacher-child interactions in two settings with twenty-one young children who had mental ages between nine and thirty-five months (mean = 19.2) and chronological

---

1. Nutrition interventions, because much mild retardation in particular appears to result from poor diet

2. A rich variety of activities providing stimulation

3. Multisensory input, because when young children with mental retardation hear, see, and touch things, they learn more, and faster

4. Applied behavior analysis, because it helps to clarify for the child what behaviors are desired

5. Modeling, because studies by Albert Bandura and by Marc Gold demonstrated that showing a child what is desired may be the clearest, most direct means of instruction available to us

6. Instructing parents and other primary caregivers on how to use language to elaborate on directions and to explain what is wanted, rather than just repeating the injunction "No!"

7. Encouraging children to explore, limiting caregiver control to essential constraints

---

FIGURE 15.1 What works: mental retardation

ages between two and eight years (mean = 4.5), Hodapp, Evans, and Ward (1989) found that teachers typically matched their language to the child's response to the preceding request or situation, moving up or down in communication complexity depending on how the child behaved. If a child responded appropriately to one request, the teacher would ask for a higher-level response; if a child's acted inappropriately the teacher repeated the same request or made a lower-level request.

Particularly helpful to many children with Down syndrome is the personal computer (PC). PCs equipped with speech synthesis (computer talk) are especially valuable, because the computer's monotonous "voice" gives equal emphasis to each phoneme. The hearing impairment that is common in children with Down syndrome often causes them to miss word endings, prepositions, and other sentence elements that are spoken rapidly, in higher pitches, and merged into other words (as "howdjadue" for "how do you do?"). The computer will pronounce each sound with the same speed and at much the same pitch, making it much easier for children with Down syndrome to hear, attend to, and learn these sounds and parts of speech (Adler & Drew, 1988).

Ironically, then, the preferred speech synthesis hardware and software system for use with children who have Down syndrome is one of the older, less sophisticated ones. Newer, state-of-the-art speech synthesis systems that produce high-quality speech with greater variability in pitch are less suitable, because children who have Down syndrome often display mild to moderate hearing losses. To some extent, properly fitted hearing aids may help the child understand even the newer, more variegated speech synthesis systems.

Early infant stimulation and continued high-quality communication interaction make a tremendous difference to young children who are mentally retarded. This kind of early and rich stimulation, combined with use of technology discussed in Chapter 10, is having a profound impact on children who are mentally retarded today, as compared with years past. PCs presenting information both auditorially and visually can be very helpful to young children who are mentally retarded. Multimedia presentations offer the child redundancy, or the same information in different forms; and this redundancy appears to help many young children

The PC equipped with speech synthesis appears to be unusually helpful for many young children with cognitive development needs. The monotone of inexpensive synthesizers seems to be understandable for many children with Down syndrome, even when most speech is not fully comprehensible.

with mental retardation to learn. Interactivity is another feature of many educational software programs; these programs present information, request a response, and react to that answer by branching into one of several next steps. And of course the program has no emotions; it does not become impatient with a slow child, nor angry with an error-prone child.

Curriculum

Mental Retardation. Programming for young children with moderate and severe mental retardation tends to focus on maximizing the children's cognitive achievements. Such programs stress development of language and conceptual foundations for later learning. They also emphasize adaptive behavior, helping children to learn age-appropriate behavior that may accelerate social acceptance by nonretarded classmates in K–12.

Curriculum in ECSE is quite similar across the nation (Graham & Bryant, 1993; Goodman, 1992). Especially with young children having severe needs, a highly structured program is common. The curriculum is constructed, in large part, from assessment findings (see Chapter 7): Items missed on standardized tests or identified by parents or other caregivers as not yet achieved become the basis for instruction. To illustrate, when the author visited the Variety Preschoolers Workshop in Syosset, New York, which uses a proprietary assessment instrument called "The 5 P's," the center's psychologist stated forthrightly, "The items (identified by parents and teachers) become the program."

Perhaps nowhere is this tendency to teach from test results more apparent than in curricula used with young children with mental retardation. Each day in an ECSE program for such children is remarkably like all other days. The day begins with attendance (who is present, what everyone's name is), calendar work (the day of the week, special days coming up), circle time (preacademic instruction in colors, numbers, shapes, and so on), snack time (social interaction), recess or recreation (gross motor activity), and art time (fine motor activity).

Much intervention with young children with mental retardation features **direct instruction**, or didactic, teacher-directed activities. Although such teacher interventions are sometimes controversial in early childhood, Bredekamp (1993b) explained that they do not necessarily violate "developmentally appropriate practice" (DAP). Bredekamp noted that although the overall emphasis in DAP is on early childhood (EC) staff following children and facilitating child-directed activities, there is a time and a place for direct instruction, especially where research has shown it to be effective. Children with disabilities or delays in the domain of cognitive development are in particular need of intensive assistance in language and in concept development.

Direct instruction facilitates development in the cognitive domain because it targets precisely those concepts the child has not yet mastered, offers immediate teacher or other professional guidance on those ideas, and gives the child assisted practice in applying the concepts. In addition, direct instruction saves considerable time, an important consideration. A child-care worker who implements DAP principles in their pure form might follow a child for many weeks, even months, before serendipitously coming across an opportunity to facilitate learning of a particular concept. With direct instruction, by contrast, the ECSE worker introduces the concept when she believes the child is ready for it, when the necessary materials are at hand, and when opportunities to practice the key ideas are available.

That children with Down syndrome benefit from such early intervention has been documented by Brinkworth (1975), Connolly, Morgan, and Russell (1984), and Sharav and

direct instruction is structured, teacher-led instruction. It often is contrasted to less didactic, more interactive approaches to learning, such as "developmentally appropriate practice."

Schlomo (1986). The latter two experiments were longitudinal studies of center-based and home-based early intervention programs. Neither, however, used control groups, so the reported benefits cannot definitely be attributed to the programmatic instruction.

Other questions about the direct-instruction approach were raised in Joan Goodman's book, *When Slow Is Fast Enough* (1992). Goodman is a psychologist who came to ECSE from a background in EC. While visiting twenty ECSE programs for children with moderate mental retardation, Goodman was surprised by the extent to which ECSE teachers used applied behavior analysis and other aspects of direct instruction. Knowing that such children characteristically have short attention spans and limited memory, Goodman expected the teachers to be much less didactic and controlling than they were. That is why she titled her book chapter on methods, "Curriculum and Instruction: Teachers versus Students."

It is a good title. The dilemma facing ECSE professionals who work with young children with moderate or severe mental retardation is what the focus should be. Many parents of such children push hard for a socialization agenda, believing that if their children are exposed to nondisabled children, under controlled conditions, their children will in time come to be accepted. Such social acceptance often is of urgent importance to parents. The ECSE professionals Goodman observed believed, instead, that preacademics was the proper focus. These young children had so very much information to learn, in such a short time, they contended, that nothing short of carefully planned, strongly controlled instruction would succeed.

The curricula used in these programs with children with moderate or severe mental retardation is qualitatively as well as quantitatively different from those used in prekindergarten programs for nondisabled children. Goodman memorably describes how ECSE teachers worked with their young charges, day after day, month after month, on the same preacademic areas— the day of the week, colors, shapes, and so on. Mainstreamed settings in which children with and without disabilities are mixed could not, and would not, allow such almost-endless repetition. They would move, firmly and rapidly, on to new areas of learning, inevitably leaving the child with retardation behind.

After almost two years on the road visiting ECSE programs, Goodman longed to see more flexibility, more freedom, more spontaneity. Yet, in the end, she concluded that the teachers she had observed had good reasons for acting as they did. The research evidence, Goodman concluded, is that applied behavior analysis does help young children with mental retardation to learn preacademics. More progressive approaches appear, however, to help these children more in the areas of social interaction and problem solving. The issue comes down to a value judgment. What is it that a program wants to accomplish? If the goal is to give young children the preacademics they need to succeed in the next environment, a direct-instruction method may be the approach of choice. However, if the aim is to nourish curiosity and self-confidence in these children, a more developmental approach may be indicated.

In addition to classroom instructing, multidisciplinary early intervention should include physical and occupational therapy to assist with normal developmental tasks and also deal with hypotonia in musculature. That need is especially urgent for young children who have Down syndrome, which often causes hypo- or hypertonia as well as mental retardation. Speech and language services can also be very helpful in accelerating acquisition of intelligible speech and practical language to express needs and desires. Both home-based and center-based strategies should be pursued.

The evidence is that multidisciplinary interventions—including physical and occupational therapy, speech and language pathology, multimedia PC programs, and direct instruction— can lead to remarkable gains among young children with mental retardation. The ECSE worker needs to maintain the focus on the "whole child." These children need assistance not only in cognitive development but, just as urgently, in communication, physical, social or emotional, and adaptive development as well. That is why the multidisciplinary team approach is critical in planning ECSE programming for children with mental retardation.

Learning Disabilities. The new evidence on neurological bases for some LD already is suggesting intervention strategies. Dr. Tallal, working with young children who have language impairments, reported that when these children used computer speech synthesis to listen to the sounds, they understood far better than they could understand the same sounds in real-time, human speech. That is because the computer can artificially stretch out (slow down) the initial *b* and *d* sounds, making it possible for children with LD to distinguish them (Blakeslee, 1991b).

Similarly, Dr. Livingstone, who headed the Harvard study on magno and parvo cells, reported that despite the preliminary nature of the findings, she believed that early intervention while the brain's plasticity is working in the child's favor may assist in alleviating LD by the time children enter kindergarten (Blakeslee, 1991b). Because magno cells do not process color (that is handled by the smaller parvo cells), the use of color filters (a controversial technique in teaching dyslexic individuals to read) may be indicated by this study. In effect, the use of color would route the information to parvo, rather than magno, cells, thus using brain cells that are normal in dyslexics.

If Tallal, Livingstone, and their colleagues are correct that for many young children with LD a central problem is in processing rapidly changing sensory input, one implication for intervention may be to alter the *temporal* nature of information in ECSE programs. Recall that in Tallal's study, even young children with severe language impairments performed well when auditory, visual, or tactual information was presented at a slow pace. The vehicle most readily available to ECSE programs for temporal variation of visual and auditory information is the PC. Additionally, PCs can accept even very slow typing, and computer speech recognition systems can accept slower-than-normal speech production. These tools might be explored in ECSE programs serving children with severe language and other disabilities.

Other implications are more controversial. The Harvard work may give new life to vision-based interventions for children with LD. As Livingstone and her colleagues implied, intensive EC interventions that help children to use their parvocellular system for reading readiness and early reading tasks may assist children with dyslexia to learn to read much faster and much better. Mary Williams of the University of New Orleans has experimented with color filters. She found that blue light filters helped some 80 percent of her dyslexic subjects, while red filters helped some 8 percent. The filters are pieces of transparent colored plastic, and as such are readily and inexpensively available to ECSE programs. It is possible, she reported, that California psychologist Helen Irlen has a point. Harshly criticized since she began offering colored lenses to dyslexic individuals in 1983, Irlen insisted that the lenses help her patients, although she says she does not know why (Blakeslee, 1991b).

Fragile X Syndrome. This condition was relatively recently identified, so not much is known about working with children who have fragile X syndrome. Freund (1994), for example, observed, "No unique or specific interventions for young Fragile X children have been identified through research" (p. 43). She did, however, indicate that adaptive behavior interventions are urgently important with such children: "[A]daptive social development . . . is probably the single-most important issue of development for the developmentally delayed Fragile X child" (p. 43). Adaptive development is considered in Chapter 17.

Suggestions made elsewhere in this book on interventions with children who have similar problems, albeit due to other conditions, may help. Extreme hyperactivity is an example. Helping children with fragile X syndrome often involves use of prescription drugs such as Ritalin and Dexedrine to control hyperactivity; the same medications are also used with children diagnosed as having Attention Deficit Hyperactivity Disorder (ADHD). Because many young children with fragile X syndrome display autistic behaviors, some of the interventions suggested by Frith (1993) may help (see Chapter 17). Offering lessons visually, especially on computer, seems to help as well.

Family counseling is an important intervention when a child is diagnosed as having fragile X syndrome. That is because the inheritance pattern is such that the condition is not merely passed on from parent to child but will occasionally worsen from generation to generation. That is not always true. In some instances, the error pattern shrinks (the number of repeats becomes smaller in child than in parent). It is not yet known why that occurs. However, once the mechanisms causing this error correction to take place are discovered, it may be just a short step to genetic therapy for fragile X syndrome.

WORKING WITH PARENTS

The key to helping children with cognitive development needs is close program-family ties. Although research does not support the use of traditional "parent training" approaches, the Division for Early Childhood's "recommended practices" strongly support empowering parents to solve their own problems. Courtesy of Beach Center on Families and Disability, University of Kansas.

ECSE workers may suggest ways to provide stimulation for young children at home, particularly in families where parents are not well educated. As Craig Ramey's Project CARE showed, efforts by early intervention and preschool specialists to help members of low-SES families can have dramatic results. A related approach ECSE specialists may suggest to parents is that of linguistic elaboration.

Although Ramey worked with families of young children believed to be at risk for delays in cognitive development, it must be emphasized here that cognitive development during the first six years of life is of crucial significance for *all* young children. To illustrate, consider a three-year-old child who is deaf. Unless parents and other family members act aggressively to create in the home a rich environment that provides visual information and stimulation to the child, the child will not develop normally in the cognitive domain. That is why the IDEA emphasizes that all young children should be helped, as appropriate, in all five domains of development.

Also helpful, research suggests, is specific information answering parents' questions. Fragile X syndrome, for example, can be frightening for many families. In particular, women who learn that they are carriers of the genetic defect responsible for the condition need counseling to understand their options. Families who have one child with Down syndrome understandably want to know what the likelihood is that future children will also be affected. This kind of genetic counseling will likely become an increasingly important function of ECSE programs, as more and more families turn to ECSE professionals for knowledgeable guidance in dealing with these troubling questions. Chapter 18 explores these issues in detail.

SUMMARY

Cognitive development depends heavily upon environmental influences. Young children grow intellectually when they are given frequent and ample opportunities to explore; when they are surrounded by visual, auditory, and tactile stimulation; and when they receive explanations rather than just orders or directions. On the other hand, when they are over-protected (perhaps by worried parents), when they are deprived of intellectual stimulation (perhaps because of deafness or because of parental neglect), and when they hear and see little linguistic interaction between adults, their cognitive development is slowed.

Much of the most interesting work on LD today is being done in fields related to neurology. Findings that visual, auditory, and/or tactual mechanisms may be off in some people with LDs suggest new assessment approaches and new intervention methodologies. As exciting as these discoveries are, the likelihood is that such neurological bases are involved only in a minority of cases of LDs. As Shaywitz showed, some learning disabilities may not be distinct conditions at all but rather variations within the normal range of cognitive abilities. Despite this new work on LD in young children, the large number of parents of under-six children who told census takers that they believed their children had LDs remains intriguing. Follow-up research is needed to understand better why so many parents make such reports. Is it because large numbers of pediatricians and other primary medical care providers are diagnosing LDs in preschool-age children? Is it due, rather, to parental preference for the term "learning disability" over "mental retardation"? Or is it due to parental observation of clumsiness, perceptual disorders, and other indicators pointing toward possible LDs?

The PC can be of considerable value to young children who are mentally retarded or learning disabled. The computer's ability to present information at variable speeds and in multiple modes—visually and auditorially, in words and pictures, in colors, and in moving scenes—is one reason. The interactive nature of many of today's computer programs is another. And the computer's infinite patience is a third. Despite its potential, the PC has yet to become a fixture in even a large minority of American homes, and seems to be most conspicuously absent in low-SES households.

QUESTIONS FOR REFLECTION

1. What are some early indications of possible learning disabilities?
2. Explain, in your own words, what "metacognition" means.
3. How might timing delays (auditory lags), as reported by Tallal, lead to problems in learning what one hears?
4. What teaching strategies are suggested by the idea that much learning disability involves temporal information processing problems?
5. Why is low socioeconomic status associated with mild mental retardation?
6. Give at least three characteristics of Down syndrome.
7. Why does fragile X manifest itself in boys rather than in girls?
8. What informal tests of learning disabilities does Tallal's work suggest?
9. What kinds of interventions appear to help in preventing mild mental retardation?
10. Describe "direct instruction" and explain why it is often used with young children with mental retardation.

Social or Emotional Development

Testifying before the U.S. Senate Subcommittee on Disability Policy in 1989, Steve Forness said, on behalf of the National Mental Health Special Education Consortium:

> [W]e simply do not know enough about identifying and serving children [with emotional disturbance] in our public schools. Three of five of these children are in restrictive school settings. As a matter of fact, we are using out-of-school placements for these children half again as much as any other major category of special education. We are taking them out of their homes and even out of their communities in order to serve them, rather than developing school-based programs. Two out of five children we serve drop out of school before graduation. It is the highest dropout rate of all ten categories of special education. Something is not working. . . . There is a shortage of teachers in this category and it is the worst of all ten categories in special education. It is especially critical in recruiting minority teachers. Thirty percent of our teachers leave after three or four years, because of the stress of this job. (Forness, 1989, pp. 186–187)

OVERVIEW

Delays in and limitations of social or emotional development are important to early childhood special education (ECSE) personnel for two reasons. First, the domain is important in itself—and has, as Dr. Forness told the Senate, received relatively less attention from special educators than have other kinds of disabilities. Speaking on behalf of the Council for Exceptional Children (CEC), Frederick Weintraub told the Senate at the same hearing, "It is generally agreed that this area (emotional development) is probably the most problematic in special education and the area that historically has gotten the least national attention and leadership" (Weintraub, 1989, p. 30). Children with social or emotional disorders need help to be successful in ECSE programs—and later in school as well. Fortunately, well-established principles of modifying inappropriate behavior are available for use in early childhood (EC) programs.

The domain of social or emotional development is much broader than is the Part B category "emotionally disturbed." For this reason, ECSE programs have an opportunity to serve many young children who have important needs but who may not qualify for needed services after they leave preschool (Campbell, 1990). The ECSE focus on family services allows professionals to intervene in families much more readily than does the more child-centered focus of elementary and secondary education. Family services during the early childhood years can help parents to understand how social and emotional development occurs, to learn ways of stimulating appropriate behavior, and to acquire competence in using nonpunitive methods to control behavior. By intervening early, with both the child and the family, ECSE programs may prevent or at least ameliorate severe social or emotional problems.

If allowed to continue, on the other hand, these problems may become much worse. According to the U.S. Department of Education's *Fifteenth Annual Report* (1993b, Table 1.9, p. 28), students with serious emotional disturbance have the lowest rate of graduation of any category of students with disabilities. The National Longitudinal Transition Study in Special Education (NLTS), reported upon in the *Fourteenth Annual Report* (U.S. Department of Education, 1992c), showed that these children and youth have the highest absenteeism rates of all children with disabilities and that close to half (45 percent) received at least one failing grade during the most recent school year.

The domain of social or emotional development is important to ECSE professionals for another reason. Children with established conditions or delays in other domains of early childhood development may also have social or emotional problems. These may occur, for example, when a child who is blind arrives at a day-care center or preschool program not having had the kinds or amount of social interaction other children take for granted. This child's experiential deprivation may surface as age-inappropriate behavior, including excessive withdrawal, self-stimulation, and other indicators that the child needs assistance in social and emotional growth. Similarly, children with severe physical disabilities may have had years of hospitalization; their experiences, the lives they have lived, are very different from those of most children. That their behavior, too, should differ is no surprise. Third, these children may have health problems or physical conditions placing them at risk for accidents or illnesses even in ordinary, everyday activities; parental worries, often internalized by the child, may lead them to avoid activity and fear social interaction. These children are not emotionally disabled, but their behavior may be similar in some ways to the behavior of children who are.

Del'Homme and her colleagues (1994) made a related point. Structured settings are more likely to evoke acting-out behavior than are less formal situations, such as free play. Because many ECSE programs are carefully planned, tightly scheduled, highly structured environments—because, to use the words of Wolery and Sainato (1993), such approaches "cause rapid learning and use of important skills" (p. 53)—they may occasion more externalizing behavior than might more relaxed settings. Del'Homme et al. make the point that "it may be that difficulties experienced in instructional contexts reflect a lack of experience with the demands of this setting, rather than a developing behavior disorder" (p. 230). That is, acting-out behavior may be a normal response from a child rather than a symptom of some underlying disability.

This reinforces a central theme of this book: ECSE programs should assess social or emotional development in *all* young children and should consider interventions appropriate for all of them, not merely those showing disabilities, delays, or deviations primarily in the social or emotional development domain. Indeed the multidisciplinary approach required by the Individuals with Disabilities Education Act (IDEA) mandates that members of the multidisciplinary team perform an assessment of social or emotional development in all young children and that services be provided, as appropriate, in this domain even if the child's primary needs are in some other domain of development.

However, social or emotional development in early childhood is of most concern in one or both of two instances. One is when social or emotional problems interfere with the child's own learning; an example is a child whose thumb sucking is so excessive that she rarely participates in activities requiring the use of both hands. The second is when these problems interfere with learning by other children; an obvious example is when a child's temper tantrum disrupts a group activity. Although social or emotional disorders, delays, and deviations are challenging for ECSE professionals, the evidence is that real progress can often be made in this domain. To illustrate, what is now the Early Education Program for Children with Disabilities (EEPCD), then called the Handicapped Children's Early Education Program (HCEEP), followed the development in the mid-1970s of 9,600 children with many different disabilities who had been served in HCEEP programs. While longitudinal outcomes revealed progress in many areas, the greatest gains were achieved in the area of personal and social skills (General Accounting Office, 1979).

This chapter explores common problems in the social or emotional development domain and discusses techniques ECSE workers may use to alleviate behavior problems. The chapter's treatment of intervention focuses heavily on applied behavior analysis (behavior modification) because of this approach's demonstrated utility with children who have social or emotional problems (Wolery, Bailey, & Sugai, 1988). (The following chapter discusses a variation on that approach: cognitive behavior modification.) The chapter concludes with some suggestions on working with parents.

PREVALENCE

Social or emotional conditions were reported by parents in the Survey on Income and Program Participation (SIPP) study for 42,000 of the 851,000 under-six children identified as having conditions leading to limitations (disabilities), that is, 4.9 percent of all children in that age range who had any disability. The conditions parents identified included emotional disturbance and conduct disorders. These are children for whom social or emotional limitations were identified as first (primary) conditions. In addition, of the 216,000 under-six children for whom two conditions were identified, social or emotional limitations were reported for 29,000 (13 percent); that makes social or emotional limitations the number-two secondary impairment in this population. All told, 71,000 children under six years of age were classified as having limitations of social or emotional development as their first or second condition.

To place these numbers in perspective, social or emotional limitations were reported only about one-fourth as often as were limitations of physical development. In part, this may reflect the difficulty of establishing social or emotional delay much before five years of age. In part, too, it comports with other evidence that social or emotional problems are unusual in young children, particularly as compared to adolescents and young adults. The U.S. Department of Education (1993b, p. 5) reported that about 1 percent of school-age children and 8.9 percent of special education elementary and secondary students were classified as emotionally disturbed. That the prevalence in the early childhood years is approximately half that of the elementary and secondary school-age populations (4.9 versus 8.9 percent) is consistent with the idea that these kinds of problems tend to be diagnosed after the early childhood years. Both sets of figures may be too low (Silver, 1988). One review of epidemiological studies suggests that 8 to 10 percent of children and youth may have social or emotional disorders (Brandenburg, Friedman, & Silver, 1987).

Many parents of preschool and school-age children resist the "emotionally disturbed" label. Such parental preferences may result in under-reporting of actual instances.

DEVELOPMENTAL DELAYS

States define "developmental delays" to include behavior that is not age-appropriate. For example, a one-year-old may cling to her mother when dropped off at a nursery school or day-care center. Were a five-year-old to display this same fear of separation from the mother, however, it would clearly be age-inappropriate; most five-year-olds display more independence, especially in public settings. The delays may be expressed in terms of time, as in that example, in which behavior appears at least twelve months after it normally ceases. They may also be expressed in ways state rules require, as deviations from the mean on standardized tests, or in percentage terms. Despite the fact that state regulators may write such standards into state guidelines, the usefulness of these rules is questionable. Very few tests of social or emotional behavior are available for use with early childhood populations.

For this reason, informed clinical opinion is particularly important in establishing eligibility for services. Many states look to expert diagnosticians to interpret such terms as "persists" (as in inappropriate behavior) or "interferes" (with the child's own or other children's activities). Clinicians draw upon what we know about normal development in making such decisions. Social or emotional delays rarely are reported by parents of infants and toddlers; parental concerns in the birth-to-two period focus much more on sleeping and feeding problems. However, during the early preschool-age period, especially from ages three to four, parental complaints about behavior rise very sharply. Parents who accepted willfulness, disobedience, and impulsivity as "to be expected in the 'terrible twos'" become concerned when these patterns persist.

The assessor faces a difficult task in evaluating such complaints. Major developmental changes take place, featuring (in most young children) a sharp decline in aggressive and destructive behaviors between the ages of three and four (Tynan & Nearing, 1994). On the one hand, volatility in behavior is very common between the ages of three and six, and changes are both abrupt and short-lived. What may appear at first glance to be developmental delays often are very normal variations in development. For these reasons, assessors may be reluctant to pronounce a delay, preferring to tell the parents to "wait—it will take care of itself." On the other hand, however, children whose behavior does not change spontaneously may have real problems that, left untreated, seriously impair later school performance.

Established Conditions

A number of conditions are recognized by states as established. Differentiating them is not always as easy as is naming them. Problems of definition and of evaluation and assessment are pervasive in the domain of social or emotional development.

Children with emotional disturbance are eligible for early intervention and preschool special education services in many states. Some states recognize conduct disorders as "established," and some accept Attention Deficit Hyperactivity Disorder (ADHD). Also recognized in some states are infants, toddlers, and preschoolers diagnosed as having other varieties of mental illness. Part B preschool eligibility in most states is recognized by means of one of the ten conditions recognized in section 601(a) of the IDEA; one is "emotional disturbance."

Emotional disturbance (ED) is recognized as a disability under section 602 in the IDEA. A 1977 regulatory definition (there is no statutory definition), which appears below, remains the official definition of "emotional disturbance" (U.S. Department of Health, Education, and Welfare, 1977, p. 42478):

> *(i)   The term means a condition exhibiting one or more of the following characteristics over a long period of time and to a marked extent, which adversely affects educational performance: (A) An inability to learn which cannot be explained by intellectual, sensory, or health factors; (B) An inability to build or maintain satisfactory relationships with peers and teachers; (C) Inappropriate types of behavior or feelings under normal circumstances; (D) A general pervasive mood of unhappiness or depression; or (E) A tendency to develop physical symptoms or fears associated with personal or school problems.*
>
> *(ii) The term includes children who are schizophrenic. The term does not include children who are socially maladjusted unless it is determined that they are seriously emotionally disturbed.*

Notice the use of the word "or" in the above definition between statements (D) and (E); any one of these five behaviors or characteristics may suffice to qualify a child as eligible.

Conduct disorders include a range of emotional conditions causing limitations in social or emotional development, particularly with respect to socially approved behavior. One could say that the problem is one of undersocialization: The child has not internalized, or has not made habitual, the kinds of behaviors and attitudes that society tries to instill in all of us. Children with conduct disorders use aggression as a routine means of getting their way. Children who respond to authority figures by doing what they are told not to do, and refusing to do what they are asked to do, may also be socially or emotionally delayed. Serious problems may be indicated when children display emotions that are inappropriate for a situation: a child who laughs when most children would cry, for example, or one who becomes inconsolably depressed when most children would cry briefly and recover quickly. A very different kind of conduct disorder occurs when young children withdraw from social contact with both adults and other children. While occasional withdrawal is normal (and may

emotional disturbance (ED) is a category recognized under the IDEA. Sometimes referred to as "emotional and behavioral disorders," ED refers to behavior in children that is age-, culturally, and/or situation-inappropriate and interferes with their education and/or that of other children.

conduct disorders include a range of emotional conditions affecting behavior. Children appear to be "undersocialized" in that they often do not exhibit socially approved behavior.

Attention Deficit Hyperactivity Disorder (ADHD) is a diagnosis made when impulsivity and hyperactivity are present together with distractibility and short attention spans.

Attention Deficit Disorder (ADD) is a diagnosis reached when a child is "unavailable for learning" due to distractibility and short attention spans. The diagnosis is used if hyperactivity is not present (see ADHD).

reflect problems at home), children who persist in isolation, actually turning away from other children and from adults, may require professional help.

Attention deficits are controversial in ECSE. As with LD, diagnosis is largely a matter of testing the child for other conditions or problems, settling on attention deficit only after other labels have been rejected as inappropriate (Lerner, Lowenthal, & Lerner, 1995). *The Diagnostic and Statistical Manual of Mental Disorders–Fourth Edition* (*DSM-IV*) (1994) recognizes three kinds of attention disorders (Figure 16.1). **Attention Deficit Hyperactivity Disorder (ADHD)** is described as a condition characterized by short attention span, hyperactivity and impulsivity, and distractibility. Without hyperactivity, an attention deficit usually would be characterized as **Attention Deficit Disorder (ADD)**, although the *DSM-IV* allows use of a third diagnosis of combined or otherwise unspecified attention disorder. According to the *DSM-IV*, symptoms should appear prior to age six or seven. According to Goodman and Poillion (1992), the behaviors often first surface at about age three or four.

Attention deficits may occur together with other conditions. Children with ADHD or ADD may also have conduct disorders. Children who take medication (sedatives or anticonvulsants) to control epileptic seizures may develop what appears to be an attention deficit as a side effect of the drugs (Ariel, 1992). Similarly, children may have learning disabilities in addition to attention deficits. For all of these reasons, reaching a diagnosis of attention deficit challenges even experts in the field (Blau, 1993; Divoky, 1989; Kohn, 1989).

The distinction between LD and attention disorders is clear in theory—LD affects information processing (the information is attended to and perceived, but the third step of analyzing and interpreting information somehow goes awry) while ADHD and ADD affect attention (the information never is received, so it can neither be perceived nor processed). However, in practice, psychologists seldom can see into a young child's mind well enough to make that distinction. The outward effects that can be observed are similar in both instances: The child is not learning despite sensory integrity and adequate instruction.

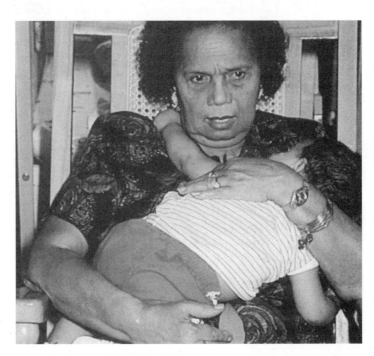

Fear of strangers is normal in very young children.

A. Either 1 or 2:

    (1) Inattention: At least six of the following symptoms of inattention have persisted for at least six months to a degree that is maladaptive and inconsistent with developmental level:

        (a) Often fails to give close attention to details or makes careless mistakes in school-work, work, or other activities.

        (b) Often has difficulty sustaining attention in tasks or play activities.

        (c) Often does not seem to listen to what is being said to him or her.

        (d) Often does not follow through on instructions and fails to finish schoolwork, chores, or duties in the workplace (not due to oppositional behavior or failure to understand instructions).

        (e) Often has difficulties organizing tasks and activities.

        (f) Often avoids or strongly dislikes tasks (such as schoolwork or homework) that require sustained mental effort.

        (g) Often loses things necessary for tasks or activities (e.g., school assignments, pencils, books, tools, or toys).

        (h) Is often easily distracted by extraneous stimuli.

        (i) Often forgetful in daily activities.

    (2) Hyperactivity-Impulsivity: At least six of the following symptoms of hyperactivity-impulsivity have persisted for at least six months to a degree that is maladaptive and inconsistent with developmental level:

    Hyperactivity:

        (a) Often fidgets with hands or feet or squirms in seat.

        (b) Leaves seat in classroom or in other situations in which remaining seated is expected.

        (c) Often runs about or climbs excessively in situations where it is inappropriate (in adolescents or adults, may be limited to subjective feelings of restlessness).

        (d) Often has difficulty playing or engaging in leisure activities quietly.

        (e) Often talks excessively.

        (f) Often acts as if "driven by a motor" and cannot remain still.

    Impulsivity:

        (g) Often blurts out answers to questions before the questions have been completed.

        (h) Often has difficulty waiting in lines or awaiting turn in games or group situations.

        (i) Often interrupts or intrudes on others.

B. Onset no later than seven years of age.

C. Symptoms must be present in two or more situations (e.g., at school, work, and at home).

D. The disturbance causes clinically significant distress or impairment in social, academic, or occupational functioning.

E. Does not occur exclusively during the course of a Pervasive Developmental Disorder, Schizophrenia, or other Psychotic Disorder, and is not better accounted for by a Mood Disorder, Anxiety Disorder, Dissociative Disorder, or a Personality Disorder.

Code based on type:
314.00 Attention-deficit/Hyperactivity Disorder, Predominantly Inattentive Type; if criterion A(1) is met but not criterion A(2) for the past six months.

(continued)

314.01 Attention-deficit/Hyperactivity Disorder, Predominantly Hyperactive-Impulsve Type; if criterion A(2) is met but not criterion A(1) for the past six months.
314.01 Attention-deficit/Hyperactivity Disorder, Combined type; if both criteria A(1) and A(2) are met for the past six months.

Source: American Psychiatric Association. (1994) *Diagnostic and statistical manual of mental disorders* (4th ed.) Washington, DC: Author.

FIGURE 16.1 DSM-IV Criteria for AD/HD

In fact, there is considerable controversy over whether ADHD and ADD are separate disorders and not variations on some other conditions (Bee, 1989; McNellis, 1987; Reid, Maag, & Vasa, 1994). To illustrate, widely reported "symptoms" of attention deficit include actions—blurting out answers without waiting to hear the whole questions, not taking turns in play time, being distracted by sights and sounds—that also could be ascribed to many other causes. One few parents readily accept is their own child-rearing practices, including neglect, as when both parents work at demanding jobs and give the child little attention. To the extent that it is a distinct disorder, no cure for attention deficit has been found.

ADHD in particular has attracted considerable mass-media attention in recent years, including 1994 cover stories in *Time* and *New York* magazines. Despite its current popularity as an explanation for socially unacceptable behavior, experts caution that very little is known about attention deficits. Some evidence suggests that ADHD does in fact run in families; it is also reported to occur much more often among boys than among girls (Reid et al., 1994). These findings suggest that ADHD may be inherited. However, the precise mechanism involved has yet to be identified.

At present, the IDEA includes neither ADHD nor ADD as a separate category under Part B. Infants and toddlers with either diagnosis may be served under Part C if the state recognizes their condition; meanwhile, preschool-age children may be provided with a free, appropriate public education under section 504 of the Rehabilitation Act (see Chapter 6). Figure 16.1 presents the *DSM-IV* criteria for AD/HD.

Aggressive behavior in particular is more common among boys than among girls. Withdrawal, however, may be more common in girls. ECSE workers should not fall into the trap of thinking that children with social or emotional problems are usually boys. In fact, withdrawal can be an indicator of emotional conditions much more severe than is suggested by some aggressive behaviors.

ASSESSMENT

The U.S. Department of Education's regulations for early intervention programs (1993a) defined the assessment role as part of "psychological services" in section 303.12, using this language:

> (i) *Administering psychological and developmental tests and other assessment procedures;*
> (ii) *Interpreting assessment results;*
> (iii) *Obtaining, integrating, and interpreting information about child behavior, and child and family conditions related to learning, mental health, and development.*

There are few standardized tests of social or emotional development appropriate for use with young children. Aydlett (1993), for example, expressed concern about the lack of instruments for assessing infant interactions with parents and professionals. Rather, ECSE workers need to rely on informed clinical opinion. Assessment focuses on the necessarily subjective process of determining whether delays exist or deviations are present. The subjectivity arises because what one professional considers normal behavior is not considered so by another; each brings his social and cultural values to the assessment process. These facts highlight the need for repeated (serial) assessments, performed over time, so that a more complete picture may be obtained.

Del'Homme et al. (1994) recommended use of the *Systematic Screening for Behavior Disorders* (SSDB; Walker & Severson, 1990) instrument. The SSDB, designed to assist in assessment of children who are at risk for social or emotional limitations, allows observers to identify maladaptive behaviors as externalizing or internalizing and to compile estimates of how frequent such behaviors are. They reported that the instrument appears to produce a "conservative measure" of the number of children at risk for behavior or emotional problems.

Another scale, *Child Behavior Checklist* (CBCL; Achenbach, 1992) is recommended by Tynan and Nearing (1994). The scale is an 83-item questionnaire with which parents identify and rate the severity of externalizing and internalizing behaviors of their infant or toddler. Tynan and Nearing suggest that a third instrument, the *Preschool Behavior Questionnaire* (PBQ; Campbell, 1987) be used with three- to five-year-olds. Similar in format to the CBCL, this scale includes items helping to assess preschool-age children with respect to aggressive, hyperactive, and fearful or anxiety-based behaviors.

The first step in assessment of social or emotional behavior must be to ascertain that no organic cause exists for the behavior. A frequent cause of apparent "willful disregard of authority," to illustrate, is a hearing loss; the child literally does not hear the authority figure's requests or commands. Some social or emotional problems have a physical cause and must be treated differently, perhaps with medication. A few children are hyperactive for chemical reasons; most are not, but those who are may need medical treatment.

After organic causes have been ruled out, the focus in assessment of social or emotional development is on degrees of difference. The question is one of whether and to what extent behavior is significantly different from age-appropriate norms. Cultural norms are relevant here. A Hispanic American or African American child may display more cooperative behavior than a white child because of cultural and familial emphasis on group relations. There may be a corresponding reluctance to compete on an individual basis. Similarly, children from low-socioeconomic status (SES) families headed by parents with low education attainment levels may not articulate their feelings as well as may children from middle- and high-SES, well-educated families. This disparity may reflect the greater use in well-educated families of verbalized rationales and elaborated-upon commands as child-management techniques, in contrast to the use of much more directive language in less educated families. Variations of these kinds are well within cultural norms and expectations.

Guidelines helpful in assessing behavior include the indicators appearing in Figure 16.2. Notice the comparative nature of these assessment measures.

The indicators in Figure 16.2 are matters of interpretation. Looking at disruptive behavior, withdrawal, age-inappropriate parallel play, attention-getting behavior, and so on, the assessor is trying to answer the question, "How much is too much?" A preschool teacher with twenty children in her class may regard some acting-out behavior as more than she can handle, given her other responsibilities. That is not the primary issue for a psychologist or other assessment professional, however. The assessor is more concerned with whether a given behavior is so dif-

1. **Persistence.** If an activity persists much longer with one child than it does with most children, concern is warranted. All children fight at times; fighting as a primary means of responding to conflicts with other children, and fighting as a daily occurrence, however, are not normal.

2. **When Displayed.** Behavior that is very normal in response to abnormal circumstances is not normal if it continues over a long period of time and is displayed under normal circumstances. Withdrawal behavior and shyness are very normal when a child returns to an ECSE program after an extended absence due to illness or hospitalization. The same withdrawal patterns appear in a very different light when displayed in more typical situations.

3. **Severity.** Aggressive behavior that is excessive in kind or duration may signal social or emotional problems. While all children will at times hit other children, violent battering of another child is not normal.

4. **Response to Intervention.** When the ECSE worker or parent has used standard procedures to stop a behavior, yet it continues unabated, concern is warranted.

5. **Interference with Own Activities.** One of the most important indicators of social or emotional problems occurs when the child's own learning and play activities are disrupted or halted altogether because of the behavior.

6. **Interference with Others' Activities.** A related indicator is when other children cannot play or engage in a learning activity due to one child's behavior.

FIGURE 16.2 Assessing behavior in young children

ferent from that of other children that intervention is required. A good example is the infant's ability to attend to things and events. Serious deficits in that area will interfere with education and therapy. Modulation of behavior is another example; a young child who moves quickly from laughing to crying will unnerve other children, leading to his social isolation. More attenuated moves over a period of time, in this case from laughing to smiling to sitting quietly to shifting to frowning to crying, are more acceptable to other children.

The next step is to watch the child over a period of time, in different settings. Is behavior triggered by some particular event? Does it occur at home, at school, or both? How frequent is the behavior? This monitoring helps the assessor create a *baseline*, or measure of existing behavior. It also helps the assessor to isolate what the people around the child do immediately before the undesired behavior occurs. Bearing in mind the old saw, "children learn what they live," the assessor watches how parents and ECSE workers themselves behave both before and after instances of undesired behaviors. The emphasis is upon the behavior: What is happening, when, and in response to what antecedents and what consequences?

Observing behavior is important for another reason. Such labels as ADHD may be discarded if the child displays consistent attention to a task—any task, even watching television—so the first step is very careful observation. Watching the child in different settings also helps to differentiate similar conditions, something that is particularly important when the examiner suspects ADHD or a conduct disorder. Diagnosis of social or emotional conditions often involves testing for one possible disorder after another, ruling each out, and then settling on the most likely condition (Goodman & Poillion, 1992; Reid et al., 1994).

Often, the assessor will learn that the child is responding quite normally to abnormal circumstances. The problem frequently is the parents' behavior, and sometimes it is the ECSE

Turning to a trusted care-giver at times of distress is normal. Persistent clinging, however, is not—and signals possible need for treatment.

worker's behavior. These adults may be encouraging inappropriate behavior by attending to it. Some parents, for example, unwittingly trigger acting-out behavior by withholding attention until the behavior forces them to pay attention to the child. At times, ECSE workers will also lavish attention on a misbehaving child. What is happening here is readily explained. The child is responding quite appropriately to the signals he is getting. At other times, though, the assessor will see that both parent and professional are doing what they should be doing. They are attending to good behavior and ignoring bad behavior. Still the misbehaving persists. Now there is a problem, and the focus of the problem is the child. Having ruled out organic and environmental causes for behavior, the assessor is now ready for a formal evaluation. Referral to a clinic specializing in behavior disorders may be necessary. Such referral should not be made until other causal factors have been eliminated (Wolery et al., 1988).

Very helpful diagnostic guidelines, *Diagnostic Classification of Mental Health and Developmental Disorders of Infancy and Early Childhood* (1994), together with *The DC:03 Casebook* (1997), have been issued by Zero to Three, the National Center for Infants, Toddlers and Families, in Washington, D.C. The *Casebook* offers twenty-four case reports illustrating how the classification system may be used. This system is markedly different from earlier ones. It looks for atypical behaviors rather than just for delays in development. Especially of concern is self-regulation, including hyperactivity, underactivity, impulsivity, and other deviations from normal behavior.

Diagnosis of ADHD in particular is challenging for assessors. Suggestions have been made by Barkley, whose 1990 book *Attention Deficit Hyperactivity Disorder: A Handbook for Diagnosis and Treatment* is a comprehensive text on the subject, and by Tynan and Nearing (1994). The most important indicator to look for, these authors agree, is family history: ADHD tends to run in families, probably because it is inherited. Other risk factors known to be associated with ADHD are low birthweight, parental substance abuse (especially maternal use in pregnancy), low parental education attainment levels, low SES, and single-parent status. Of these, the only factor directly associated with ADHD (and not with other conditions such as mental retardation or learning disability) is familial ADHD.

A second indicator is resistance to reinforcers that normally work to control aggressive behavior. Experience in ECSE programs that serve young children with ADHD indicates that even these powerful interventions may fail to alter behavior in children having this condition. However, before concluding that "behavior modification doesn't work," program staff should consult with an expert on applied behavior analysis to ascertain that everything has been done correctly and that nothing else in the extensive repertoire of reinforcers remains to be tried.

Finally, parent reports can be very helpful in differentiating ADHD from other conditions related to social or emotional development. There often is a distinctive flavor to mothers' complaints about behavior of children with ADHD. Pediatric neurologist Bruce Roseman, to illustrate, told reporter Claudia Wallis: "You ask, 'Mrs. Smith, how about the terrible twos?' She'll start to cry, 'You mean the terrible twos, threes, fours, the awful fives, the horrendous sixes, the God-awful eights, the divorced nines, the I-want-to-die tens!'" (Wallis, 1994, p. 47).

INTERVENTION

The IDEA's requirement that multidisciplinary teams carry out both assessment and intervention has important implications for ECSE programs. Perhaps the most central is that *all* young children in ECSE programs be considered both for assessment and for intervention in the domain of social or emotional development. This process can become expensive. The approach dictates that children with communication-related disabilities or delays, as well as children with concerns primarily cognitive or physical in nature, be assessed on social or emotional development as well as in their primary domain of need. It also requires that early intervention or preschool special education and related services to prevent problems or to accelerate development in the social or emotional domain be reviewed for inclusion in the individualized family service plan (IFSP) or individualized education program (IEP).

The U.S. Department of Education's regulations for early intervention programs described the service provision component of "psychological services" in section 303.12 as follows:

> *(iv) Planning and managing a program of psychological services, including psychological counseling for children and parents, family counseling, consultation on child development, parent training, and education programs.*

Especially when a child is displaying delays, deviations, or disabilities in the domain of social or emotional development, parental resistance to psychological counseling may be strong. The adoption of an attitude of nonjudgmental, cooperative searching is central to success in this area. ECSE personnel need to focus on the behavior. Although it may be tempting to seek psychological bases for inappropriate behaviors, the initial attention should instead be on the specific behaviors that are situation-inappropriate. By attending to these rather than to the child or even the parents, ECSE personnel can avoid premature and inappropriate blaming. Even when program staff discover that a child's behavior has emerged as a direct result of inappropriate parental reinforcements, the focus must remain firmly on the behavior itself ("George took Sam's drink at lunch today") rather than on the child ("George upset all of us today") or on the parents ("Can't you teach him to leave other children's things alone?").

Children who display inappropriate behavior should not be labeled—whether "emotionally disturbed," "conduct disordered," "schizophrenic," or "ADHD"—except in rare cases, and even then with great care. Similarly, labels should never be used as excuses. Even children with severe conduct disorders can learn to behave appropriately. Making excuses for the child ("He is, after all, emotionally disturbed") solves nothing. It does not help the child, nor does it reduce future occurrences—indeed it increases them. And it does not deal with the most frequent real reason for misbehavior—that the child does not know what to do, does not have the skills to perform a task, and finds an outlet for his frustration in acting out. Even if the child is hyperactive or aggressive, the hyperactive behaviors and the aggressive behaviors still have to be dealt with and, in time, eliminated.

With respect to ADHD, experts recommend that ECSE workers follow the principles of applied behavior analysis that are discussed in the next section. Also frequently recommended for children with ADHD is use of stimulant medications such as Ritalin, Dexedrine, and Cylert, which have the paradoxical effect in these children of reducing rather than increasing activity levels. Some thirty-five years of experience in using Ritalin with hyperactive children supports its selection (Barkley, 1990; Fiore, Becker, & Nero, 1993). However, many parents and professionals are understandably reluctant to use strong medication with young children. Certainly, behavior measures should be tried before drugs are used.

That holds true for most conditions related to social or emotional development. Most disabilities in this domain do not have well-established organic (physical) causes and therefore should not be treated medically. Drugs such as Ritalin and Dexedrine may also have side effects such as weight loss, insomnia, and increased blood pressure. If medication is used, then, ECSE workers should monitor the child closely and alert a physician if such effects occur.

Thomas and Tidmarsh (1997) urged ECSE workers to create a safe environment for the children and to encourage parents, when appropriate, to seek marital and other counseling services. They offered three case studies to illustrate effective intervention techniques.

Perhaps the single most important intervention ECSE workers can use is to look for positive behavior and attend to it. This is something we all know we should do; but it is also something we very rarely actually do. Parents and professionals alike are routinely astonished when they view videotapes of their own interactions with children, showing how they (unintentionally) regulate children's activities. Appropriate behavior exhibited by the child many, many times during the videotaped session almost never arouses comment by the parent or professional. Inappropriate behavior, by contrast, frequently brings immediate and total attention from the parent or professional. After watching such a videotape, many adults understand why children misbehave.

This illustrates a point made in the Assessment section; often the source of the problems lies not with the child, but rather is in the child's environment. The problems may be our own behaviors. It is urgently important to broaden the focus of inquiry beyond just the child and to examine ourselves and our own behavior as well. People's attention is drawn to sudden, unexpected, and disruptive behavior; that is why many children display it: to get attention. Some researchers have even postulated that disruptive behavior is seven times more likely to get our attention as is appropriate behavior (Strain, Lambert, Kerr, Stagg, & Lenker, 1983).

Applied Behavior Analysis

Well-established procedures that work very well in helping children to develop, maintain, and generalize appropriate behavior are available for use in ECSE programs (Figure 16.3). The principles of applied behavior analysis themselves are readily learned. They are summarized in many texts ECSE professionals have read or can easily secure (i.e., Wolery et al., 1988). Virtually any good text on educational psychology includes an introduction to behavior theory (i.e., Woolfolk, 1990); of course, more thoroughgoing treatments on educational uses of applied behavior analysis are also available (e.g., Jenson, Sloane, & Young, 1988). For a comprehensive review of behavior therapy techniques with children, see Witt, Elliott, and Gresham's thick *Handbook of Behavior Therapy in Education* (1988), which includes material on what kinds of behavior interventions tend to be acceptable to parents, teachers, and children; a review of legal issues involved in applied behavior analysis, including placement changes; and effects of different interventions with children having a variety of severe conditions. The discussion here is limited to highlights, showing how the techniques relate to work in ECSE programs.

The core concept behind applied behavior analysis is so basic as to be banal: If you want to see more of something, attend to it. For example, when a child plays successfully with another child for five successive minutes, the adult should pay attention to the child. This may take the form of walking over to the child, touching his shoulder, and saying something like, "Glad to see you two are getting along so well," or even giving the child a hug. Once the child's behavior becomes routine, or habitual, it may be reinforced by allowing him to engage in a preferred activity. Later, such privileges should be contingent on the child's playing for ten, then twenty, minutes at a stretch.

---

1. **Baseline.** Document behavior in discrete time periods (1-, 5-, 10-minute intervals, and so on) in different settings, with different caregivers and different children. How frequently is unacceptable behavior exhibited? After what antecedent events? Prior to what subsequent events?

2. **Attend to Desired Behavior.** Give the child your attention when he does things you approve. It may be just a glance, a smile, a pat on the back. The key is to attend *immediately,* so that the child connects the behavior to the attention.

3. **Ignore Undesired Behavior.** As difficult as this step is, it is essential that the child *not* receive your attention after unacceptable behavior. Wait until desired behavior reappears, and then give the child your attention.

4. **Attend to Incompatible Behavior.** To decrease unacceptable activities, reinforce alternative actions. Let the child know that these other behaviors are more acceptable options.

5. **Shape Behavior.** If the child cannot do what you want, attend to whatever he *can* do that approximates what you desire. Later, expect more before you grant the child your attention.

6. **Maintain Behavior.** Intermittent, unpredictable reinforcement maintains behavior. Once desired behavior is established, attend to it only on occasion or seemingly at random.

7. **Generalize Behavior.** After acceptable behavior is well-established in the presence of an ECSE staff member, reinforce it when another worker is there. Later, generalize to other settings as well.

FIGURE 16.3 Altering behavior in young children

This example illustrates several key principles of applied behavior analysis. The first and most important is that behavior that is rewarded, or reinforced, increases in frequency. Neither parents nor ECSE professionals can reinforce behavior until they understand what a child considers to be rewarding. You must understand the child. Some children find personal attention from a caregiver or teacher to be rewarding, but some find it distracting, or even annoying. For some children the opportunity to play with other children is reinforcing, while for others the chance to play alone is preferable. Applied behavior analysis teaches that a *reinforcer* is anything that increases the frequency of the behavior it follows. No one knows what will reinforce a given child's behavior until he sees what the child does.

Reinforcers have several characteristics. First, they must follow behavior *immediately*. If they do not come until some time after the desired behavior is exhibited, that behavior may not be reinforced. Second, to establish a new behavior and to make it habitual, reinforcers must follow behavior *consistently*.

shaping is a method of successive approximations in which only ever-more-accurate behaviors are reinforced.

Also illustrated by the example is **shaping**. Applied behavior analysis teaches that behaviors must be within the child's repertoire. The child must be able to do what we expect from him. If the child is unable to do that—for example, to play with another child for a twenty-minute period—we must identify what *is* within the child's behavior repertoire. The first time this behavior is exhibited when we want it, it should be reinforced. Once it appears consistently and regularly, as when a child routinely plays for five minutes without acting out, it is time to shift our attention. Now, only successful play of ten or more minutes will be reinforced. After the child manages that level of interactive play, the time period again is lengthened. This concept of shaping is an extremely powerful one for use with children who have social or emotional behavior problems. It allows us to reinforce *something*, while working steadily toward the ultimate goal.

The example also brings up something known as the Premack principle (Premack, 1959). Stated one way, the Premack principle tells us that a more preferred activity reinforces a less preferred activity. But how does one know which activity is more, or less, preferred? The answer is, by watching the child during unregulated times. What does the child most often do? This helps us to understand the Premack principle as meaning that a more frequent activity will reinforce a less frequent one. In the example, a child was given permission to do something he liked after consistently demonstrating successful play with another child.

Giving such permission is an example of an *intrinsic* reinforcer. Play is something the child already prefers to do. Later, an *extrinsic* reinforcer may be introduced. Extrinsic reinforcers stand for, or represent, intrinsic ones. For example, the child may be told that permission has been granted to do the preferred activity, but later on in the day. The promise stands in place of the activity. A token may accomplish this purpose.

Reinforcers may be positive or negative. In positive reinforcement, something is given or presented to the child. In the example, permission was granted to play, or a token was given. In negative reinforcement, something the child dislikes is taken away or removed. The effect of negative reinforcement may be illustrated by lunchtime or recess time: In both cases, children are released from the regulations imposed during supervised activities. In negative reinforcement, such release is made contingent upon successfully performing a desired behavior. The child is freed from supervision after, say, sitting quietly throughout story time. Because these terms are so often misunderstood, they are probably better called presentation reinforcers and removal reinforcers. The bottom line is the same in both instances: The preceding behavior increases. Both presentation and removal reinforcers, or positive and negative reinforcers, increase desired behavior.

What does an ECSE worker do if he wishes to decrease behavior (that is, make it less frequent)? The best way may be to reinforce an *incompatible behavior*. In this approach, reinforcement is given to an activity that the child cannot do while also displaying the undesired behavior.

Meanwhile, the undesired behavior is ignored. Ignoring misbehavior is very important. It must not be reinforced in any way. Systematically ignoring behavior is called *extinction*. Extinction works; it is a useful technique. However, practicing extinction can try the patience of ECSE workers and parents. To understand why extinction often takes so long to be effective, consider the activity of gambling. People go to Atlantic City, Las Vegas, or other places that support gambling because they expect to be reinforced, that is, to win money. Even in the face of a long string of losses, most people persist in gambling behavior; after a time, they are rewarded with a win. They are thus being *intermittently* reinforced.

Establishing behavior requires that reinforcement occur both immediately and consistently. Different rules apply when one wants to *maintain* a behavior. Fortunately, it is not necessary to continue to reinforce behavior every time it occurs. In fact, better results come from making reinforcement less predictable. Reinforcement schedules may be varied in several ways. One is to reinforce after set periods of time (say, every ten minutes); another is to reinforce after a certain number of responses (say, five correct answers). Perhaps the best method of maintaining an established behavior is to reinforce at random, that is, at unexpected intervals or rates. The child never knows, and cannot figure out, when reinforcement next will occur. This is exactly the situation the gambler experiences: He anticipates reinforcement, but has no way of knowing when it will occur.

Unfortunately, the same principles that govern maintenance of behavior apply when one attempts to extinguish undesired behavior. Such actions persist in the face of well-spaced-out, even random reinforcers. The behavior does not finally extinguish until a period of time without any reinforcement, often a very long time.

Once desired behaviors have been established and maintained, the issue becomes one of *generalization*. A child may exhibit appropriate behavior with one teacher but not with another. Similarly, getting the child to behave appropriately in ECSE programs does little good if the child continues inappropriate behaviors at home. Generalization is an important concern. It should be part of any ECSE worker's plan when modifying a child's behavior. Generalization is best accomplished after a behavior is established and maintained in one setting.

Vaughn, Bos, and Lund (1986) suggested that the first step in generalizing is to vary the reinforcer: Introduce a different reinforcer, perhaps a promise in place of immediate permission to do a preferred activity; or use verbal praise in place of either. Second, vary the cue (prompt) that is expected to trigger the desired behavior. The same response may be used in another situation, for example, when the child is playing with a different child. Third, show the student another response, and reinforce that. This helps the child to develop alternative, but equally acceptable, behaviors. The response may also be changed by reducing the time allowed for completion. Fourth, vary the presenter. The child should learn that the behavior itself will be reinforced, even if the original presenter is not there. And fifth, reinforce the same behavior in a different setting, perhaps at the home during a home visit.

Interaction with other children is a major concern in ECSE. While interaction skills may be taught, at least with respect to a specific situation, getting children with severe disabilities to display those same skills in other settings is often difficult. To illustrate, using prompts and rewards, Cone and his associates taught boys with mental retardation to toss a ball to one another. While the children learned at least parts of the task, they did not perform their

Young children frequently become upset when another child cries.

new skills in any location other than that in which they originally had been taught. Cone's intent had been to give the boys social interaction skills valued by other children (in this case, ball-playing abilities). The researchers found, however, that the skills, once learned, did not transfer to other situations and did not appear to increase the boys' social acceptance by others (Cone, Anderson, Harris, Goff, & Fox, 1988). Lovaas (1987), reporting on his work with children who have autism, expressed a similar worry about generalization: Each behavior had to be taught in each setting in which its display was expected. These generalization problems are especially significant in the area of social behavior, because each situation is different.

Social interaction is, by its very nature, a fluid process requiring rapid adaptation to different people, different topics of conversation, and different roles; for these reasons, it may not lend itself well to traditional applied behavior analysis techniques. *Cognitive behavior modification,* however, because it focuses upon teaching children how to assess and respond to different situations, may prove to be more successful; cognitive behavior modification is described in the next chapter.

Another principle of applied behavior analysis used with children is "time out." In time out, a child is removed from an area in which reinforcement is possible and placed into one in which no reinforcement is possible. The technique should be used with caution, and by trained personnel. Time out works best when an entirely separate area is used, preferably another room. The Variety Preschoolers Workshop has found that such a room should be very softly lit, with approximately the amount of light that remains after sundown. It should be padded and soundproofed to remove any stimulation through sound; and there should be no interesting objects or toys. The idea is to remove any possible source of stimulation or reinforcement.

ECSE workers must bear several things in mind about time out. First, the ground rules must be clearly understood by everyone—parent, child, and ECSE worker alike. Those rules must be objective, they must be few, and they must be explained to the point of being clearly understood in advance. First, when a rule is broken, the ECSE worker should say firmly, "I cannot allow you to do that" and escort the child out. Hard as it may be to do, the ECSE worker should give an absolute minimum of attention to the undesired behavior. Second, time out must be used only as a last resort, after classroom or playroom management techniques have failed to control behavior. Third, it must be used for short periods of time (up to and seldom exceeding five minutes). Fourth, the child must be returned to the playroom or classroom immediately after time out. During the trip back, ECSE workers should give the child prompts, cues, or suggestions on what activities will be approved upon reentry to the classroom or playroom. It is very important, as well, that ECSE workers monitor the child's actions upon return, immediately reinforcing any appropriate behaviors (Bloch, 1993).

Both Part C and Part B contain **stay-put** provisions, prohibiting changes in placement or in patterns of service delivery without prior parental permission. Excessive use of time-out rooms may constitute such a *change in placement*. The issue of what is a placement change was explored in depth in a 1988 Supreme Court decision, *Honig v. Doe*. The case concerned two emotionally disturbed boys who had been expelled from school. The Supreme Court based its decision on the Part B stay-put provision, ruling that a child may be suspended for several days (up to ten). That suspension may trigger review of the appropriateness of the placement, which may then be changed after parental notification and consent. While this review is occurring, the child stays put in the existing educational placement, or in an alternative placement to which the parents concur (Yell, 1989).

stay-put is an important due-process right under Part B of the Individuals with Disabilities Education Act (IDEA). While a dispute is pending, the child with a disability is to continue receiving a free, appropriate public education and is to remain in the current placement.

Other Interventions

Beyond applied behavior analysis, ECSE workers may find that *structuring the environment* to maximize learning opportunities is a good response to social or emotional needs. A structured environment has discrete areas designated for specific activities. This often helps young children with social or emotional conditions, because the setting itself provides clues as to what behavior is expected and what will be tolerated. Such a play area or classroom could also include locations in which children may be observed discreetly yet effectively; when some children may attack or otherwise harm other children, it is essential that childcare workers be able to catch such behavior immediately and respond quickly. A structured environment, too, provides continuity from day to day, giving children who need predictability and structure some scaffolding upon which to hang the changes each day inevitably brings.

ECSE workers may also draw upon the power of *peer-group interactions* to help young children with social or emotional conditions or needs. Young children, including those with behavior needs, often value other children's approval and friendship; these desires for peer acceptance may moderate even some behaviors adult caregivers find hard to control. The ECSE worker's task with small groups is twofold. First, he must give all children in the group effective tactics for responding to unacceptable behavior when it occurs; they must know how to react when threatened physically or verbally. Second, he must suggest to the child demonstrating such behavior what alternative actions may lead to the desired result. Ladd and Mize (1983) suggested that caregivers offer children specific strategies for gaining and keeping other children's support. Often, behavior that is unacceptable results because a child just does not know other ways of gaining peer acceptance. The motivating factor for the child in this case is approval from other children. That is a powerful change agent.

For the same reason, *modeling* is an effective way of teaching acceptable ways of responding to frustration. One of the major arguments given by proponents of integration of children with and without disabilities is that the former will be exposed, every day, to the kinds of behavior that children with no disabilities display. The hope is that they will then display such behavior themselves. The same holds true when children with and without behavior or emotional needs are integrated. Modeling will be discussed further in the next chapter.

Giving the child a sense of security may be most important. When young children know that ECSE workers may disapprove of discrete behaviors but understand that this disappointment is specific to the behavior and not to the child, they may become more open to program staff efforts to change those behaviors. Both the Division for Early Childhood (DEC) and National Association for the Education of Young Children (NAEYC) recommended practices emphasize accepting and supporting children so that they will gain a sense of belonging.

Interagency Coordination

Children with social or emotional disorders and their families are particularly in need of services from a broad range of agencies, including child welfare or child protection agencies, mental health agencies, and education agencies, among others. The coordination problems are severe. Even elementary and secondary schools, which have had twenty years' experience serving children and youth with emotional disturbances, have yet to create smooth-running networks of interagency service coordination (Knitzer, 1988; Friedman, Silver, Duchnowski, Kutash, & Eisen, 1988). Knitzer (1988) reported that more than 250,000 children of all ages are in out-of-home care placements made by child welfare agencies, either at the parents' request or by court order. State custody (including foster care and adoption) commonly follows reports of child abuse or neglect, but it also comes into effect at times when overburdened families find themselves without alternative options to care for a child; making a bad situation worse, many child welfare agencies will not assume financial responsibility for such placements unless a transfer of custody occurs.

WORKING WITH PARENTS

Parents are often sensitive to delays, deviations, and disabilities in the area of social or emotional development. They feel that ECSE workers will blame them for anything that goes wrong; and for this reason they may deny problems, withhold cooperation, and even withdraw the child from the program. The Variety Preschoolers Workshop has shown that ECSE workers can deal with these understandable parental concerns by adopting a nonjudgmental posture. Particularly while the initial evaluation and assessment process is taking place, program staff should take the position that they are interested in the behavior itself, the extent to which it is manifested in different settings, and the degree to which it may be modified with standard interventions. This focus on specific behavior is in contrast to any blame placing. The attention is thus not on a "bad" child but rather on specific behaviors ("Under what circumstances does he cry quickly, with little apparent provocation?").

In working with parents it is also helpful to videotape sessions during which they interact with their children. As mentioned earlier in this chapter, most people (professionals as well as laypeople) truly are not aware just how little attention they give to behavior they like. By videotaping a session and playing it back later, ECSE personnel can help parents literally see what they are doing. The aim, again, is not one of blame, but rather one of discovery. Such taping sessions should be followed by simple instructions in the basics of applied behavior analysis. The core principles are readily understood and in most cases easily applied. The key seems to be personal awareness. When the parent is more conscious of himself as being able to control reinforcements and understands that behaviors that are reinforced appear more frequently, he often becomes quite expert at providing selective attention and dispensing other reinforcers according to a schedule. Following these principles becomes its own reward for parents, as they see improvements in the child's behavior and as their family lives become more enjoyable.

In this context, recognition of cultural norms is important. In general, African American mothers tend to withhold praise and other rewards for appropriate behavior, out of a fear of spoiling the child. They will use punishment more readily and more frequently, as a rule, than will white or Hispanic American mothers (Ford, 1992; Franklin 1992). One consequence of punishment as a means of controlling behavior is that displacement may occur; that is, the child may act out in other ways. ECSE workers might call this phenomenon to the attention of African American parents and offer suggestions on ways to handle it. Asking parents to completely alter their child-rearing practices in order to conform to principles of applied behavior analysis, however, may be going too far. It may be more appropriate to discuss with parents alternative ways of responding to inappropriate behavior, suggesting rather than insisting that they use presentation and removal reinforcement as preferred options to punishment. With Hispanic American parents, ECSE workers must also be sensitive to cultural values. In general, Hispanic American families will look internally, within the family for solutions, rather than to external sources such as ECSE programs. This bias toward self-reliance should be respected. An identical amount and kind of assistance may be rejected by a Hispanic American family and accepted by an African American family.

S UMMARY

Delays or disabilities in the social or emotional development domain are relatively uncommon in the early childhood years. Young children may have social or emotional problems, but these may not appear to be serious until years later. Social or emotional delays or limitations may also emerge as a secondary consequence of a physical, cognitive, or other disability. This is particularly likely where parents or other primary caregivers feel sorry for the child and abandon the usual disciplinary and other child-management procedures; but problems may also occur when young children with disabilities become frustrated, angry, or even depressed due to their difficulties. That is especially common when the physical or other disability is acquired rather than congenital.

EC programs work much more closely with families than do most elementary and secondary schools. The family focus of ECSE programs gives professionals important opportunities to intervene in the family to prevent, ameliorate, or eliminate inappropriate behaviors; elementary or secondary school staff may find it much more difficult to take the same steps, because these programs do not have the same family orientation. ECSE programs have another important advantage. The enabling legislation in both Part C and preschool Part B permits ECSE programs to serve children with delays in social or emotional development. Elementary and secondary programs, by contrast, are limited to serving a much more narrowly constructed category, that of "emotional disturbance." Third, ECSE programs have a mandate to provide multidisciplinary assessment and services in all five domains of development, even when a child has a disability or delay only in one such domain. All young children are entitled to multidisciplinary assessment in each domain and to services, whether early intervention services or preschool related services, in any domain in which assistance appears to be appropriate and to which parents agree. For these three reasons, EC programs have a unique role to play in this domain.

QUESTIONS FOR REFLECTION

1. Why might children with emotional disorders act out more in structured environments than in free-play settings?

2. Distinguish between ADD and ADHD.

3. In your own words, explain the difference between "externalizing" and "internalizing" behaviors.

4. Explain how "the exclusion factor" works in defining emotional disturbance.

5. Why is it important to observe behavior in different settings before making a decision about the label emotional disturbance or about ADHD?

6. How can ECSE workers overcome parental resistance to discussion of emotional problems in children?

7. According to the text, children most often act out because they lack what?

8. Although Ritalin often helps children who have ADHD, the text recommends using something else first. What is that?

9. Explain "shaping" and give an example of how you might use this technique.

10. In your own words, explain the difference between positive and negative reinforcement.

Adaptive Development

The data suggest that the young child should be prepared for kindergarten by incorporating into preschool experiences skills that develop a sense of independence through self-help, understanding, following classroom rules and routines, and working independently. . . . Children's initial success in a school environment can be attributed to the level that they can feed, toilet, comply with routines, understand/initiate conversation, and have a foundational knowledge of who they are. (Johnson, Gallagher, Cook, & Wong, 1995, pp. 326, 325)

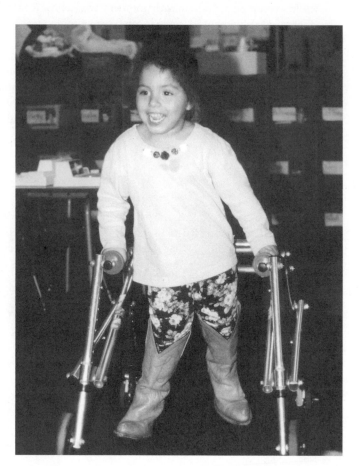

OVERVIEW

The final domain is that of *adaptive development.* Sometimes referred to as "self-help," this domain actually is much broader than that. It relates to a young child's ability to display age-appropriate self-care and other behaviors in such a way as to adapt meaningfully to different circumstances. In adaptive development, the principal concern is with behavior that is both situation-appropriate and personally appropriate.

Young children are expected, before they enter elementary school, to demonstrate a number of behaviors. These include dressing and feeding themselves, exercising safety precautions when crossing streets, playing interactively with other children, observing program regulations, obeying authority figures such as early childhood special education (ECSE) personnel, and using restroom facilities appropriately. Also important is how language is used. Dramatic divergences may occur in children with autism, for example, between language development and how it is expressed. Children with autism may have great difficulty expressing the language they learn, and may for that reason be misunderstood as having no useful language. Although these areas of adaptive development are important, self-help remains a central component of adaptive behavior, one we should not lose sight of as we expand our horizons to incorporate other kinds of behavior.

This chapter considers AIDS, autism, epilepsy, fetal alcohol syndrome, and vulnerable child syndrome (children with mothers who abuse controlled substances). Each affects adaptive development. Because it can be so helpful in teaching adaptive behaviors, the intervention of cognitive behavior modification is described in this chapter. All children referred for testing, not only those with disabilities or delays in adaptive behavior, should be assessed in this domain and should receive early intervention, preschool special education, and related services in the area of adaptive development if appropriate and if approved by parents. The Individuals with Disabilities Education Act (IDEA) calls for multidisciplinary teams in assessment, in development of individualized family service plans (IFSPs), and in delivery of services.

PREVALENCE

No one disability is linked directly to this domain. The 1991–1992 Survey of Income and Program Participation (SIPP) study (Bowe, 1994) estimated the birth-to-five population of children with conditions that Bowe interpreted as being related to adaptive development at

Adaptive development includes learning how to handle distress in other children. Here a boy looks to a caregiver to help a playmate. Such behavior is normal.

43,000, or some 5 percent of all birth-to-five children with any kind of limitation. Bowe included children with epilepsy and other seizure-related disorders and children with autism in the adaptive development category. Categorization of children in that study was difficult, because very little information was available about the children's needs. Notably, children with delays or established conditions affecting other areas of development may also have needs in the area of adaptive development, but no data about such needs were collected in the SIPP study.

It is common for parents to excuse adaptive behavior delays or deviations in children with developmental delays or established conditions in other areas, reasoning that the child has other, much more important concerns. For this reason, parents may have underreported adaptive limitations to SIPP interviewers. It is important that ECSE staff impress upon parents the critical role adaptive behavior plays in academic success in elementary school and in social acceptance by other children, particularly nondisabled children. As the earlier discussion of social behaviors illustrates, adaptive behavior is crucially important to success in integrated settings. Stating it differently, as Allen (1992) did: "The more proficient they become in caring for their personal needs, the less likely it is they will be placed in segregated classes" (p. 219). Spodek, Saracho, and Lee (1984) made the same point: Frequently it is not the academic challenges of integrated programming that cause children to fail in such settings but rather the social and adaptive requirements that they cannot meet.

DEVELOPMENTAL DELAYS

States may express developmental delays in adaptive behavior as age-inappropriate behavior, using twelve-month or percentage delays for milestones like "ties own shoes" or "is toilet trained." Although some states may use measures based on standard deviations (S.D.s), such standards often are inappropriate in this area. The usefulness of S.D. is a direct function of the availability of standardized tests that provide means and S.D. with which to compare individual scores. Few such measures are available in this area of development. The most appropriate indicators are those that look to behavior as it relates to specific situations.

ESTABLISHED CONDITIONS

As suggested earlier, no established condition is unique to the domain of adaptive behavior. Rather, conditions that almost invariably delay development in other domains, as cerebral palsy does in physical and communication development, also may affect adaptive development. This chapter discusses several additional conditions that appear to relate more closely to adaptive than to the other four domains of development.

fetal alcohol syndrome (FAS) results from maternal abuse of alcohol during pregnancy and has three dimensions: facial characteristics, physical growth, and neurological aspects. In fetal alcohol effect (FAE), one or two kinds of symptoms, but not all three, are present.

Fetal Alcohol Syndrome

Fetal alcohol syndrome (FAS) is a complex of developmental effects caused by maternal use of alcohol during pregnancy. Olson (1994) suggested that the syndrome includes three kinds of symptoms: facial abnormalities, growth problems, and neurological impairments (Figure 17.1). Many infants with FAS are premature, with low birthweight. The first set of characteristics is facial, including a small head and underdeveloped eyes that appear "too far

1. Physical, especially facial, features—including short eye slits that make eyes appear to be set far apart, a flat midface, and a thin upper lip.

2. A growth deficiency (height, weight), placing the child in the lowest tenth of age norms.

3. Evidence of central nervous system (CNS) dysfunction, including hyperactivity, seizures, attention deficits, and microcephaly.

—adapted from Olson (1994)

FIGURE 17.1 Fetal alcohol syndrome indicators

apart." The ears may be prominent and unusually low. There often is a thin, long, or smooth upper lip. The second area is permanent growth retardation (stunted growth). The child may be limited in walking, and heart defects are common. Many children with FAS have difficulty sleeping through the night. Finally, neurological conditions may include mental retardation, hyperactivity, and speech impairments. FAS is a major cause of mental retardation in children; there are discernible differences between the brains of infants with and without FAS; infants with FAS have fissures that are notably more smooth than normal. Some children with FAS have seizures.

It is obvious from this discussion that FAS may affect cognitive and physical development. Yet the connection with adaptive development is a strong one. A particular problem of many children with FAS is learning cause and effect; they may need to learn safety rules by rote, for example, and may not understand the reasons behind rules governing social behavior. Kolata (1989) reported severe cause-and-effect deficits among Native Americans who engage in heavy drinking. The implications for teaching adaptive behavior are obvious: Applied behavior analysis or other behavior therapy approaches are necessary because just

Facial abnormalities typical of fetal alcohol syndrome (FAS) include characteristic eyes, ears, and smooth upper lip.

1. Observe the child carefully, in many different situations. She will show you what works for her.

2. Because FAS frequently results from parental substance abuse, ECSE workers should help family members obtain counseling and other help from community resources.

3. Identify and eliminate, where possible, excess stimulation of the child. Both at home and in the program, overstimulation may trigger hyperactivity and attention problems.

4. Use direct instruction to teach the child specific, concrete behaviors that other children may learn in less formal ways. Examples include showing her how to behave in social situations with family members and how to entertain herself when bored.

5. Adopt cognitive behavior modification strategies, including explicit explanations of what is desired and why, so that the child understands when behavior is reinforced or results in punishment.

—adapted from Olson (1994)

FIGURE 17.2 Intervention: FAS

telling the child what to do often does not suffice. In *fetal alcohol effect (FAE)*, children exhibit symptoms in one or two of the three categories. FAE usually has much less severe consequences for the child. See Figure 17.2 for intervention ideas for use with children having FAS or FAE.

Vulnerable Child Syndrome

vulnerable child syndrome (VCS) is an attempt to describe the condition of children exposed prenatally to cocaine, heroin, and other controlled substances, formerly called "crack babies."

Vulnerable child syndrome (VCS) (after Frank, 1990) includes children exposed prenatally to cocaine, heroin, and other controlled substances. Shortly after cocaine came into widespread use in the United States in 1985, neonatal intensive care unit (NICU) intervention specialists and child-care workers noticed effects in infants and toddlers born of cocaine-abusing mothers. The first reports suggested alarming numbers of such children—and a baffling variety of symptoms. (*Newsweek*'s February 12, 1990, issue, for example, focused on "The Crack Children," claiming that 11 percent of all newborns, or 375,000 infants annually, were displaying growth abnormalities, difficulty in concentrating, and a host of birth defects.) In the initial hysteria, the term "crack babies" came into widespread use. However, later research has established that the environmental quality of postnatal life for these infants may contribute much more to their problems than the mother's substance abuse during pregnancy (Frank, 1990; Williams & Howard, 1993). That is because adults addicted to illegal drugs may be so preoccupied with supporting their drug habits that they do not provide the infant with adequate nutrients and a safe, clean home environment, not to mention intellectual and sensory stimulation throughout the day (Chapman & Elliott, 1995).

The cocaine connection is not necessarily only with the mother. A 1991 report in the *Journal of the American Medical Association* suggested that cocaine binds to sperm and therefore may be carried by the sperm to the egg during fertilization (Yazigi, Odem, & Polakoski, 1991). Earlier work had shown neurological damage in children of male cocaine abusers. Neonates (birth to twenty-eight days) prenatally exposed to cocaine and other toxic substances may respond poorly to caregivers, appear irritable and tremulous, and not track human faces as other newborns do (Williams & Howard, 1993). Others show no immediate effects (Griffith, 1990). Little is known about postinfancy effects. However, as they get older, many of these young children test within normal ranges for intelligence, although they demonstrate limitations in ability to concentrate, in interactions with other children, and in adapting to new environments (Chasnoff, 1989a, b; Miller, 1997; Williams & Howard, 1993).

AIDS

AIDS (acquired immune deficiency syndrome) is a condition in which the body's immune system fails. It is widely believed to be caused by the human immunodeficiency virus (HIV).

human immunodeficiency virus (HIV) is the virus associated with, and widely believed to cause, AIDS.

AIDS, or acquired immune deficiency syndrome, is widely accepted by states as an established condition. AIDS is believed to be caused by the **human immunodeficiency virus (HIV)**. Detecting the disease in infants and very young children is problematic. Young children may be carriers of the mother's transferred antibodies, and thus test positive for the virus until thirteen or fifteen months of age, or perhaps as late as eighteen months (Rathlev, 1994). During this period, children may passively carry maternal antibodies, but that does not mean that they themselves are infected.

In fact, only a small minority of infants, toddlers, and preschoolers born to HIV-positive mothers will develop AIDS. A strong majority (two-thirds to three-quarters) are not themselves infected (Rathlev, 1994). Caroline Johnson, of Children's Hospital, in Oakland, California, which has had more experience than have most programs with pediatric AIDS, estimated that about one-third of infants born to HIV-positive mothers are infected (Johnson, 1993). If the mother takes the drug AZT during pregnancy, she can dramatically cut the risk of transmitting the disease to her fetus (Sack, 1994).

Initial symptoms in children include respiratory and other infections, failure to thrive, chronic diarrhea, and delays in linear growth (Johnson, 1993). As of September 1977, 7,000 cases of AIDS in children had been reported to the Atlanta-based Centers for Disease Control and Prevention (CDC); that was 1 percent of the 25,000 cases in Americans of all ages reported to the CDC in the first nine months of 1997.

About one in four HIV-infected infants will develop AIDS before the age of one year; most others will develop symptoms during the second year of life, or shortly thereafter. Far more children are infected with the virus than display symptoms of AIDS. In fact, HIV infection is widely believed to be, or about to become, the single most prevalent developmental disability in children (Johnson, 1993; Rosen & Granger, 1992).

Generalized developmental delays are common in children who have pediatric AIDS. Johnson (1993) reported motor and speech delays or regressions, as well as delay or regression in social smiling. Especially in cases of vertical transmission from mother to child, psychological devastation can occur, as the mother despairs both for herself and for her child. Social stigma adds to their problems. Commonly, the social support system the mother had developed begins to disappear. Lesar and Maldonado (1994) reported that about 20 percent to 40 percent of HIV-positive children require foster home placement or other alternative living arrangements because the mother is preoccupied with her own illness. When the mother becomes unable to continue to care for the child, surrogates, including relatives and friends, assume that responsibility; frequently, these surrogates know little about AIDS. As the child's health continues to deteriorate, surrogates often become depressed and angry.

Survival rates to age fifteen and beyond have been reported. Commented Johnson (1993), "Children with HIV infection no longer are dying after a few short months but rather are living and coping with a chronic illness" (p. 7). She reported attentional deficits, withdrawal, and regression in motor behavior as common developmental effects of the virus on young children. The fact that life expectancy for young children infected with the virus is lengthening, in addition to the growing number of children infected, means that ECSE programs need to prepare themselves to handle substantial numbers of HIV-infected young children. Preventive procedures should be followed as a matter of everyday practice. Lesar and Maldonado (1994) reported that as of early 1994, "There is no documented case of a teacher, day-care provider, or uninfected child contracting HIV from a child who is HIV positive or who has AIDS" (p. 78). This appears largely due to protective measures, which should not be relaxed in light of the absence of reported transmissions.

Perhaps the first step is for ECSE program staff and volunteers to educate themselves about the disease, how it is transmitted, and how it affects not only child development but also the mother-child relationship. Although confidentiality rules prevent disclosure of any given child's HIV status, program administrators need to take steps to protect staff, volunteers, and children themselves. Program staff and volunteers may be instructed to assume that one or more children is infected and to follow such precautions as wearing gloves whenever blood may be present. Alternatively, staff and volunteers may be told that one or more children in a program have tested positive for the virus, without identifying which child(ren). The point is that standard procedures for handling cuts and other instances in which blood is spilled should be followed even if no child in the program is known to have the virus (Rathlev, 1994).

Epilepsy

epilepsy is a physical condition producing irregular electric discharges in the brain. There are actually several types of epilepsy, many caused by head injuries.

Often caused by head injuries, as in traumatic brain injury (Chapter 13), **epilepsy** is a physical condition producing irregular electrical discharges in the brain. There are actually several epilepsies, some much more serious than others. Seizures, whether *tonic-clonic* (formerly grand mal), or more modest types, may cause a child to break the rules of social behavior, for example in story time or quiet time, and may also interfere with learning. For these reasons, epilepsy is discussed in this chapter. The 1991–1992 SIPP found that about 3 percent of under-six children with a disability had epilepsy, or epilepsy-like seizures, as a primary (first) condition. To place the 25,000 prevalence estimate in context, epilepsy is one of the least common of the parent-identified conditions of these children. The Epilepsy Foundation of America estimates that two to two-and-a-half million Americans of all ages have epilepsy.

In an excellent brief discussion of pediatric epilepsy, Brunquell (1994) noted that epilepsy occurs at a rate among infants of one per thousand, much higher than the rates among older people. He explained that a single seizure does not indicate epilepsy. Rather, epilepsy is characterized by recurrent, unprovoked seizures. Each of us has a seizure threshold, Brunquell reported; epilepsy, then, may be understood as a condition in which the threshold is lower than it is with most people. His article goes into considerable detail to explain how different epilepsies are diagnosed and how medication for each is selected. Brunquell estimated that about 30 percent of individuals with epilepsy cannot achieve satisfactory control of seizures through medication. For these people, surgery may be an option. New, far more sophisticated surgical interventions, Brunquell reported, are as helpful for young children as for older individuals.

Epilepsy seizures range from the generalized tonic-clonic seizures in which electrical storms in the brain trigger loss of consciousness to the brief, transient "absence" (formerly petit mal) seizures that look more like blinking or daydreaming and last for seconds. One complex, Lennox-Gastaut syndrome, affects about 20,000 children in the United States. It causes massive, repeated seizures, as many as 100 to 200 per hour and if not treated, usually leads to mental retardation. As should be evident from this range of symptoms, epilepsy is not one condition but rather a variety of disorders. Common causes include blows to the head, as in automobile accidents, and heredity. Frequently, though, no cause can be located.

About 85 percent of seizures can now be controlled with medication. However, many drugs have important side effects. Dilantin can disrupt coordination; Tegretol can produce blurred vision; Depakene can cause hair loss. Other drugs used include Zlonopin, Zarontin, Depakote, Mysoline, and Tranxene. About half of all Americans with epilepsy benefit from medications introduced before 1980, including Dilantin and Tegretol. The more than one million Americans of all ages who could not be helped with those drugs may benefit from the newer Lamotrigine and Gapapentin, which were approved for general use by the Food and Drug Administration in late 1993. A third new drug, Felbamate (Felbatol), appears to help some children with Lennox-Gastaut syndrome, the brutally severe form of epilepsy. However, reports surfaced in August 1994 linking Felbamate to aplastic anemia, for which reason Garten-Wallace, the drug's maker, urged doctors to stop prescribing it until more testing could be done.

Autism

autism is a condition affecting communication, imagination, and socialization. Its most prominent characteristic is an "autistic aloneness" in which children appear to avoid and even to reject social interaction.

About one child in every 2,000 has **autism**, although current diagnostic criteria result in a higher rate, some one or two per 1,000 population, or about the same as Down syndrome (Frith, 1993). Autism or autistic-like behavior was reported at a 2 percent rate in the SIPP study. The SIPP projected 18,000 children under age six with autism or autistic-like conditions.

Following Wing (1981), Frith (1993) described autism as having three dimensions: impairments in communication, imagination, and socialization. Parents most often first notice delays in language and speech, and it is usually for that reason that they bring the child to a pediatrician, and later to a speech and hearing clinic, for assessment. Other speech-related problems, such as muteness and *echolalia* (meaningless repetition), are readily observed, as well. Children of all kinds imitate; there is nothing unusual about a three-year-old occasionally exhibiting echolalic-like speech. Children with autism, however, may be echolalic until age five or six, alarming their parents; the echolalia is not occasional but rather is a common occurrence. Immediate echolalia is a key symptom of autism.

The most prominent characteristic of autism is not speech and language delay, however, but rather an "autistic aloneness" (Frith, 1989, 1993). There is an aversion of the eyes and a lack of responsiveness to others as people. The child does not seem to understand what is said to her, does not look up when called, seems to "look through" people. Children with autism do not use gaze for communication; this seems not to be a matter of avoiding eye contact but rather of not using eye contact as expected. Frith (1993) noted that young children with autism do not engage in "shared attention," as when they point to something of interest so as to engage a caregiver's attention to it. When infants and toddlers point to something only when they want it, Frith (1993) commented, this may be one of the earliest indications of autism.

During the second to the fifth year of life, most children engage in pretend play virtually every day. Children with autism do not, Frith (1993) said: "Autistic children cannot understand pretense and do not pretend when they are playing" (p. 112). They may also seem to be overselective, screening out some cues, attending only to a few isolated cues. In addition, often there is self-injurious behavior. O. Ivar Lovaas, an expert on childhood autism, suspected that the child is attempting to communicate something—perhaps "You haven't fulfilled my needs, you haven't taught me a more appropriate way to interact" (Lovaas, 1989, p. 5).

A frequent class of symptoms is an obsessive desire for sameness, a rigid repetition of certain activities. This rarely occurs in other childhood disabilities. There are very narrow, intense interests and stereotypical movements. These symptoms help us to distinguish autism from emotional disturbance or mental illness. In addition, autism does not feature "hearing voices" or a conviction that the environment holds personal messages; nor does it first develop in adolescence or adulthood. (Those symptoms are characteristic of schizophrenia.)

Autism may be caused by fragile X syndrome, which is also associated with varying degrees of mental retardation (see Chapter 15). Other causes for autism are unknown. The condition is physical, though; among other indicators of that, about one-quarter to one-third of children with autism will develop seizures during adolescence. Additionally, there is a high proportion of perinatal (during pregnancy or birth) brain damage, again not always traceable to an identifiable cause. Electroencephalogram (EEG) patterns are abnormal. Finally, there may be a genetic predisposition in that, at times, both twins will have it. Frith (1993) stated that the likelihood that two members of the same family will have autism is greater than would be expected from chance alone by a factor of 50 to 100.

Whatever the causes, autism is a severe disability. Josh Greenfield (1972) described the kinds of behaviors that many parents find so disturbing:

> *At the age of four, Noah is neither toilet-trained nor does he feed himself. He seldom speaks expressively, rarely employs his less-than-a-dozen-word vocabulary. His attention span in a new toy is a matter of split seconds, television engages him only for an odd moment occasionally, he is never interested in other children for very long. His main activities are lint-catching, thread pulling, blanket-sucking, spontaneous giggling, inexplicable crying, bed-bouncing, eye-squinting, wall-hugging, circle-walking, and incoherent babbling addressed to his finger-flexing right hand.*
>
> *But two years ago, Noah spoke in complete sentences, had a vocabulary of well over 150 words, sang the verses of his favorite songs, identified the objects and animals in his picture books, was all but toilet-trained, and practically ate by himself.* (p. 3–4)

In 1990, Congress added autism as a distinct category qualifying for assistance under Part B. The condition previously had been subsumed, in U.S. Department of Education reports, under "emotional disturbance" or "other health impaired." The 1990 addition of autism as a separate category reflected growing recognition that autism is fundamentally different from social or emotional conditions. For one thing, the symptoms do not disappear; people do not "grow out of it." For another, psychotherapy and other traditional means of dealing with emotional disturbance seldom work with children who are autistic (Lovaas, 1989).

However, young children with autism may have more potential for growth than is generally recognized. Zelaro (1997), using innovative means of assessment, argued that many such children may be born with near-normal levels of intelligence. In his view, some become mentally retarded because of "their disturbed behavior, delayed object use, and extreme expressive language delays" (p. 11). Professionals in ECSE are well-advised to wait for replication by other researchers before accepting Zelaro's ideas. If he proves to be correct, however, ECSE workers will be challenged to recognize, and then to preserve, the intact cognitive abilities of the children.

ASSESSMENT

The domain of adaptive behavior is a broad one, encompassing many kinds of activities and situations. The interest in early childhood is evaluating the extent to which a child performs activities that are both age-appropriate and situation-appropriate. It is necessary to include in this work a recognition of cultural variables, in that behavior culturally valued in one family (i.e., individual competence, competitiveness) may not be valued in a second family, which may instead place emphasis on interpersonal relations, cooperation, and group problem solving. Given these variables, professional judgment or informed clinical opinion is particularly critical in assessing adaptive development.

Children whose disabilities or delays appear to be primarily related to another domain nonetheless should be assessed and helped in the domain of adaptive development. Freund (1994), to illustrate, called adaptive development the single most critical area of intervention for children with fragile X syndrome, an inherited condition that often leads to mental retardation (see Chapter 15). Similarly, children with losses of hearing or vision may be overprotected by parents, who thus prevent them from learning how to behave independently in different situations. Those skills are essential for successful integration in K–12 programs. Young children with severe physical disabilities may need special help in gaining physical access to different parts of the community so that they can learn to get around independently.

Some standardized instruments are available for use in the early childhood years. One of the most commonly used measures of adaptive behavior is the Vineland Adaptive Behavior Scales (Sparrow, Balla, & Cichetti, 1984). This instrument provides a general overview of adaptive behavior, including daily living skills, communication, socialization, and motor skills. It uses a semistructured interview format and may be responded to by a teacher, caregiver, or parent. Results may be expressed as standard scores and as age-equivalent scores. Interrater reliability, internal consistency, and concurrent validity indicate that this is a good instrument for use with young children who have developmental delays or disabilities.

The Brazelton Neonatal Behavioral Assessment Scale (Brazelton, 1984) and the Index of Neurobehavioral Dysfunction (Cole, 1996) have been used with infants suspected of prenatal exposure to alcohol or drugs. The Brazelton instrument in particular is widely used during the first month of life to assess head turning, reflex action, and reaction to stimuli.

The Bayley Scales of Infant Development (second edition) include measures of adaptive development. The original Bayley Scales were widely used for this purpose; the 1993 edition appears to be helpful, as well, but it is too new as yet to be established as a valid and reliable instrument. The Carolina Record of Individual Behavior (Simeonsson et al., 1982) rates a child's interaction with the environment. The clinician observes the child's behavior and rates its appropriateness. Test-retest reliabilities are reported that are well within acceptable ranges. The Battelle Developmental Inventory contains an adaptive behavior subscale as well as personal-social, gross and fine motor, and communication measures.

Both delays and deviations may be noted. Delays occur when behavior is appropriate, but for a younger age period. Parallel play, to illustrate, is appropriate for two-year-olds but not for five-year-olds. Deviations, however, are forms of behavior that are fundamentally different from those displayed by nondisabled children under six. Disinterest in self-dressing, for example, is atypical in young children; even two-year-olds want to at least help dress themselves. Self-stimulation in public is another deviation, as is aimless wandering in the halls during breaks in scheduled activities.

However demanding assessment in the domain of adaptive development may be, the IDEA looks to ECSE programs to assess each eligible child in this domain as in the others. That is crucial. Children whose primary needs lie in another domain nonetheless should also be assessed in the area of adaptive behavior. Program staff should be particularly alert to instances in which primary caregivers, whether parents or other adults, unwittingly retard a young child's development in this domain by overprotecting the child and by not expecting the child to perform self-care and other activities that are part of age-appropriate behavior.

With respect to children with autism, assessment involves looking for indicators of this unusual condition. About 50 percent of children with autism have no functional oral language (Frith, 1989). In fact, many have extreme difficulty with expressive communication of any kind. The literature suggests that as many as 70 percent of all children with autism have mental retardation, about 40 percent in the 40–50 IQ range and another 30 percent in the 50–70 IQ range (Frith, 1989, 1993). However, it has long been noted that the IQ profile is a jagged one, with children scoring high in some areas, low on others; the children are sometimes said to have "splinter skills." In particular, communication-based measures, including reading comprehension, are typically low; by contrast, scores on design tasks such as copying a figure are often high. What that means, however, is not known.

Frith (1993) suggested that the underlying problem in autism may be related to "the ability to think about thoughts or to imagine another individual's state of mind" (p. 112). That is, what many educators call *metacognition,* or the process of examining one's own and others' ways of thinking and learning, appears to go awry in autism. Lack of shared attention and pretend play, Frith indicated, are observable indicators of such a metacognitive deficit. When young children do not seek to engage a caregiver or other child in attending to an interesting object, and when they do not engage in pretend play with toys, assessors should take note. Frith also suggests that the communicative, socialization, and imagination deficits associated with the condition be studied as possible indicators of autism. These include echolalia, nonuse of eye contact as expected, "autistic aloneness," and selective attention only to some elements of sensory input.

Zelaro (1997), insisting that "conventional tests of infant-toddler development confound the measures used to infer mental ability with the child's disability" (p. 1), offered "a new approach" to assessing central information processing capabilities. The methods remain controversial pending additional research. Zelaro himself recognized the likelihood that his findings would need to be replicated before they would lead to changes in early childhood special education practice.

INTERVENTION

Virtually all young children with disabilities, delays, or deviations in behavior can learn at least some adaptive behaviors. Children who are HIV-positive may live for years without significant symptoms; children with AIDS also may have years of productive learning. An important "staff memorandum" prepared by the U.S. Department of Education's Office for Civil Rights (OCR) confirmed that children with AIDS are entitled to a free, appropriate public education, pursuant to section 504 of the Rehabilitation Act (OCR Staff Memorandum, 16 EHLR 712, 1990; Supplement 266, June 1, 1990). That includes training and assistance in functioning independently both at home and in ECSE programs.

Other children with very severe physical disabilities, or severe mental retardation, can learn skills of helping others to help them. Adaptive behavior skills may be taught by early childhood special educators and other ECSE professionals. The contributions an occupational therapist may make should not be overlooked. Occupational therapists teach adaptive behaviors as part of their professional responsibilities. To illustrate, the federal regulations for early intervention (U.S. Department of Education, 1993a) defined occupational therapy in section 303.12(8) as follows:

> [S]ervices to address the functional needs of a child related to adaptive development, adaptive behavior and play, and sensory motor and postural development. These services are designed to improve the child's functional ability to perform tasks in home, school, and community settings. . . .

Effective intervention in the domain of affective development begins, as it does in all domains, with IFSPs and individualized education programs (IEPs). It is imperative that these written plans identify the child's needs and specify precisely what kinds of instruction will be attempted. Goals and objectives must be written that are concrete and measurable. Minchnowicz, McConnell, Peterson, and Odom (1995), examining the IEPs of 163 children participating in ECSE programs in two states, echoed other researchers when they wrote, "The strongest conclusion suggested by this study is that the overall quality of IEP social objectives is poor" (p. 279). In particular, they found, social objectives were "immeasurable as written" (p. 279).

An obviously important capability in childhood is the ability to play games. Raschke, Dedrick, Heston, and Farris (1996) illustrated how one board game, "Candy Land," could be adapted so that young children with moderate and severe disabilities could play it. The goal was written as follows: "Given the Milton Bradley game, Candy Land, 3 to 6 students, and the verbal cue, 'You are to play the game until everyone finishes,' the students will be able to correctly play the game on three consecutive occasions" (p. 29). Objectives then were prepared, twelve in number, identifying subskills required to meet the goal. The teachers watched the children attempting to play the game and in that way identified the problems the game posed for them. Each problem had to be solved. For example, a child's picture was taped to a game piece so that the child would remember which piece was hers. In the end, twenty-two of the twenty-four students Raschke et al. studied, met the goal.

Whether early childhood special educators, occupational therapists, or others do the teaching, some techniques are particularly suited to instruction in adaptive behavior. One is to take full advantage of the opportunity teaching adaptive behaviors offers to introduce and practice other concepts and behaviors. In many instances, adaptive behavior sessions are both frequent and lengthy; a considerable amount of the time children are in ECSE settings is often given over to instruction in adaptive behavior. Language is a good example. When children are learning self-care, self-dressing, and self-eating behaviors, they tend to give their full attention to the task. Such situations offer ECSE workers an ideal opportunity to introduce new words describing the activities being performed, the feelings the child has during those activities, and the implements being used. Conceptual information necessary for development may also be taught; during instruction in self-feeding, for example, children may be taught sequence, color, number, and other things, in addition to food groups.

A technique important to instruction in the adaptive development domain is applied behavior analysis, which was discussed in the previous chapter. Those techniques certainly are applicable in the domain of adaptive behavior as well. However, since the cardinal principles of adaptive behavior are the ability to size up a situation, select appropriate behaviors to match that situation's expectations or demands, and flexibly implement that plan with modifications as the changing situation demands, a variation on applied behavior analysis

cognitive behavior modification stresses the importance of teaching the child ways of thinking about situations, in the belief that learning is a change in the *capacity* to behave in a certain way.

may prove especially helpful. That variation is called **cognitive behavior modification.** The major advantage of cognitive behavior modification is that it can be used to alter not only the child's behavior but also the child's thinking behind that behavior. That can be extremely helpful in the case of impulsive children, children who use aggression as their primary coping mechanism for frustration of all kinds, children with other emotional or behavior disorders, and children with adaptive behavior limitations.

This approach focuses as much on faulty thinking skills as it does on behavior. It includes training for children in self-monitoring, problem solving, and relaxation (Reid, Maag, & Vasa, 1994). Children are offered suggestions both on analytical skills and on specific activities. McEvoy and Odom (1987), for example, helped preschool-age children with behavior disorders to learn more socially acceptable ways of doing things, together with information on how to select from among several interaction strategies.

A great deal of research evidence now supports cognitive behavior modification (Witt, Elliott, & Gresham, 1988; Woolfolk, 1990), but the evidence is more mixed on its effectiveness with children having adaptive and/or emotional or social conditions or delays (Fiore, Becker, & Nero, 1993; Reid et al., 1994). The technique remains promising for such uses because it helps to alter the way a child *thinks* about situations and responds to them. The basic principles of applied behavior analysis outlined in the previous chapter apply as well in cognitive behavior modification. One of those is that behavior that is reinforced increases in frequency. An important assumption of applied behavior analysis generally is that behavior must be demonstrated; one cannot study, and certainly cannot modify, behavior that is never shown. If a child does not display behavior, she cannot be reinforced—and therefore does not learn the desired behavior. Traditional applied behavior analysis has great difficulty with situations in which learning occurs without behavior.

Cognitive behavior modification, however, can readily explain such occurrences. What about instances in which behavior increases—that is, learning occurs—without being reinforced? That is the question Albert Bandura (1977) forced us to consider. What Bandura did was to challenge the whole foundation of applied behavior analysis by showing that behavior need not be demonstrated in order for learning to occur. In a series of studies, Bandura illustrated what he called *social learning.* First, he created some videotapes and films in which children did certain things and were reinforced for doing so. These "models" performed desired behavior. The subjects in Bandura's studies watched the videotape or film. After it was shown, Bandura observed their behavior. They clearly had learned that certain behaviors were desired (would be reinforced).

Over a period of years, Bandura established some rules governing social learning. One is that attention is necessary. A second is that children must have an opportunity to display the desired behavior (e.g., practice it). A third is that these children are being *vicariously* reinforced when they observe models being rewarded. In effect, Bandura said, the children were learning without performing behavior because their thinking processes were being altered. They were learning, and being reinforced, mentally. Vaughn, Ridley, and Bullock (1984) used puppets to model desired behavior to young children. Again, vicarious reinforcement was taking place (the children identified with the puppets, saw them do things and be rewarded for doing them, and learned from that process that certain behaviors would be reinforced).

Modeling is a major component of cognitive behavior modification. Children are asked to attend to behavior that is being modeled. As Lovaas (1989) points out, adults can start this process—they can model desired behavior—but other children need to model it as well for it to be established and maintained. In cognitive behavior modification, another step is

modeling occurs when a child watches a high-status "model" perform positive actions and be reinforced for doing so. The child is vicariously reinforced by watching the model be rewarded.

taken. The adults, and often other children as well, talk through the steps they are taking. They articulate out loud what their thinking processes are—what they are doing, and in what order. Thus, children learn not only what to do but also how to think about it. They are encouraged to duplicate the modeled behavior. At first, particularly with young children, this may be done with *overt* talking out, but later it becomes *covert* talking out, for example talking to oneself silently, as the task is performed.

These techniques may be used to teach many adaptive behaviors. Modeling is particularly important. One benefit of integrating of children with and without disabilities is the ready availability for the former of examples of developmentally appropriate behavior by the latter; children with disabilities, delays, or deviations in behavior are exposed daily to how children with no disabilities do these things (Allen, 1992). That is why Lovaas was so concerned that young children with autism be integrated into regular preschool, kindergarten, and elementary school programs. It is only by being with, observing, and being socialized by children with no disabilities that appropriate behaviors are modeled, learned, and practiced until they become habitual.

Whether the adaptive behaviors at issue have to do with self-care, self-feeding, self-dressing, or self-regulation of desires, instruction may best be accomplished by observing the rules of cognitive behavior modification. The ECSE worker should model the desired behavior. While doing so, she should talk through that behavior—verbalizing what is being done, in what sequence, and why it is being done in that way. The conjunction of physical modeling with verbalized thinking processes helps young children see not only what behavior is acceptable but also how to think about the behavior itself.

If "developmentally appropriate adaptive behavior" means anything, it means doing what is expected in a particular situation. In play, that means assessing a situation before seeking entry into a group. In self-care, it means anticipating needs before they become uncontrollable (as in the need to go to the bathroom). In these and other situations, the child needs to be able to think through and analyze a situation. The next step is to identify alternative behaviors, or options, and to determine which are acceptable in that situation. The child then formulates and carries out a plan of action. While doing so, she notes the reactions of other children and modifies behavior accordingly. All of these are cognitive steps that children need to learn in order to demonstrate acceptable adaptive behavior.

An example of this is given by Trawick-Smith (1992). Observing the play behaviors of "influential" preschoolers, he found that they made more efforts to persuade than did "dominant" (physically stronger) or "low-status" children. They offered reasons for complying with their recommendations. And they tailored their conversational style and content to other children, using different means with different children. Trawick-Smith illustrates the successful behavior of one child (Z) in overcoming objections from another child (K):

> K: *"I'm building a farm here. Let's say this is a farm."*
> Z: *"No, this is a museum where paintings are. See, K?"*
> K: *"No. It's a farm."*
> Z: *"No, 'cause there's not enough room for a whole farm. Let's say it's a museum where farm animals can go. They can go to the museum, okay? See? (Begins placing farm animals in his structure)*
> K: *"Okay."* (Trawick-Smith, 1992, p. 107)

As this example shows, Z gave reasons why K should yield to his plan. Trawick-Smith suggested that persuasiveness is at least in part a function of how often one tries to persuade others. He cited Scarlett (1983) to the effect that children who win acceptance from other children try to "influence or structure how peers behave." Dominant children, by contrast, use physical presence or verbal commands to get their way. Persuasive children use such tactics, but sparingly. Such antagonistic or angry actions or statements are less effective than well-thought-out reasons.

Trawick-Smith raised the issue of whether these negotiating skills can be taught (or learned). He noted that persuasive children use persuasion frequently, thus getting practice in the technique. Trawick-Smith suggested that they become better over time (practice makes perfect). He also endorsed Ladd and Mize's (1983) findings that one can teach children to be more persuasive by presenting them with strategies, giving them opportunities to practice those approaches, and offering feedback to the child on how the strategies appear to have been received by other children. The first step appears particularly important, Trawick-Smith said, because his work suggests that persuasive children use a variety of strategies, choosing from among a repertoire the approach most likely to work in a given situation. "Through modeling, prompting, or direct instruction children might be presented with a range of effective persuasive strategies. . . . Besides teaching initiating behaviors, interventions should promote competence in responding to others' initiatives" (p. 111).

Applied behavior analysis and cognitive behavior modification may be especially helpful with children who have VCS. These children need structured environments and one-on-one direct instruction. Those children with VCS who exhibit extreme sensitivity to sensory input (whether being touched, hearing noises, or other stimulation) may be helped if stimulation is initially reduced. Sensory input is then gradually increased, and the child is given an opportunity to adjust (habituate) to the new level before stimulation again is increased (Williams & Howard, 1993).

Autism

Interventions to help children with autism remain few and far between. *Preschool Education Programs for Children with Autism* (Harris & Handleman, 1993) is a recent text offering concrete suggestions drawn from the experience of ten preschool education service providers. Research-validated approaches, however, remain elusive. Applied behavior analysis work by Lovaas (1987) suggested that rigorous, extended applications of the principles of

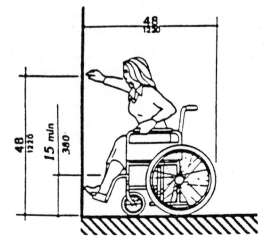

Making sure objects are reachable is a small but important step toward facilitating adaptive behavior for children who have physical disabilities.

Source: U.S. Architectural and Transportation Barriers Compliance Board (1991). Americans with Disabilities Act Accessibility Guidelines. *Federal Register,* 56(144), July 26, p. 35476.

applied behavior analysis might produce spectacular results with very young (eighteen months to five years) children with autism. A few years later, much excitement was created by observational reports (Biklen & Schubert, 1991; Crossley & Remington-Gurney, 1992) suggesting that children with autism could learn more, and communicate better, using "facilitated communication," than anyone had previously believed. Both breakthroughs have become controversial in the light of further experimental work.

Ivar Lovaas at UCLA demonstrated a home-based, one-to-one approach that restructures a child's home environment to make it functional for a child with autism. The project's aims were to demonstrate behavioral interventions useful with young children who have autism. Beginning as early as eighteen months, and continuing as late as five years of age, the Young Autism Project featured as many as forty hours per week of applied behavior analysis intervention. Staff and parents met at a clinic weekly for about two hours; virtually all other work was performed in the home. UCLA graduate students, parents, and even neighbors or relatives worked with the children.

In a 1987 article describing the outcomes of his work, Lovaas reported on nineteen young children who participated in the project for two or more years. Half had entered regular elementary school and tested normal or above normal on IQ tests; most of the others entered special education classes in regular public schools and tested mildly retarded. Comparing the experimental subjects with control-group children who received just ten hours weekly of intervention, Lovaas reported an average IQ gain of 30 points over two years (Lovaas, 1987). He contended that very intensive treatment is essential for progress with young children who have autism: "You're not going to do a lot with less than thirty hours of one-to-one training a week" (Lovaas, 1989, p. 9). He added: "But they didn't start playing with other kids; they didn't become emotionally attached to their parents; they didn't simultaneously learn to put on their pants or learn to go to the toilet" (Lovaas, 1989, p. 4). He further pointed out that the children had learned only after direct instruction in each specific activity; they demonstrated very little generalization from one setting to another or from one task to a similar task. Nonetheless, he insisted that the approach showed that applied behavior analysis could help even children with severe autism. Looking to the next stage, he urged that children with autism not only be integrated into regular classes insofar as possible but be directly taught how to watch what the other children do:

> *Mainstreaming is absolutely essential, because if you get the children hooked on normal peers and developing friendships, they won't regress once you stop treatment; then the development is in the hands of the child's friends. Adults can help a child get started, but it's other children that make a child normal, not adults.* (Lovaas, 1989, p. 2)

Despite his own qualifications about what his project demonstrated, Lovaas's reports elicited much skepticism from other researchers. Schopler, Short, and Mesibov (1989), for example, criticized Lovaas's choice of outcome measures, criteria for subject selection, and other aspects of his experimental design. Lovaas and his colleagues Smith and McEachin (1989) replied, defending their methods. What neither Schopler et al. nor Lovaas et al. noted was another concern with the Los Angeles work: Providing forty hours weekly of intensive intervention at the homes of young children is so difficult, and so costly, that few ECSE programs or university programs not supported by research grants will be able to replicate it.

Even greater skepticism greeted reports a few years later about a process that Rosemary Crossley of the DEAL Communication Centre in Victoria, Australia, dubbed **facilitated communication**, in which children with autism type on personal computers while a care-

facilitated communication is a controversial method in which children with autism type on personal computers while a caregiver or teacher touches them. The touching is the "facilitated" part of the communication.

giver or teacher touches them. Facilitated communication begins with the therapist placing her hands directly over the child's hands. The caregiver initiates the motion of the child's hands to the computer's keyboard and helps the child to isolate one finger for typing. After a key is touched, the facilitator quickly moves the hands back so as to prevent repeat-keying. This is the "facilitation" component of the process.

Facilitated communication is a technique that relies heavily on that personal assistance of a facilitator who touches the child while typing is occurring. Crossley explained that non-speaking children who have autism tend to display difficulty using their hands, in particular pointing effectively. There may be hypotonia (muscle floppiness) or hypertonia (excessive muscle contraction). She and Douglas Biklen of Syracuse University (who brought the technique to the United States) contended that this physical contact is necessary to ensure the child that success is possible or to slow the child down (Biklen & Schubert, 1991; Makarushka, 1991).

The results Crossley reported in Australia, and that Biklen later repeated, were nothing short of astounding. Children with no prior communication history quickly typed messages that gave the lie to almost every assumption about their intellectual capabilities. Child after child typed, some at the very first session with the computer, "I am not retarded." Others provided detailed explanations of their feelings and showed empathy for the feelings of others, including their parents. The typed messages tended to be in correct English. Said Biklen: "What the students are telling us is that they don't want to have autism, and that they want to be able to talk. And these are things that are probably not going to change" (Makarushka, 1991, p. 33).

All of this—the introspection, the communication ability, and the metacognition—violated every precept Frith (1989, 1993) and others had advanced in explaining autism. Skepticism greeted Crossley's and Biklen's reports, especially from researchers who noted that no experimental work had been conducted with the method. Despite growing doubts about their claims, Crossley and Biklen initially declined to subject the technique to controlled, experimental verification.

Others were not so hesitant. At the O.D. Heck Developmental Center in Schenectady, New York, Douglas Wheeler and his colleagues designed and conducted a rigorous test of the

According to Uta Frith, pretend play does not occur among young children with autism.

1. Give children with autism love. These children do need love, even if this does not appear to be true.

2. Offer a structured environment—firm, calm, reassuring. Children with autism need structure.

3. Directly teach children how to read other people's body language, how to make people be friendly.

4. Directly teach metacognitive skills (understanding one's own and others' thought processes).

5. Teach by overteaching, by calling attention to cues the child may have overlooked. Children with autism at times are overselective and attend to only a few cues.

6. Use sign language. Signs force children to watch you.

—adapted from Frith (1989, 1993)

FIGURE 17.3 What works: autism

method (Wheeler, Jacobson, Paglieri, & Schwartz, 1993). Studying twelve individuals with autism and nine facilitators as they typed labels for different pictures, Wheeler et al. found that "the only 'correct' labels were for pictures shown to the facilitators and not shown to the participants" (p. 49). In not even one instance was the picture shown to the person with autism correctly labeled through facilitated communication. The experimenters could come up with no explanation for these results other than that the facilitators were determining what was typed, albeit virtually always without knowing they were doing so. In quick succession, experimental studies showing the same kind of facilitator dominance were reported by Moore, Donovan, Hudson, Dykstra, and Lawrence (1993) and by Smith and Belcher (1993). These findings cast serious doubt on the validity of facilitated communication.

Despite these setbacks, the search for "solutions" goes on. Nickel (1996) discussed parental motivations for pursuing controversial therapies. He suggested that ECSE workers tell parents up front about such approaches and acknowledge frankly their professional skepticism about them. Nickel provided a brief set of questions parents might be asked to review when they are considering nonstandard treatments. These questions help parents to examine their motivations (e.g., are they desperately seeking a "cure"?) and to evaluate claims made about nontraditional interventions (e.g., have truly independent experts recommended this approach for children like our child?).

What are ECSE workers and parents to make of all this? Tellingly, Uta Frith—a renowned authority on autism—discussed neither the work of Crossley and Biklen, nor that of Lovaas, in her mid-1993 *Scientific American* article about autism. Frith did agree with Lovaas (1987) that child-care workers and parents need to teach children who have autism virtually everything. Frith (1989, 1993) recommended that the children be taught how to read body language, so as to understand nonverbal communication. She added in her 1989 book that use of sign language with this population can help, in part because sign language can be understood only if the child makes eye contact with teachers and peers; children with autism tend to have difficulty making and maintaining eye contact. Other than these few points of concurrence, the research evidence has little to offer ECSE workers and parents other than Frith's repeated urges that these children need love, want it, and (even if they are not showing this) respond positively to it.

WORKING WITH PARENTS

As noted earlier, parents sometimes excuse young children with disabilities from performing self-care activities, out of a concern that the child "has so much else to worry about." Other parents may do these things for the child in the mistaken belief that they are helping. Either pattern—excusing or overdoing—harms the child. It also interferes with, and delays success in, ECSE program efforts to teach adaptive behavior. Adaptive behaviors are among the most likely to be the subject of adult attention both at home and in EC programs. Thus, parental and ECSE worker cooperation is essential. ECSE workers should emphasize to parents that it is essential for young children with disabilities to master these self-help and other adaptive behaviors. They are critical to success in integrated settings, for example. And they are as developmentally appropriate as anything can be.

Children in the early childhood years are driven (no other word seems sufficient to describe it) to master self-control skills. From the first attempt to sit, or walk, or run, children in the early childhood years demonstrate persistence that is far beyond the capacity of many of their caregivers; children will practice a new skill for days and weeks on end, persisting in the face of almost certain frustration. To stop the child from doing that because the adult feels frustration is a disservice to the child. This point needs to be made with emphasis, not only to parents but also to any ECSE worker who does things that children are trying to do by themselves.

With children who have severe disabilities adults should limit their assistance to what is necessary and unavoidable. Let us illustrate with a child who has cerebral palsy. Before dressing, this child may need assistance in putting on braces. The adult's role should be as restricted as possible. If the braces are located in another area that the child cannot travel to, the adults may bring the braces to a point within the child's reach; however, a better solution

The "autistic aloneness" characteristic of autism includes nonuse of eye contact for communication purposes. There is an avoidance of direct gaze.

is to establish a permanent place for keeping braces that is readily within the child's reach. If the braces require strapping, the adult may perform that task after the child has placed the braces on her legs; again, however, there are better solutions. Braces that may be attached with Velcro straps offer a solution that even children with severe cerebral palsy can strap.

Other examples are legion. Allen (1989) illustrated appropriate assistance by noting that adults may help children who have difficulty putting on their own coats by placing the coat on a child-size chair; by sitting in the chair and reaching each arm back in sequence, the child can put on the coat. Such assistance—limiting the adult involvement to simply placing the coat on the chair back—is much more suitable than actually putting the coat on the child. Watson (1973) showed how *chaining* could be used to teach children how to take off T-shirts. The child first learns to do the final step of the process (in this case, removing the shirt from the left wrist and hand); once this is learned, the preceding step is added. Continuing backward, the child eventually demonstrates the entire process. Watson showed how the technique could be used for entire dressing patterns. At first, the adult completely dresses the child except for her shoes; she must put on her shoes to be reinforced. Later, after that is learned, the child must put on both socks and shoes; later, of course, pants, shirts, and other items of clothing are added.

Young children are powerfully driven to perform self-care and many other adaptive activities for good reasons. Being able to perform these activities is one of the child's first demonstrations of independence from caregivers. That move toward independence is itself developmentally important. Parent and professional alike are well advised to think through how minimal their support might be, what kinds of assistive technology devices and services might be useful, and what kinds of behavior techniques might accelerate the child's learning. Those kinds of planning activities are far more helpful to a child with a disability, delay, or deviation in behavior than is direct assistance in performing adaptive behaviors.

The challenge for parents of children with autism is sobering by any measure. Lovaas (1987) and Kozloff and his associates (1988) cautioned that parenting with young children who are autistic is a demanding, full-time job. Kozloff et al. (1988), reviewing almost twenty years of their efforts to train parents of children with autism, concluded that it not only can be done but that it is an essential element of an overall approach to helping children with autism. Parents reported real progress in their children's behavior as a result of the applied behavior analysis techniques they used. These changes, in turn, renewed parental enthusiasm for the interventions. Other experts, however, echoed Lovaas (1987) in pointing to significant problems in achieving generalization of training with children with autism. Progress made at home does not seem to translate to similar progress in other settings, nor do advances in school transfer to the home (Schriebman, 1988).

SUMMARY

Delays in adaptive development are characteristic of children with mental retardation and emotional disturbance and indeed are central to the definitions of those terms. The availability of a fifth domain, that of adaptive development, allows ECSE programs to serve young children who are neither mentally retarded nor emotionally disturbed but who for other reasons, perhaps because of parental neglect or poor child-management techniques, have yet to acquire the kinds of adaptive behaviors necessary for formal schooling.

This chapter discussed a number of conditions often associated with delays in adaptive development. AIDS is one; young children who are HIV-infected or who have developed the symptoms of AIDS often display delays or even regressions in adaptive behavior. The neurological impairments common to children with FAS similarly lead to difficulties in adaptive development. To the extent that such children's primary caregivers abuse alcohol, the home environment may be one of little appropriate stimulation, leading to delays in adaptive development. Similarly, while questions persist as to what permanent effects, if any, VCS produces, there is little doubt that drug addiction in primary caregivers dramatically reduces the attention many give to adaptive development in their children. Seizures resulting from epilepsy interfere with a child's ability to attend to program activities; those seizures may also disrupt the attention of other children to program tasks.

As an intervention technique, cognitive behavior modification combines direct instruction with well-established techniques of promoting desired behaviors. The method is particularly well suited to adaptive development because of the demands of this domain: Children must assess each new situation, weigh alternative behaviors, determine which is most situation-appropriate, implement that approach, and react to how it is received by others. The flexibility all of these tasks require is best taught by helping children to talk through behavioral alternatives and to explain or justify their behaviors as appropriate. Even though he achieved success in Los Angeles with many young children who have autism, Lovaas (1987, 1989) recognized that replications in other programs will be limited, both because the required early childhood intervention is so extreme (more than forty hours weekly) and because even with this intensive treatment, many children are not ready for integration when they enter school.

The domain of adaptive development is vital not only to children displaying delays or deviations in behaviors related to this domain but to all young children. Experience with applying what Salisbury and Vincent (1990) called the "criterion of the next environment" teaches ECSE workers to emphasize the acquisition during the preschool years of the kinds of adaptive behaviors necessary for success in K–12 programs. Often, the extent to which children with disabilities are able to integrate successfully in regular classrooms is a direct function of the degree to which they have mastered the demands of adaptive development. That is, their ability to care for themselves and to respond appropriately to new and challenging situations is crucial to successful integration in kindergarten and in elementary school.

Questions for Reflection

1. In your own words, what is "adaptive development"?

2. What are the three kinds of indicators of FAS?

3. How might problems in learning cause-and-effect manifest themselves in young children?

4. How do alcohol and illegal drugs, when used by a mother during pregnancy, differentially affect young children?

5. Explain why it would be wrong to assume that children of an AIDS-infected mother are also infected.

6. Give an example of "echolalia."

7. Explain why autism is not an emotional disturbance.

8. Differentiate cognitive behavior modification from applied behavior analysis.

9. How could you use modeling to change a child's behavior?

10. What practical realities might hinder an ECSE program from adopting Lovaas's approach to autism in young children?

Early childhood special education (ECSE) is a fast-growing field, alive with excitement and controversy. Chapter 18 surveys some pressing concerns of ECSE workers, including program issues (inclusion, excellence, categories, and labels), ethics (prenatal screening and other services, alcohol and drug abuse by parents, testing, and privacy), and costs (the high cost of comprehensive programs, cost-effectiveness). How ECSE as a field resolves these questions will tell a great deal about the field and its future, especially given the growing pressure from all levels of government—federal, state, and local—to contain program costs. Will it be possible to maintain and to improve service quality despite such pressure?

As a still-growing field, ECSE also faces a mounting volume of data. A quick glance at the References section of this book will illustrate this; most references are from 1992 or later, yet many hundreds of articles, books, and other sources are included. In fact, a few thousand such publications were reviewed while this text was being written. The ever-increasing number of studies, journal articles, program descriptions, and legislative and judicial decisions threatens at times to become overwhelming.

Assisting the ECSE worker to keep up with this flood of information is a wide variety of organizations specializing in one or another aspect of ECSE or some related field. A growing number of books synthesize state-of-the-art knowledge in different aspects of the field, further helping professionals and paraprofessionals to keep up with developments. And a mushrooming number of self-help and advocacy organizations have emerged over the past fifteen years to offer much-needed resources for professionals, paraprofessionals, parents, and others interested in ECSE-related issues. Some of these are described in the Resources section at the end of this book.

The reader should recognize that this Resources section could easily have been double or even triple the size it is. To illustrate, *Exceptional Parent* magazine annually publishes a list of statewide organizations specializing in technology for people with disabilities; rather than reprint the more than fifty listings, the Resources section alerts the reader to the magazine's yearly compilation. Another example: the Technical Assistance for Parents Program (TAPP) includes seven centers; the Resources section notes just two of these but at the same time tells the reader how to contact the others.

The reader also must bear in mind that addresses of organizations change—frequently. In the event that an envelope of yours is returned, stamped "forwarding order expired" by the U.S. Postal Service, you will probably be able to find the new address by contacting one of the related resources listed.

Especially helpful are NEC*TAS, a federally funded resource center in North Carolina, and the National Information Center for Children and Youth with Disabilities in Washington, D.C. Both these organizations maintain up-to-date databases of organizations, including telephone and, often, fax numbers as well.

Issues in Early Childhood Special Education

The question of how much we try to fix up and how much we allow to let be is part of a greater, ancient dispute about rearing children. And, because it engages questions of serious social and personal values, it is as intractable as it is fundamental. (Goodman, 1992, p. 5)

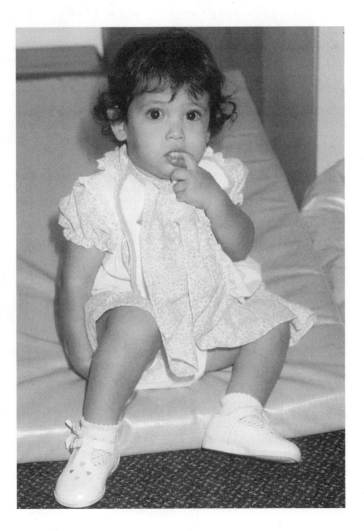

OVERVIEW

Issues are questions on which equally well-informed individuals have honest divergences of opinion. In early childhood special education (ECSE), there are many such questions. This chapter considers ethical issues such as whether the Individuals with Disabilities Education Act's (IDEA) entitlement of services for very young children should be extended downward from birth to some period prior to birth. With the increasing survival rates of premature infants, questions are arising about what kinds of services are appropriate or reasonable when such infants have very severe, life-threatening conditions. Also considered is a family's right to refuse even the most initial services such as testing and referral. This right is ensured under Part C, yet some advocates are concerned that it may have the effect of depressing demand for services. When disability is caused by parental (usually maternal) abuse of alcohol or drugs, particularly difficult ethical questions arise. With large numbers of such children being served in ECSE programs today, and with more and more being added every year, these considerations are important for us to address.

Genetic engineering and prenatal identification of disability in the fetus, together with the Human Genome Project, raise important ethical issues. Today, prenatal identification of disability in the fetus leaves the mother with a difficult, all-or-none choice of aborting the fetus or continuing with the pregnancy. Within a few years, however, it is likely that she will have a third choice—authorizing gene therapy and other medical interventions to alleviate, or even eliminate the disability.

Programmatic issues also are lively in ECSE. One discussed throughout this book is inclusion; it remains an issue of powerful emotional appeal despite the fact the federal statute does not explicitly authorize such cookie-cutter approaches. Parental concerns about labeling or categorizing children, which may cause them to decline early intervention services, may also lead them to resist referral from Part C programs to preschool Part B programs. Again, these considerations may limit the kinds and amount of services children receive to meet their unique needs. Finally, costs are a continuing concern in ECSE.

ETHICAL ISSUES

Members of ECSE multidisciplinary teams, including psychologists, social workers, physicians, nurses, early childhood educators, and other professionals, frequently are called upon to provide informed opinions on difficult ethical questions. The likelihood is that as science and technology advance, the number of such questions will increase rather than decrease. Although ethical dilemmas seldom have ready solutions, information is available to assist ECSE workers in thinking about such issues and in advising fellow professionals and family members.

Prenatal Services?

Recent advances in genetics and medicine suggest that services to families before a child is born may be both effective and cost-effective, especially in cases where intervention prior to birth may be in the best interests of both family and child. Today's fetal tests can help to identify more than two hundred disabling conditions in early pregnancy. Women today sometimes consider themselves to be "temporarily pregnant" until they learn about the genetic makeup of the fetus they are carrying, not only its sex but increasingly the likelihood that birth may bring with it mental or physical disabilities. Because fairly simple tests performed during pregnancy can identify possible disabilities, many women request such tests (Bartels, LeRoy, & Caplan, 1992; Langlors, 1992). These tests may be especially important for high-risk women, who tend to underutilize prenatal services and who are also more likely to give birth to children with disabilities (Arcia & Gallagher, 1993; Arcia, Keyes, Gallagher, & Herrick, 1993). Prenatal services may encourage these women to seek appropriate care, earlier, for their infants.

Whatever their benefits, prebirth services are not authorized under the IDEA. Justification for using IDEA monies to perform prebirth testing on, for example, HIV, can be questioned on the grounds that the clear majority of such instances involve a fetus that has no disability. The IDEA authorizes services for children from birth, or from initial diagnosis of a disability or identification of a delay. Eligibility under Part C is limited to instances in which infants or toddlers have disabilities or documented delays. In addition, a positive test for HIV means that the mother has HIV, but not necessarily that the infant does. Most infants born to HIV-positive mothers are not HIV-positive. In effect, then, the HIV testing now being done in some forty-four states identifies HIV-positive status in new mothers rather than in infants (Sack, 1994; Johnson, 1993). In instances other than HIV, prenatal tests cannot yet ascertain with certainty that a fetus has a disabling condition, nor can they predict how severe that condition might be (Bartels et al., 1992; Hubbard & Wald, 1993). Accordingly, providing IDEA-funded prenatal services might result in public funds being expended on children and their families when no disability or delay is present and none will occur.

Fetal tests include (1) early amniocentesis, which may be performed during the first two weeks of pregnancy; (2) **chorionic villus sampling (CVS)**, which may be done at nine to eleven weeks; (3) a blood test for **alpha-fetoprotein (AFP)**, a protein produced by the fetus, which may be performed at sixteen to eighteen weeks; (4) **amniocentesis**, which may be done at about the same time (fifteen to eighteen weeks); and (5) ultrasound, currently performed on more than half of all pregnant women, once at eighteen to twenty-two weeks and again at thirty-one to thirty-three weeks. Early amniocentesis, CVS, ultrasound, and the AFP test all may be done during the first trimester, when abortion is safest. If disability is discovered, women electing to continue the pregnancy may receive early counseling, which may greatly assist them in preparing to raise a child with a disability. Although the AFP test is widely recommended for all pregnant women, these and other tests remain voluntary on the part of the woman. They usually cannot provide certainty that the fetus would be born with a disability, and they can virtually never predict the severity of any such disability. In **genetic counseling**, the woman is told that the fetus may have a disability (usually, she is given a percentage chance, such as 20 percent or 50 percent) and that no one knows how severe the condition, if indeed it exists, will be. Mental retardation, for example, ranges from mild to profound, yet none of these tests can specify which of these very different levels is probable or even possible (Bartels et al., 1992; Langlors, 1992; Hubbard & Wald, 1993; Waldholz, 1989).

The AFP test may suggest problems with the brain or spinal cord (very high levels of AFP) or Down syndrome (very low levels). Early amniocentesis and regular amniocentesis involve inserting a long needle through the abdomen and into the uterus, removing amniotic fluid, and then analyzing chromosomes from fetal cells. The procedures may suggest Down syndrome, Tay-Sachs disease, cystic fibrosis, sickle cell anemia, and many other conditions. CVS involves collecting placental cells by inserting a catheter through the cervix or

chorionic villus sampling (CVS) is a fetal test involving collection of placental cells by inserting a catheter through the cervix or the abdomen. It provides the same information as amniocentesis does.

alpha-fetoprotein test (AFP) is a blood test performed during pregnancy. If low levels of the protein are found, this suggests that the fetus may have Down syndrome.

amniocentesis is the oldest fetal test and is performed during the second trimester of pregnancy. A newer version, sometimes called "early amnio," can be used within the first weeks of pregnancy.

genetic counseling is nondirective counseling and provision of information, often to prospective parents, about genetics and the likelihood that a fetus has certain characteristics.

the abdomen. This test provides the same information as do early amniocentesis and regular amniocentesis, but there is some evidence that it may increase the risk of limb deformities in the fetus, especially if done prior to the ninth week. Sonograms (ultrasound) are noninvasive, quick, and have few if any side effects. They can detect many birth defects, including spina bifida; Down syndrome; and severe brain, heart, lung, and kidney problems. One advantage of ultrasound is that costs are much lower than with other methods ($200 or so, versus $900 to $1000) (Ewigman, Crane, Frigoletto, LeFevre, Bain, McNellis, & the RADIUS Study Group, 1993).

Some critics contend that the availability of such fetal tests encourages abortion. Actually, the tests remain entirely voluntary on the part of the women. In addition, many women continue with pregnancy even when presented with evidence that the fetus may have a disability. A 1993 study of 15,000 low-risk pregnant women found that those who received ultrasound scans prior to twenty-four weeks' gestation did not elect abortion more often than did other pregnant women (Allen, Donohue, & Dusman, 1993).

Genetic Engineering

Ashi DeSilva and Cindy Cutshall, two preteens who live near Cleveland, Ohio, are two of the first children to benefit from gene therapy. Cindy and Ashi were born with a defective gene that could not tell their bodies to make a critical enzyme. Without that substance, T-cells died off, crippling the disease-fighting immune system and leaving them vulnerable to potentially fatal infections. The condition, which is very rare, is called ADA deficiency, the lack of an enzyme called adenosine deminase. It has long been known to result from a very specific biological problem, one that researchers thought they could resolve. (So many researchers worked on the problem that one wag said there were more researchers in ADA than patients.)

Ashi spent her entire first year of life fighting off colds; she was constantly on antibiotics. At two, she was too weak to walk across the living room. Shortly thereafter, the family learned that she had ADA deficiency. On September 12, 1990, just after her fourth birthday, she received the ADA gene at the National Institutes of Health (NIH), in Bethesda, Maryland. Some blood was removed so that her remaining T-cells could be injected with the ADA gene that makes the missing enzyme. The treated cells were then infused into her veins. This happened in seven separate treatments over about a year. Today, Ashi has fully recovered.

Cindy got pneumonia about every other month. At one point, she was unable to exercise even for five minutes. Using PEG-ADA, an experimental drug, helped, but not enough. In January 1991 she, too, received the ADA gene at NIH. Now she plays baseball for hours at a time, and rarely gets infections.

Similar interventions may soon help children with muscular dystrophy (MD). Writing in the journal *Nature,* geneticist Jeffrey Chamberlain of the University of Michigan and his colleagues described placing dystrophin-making genes into mice embryos (Cox, Cole, Matsumura, Phelps, Hauschka, Campbell, Faulkner, & Chamberlain, 1993). Dystrophin is the protein that is missing in individuals who have Duchenne MD. The mice, which would otherwise have been born with MD, escaped the disease. The researchers are now studying use of disarmed versions of the adenovirus, ordinarily a cause of the common cold, as a potential carrier for the engineered gene in humans. Some human studies already have begun (Baskin, 1991; Pekkanen, 1991).

genetic engineering, also called gene therapy, is a process in which interventions are effected to eliminate or at least alleviate a condition. Prior to gene therapy, a pregnant woman had only two choices in responding to fetal test results: Proceed to term, or abort the fetus. Genetic engineering gives her a third option: to "fix" the fetus.

A woman has two choices if test results suggest that the fetus may be born with a disability: to abort, or to continue to term. A third possible option, **genetic engineering** or gene therapy, in which interventions are effected to eliminate or at least alleviate the condition, is just now emerging.

Gene therapy promises to allow doctors to remove faulty genes and replace them with normal genes. If we could do that, should we be doing so, knowing that it would surely lead, for people with enough money to afford it, to designer babies (Cowley, 1990)? That is, once the method becomes available, what is to stop people from designing a fetus precisely to match their desires—for example, with genes for high intelligence, athletic ability, and so on? That question, in turn, leads to others. Should society make genetic engineering available to poor people as well, on the grounds that it not only enhances the quality of life for affected individuals and their families but also may save taxpayers large sums of money? The federal government alone already spends more than $100 billion annually on programs for people with disabilities (for brief and readable synopses of these programs, see *Summary of Existing Legislation Affecting People with Disabilities*, 1992). States spend even more on disability each year. With such an obvious financial interest in preventing and eliminating disability, should government use Medicaid, for example, to fund genetic engineering? A related question is whether individuals with disabilities themselves have a right to genetic engineering, once it becomes feasible (Cowley, 1990; Kolata, 1990).

In an important cautionary note, Harvard University professor emerita of biology Ruth Hubbard and writer Elijah Wald suggested, in *Exploding the Gene Myth* (1993), that the state of the art in both molecular genetics and genetic engineering is very far from the point it will have to reach before we can talk about using genetics to cure disabilities. Hubbard and Wald pointed out that most characteristics in humans, including disabilities, are based not on one or even a few genes but on hundreds, even thousands.

Alcohol and Drugs

About 10 million Americans abuse drugs regularly, of whom some 5.5 million are women. Some 3 million of these women are of childbearing age. Annually, they give birth to about 500,000 children prenatally exposed to drugs. Although some studies have found effects persisting as late as age three or four, the current evidence seems to be that the effects of prenatal exposure to controlled substances may not be as permanent as those from prenatal exposure to alcohol. These findings must be read with caution, however, because programs have as yet little experience with the long-term effects of cocaine.

There is some evidence, as yet inconclusive, that paternal abuse of alcohol and drugs may also affect fetal development. When the father drinks or uses controlled substances in the hours or days prior to conception, it is possible that his sperm may be affected. Sperm may carry—and be damaged by—as many as eighty **teratogens** (harmful substances), including alcohol. The evidence remains far less conclusive, however, than is the evidence on maternal use of the same substances, whether just prior to or after conception.

teratogens are harmful substances, including alcohol and controlled substances, that can cause disabilities or other health impairments.

When children become disabled or have developmental delays due to maternal or paternal abuse of alcohol or drugs, there is a strong temptation to blame the parents. It is important to bear in mind that the blame game does not solve any problems. Rather, efforts should focus on assisting the child to learn and providing support to the family in its efforts to reduce consumption. The parents' right to privacy must also be respected. Perhaps the most significant and lasting effects on children are related to lifestyle. Mothers using controlled substances may neglect nutrition, heat, and cleanliness in the home, focusing instead on getting high. Peripatetic lifestyles, the absence of the father, chronic lack of money, and other similar factors may harm the child more than exposure to the drug itself.

Genetic Discrimination

Prenatal testing raises questions about invasion of privacy and other kinds of discrimination on the basis of genetics. These issues are far broader than HIV, alcohol, and drugs. To illustrate, consider fragile X syndrome, which was discussed in Chapter 15. Should all members of a family be tested if one person develops the symptoms known to be associated with the syndrome? The questions are particularly disturbing with respect to women, who rarely show symptoms of fragile X syndrome but who are carriers. Being a carrier should not affect these women except when they make decisions related to childbearing. One could imagine a future in which these women would be told they must abort all their male children. And what about their medical records? Who has a right to see those records (Freund, 1994)? Paul Billings, an internal medicine specialist at Veterans Administration hospital in Palo Alto, California, raised the spectre of possible discrimination on the basis of test results: "For those who are fragile X positive, it could eliminate their health insurance [and] life insurance." Bioethicist John Fletcher of the University of Virginia countered that testing may help family members: "Fragile X is a disease. If you know what the cause is, it helps explain what happened" (Billings and Fletcher were quoted in Cooke, 1993, p. 7).

Alper, Natowicz, and Ard (1993) defined **genetic discrimination** as follows:

discrimination against an individual or against members of the individual's family solely because of real or perceived differences from the typical ("normal") genetic composition of that individual. Genetic discrimination is a subset of disability discrimination because the individuals who suffer the discrimination are perceived to have a disability. (p. 27)

genetic discrimination is decision making on the basis of an individual's real or perceived genetic characteristics.

They expected such discrimination to increase because of the growing number of predictive tests, because electronic storage and retrieval is continuing to advance in power and utility, and because the growing interconnections of the nation's health care system make it much easier for health care professionals, insurers, employers, and even educators to get genetic data on virtually any American.

According to the U.S. Equal Employment Opportunity Commission (EEOC), the Americans with Disabilities Act (see Chapter 5) forbids genetic discrimination. In addition, about two dozen states bar employers and insurers from using genetic information in discriminatory ways.

Mapping DNA

Molecular genetics is finding more genetic bases for disabilities at an almost breakneck pace. Nearly every week brings another journal article about some new discovery. The federal government's Human Genome Project is a $3 billion, fifteen-year venture to map the entire deoxyribose nucleic acid (DNA) structure in all twenty-three human chromosomes (Langlors, 1992; Watson, 1990). Administered by the National Institutes of Health and the U.S. Department of Energy, the research effort aims to locate all 100,000+ human genes and to identify their functions. Scientists have found a gene, the protein, or a genetic marker for more than 200 disabilities, among them cystic fibrosis, dyslexia, multiple sclerosis (MS), schizophrenia, Huntington's disease, sickle-cell anemia, Down syndrome, Parkinson's disease, and Alzheimer's disease. The twenty-first chromosome, for example, is linked both to Down syndrome and to one form of Alzheimer's disease, the fourth to Huntington's disease and one form of MD. Fragile X syndrome is tied to the X chromosome, as is Duchenne MD (Cox et al., 1993). In many cases, a test for the presence of such genes has been developed and is available for use during pregnancy even within the first few weeks of gestation, and at almost any time thereafter (Baskin, 1991; Pekkanen, 1991; Van Dyke & Lin-Dyken, 1993).

These tests raise a host of difficult questions. Now that geneticists can identify many disabilities in genes, who has a right to see the results of such tests? Does a prospective bride have the right to know that her husband-to-be has genetically caused MS and might someday become unable to work? Does a health insurance carrier have the right to know that an applicant has a predisposition to a serious medical condition? Does a father-to-be have the right to know the genetic test information being used by the mother-to-be in deciding whether or not to continue with the pregnancy (Bartels et al., 1992; Hubbard & Wald, 1993)?

These are ethical questions, not scientific ones. The Human Genome Project recognizes this and allocates 5 percent of its annual budget to support a study of the ethical, legal, and social implications of genetic research (Watson, 1990). In an excellent overview of the ethical questions with which many women and professionals wrestle, Otten (1989) pointed out that most medical ethicists and other professionals pregnant women may consult will adopt a nondirective pose—providing factual information, but leaving the choice to the woman. As Otten illustrated with several telling examples, the more genetic information women secure, the more difficult their choices seem to become. However, ECSE professionals should continue to limit themselves to nondirective counseling, because family decisions properly revolve around personal and religious values. Team members may explain what disabilities are and how these affect young children, as well as what can be done to help such children.

People have difficulty dealing with the kinds of information now available. What does it mean, for example, to say that there is a 10 percent chance of a fetus being born with Down syndrome? Is that a low probability, or a high one? Particularly because current techniques cannot predict the severity of a disability, people are left to cope with uncertainty. It may be helpful for prospective parents to meet with professionals, such as ECSE team members, to discuss what a given disability or other health condition might mean, how it would affect the child, and how it would change their family life. Clear, objective explanations can help to alleviate fears and assist prospective parents in making rational, informed decisions.

PROGRAMMATIC ISSUES

What Is an "Appropriate" Medical Intervention?

As more and more premature babies survive the challenging first year of life, difficult ethical questions emerge as to what are "appropriate" or "reasonable" levels of intervention, particularly with respect to medical treatment. According to a study at Johns Hopkins Hospital (Allen et al., 1993), premature babies born at twenty-five weeks' gestation usually survive with few major problems, those born prior to twenty-two weeks seldom survive, and those born at twenty-two to twenty-four weeks frequently survive but with significant health problems. The review of 142 babies born at twenty-two to twenty-five weeks found that only 2 percent of babies born at twenty-three weeks escaped disabilities, compared to 21 percent born at twenty-four weeks and 69 percent born at twenty-five weeks. Medical technology today allows survival even of extremely premature babies, although usually with severe health problems.

With such infants, the question emerges of what is indicated as appropriate medical treatment? That is, what is reasonable intervention? The issues were highlighted in the Baby K case, involving a baby born with anencephaly on October 13, 1992. A prenatal exam early in the pregnancy had shown that the baby was likely to be born with this condition. The mother elected to continue with the pregnancy, however. According to her physicians, the baby was born lacking most brain cells, was unable to hear or see, and felt no pain. Given almost no chance of survival beyond six months, the baby unexpectedly lived for well over a year. At that point, in late 1993, the Virginia hospital caring for her sought assurance from a federal district court that it would not violate any federal laws were it to withhold lifesaving intervention the next time the child required treatment to remain alive. The baby's mother opposed the hospital, insisting that all possible interventions be attempted. The issue was not cost, the hospital said; the mother's insurance remained adequate to cover most expenses. Rather, the hospital's concern was that further intervention most likely would be futile.

The Baby K case raises difficult questions. Helping to frame our decisions in such cases is the Child Abuse Prevention and Treatment Act, as amended by PL 98-457 on October 9, 1984. The district court used this act in ruling for the mother that treatment be continued.

The statute is based upon section 504 of the Rehabilitation Act of 1973, PL 93-112, which bars discrimination in any program or activity receiving or benefiting from federal financial assistance, as the Virginia hospital did. The ADA similarly prohibits discrimination, even for entities that do not receive or benefit from any federal funds. The question becomes: What is discrimination? This issue was tested in the early 1980s, in a case known as Baby Doe: The federal government sued in court to stop a hospital from withholding treatment for an infant with a severe disability, claiming a violation of section 504. The Congress codified its interpretation of how section 504 applies to cases like this in PL 98-457. Part B—Services and Treatments for Disabled Infants—offers a new definition of the phrase child abuse and neglect:

> [T]he term "withholding of medically indicated treatment" means the failure to respond to the infant's life-threatening conditions by providing treatment (including appropriate nutrition, hydration, and medication) which, in the treating physician's or physicians' reasonable medical judgment, will be most likely to be effective in ameliorating or correcting all such conditions, except that the term does not include the failure to provide treatment (other than appropriate nutrition, hydration, or medication) to an infant when, in the treating physician's or physicians' reasonable medical judgment,
> (A) the infant is chronically and irreversibly comatose;
> (B) the provision of such treatment would (i) merely prolong dying, (ii) not be effective in ameliorating or correcting all of the infant's life-threatening conditions, or (iii) otherwise be futile in terms of the survival of the infant; or
> (C) the provision of such treatment would be virtually futile in terms of the survival of the infant and the treatment itself under such circumstances would be inhumane. (section 121[3])

Generally, then, it is discrimination if medically indicated and appropriate care is withheld because the child has a disability. One cannot make quality-of-life decisions based upon some measure of which lives are worth living and which are not. On the other hand, this codification of section 504's application to medical care does make clear that there is no obligation to provide futile care or to prolong life for the sake of prolonging life.

Identification and Referral

Part C of the IDEA expressly grants to families the right to refuse any early intervention services without prejudicing their rights to other services, or to the same services at a later date. As implemented in some states, this includes referral for testing as well as the initial referral for services. Some advocates are concerned that family members do not understand, and are not willing to face, the reality that their child has a disability or a developmental delay. If we do in fact honor the parents' absolute right to deny or defer services, we may harm the child in the interests of protecting the parents' right to make decisions affecting the family. One solution to such problems is for ECSE workers to take the time to counsel, educate, and reassure family members.

Categories and Labels

Part C recognizes the difficulty of labeling young children and specifically allows states to avoid it. Under Part B, states may elect to continue not labeling children until they turn ten years of age. As discussed earlier, labeling has long been a concern. As far back as 1976, for example, mislabeling of children in Head Start programs attracted congressional attention. LaVor and Harvey (1976), for example, cited a Senate committee report on the problems reported when Head Start programs were first required to include children with disabilities (then called handicapped children) in their service populations:

> *Mislabeling of children to meet a congressional mandate is a gross violation of the law and a grave injustice both for those children who are so labeled and those who will outgrow their conditions, but may not outgrow the labels; as well as for those handicapped children who, because the opportunities for enrollment [in Head Start] have been filled, will not be able to benefit from the substantial services that Head Start offers.* (p. 230)

The concerns continue today, largely unabated. Considerable controversy remains over such labels as Attention Deficit Hyperactivity Disorder and learning disability (Goodman & Poillion, 1992; Reid, Maag, & Vasa, 1994). A possible compromise, as suggested in an earlier chapter, is to label the service, not the child; yet this, too, has pitfalls. The issue at present is not so much whether to use labels, but rather in what circumstances to use them. Labels are appropriate for use when required to facilitate clear communication with parents, to report to funding agencies, and in professional writing, as when reporting upon a research study (Goodman, 1992). In other instances, it is best to avoid labels, focusing instead upon individual children and their needs.

Procedural Safeguards

Parents enjoy the right under Part B's section 615 to recover their attorney's fees if they are the prevailing party in federal district court. However, Part C does not contain any such attorneys'-fees provision. The conspicuous absence of the provision in Part C appears due to political considerations: The Congress, in enacting Part C, wanted to avoid imposing seemingly excessive burdens on the states.

Interagency Agreements

The interdisciplinary nature of early intervention services makes it more difficult for states to carry out Part C than, for example, preschool special education services. Part C authorizes a wide range of family and child services, spanning the jurisdictions of many different agencies. Any one early intervention program may need to work with as many as ten, or even more, different state agencies to certify its staff as approved for service delivery under Part C. Client eligibility standards, which typically differ from agency to agency, need to be made consistent enough for each family to qualify for the full range of appropriate services. Funding arrangements must be worked out so that each agency—on the state, county, and local levels—bears its appropriate burden and interagency cooperation becomes feasible.

Personnel requirements for specialists in early intervention may pose another problem. Existing qualifications for, say, speech pathologists may suffice or, if necessary, be modified to create a new subspecialty in speech therapy with infants and toddlers. Coordination between two or even more state agencies may be required before qualifications for licensing or certification in that subspecialty are established.

Although the states have by now about fifteen years' experience in grappling with such issues, interagency coordination remains an important issue in ECSE, particularly because of mounting cost pressures in many states and counties (see Costs section later in chapter).

Inclusion

The IDEA holds forth two preeminent values: individualization and appropriateness. The act's opening statement of purpose in section 601 ensures children a free, appropriate public education. Both special education and early intervention services are to be appropriate, and placements in natural environments or least restrictive environments are authorized only "to the maximum extent appropriate." Similarly, each infant and toddler with a disability is entitled to an individualized plan, as is each three- to five-year-old child with a disability.

These considerations seem to militate against sweeping implementation of inclusion policies. Inclusion advocates argue that children with disabilities are entitled, as a civil right, to services in the mainstream of American society. However, the IDEA subordinates this right to what it regards as a superordinate one: the right to services that meet children's unique needs, that is, are appropriate.

The emotional appeal of inclusion often threatens to overwhelm these legal niceties. The word itself is an inviting one, conjuring up images of democracy, equality, and opportunity. It is quite possible that emotion will prevail, in practice if not in law, unless parents and professionals hold fast to the values that the IDEA celebrates, namely, the belief that the unique needs of individual children supersede any mass-produced, one-size-fits-all solution, even one as instinctively attractive as inclusion. Many early childhood (EC) programs hire workers who have as little as eight to fifteen *hours* of training—far below the "highest standards of the state" that the IDEA sets for ECSE programs. Twenty states allow infant-to-caregiver ratios above the 4-to-1 recommended by the National Association for the Education of Young Children (NAEYC). These are not trivial concerns. They should give pause to inclusion advocates.

This is not to say that ECSE professionals should in any way relax their vigilance against unnecessary segregation of children. Just as mindless inclusion does a disservice to children, so too does needless segregation. An important issue shaping the future of ECSE is how the field will balance integration and service appropriateness. Nowhere is that challenge more evident than with children who are deaf.

Deafness Is Different

Young children who are deaf have needs that are qualitatively different from those of children with most other disabilities. The whole concept of integration, whether one calls it mainstreaming, least restrictive environment, inclusion, or something else, carries a fundamentally different meaning when applied to children who are deaf (Dolnick, 1993). The first and most obvious reason for this is that because such children cannot hear and understand conversational speech through the ear alone, simply placing them in a room alongside children who can hear does nothing to advance interaction. A deaf child placed in a regular nursery or preschool program will likely be ill-served unless teachers, aides, and classmates practice special communication methods throughout the day (Antia, Kreimeyer, & Eldredge, 1994). These researchers found that integration benefits faded once social-support intervention ended.

The second, less obvious reason is that the primary challenge in early intervention and preschool special education for young children who are deaf is to help them acquire language. If they learn English, especially if they master reading, they will be well-positioned for success in K–12 schools. That is particularly true as technology improves in its ability to convert speech to text. In fact, speech recognition technologies promise to revolutionize the lives of people who are deaf, but *only* if they can read, and read well. Similarly, closed captions have opened up television for enjoyment by people who are deaf, and soon will do so even for theatrical movies; again however, their use requires very well developed reading skills. For these reasons, the emphasis in programming for birth-to-five children who are deaf must be on acquisition of the English language.

These considerations bother some ECSE workers, because they appear to call for separate programming for young children who are deaf. But the IDEA's statutory requirements for an appropriate education and for individualized programming mean little unless ECSE staff are flexible enough to recognize that the children's unique needs, not program philosophy, should dictate how services are delivered.

Excellence

Children are guaranteed an appropriate education under Part B and appropriate services under Part C. Should the quality be better than just appropriate? Should children be provided not just with access to services, which is guaranteed today, but with excellence? Will America extend its commitment to quality in education to include young children with disabilities? Former U.S. Department of Education Assistant Secretary Robert R. Davila, then the nation's top special educator, noted that, in his view, the goal was a realistic one but that important questions had to be answered first. "What is a quality education?" asked Davila. "For a child who is seriously emotionally disturbed? For one who is profoundly retarded? Can we agree upon standards for measuring whether a school is giving them an education that is in fact 'excellent'?" (Davila, 1991).

Attention to quality issues has increased recently in the special education literature (Audette & Algozzine, 1992; Bruininks, Thurlow, & Ysseldyke, 1992; Ysseldyke, Thurlow,

& Bruininks, 1992). Much of this new work comes as special educators address ways in which special education may benefit from education reform efforts, including the administration's "Goals 2000" program. More relevant to ECSE is the new focus upon student outcomes and upon applying principles of biofeedback to service programs. In these efforts, outcomes are used to feed back into school programs information that helps teachers and administrators to improve future outcomes. Similar steps may be taken in ECSE using data obtained on how children who have graduated from ECSE programs perform in kindergarten and in elementary grades. Such data may highlight areas in which ECSE programs need to expand or otherwise change services.

Family-Focused versus Family-Centered

Early intervention and preschool special education must, by statute, be family-focused. In recent years, the professional literature has emphasized one side of the picture, what it calls a family-centered approach. So much stress has been placed on valuing and empowering the family that now there is a risk of denigrating the role of the ECSE worker. It is important to recall that the word "family-centered" does not appear in the legislation. In several instances, though, the family is given specific authority over what will be done, how it will be done, and even whether it will be done. These provisions, taken together, make Part C exceptional as one of only a few federal laws that focus on families as decision-making entities. However, while Part C focuses on the family to an extent unprecedented in federal legislation, it does not turn over to the parents all decision-making authority. The legislation's objective, rather, is to foster a partnership between families and ECSE programs (Goodman, 1994).

A family focus challenges professionals and service agencies to change the ways in which they have been working with families. The statute envisions a *partnership* between families and ECSE programs (Goodman, 1994). How to implement this partnership continues to be an issue. One thing literature teaches, however, is that ECSE professionals should not try to turn parents into "teachers at home." But that is precisely what many do. Boyce, White, and Kerr (1993) observed, "[S]ervice providers report that more time is spent instructing parents in intervention procedures than in providing other types of services to parents" (p. 330). A study by Mahoney and O'Sullivan (1990) of early intervention programs for children who are mentally retarded found parent training on professional techniques used by mental retardation specialists to be the intervention approach of choice.

The professional literature correctly calls the attention of ECSE workers to the importance of changing their focus. Many were trained under a different philosophy, one in which the professional was considered the individual who had the expertise, who was authorized by law to make programmatic decisions, and who bore responsibility for carrying out statutory requirements. The family focus, however, calls for these professionals to become reflective practitioners who balance their expert knowledge with a conscious recognition that they do not always understand, or appreciate, the values and concerns of individual families. In a family-focused program, reflection causes the professional to seek to involve parents in an exercise in shared responsibility (Sokoly & Dokecki, 1992). That is, the family is understood as having the privilege, as well as the right, to take part in making those decisions that the family says it wants to help make. This is not what many ECSE workers were taught during their training, however. That is why ECSE leaders now feel it is necessary to place so much emphasis on family involvement.

We must not go to the other extreme, however, and abdicate all professional responsibility in the name of empowering the family (Goodman, 1994). There are many things the family should look to professionals to decide, among them assessment techniques, specific intervention strategies, and other means to family-identified goals. Parents and professionals should jointly discuss and decide upon the objectives to be reached via those means. Ideally, then, the ECSE professional seeks to provide honest, comprehensive information to families so that they have a knowledge base upon which to build. The professional also seeks to understand the family's values and concerns so that he may suggest ways to satisfy those values and resolve those concerns. Such information sharing then becomes a prelude to open discussion of alternatives. If the professional has been open, honest, and forthright, parents will develop a sense of trust in him that facilitates joint decision making. That is the goal of the IDEA—and the challenge for all of us in ECSE.

The Role of Adults with Disabilities

Multidisciplinary team members in ECSE rarely include people who themselves have disabilities. Program administrators desiring to arrange for staff training on the ethics of genetics, on genetic counseling, and on the psychosocial impact of genetic information on families and individuals should incorporate the perspectives of individuals with disabilities. That is because adults with disabilities offer perspectives not otherwise available to members of the team. If we as a society were to decide that aborting fetuses on the basis of genetic information is acceptable, or even desirable, what does that say about our ability as a society to accept those individuals already among us who have these disabilities? Could we maintain the cognitive dissonance of asserting potential disability justifies abortion while simultaneously claiming that people with existing disabilities who live among us are entitled to just as much respect and equal civil rights as others? That would be a difficult balancing act for any of us.

Adults with disabilities who have been active in advocating for implementation and enforcement of the ADA and other disability rights legislation tend to view disability itself as less handicapping than attitudinal, architectural, transportation, housing, and other societal barriers. Adrienne Asch (1993) of Wellsley College, who is blind, offers a view widely held among adults with disabilities when she writes that she views the new research on genetics with concern and apprehension:

> [S]ome of us are convinced of subtle and not-so-subtle bias against disabled people by some geneticists who do the science and by some genetic counselors who translate science to the public seeking information. Our discomfort arises out of the knowledge that when information about life with disability is described at all, it usually is in a description filled with gloom and tragedy and limited opportunities completely at odds with the views of the disability rights movement and of the legislators and professionals whose work supports movement goals. Rather, the whole genetics enterprise is permeated by the medical model of disability—linking every difficulty to the physiological characteristics of the condition and not to any characteristics of the society in which people with the condition live their lives. (pp. 3–4)

William Roth (1993) of the State University of New York at Albany concurs. Disability, such as his cerebral palsy "is not a disaster," he wrote, adding that the environment often matters more than genetics:

> A poor person may live in a house of lead paint, inadequate plumbing, poor temperature control, etc., and may not be able to afford the medical services for children that are the true

triumph of modern medicine. Although we are learning that more disabilities are genetic, environments do matter, often decisively. (p. 25)

Offering such views is but one of many ways in which adults with disabilities could contribute to ECSE programs throughout the nation. Hirsch (1993) suggested that Interagency Coordinating Councils (ICCs), whether on the state or local level, could benefit from adult members who themselves have disabilities. The perspective of these individuals would add much to ICC discussions, she believed, because ECSE personnel persist in regarding children with disabilities as "passive, as object-like, or at least as the kinds of human beings who are incapable of having any insights into their own situation" (p. 33). Hirsch contended that similar attitudes have pervaded special education for decades, and that the products of those attitudes, today's adults with disabilities, are sensitive to such paternalism and able to make others aware of it as well. Adults with disabilities also bring firsthand knowledge of what people with disabilities need to know, and do, in order to live independently in today's society. Such knowledge can inform ECSE programs, Hirsch said, and also help parents gain insights into what kinds of lives their children likely will lead. For these reasons, Hirsch observed, "[d]isability advocates could bring a new perspective to the education of disabled children, a perspective that would be likely to increase disabled students' motivation and help prepare them for adult life" (p. 33).

She was concerned, however, that when adults with disabilities have volunteered their expertise and time, they "have been met with strong resistance in some school districts" (p. 33). Turnbull and Turnbull (1993) concurred with Hirsch, adding that adults with disabilities place much greater emphasis on self-determination and independence than do parents or professionals. Such a perspective is necessary, they wrote, to help overcome the decades-old paternalism that to date has characterized special education at all levels.

However, the views of adults with disabilities on the ethical questions discussed here are not monolithic (Shapiro, 1993). Many disability rights activists have mixed feelings about prenatal services, testing, and genetic engineering. They differ on other matters, as well. The statement is sometimes made that "no one could oppose efforts to cure disabilities." But some people do. There are, for example, many adults who are deaf who oppose research to cure deafness. They believe that such research makes the statement that they are inferior to other people and that they should be "fixed" in order to become as good as others. For this reason, some even talk about wanting to firebomb research labs to stop the research. Others actively opposed the creation in 1988 of the National Institute on Deafness and Other Communication Disorders (NIDOCD), the first new NIH institute in more than a decade, on the same grounds (Commission on Education of the Deaf, 1988; Bowe, 1991b). Such radical views are not shared by all adults with hearing impairments. Certainly, members of the Association of Late Deafened Adults would be unlikely to espouse such sentiments (Bowe, 1991b).

While many adults with disabilities have much to contribute to ICCs and to ECSE programs, it is important not to overestimate what the average adult with a disability knows about federal and state laws on disability, special education, and related programs. A 1993 survey by the polling firm Louis Harris and Associates found that only 29 percent of adults with disabilities knew about even the landmark ADA. The poll was conducted three years following its enactment in 1990 (National Organization on Disability, Harris & Associates, 1993). An earlier study by the same polling firm found that even smaller proportions of adults with disabilities were familiar with what is now the IDEA (then the Education of the Handicapped Act). Harris interpreted these data as suggesting that the undereducation endemic among adults with disabilities, combined with their relative difficulty in gaining access to information (often because of sensory or mental limitations), restricts their ability to learn about such laws (ICD/Harris, 1986).

Perhaps the best way to identify individuals with disabilities who are familiar with the IDEA and other federal and state statutes, and who may also be willing to serve on ICCs or otherwise become involved in ECSE programs, is to contact a local Independent Living Center (ILC). There are about 500 such centers nationwide. Virtually all are community-based, nonprofit organizations that are governed by adults with disabilities; in most, people with disabilities hold policy-making staff positions as well. Many centers are funded through title VII of the Rehabilitation Act, PL 102-569, while others are state-funded. Their principal activities are local advocacy (pressuring municipalities to remove architectural, transportation, and communication barriers, for example), peer counseling (in which experienced counselors, themselves individuals with disabilities, guide adults with disabilities through personal crises), and information and referral (in which centers share resources with callers and visitors, enabling these consumers to identify community programs that provide services they need). The Independent Living Research Utilization project (ILRU, 2323 S. Shepherd, Suite 1000, Houston, TX 77019) offers a regularly updated directory of ILCs. (It also offers a *Guide to Planning Accessible Meetings,* a compendium of practical suggestions on how to make conferences, meetings, and even large conventions accessible to and usable by people with disabilities.)

RESEARCH ISSUES

Inconclusive Research

The most comprehensive and best-controlled research on early intervention and preschool special education to date has been disturbingly inconclusive as Chapter 3 showed. Even when tackling such seemingly incontrovertible statements as the earlier, the better and the more intensive, the better, researchers seem unable to provide the kinds of affirmative answers that practitioners and parents alike anticipated. Evidence that the earlier intervention begins, the more successful it will be remains far from conclusive (Boyce, Smith, Immel, Casto, & Escobar, 1993; Casto & Mastropieri, 1986a). On the seemingly noncontroversial question of whether more intensive treatment produces better results, research again has come up empty-handed (Innocenti & White, 1993; Parette et al., 1991).

Why has experimental research to date been so unable to provide evidence in support of early intervention and preschool special education? McWilliam and Bailey (1993) argued that one reason is the complexity of early intervention. Work with children under six features many goals and objectives—among them social, emotional, intellectual, physical, and other kinds of development, as well as family support; yet the typical experimental research study assesses only one, or at most two, kinds of outcomes. These authors contended that early intervention may indeed produce significant and long-lasting effects but that these may be in areas the researchers did not study.

Qualitative Research

One response to the inconclusiveness of controlled research to date has been an explosion of qualitative research studies. These investigations do not attempt to control extraneous sources of variance but rather report on what the researcher sees happening in a given setting.

While such studies have given us much useful information, it is nonetheless true that qualitative research can mislead practitioners and parents.

Nowhere is this more painfully evident than in the field of facilitated communication with children who have autism. The initial reports (Crossley & Remington-Gurney, 1992; Biklen, 1990; Biklen & Schubert, 1991) excited tremendous interest. Each was a qualitative (nonexperimental) study; the reports presented what the writer saw happening. As word spread, thousands of people learned the techniques of facilitated communication, many of them at Biklen's Syracuse University Facilitated Communication Institute (Crossley, 1993).

Yet when controlled studies were conducted, the initial appeal of facilitated communication began to fade. Perhaps most devastating were the experiments conducted at the O. D. Heck Developmental Center in Schenectady, New York (Wheeler, Jacobson, Paglieri, & Schwartz, 1993). Twelve people living at the center and nine facilitators were tested in a double-blind experiment, in which the facilitators sometimes saw the same pictures as the autistic individuals but sometimes saw different pictures. At other times, only the person with autism was shown a picture or given a topic to discuss; in these cases, the facilitator remained unaware of the information known to the individual with autism. The study showed that when the facilitator had incorrect knowledge, or no knowledge, of the picture or topic, facilitated communication was not on target. In fact, when the individual with autism was shown a different picture than the one given to the facilitator, the facilitated communication almost invariably was about the picture seen only by the facilitator. The evidence from the O. D. Heck study strongly suggested that facilitator influence, albeit usually unconscious on the part of the facilitator, was nonetheless an unavoidable consequence of facilitated communication.

In the months and years following the O. D. Heck study, numerous other reports of controlled experiments on facilitated communication were published (Donnellan, Sabin, & Majure, 1992; Eberlin, McConnachie, Ibel, & Volpe, 1993; Moore, Donovan, & Hudson, 1993; Moore, Donovan, Hudson, Dykstra, & Lawrence, 1993; Smith & Belcher, 1993). These studies reinforced the doubts raised by the O. D. Heck study, finding that evidence of facilitator influence over the content of facilitated communication was all but undeniable.

Although qualitative research in this instance led to very controversial reports, the method remains one that has much to offer ECSE workers. Yet the contributions of controlled, scientific study remain necessary to corroborate reports from observational studies, even if they at first yield inconclusive, or even negative, results.

MONEY ISSUES

Costs

Early intervention services for infants, toddlers, and families can be expensive. Perry (1993) reported that such services average some $5,000 per year per child in some states, with costs ranging from as low as $4,000 for some children with communication delays or disabilities to as high as $15,000 for some children with multiple and severe needs. Costs often are high because programs must not only compensate staff who identify the full range of approved service delivery agencies and complete the often voluminous paperwork needed for referrals, they must also pay full- and part-time professional and paraprofessional services personnel, as well as consultants and contractors who deliver highly specialized therapy or other services. Because many of these professionals work one-on-one with infants and toddlers, costs per child are high. In addition, transportation services may be as expensive for half-day programs as for full-day programs. All this results in a very high cost per child.

Warfield (1995) suggested that home visits appear to be especially helpful with mother-child interactions because they reduce parental stress. However, home visits cost about 2.5 times as much as group services. This introduces the issue of cost-effectiveness, to which we now turn.

Cost-Effectiveness

Research to date has been unable to establish the cost-effectiveness of early intervention and preschool special education. Longitudinal studies far outpacing anything done to date are required to do that. In all likelihood, twenty-year tracking studies will be necessary, because the cost-effectiveness of services ultimately depends on what the recipients of those services do. The major question is whether people with disabilities who receive early intervention and preschool special education will do any better in their post–high school years than do today's young adults with disabilities, most of whom did not benefit from services of the kind now available for children from birth to five.

It is difficult to see how they could do any worse. Today, twice as many adults with disabilities depend on federal and state handouts, notably Supplemental Security Income (SSI) and Medicaid, as support themselves by working. Of the estimated thirteen million adults of working age (sixteen to sixty-four) who have work-related disabilities, about eight million receive some kind of federal subsidy, while just four million work full- or part-time (Bowe, 1993c). In fact, if one were to heed Woodward and Bernstein's motto when reporting Watergate, "follow the money," one would discover that the federal government spends *fifteen times* as much on SSI and Social Security Disability Insurance as it does on early intervention, special education, rehabilitation, civil rights, and related programs designed to help people with disabilities to become more independent. When Medicaid and Medicare are added, which they must be as components of welfare-type subsidies for nonworking persons with disabilities, the imbalance amounts to a staggering forty to one.

In time, ECSE will be looked to as one of the most important means by which federal and state governments may increase independence among Americans with disabilities and decrease their reliance on public support. We will realize the full benefits of that, however, only if ECSE succeeds in resisting short-term cost-cutting pressures in the interests of longer-term paybacks and other compelling public interests.

SUMMARY

The field of ECSE promises to be a lively one in the years ahead. How we resolve the difficult ethical questions that confront us today matters greatly. How we balance concerns about costs against concerns about quality will make a great difference, as well. The likelihood is that both kinds of decisions will become harder, not easier, as the years go by. In ethics, that is because as we learn ever more about the genetic code and how it affects the fetus, our knowledge seems to increase uncertainty, rather than decrease it (Bartels et al., 1992; Kolata, 1992a; Van Dyke & Lin-Dyken, 1993). Cost questions, similarly, become more pressing as ECSE continues to serve larger numbers of children, including more and more children with severe disabilities. The probability is that convincing data on the cost-effectiveness of ECSE will not appear for a number of years, however, making decisions of fund allocation difficult at all levels of government.

Meanwhile, ECSE faces difficult questions about what its goals are, and should be. Does following a family-focused philosophy mean always acceding to the desires of the family, even when the interests of the child are best met in ways the family resists? Are ECSE programs in the business of providing the best possible services, or only those that are good enough? Will ECSE find meaningful roles for adults with disabilities to play, so that the field will benefit from the unique insights of these individuals, as have the fields of rehabilitation and independent living, both of which involve adults with disabilities in all major decisions?

The good news is that on so many fronts—earlier and earlier identification of disability, more and better early intervention techniques and strategies, ever more powerful yet less expensive technologies, and so on—we have made impressive progress. Today, ECSE has much more to offer young children with disabilities or developmental delays, and their families, than was the case just a few years ago. As we confront the challenging issues outlined in this chapter, and as we reflect upon ECSE's rich history, we may find assurance in the profession's impressive record of doing good well. Despite growing cost pressures, inconclusive research, and the stress of operating in a multidisciplinary, interagency environment, ECSE has done its work and done it well. That bodes well for our future, very well indeed.

QUESTIONS FOR REFLECTION

1. What in the IDEA's definition of "infants and toddlers" forbids prebirth services? (If necessary, reread the definition, which appears in Chapter 2.)

2. What factors other than parental drug abuse itself might lead to delays in development among young children?

3. In your own words, define "genetic discrimination."

4. Is there a basis for outlawing genetic discrimination in the Americans with Disabilities Act? (If necessary, reread the description of the ADA in Chapter 5.)

5. What does "nondirective" counseling mean? Think of yourself as a counselor. Could you be 100 percent nondirective?

6. Why is deafness "different" when it comes to approaches such as inclusion?

7. What does the word "appropriate" mean to you? (If necessary, reread the discussion in Chapter 8.) Why would the IDEA have to be changed if we decided that our goal in ECSE is to provide an "excellent" service rather than an "appropriate" one?

8. What kinds of unique contributions to an ECSE program might be made by an adult who himself is a person with a disability?

9. Why does it matter if an ECSE program is "cost-effective"? Should it matter?

10. What is an independent living center? How could one be helpful to an ECSE program?

Resources

A tremendous number of books, journals, agencies, and organizations are available to assist early childhood special education (ECSE) workers and parents. The resources listed and described in this chapter have proven useful to the author; however, no endorsement should be implied. Addresses given were accurate when the book went to press. Phone numbers change too frequently (especially area codes and exchange numbers) to be helpful in a book like this.

The World Wide Web (WWW) has become an increasingly vital tool for people seeking information. The field of early childhood special education certainly is no exception. A vast wealth of material relevant to the topics discussed in this book is available on-line. Much of it is valuable; some of it is worthless. How to tell the difference? A few comments may help the reader.

A good rule of thumb is to begin your search at the Web site of a well-respected national organization that specializes in the topic of interest to you. For example, you might surf to the Web site of the National Early Childhood Technical Assistance System (NEC*TAS) at www.nectas.unc and then, after reaching that site, look for "hot links" or connections to other sites. Similarly, the Council for Exceptional Children (www.cec.sped.org) and CEC's Division for Early Childhood (www.dec-sped.org) are excellent starting points, as is the U.S. Department of Education (www.ed.gov). A reputable Web site generally will list only respectable resources, avoiding those that have questionable validity. You may also bring a Web site about which you have questions to the attention of a professor, teacher, or other scholar whose opinion you trust, asking her to evaluate the site and the information it offers.

The Web is very new—few people were using it even five years ago. For this reason, no one really knows whether Web site addresses will remain constant or will change as often as phone numbers now do. One good piece of news: Most Web sites that change their addresses maintain a "poster" at the old address, advising you of the address change and offering you a hot link to the new address. At any rate, this book gives you mailing addresses along with Web site addresses so that even if a Web site moves or disappears, you can still reach the organization you want to contact.

BOOKS

General

Allen, K. E., & Schwartz, I. S. (1996). *The exceptional child: Main-streaming in early childhood education* (3rd ed.). Albany, NY: Delmar.

This 356-page text explains, in highly readable language and with numerous illustrations, how early childhood (EC) programs may integrate young children with disabilities. Chapters on behavior, communication, and other domains of development offer practical suggestions.

Guralnick, M. J. (Ed.). (1997). *The effectiveness of early intervention.* Baltimore: Paul H. Brookes.

Guralnick, a highly respected researcher with the University of Washington, compiled this collection of twenty-five review articles, most of which examine research on specific disabilities or at-risk status. The text is a good resource for current information on what we know about intervention.

Levine, J., Murphy, D., & Wilson, S. (1993). *Getting men involved: Strategies for early childhood programs.* New York: Scholastic.

In this trade paperback, Levine, director of The Fatherhood Project at the Families and Work Institute in New York City and his two coauthors offer suggestions drawn from fourteen EC programs around the nation on how to get fathers as well as mothers involved in services for young children. In one EC program, the (mostly male) bus drivers doubled as classroom volunteers. They also conducted outreach to fathers of the children. Other programs created men's groups at which fathers exchanged ideas and feelings.

Mathews, J. (1992). *A mother's touch: The Tiffany Callo story.* New York: Henry Holt.

Tiffany Callo wanted to raise her two children, but public social services agencies made that almost impossible for her, viewing her cerebral palsy as a condition that rendered her unfit to be a mother. Mathews's story offers, in very readable form, a penetrating look both at the lives of people with disabilities and at the often paternalistic attitudes of the "system" of social welfare agencies as seen from the perspective of an adult with a disability. Highly recommended for ECSE workers as a "window" through which to see how "patients" and "clients" often see social services agencies and how people with disabilities often are capable of doing far more than the "system" gives them credit for—or even allows them to do. The story also illustrates how disability issues are intertwined in often unexpected ways.

McLean, M., Bailey, D. B., & Wolery, M. (1996). *Assessing infants and toddlers with special needs* (2nd ed.). Englewood Cliffs, NJ: Merrill.

This 580-page hardcover text introduces testing, examines how assessment is done with very young children, and explores techniques of child and family assessment.

Shapiro, J. (1993). *No pity.* New York: Times Books/Random House.

U.S. News & World Report writer Joseph P. Shapiro offers a readable account of the disability rights movement, from its beginnings in the 1960s to the early 1990s. Helpful on attitudes of people with disabilities, as well as federal rights.

Wolery, M., Bailey, D., & Sugai, G. (1988). *Effective teaching: Principles and procedures of applied behavior analysis with exceptional students.* Boston: Allyn & Bacon.

This 535-page text teaches applied behavior analysis and shows how it may be used to analyze and change children's behavior to reduce inappropriate behavior and to increase desired behavior.

ADHD

Barkley, R. (1990). *Attention Deficit Hyperactivity Disorder: A handbook for diagnosis and treatment.* New York: Guilford.

A professional text, highly regarded for its comprehensiveness and accuracy.

Latham, P. S., & Latham, P. H. (1992). *Attention Deficit Disorder and the law: A guide for advocates.* Washington, DC: JKL Communications (1016 16th St. NW, Washington, DC 20036).

A primer for educated laypeople on how ADHD and related disorders are addressed in federal and state statutes.

Lerner, J., Lowenthal, B., & Lerner, S. (1995). *Attention Deficit Disorders: Assessment and teaching.* Pacific Grove, CA: Brooks/Cole.

A brief, readable introduction to ADD and ADHD.

AIDS

Duh, S. (Ed.). (1991). *Blacks and AIDS: Causes and origins.* Newbury Park, CA: Sage Publications.

In this book, Dr. Duh offers a readable and thorough discussion of AIDS, including prenatal exposure. He explores whether AIDS has a genetic basis in the black community, concluding that the unusually high rates of AIDS among African Americans are more likely due to the same factors that lead to greater disability in this minority group, notably low SES and lack of access to health care.

Walker, R. S. (1991). *AIDS today, tomorrow: An introduction to the HIV epidemic in America.* Atlantic Highlands, NJ: Humanities Press International.

This 187-page book offers an excellent introduction for laypeople of how AIDS is transmitted, how it is treated in American society, and how the epidemic may be contained. The text is a wide-ranging, very readable introduction to the many aspects of working with people who have, or are at risk of getting, AIDS.

Autism

Frith, U. (1989) *Autism: Explaining the enigma.* Cambridge, MA: Basil Blackwell.

Although now somewhat dated, this text remains a standard reference. Uta Frith is a world-recognized expert on autism. In this book she offers readable, concrete information about the puzzling disorder.

Harris, S. L., & Handleman, J. S. (Eds.). (1993). *Preschool education programs for children with autism.* Austin, TX: PRO-ED.

In 250 pages, this book offers child-care workers and early childhood special educators concrete suggestions for working with young children who have autism. Ten contributors, many themselves direct service providers, contribute practical ideas on assessment, curriculum, and other issues.

Cerebral Palsy

Gerales, E., & Ritter, T. (Eds.). (1991). *Children with cerebral palsy: A parent's guide.* Rockville, MD: Woodbine House.

This text focuses on early intervention with young children who have cerebral palsy. Elaine Gerales, a parent herself, keeps the book focused on families. Physicians and other practitioners offer practical suggestions.

Deafness and Hearing Impairment

Legal rights of hearing impaired people. (1992). Washington, DC: Gallaudet University Bookstore.

A brief summary of federal and state laws affecting deaf and hard-of-hearing Americans.

Diversity

Harry, B. (1992). *Cultural diversity, families, and the special education system: Communication and empowerment.* New York: Teachers College Press.

This 278-page book focuses on the daily lives of families in racial and cultural minority groups. Harry offers ethnographic portraits of a dozen Puerto Rican families in an effort to convey the realities of their lives and how disability is perceived in terms of cultural realities.

Galanti, G. (Ed.). (1991). *Caring for patients from different cultures: Case studies from American hospitals.* Philadelphia: University of Pennsylvania Press.

Drawing from a decade of experience in teaching nursing students to work in multicultural settings, the editor brings together highly readable, very insightful perspectives on how people from different racial and ethnic minority groups perceive time, money, personal contact, family structure, gender roles, and other issues relevant to successful work with families. In just 138 pages, the book raises, and offers detailed suggestions about, issues of vital importance to ECSE workers who want to empower families.

Families

Dunst, C., Trivette, C., & Deal, A. (1993). *Supporting and strengthening families: Methods, strategies, and outcomes.* Cambridge, MA: Brookline Books.

A text for ECSE workers on providing supports as well as services to families with young children who have disabilities or developmental delays.

Left, P., & Walizer, E. (1992). *Building the healing partnership: Parents, professionals, and children with chronic illnesses and disabilities.* Cambridge, MA: Brookline Books.

In this book, a parent joins a child psychiatrist to talk about how parents now play a much more decisive and directive role in child care than was true just a few years ago. The points are made through brief vignettes, making the text readable for parents as well as for professionals.

Meyer, D., & Vadasy, P. (1996). *Living with a brother or sister with special needs: A book for sibs* (2nd ed.). Seattle, WA: University of Washington Press.

First published in 1985, this book has been well-received. It offers readable explanations of major disabilities that were discussed in this text, as well as information about special education.

Genetics and Ethics

Bartels, D., LeRoy, B., & Caplan, A. (1992). *Prescribing our future: Ethical challenges of genetic counseling.* New York: Aldine De Gruyter.

This 186-page book offers a lay view of genetic counseling, including its history, training for genetic counselors, and applications.

Blank, R. (1992). *Mother and fetus: Changing notions of maternal responsibility.* Westport, CT: Greenwood Press.

In 207 pages, Robert Blank discusses the rights of women to abort or continue to term versus the rights of the fetus and of society at large. His concern is with those relatively few, but frequently litigated, cases where the interests of mother and fetus diverge. The book's major contribution is that it addresses difficult ethical issues head-on and offers a way of thinking about these.

Dorris, M. (1989). *The broken cord: A family's ongoing struggle with fetal alcohol syndrome.* New York: Harper & Row.

An outstanding introduction to FAS and FAE from the point of view of Michael Dorris, who adopted a Native American child who turned out to have had an alcoholic mother.

Kevles, D., & Hood, L. (Eds.). (1993). *The code of codes: Scientific and social issues in the Human Genome Project.* Cambridge, MA: Harvard University Press.

This 396-page volume includes contributions by James Watson and other luminaries in human biology. It offers a current, up-to-date, and exciting perspective on the fifteen-year, $3 billion project to map all 100,000-odd genes in human DNA. The book is especially helpful on the ethics of how to use genetic information. The book is most readable for individuals who have at least a college education. ECSE workers who take the time to familiarize themselves with its content should have little difficulty explaining it to interested parents and paraprofessionals who would find the book rough going.

Learning Disabilities

Latham, P. S., & Latham, P. H. (1993). *Learning disabilities and the law.* Washington, DC: JKL Communications (1016 16th St. NW, Washington, DC 20036).

Readable explanation of how federal and state laws affect individuals with learning disabilities.

Smith. S. (1991). *Succeeding against the odds: Strategies and insights from the learning disabled.* Rockville, MD: Woodbine.

In 300 pages, Smith describes how adults with learning disabilities cope with everyday life, including employment, college, and community shopping and banking. Some tactics they use may also prove helpful to young children with similar disabilities.

Technology

Lazarro, J. (1993). *Adaptive Technologies for learning & work environments.* Chicago: American Library Association.

This book provides a helpful overview of computer-related products and services and then shows how hardware and software can help people with hearing, vision, mobility, and other disabilities.

Lindsey, J. D. (Ed.). (1993). *Computers and exceptional individuals* (2nd ed.). Austin, TX: PRO-ED.

Another helpful guide on technology, including discussion of telecommunications, augmentative communication, and multimedia.

JOURNALS

Behavioral Disorders. Focuses on emotional and behavior-related disabilities and conditions. Division for Children with Behavior Disorders, Council for Exceptional Children, 1920 Association Drive, Reston, VA 22091.

Early Childhood Research Quarterly. Peer-reviewed journal for professionals. Sponsored by the National Association for the Education of Young Children. It is published by Ablex Publishing Corporation, 355 Chestnut Street, Norwood, NJ 07648. Editorial offices are at 1267 Child Development and Family Studies Building, Purdue University, West Lafayette, IN 47907-1267.

Exceptional Children. General special education journal featuring refereed articles. Council for Exceptional Children, 1920 Association Drive, Reston, VA 22091.

Exceptional Parent. A readable journal for parents of children with disabilities. Each year, the journal issues its "Annual Guide to Products and Services," an excellent resource on technology as well as services for children and families, including "800" numbers. Psy-Ed Corporation, P.O. Box 300, EP, Denville, NJ 07834.

Infants and Young Children. Journal on medical and other early interventions. Four times each year, this journal provides articles of practical importance for ECSE programs and personnel. Aspen Publishers, 7201 McKinne Circle, Frederick, MD 21701.

Journal of Early Intervention. Journal on working with infants and toddlers. A quarterly publication by the Division for Early Childhood, Council for Exceptional Children. Formerly called the *Journal of the Division for Early Childhood.* Council for Exceptional Children, 1920 Association Drive, Reston, VA 22091.

Journal of Special Education. General special education journal featuring refereed articles. PRO-ED, 8700 Shoal Creek Boulevard, Austin, TX 78757-6897.

Journal of Special Education Technology. Focuses on assistive and instructional devices and software. Attention: Herb Rieth, Editor, Peabody College of Vanderbilt University, Box 328, Nashville, TN 37203.

Ragged Edge. Tabloid written by adults with disabilities. "The" authoritative voice of disability advocates, the *Rag* is an outspoken, often radical voice protesting against paternalism. Indispensable for "the consumer viewpoint" on disability issues. The Disability Rag, P.O. Box 145, Louisville, KY 40201.

Teaching Exceptional Children. A readable, practice-oriented magazine for special education teachers. Council for Exceptional Children, 1920 Association Drive, Reston, VA 22091.

Topics in Early Childhood Special Education. Quarterly journal having three issues annually on selected topics and one "open." PRO-ED, 8700 Shoal Creek Boulevard, Austin, TX 78757-6897.

DIRECTORIES

Directory of national information sources on disabilities. Silver Spring, MD: NARIC and ABLEDATA, 8455 Colesville Road, #935, Silver Spring, MD 20910-3319.

Resource directory of more than five hundred organizations of and for people with disabilities, including what they do, who they serve, and what publications or other information they offer.

ILRU Directory of independent living programs. Houston, TX: Independent Living Resource Utilization Project, 2323 S. Shepherd #1000, Houston, TX 77019.

Excellent directory of some five hundred centers for independent living, most of which are local self-help groups. By law, these centers must be governed and operated by adults with disabilities. The ILCs are excellent sources of names of local advocates who are individuals with disabilities and who may be interested in providing consumer perspectives on ECSE programs and/or on individual families.

State Resource Sheet. Washington, DC: National Information Center for Children and Youth with Disabilities, P.O. Box 1492, Washington, DC 20013.

A very helpful service from this federally funded center, these "State Resource Sheets" offer regularly updated information on disability-related organizations and agencies within a particular state.

White, B., & Madara, E. (Eds.) *The self-help sourcebook: Finding and forming mutual aid self-help groups.* Denville, NJ: American Self-Help Clearinghouse, Riverside Medical Center, Denville, NJ 07834.

Excellent directory of self-help support groups, this text is updated every two years (the latest, seventh, edition is 1998; the next will be published in 2000). Provides addresses, telephone numbers, and brief descriptions of more than six hundred national, state, and local self-help organizations, many of which focus on a particular disability or health condition. Very highly recommended for ECSE programs because it will help so many parents to link up with other families having children with similar needs.

INFORMATION SOURCES

Federal

Administration on Developmental Disabilities
U.S. Department of Health and Human Services
200 Independence Avenue SW
Washington, DC 20201
www.hhs.gov
The federal agency coordinating state-run programs for children with severe and multiple needs.

Architectural and Transportation Barriers
  Compliance Board
1331 F Street NW #1000
Washington, DC 20004-1111
www.access-board.gov
  A small, independent federal agency offering guidelines on accessibility in construction and transportation.

Department of Education
400 Maryland Avenue SW
Washington, DC 20202
www.ed.gov.
  The federal agency responsible for administering the IDEA and other laws providing services to people with disabilities.

Department of Housing and Urban Development
451 7th Street NW
Washington, DC 20410
www.hud.gov
  The federal agency responsible for implementation of PL 100-407, the Fair Housing Amendments Act of 1990.

Department of Justice
Office of the Americans with Disabilities Act
Civil Rights Division
P.O. Box 66118
Washington, DC 20035-6118
www.usdoj.gov
  The federal office responsible for implementation of ADA titles II (on state and local government) and III (on places of public accommodation).

Department of Transportation
400 7th Street NW
Washington, DC 20590
www.fta.dot.gov
  The federal office responsible for implementation of ADA transportation requirements.

Equal Employment Opportunity Commission
1801 L Street NW
Washington, DC 20507
www.eeoc.gov
  The federal agency responsible for implementation of ADA title I (on employment).

Federal Communications Commission
1919 M Street NW
Washington, DC 20554
www.fcc.gov
  The federal agency responsible for implementation of ADA title IV (on telecommunications) and PL 101-431, the Television Decoder Circuitry Act of 1990 (on caption decoders in commercial TV sets).

National Council on Disability
1331 F Street, NW, #1050
Washington, DC 20004
www.ncd.gov
> A small, independent federal agency that advocates for laws on behalf of people with disabilities.

National Institutes of Health
Bethesda, MD 20892
www.nih.gov
> The NIH sponsor research on hearing (National Institute on Deafness), aging and age-related disabilities (National Institute on Aging), and so on.

Social Security Administration
6401 Security Boulevard
Baltimore, MD 21235
> The federal agency responsible for administering Social Security Disability Insurance (SSDI) and Supplemental Security Income (SSI)

General

Consortium for Citizens with Disabilities
c/o The ARC
1522 K Street NW
Washington, DC 20005
www.radix.net/~ccd
> An association of Washington-based advocacy groups, CCD has a task force on special education issues.

Division for Early Childhood
Council for Exceptional Children
1920 Association Drive
Reston, VA 22091-1589
www.dec-sped.org
> DEC is the division of CEC that focuses on ECSE. An association of special educators and related services personnel, CEC is a long-standing advocate for special education and early intervention.

Edward Mazique Parent/Child Center
1719 13th Street NW
Washington, DC 20009
> A direct services center specializing in services for families from ethnic and racial minority groups.

ERIC Clearinghouse on Elementary and Early Childhood Education (ERIC/EECE)
University of Illinois
805 West Pennsylvania Avenue
Urbana, IL 61801
> Offers on-line and off-line articles on curriculum, diversity, and other topics.

Independent Living Research Utilization Program
2323 S. Shepherd #1000
Houston, TX 77019
> A research and training project focusing on independent living centers for adults with disabilities, the ILRU Program offers an excellent *Guide to Planning Accessible Meetings*, in addition to its indispensable annual directory of ILCs.

National Association for the Education of Young Children
1509 16th Street, NW
Washington, DC 20036
www.naeyc.org
> An association promoting EC services and "developmentally appropriate practice."

National Association of State Directors of Special Education
1800 Diagonal Road, Suite 320
King Street Station 1
Alexandria, VA 22314
> An association of state special education agency directors, NASDSE coordinates information sharing among directors and represents them in Washington. Excellent source of names, titles, addresses, and telephone numbers of state agency officials.

National Center for the Early Childhood Workforce
733 15th Street NW, #1037
Washington, DC 20005
> Advocates for EC professionals and paraprofessionals, including political awareness and voter registration activities.

National Early Childhood Technical Assistance System
Suite 500, NationsBank Plaza
137 East Franklin Street
Chapel Hill, NC 27514
www.nectas.unc.edu
> NEC*TAS is a federally funded center on ECSE. Each year, it issues numerous reports on issues important to the field. It also maintains current and comprehensive contact information about Part C and preschool Part B programs in the states, for which reason it is an excellent source of names, addresses, telephone and fax numbers, and so on for parents and professionals alike.

National Easter Seals Society
230 West Monroe Street, #1800
Chicago, IL 60606-4802
www.seals.com
> NESS and its two hundred affiliates nationwide are private, nonprofit providers of services for children and adults with physical disabilities.

National Resource Center for Paraprofessionals in Education and Related Human Services
33 West 42nd Street, Room 620N
New York, NY 10036
> Specializes in providing readable resource materials targeted at paraprofessionals.

Zero to Three, National Center for Clinical Infant Programs
734 15th Street NW #1000
Washington, DC 20005
           or
2000 14th Street North, Suite 380
Arlington, VA 22201
> Specialists in serving infants and toddlers with developmental delays or at risk for delays. Zero to Three hosts important conferences on Part C-related issues, usually in Washington, DC.

Lawyers and Legal Advocacy

Disability Rights Education and Defense Fund
2212 6th Street
Berkeley, CA 94702
> A private advocacy organization of and for people with disabilities, DREDF has been active in advocating for human and civil rights for Americans with disabilities. It offers legal representation and cocounsel in selected cases.

Public Interest Law Center of Philadelphia
125 S. 9th Street #700
Philadelphia, PA 19107
> PILCOP has worked with families and children with disabilities for more than twenty years, notably in the landmark *PARC v. Commonwealth of Pennsylvania* case. It specializes in class-action suits.

ADHD

Attention Deficit Disorder Association
PO Box 972
Mentor, OH 44061
> A national organization providing information on ADHD and related disorders.

ADDult Support Network
2620 Ivy Place
Toledo, OH 43613
> A national support group of individuals with ADHD and related disorders, the Network is affiliated with the ADDA (above).

Attention Deficit Information Network, Inc.
475 Hillside Avenue
Needham, MA 02194
> AD-IN is a good information and referral source for support groups, experts, and information about ADHD.

Children and Adults with Attention Deficit Disorder
499 Northwest 70th Avenue, #101
Plantation, FL 33317
www.chadd.org

> A national support and information organization with more than 450 parent group affiliates, CH.A.D.D. has grown to 21,000 members since it was formed in 1988.

The Association for the Advancement of Behavior Therapy
15 West 36th Street
New York, NY 10018
> An information source on ADHD.

AIDS

AIDS Action Council
1875 Connecticut Avenue NW #700
Washington, DC 20009
> Representing some nine hundred community groups, the council promotes legislation protecting people with AIDS and advocates for more research and better care.

National AIDS Clearinghouse
P.O. Box 6003
Rockville, MD 20849-6003
> This information service offers materials in Spanish as well as English, and operates a hot line. The clearinghouse is sponsored by the Atlanta-based Centers for Disease Control and Prevention.

Autism

Autism Society of America
7910 Woodmont Avenue, Suite 650
Bethesda, MD 20814–3015
> With more than 185 chapters nationwide, the ASA offers factual information about autism, and urges research and treatment advances.

Blindness and Low Vision

American Council of the Blind
1155 15th Street NW #720
Washington, DC 20005
www.acb.org
> A consumer organization of blind and low-vision adults, ACB has fifty-two state or regional chapters and about two dozen affiliates. An excellent source of information about the consumer perspective.

American Foundation for the Blind
11 Penn Plaza #300
New York, NY 10001
www.afb.org/afb
> Founded by Helen Keller, this organization advocates on behalf of people who are blind. It offers a wealth of information about

blindness and low vision and sponsors a National Technology Center.

The Lighthouse, Inc.
111 East 59th Street
New York, NY 10022

The Lighthouse offers consumer products for blind and low-vision persons and annually publishes a catalog describing them. It purchased the American Foundation for the Blind's consumer products business in mid–1994.

National Federation of the Blind
1800 Johnson Street
Baltimore, MD 21230
www.nfb.org

A national organization competing with ACB, the federation claims to be "the voice of the organized blind." Another excellent source for consumer views.

Cerebral Palsy

United Cerebral Palsy Associations, Inc.
1660 L Street NW, #700
Washington, DC 20036
www.ucpa.org

A private organization with 183 affiliates nationwide.

Cystic Fibrosis

Cystic Fibrosis Foundation
6931 Arlington Road
Bethesda, MD 20814
E-mail: info@cff.org
www.cff.org

The authoritative source on cystic fibrosis.

Cystic Fibrosis Research Inc.
560 San Antonio Road #103
Palo Alto, CA 94306-4349
E-mail: cfri@ix.netcom.com
www.cfri.org

A major source of funding for, and information about, research on prevention and amelioration of cystic fibrosis.

Deafness and Hearing Impairment

National Association of the Deaf
814 Thayer Avenue
Silver Spring, MD 20910
www.nad.org

A consumer organization with state chapters nationwide.

Telecommunications for the Deaf, Inc.
8719 Colesville Road
Silver Spring, MD 20910

A consumer and industry association interested in technology for communication-impaired people.

Self Help for Hard of Hearing People
7800 Wisconsin Avenue
Bethesda, MD 20814

A consumer association with state and local chapters throughout the nation.

Diabetes

American Diabetes Association
505 Eighth Avenue, 21st Floor
New York, NY 10018
www.diabetes.org

Offers brochures on diabetes.

Juvenile Diabetes Foundation
432 Park Avenue South
New York, NY 10016-8013
www.jdfcure.org

Founded in 1971, it has 128 chapters in North America and funds the Diabetes Research Foundation.

Epilepsy

Epilepsy Foundation of America
National Epilepsy Library
4351 Garden City Drive
Landover, MD 20785
www.efa.org

A private organization providing information and advocacy services for people with epilepsy.

Families

Association for the Care of Children's Health
7910 Woodmont Avenue, #300
Bethesda, MD 20814

In addition to its regularly updated *Parent Resource Directory,* the ACCH links parents of children with disabilities or developmental delays for parent-to-parent networking and mutual support. It also offers a guidebook for developing IFSPs.

Beach Center on Families and Disability
Bureau of Child Research
University of Kansas
4138 Haworth Hall
Lawrence, KS 66045
www.lsi.ukans.edu/beach

A federally funded research and training center, Beach focuses on childhood disability. Its directors, H. R. and Ann Turnbull, are experts on special education law.

Children's Defense Fund
25 E Street, NW
Washington, DC 20001

An outstanding public-interest advocacy group, CDF has a long-standing interest in lobbying for children with disabilities. It publishes low-cost (most under $6) publications on how to be an advocate, how to use the mass media, and how to lobby and raise funds for programs.

Estate Planning for People with Disabilities
3100 Arapahoe Avenue #112
Boulder, CO 80303

A national organization focusing on assistance in financial planning to families with a child, sibling, or other family member who has a disability. Some 130 local estate-planning teams (including CPAs) in forty-four states are available to help families plan.

National Information Center for Children and Youth with Disabilities
P.O. Box 1492
Washington, DC 20013
www.nichcy.org

A federally funded center that offers readable information and referral services especially for families. Single copies of its many publications are free.

Parents Helping Parents
535 Race Street #140
San Jose, CA 95126

A family-directed resource center for parents, PHP offers information and referral for parents with children who have disabilities.

Technical Assistance for Parent Programs
c/o Federation for Children with Special Needs
95 Berkeley Street, Suite 104
Boston, MA 02116

Federally funded center that supports parent-to-parent communication and mutual-help groups. TAPP offers information and publications for parent-based organizations and for families. Also refers parents to one of four regional centers and three focus centers. The focus center on early childhood: Pilot Parent Partnerships, 2150 E. Highland Avenue #105, Phoenix, AZ 85106. On technology: PLUK, 1500 N. 30th, Billings, MT 59101.

Fragile X

National Fragile X Foundation
1441 York Street #215
Denver, CO 80206
www.fragilex.org

An information resource on genetic testing, family needs, and family counseling support groups and experts, the foundation is a good source of information about this disorder.

Learning Disability

Learning Disabilities Association of America
4156 Library Road
Pittsburgh, PA 15234
www.ldanatl.org

A parent-based group offering information and advocacy for children, youth, and adults with dyslexia and other learning disabilities. Formerly called ACLD.

Orton Dyslexia Society
The Chester Building #382
8600 LaSalle Road
Baltimore, MD 21286-2044
www.ods.org

A private group specializing in dyslexia, the Orton Society has forty-three affiliates or volunteer branches staffed by professionals who can offer referrals to evaluators and tutors.

Mental Illness

American Psychological Association
1200 17th Street NW
Washington, DC 20036

A professional association for psychologists, the APA includes sections for those working in public schools and related programs.

American School Counseling Association
5999 Stevenson Avenue
Alexandria, VA 22304

Specializing more in school-related needs than the APA does, the ASCA includes as members counselors who are not psychologists.

Judge David L. Bazelon Center for Mental Health Law
1101 15th Street NW #1212
Washington, DC 20005-5002

Known until 1993 as The Mental Health Law Project, this nonprofit organization has advocated for many years on disability rights and special education issues, not restricting itself to mental health.

National Alliance for the Mentally Ill
200 N. Glebe Road #1015
Arlington, VA 22203

The alliance is a self-help, consumer organization run principally by individuals who themselves are mentally ill or mentally restored. It advocates for better treatment and greater rights.

Support groups affiliated with the alliance offer help to families and to individuals alike.

Muscular Dystrophy

Muscular Dystrophy Association
3300 E. Sunrise Drive
Tucson, AZ 85718
www.mda.org
> Sponsors the Labor Day telethon that helps support research, service, and information programs.

Other Physical Disabilities

American Amputee Foundation
P.O. Box 250218
Hillcrest Station
Little Rock, AR 72225
> The foundation provides information and referral for people with amputation and their families.

American Occupational Therapy Association
4720 Montgomery Lane
P.O. Box 31200
Bethesda, MD 20842-1220
> An association of occupational therapists, AOTA seeks to educate its members and to advance the profession.

American Physical Therapy Association
1111 North Fairfax Street
Alexandria, VA 22314-1488
> The APTA features counts among its members some 57,000-odd PT professionals, as well as students. It seeks to increase public understanding of physical therapy.

Americans Disabled for Attendant Programs Today
3005 West Gill Place
Denver, CO 80219
> An advocacy organization comprising disability activists, ADAPT urges profound change in national and state medical care policies, advocating specifically for giving control of attendant care services to consumers themselves. A good source of adults with disabilities who may be willing to serve as mentors or advisers in ECSE programs.

Rare Disorders

National Organization for Rare Disorders
100 Route 37, P.O. Box 8923
New Fairfield, CT 06812-8923
www.pcnet.com/~orphan/
> A voluntary federation of chapters concerned with "orphan diseases," NORD is an excellent resource for information about unusual genetic and other conditions.

Respite Services

National Resource Center for Respite and Crisis Care Services
Chapel Hill Training-Outreach Project
800 Eastowne Drive #105
Chapel Hill, NC 27514
www.chtop.com
> The "ARCH" focuses on respite care, an allowable entry intervention service under the IDEA's Part C.

Retardation

The ARC
of the United States
500 East Border Street #300
Arlington, TX 76010
www.thearc.org
> A private, nonprofit association of affiliates providing services, information, research, and advocacy on behalf of people with retardation. The ARC (formerly Association for Retarded Citizens/United States) has 1,200 chapters or affiliates.

National Down Syndrome Society
666 Broadway
New York, NY 10012
www.ndss.org
> Sponsors research, information, and outreach on behalf of children and adults with Down syndrome.

Speech and Language

American Speech-Language-Hearing Association
10801 Rockville Pike
Rockville, MD 20852
> A professional organization for speech, language, and hearing pathologists and for audiologists.

American Cleft Palate Association
University of Pittsburgh
331 Falk Hall
Pittsburgh, PA 15261
> A private association offering information about speech disorders due to cleft palate.

Spina Bifida

Spina Bifida Association of America
4590 MacArthur Boulevard NW, #250
Washington, DC 20007-4226
www.sbaa.org
> With more than a hundred chapters and affiliates, SBAA offers support for parents and other family members of individuals with spina bifida. It provides information on treatment, education, and social and medical services as well.

Traumatic Brain Injury

Brain Injury Association
1776 Massachusetts Avenue NW #100
Washington, DC 20036
www.biausa.org
    A private organization advocating for laws benefiting people with TBI. The foundation is affiliated with more than four hundred support groups nationwide.

New Medico Head Injury System
14 Central Avenue
Lynn, MA 01901
    Publishes *Headlines*, a quarterly magazine that offers good coverage of TBI, including cases among children. For example, the September/October 1993 issue was devoted to "neurological insult in young children." It also offers a free, fifty-two-page booklet, *Understanding Brain Injury*, which describes TBI, seizures, and the brain in clear and objective fashion.

References

Aaronson, D. W., & Rosenberg, M. (1985). Asthma: General concepts. In R. Paterson (Ed.), *Allergic diseases.* Philadelphia: J. B. Lippincott.

Abeson, A. (1972). Movement and momentum: Government and the education of handicapped children. *Exceptional Children, 39,* 63–66.

Abeson, A., Burgdorf, R., Casey, P., Kunz, J. & McNeil, W. (1975). Access to opportunity. In N. Hobbs (Ed.), *Issues in the classification of children,* (Vol. 2, pp. 270–292). San Francisco: Jossey-Bass.

Abeson, A., & Zettel, J. (1977). The end of the quiet revolution: The Education for All Handicapped Children Act of 1975. *Exceptional Children, 44,* 115–128.

Accardo, P. J., & Capute, A. J. (1979). Parent counseling. In P. J. Accardo & A. J. Capute (Eds.), *The pediatrician and the developmentally delayed child* (pp. 167–177). Baltimore: University Park Press.

Achenbach, T. M. (1992). *Manual for the Child Behavior Checklist 2/3 and 1992 profile.* Burlington, VT: University of Vermont Department of Psychiatry.

Adler, J., & Drew, L. (1988). Waking sleeping souls. *Newsweek,* March 28, pp. 70–71.

Adult Learning & Literacy (ALL.) Bulletin, 5(6). (1993). Family literacy issue, December.

Affleck, G., McGrade, B., McQueeney, M., & Allen, D. (1992). Promise of relationship-focused early intervention in developmental disabilities. *Journal of Special Education, 26,* 413–430.

Affleck, G., Tennen, H., Rowe, J., Roscher, B., & Walker, L. (1989). Effects of formal support on mothers' adaptation to the hospital-to-home transition of high-risk infants: The benefits and costs of helping. *Child Development, 60,* 488–501.

Alberto, P. A., Briggs, T., & Goldstein, D. (1983). Managing learning in handicapped infants. In Garwood, S. G., & Fewell, R. R. (Eds.), *Educating handicapped infants: Issues in development and intervention* (pp. 417–454). Rockville, MD: Aspen Systems Corporation.

Allen, K. E. (1992). *The exceptional child: Mainstreaming in early childhood education.* Albany, NY: Delmar.

Allen, K. E., & Marotz, L. (1989). *Developmental profiles, birth to six.* Albany, NY: Delmar.

Allen, M. C., Donohue, P. K., & Dusman, A. E. (1993). The limit of viability: Neonatal outcome of infants born at 22 to 25 weeks' gestation. *New England Journal of Medicine, 329*(22), 1597–1601.

Alliance for Public Technology. (1993). *Technologies of freedom: Tutorial notebook.* Washington, DC: Author.

Allison, M. (1992). The effects of neurologic injury on the maturing brain. *Headlines, 3*(5), 2–6, 9–10.

Alper, J., Natowicz, M., & Ard, C. (1993). Discrimination on the basis of perceived genetic disabilities. *Disability Studies Quarterly, 13*(3), 27–30.

American Association of Colleges of Teacher Education. (1988). *Teacher education pipeline: Schools, colleges and departments of education enrollments by race and ethnicity.* Washington, DC: Author.

American Association on Mental Retardation. (1992). *Mental retardation: Definition, classification, and systems of support.* Washington, DC: Author.

American Psychiatric Association. (1994). *Diagnostic and statistical manual of mental disorders* (4th ed.). Washington, DC: Author.

Anastasiow, N. (1981). Early childhood education for the handicapped in the 1980's: Recommendations. *Exceptional Children, 47*(4), 276–282.

Anderson, S. M. (1989). Secondary neurologic disability in myelodomengingocele. *Infants and Young Children, 1*(1), 9–21.

Antia, S., Kreimeyer, K., & Eldredge, N. (1994). Promoting social interaction between young children with hearing impairments and their peers. *Exceptional Children, 60*(3) 262–275.

Appl, D. (1996). Recognizing diversity in the early childhood classroom. *Teaching Exceptional Children, 28*(4), 22–25.

Aram, D. M., Morris, R., & Hall, N. E. (1992). The validity of discrepancy criteria for identifying children with developmental learning disorders. *Journal of Learning Disabilities, 25*(9), 549–554.

Arcia, E., & Gallagher, J. J. (1993). Who are underserved by early intervention? Can we tell? *Infant-Toddler Intervention, 3(2),* 93–100.

Arcia, E., Keyes, L., Gallagher, J., & Herrick, H. (1992). *Potential underutilization of Part H services: An empirical study of national demographic factors.* Chapel Hill: University of North Carolina Policy Studies Project.

Arcia, E., Keyes, L., Gallagher, J., & Herrick, H. (1993). National portrait of sociodemographic factors associated with underutilization of services: Relevance to early intervention. *Journal of Early Intervention, 17*(3), 283–297.

Ariel, A. (1992). *Education of children and adolescents with learning disabilities.* New York: Merrill.

Arnst, C. (1994). Trying to knock the wind out of asthma. *Business Week,* June 20, 184–185.

Asch, A. (1993). The human genome and disability rights: Thoughts for researchers and advocates. *Disability Studies Quarterly, 13*(3), 3–5.

Association for the Care of Children's Health. (1992). Guidelines for facilitating father support groups. *ACCH Network, 9*(4), 2.

Audette, B., & Algozzine, B. (1992). Free and appropriate education for all students: Total quality and the transformation of American public education. *Remedial and Special Education, 13*(6), 8–18.

Audit finds day-care safety flaws. (1994). *Newsday,* January 24, p. 13.

Aydlett, L. A. (1993). Assessing infant interaction skills in interaction-focused intervention. *Infants and Young Children, 5*(4), 1–7.

Badger, E. (1981). *Infant/toddler: Introducing your child to the joy of learning.* New York: McGraw Hill.

Bailey, D. B. (1989). Issues and directions in preparing professionals to work with young handicapped children and their families. In J. J. Gallagher, P. L. Trohanis, & R. M. Clifford (Eds.), *Policy implementation and PL 99-457: Planning for young children with special needs* (pp. 97–132). Baltimore: Paul H. Brookes.

Bailey, D. B. (1991). Issues and perspectives on family assessment. *Infants and Young Children, 4*(1), 26–34.

Bailey, D. B. (1997). Evaluating the effectiveness of curriculum alternatives for infants and preschoolers at high risk. In M. J.

Guralnick (Ed.), *The effectiveness of early intervention.* Baltimore: Paul H. Brookes.

Bailey, D. B., Buysse, V., Edmondson, R., & Smith, T. M. (1992). Creating family-centered services in early intervention: Perceptions of professionals in four states. *Exceptional Children, 58*(4), 298–309.

Bailey, D. B., Buysse, V., & Palsha, S. A. (1990). Self-ratings of professional knowledge and skill in early intervention. *Journal of Special Education, 23,* 423–435.

Bailey, D. B., & McWilliam, P. J. (1990). Normalizing early intervention. *Topics in Early Childhood Special Education, 10*(2), 33–47.

Bailey, D. B., & McWilliam, P. J. (1993). The search for quality indicators. In P. J. McWilliam & D. B. Bailey (Eds.), *Working together with children and families: Case studies in early intervention.* (pp. 3–20). Baltimore: Paul H. Brookes.

Bailey, D. B., McWilliam, P. J., & Winton, P. J. (1992). Building family-centered practices in early intervention: A team-based model for change. *Infants and Young Children, 5*(1), 73–82.

Bailey, D. B., Palsha, S. A., & Simeonsson, R. J. (1991). Professional skills, concerns, and perceived importance of work with families in early intervention. *Exceptional Children, 58*(2), 156–165.

Bailey, D. B., & Simeonsson, R. J. (1988). Assessing needs of families with handicapped infants. *Journal of Special Education, 22*(3), 117–127.

Bailey, D. B., Simeonsson, R. J., Yoder, D., & Huntington, G. (1990). Preparing professionals to serve infants and toddlers with handicaps and their families: An integrative analysis across eight disciplines. *Exceptional Children, 57*(1), 26–35.

Bailey, D. B., & Wolery, M. (1984). *Teaching infants and preschoolers with handicaps.* Columbus, OH: Merrill.

Ballard, J., and Zettel, J. (1977). Public Law 94-142 and section 504: What they say about rights and protections. *Exceptional Children, 44*(3), 177–184.

Bandura, A. (1977). *Social learning theory.* Englewood Cliffs, NJ: Prentice Hall.

Barkley, R. (1990). *Attention Deficit Hyperactivity Disorder: A handbook for diagnosis and treatment.* New York: Guilford.

Barnett, S. A. (1992). Design comes of age. *Newsday,* June 11, pp. 73–75, 83.

Baroni, M., Tuthill, P., Feenan, L., & Schroeder, M. (1994). Technology-dependent infants and young children: A retrospective case analysis of service coordination across state lines. *Infants and Young Children, 7*(1), 69–78.

Barraga, N. C. (1983). *Visual handicaps and learning* (Rev. ed.). Austin, TX: Exceptional Resources.

Bartels, D., LeRoy, B., & Caplan, A. (1992). *Prescribing our future: Ethical challenges of genetic counseling.* New York: Aldine De Gruyter.

Baskin, Y. (1991). Finding the cause of muscular dystrophy. *World Book Health and Medical Annual*, 170–183.

Batshaw, M., & Perrett, Y. (Eds.). (1992). *Children with disabilities: A medical primer.* Baltimore: Paul H. Brookes.

Bayley, N. (1969). *Bayley Scales of Infant Development.* San Antonio, TX: The Psychological Corporation.

Bayley Scales of Infant Development: Second edition. (1993). San Antonio, TX: The Psychological Corporation.

Beck, L. R., Hammond-Cordero, M., & Poole, J. (1994). Integrated services for children who are medically fragile and technology dependent. *Infants and Young Children*, 6(3), 75–83.

Bee, H. (1989). *The developing child.* New York: Harper & Row.

Begley, S. (1992). A new genetic code: The ABC's of DNA are changing radically. And that can bring tragedy. *Newsweek*, November 2, 77, 78.

Behl, D., White, K. R., & Escobar, C. M. (1993). New Orleans early intervention study of children with visual impairments. *Early Education and Development*, 4(4), 256–274.

Behr, J. (1991). Testimony before the Subcommittee on Disability Policy, March 15. *Senate report S. hrg. 102-133.* Washington, DC: U.S. Government Printing Office, 29–33.

Bellamy, G. T. (1987). OSEP memorandum to state school officers. (December 8) Unpublished document. Washington, DC: U.S. Department of Education, Office of Special Education Programs.

Benn, R. (1991). *A state wide definition of eligibility under P.L. 99-457, Part H: A final research report.* Detroit, MI: Merrill-Palmer Institute.

Bennefield, R., & McNeil, J. (1989). *Labor force status and other characteristics of persons with a work disability: 1981 to 1988.* Washington, DC: U.S. Government Printing Office.

Bennett, T., & Watson, A. L. (1993). A new perspective on training: Competence building. *Journal of Early Intervention*, 17(3), 309–321.

Benson, A. M., & Lane, S. J. (1993). The developmental impact of low-level lead exposure. *Infants and Young Children*, 6(2), 41–51.

Bigge, J. (1988). *Curriculum-based instruction for special education students.* Mountain View, CA: Mayfield Publishing.

Biklen, D. (1985). *Achieving the complete school.* New York: Teachers College Press.

Biklen, D. (1990). Communication unbound: Autism and praxis. *Harvard Educational Review*, 60(3), 291–314.

Biklen, D. (1992). *Schooling without labels.* Philadelphia. Temple University Press.

Biklen, D., Morton, M., Gold, D., Berrigan, C., & Swaminathan, S. (1992). Facilitated communication: Implications for individuals with autism. *Topics in Language Disorders*, 12(4), 1–28.

Biklen, D., & Schubert, A. (1991). New words: The communication of students with autism. *Remedial and Special Education*, 12(6), 46–57.

Birth defects lessened by folic acid, study shows. (1992). *Newsday*, December 24, 17.

Blackman, J. A. (1990). *Medical aspects of developmental disabilities in children birth to three* (2nd ed.). Rockville, MD: Aspen.

Blakeslee, S. (1991a). Brain yields new clues on its organization for language. *New York Times*, September 10, C1, C10.

Blakeslee, S. (1991b). Study ties dyslexia to brain flaw affecting vision and other senses. *New York Times*, September 15, pp. 1, 30.

Blank, R. (1992). *Mother and fetus: Changing notions of maternal responsibility.* Westport, CT: Greenwood Press.

Blau, M. (1993). A.D.D.: The scariest letters in the alphabet. *New York*, December 13, pp. 45–51.

Bloch, J. S. (1993). Personal communication, August 5.

Bloch, J. S., & Seitz, M. (1985). *Empowering parents of disabled children: A family exchange center.* Syosset, NY: Variety Preschoolers Workshop.

Bloch, J. S., & Seitz, M. (1989). Parents as assessors of children: A collaborative approach to helping. *Social Work in Education*, July, 226–244.

Bluma, S., Shearer, M., Frohman, A., & Hillard, J. (1976). *Portage guide to early education.* Portage, WI: Cooperative Educational Service Agency #12.

Board of Education, Hendrick Hudson School District v. Rowley 458 U.S. 176, 181 (1982).

Bos, C. S., & Vaughn, S. (1988). *Strategies for teaching students with learning and behavior problems.* (2nd ed.). Boston: Allyn and Bacon.

Bowe, F. (1978). *Handicapping America.* New York: Harper & Row.

Bowe, F. (1985a). *Black adults with disabilities.* Washington, DC: President's Committee on Employment of People with Disabilities.

Bowe, F. (1985b). *Disabled adults of Hispanic origin.* Washington, DC: President's Committee on Employment of People with Disabilities.

Bowe, F. (1988). Why seniors don't use technology. *Technology Review*, 91(6), 34–40.

Bowe, F. (1990). Demography, politics and disability. *Disability Studies Quarterly, 10*(3), 19–20.

Bowe, F. (1991a). Access to telecommunications: The views of blind and visually impaired adults. *Journal of Visual Impairment and Blindness, 85*(8), 328–331.

Bowe, F. (1991b). *Approaching equality.* Silver Spring, MD: T. J. Publishers.

Bowe, F. (1992a). *Equal rights for Americans with disabilities.* New York: Franklin Watts.

Bowe, F. (1992b). Radicalism v. reason. In D. F. Moores, M. Walworth, & T. J. O'Rourke (Eds.). *A free hand.* Silver Spring, MD: T. J. Publishers.

Bowe, F. (1993a). Preface. In M. Scherer, *Living in the state of stuck: How assistive technologies affect the lives of people with disabilities.* (xi–xiv). Cambridge, MA: Brookline Books.

Bowe, F. (1993b). Getting there: Update on recommendations by the Commission on Education of the Deaf. *American Annals of the Deaf, 138*(3), 304–308.

Bowe, F. (1993c). Statistics, politics, and employment of people with disabilities. *Journal of Disability Policy Studies, 4*(2), 83–91.

Bowe, F. (1994). Population estimates: Birth-five children with disabilities. *Journal of Special Education, 28*(4), 28–37.

Bowe, F. (in press). *Physical, Sensory, and Health Disabilities: An introduction.* Columbus, OH: Merrill.

Bowman, B. (1992). Who is at risk for what and why. *Journal of Early Intervention, 16*(2), 101–108.

Boyce, G. C., Smith, T. B., Immel, N., Casto, G., & Escobar, C. (1993). Early intervention with medically fragile infants: Investigating the age-at-start question. *Journal of Early Education and Development, 4*(4), 327–345.

Boyce, G. C., White, K. R., & Kerr, B. (1993). The effectiveness of adding a parent involvement component to an existing center-based program for children with disabilities and their families. *Early Education and Development, 4*(4), 327–345.

Braden, J., Maller, S., & Paquin, M. (1993). The effects of residential versus day placement on the performance IQs of children with hearing impairment. *Journal of Special Education, 26*(4), 423–433.

Brandenburg, N. A., Friedman, R. M., & Silver, S. (1987). *The epidemiology of childhood psychiatric disorders: Recent prevalence findings and methodologic issues.* Tampa, FL: Florida Mental Health Institute.

Brandt, P. (1993). Negotiation and problem-solving strategies: Collaboration between families and professionals. *Infants and Young Children, 5*(4), 78–84.

Brault, L. (1992). Achieving integration for infants and toddlers with special needs: Recommendations for practice. *Infants and Young Children, 5*(2), 78–85.

Brazelton, T. (1984). *Neonatal Behavioral Assessment Scale.* Philadelphia: Lippincott.

Brazelton, T. B., & Cramer, B. G. (1990). *The earliest relationship: Parents, infants and the drama of early attachment.* Reading, MA: Addison-Wesley.

Bredekamp, S. (Ed.). (1987). *Developmentally appropriate practice in early childhood programs serving children from birth through age 8: Expanded edition.* Washington, DC: National Association for the Education of Young Children.

Bredekamp, S. (1993a). Myths about developmentally appropriate practice: A response to Fowell and Lawton. *Early Childhood Research Quarterly, 8,* 117–119.

Bredekamp, S. (1993b). The relationship between early childhood education and early childhood special education: Healthy marriage or family feud? *Topics in Early Childhood Special Education, 13*(3), 258–273.

Bredekamp, S., & Copple, C. (Eds.). (1997). *Developmentally appropriate practice in early childhood programs: Revised edition.* Washington, DC: National Association for the Education of Young Children.

Bricker, D., & Slentz, K. (1990). Personnel preparation: Handicapped infants. In M. Wang, H. Walberg, & M. Reynolds (Eds.), *Handbook of special education research and practice.* Oxford, England: Pergamon.

Bricker, D., & Squires, J. (1989). Low cost system using parents to monitor the development of at-risk infants. *Journal of Early Intervention, 13,* 50–60.

Bricker, D., Squires, J., Kaminski, R., & Mounts, L. (1988). The validity, reliability and cost of a parent-completed questionnaire system to evaluate at-risk infants. *Journal of Pediatric Psychology, 13*(1), 55–68.

Bricker, D., & Veltman, M. (1990). Early intervention programs: Child-focused approaches. In S. J. Meisels & J. P. Shonkoff (Eds.), *Handbook of early childhood intervention* (pp. 373–399). New York: Cambridge University Press.

Brinker, R., Frazier, W., & Baxter, A. (1992). Maintaining involvement of inner city families in early intervention programs through a program of incentives: Looking beyond family systems to societal systems. *OSERS News in Print, 4*(3), 8–17.

Brinkworth, R. (1975). Early treatment and training for the infant with Down syndrome. *Royal Society of Health, 2,* 75–78.

Brittan (CA) Elementary School District. (1990). *Education for the Handicapped Law Report,* 16 EHLR 1226. (Now *Individuals with Disabilities Education Law Report.*)

Brockenbrough, K. (1991). Preparing personnel for pluralism. *NEC*TAS Notes,* August 26. Chapel Hill, NC: National Early Childhood Technical Assistance Center.

Brodsky, P., Brodsky, M., Lee, H., & Sever, L. (1986). Two evaluation studies of Reitan's REHABIT program for the retraining of brain dysfunctions. *Journal of Perceptual and Motor Skills, 63,* 501–502.

Brody, J. E. (1991). A quality of life determined by a baby's size. *New York Times,* October 1, A1, A20.

Bronfenbrenner, U. (1979). *The ecology of human development: Experiments by nature and design.* Cambridge, MA: Harvard University Press.

Bronfenbrenner, U. (1989). Ecological systems theory. *Annals of Child Development, 6,* 187–249.

Bronowski, J. (1973). *The ascent of man.* Boston: Little, Brown.

Brown, S. C. (1986). Etiological trends, characteristics, and distributions. In A. N. Schildroth & M. A. Karchmer (Eds.), *Deaf children in America* (pp. 33–54). San Diego, CA: College Hill Press.

Brown, W., & Brown, C. (1993). Defining eligibility for early intervention. In W. Brown, S. K. Thurman, & L. F. Pearl (Eds.), *Family-centered early intervention with infants and toddlers: Innovative cross-disciplinary approaches* (pp. 21–42). Baltimore: Paul H. Brookes.

Brown, C. W., Perry, D. F., & Kurland, S. (1994). Funding policies that affect children: What every early interventionist should know. *Infants and Young Children, 6*(4), 1–12.

Brown, W., & Rule, S. (1993). Personnel and disciplines in early intervention. In W. Brown, S. K. Thurman, & L. F. Pearl (Eds.), *Family-centered early intervention with infants and toddlers: Innovative cross-disciplinary approaches.* (pp. 245–268) Baltimore: Paul H. Brookes.

Bruder, M. B. (1997). The effectiveness of specific educational/developmental criteria for children with established conditions. In M. J. Guralnick (Ed.), *The effectiveness of early intervention.* Baltimore: Paul H. Brookes.

Bruder, M. B., Lippman, C., & Bologna, T. M. (1994). Personnel preparation in early intervention: Building capacity for program expansion within institutions of higher education. *Journal of Early Intervention, 18*(1), 103–110.

Bruininks, R., Thurlow, M., & Ysseldyke, J. (1992). Assessing the right outcomes: Prospects for improving education for children with disabilities. *Education and Training in Mental Retardation, 27*(2), 167–175.

Bruner, J. (1966). *Toward a theory of instruction.* New York: Norton.

Bruner, J. (1981). The social context of language acquisition. *Language and Communication, 1,* 155–178.

Brunquell, P. J. (1994). Listening to epilepsy. *Infants and Young Children, 7*(1), 24–33.

Buysse, V., & Bailey, D. (1993). Behavioral and developmental outcomes in young children with disabilities in integrated and segregated settings: A review of comparative studies. *Journal of Special Education, 26*(4), 434–461.

Calem, R. E. (1992). Coming soon: The PC with ears. *New York Times,* August 30, p. 9.

Campbell, P. H. (1991). Evaluation and assessment in early intervention for infants and toddlers. *Journal of Early Intervention, 15*(1), 36–45.

Campbell, S. B. (1987). Parent referred problem three year olds: Developmental changes in symptoms. *Journal of Child Psychology and Psychiatry, 28,* 835–846.

Campbell, S. B. (1990). *Behavioral problems in preschool children.* New York: Guilford Press.

Cardon, L. R., Smith, S. D., Fulker, D. W., Kimberling, W. J., Pennington, B. F., & DeFries, J. C. (1994). Quantitative trait locus for reading disability on chromosome 6. *Science, 266,* 276–279.

Carnegie Corporation of New York. (1994). *Starting points: Meeting the needs of our youngest children.* New York: Author.

Carpenter, R., Mastergeorge, A., & Collins, T. (1983). The acquisition of communicative intentions in infants eight to fifteen months of age. *Language and Speech, 26,* 101–116.

Carta, J. J., Schwartz, I. S., Atwater, J. B., & McConnell, S. R. (1991). Developmentally appropriate practice: Appraising its usefulness for young children with disabilities. *Topics in Early Childhood Special Education, 11*(1), 1–20.

Carter, K. (1983). Comprehensive preliminary assessment of low vision. In R. T. Jose (Ed.), *Understanding low vision.* New York: American Foundation for the Blind.

Casto, G., & Mastropieri, M. A. (1986a). The efficacy of early intervention programs: A meta-analysis. *Exceptional Children, 52*(5), 417–424.

Casto, G., & Mastropieri, M. A. (1986b). Much ado about nothing: A reply to Dunst and Snyder. *Exceptional Children, 53*(3), 277–279.

Casto, G., & White, K. R. (1985). The efficacy of early intervention programs with environmentally at-risk infants. *Journal of Children in Contemporary Society, 17,* 37–48.

Cavallaro, S., & Porter, R. (1980). Peer preferences of at-risk and normally developing children in a preschool mainstream classroom. *American Journal of Mental Deficiency, 84*(4), 357–366.

Center for Accessible Housing. (1992). *Recommendations for accessibility standards for children's environments.* Washington, DC: U.S. Architectural and Transportation Barriers Compliance Board.

Centers for Disease Control and Prevention. (1992). Recommendations for the use of folic acid to reduce the number of cases of spina bifida and other neural tube defects. *Morbidity and Mortality Weekly Report, 41,* Number RR-14, September 11.

Chaikind, S., Danielson, L., & Brauen, M. (1993). What do we know about the costs of special education? A selected review. *Journal of Special Education, 26*(4), 344–370.

Chandler, L., Andrews, M., & Swanson, M. (1981). *The movement assessment of infants.* Rolling Bay, WA: Infant Movement Research.

Chapman, J. W. (1992). Learning disabilities in New Zealand: Where kiwis and kids with LD can't fly. *Journal of Learning Disabilities, 25,* 362–370.

Chapman, J., & Elliott, K. (1995). Preschoolers exposed to cocaine: Early childhood special education and Head Start preparation. *Journal of Early Intervention, 19*(2), 118–129.

Charlesworth, R. (1992). *Understanding child development* (3rd ed.). Albany, NY: Delmar.

Charmatz, M. (1993). Legal defense fund. *Broadcaster,* May, 17.

Chasnoff, I. J. (1989a). Cocaine, pregnancy, and the neonate. *Women & Health, 15*(3), 23–35.

Chasnoff, I. J. (1989b). National Epidemiology of Perinatal Drug Use. Paper presented at Drugs, Alcohol, Pregnancy and Parenting Conference, July, Spokane, WA.

Chen, D., Brekken, L., & Chan, S. (1997). Project CRAFT: Culturally Responsive and Family-focused Training. *Infants and Young Children, 10*(1), 61–73.

Chinn, P., & Hughes, S. (1988). Representation of ethnic minorities in special education for the mentally retarded and learning disabled. In L. Olion (Chair), *Reaching new horizons.* Council for Exceptional Children Symposia on the Education of Culturally Diverse Children, Denver.

Chinn, P., & Selma, H. (1987). Representation of minority students in special education classes. *RASE, 8,* 41–46.

Chomsky, N. (1957) *Syntactic structures.* The Hague: Mouton.

Chomsky, N. (1968). *Language and mind.* New York: Harcourt Brace Jovanovich.

Christian, B. T. (1983). A practical reinforcement hierarchy for classroom behavior modification. *Psychology in the Schools, 20,* 83–84.

Clark, T. C., & Watkins, S. (1985). *SKI*HI Curriculum:* Fourth edition. Logan, UT: SKI*HI Institute at Logan State University.

Clarkson, R. L., Vohr, B. R., Blackwell, P. M., & White, K. R. (1994). Universal infant hearing screening and intervention: The Rhode Island program. *Infants and Young Children, 6*(3), 65–74.

Clements, D. H., & Nastasi, B. K. (1992). Computers and early childhood education. In M. Gettinger, S. N. Elliot, & T. R.

Kratochwill (Eds.), *Advances in school psychology: Preschool and early childhood treatment directions* (pp. 187–246). Hillsdale, NJ: Lawrence Erlbaum.

Clements, D. H., Nastasi, B. K., & Swaminathan, S. (1993). Young children and computers: Crossroads and directions from research. *Young Children,* January, pp. 56–64.

Clifford, R. (1991). *State financing of services under P.L. 99-457, Part H.* Chapel Hill, NC: Carolina Policy Studies Program, University of North Carolina.

Clifford, R., Bernier, K. Y., & Harbin, G. (1993). *Financing Part H services: A state level view.* Chapel Hill, NC: Carolina Policy Studies Program.

Cohen, S., Semmes, M., & Guralnick, M. (1979). Public law 94-142 and the education of preschool handicapped children. *Exceptional Children, 45*(4), 279–285.

Cole, J. (1996). Intervention strategies for infants with prenatal drug exposure. *Infants and Young Children, 8*(3), 35–39.

Cole, K. N., Dale, P. S., & Mills, P. S. (1991). Individual differences in language delayed children's responses to direct and interactive preschool instruction. *Topics in Early Childhood Special Education, 11,* 99–124.

Cole, K. N., Dale, P. S., & Mills, P. S., & Jenkins, J. R. (1993). Interaction between early intervention curricula and student characteristics. *Exceptional Children, 60*(1), 17–28.

Coleman, L. (1993). A method for studying the professional practical knowledge of service providers. *Journal of Early Intervention, 17*(1), 21–29.

Commission on Education of the Deaf. (1988). *Toward equality: Education of the deaf.* Washington, DC: U.S. Government Printing Office.

Commission on the Financing of a Free and Appropriate Education for Special Needs Children. (1983). Unpublished report to the Subcommittee on Select Education, U.S. House of Representatives, March.

Cone, J. D., Anderson, J. A., Harris, F. C., Goff, D. K., & Fox, S. R. (1988). Developing and maintaining social interaction in profoundly retarded young males. *Journal of Abnormal Child Psychology, 6,* 351–360.

Congressional Research Service. (1986). *Preschool programs for the education of handicapped children: Background, issues, and federal policy options.* Washington, DC: Library of Congress.

Connolly, B. H., Morgan, S. B., & Russell, F. F. (1984). Evaluation of children with Down syndrome who participated in an early intervention program. *Physical Therapist, 64,* 1515–1518.

Connolly, B. H., Morgan, S. B., Russell, F. F., & Fulliton, W. L. (1993). A longitudinal study of children with Down syndrome who experienced early intervention programming. *Physical Therapist, 73*(3), 170–179.

Cooke, R. (1993). Fragile-X: Genetic screenings raise new hopes of treatment, and a whole new set of problems. *Newsday,* May 30, 7, pp. 58–59.

Cooley, W. C., & Graham, J. M. (1991). Down syndrome: An update and review for the primary paediatrician. *Clinical Paediatrics, 30*(4), 233–253.

Corsaro, W. A. (1985). *Friendships and peer culture in the early years.* Norwood, NJ: Ablex.

Coster, W. J., & Haley, S. M. (1992). Conceptualization and measurement of disablement in infants and young children. *Infants and Young Children, 4*(4), 11–22.

Council for Exceptional Children. (1993). CEC policy on inclusive schools and community settings. *Teaching Exceptional Children,* Supplement, *25*(4), May.

Cowley, G. (1990). Made to order babies. *Newsweek,* special edition, Winter/Spring, pp. 94–95, 98, 100.

Cox, G. A., Cole, N. M., Matsumura, K., Phelps, S. F., Hauschka, S. D., Campbell, K. P., Faulkner, J. A., & Chamberlain, J. S. (1993). Overexpression of dystrophin in transgenic *mdx* mice eliminates dystrophic symptoms without toxicity. *Nature, 364*(6439), 725–729.

Crossley, R. (1992). Getting the words out: Case studies in facilitated communication training. *Topics in Language Disorders, 12*(4), 46–59.

Crossley, R. (1993). Facilitated communication training in North America. *International Exchange of Experts and Information in Rehabilitation,* special issue, 1–11.

Crossley, R., & Remington-Gurney, J. (1992). Getting the words out: Facilitated communication training. *Topics in Language Disorders, 12*(4), 29–45.

Cruickshank, W. (Ed.). (1976). *Cerebral palsy: A developmental disability* (3rd ed.). Syracuse, NY: Syracuse University Press.

Cryer, D., Harms, T., & Bourland, B. (1987a). *Active learning for infants.* Menlo Park, CA: Addison-Wesley.

Cryer, D., Harms, T., & Bourland, B. (1987b). *Active learning for ones.* Menlo Park, CA: Addison-Wesley.

Culbertson, J. L., & Willis, D. J. (Eds.). (1993). *Testing young children: A reference guide for developmental, psychoeducational, and psychosocial assessments.* Austin, TX: PRO-ED.

Cystic Fibrosis Foundation. (1998). *Facts About Cystic Fibrosis* [On-line pamphlet]. Available: www.cff.org/factsabo.htm

Damage from lead exposure is permanent, study indicates. (1990). *Washington Post,* January 11, A8.

Damasio, H., & Damasio, A. (1989). *Lesion localization in neuropsychology.* New York: Oxford University Press.

Danaher, J. (1992). Preschool special education eligibility classifications and criteria. *NEC*TAS Notes* no. 6, November.

Davila, R. R. (1991). Personal communication, August 12.

Davila, R. R. (1993). Personal communication, May 24.

DC:03 casebook. (1997). Washington, DC: ZERO TO THREE.

DeGangi, G., Royeen, C. B., & Wietlisbach, S. (1992). How to examine the individualized family service plan: Preliminary findings and a procedural guide. *Infants and Young Children, 5*(2), 42–56.

Deitz, S. J., & Ferrell, K. A. (1993). Early services for young children with visual impairment: From diagnosis to comprehensive services. *Infants and Young Children, 6*(1), 68–76.

Del'Homme, M. A., Sinclair, E., & Kasari, C. (1994). Preschool children with behavioral problems: Observation in instruction and free play contexts. *Behavioral Disorders, 6*(3), 221–232.

Diagnostic classification of mental health and developmental disorders of infancy and early childhood. (1994). Washington, DC: ZERO TO THREE.

Division for Early Childhood Task Force. (1993). *DEC recommended practices: Indicators of quality in programs for infants and young children with special needs and their families.* Pittsburgh, PA: Council for Exceptional Children, Division for Early Childhood.

Division of Assistance to States. (1979). Policy letter to Harold Burke (January 30). Unpublished memorandum from what is now the Office of Special Education Programs. Washington, DC: U.S. Department of Health, Education, and Welfare.

Divoky, D. (1989). Ritalin: Education's fix-it drug? *Phi Delta Kappan, 70*(8), 599–605.

Doctors are target of campaign to stop drinking during pregnancy. *The Nation's Health,* May/June, 20.

Dolnick, E. (1993). Deafness as culture. *The Atlantic Monthly, 272*(3), 37–53.

Donnellan, A., Sabin, L., & Majure, L. (1992). Facilitated communication: Beyond the quandary to the questions. *Topics in Language Disorders, 12*(4), 69–82.

Dore, J. (1974). A pragmatic description of early language development. *Journal of Psycholinguistics Research, 4,* 343–351.

Dorris, M. (1989). *The broken cord: A family's ongoing struggle with fetal alcohol syndrome.* New York: Harper & Row.

Duane, D. D., & Leong, C. K. (1985). *Understanding learning disabilities: International and multidisciplinary views.* New York: Plenum Press.

Duara, R., Kushch, A., Gross-Glenn, K., Barker, W. W., Jallad, B., Pascal, S., Lowenstein, D. A., Sheldon, J., Rabin, M., Levin, B., & Lubs, H. (1991). Neuroanatomic differences between dyslexic and normal readers on magnetic resonance imaging scans. *Archives of Neurology, 48,* 410–416.

Duh, S. (Ed.). (1991). *Blacks and AIDS: Causes and origins.* Newbury Park, CA: Sage Publications.

Duncan, J. G. (1993). Personal communication, May 24.

Dunst, C. J. (1981). *Infant learning: A cognitive-linguistic intervention strategy.* Hingham, MA: Teaching Resources.

Dunst, C. J., Johanson, C., Trivette, C.M., & Hamby, D. (1991). Family-oriented early intervention policies and practices: Family-centered or not? *Exceptional Children, 58*(2), 115–126.

Dunst, C. J., & Snyder, S. W. (1986). A critique of the Utah State University early intervention meta-analysis research. *Exceptional Children, 53*(3), 269–276.

Dunst, C. J., & Trivette, C. M. (1988). An enablement and empowerment perspective on case management. *Topics in Early Childhood, 8,* 87–102.

Dunst, C., Trivette, C. M., & Deal, A. (1993). *Supporting and strengthening families: Methods, strategies, and outcomes.* Cambridge, MA: Brookline Books.

Durenberger, D. (1991). Statement before Subcommittee on Disability Policy, March 15. *Senate report S. hrg. 102-133.* Washington, DC: U.S. Government Printing Office, 19.

Dyslexia may be tied to brain's last fetal stages. (1993). *Newsday,* August 26, p. 65.

Eaton, B. (1997). Personal communication, February 7.

Eberlin, M., McConnachie, G., Ibel, S., & Volpe, L. (1993). Facilitated communication: A failure to replicate the phenomenon. *Journal of Autism and Developmental Disorders, 23*(3), 507–529.

Education Commission of the States. (1989). A close look at the shortage of minority teachers. *Education Week,* May, 29.

Emihovich, C., & Miller, G. (1988). Effects of Logo and CAI on black first graders' achievement, reflectivity, and self-esteem. *The Elementary School Journal, 88,* 473–487.

Enscher, G., Blatt, B., & Winschel, J. (1977). Head Start for the handicapped: Congressional mandate audit. *Exceptional Children, 43*(4), 202–210.

Epps, E. G. (1974). Situational effects in testing. In L.P. Miller (Ed.), *The testing of black students: A symposium* (pp. 17–29). Orlando, FL: Harcourt Brace Jovanovich.

Erikson, E. (1963). *Childhood and society* (2nd ed.). New York: Norton.

Erwin, E. J. (1994). Social competence in young children with visual impairments. *Infants and Young Children, 6*(3), 26–33.

Escobar, C. M., Barnett, W. S., & Goetze, L. D. (1994). Cost analysis in early intervention. *Journal of Early Intervention, 18*(1), 48–63.

Ewigman, B. G., Crane, J. P., Frigoletto, F. D., LeFevre, M. L., Bain, R. P., McNellis, D., & the RADIUS Study Group. (1993). *Effects of prenatal ultrasound screening on perinatal outcome.* New England Journal of Medicine, *329*(12), 821–827.

Experimental maternal blood test for fetal ills. (1991). *New York Times,* October 9, C14.

Fagan, J., & Singer, L. (1983). Infant recognition memory as a measure of intelligence. In L. Lipsett (Ed.), *Advances in infant research* (Vol. 2, pp. 31–78). Norwood, NJ: Ablex.

Farran, D. C. (1990). Effects of intervention with disadvantaged and disabled children: A decade review. In S. J. Meisels & J. P. Shonkoff (Eds.), *Handbook of early childhood intervention.* New York: Cambridge University Press.

Farran, D. C., Kasari, C., Comfort, M., & Jay, S. (1986). *Parent/Caregiver Involvement Scale.* (Revision of *Parent-Child Interaction Scale,* 1980, 1981, 1984) (D. C. Farran, Center for Development of Early Education, Kamehameha Schools, Bishop Estate, Honolulu, HI 96817.)

Fenichel, G. M., Mendell, J. R., Moxley, R. T., Griggs, R. C., Brooke, M. H., Miller, J. P., Pestronk, A., Robison, J., King, W., Sigore, L., Pandya, S., Florence, J., Schierbecker, J., & Wilson, B. (1991). A comparison of daily and alternate-day prednisone therapy in the treatment of Duchenne muscular dystrophy. *Archives of Neurology, 48,* 575–579.

Ferguson, P., Ferguson, D., & Taylor, S. (Eds.). (1992). *Interpreting disability: A qualitative reader.* New York: Teachers College Press.

Ferrell, K. A. (1984). The editors talk. *Education of the Visually Handicapped, 16,* 43–46.

Fetal tissue transplants—and hope. (1992). *New York Times,* December 5, p. 18.

Fewell, R. R. (1991). Trends in the assessment of infants and toddlers with disabilities. *Exceptional Children, 58*(2), 166–173.

Fewell, R. R., & Glick, M. P. (1993). Observing play: An appropriate process for learning and assessment. *Infants and Young Children, 5*(4), 35–43.

Fewell, R. R., & Vadasy, P. F. (1983). *Learning through play: A resource manual for teachers and parents.* Hingham, MA: Teaching Resources.

Figueroa, R. A. (1990). Assessment of linguistic minority group children. In C. R. Reynolds & R. W. Kamphaus (Eds.), *Handbook of psychological and educational assessment of children; Vol. 1. Intelligence and achievement* (pp. 671–696). New York: Guilford.

Fiore, T., Becker, E., & Nero, R. (1993). Educational interventions for students with attention deficit disorder. *Exceptional Children, 60*(2), 163–173.

Fisher, F. D. (1992). What the coming telecommunications infrastructure could mean to our family. In *A national information network: Changing our lives in the 21st century.* (pp. 1–18). Nashville, TN, and Queenstown, MD: Northern Telecom Inc. and the Aspen Institute.

Fletcher, J. M. (1992). The validity of distinguishing children with language and learning disabilities according to discrepancies with IQ: Introduction to the special series. *Journal of Learning Disabilities, 25*(9), 546–548.

Flinchum, B. M. (1975). *Motor development in early childhood.* St. Louis, MO: Mosby.

Florida Department of Education. (1988). *Building standards for educational facilities for handicapped children.* Tallahassee, FL: Author.

Flowers, D. L., Wood, F. B., & Naylor, C. E. (1991). Regional cerebral blood flow correlates of language processes in reading disability. *Archives of Neurology, 48,* 637–643.

Folio, M. R., & Fewell, R. R. (1983). *Peabody Developmental Motor Scales and Activity Cards.* Allen, TX: DLM Teaching Resources.

Ford, B. (1992). Multicultural education training for special educators working with African-American youth. *Exceptional Children, 59*(2), 107–114.

Forness, S. (1989). Testimony. *S. hrg. report 101-287.* (186–200). Washington, DC: U.S. Government Printing Office.

Fowell, N., & Lawton, J. (1992). An alternative view of appropriate practice in early childhood education. *Early Childhood Research Quarterly, 7,* 53–73.

Fowler, S. A., Chandler, L. K., Johnson, T. E., & Stella, M. E. (1988). Individualizing family involvement in school transitions: Gathering information and choosing the next program. *Journal of the Division for Early Childhood, 12,* 208–216.

Fowler, S. A., Schwartz, I., & Atwater, J. (1991). Perspectives on the transition from preschool to kindergarten for children with disabilities and their families. *Exceptional Children, 58*(2), 136–145.

Fox, H., Wicks, L., McManus, M., & Newacheck, P. (1992). Private and public health insurance for early intervention services. *Journal of Early Intervention, 16*(2), 109–122.

Fraiberg, S. (1968). Parallel and divergent patterns in blind and sighted infants. *The Psychological Study of the Child, 23,* 264–300.

Fraiberg, S. (1970). Interventions in infancy. *Journal of the American Academy of Child Psychiatry, 10*(3) 381–405.

Fraiberg, S. (1975). The development of human attachments in infants blind from birth. *Merrill-Palmer Quarterly, 21,* 315–334.

Fraiberg, S. (1977). *Insights from the blind: Comparative studies of blind and sighted infants.* New York: Basic Status in Books.

Fraiberg, S., & Freedman, C. A. (1964). Studies in the ego development of the congenitally blind child. *The Psychoanalytic Study of the Child, 19,* 113–169.

Fraiberg, S., Smith, M., & Adelson, E. (1969). An educational program for blind infants. *Journal of Special Education, 3*(2), 121–139.

Frank, D. A. (1990). Infants of substance abusing mothers: Demographics and medical profile. Paper presented at Babies & Cocaine Conference, August, Washington, DC.

Frankenburg, W. K., Dodds, J. B., Archer, P., Bresnick, B., Maschka, P., Edelman, N., & Shapiro, H. (1990). *Denver II screening manual.* Denver, CO: Denver Developmental Materials.

Franklin, M. (1992). Culturally sensitive instructional practices for African-American learners with disabilities. *Exceptional Children, 59*(2), 115–122.

Freeman, B. J. (1993). The syndrome of autism: Update and guidelines for diagnosis. *Infants and Young Children, 6*(6), 1–11.

Freud, S. (1933). New introductory lectures on psychoanalysis. In J. Strachy (Ed., Trans.), *The complete psychological works* (Vol. 22). New York: Norton.

Freund, L. S. (1994). Diagnosis and developmental issues for young children with Fragile-X syndrome. *Infants and Young Children, 6*(3), 34–45.

Freundlich, N. (1992). What gene-splicing can do for the lowly seaweed. *Business Week,* October 5, p. 107.

Friedman, R., Silver, S., Duchnowski, A., Kutash, K., & Eisen, M. (1988). *Characteristics of children with serious emotional disturbances identified by public systems as requiring services.* Tampa, FL: Florida Mental Health Institute.

Friend, T. (1991). Sperm may carry cocaine to egg. *USA Today,* October 9.

Friend, T. (1993). Gene defects in 'Bubble Boy,' other ills found. *USA Today,* April 9, D1.

Frith, U. (1989). *Autism: Explaining the enigma.* Cambridge, MA: Basil Blackwell.

Frith, U. (1993). Autism. *Scientific American,* June, 108–114.

From ADA to empowerment: The report of the Task Force on the Rights and Empowerment of Americans with Disabilities. (1991). Washington, DC: Task Force.

Fuchs, D., Featherstone, N., Garwick, D., & Fuchs, L. (1984). Effects of examiner familiarity and task characteristics on speech and language-impaired children's test performance. *Measurement and Evaluation in Guidance, 16*(4), 198–204.

Fuchs, D., Fuchs, L., Benowitz, S., & Barringer, K. (1987). Norm-referenced tests: Are they valid for use with handicapped students? *Exceptional Children, 54*, 263–272.

Fuchs, D., Fuchs, L., Garwick, D., & Featherstone, N. (1983). Test performance of language-handicapped children with familiar and unfamiliar examiners. *Journal of Psychology, 1214*, 37–46.

Furuno, S., O'Reilly, A., Hosaka, C., Inatsuka, T., Allman, T., & Ziesloft, B. (1985). *Hawaii Early Learning Profile* (HELP) (Rev. ed.). Palo Alto, CA: VORT Corp.

Galaburda, A. M., Menard, M. T., & Rosen, G. D. (1994). Evidence for aberrant auditory anatomy in developmental dyslexia. *Proceedings of the National Academy of Sciences, 91*, 8010–8013.

Galanti, G. (Ed.). (1991). *Caring for patients from different cultures: Case studies from American hospitals.* Philadelphia: University of Pennsylvania Press.

Gallagher, J. (1972). The special education contract for mildly handicapped children. *Exceptional Children, 28*, 527–535.

Gandell, T., & Laufer, D. (1993). Developing a telecommunications curriculum for students with physical disabilities. *Teaching Exceptional Children, 25*(2), 26–28.

Garcia, E., & McLaughlin, B. (1995). *Meeting the challenge of linguistic and cultural diversity in early childhood education.* New York: Teachers College Press.

Garshelis, J. A., & McConnell, S. R. (1993). Comparison of family needs assessed by mothers, individual professionals, and interdisciplinary teams. *Journal of Early Intervention, 17*(1), 36–49.

Gay, G. (1989). Ethnic minorities and educational equality. In J. Banks and C. Banks (Eds.), *Multicultural education: Issues and perspectives* (pp. 167–188). Boston: Allyn & Bacon.

Gelman, D. (1990). How the brain recovers. *Newsweek*, April 9, 48–50.

Gene behind retardation found. (1991). *Newsday*, May 30, 6.

General Accounting Office. (1979). *The Comptroller General's report: Early childhood and family development programs improve the quality of life for low income families.* Washington, DC: Author.

Gerales, E., & Ritter, T. (Eds.). (1991). *Children with cerebral palsy: A parent's guide.* Rockville, MD: Woodbine House.

Gesell, A. (1925). *The mental growth of the preschool child: A psychological outline of normal development from birth to the sixth year.* New York: Macmillan.

Getting on the electronic highway. (1994). *Teaching Exceptional Children, 26*(2), Winter, 64–71.

Gibbs, E. D. (1990). Assessment of infant mental ability: Conventional tests and issues of prediction. In E. D. Gibbs & D. M. Teti (Eds.), *Interdisciplinary assessment of infants: A guide for early intervention professionals* (pp. 77–90). Baltimore: Paul H. Brookes.

Glass, G. V. (1976). Primary, secondary, and meta-analysis of research. Educational Researcher, *5*(10), 3–8.

Glass, G. V., McGaw, B., & Smith. M. L. (1981). *Meta-analysis in social research.* Newbury Park, CA: Sage.

Glass, P. (1993). Development of visual function in preterm infants: Implications for early intervention. *Infants and Young Children, 6*(1), 11–20.

Gliedman, J., & Roth, W. (1980). *The unexpected minority.* New York: Harcourt Brace Jovanovich.

Goetze, L. D., Immel, N., Escobar, C. M., Gillette, Y., Coury, D., & Hansen, N. (1993). Does more intensive neonatal intensive care unit follow-up service result in better outcomes? A cost-effective analysis. *Early Education and Development, 4*(4), 275–289.

Goodman, G., & Poillion, M. J. (1992). ADD: Acronym for any dysfunction or difficulty. *Journal of Special Education, 26*(1), 37–56.

Goodman, J. (1992). When slow is fast enough: Educating the delayed preschool child. New York: Guilford Press.

Goodman, J. (1994). 'Empowerment' versus 'best interests': Client-professional relationships. *Infants and Young Children, 6*(4), vi–x.

Goodman, J., & Bond, L. (1993). The individualized education program: A retrospective critique. *Journal of Special Education, 26*(4), 408–422.

Gore, A. (1993). Remarks by Vice President Al Gore at the National Press Club, December 21. Unpublished speech, transcript from the White House, Office of the Vice President.

Gottlieb, J., & Davis, J. (1973). Social acceptance of EMR children during overt behavioral interactions. *American Journal of Mental Deficiency, 78*(2), 141–143.

Graham, M., & Bryant, D. (1993). Developmentally appropriate environments for children with special needs. *Infants and Young Children, 5*(3), 31–42.

Greenfield, J. (1972). *A child called Noah.* New York: Holt, Rinehart & Winston.

Griffith, D. R. (1990). The effects of perinatal drug exposure on child development: Implications for early intervention and education. Paper presented at Babies & Cocaine Conference, November, San Francisco, CA.

Guralnick, M. J. (1980). Special interaction among preschool handicapped children. *Exceptional Children, 46*, 248–253.

Guralnick, M. J. (1990). Early childhood mainstreaming. *Topics in Early Childhood Special Education, 10*(2), 1–17.

Guralnick, M. J. (1991). The next decade of research on the effectiveness of early intervention. *Exceptional Children, 58*(2), 174–183.

Guralnick, M. J. (1993). Second generation research on the effectiveness of early intervention. *Early Education and Development, 4*(4), 366–378.

Guralnick, M. J. (Ed.). (1997). *The effectiveness of early intervention.* Baltimore: Paul H. Brookes.

Hall, S. S. (1989). The gene boy. *Hippocrates*, November/December, 75–76, 78, 80–82.

Hallahan, D. P. (1992). Some thoughts on why the prevalence of learning disabilities has increased. *Journal of Learning Disabilities, 25*(8), 523–528.

Halverson, L. E. (1971). The significance of motor development. In G. Engstrom (Ed.), *The significance of the young child's motor development* (pp. 17–33). Washington, DC: National Association for the Education of Young Children.

Hanft, B., & Feinberg, E. (1997). Toward the development of a framework for determining the frequency and intensity of early intervention services. *Infants and Young Children, 10*(1), 27–37.

Hanft, B., & Royeen, C. B. (1991). Commentary. *Infants and Young Children, 4*(2), 8–11.

Hanft, B., & Striffler, N. (1995). Incorporating developmental therapy in early childhood programs: Challenges and promising practices. *Infants and Young Children, 8*(2) 37–47.

Hanline, M. F., & Knowlton, A. (1988). A collaborative model for providing support to parents during their child's transition from infant intervention to preschool special education public school programs. *Journal of the Division for Early Childhood, 12,* 116–125.

Harbin, G., Gallagher, J., & Terry, D. (1991). Defining the eligible population: Policy issues and challenges. *Journal of Early Intervention, 15*(1), 13–20.

Harkin, T. (1989). Opening statement, April 2. *S. hrg. 101-287.* Washington, DC: U.S. Government Printing Office, 1–2.

Harms, T., Clifford, R. M., & Bailey, D. B. (1986). *Special needs items for the ECERS.* Chapel Hill, NC: Frank Porter Graham Child Development Center.

Harms, T., Clifford, R. M., & Cryer, D. (1980). *Early Childhood Environment Rating Scale.* New York: Teachers College Press.

Harms, T., Cryer, D., & Clifford, R. M. (1989). *The Infant/Toddler Environment Rating Scale.* New York: Teachers College Press.

Harnshaw, J., Scheiner, A., Moxley, A., et al. (1976). School failure and deafness after silent congenital cytomegalovirus infection. *New England Journal of Medicine, 295,* 468–470.

Harrigan, S. (1992). 'Jerry's Orphans.' *Newsday,* August 28, 1, 3, 35.

Harris & Associates. (1989). *The ICD survey III: A report card on special education.* New York: International Center for the Disabled.

Harris, S. L., & Handleman, J. S. (Eds.). (1993). *Preschool education programs for children with autism.* Austin, TX: PRO-ED.

Harry, B. (1992a). *Cultural diversity, families, and the special education system: Communication and empowerment.* New York: Teachers College Press.

Harry, B. (1992b). Restructuring the participation of African-American parents in special education. *Exceptional Children, 59*(2), 123–131.

Hart, B., & Risley, T. (1968). Establishing use of descriptive adjectives in the spontaneous speech of disadvantaged preschool children. *Journal of Applied Behavior Analysis, 8,* 411–420.

Hart, V. (1986). Testimony before the Subcommittee on Select Education, July 24. *House Report 99-120.* Washington, DC: U.S. Government Printing Office, 144–155.

Hartshorne, T. S., & Boomer, L. W. (1993). Privacy of school records: What every special education teacher should know. *Teaching Exceptional Children, 25*(4), Summer, 32–35.

Hauger, S. (1992). Electronic service delivery and persons with disabilities. (November 9) Unpublished document. Blacksburg, VA: Draft report to U.S. Congress Office of Technology Assessment.

Head Start: The emotional foundations of school readiness. (1992). Arlington, VA: ZERO TO THREE/National Center for Clinical Infant Programs.

Healy, A., Keesee, P., & Smith, B. (1989). *Early services for children with special needs: Transactions for family support.* Baltimore: Paul H. Brookes.

Hebbeler, K. M., Smith, B. J., & Black, T. L. (1991). Federal early childhood special education policy: A model for the improvement of services for children with disabilities. *Exceptional Children, 58*(2), 104–112.

Heckman, M., & Rike, C. (1994). Westwood Early Learning Center: A framework for integrating young children with disabilities. *Teaching Exceptional Children, 26*(2), 30–35.

Heekin, S. (1993). *Section 619 profile: Fourth edition.* Chapel Hill, NC: NEC*TAS.

Hehir, T. (1993). Letter to Peter J. Seiler, November 19. Policy letter, Office of Special Education Programs, U.S. Department of Education.

Heriza, C., & Sweeney, J. (1994). Pediatric physical therapy: Part I. Practice Scope, scientific basis, and theoretical foundation. *Infants and Young Children, 7*(2), 20–32.

Heriza, C., & Sweeney, J. (1995). Pediatric physical therapy: Part II. Approaches to movement dysfunction. *Infants and Young Children, 8*(2), 1–14.

Hilts, P. J. (1992). Congress urged to lift ban on fetal-tissue research. *New York Times*, May 27, A12.

Hirsch, K. (1993). Disabled adults: An untapped resource for the education of disabled children. *Disability Studies Quarterly*, *13*(4), 32–34.

Hirshoren, Al, & Umansky, W. (1977). Certification for teachers of preschool handicapped children. *Exceptional Children*, *44*(3), 191–193.

Hobbs, N. (Ed.). (1975). *Issues in the classification of children.* San Francisco: Jossey-Bass.

Hodapp, R. M., Evans, D. W., & Ward, B. A. (1989). Communicative interaction between teachers and children with severe handicaps. *Mental Retardation*, *27*(6), 388–395.

Holder-Brown, L., & Parette. H. P. (1992). Children with disabilities who use assistive technology: Ethical considerations. *Young Children*, *47*(6), 73–77.

Honey, M., & Henriquez, A. (1993). *Telecommunications and K–12 educators: Findings from a national survey.* New York: Bank Street College of Education, Center for Technology in Education.

Horn, W. (1993). Putting parents first. *Wall Street Journal*, May 28, A10.

Hubbard, R., & Wald, E. (1993). *Exploding the gene myth.* New York: Beacon.

Hudson, A., Malita, B., & Arnold, W. (1993). Brief report: A case study assessing the validity of facilitated communication. *Journal of Autism and Developmental Disorders*, *23*(1), 165–173.

Hughes, M., & Macleod, H. (1986). Part II: Using Logo with very young children. In R. Lawler, B. Boulay, M. Hughes, & H. Macleod (Eds.), *Cognition and computers: Studies in learning* (pp. 179–219). Chichester, England: Ellis Horwood Limited.

Humphreys, R. (1989). Patterns of pediatric brain injury. In M. Miner & K. Wagner (Eds.), *Neurotrauma 3: Treatment, rehabilitation and related issues* (pp. 115–126). Stoneham, MA: Butterworth.

Hutchins, J. (1994). A guide to purchasing a caption decoder-equipped TV set. *GA-SK, 12*(2), 1, 8. (Newsletter published by Telecommunications for the Deaf Inc., 8719 Colesville Road, Suite 300, Silver Spring, MD 20910)

ICD/Harris & Associates. (1986). *The ICD Survey of disabled Americans: Bringing disabled Americans into the mainstream.* New York: International Center for the Disabled.

Individuals with Disabilities Education Act, 20 U.S.C. 1400, as amended by PL 102-119, the IDEA amendments of 1991.

Infant Health and Development Program. (1990). Enhancing the outcomes of low-birth-weight, premature infants. *Journal of the American Medical Association*, *263*, 3035–3042.

Innocenti, M. S., Hollinger, P. D., Escobar, C. M., & White, K. R. (1993). The cost-effectiveness of adding one type of parent involvement to an early intervention program. *Early Education and Development*, *4*(4), 306–326.

Innocenti, M. S., & White, K. R. (1993). Are more intensive early intervention programs more effective? A review of the literature. *Exceptionality*, *4*(1), 31–50.

Internet access points to ERIC. (1993). *The ERIC Networker* 4.1, July.

Ireton, H., & Thwing, E. (1974a). *The Early Child Development Inventory.* Minneapolis, MN: Behavior Science Systems.

Ireton, H., & Thwing, E. (1974b). *Manual for the Minnesota Child Development Inventory.* Minneapolis, MN: Behavior Science Systems.

Ireton, H., & Thwing, E. (1974c). *Minnesota Infant Development Inventory.* Minneapolis, MN: Behavior Science Systems.

Ireton, H., & Thwing, E. (1974d). *Minnesota Pre-Kindergarten Development Inventory.* Minneapolis, MN: Behavior Science Systems.

Ireton, H., & Thwing, E. (1974e). *Minnesota Preschool Inventory.* Minneapolis, MN: Behavior Science Systems.

Jenkins, J. R., Cole, K. N., Dale, P. D., & Mills, P. E. (1989). *A longitudinal comparison of two preschool instruction models.* (Final report no. G008400646, for U.S. Department of Education.) Seattle, WA: University of Washington, Experimental Education Unit WJ-10.

Jenkins, J. R., & Sells, C. J. (1984). Physical and occupational therapy: Effects related to treatment, frequency, and motor delay. *Journal of Learning Disabilities*, *17*, 89–95.

Jenkins, J. R., Sells, C. J., Brady, D., Down, J., Moore, B., Carman, P., & Holm, R. (1982). Effects of occupational and physical therapy in a school program. *Physical and Occupational Therapy in Pediatrics, 4*, 19–29.

Jenson, W. R., Sloane, H. N., & Young, K. R. (1988). *Applied behavioral analysis in education: A structured approach.* Englewood Cliffs, NJ: Prentice Hall.

Johns, N., & Harvey. C. (1993). Training for work with parents: Strategies for engaging practitioners who are uninterested or resistant. *Infants and Young Children*, *5*(4), 52–57.

Johnson, C. B. (1993). Developmental issues: Children infected with the human Immunodeficiency Virus. *Infants and Young Children*, *6*(1), 1–10.

Johnson, J. E., & Johnson, K. M. (1992). Clarifying the developmental perspective in response to Carta, Schwartz, Atwater, and McConnell. *Topics in Early Childhood Special Education*, *12*(4), 439–457.

Johnson, K. M., & Johnson, J. E. (1993). Rejoinder to Carter, Atwater, Schwartz, and McConnell. *Topics in Early Childhood Special Education, 13*(3), 255–257.

Johnson, L. J., Gallagher, R. J., Cook, M., & Wong, P. (1995). Critical skills for kindergarten: Perceptions from kindergarten teachers. *Journal of Early Intervention, 19*(4), 315–349.

Johnson, L. J., Kilgo, J., Cook, M. J., Hammitte, D. J., Beauchamp, K., & Finn, D. (1992). The skills needed by early intervention administrators/supervisors: A study across six states. *Journal of Early Intervention, 16*(2), 136–145.

Johnson, L. J., & LaMontagne, M. J. (1993). Using content analysis to examine the verbal or written communication of stakeholders within early intervention. *Journal of Early Intervention, 17*(1), 73–79.

Johnson-Martin, N. M., Jens, K. G., & Attermeier, S. A. (1986). *The Carolina curriculum for handicapped infants and infants at risk.* Baltimore: Paul H. Brookes.

Jones, L. E. (1988). The free limb scheme and the limb-deficient child in Australia. *Australian Paediatric Journal, 24*(5), 290–294.

Kakalik, J., Furry, W., Thomas, M., & Carney, M. (1981). *The costs of special education* (a Rand Note). Santa Monica, CA: Rand Corporation.

Kantor, R., Elgas, P. M., & Fernie, D. E. (1993). Cultural knowledge and social competence within a preschool peer culture group. *Early Childhood Research Quarterly, 8*, 125–147.

Kaplan-Sanoff, M., Parker, S., & Zuckerman, B. (1991). Poverty and early childhood development: What do we know, and what should we do? *Infants and Young Children, 4*(1), 68–76.

Kauffman, J. (1993). How we might achieve the radical reform of special education. *Exceptional Children, 60*(1), 6–16.

Kaufman, A. S., & Kaufman, N. L. (1983). *K–ABC administration and scoring manual.* Circle Pines, MN: American Guidance Service.

Keeney, S. M. (1994). Going back to school. *REHAB Management, 7*(1), 24–28.

Kelly, J. (1991). A question of concentration. *Newsday*, March 2, 15–17.

Kemp, D. T. (1978). Stimulated acoustic emissions from within the human auditory system. *Journal of the Acoustic Society of America, 64*, 1386–1391.

Kenny, T. J., & Culbertson, J. L. (1993). Developmental screening for preschoolers. In J. L. Culbertson, & D. J. Willis. (Eds.), *Testing young children: A reference guide for developmental, psychoeducational, and psychosocial assessment.* Austin, TX: PRO-ED.

Kerlinger, F. N. (1986). *Foundations of behavioral research* (3rd ed.). New York: Holt, Rinehart & Winston.

Kermoian, R., & Campos, J. J. (1988). Locomotor experience: A facilitator of spatial cognitive development. *Child Development, 59*, 908–917.

Kevles, D., & Hood, L. (Eds.). (1993). *The code of codes: Scientific and social issues in the Human Genome Project.* Cambridge, MA: Harvard University Press.

Kingsley, J., & Levitz, M. (1994). *Count us in: Growing up with Down syndrome.* New York: Harcourt Brace.

Kirk, S. A. (1963). Behavior, diagnosis and remediation of learning disabilities. In *Proceedings of the annual meeting of the conference on exploration into the problems of the perceptually handicapped child* (Vol. 1). Chicago: Perceptually Handicapped Children.

Kirsch, I. S., Jungeblut, A., Jenkins, L., & Kolstad, A. (1993). *Adult literacy in America.* Washington, DC: U.S. Government Printing Office.

Klein, J. W. (1975). Mainstreaming the preschooler. *Young Children*, July, 317–327.

Knitzer, J. (1988). Policy perspectives on the problem. In J.G. Looney (Ed.), *Chronic mental illness in children and adolescents* (pp. 53–71). Washington, DC: American Psychiatric Press.

Kochanek, T. T., & Buka, S. L. (1991). Using biologic and ecologic factors to identify vulnerable infants and toddlers. *Infants and Young Children, 4*(1), 11–25.

Koegel, R. L., & Mentis, M. (1985). Motivation in childhood autism: Can they or won't they? *Journal of Child Psychology and Psychiatry, 26*, 185–191.

Kohlberg, J., & Mayer, R. (1972). Development as the aim of education. *Harvard Educational Review, 42*, 449–496.

Kohlberg, L. (1984). *Essays on moral development.* San Francisco: Harper & Row.

Kohlberg, L., with DeVries, R., Fein, G., Hart, D., Mayer, R., Noam, G., Snarney, J., & Wertsch, J. (1987). *Child psychology and childhood education: A cognitive developmental view.* New York: Longman.

Kohn, A. (1989). Suffer the restless children. *The Atlantic Monthly, 264*(5), 90–100.

Kolata, G. (1989). A new toll of alcohol abuse: The Indians' next generation. *New York Times*, July 19, A1, D24.

Kolata, G. (1990). Why gene therapy is considered scary, but cell therapy isn't. *New York Times*, September 16, E5.

Kolata, G. (1992a). Genetic defects detected in embryos just days old. *New York Times*, September 24, A1, B10.

Kolata, G. (1992b). Study reports dyslexia is not unalterable, as experts have been assuming. *New York Times*, January 16, A18.

Kontos, S., & File, N. (1992). Conditions of employment, job satisfaction, and job commitment among early intervention personnel. *Journal of Early Intervention, 16*, 155–165.

Kostlenik, M. J. (1992). Myths associated with developmentally appropriate programs. *Young Children, 47*, 17–23.

Kozloff, M. A., Helm, D. T., Cutler, B. C., Douglas-Steele, D., & Scampini, L. (1988). Training programs for families of children with autism or other handicaps. In R. DeV. Peters & R. J. McMahon (Eds.), *Social learning and systems approach to marriage and the family* (pp. 217–250). New York: Brunner/Mazel.

Kozma, I., & Balogh, E. (1995). A brief introduction to conductive education and its application at an early age. *Infants and Young Children, 8*(1), 68–74.

Krajicek, M., & Tompkins, R. (Eds.). (1993). *The medically fragile infant.* Austin, TX: PRO-ED.

Kramer, S. J., & Williams, D. R. (1993). The hearing-impaired infant and toddler: Identification, assessment and intervention. *Infants and Young Children, 6*(1), 35–49.

Krauss, M. W., Upshur, C. C., Shonkoff, J. P., & Hauser-Cram, P. (1993). The impact of parent groups on mothers of infants with disabilities. *Journal of Early Intervention, 17*(1), 8–20.

Kreutz, D. (1993). Seating and positioning for the newly injured. *REHAB Management, 6*(1), 67–75.

Kubler-Ross, E. (1969). *On death and dying.* New York: Macmillan.

Kuzemko, J. A. (1980). *Asthma in children.* Baltimore: University Park Press.

Kyes, K. (1994). Funding for assistive technologies: A conversation with Allan I. Bergman. *REHAB Management,* June/July, 26, 28, 30–31.

LaBlance, G., Steckol, K., & Smith, V. (1994). Stuttering: The role of the classroom teacher. *Teaching Exceptional Children, 26*(2), 10–12.

Ladd, G. W., & Mize, J. (1983). A cognitive-social learning model of social-skill training. *Psychological Review, 90*, 127–157.

Langlors, S. (1992). Genetic diagnosis based on molecular analysis. *Pediatric Clinics of North America, 39*, 91–105.

Lantos, J., & Kohrman, A. (1992). Ethical aspects of home care. *Pediatrics, 89*, 920–924.

LaPlante, M., Hendershot, G., and Moss, A. (1992). Assistive technology devices and home accessibility features: Prevalence, payment, need, and trends. *Advance Data from Vital and Health Statistics, 217*, September 16. Hyattsville, MD: National Center for Health Statistics.

Lary, J., & Edmonds, L. (1996). Prevalence of spina bifida at birth—United States, 1983–1990. A comparison of two surveillance systems. *Morbidity and Mortality Weekly Report, 45*, Number SS-2, April 19.

Latham, P. S., & Latham, P. H. (1992). *Attention Deficit Disorder and the law: A guide for advocates.* Washington, DC: JKL Communications.

LaVor, M., & Harvey, J. (1976). Headstart, Economic Opportunity, Community Partnership Act of 1974. *Exceptional Children, 43*, 227–230.

Law, M., Cadman, D., Rosenbaum, P., Walter, S., Russell, D., & DeMateo, C. (1991). Neurodevelopmental and upper-extremity inhibitive casting for children with cerebral palsy. *Developmental Medicine and Child Neurology, 33*, 379–387.

Lazarro, J. J. (1993). *Adaptive technologies for learning and work environments.* Chicago: American Library Association.

Leary, W. E. (1993). U.S. panel backs testing all babies to uncover hearing losses early. *New York Times,* March 10, C12.

Left, P., & Walizer, E. (1992). *Building the healing partnership: Parents, professionals, and children with chronic illnesses and disabilities.* Cambridge, MA: Brookline Books.

Legal rights of hearing impaired people. (1992). Washington, DC: Gallaudet University.

Lenihan, J. (1977). Disabled Americans: A history. *Performance, 27*(5-6-7). (Ceased publication; contact President's Committee on Employment of People with Disabilities, Washington, DC, for copies.)

Leone, P. E. (1985). Suspension and expulsion of handicapped pupils. *Journal of Special Education, 19*(1), 111–121.

Lerner, J., Lowenthal, B., & Lerner, S. (1995). *Attention deficit disorders: Assessment and teaching.* Pacific Grove, CA: Brooks/Cole Publishing.

Lesar, S., & Maldonado, Y. A. (1994). Infants and young children with HIV infection: Service delivery considerations for family support. *Infants and Young Children, 6*(4), 70–81.

Levine, J., Murphy, D., & Wilson, S. (1993). *Getting men involved: Strategies for early childhood programs.* New York: Scholastic.

Levine, M. N. (1986). Psychoeducational evaluation of children and adolescents with cerebral palsy. In P. J. Lazarus & S. S. Strichart (Eds.), *Psychoeducational evaluation of children and adolescents with low-incidence handicaps* (pp. 267–284). Orlando, FL: Grune & Stratton.

Lewis, P. H. (1992). So the computer talks. Does anyone want to listen? *New York Times,* October 4, p. 9.

Lie, R. T., Wilcox, A. J., & Skjerven, R. (1994). A population-based study of the risk of recurrence of birth defects. *New England Journal of Medicine, 331*(1), 1–4.

Linder, T. W. (1990). *Transdisciplinary play-based assessment: A functional approach to working with young children.* Baltimore: Paul H. Brookes.

Linder, T. W. (1993). *Transdisciplinary play-based assessment.* Baltimore: Paul H. Brookes.

Lindsey, J. D. (Ed.). (1993). *Computers and exceptional individuals.* Austin, TX: PRO-ED.

Little Soldier, L. (1992). Working with Native American children. *Young Children, 47*(6), 15–21.

Livingstone, M. S., Rosen, G. D., Drislane, F. W., & Galaburda, A. M. (1991). Physiological and anatomical evidence for a magnocellular defect in developmental dyslexia. *Proceedings of the National Academy of Sciences, 88,* 7943–7947.

Lockwood, S. (1994). Early speech and langue indicators for later learning problems: Recognizing a language organization disorder. *Infants and Young Children, 7*(2), 43–52.

Lovaas, O. I. (1987). Behavioral treatment and normal educational and intellectual functioning in young autistic children. *Journal of Consulting and Clinical Psychology, 55*(1), 3–9.

Lovaas, O. I. (1989). Interview. *Focus on Autistic Behavior, 4*(4), 1–11.

Lovaas, O. I., Smith, T., & McEachin, J. (1989). Clarifying comments on the young autism study: Reply to Schopler, Short, and Mesibov. *Journal of Consulting and Clinical Psychology, 57*(1), 165–167.

Lozes, M. H. (1988). Bladder and bowel management for children with myelomeningocele. *Infants and Young Children, 1,* 52–62.

Luckasson, R., Coulter, D., Polloway, E., Reiss, S., Shalock, R., Snell, M., Spitalnik, D., & Stark, J. (1993). *Mental retardation: Definitions, classification, and systems of support* (9th ed.). Washington, DC: American Association on Mental Retardation.

Ludlow, B. L. (1994). Using distance education to prepare early intervention personnel. *Infants and Young Children, 7*(1), 51–59.

Lutkenhoff, M., & Oppenheimer, S. (1996). *SPINAbilities: A young person's guide to spina bifida.* Bethesda, MD: Woodbine.

MacFarland-Smith, J., Schuster, J. W., & Stevens, K. B. (1993). Using simultaneous prompting to teach expressive object identification to preschoolers with developmental delays. *Journal of Early Intervention, 16*(4), 50–60.

Madden, J. (1993) Psychological adjustment following SCI. *REHAB Management, 6*(2), 67–70.

Mahoney, G., & O'Sullivan, P. (1990). Early intervention practices with families of children with handicaps. *Mental Retardation, 28,* 169–176.

Mahoney, G., O'Sullivan, P., & Fors, S. (1989). The family practices of service providers for young handicapped children. *Infant Mental Health Journal, 10,* 75–83.

Makarushka, M. (1991). The words they can't say. *New York Times Magazine,* October 6, 32, 33, 36, 70.

Malina, R. M. (1982). Motor development in the early years. In S. G. Moore & K. Cooper (Eds.), *The young child: Reviews of research* (Vol. 3, pp. 211–229). Washington, DC: National Association for the Education of Young Children.

Manegold, C. S. (1994). Special pupils, regular classes, thorny issues. *New York Times,* January 26, A19.

Marlow, M. (1991). Statement at March 15 hearing on Part H reauthorization, U.S. Senate Subcommittee on Disability Policy. *Senate report S. hrg. 102-133.* Washington, DC: U.S. Government Printing Office, 21–25.

Martin, A. (1988). Screening, early intervention, and remediation: Obscuring children's potential. *Harvard Educational Review, 58*(4), 488–502.

Martin, S. L., Ramey, C.T., & Ramey, S. (1990). The prevention of intellectual impairment in children of impoverished families: Findings of a randomized trial of educational day care. *American Journal of Public Health, 80*(7), 844–847.

Maslow, A. H. (1954). *Motivation and personality.* New York: Harper & Row.

Massoulos, C. G. (1988). Acceptance and rejection of friendships in peer culture within an early childhood setting: An observational study approach. Unpublished doctoral dissertation, Ohio State University, Columbus, OH.

Mathews, J. (1992). *A mother's touch: The Tiffany Callo story.* New York: Henry Holt.

McCall, R. (1976). Toward an epigenetic conception of mental development in the first three years of life. In M. Lewis (Ed.), *Origins of intelligence: Infancy and early childhood.* New York: Plenum.

McCarthy, D. (1972). *McCarthy Scales of Children's Abilities.* San Antonio, TX: The Psychological Corporation.

McCollum, J. (1987). Early interventionists in infant and early childhood programs: A comparison of preservice training needs. *Topics in Early Childhood Special Education, 7*(2), 24–35.

McCormick, J. (1993). The enabled computer: Computing for the physically challenged. *Computer Monthly,* January, 202–203.

McCormick, M. C. (1989). Long-term follow-up of infants discharged from neonatal intensive care units. *Journal of the American Medical Association, 261*(12), 1767–1772.

McDermott, R. P., & Church, J. (1976). Making sense and feeling good: The ethnography of communication and identity work. *Communication, 2*, 121–142.

McEvoy, M. A., & Odom, S. L. (1987). Social interaction training for preschool children with behavior disorders. *Behavioral Disorders, 12*, 242–251.

McGinnis, E., & Goldstein, A. (1990). *Skill-streaming in early childhood: Teaching prosocial skills to the preschool and kindergarten child.* Champaign, IL: Research Press.

McLean, M., & McCormick, K. (1993). Assessment and evaluation in early intervention. In W. Brown, S. K. Thurman, & L. F. Pearl (Eds.), *Family-centered early intervention with infants and toddlers: Innovative cross-disciplinary approaches.* Baltimore: Paul H. Brookes.

McLean, M., & Odom, S. (1993). Practices for young children with and without disabilities: A comparison of DEC and NAEYC identified practices. *Topics in Early Childhood Special Education, 13*(3), 274–292.

McNeil, J. (1993a). *Americans with disabilities: 1991–1992.* U.S. Bureau of the Census, Current Population Reports, P-70-33. Washington, DC: U.S. Government Printing Office.

McNeil, J. (1993b). Census Bureau data on persons with disabilities: New results and old questions about validity and reliability. Unpublished paper presented at June 17–19 meeting of Society for Disability Studies.

McNeil, J. (1997). *Americans with disabilities: 1994–1995.* U.S. Bureau of the Census, Current Population Reports, P70-61. Washington, DC: U.S. Department of Commerce.

McNellis, K. L. (1987). In search of the attentional deficit. In S. J. Ceci (Ed.), *Handbook of cognitive, social, and neuropsychological aspects of learning disabilities* (Vol. II). Hillsdale, NJ: Lawrence Erlbaum Associates.

McNulty, B. (1991). Testimony before the Subcommittee on Disability Policy, March 15. *Senate report S. hrg. 102-133.* Washington, DC: U.S. Government Printing Office, 89–93.

McWilliam, P. J., & Bailey, D. B. (1992). *Children, families, and communities of caring: Case studies in early intervention.* Baltimore: Paul H. Brookes.

McWilliam, P. (1993). Real-world challenges to achieving quality. In P. McWilliam, & D. B. Bailey (Eds.). below cite, pp. 21–32.

McWilliam, P. J., & Bailey, D. B. (Eds.). (1993). *Working together with children and families: Case studies in early intervention.* Baltimore: Paul H. Brookes.

Mental retardation and its genetic path. (1991). *Insight*, March 18, p. 50.

Meyer, D., & Vadasy, P. (1996). *Living with a brother or sister with special needs: A book for sibs* (2nd ed.). Seattle, WA: University of Washington Press.

Miller, H. (1997). Prenatal cocaine exposure and mother-infant interaction: Implications for occupational therapy intervention. *American Journal of Occupational Therapy, 51*(2), 119–131.

Miller, W. (1989). Obstetrical issues. Paper presented at July Spokane (WA) conference on Drugs, alcohol, pregnancy and parenting: An intervention model.

Mills, J. (1994). Computer age tots trade toy blocks for software. *New York Times*, February 13, 1, 32.

Mills v. Board of Education of the District of Columbia, 348 F. Supp. 866 (D.D.C. 1972). Civil action 193–71.

Minchnowicz, L. L., McConnell, S. R., Peterson, C. A., & Odom, S. L. (1995). Social goals and objectives of preschool IEPs: A content analysis. *Journal of Early Intervention, 19*(4), 273–282.

Minke, K. M., & Scott, M. M. (1993). The development of individualized family service plans: Roles for parents and staff. *Journal of Special Education, 27*(1), 82–106.

Moore, M., Strang, E., Schwartz, M., & Braddock, M. (1988). *Patterns in special education service delivery and cost.* Washington, DC: Decision Resources Corporation.

Moore, S., Donovan, B., & Hudson, A. (1993). Brief report: Facilitator-suggested conversational evaluation of facilitated communication. *Journal of Autism and Developmental Disorders, 23*(3), 541–549.

Moore, S., Donovan, B., Hudson, A., Dykstra, J., & Lawrence, J. (1993). Brief report: Evaluation of eight case studies of facilitated communication. *Journal of Autism and Developmental Disorders, 23*(3), 531–539.

Moores, D. F. (1982). *Educating the deaf: Psychology, principles, and practices* (2nd ed.). Dallas, TX: Houghton Mifflin.

Moores, D. F. (1991). Dissemination of a model to create least restrictive environments for deaf students. Final report, Grant G008720128, Project 84133. Washington, DC: Gallaudet Research Institute, Gallaudet University.

Moores, D. F. (1993). Total inclusion/zero reject models in general education: Implications for deaf children. *American Annals of the Deaf, 138*(3), 251.

Msall, M., DiGaudio, K., & Malone, A. (1991). Health, developmental, and psychosocial aspects of Down syndrome. *Infants and Young Children, 4*(1), 35–43.

Mueller, F. (1992). Telecommunications. *Teaching Exceptional Children, 25*(1), 8–11.

Murray, A. D. (1992). Early intervention program evaluation: Numbers or narratives? *Infants and Young Children*, *4*(4), 77–88.

Musick, J. S. (1994). Grandmothers and grandmothers-to-be: Effects on adolescent mothers and adolescent mothering. *Infants and Young Children*, *6*(3), 1–9.

Mutant gene plays role in some diabetes cases. (1992). *Newsday*, April 23, p. 19.

National Association for the Education of Young Children and National Association of Early Childhood Specialists in State Departments of Education (NAEYC & NAECS/SED). (1991). Guidelines for appropriate curriculum content and assessment in programs serving children ages 3 through 8. *Young Children*, *46*(3), 21–38.

National Association of State Directors of Special Education. Report, legislative and action initiatives. (1986). Unpublished report. Washington, DC: Author, March 26.

National Clearinghouse for Professions in Special Education. (1988). *Information on personnel supply and demand: The supply of minority teachers in the United States.* Reston, VA: The Council for Exceptional Children.

National Council on Disability. (1993a). *Meeting the unique needs of minorities with disabilities.* Washington, DC: Author.

National Council on Disability. (1993b). *Serving the nation's students with disabilities: Progress and prospects.* Washington, DC: Author.

National Council on Disability. (1993c). *Study on the financing of assistive technology devices and services for individuals with disabilities.* Washington, DC: Author.

National Head Injury Foundation. (1990). *National directory of head injury rehabilitation services.* Southborough, MA: Author.

National Joint Committee on Learning Disabilities. (1988). Unpublished letter to NJCLD member organizations. For copies, contact Learning Disabilities Association of America, 4156 Library Road, Pittsburgh, PA 15234.

National Organization on Disability and Harris & Associates. (1993). *The attitudes of disabled people on political and other issues.* Washington, DC: First Author.

Nazzo, J., & Sabo, D. (1991). Screening in audiology: Principles and practices. Presented at ASHA annual convention, November, Nashville, TN.

Neisworth, J. T., & Bagnato, S. J. (1992). The case against intelligence testing. *Topics in Early Childhood Special Education*, *12*(1), 1–20.

Neisworth, J. T. (1993). Assessment. In DEC Task Force, *op cit.*, 11–16.

New OCR memorandum. (1990). *Education for the Handicapped Law Report*, supplement 266, June 1, 170. [Now *Individuals with Disabilities Education Law Report*; see also OCR staff memorandum below.]

New OCR rulings. (1991). *Individuals with Disabilities Education Law Report*, *17*(14) IDELR 104–106.

Newborg, J., Stock, J. R., Wnek, L., Guidubaldi, J., & Svinicki, J. (1984). *Battelle Developmental Inventory.* Allen, TX: DLM Teaching Resources.

Newman, M. (1993). End of an era. *Newsday*, March 31, Part II, pp. 60–61, 68.

Nickel, R. E. (1992). Disorders of brain development. *Infants and Young Children*, *5*(1), 1–11.

Nickel, R. E. (1996). Controversial therapies for young children with developmental disabilities. *Infants and Young Children*, *8*(4), 29–40.

Noble, B. (1993). Hearing-aid phone rules are delayed. *New York Times*, April 16, D1–D2.

Noonan, M. J., & Kilgo, J. L. (1987). Transition services for early age individuals with severe mental retardation. In R. N. Iacone & R. A. Stodden (Eds.), *Transition issues and directions* (pp. 25–37). Reston, VA: Council for Exceptional Children.

Novaco, R. (1975). *Anger control: The development and evaluation of an experimental treatment.* Lexington, MA: D. C. Heath.

OCR staff memorandum. (1990). *Education for the Handicapped Law Report*, 16 EHLR 712. [Now *Individuals with Disabilities Education Law Report*; see New OCR memorandum above.]

Oddone, A. (1993). Inclusive classroom applications. *Teaching Exceptional Children*, Fall 1993, 74–75.

Odom, S. L., & McEvoy, M. A. (1990). Mainstreaming at the preschool level: Potential barriers and tasks for the fields. *Topics in Early Childhood Special Education*, *10*(2), 48–61.

Odom, S. L., & McLean, M. E. (1993). Establishing recommended practices for programs for infants and young children with special needs and their families. In DEC Task Force, *op cit.*, 1–10.

Odom, S. L., McLean, M. E., Johnson, L. J., & LaMontagne, M. J. (1995). Recommended practices in early childhood special education: Validation and current use. *Journal of Early Intervention*, *19*(1), 1–17.

Ojemann, G. A. (1983). Brain organization for language from the perspective of electrical stimulation mapping. *The Behavioral and Brain Sciences*, *6*, 189–206.

Okie, S. (1990). Smoking crack cocaine may cause strokes in young people. *Washington Post*, September 12, A6.

Olson, H. C. (1994). The effects of prenatal alcohol exposure on child development. *Infants and Young Children*, 6(3), 10–25.

Olson, M. (1987). Early intervention for children with visual impairments. In M. J. Guralnick & F. C. Bennett (Eds.), *The effectiveness of early intervention for at-risk and handicapped children* (pp. 318–321). Orlando, FL: Academic Press.

Oster, P. (1992). The Dutch try a little withdrawal. *Business Week*, December 14, 4.

Otten, A. (1989). Parental agony. *Wall Street Journal*, March 8, A1, A8.

Page, T. J., & Chew, M. B. (1993) Rethinking TBI. *REHAB Management*, 6(2), 53–64.

Papert, S. (1993). *The children's machine: Rethinking school in the age of the computer.* New York: Basic Books.

Parette, H. P., Hendricks, M. D., & Rock, S. L. (1991). Efficacy of therapeutic intervention intensity with infants and young children with cerebral palsy. *Infants and Young Children*, 4(2), 1–19.

Parette, H. P., Hourcade, J. J., & VanBiervliet, A. (1993). Selection of appropriate technology for children with disabilities. *Teaching Exceptional Children, 25*(3), 18–22.

Parker, S., Greer, S., & Zuckerman, B. (1988). Double jeopardy: The impact of poverty on early childhood development. *Pediatric Clinics of North America, 35*, 1227–1239.

Parker, S. B. (1991). Changes in the way Social Security evaluates claims for childhood disability benefits. *Journal of Disability Policy Studies, 2*(2), 77–86.

Pear, R. (1992). U.S. orders testing of poor children for lead poisoning. *New York Times*, September 13, 1, 42.

Pearl, L. (1993). Providing family-centered early intervention. In W. Brown, S. Thurman, & L. Pearl. (Eds.), *Family-centered early intervention with infants and toddlers: Innovative cross-disciplinary approaches* (pp. 81–101). Baltimore: Paul H. Brookes.

Pedhazur, E. J., & Schmelkin, L. P. (1991). *Measurement, design, and analysis: An integrated approach.* Hillsdale, NJ: Lawrence Erlbaum Associates.

Pekkanen, J. (1991). Genetics: Medicine's amazing leap. *Reader's Digest*, September, 23–32.

Pennington, F. B., Gilger, J. W., Olson, R. K., & DeFries, J. C. (1992). The external validity of age- versus IQ-discrepancy definitions of reading disability: Lessons from a twin study. *Journal of Learning Disabilities, 25*(9), 562–565.

Pennsylvania Association for Retarded Children v. Commonwealth of Pennsylvania, David H. Kurtzman et al., 334 F. Supp. 1257 (E.D. Pa. 1972), civil action no. 71-42 (3 Judge Court, E.D. Pennsylvania, 1971), Order, injunction, and consent agreement.

Perelman, L. (1992). *School's out: Hyperlearning, the new technology, and the end of education.* New York: William Morrow.

Perry, D. (1993). *Projecting the costs of early intervention services: Four states' experiences.* Chapel Hill, NC: NEC*TAS.

Perry, M., & Garber, M. (1993). Technology helps parents teach their children with developmental delays. *Teaching Exceptional Children, 25*(2), 8–11.

Peters, M. T., & Heron, T. E. (1993). When the best is not good enough: An examination of best practice. *Journal of Special Education, 26*(4), 371–385.

Piaget, J. (1962). *Play, dreams and imitation in childhood.* New York: Norton.

Piaget, J., & Inhelder, B. (1969). *The psychology of the child.* New York: Basic Books.

Plugging into the 'Net.' (1993). *The ERIC Review, 2*(3), Winter.

Port, O. (1992). Unscrambling genetic codes: A progress report. *Business Week*, November 9, 109.

Premack, D. (1959). Toward empirical behavior laws. *Psychological Review, 66*(4), 219–233.

Prizant, B., Audet, L., Burke, G., Hummel, L., Maher, S., & Theadore, G. (1990). Communication disorders and emotional/behavioral disorders in children. *Journal of Speech and Hearing Disorders, 55*, 179–192.

Prizant, B., & Wetherby, A. M. (1993). Communication and language assessment for young children. *Infants and Young Children, 5*(4), 20–34.

Prizant, B., Wetherby, A., & Roberts, J. (1993). Communication problems in infants and toddlers. In C. Zeanah (Ed.), *Handbook of mental health.* New York: Guilford.

Raab, M. M., Davis, M. S., & Trepanier, A. M. (1993). Resources versus services: Changing the focus of intervention for infants and young children. *Infants and Young Children, 5*(3), 1–11.

Rabin, R. (1989). Warnings unheeded: A history of child lead poisoning. *American Journal of Public Health, 79*(12), 1668–1774.

Rall, D. P. (1994). Test kids' blood for lead. *New York Times*, January 24, A15.

Ramey, C. T., Bryant, D. M., Wasik, B. H., Sparling, J. J., Fendt, K. H., & LaVange, L. M. (1992). Infant health and development program for low birth weight, premature infants: Program elements, family participation, and child intelligence. Pediatrics, 3, 454–465.

Ramey, C. T., & Ramey, S. L. (1992). Effective early intervention. Mental Retardation, 30(6), 337–345.

Rapport, M. (1996). Legal guidelines for the delivery of special health care services in schools. *Exceptional Children, 62*(6), 537–549.

Raschke, D. B., Dedrick, C. V., & Hanus, K. (1991). Adaptive playgrounds for all children. *Teaching Exceptional Children,* Fall, 25–28.

Raschke, D. B., Dedrick, C. V., Heston, M. L., & Farris, M. (1996). Everyone can play: Adapting the Candy Land board game. *Teaching Exceptional Children,* Summer, 28–33.

Rathlev, M. (1994). Universal precautions in early intervention and child care. *Infants and Young Children,* 6(3), 54–64.

Raver, S. (1991). *Strategies for teaching at-risk and handicapped infants and toddlers: A transdisciplinary approach.* New York: Merrill.

Ray, J. (1974). Ethological studies of behavior in delayed and non-delayed toddlers. Paper presented at the annual meeting of the American Association on Mental Deficiency, Toronto.

Reganick, K. A. (1994). Using computers to initiate active learning for students with severe behavior problems. *T.H.E. Journal,* June, 72–74.

Reid, R., Maag, J., & Vasa, S. (1994). Attention deficit hyperactivity disorder as a disability category: A critique. *Exceptional Children,* 60(3), 198–214.

Repetto, J., & Correa, V. (1996). Expanding views on transition. *Exceptional Children,* 62(6), 551–563.

Riko, K., Hyde, M. L., & Alberti, M. B. (1985). Hearing loss in early infancy: Incidence, detection and assessment. *Laryngoscope,* 85, 137–143.

Roberts, J., & Crais, E. (1989). Assessing communication skills. In D. Bailey & M. Wolery (Eds.), *Assessing infants and children with handicaps.* Columbus, OH: Merrill.

Robinson, C., & Fieber, N. (1988). Cognitive assessment of motorically impaired infants and preschoolers. In T. Wachs, & R. Sheehan (Eds.), *Assessment of young developmentally disabled children* (pp. 127–162). New York: Plenum.

Roizen, N. (1997). New advancements in medical treatment of young children with Down syndrome: Implications for early intervention. *Infants and Young Children,* 9(4), 36–42.

Rosen, S., & Granger, M. (1992). Early interventions and school programs. In A. Crocker, H. Cohen, & T. Kastner (Eds.), *HIV infection and developmental disabilities.* Baltimore: Paul H. Brookes.

Rosenkoetter, S. E. (1992). Guidelines from recent legislation to structure transition planning. Infants and Young Children, 5(1), 21–27.

Rosenthal, E. (1990). When a pregnant woman drinks. *New York Times Magazine,* February 4, pp. 30, 31, 49, 61.

Rosenthal, E. (1991). As more tiny infants live, choices and burden grow. *New York Times,* September 29, pp. 1, 26.

Rosetti, L. (1986). *High-risk infants: Identification, assessment and intervention.* Boston: Little, Brown.

Rosetti, L. (1990). *Infant-toddler assessment: An interdisciplinary approach.* Baltimore: University Park Press.

Ross, D. (1985). Social competence in kindergarten: Applications of symbolic interaction theory. Paper presented at the annual meeting of the American Educational Research Association, Chicago, April.

Ross, L. (1995). Connect with kids and parents of different cultures. *Instructor,* July/August, 51–53.

Roth, W. (1993). Disability, genetics, and post-modern medicine. *Disability Studies Quarterly,* 13(3), 24–27.

Roush, J., Harrison, M., Palsha, S., & Davidson, D. (1992). A national survey of educational preparation programs for early intervention specialists. *American Annals of the Deaf,* 137(5), 425–430.

Rowley-Kelly, F., & Reigel, D. (Eds.). (1993). *Teaching the student with spina bifida.* Baltimore: Paul H. Brookes.

Royeen, C. (1992). A glimpse of the human experience: Parenting infants and toddlers who are disabled. *Infants and Young Children,* 5(2), 65–57.

Rucker, R. (1991). Statement at March 15 hearing on Part H reauthorization, U.S. Senate Subcommittee on Disability Policy. *Senate report S. hrg. 102-133.* Washington, DC: U.S. Government Printing Office, 75–87.

Sack, K. (1994). Battle lines drawn over newborn H.I.V. disclosure. *New York Times,* June 26, 23, 29.

Safer, N. D., & Hamilton, J. L. (1993). Legislative context for early intervention services. In W. Brown, S. K. Thurman, & L. F. Pearl (Eds.), *Family-centered early intervention with infants and toddlers: Innovative cross-disciplinary approaches* (pp. 1–19). Baltimore: Paul H. Brookes.

Salisbury, C. L. (1991). Mainstreaming during the early childhood years. *Exceptional Children,* 58(2), 146–155.

Salisbury, C., & Vincent, L. J. (1990). Criterion of the next environment and best practices: Mainstreaming and integration 10 years later. *Topics in Early Childhood Special Education,* 10(2), 78–89.

Sanford, A. R., & Zelman, J. G. (1987). The learning accomplishment profile. In D. B. Bailey & M. Wolery (Eds.), *Assessing infants and preschoolers with handicaps.* Columbus, OH: Merrill.

Sawyer, R. J., & Zantal-Wiener, K. (1993). Emerging trends in technology for students with disabilities. *Teaching Exceptional Children,* 26(1), 70–76.

Scarlett, W. G. (1983). Social isolation from agemates among nursery school children. In M. Donaldson, R. Grieve, & C.

Pratt (Eds.), *Peer relationships and social skills in childhood* (pp. 34–45). New York: Guilford.

Scherer, M. J. (1993). *Living in the state of stuck: How technology impacts the lives of people with disabilities.* Cambridge, MA: Brookline Books.

Schmeck, H. (1988). Defect in muscle disease pinpointed. *New York Times*, December 23.

Schneider, J., & Chasnoff, I. (1987). Cocaine abuse during pregnancy: Its effects on infant motor development—A clinical perspective. *Topics in Acute Care and Trauma Rehabilitation, 2,* 59–69.

Scholl, G. (Ed.). (1986). *Foundations of education for blind and visually handicapped children and youth: Theory and practice.* New York: American Foundation for the Blind.

Schopler, E., Short, A., & Mesibov, G. (1989). Relation of behavioral treatment to "normal functioning": Comment on Lovaas. *Journal of Consulting and Clinical Psychology, 57*(1), 162–164.

Schrag, J. A. (1990a). Memorandum to lead agency directors and Part H contact persons. March 20. Unpublished memorandum. Washington, DC: U.S. Department of Education, Office of Special Education Programs.

Schrag, J. A. (1990b). Memorandum to state school officers. May 8. Unpublished memorandum. Washington, DC: U.S. Department of Education, Office of Special Education Programs.

Schrag, J. A. (1990c). Memorandum to Part H coordinators. June 1. Unpublished memorandum. Washington, DC: U.S. Department of Education, Office of Special Education Programs.

Schriebman, L. (1988). Parent training as a means of facilitating generalization of autistic children. In R. H. Horner, S. Dunlap, & R. I. Koegel (Eds.), *Generalization and maintenance: Life-style changes in applied settings* (pp. 21–40). Baltimore: Paul H. Brookes.

Schrier, E. (1990). The future of access and technology for blind and visually impaired people. *Journal of Visual Impairment and Blindness, 84*(10), 520–523.

Schroeder, P. (1993). Personal communication, May 28.

Schumacker, H. R., Klippel, J. H., & Robinson, D. R. (Eds.). (1988). *Primer on the rheumatic diseases* (9th ed.). Atlanta, GA: Arthritis Foundation.

Scott, T., Cole, M., & Engel, M. (1992). Computers and education: A cultural constructivist perspective. In G. Grant (Ed.), *Review of research in education* (pp. 191–251). Washington, DC: American Educational Research Association.

Selikowitz, M. (1990). *Down syndrome: the facts.* Oxford, England: Oxford University Press.

Setoguchi, Y., & Rosenfelder, R. (1982). *The limb deficient child.* Springfield, IL: Charles C. Thomas.

Sexton, D., Snyder, P., Wolfe, B., Lobman, M., Stricklin, S., & Akers, P. (1996). Early intervention inservice training strategies: Perceptions and suggestions from the field. *Exceptional children, 62*(6), 485–495.

Shackelford, J. (1992). State/jurisdiction eligibility definitions for Part H. *NEC*TAS Notes*, (5), October.

Shaer, C. (1997). The infant and young child with spina bifida: Major medical concerns. *Infants and Young Children, 9*(3), 13–25.

Shapiro, J. (1993). *No pity.* New York: Times Books/Random House.

Sharav, T., & Schlomo, L. (1986). Stimulation of infants with Down syndrome: Long-term effects. *Mental Retardation, 24,* 81–86.

Shaywitz, S. E., Escobar, M. D., Shaywitz, B. A., Fletcher, J. M., & Makuch, R. (1992). Evidence that dyslexia may represent the lower tail of a normal distribution of reading ability. *New England Journal of Medicine, 326*(3), 145–150.

Shaywitz, S. E., & Shaywitz, B. A. (1988). Attention Deficit Disorder: Current perspectives. In J. E. Kavanagh & J. Truss (Eds.), *Learning disabilities: Proceedings of the national conference* (pp. 369–456). Parkton, MD: York Press.

Sherman, R. (1991). Employer use of genetic test to be restricted? *National Law Journal,* November 25, 15, 18.

Shonkoff, J. P., & Hauser-Cram, P. (1987). Early intervention for disabled infants and their families: A quantitative analysis. *Pediatrics, 80*(5), 650–658.

Shonkoff, J., & Meisels, S. (1991). Defining eligibility for services under PL 99-457. *Journal of Early Intervention, 15*(1), 21–25.

Sigman, M., Cohen, S., Beckwith, L., & Parmelee, A. (1986). Infant attention in relation to intellectual abilities in childhood. *Developmental Psychology, 22,* 788.

Silver, S. (1988). The scope of the problems in children and adolescents. In J. G. Looney (Ed.), *Chronic mental illness in children and adolescents* (pp. 39–52). Washington, DC: American Psychiatric Press.

Silverstein, R. (1989). A window of opportunity: PL 99-457. In *The intent and spirit of P.L. 99-457: A sourcebook* (pp. A1–A7). Washington, DC: National Center for Clinical Infant Programs. An edited version of a speech by Mr. Silverstein, November 3, 1988, at the national meeting of Project Zero to Three.

Simeonsson, R. J., Huntington, G. S., Short, R. J., & Ware, W. (1982). The Carolina record of individual behavior: Characteristics of handicapped children. *Topics in Early Childhood, 2*(2), 43–55.

Skinner, B. F. (1953). *Science and human behavior.* New York: Macmillan.

Slaughter, D. (1983). Early intervention and its effects on maternal and child development. *Monographs of the Society for Research in Child Development, 48*, serial 202.

Smith, A. (1986). Testimony before the Subcommittee on Select Education, July 23. *House report 99-120.* Washington, DC: U.S. Government Printing Office, 123–135.

Smith, B. (1986). Testimony before the Subcommittee on Select Education, July 23, 1986. *House report 99-120.* Washington, DC: U.S. Government Printing Office, 92–93.

Smith, M., & Belcher, R. (1993). Brief report: Facilitated communication with adults with autism. *Journal of Autism and Developmental Disorders, 23*(1), 175–183.

Smith, R. (1994). No more child's play. *REHAB Management, 7*(1), 40, 42.

Smith, S. (1991). *Succeeding against the odds: Strategies and insights from the learning disabled.* Rockville, MD: Woodbine House.

Snow, R. E. (1989). Aptitude-treatment interaction as a framework for research on individual differences in learning. In P. L. Ackerman, R. J. Sternberg, & R. Glaser (Eds.), *Learning and individual differences* (pp. 13–59). New York: W. H. Freeman.

Social Security Administration. (1991). Supplemental Security Income; Determining eligibility for a child under age 18; final rule with request for comments. *Federal Register*, February 11, 5534-5565.

Social Security Administration. (1997a). CFR Correction. *Federal Register, 62*(130), 36460.

Social Security Administration (1997b). *The definition of disability for children.* SSA Publication No. 05-11053. July. Baltimore: Author.

Sokoly, M. M., & Dokecki, P. R. (1992). Ethical perspectives on family-centered early intervention. *Infants and Young Children, 4*(4), 23–32.

Sontag, J. C., & Schacht, R. (1994). An ethnic comparison of parent participation and information needs in early intervention. *Exceptional Children, 60*(5), 422–433.

Souders, R. (1993). I was forced to find my gifts. *Parade Magazine*, March 21, 11, 12.

Sparling, J. J., & Lewis, I. S. (1979). *Learning games for the first three years: A guide to parent-child play.* New York: Walker.

Sparling, J. J., & Lewis, I. S. (1985). *Partners for learning.* Lewisville, NC: Kaplan Press.

Sparling, J. J., Lewis, I. S., & Neuwirth, S. (1993). *Early partners.* Lewisville, NC: Kaplan Press.

Sparrow, S., Balla, D., & Cichetti, D. V. (1984). *Vineland Adaptive Behavior Scales—Expanded form.* Circle Pines, MN: American Guidance Service.

Specter, M. (1987). New muscular dystrophy treatment delays loss of ability to walk. *Washington Post*, August 6, A13.

Spina Bifida Association of America. (1997). Facts about spina bifida. www.sbaa.org

Spodek, B., Saracho, O. N., & Lee, C. L. (1984). *Mainstreaming young children.* Belmont, CA: Wadsworth.

Squires, S. (1993). Hearing problems frequently undetected. *Washington Post*, March 4, Health.

Stehli, A. (1991). *The sound of a miracle: A child's triumph over autism.* New York: Doubleday.

Stevenson, J., & Richman, N. (1976). The prevalence of language delay in a population of three-year-old children and its association with general retardation. *Developmental Medicine and Child Neurology, 18*, 431–441.

Strain, P. S. (1990). LRE for preschool children with handicaps: What we know, what we should be doing. *Journal of Early Intervention, 14*, 291–296.

Strain, P. S., Lambert, D. L., Kerr, M. M., Stagg, V., & Lenker, D. (1983). Naturalistic assessment of children's compliance to teacher's requests and consequences for compliance. *Journal of Applied Behavior Analysis, 16*, 2143–2149.

Strain, P. S., & Smith, B. J. (1986). A counter-interpretation of early intervention effects: A response to Casto and Mastropieri. *Exceptional Children, 53*(3), 260–265.

Striffler, N. (1993). The changing role of speech-language pathologists and audiologists. *Disability Studies Quarterly, 13*(4), 16–18.

Stuckless, E. R. (1992). Reflections on bilingual, bicultural, education for deaf children. *American Annals of the Deaf, 136*(3), 270–272.

Summary of existing legislation affecting people with disabilities. (1992). Washington, DC: U.S. Department of Education.

Sutton, R. (1990). Independence days. *Washington Post*, October 22, B5.

Swan, W. (1980). The Handicapped Children's Early Education Program. *Exceptional Children, 47*(1), 12–16.

Swan, W., & Morgan, J. (1993). *Collaborating for comprehensive services for young children and their families: The local interagency coordinating council.* Baltimore: Paul H. Brookes.

Talan, J. (1990). How lead destroys lives. *Newsday*, January 11, 15.

Talan, J. (1994). Fetus, stress link? *Newsday*, February 8, 70, 73.

Tallal, P., Stark, R. E., & Mellits, D. E. (1985). Identification of language-impaired children on the basis of rapid perception and production skills. *Brain and Language, 25*, 314–322.

Tayler, L. (1992). Computer the voice, ears for defendant. *Newsday*, February, 14, p. 22.

Teller, D. Y., McDonald, M., Preston, K., Sebris, S., & Dobson, V. (1987). Assessment of visual acuity in infants and children: The acuity card procedure. *Developmental Medicine and Child Neurology, 28*, 779–789.

Teplin, S. (1995). Visual impairment in infants and young children. *Infants and Young Children, 8*(1), 18–51.

Thiele, J., & Hamilton, J. (1991). Implementing the early childhood formula: Programs under PL 99-457. *Journal of Early Intervention, 15*(1), 5–12.

Thomas, J., & Tidmarsh, L. (1997). Hyperactive and disruptive behaviors in very young children: Diagnosis and intervention. *Infants and Young Children, 9*(3), 46–55.

Thompson, L. (1988). New understanding of muscular dystrophy. *Washington Post*, January 5.

Thorndike, R. L., Hagen, E. P., & Sattler, J. M. (1986). *Stanford-Binet Intelligence Scale: Fourth edition*. Chicago: Riverside.

Thurman, K. (1999). "Book review." *Journal of Early Intervention, 22*(1), 90–92.

Thurman, S. K., & Gonsalves, S. V. (1993). Adolescent mothers and their premature infants: Responding to double risk. *Infants and Young Children, 5*(4), 44–51.

Timothy W. v. Rochester (NH) School District. (1989). 875 F. 2d 954 (1st Circuit), *cert. denied* 110 S. Ct. 519.

Tingley, C. (1988). *Down syndrome: A resource handbook*. Boston: College-Hill (now PRO-ED).

Trawick-Smith, J. (1992). A descriptive study of persuasive preschool children: How they get others to do what they want. *Early Childhood Research Quarterly, 7*, 95–114.

Trohanis, P. (1989). Testimony before the Subcommittee on the Handicapped. *S. Hrg. 101-287*. Washington, DC: U.S. Government Printing Office, 48–73.

Turnbull, A., & Turnbull, R. (1993). Enhancing beneficial linkages across the life span. *Disability Studies Quarterly, 13*(4), 34–36.

Turnbull, H. R. (1990). *Free appropriate public education: Law and interpretation*. Denver, CO: Love.

Turnbull, H. R., & Turnbull, A. P. (1991). Procedural safeguards under Part H: How judicial interpretations of Part B may affect Part H. *Journal of Early Intervention, 15*(1), 80–88.

Tynan, W. D., & Nearing, J. (1994). The diagnosis of attention deficit hyperactivity disorder in young children. *Infants and Young Children, 6*(4), 13–20.

U.S. Architectural and Transportation Barriers Compliance Board. (1986). *Recommendations for accessibility to serve physically handicapped children in elementary schools*. Washington, DC: Author.

U.S. Architectural and Transportation Barriers Compliance Board. (1997a). *Americans with Disabilities Act guidelines: Children's elements*. Washington, DC: Author.

U.S. Architectural and Transportation Barriers Compliance Board. (1997b). *Regulatory negotiation committee on accessibility guidelines for play facilities: Final report*. Washington, DC: Author.

U.S. Congress, House of Representatives. (1986). *Hearing report 99-120*. Education of the Handicapped Act amendments of 1986, Committee on Education and Labor. Washington, DC: U.S. Government Printing Office.

U.S. Congress, House of Representatives. (1986). *House report 99-860*. Education of the Handicapped Act amendments of 1986, Committee on Education and Labor. Washington, DC: U.S. Government Printing Office.

U.S. Congress, House of Representatives. (1990). *House report 101-787*. Education of the Handicapped Act amendments of 1990, Conference Report. Washington, DC: U.S. Government Printing Office.

U.S. Congress, House of Representatives. (1991). *House report 102-198*. Individuals with Disabilities Education amendments of 1991, Committee on Education and Labor. Washington, DC: U.S. Government Printing Office.

U.S. Congress, Senate. (1975). *Senate report 94-168*. Education for All Handicapped Children Act, Committee on Labor and Public Welfare. Washington, DC: U.S. Government Printing Office.

U.S. Congress, Senate. (1989a). *Senate hearing report 101-287*. Subcommittee on Disability Policy, Committee on Labor and Human Resources. Washington, DC: U.S. Government Printing Office.

U.S. Congress, Senate. (1989b). *Senate report 101-204*. Individuals with Disabilities Education Act amendments of 1989, Committee on Labor and Human Resources. Washington, DC: U.S. Government Printing Office.

U.S. Congress, Senate. (1991). *Senate Report 102-84*. Individuals with Disabilities Education Act amendments, Committee on Labor and Human Resources. Washington, DC: U.S. Government Printing Office.

U.S. Department of Education. (1984). *Sixth annual report to Congress on implementation of Public Law 94-142: The Education for All Handicapped Children Act*. Washington, DC: Author.

U.S. Department of Education. (1985). *Seventh annual report to Congress on implementation of Public Law 94-142: The Education for All Handicapped Children Act.* Washington, DC: Author.

U.S. Department of Education. (1999). Assistance to States for the Education of Children with Disabilities and the Early Intervention Program for Infants and Toddlers with Disabilities: Final Regulation. *Federal Register,* March 12, 1999, 12405–12672.

U.S. Department of Education. (1992a). Assistance to States for the Education of Children with Disabilities Program and Preschool Grants for Children with Disabilities: Final rule. *Federal Register,* September 29, 1992, 44794–44852.

U.S. Department of Education. (1992b). Assistance to States for the Education of Children with Disabilities Program and Preschool Grants for Children with Disabilities: Correction; final rule. *Federal Register,* October 27, 1992, 48694–48704.

U.S. Department of Education. (1993a). Early Intervention Program for Infants and Toddlers with Disabilities; final rule. *Federal Register,* July 30, 40958–40989.

U.S. Department of Education. (1993b). *Fifteenth annual report on the implementation of the Individuals with Disabilities Education Act.* Washington, DC: Author.

U.S. Department of Education. (1992c). *Fourteenth annual report to Congress on implementation of the Individuals with Disabilities Education Act.* Washington, DC: Author.

U.S. Department of Education. (1992d). Notice of policy guidance. *Federal Register,* October 30, 57 (211), 49274–49276.

U.S. Department of Education. (1997). *Nineteenth annual report to Congress on implementation of the Individuals with Disabilities Education Act.* Washington, DC: Author.

U.S. Department of Education. (1998). *Twentieth annual report to Congress on implementation of the Individuals with Disabilities Education Act.* Washington, DC: Author.

U.S. Department of Health and Human Services. (1992). *Eighteenth annual report of the U.S. Department of Health and Human Services to the Congress of the United States on services provided to children with disabilities in the Head Start program.* Washington, DC: Author.

U.S. Office of Health, Education, and Welfare, Office of Education. (1977). Assistance to states for education of handicapped children: Procedures for evaluating specific learning disabilities. *Federal Register, 41,* pp. 65082–65085.

Upshur, C. (1991). Mothers' and fathers' ratings of the benefits of early intervention services. *Journal of Early Intervention, 15,* 345–357.

Uslan, M. (1992). Barriers to acquiring assistive technology: Cost and lack of information. *Journal of Visual Impairment and Blindness, 86*(9), 402–407.

Vadasy, P., Fewell, R., Greenberg, M., Dermond, N., & Meyer, D. (1986). Follow-up evaluation of the effects of involvement in the fathers program. *Topics in Early Childhood Special Education, 6*(1), 16–31.

Vadasy, P., Fewell, R., Meyer, D., & Greenberg, M. (1985). Supporting fathers of handicapped young children: Preliminary findings of program effects. *Analysis and Intervention in Developmental Disabilities, 5,* 125–137.

Vaidya, S., & McKeeby, J. (1984). Computer turtle graphics: Do they affect children's thought processes? *Educational Technology, 24*(9), 46–47.

Valliere, J. M. (1994). Infant mental health: A consultation and treatment team for at-risk infants and toddlers. *Infants and Young Children, 6*(3), 46–53.

Vanderheiden, G. (1992a). A standard approach for full visual annotation of auditorially presented information for users, including those who are deaf: ShowSounds. Unpublished manuscript. Trace Center, S-151 Waisman Center, University of Wisconsin-Madison.

Vanderheiden, G. (1992b). Making software more accessible for people with disabilities: A white paper on the design of software application programs to increase their accessibility for people with disabilities. Unpublished manuscript. [See Trace, above.]

Van Dyck, P. C. (1991). *Use of parental fees in PL 99-457, Part H.* Chapel Hill, NC: University of North Carolina, Frank Porter Graham Child Development Center, Carolina Policy Studies Program.

Van Dyke, D. C., & Lin-Dyken, D. C. (1993). The new genetics, developmental disabilities, and early intervention. *Infants and Young Children, 5*(4), 8–19.

Van Riper, C. (1993). *The nature of stuttering* (2nd ed.). Prospect Heights, IL: Waveland Press.

Vaughn, S. R., Bos, C. S., & Lund, K. A. (1986). . . . But they can do it in my room: Strategies for promoting generalization. *Teaching Exceptional Children, 18,* 176–180.

Vaughn, S. R., Ridley, C. A., & Bullock, D. D. (1984). Interpersonal problem solving skills training with aggressive young children. *Journal of Applied Developmental Psychology, 5,* 213–223.

Verhaaren, P. R., & Connor, F. P. (1981). Physical disabilities. In J. M. Kauffman & D. P. Halloran (Eds.), *Handbook of special education.* Englewood Cliffs, NJ: Prentice Hall.

Viadero, D. Side by side. *Teacher Magazine Reader,* n.d.

Vickers, T. (1986). Testimony before the Subcommittee on Select Education, July 23. *House report 99-120.* Washington, DC: U.S. Government Printing Office, 16–23.

Vincent, L. J. (1986). Testimony before the Subcommittee on Select Education, July 29. *House report 99-120.* Washington, DC: U.S. Government Printing Office, 341–361.

Vincent, L. J. (1992). Families and early intervention: Diversity and competence. *Journal of Early Intervention, 16,* 166–172.

Vincent, L., Brown, L., & Getz-Sheftel, M. (1981). Integrating handicapped and typical children during the preschool years: The definition of best education practice. *Topics in Early Childhood Special Education, 1*(1), 17–24.

Vincent, L. J., Salisbury, C., Walter, G., Brown, P., Gruenewald, L., & Powers, M. (1980). Program evaluation and curricular development in early childhood special education: Criterion of the next environment. In W. Sailor, B. Wilcox, & L. Brown (Eds.), *Methods of instruction for severely handicapped students* (pp. 303–328). Baltimore: Paul H. Brookes.

Volpe, J. J. (1987). *Neurology of the newborn.* Philadelphia: W. B. Saunders.

Vygotsky, L. S. (1978). *Mind in society: The development of higher psychological processes.* Cambridge, MA: Harvard University Press.

Waaland, P. (1990). Pediatric traumatic brain injury. *Special Topic Report.* The Rehabilitation Research & Training Center on Severe Traumatic Brain Injury. Richmond, VA: Medical College of Virginia.

Wade, D. (1992). Alcoholism is a disease. *Fine Line,* July/August, *1*(10).

Wagner, A. E., & Lockwood, S. L. (1994). Pervasive developmental disorders: Dilemmas in diagnosing very young children. *Infants and Young Children, 6*(3), 21–32.

Waissman, R. (1993). Ethical issues in home care treatment of a chronic illness: Analysis of the notion of responsibility. *Disability Studies Quarterly, 13*(4), 28–32.

Waldholz, M. (1989). Newer prenatal test, performed earlier on fetus, poses only slightly more risk. *Wall Street Journal,* March 9, B5.

Walker, H. M., & Severson, H. H. (1990). *Systematic screening for behavior disorders: A validated project of the national diffusion network.* Longmont, CO: Sopris West.

Walker, R. S. (1991). *AIDS today, tomorrow: An introduction to the HIV epidemic in America.* Atlantic Highlands, NJ: Humanities Press International.

Wallace, G., & Kauffman, J. M. (1986). *Teaching students with learning and behavior problems* (3rd ed.). Columbus, OH: Merrill.

Wallis, C. (1994). Life in overdrive. *Time,* July 18, pp. 42–50.

Warfield, M. E. (1995). The cost-effectiveness of home visiting versus group services in early intervention. *Journal of Early Intervention, 19*(2), 130–148.

Warren, D. H. (1984). *Blindness and early childhood development* (2nd ed., revised). New York: American Foundation for the Blind.

Wasik, B. H., Bryant, D. M., & Lyons, C. M. (1990). *Home visiting: Procedures for helping families.* Newbury Park, CA: Sage Publications.

Wasik, B. H., Ramey, C. T., Bryant, D. M., & Sparling, J. J. (1990). A longitudinal study of two early intervention strategies: Project CARE. *Child Development, 61,* 1682–1692.

Watson, J. D. (1990). The Human Genome Project: Past, present, and future. *Science, 248,* 44–49.

Watson, L. S. (1973). *Child behavior modification: A manual for teachers, nurses and parents.* New York: Pergamon Press.

Weicker, L. (1991). Letter to U.S. Senator Tom Harkin, March 15. In *Senate report S. hrg. 102-133.* Washington, DC: U.S. Government Printing Office, 12–13.

Weintraub, F. (1986). Testimony before the Subcommittee on Select Education, July 23. *House report 99-120.* Washington, DC: U.S. Government Printing Office, 23–52, 91–100.

Weintraub, F. (1989). Testimony before the Subcommittee on the Handicapped, April 3. *Senate report S. hrg. 101-287.* Washington, DC: U.S. Government Printing Office, 13–36.

Wershing, A. (1994). Making play accessible. *REHAB Management, 7*(1), 123–125.

Wetherby, A., Cain, D., Yonclas, D., & Walker, V. (1988). Analysis of intentional communication of normal children from the prelinguistic to the multi-word stage. *Journal of Speech and Hearing Research, 31,* 240–252.

Wetherby, A., & Prizant, B. (1992). Profiling young children's communicative competence. In S. Warren, & J. Reichle (Eds.), *Causes and effects in communication disorders.* Baltimore: Paul H. Brookes.

Wheeler, D., Jacobson, J., Paglieri, R., & Schwartz, A. (1993). An experimental assessment of facilitated communication. *Mental Retardation, 31*(1), 49–60.

White, K. R. (1985/1986). Efficacy of early intervention. *Journal of Special Education, 19*(4), 401–416.

White, K. R. (1988). Cost analyses in family support programs. In H. B. Weiss, & F. H. Jacobs (Eds.), *Evaluating family programs.* (pp. 429–443). New York: Aldine de Gruyter.

White, K. R. (1990). *Longitudinal studies of the effects and costs of early intervention with handicapped children.* 1989–1990 Final report. Logan, UT: Utah State University, Early Intervention Research Institute.

White, K. R. (1993). Personal communication, May 20.

White, K. R., & Behrens, T. R. (Eds.). (1993). The Rhode Island hearing assessment project: Implications for universal newborn hearing screening. (special issue) *Seminars in Hearing, 14*(1).

White, K. R., Boyce, G., Casto, G., Innocenti, M. S., Taylor, M. J., Goetze, L., & Behl, D. (1994). Comparative evaluations of early intervention alternatives: A response to commentaries by Guralnick and Telzrow. *Early Education and Development, 5*(1), 56–68.

White, K. R., & Casto, G. (1985). An integrative review of efficacy studies with at-risk children: Implications for the handicapped. *Analysis and Intervention in Developmental Disabilities, 5,* 7–31.

White, K. R., Casto, G., Mott, S. E., Barnett, W. S., Pezzino, J., Lowitzer, A. C., Eiserman, E. D., Wingate-Corey, T., Immel, N., & Innocenti, M. S. (1987). *1986–1987 annual report of the longitudinal studies of the effects and cost of early intervention for handicapped children* (Contract # 800-85-0173). Logan, UT: Early Intervention Research Institute, Utah State University. (ERIC Clearinghouse on Handicapped and Gifted Youth #ED 293–241)

White, K. R., & Immel, N. (1991). *Medicaid and other third-party payments: One piece of the early intervention financing puzzle.* Bethesda, MD: National Center for Family-Centered Care, Association for the Care of Children's Health.

White, K. R., Mastropieri, M. A., & Casto, G. (1984). An analysis of special education early childhood projects approved by the Joint Dissemination Review Panel. *Journal of the Division for Early Childhood, 9,* 11–26.

White, K. R., Taylor, M. J., & Moss, V. D. (1992). Does research support claims about the benefits of involving parents in early intervention programs? *Review of Educational Research, 62*(1), 91–125.

Wiig, E. H., & Semel, E. M. (1984). *Language assessment and intervention for the learning disabled* (2nd ed.). Columbus, OH: Merrill.

Will, M. (1986). Educating children with learning problems: A shared responsibility. Unpublished document, U.S. Department of Education, Office of Special Education Programs.

Williams, B. (1991). Testimony before the U.S. House of Representatives Subcommittee on Select Education and Civil Rights. Santa Fe, NM.

Williams, B. F., & Howard, V. F. (1993). Children exposed to cocaine: Characteristics and implications for research and intervention. *Journal of Early Intervention, 17*(1), 61–72.

Williams, H. G. (1983). Assessment of gross motor functioning. In K. D. Paget & B. A. Bracken (Eds.), *The psychoeducational assessment of preschool children* (pp. 225–260). New York: Grune & Stratton.

Williams, S. W., & Ogletree, S. M. (1992). Preschool children's computer interest and competence: Effects of sex and gender role. *Early Childhood Research Quarterly, 7,* 135–143.

Williamson, W. D., & Demmler, G. J. (1992). Congenital infections: Clinical outcome and educational implications. *Infants and Young Children, 4*(4), 1–10.

Willoughby-Herb, S. J., & Neisworth, J. T. (1982). *HICOMP Preschool Curriculum.* Columbus, OH: Merrill.

Wilson, W. M. (1992). The Stanford-Binet: Fourth edition and Form L-M in assessment of young children with mental retardation. Mental Retardation, *30*(2), 81–84.

Winerip, M. (1993). Striking up a conversation with the TV. *New York Times,* April 11, Metro Report, 23.

Wing, L. (1981). *Early childhood autism: Clinical, educational, and social aspects.* 3rd ed. New York: Pergamon Press.

Winslow, R. (1994). Lung treatment lowers mortality rate for infants by 5%, cuts hospital costs. *Wall Street Journal,* May 26, B5.

Witt, J. C., Elliott, S. N., & Gresham, F. M. (Eds.). (1988). *Handbook of behavior therapy in education.* New York: Plenum Press.

Wolery, M. (1989). Transitions in early childhood special education: Issues and procedures. *Focus on Exceptional Children, 22*(2), 1–16.

Wolery, M. (1991). Instruction in early childhood special education: "Seeing through a glass darkly... knowing in part." *Exceptional Children, 58*(2), 127–135.

Wolery, M., Bailey, D., & Sugai, G. (1988). *Effective teaching: Principles and procedures of applied behavior analysis with exceptional students.* Boston: Allyn & Bacon.

Wolery, M., Holcombe-Ligon, A., Brookfield, J., Huffman, K., Schroeder, C., Martin, C., Venn, M., Werts, M., & Fleming, L. (1993). The extent and nature of preschool mainstreaming: A survey of general early educators. *Journal of Special Education, 27*(2), 222–234.

Wolery, M., Martin, C. G., Schroeder, C., Huffman, K., Venn, M. L., Holcombe, A., Brookfield, J. & Fleming, L. A. (1994). Employment of educators in preschool mainstreaming: A survey of general early educators. *Journal of Early Intervention, 18*(1), 64–77.

Wolery, M., & Sainato, D. (1993). General curriculum and intervention strategies. In DECTask Force (1993), *op cit.,* 50–57.

Woolfolk, A. E. (1990). *Educational psychology* (4th ed.). Englewood Cliffs, NJ: Prentice Hall.

Wortham, S. (1998). *Early childhood curriculum.* Columbus, OH: Merrill.

Yazigi, R. A., Odem, R. R., & Polakoski, K. L. (1991). Demonstration of specific binding of cocaine to human spermatozoa. *Journal of the American Medical Association, 266*(14), 1956–1959.

Yell, M. L. (1989). *Honig v. Doe*: The suspension and expulsion of handicapped students. *Exceptional Children, 56*(1), 60–69.

Yesley, M. (Ed.). (1992). Ethical, legal and social implications of the Human Genome Project: A bibliography. Washington, DC: U.S. Department of Energy, Office of Energy Research.

Ysseldyke, J., Thurlow, M., & Bruininks, R. (1992). Expected educational outcomes for students with disabilities. *Remedial and Special Education, 13*(6), 19–32.

Zelaro, P. (1997). Infant-toddler information processing assessment for children with pervasive developmental disorder and autism: Part I. *Infants and Young Children, 10*(1), 1–14.

Zelazo, R. R. (1984). Learning to walk: Recognition of higher-order influences? In L. P. Lipsitt & C. Rovee-Collier (Eds.), *Advances in infancy research* (Vol. 3, pp. 251–256). Norwood, NJ: Ablex.

Zigler, E., & Muenchow, S. (1992). *Head Start: The inside story of America's most successful educational experiment.* New York: Basic Books.

Zigler, E., & Valentine, J. (1979). *Project Head Start: A legacy of the War on Poverty.* New York: Free Press.

Glossary

Accessible refers to a standard such that at least one entrance, at least one path through a facility, at least one rest room, and so on, is usable by individuals with disabilities. This standard, which applies to existing facilities or buildings, is lower than the barrier-free standard.

Accommodation, for Piaget, is a process in which new information alters a child's understanding of reality.

Adaptability, in housing, refers to the requirement in the Fair Housing Amendments Act of 1988, PL 100-430, that new, four-unit or larger multifamily housing structures be adaptable or readily changeable to meet the special needs of individuals with severe disabilities. An example is cabinets or light switches that may be easily lowered.

Adaptive development (sometimes referred to as "self-help" development) refers to a child's ability to display age-appropriate self-care and other behaviors in such a way as to adapt meaningfully to different circumstances.

Adventitious (acquired) conditions appear after birth, usually as a result of illness or accident. They differ from congenital conditions, which are present at birth.

Age at onset is a child's age when a condition begins.

Age at start is a child's age when early intervention or other services begin.

Age appropriateness is a philosophy in which activities are designed to match children's developmental stages. It is a key concept in NAEYC's Developmentally Appropriate Practice (DAP) guidelines. DEC's Recommended Practice task force suggested that programs be *chronologically* age-appropriate as well, because otherwise some young children with disabilities might wrongly be placed in settings designed for far younger children.

AIDS, or acquired immune deficiency syndrome, is a condition in which the body's immune system fails. It is widely believed to be caused by the human immunodeficiency virus (HIV).

Alpha-fetoprotein test (AFP) is a blood test performed while a woman is pregnant. If low levels of the protein are found, this suggests that the fetus may have Down syndrome.

American Sign Language (ASL) is a language using manual signs and rules for combining them. ASL is a distinct language with its own rules, in contrast to Signed English.

Americans with Disabilities Act (ADA), PL 101-336, is the landmark 1990 federal civil rights law for individuals with disabilities. The law bans discrimination in employment, local government services, transportation, places of public accommodation, and telecommunications.

Amniocentesis is the oldest fetal test, and is performed during the second trimester of pregnancy. A newer version, sometimes called "early amnio," can be used within the first weeks of pregnancy.

Analog signals are continuous, rather than discrete. Thus, an analog clock is one whose hands move continuously.

Applied behavior analysis (behavior modification) uses control of consequences to influence behavior. It differs from cognitive behavior modification in that it does not emphasize helping children understand why some actions are reinforced and others are not.

Appropriate is a term used both in Part C and in Part B of the Individuals with Disabilities Education Act (IDEA), but it is not defined precisely in the statute. It appears to mean "meets the standards of the State" and "meets the unique needs of the child."

Architectural and Transportation Barriers Compliance Board (ATBCB) is a small independent federal agency charged with monitoring accessibility at many federal buildings. The agency sometimes is referred to as the Access Board.

Assessment is the process of collecting data to use in determining how an individual child's development is proceeding in each of the five domains of development (cognitive, adaptive, physical, communication, social or emotional) or in academic areas. In family assessment, a family's resources, priorities, and concerns are identified.

471

Assimilation, for Piaget, occurs when new information is added to existing knowledge but does not change a child's view of the world.

Assistive technology devices are any products that may be used by individuals with disabilities to do things they otherwise would have difficulty doing.

Assistive technology services include assessment, selection of devices, instruction in their use, and related services to support individuals with disabilities in use of technology.

Asthma is a condition in which people have difficulty breathing because of obstructions in the airways of the lungs. It is a chronic respiratory disorder (sometimes called a chronic obstructive pulmonary disease). The U.S. Department of Education recognizes asthma as a disability when it affects a child's education.

At risk is a term used to refer to infants or toddlers who do not exhibit developmental delays but who for biological and/or environmental reasons are more likely than are most infants or toddlers to develop such delays. The concept is used only in Part C of the Individuals with Disabilities Education Act (IDEA).

Attention is the process through which a child acquires information through the senses. Learning cannot occur absent attention.

Attention Deficit Disorder (ADD) is a diagnosis reached when a child is "unavailable for learning" due to distractibility and short attention spans. The diagnosis is used if hyperactivity is not present (see ADHD).

Attention Deficit Hyperactivity Disorder (ADHD) is a diagnosis made when impulsivity and hyperactivity are present together with distractibility and short attention spans.

Audiograms are graphic displays of hearing loss along two dimensions: pitch (frequency) and intensity (volume).

Autism is a condition affecting communication, imagination, and socialization. Its most prominent characteristic is an "autistic aloneness" in which children appear to avoid and even to reject social interaction.

Autonomy versus shame and doubt is the Eriksonian stage in which toddlers learn to assume self-responsibility, including feeding and toileting activities.

B

Barrier-free, as used in relation to buildings or facilities, means that all entrances, all rooms, and all levels or floors are accessible to people with disabilities. This standard applies to new construction and to newly renovated parts of existing facilities. The standard contrasts with "accessible," which is a lower standard.

Baud rate is the speed of data transmission, in bits per second (bps). The slowest (oldest) modems use 300 baud, the fastest use 56,000 baud or even higher rates.

BBS (bulletin board system) is a computer equipped with a modem and a communications software program to which other computer modem users may connect via telephone lines.

Bit is the smallest unit of data in computing. It is expressed in 1s and 0s. Bits that together express a unit of meaning are a byte.

Blindness is 20/200 vision, or tunnel vision where central vision subtends at an angle of 20 percent or less, as measured with corrective lenses.

Byte is a computer term referring to a string of 0s and 1s that holds meaning. Today's PCs can move or transfer information in 16- or 32-bit units.

Captions are subtitles for video programming. Captions may be "open," in which case all viewers see them, or "closed," in which case caption decoders are required to make the subtitles visible.

CD-ROM stands for "Compact Disc—Read Only Memory." CD-ROM discs store information that computer users may read, scan, and search at high speed. The user may read the disc but not write to it.

Cerebral palsy (CP) is a condition in which oxygen deprivation in, or damage to, the brain limits voluntary control of muscles.

Child development associate (CDA) paraprofessionals have a credential indicating postsecondary study in child development and child care. CDA-credentialed paraprofessionals often work in Head Start programs.

Child find is the term used in both Part C and Part B of the Individuals with Disabilities Education Act (IDEA) to refer to outreach and recruitment efforts by the state to identify, screen, and serve eligible children and families.

Children with disabilities refers to children who meet the criteria in IDEA section 602(3), notably that they have a recognized disability and for that reason need special education and related services.

Chorionic villus sampling (CVS) is a fetal test involving collection of placental cells by inserting a catheter through the cervix or the abdomen. It provides the same information as does amniocentesis.

Cochlear implants are electronic devices that simulate "hearing" for children who are deaf.

Cognitive behavior modification stresses the importance of teaching the child ways of thinking about situations, in the belief that learning is a change in the *capacity* to behave in a certain way.

Cognitive development refers to age-appropriate mental functions, especially in perceiving, understanding, and knowing, that is, becoming capable of doing intellectual tasks.

Communication is the expression and reception of meaning. It may occur through speech/hearing, reading/writing, signing/seeing, gestures, or other means.

Communication development (sometimes referred to as speech and language development) refers to a young child's ability to express thoughts and feelings and to understand vocal, nonverbal, signed, or other communication by others.

Conduct disorders include a range of emotional conditions affecting behavior. Children appear to be "undersocialized" in that they often do not exhibit socially approved behavior.

Congenital conditions appear at or prior to birth; they are present at birth, as contrasted to acquired conditions.

Cost-benefit analyses look at benefits, assigning values to them, and compare those values with the costs of providing the benefits.

Cost-effective analyses look to whether one approach, or one program, provides more benefits per dollar than another.

Cultural competence (cultural sensitivity) refers to the skill and knowledge of early childhood special education workers in relating to family members from different ethnic, racial, and cultural groups.

Curriculum is a planned sequence of activities, including both content and process, through which educators change children's behavior. Curriculum is a vehicle for reaching goals and objectives as identified in individualized family service plans and individualized education programs—an ordered arrangement of individually selected learning experiences that respond to children's particular needs.

Cystic fibrosis is an inherited condition that causes mucus to build up in the lungs, compromising lung capacity and usually resulting in death by the age of thirty. Children with cystic fibrosis need to have physical therapy, get lots of exercise, and receive dietary supplements.

D

Data telephony is the transmission of information over telephone lines by means other than voice. It includes electronic mail (E-mail), fax, and computer bulletin board systems. Data telephony makes heavy use of "off-line" or "virtual time" techniques so both parties need not be on-line at the same time.

Deafness is the inability to hear and understand conversational speech through the ear alone.

Descriptive video service (DVS) transmits spoken descriptions of on-screen television action so that individuals who are blind may learn about actions they do not see.

Developmental delays are lags in child development in any one or more of the five domains (cognitive, communication, physical, adaptive, social or emotional). How much of a lag constitutes a "delay" is to be defined by each state. The term is used in both Part C and in Part B of the Individuals with Disabilities Education Act (IDEA), for section 619.

Developmental disabilities are conditions of early onset (occurring well in advance of adulthood) that require a range of diverse services or interventions. The term formerly referred to four disabilities (autism, cerebral palsy, mental retardation, and epilepsy).

Developmental plasticity is the belief that young children in particular can develop rapidly, changing their behavior—and indeed their lives—if services are provided early in life.

Developmentally appropriate services are designed to be suitable for children at particular stages of development. Thus, very short individual activities are developmentally appropriate for infants and toddlers, while lengthy large-group activities are not.

Developmentally appropriate practice (DAP) is professional work that emphasizes activities with young children that are both age-appropriate and child-focused. In DAP approaches, children are encouraged to be active learners, while professionals guide and facilitate their activities.

Deviations are behaviors that are not normal at any age. Delays in development, by contrast, feature behavior that is normal, but for children of younger ages.

Diagnosed conditions (established conditions) are disabilities or other health conditions recognized by a state as limiting or very likely to limit activities young children can do. The term is used in Part C of the Individuals with Disabilities Education Act (IDEA).

Digital signals are discrete. They are either "on" (e.g., 1) or "off" (e.g., 0). Thus, a digital clock shows 9:15 until it shifts abruptly to 9:16.

Direct instruction is structured, teacher-led instruction. It often is contrasted to less didactic, more interactive approaches to learning, such as "developmentally appropriate practice."

Discovery learning (Jerome Bruner) is an approach in which children learn things themselves as teachers structure the environment to facilitate children's discovery.

Distance learning links an instructor in one geographical location with students at other sites. Students see and hear the instructor, who in turn sees and hears them. The connections may be via satellite broadcast or, increasingly, via fiber-optic cable.

Domains are areas of development. Part C of the Individuals with Disabilities Education Act (IDEA) recognizes five such domains: adaptive, cognitive, communication, physical, and social or emotional.

Double jeopardy is a term used by some researchers to explain risks children face due to *both* biological and environmental risk factors. Children from families of low socioeconomic status tend to have more illnesses and accidents, *and* to suffer more long-lasting consequences from these, than do children from families of high socioeconomic status.

Down syndrome is the most common identifiable cause of mental retardation, accounting for perhaps one-third of all cases. In addition to mental retardation, characteristic facial features, hypotonia (floppiness in muscles), and hearing loss are common in Down syndrome.

Dyslexia is a learning disability that interferes with reading and writing, because letters seem to float across a page, reverse, or otherwise become difficult to read. Children with dyslexia display reading difficulties despite normal or near-normal intelligence and adequate opportunities to learn to read.

E

Early childhood (EC) refers to programs for young children (usually three- to five-year-olds), such as Head Start. EC as a field is broader than is ECSE. However, many EC programs serve young children with disabilities.

Early childhood educators are professionals trained in work with young children, usually children of preschool age, or three to five.

Early Childhood Special Education (ECSE) joins Part C and section 619 of Part B of the Individuals with Disabilities Education Act (IDEA). ECSE is a unified system of services for infants, toddlers, and preschool-age children with disabilities from birth to five inclusive.

Early childhood special educators are professionals trained in work with young children, methods of education, and other kinds of intervention for children with disabilities or developmental delays.

Early Education Program for Children with Disabilities (EEPCD) is the federal grant program providing discretionary support for "model" Early Childhood Special Education programs. EEPCD was formerly called the Handicapped Children's Early Education Program (HCEEP).

Early intervention refers to services for infants and toddlers, and their families, to address the special needs of very young children who have disabilities, have developmental delays, or are at risk of developmental delays. The term is used in Part C of the Individuals with Disabilities Education Act (IDEA).

Education for All Handicapped Children Act (PL 94-142) is the landmark 1975 federal law that first established the mandate that all school-age children with disabilities must receive a free appropriate public education.

Elaboration occurs when an adult (parent or teacher) "talks out" the reasoning processes, that is, elaborates upon what steps were followed in reaching a decision.

Electronic mail (E-mail) involves exchange of written messages over telephone lines.

Elementary educators are professionals trained at the B.A. or M.A. level in teaching K–6 children. They usually are state-certified as meeting state-set minimum requirements.

Emotional disturbance (ED) is a category recognized under the Individuals with Disabilities Education Act. Sometimes also referred to as "emotional and behavioral disorders," it refers to behavior in children that is age-, culturally-, and/or situation-inappropriate and interferes with their education and/or that of other children.

Empowerment is the process of helping people feel as if they are in control. It involves feelings as well as facts.

Entitlement means that infants and toddlers must receive early intervention services if they satisfy state criteria. Similarly, three- to five-year-old children must receive free preschool services to meet their unique needs if they satisfy federal and/or state eligibility standards. (The term "zero reject" expresses a similar idea, namely, that no child who meets eligibility criteria may be denied services.)

Environmental control system (ECS) enables people to operate electrical equipment via remote control, usually with the assistance of a small personal computer.

Epilepsy is a physical condition producing irregular electric discharges in the brain. There are actually several types of epilepsy, many caused by head injuries.

Evaluation is a formal process through which a child's initial and continuing eligibility for services under the Individuals with Disabilities Education Act is established. It is periodic, occurring at specific intervals. Evaluation may establish, for example, that a child qualifies for Part C services under the act as an at-risk toddler; similarly, it may establish that a child meets a state's developmental delay criteria.

Experiential deprivation occurs when young children are not allowed to confront strange, even dangerous, situations—as when parents overprotect them. According to Erikson, over-protected children may enter school still unsure of themselves, having internalized parental fears.

Extinction occurs when reinforcement is removed altogether so that behavior decreases and then ceases.

Facilitated communication is a controversial method in which children with autism type on personal computers while a care-giver or teacher touches them. The touching is the "facilitated" part of the communication.

Family-friendly programs involve parents and other family members (as defined by the family) and value their input.

Family-focused programs see families as partners with profession-als, while **family-centered** programs tend to be planned by, and conducted with, parents, guardians, and other family members, in a dominant role.

Family support groups are loosely organized bodies of parents and other family members who come together, often at an ECSE center, to share information and offer each other assistance.

Fax (short form of "facsimile") is a device that breaks down words and images (including pictures) into bits and sends them via modem over telephone lines.

Fetal alcohol syndrome (FAS) results from maternal abuse of alcohol during pregnancy and has three dimensions: facial char-acteristics, physical growth, and neurological aspects. In fetal alcohol effect (FAE), one or two kinds of symptoms, but not all three, are present.

Formative evaluation looks to process issues such as how many families apply for services, how many are served, and how many of what kinds of services are provided. Formative evaluation may take place during an activity or program, while summative evaluation tends to occur afterward.

Forward funded refers to the fact that education programs autho-rized by federal laws are funded during any given federal fiscal year for the following fiscal year. The intent is to give states and schools notice of funds availability well in advance of the start of a school year.

Fragile X syndrome is a condition resulting from damage to the X chromosome. Hyperactivity and mental retardation are com-mon symptoms in males; females are usually only carriers.

Genetic counseling is nondirective counseling and provision of information, often to prospective parents, about genetics and the likelihood that a fetus has certain characteristics.

Genetic discrimination is decision making on the basis of an indi-vidual's real or perceived genetic characteristics.

Genetic engineering, also called gene therapy, is a process in which interventions are effected to eliminate or at least alleviate a condition. Prior to gene therapy, a pregnant woman had only two choices in responding to fetal test results: Proceed to term, or abort the fetus. Genetic engineering gives her a third option: to "fix" the fetus.

Head Start is the federally supported program of services for preschool children that was begun in 1965. Most children served are from disadvantaged families; at least 10 percent of the children served must be children with disabilities.

human immunodeficiency virus (HIV) is the virus associated with, and widely believed to cause, AIDS.

Incidence is the number of new cases annually, as contrasted with prevalence, which is the total number of such cases.

Inclusion is an approach in which children with disabilities (including those with severe disabilities) are placed in rooms with, and receive services side by side with, children who have no disabilities.

Individual appropriateness is an approach in which services are customed-designed and -delivered to respond to a child's unique needs. Often, it is a concept more honored in theory than in practice, as child-care workers often find it difficult to individualize services as much as they would like.

Individualized education program (IEP) is a written document that identifies the unique needs of the child, the special educa-tion and related services needed to meet those unique needs, annual goals and short-term objectives, how the child's progress will be assessed, the date of initiation of services and the pro-jected duration of those services. The IEP is used in Part B of the Individuals with Disabilities Education Act (IDEA).

Individualized family service plan (IFSP) is a written document outlining services for infants and toddlers, and (if the families concur) their families as well. IFSPs note the infant's or toddler's development in five domains, services the child (and family) will receive, and similar information, as well as the service coordinator's name.

Individuals with Disabilities Education Act (IDEA). The IDEA is the landmark special education law in the United States. Formerly called the Education of the Handicapped Act, it includes (as Part B) PL 94-142, the Education for All Handicapped Children Act of 1975.

Infants and toddlers refers to children before they reach the age of three. Infancy begins at birth and ends with the achievement of independent walking, while toddlers are young children who have begun walking but have not yet reached the age of three. Another commonly used way to refer to this population is "birth to two inclusive," which more directly incorporates the first thirty-six months of life.

Infants and toddlers with disabilities refers to those from birth to age two inclusive who need early intervention services because they are experiencing developmental delays in adaptive, cognitive, communication, physical, and/or social or emotional development; or because they have a diagnosed condition that has a high probability of resulting in developmental delay. The term may also include, at a state's discretion, at-risk children.

Informed clinical opinion supplements formal testing and is especially valuable where suitable tests are not available. The word "clinical" refers to assessments in which the expertise of the clinician comprises at least 50 percent of the procedure.

Initiative versus guilt is the Eriksonian stage in which preschool-age children struggle between exploring for its own sake and feeling guilty for doing so.

Intensive care unit (ICU) is a hospital ward for premature, low-birthweight, and other infants needing comprehensive care. When used with infants under one month old, ICUs are called neonatal intensive care units (NICUs).

Interagency Coordinating Council (ICC) is an advisory body that gives the state Part C (infants and toddlers) lead agency information about, and support from, other key agencies in the sate. With the ICC's help, the state lead agency creates a statewide system for implementation of Part C.

Interdisciplinary services are services provided by specialists from different disciplines working together on a team (e.g., early childhood special educators and speech pathologists). The term contrasts with services that are provided by professionals representing only one discipline (*uni*disciplinary). The term *multi*disciplinary most often refers to a team (including family members) that plans and conducts assessments or evaluations. These terms are used most often in Part C of the Individuals

with Disabilities Education Act (IDEA). The term *trans*disciplinary refers to an approach in which the often artificial boundaries between disciplines or professions are transcended or ignored so as to deliver "holistic" services to a child and/or a family.

Juvenile rheumatoid arthritis is a condition in which joints become inflamed and usually appears between the ages of eighteen months and four years; it generally has few if any lasting effects on children.

Language is a formal symbol system in which words are ordered according to rules to express meaning. It may be spoken, written, or signed, and may be expressive or receptive.

Lead agency is the term used in Part C of the Individuals with Disabilities Education Act to refer to the state agency authorized to carry out the state Part C plan and to coordinate the work of other public and private agencies. In some states, the state education agency is the lead agency; in others, a health agency, social services agency, or child-care agency serves as the lead agency. Up-to-date addresses for state lead agencies are available at www.nectas.unc.edu, the Web site of the National Early Childhood Technical Assistance System, at the University of North Carolina. NEC*TAS may also be reached at 500 NationsBank Plaza, 137 E. Franklin Street, Chapel Hill, NC 27514.

Learning disabilities (LDs) are conditions interfering with or limiting academic kinds of activities. They are believed to have neurological bases. Dyslexia is an example of an LD.

Least restrictive environment is a philosophy stressing the placement of children with disabilities in appropriate settings closest (when compared with other appropriate settings) to settings used by nondisabled children. The term is used in Part B of the Individuals with Disabilities Education Act (IDEA).

Low-income threshold is similar to the poverty level but is expressed in terms of monthly income. The term was used in the Survey of Incomes and Program Participation study (see Chapter 11).

Low vision is 20/70 vision, or worse, to 20/200 vision, which is blindness.

Machine language translation is electronic translation of, for example, English-to-Spanish or French-to-English. Little or no human intervention is required. The hardware and software are in development, but it will be several years before the technology reaches general use.

Medicaid is the federal-state medical insurance program for poor individuals. Many Supplemental Security Income recipients receive Medicaid.

Medically fragile, technology-dependent children require a range of intensive medical and other services as well as specialized equipment for ventilation and feeding.

Memory is retrieval of information. Recent studies suggest that data actually are re-created, not merely retrieved from storage.

Mental retardation refers to a combination of adaptive behavior characteristic of younger age ranges and intellectual functioning significantly lower than normal, when onset occurs prior to age eighteen. The current definition stresses that mentally retarded individuals need extensive systems of support.

Metacognition is awareness of one's own behavior and ways of thinking and learning. Frith suggests that individuals with autism may be very limited in metacognition.

Modeling occurs when a child watches a high-status "model" perform positive actions and be reinforced for doing so. The child is vicariously reinforced by watching the model be rewarded.

Modem, short for MOdulator-DEModulator, converts data from analog to digital and back to analog. Modems are used in data telephony for communication at a distance.

Morphemes are the smallest units of words that carry meaning.

Multimedia personal computers can display video as well as words, sound, data, and still images.

Muscular dystrophy (MD) is a condition characterized by muscle weakness. There are several types of MD. Duchenne MD, the most serious form, is a progressive, usually fatal, condition. Other dystrophies are less serious and rarely fatal.

Natal refers to birth. **Prenatal** has to do with incidents or conditions occurring prior to birth; **perinatal** with those occurring during the birth process; and **postnatal** with those happening after birth. **Neonates** are infants during their first month after birth (from birth to twenty-eight days).

Natural environment is a philosophy emphasizing services for infants, toddlers, and their families in places that are typical or otherwise "natural." Early intervention services are to be delivered in such environments, to the extent that these are "appropriate" and meet the child's needs. The home is the usual such environment. The term is used in Part C of the Individuals with Disabilities Education Act (IDEA).

Negative reinforcement increases the frequency of the behavior it follows by removing an undesired consequence. Also called "removal reinforcement." An example is when children are released from doing daily assigned household chores when they behave appropriately during dinner.

Neonatal intensive care units (NICUs) are hospital-based facilities for newborns in the first month of life.

Occupational therapy helps children learn to perform specific tasks (brush teeth, dress, maintain good posture, and so on.) despite physical disabilities or other conditions such as Down syndrome.

Operant conditioning is a process through which behavior is altered by manipulating its consequences.

Orientation and mobility specialists help young children who are blind or have low vision learn to navigate around the home; the early intervention program; the neighborhood; and, later, the community as a whole.

Orthopedic impairments, including spinal cord injury and cerebral palsy, are recognized disabilities under the Individuals with Disabilities Education Act (IDEA).

Orthosis is a device that enhances the function of a body part, as a leg brace helps a child to walk. It contrasts with a prosthesis, which replaces a body part.

P

Paraplegia occurs when the lower limbs (legs) are affected, usually by a spinal cord injury, but the upper limbs (arms) are not.

Part B is the part of the Individuals with Disabilities Education Act (IDEA)describing how children with disabilities aged three to eighteen shall receive a free appropriate public education.

Part C is the state-operated program created in 1986 for infants and toddlers with disabilities and their families. It is an early intervention program for children under three years of age and (with family concurrence) their families.

Perception is a process in which information entering the sensory register takes on meaning, for example, is interpreted.

Phonemes are units of sound that cannot be further divided. An example is "ph" in "phoneme," expressed as /f/. The study of phonemes and the role they play in speech is called phonology.

Physical development (sometimes called motor or coordination development) is the display of age-appropriate fine motor control and gross motor control abilities.

Physical therapy helps prevent and reduce muscle atrophy and promotes musculoskeletal development.

Places of public accommodation are restaurants, hotels, motion picture and other theaters, sporting facilities, stores and shopping malls, and doctors' and lawyers' offices. Under the Americans with Disabilities Act, title III, these must be accessible to people with disabilities and offer these people equal enjoyment to that accorded to people with no disabilities.

Positive reinforcement is the presentation of a consequence that increases the frequency of the behavior it follows. Also called "presentation reinforcement," it contrasts with negative reinforcement, in which a consequence is removed.

Pragmatics is the social use of language, or the knowledge of what expressions to use in which contexts.

Preoperational stage, for Piaget, is the stage in child development just before children acquire the ability to engage in symbolic mental actions. A preoperational child, for example, cannot grasp the concept of reversibility.

Preschool-age children are children aged three to five inclusive. Most early childhood programs focus on this population.

Preschool child with a disability is a three- to six-year-old child who has one of the disabilities recognized under the Individuals with Disabilities Education Act (IDEA). The term is used in some states to avoid the need to label a child prior to elementary school. (Preschool age begins at three and ends when the child enters kindergarten or first grade, usually at about age six.)

Preschool special education refers to special education and related services to meet the unique needs of three- to five-year-olds with disabilities and, in some states, developmental delays.

Pressure sores (decubitus ulcers) develop when the child does not shift weight on a wheelchair cushion or on a bed.

Prevalence is the number of cases in a population, as contrasted to incidence, the number of new cases.

Procedural safeguards, also called due-process rights, are granted to families in both Part C and Part B. An example is the right to see all relevant records pertaining to the child.

Processing occurs when information that has been perceived is analyzed and used by an individual.

Program evaluation attempts to answer the questions: Did a program do what it promised? Did it do these things efficiently and effectively?

Prosthesis is an artificial replacement, such as a mechanical arm or knee, for a missing limb or body part.

Punishment is any consequence that decreases the frequency of the behavior it follows. One possible outcome, however, is displacement, in which some other behavior increases in frequency.

Quadriplegia occurs when all four limbs (arms and legs) are affected, usually by a spinal cord injury.

Qualitative research is an observational study and report in which nothing is manipulated or controlled.

Quantitative research usually manipulates one or more variables ("independent variables"), observing its or their effects on dependent variables. Such studies report findings as numbers, hence the name "quantitative."

Reasonable accommodation in the Americans with Disabilities Act and section 504 refers to an adjustment enabling a qualified individual with a disability to perform a task.

Related services are noninstructional support services such as transportation, therapy, and counseling. The term is used in Part B of the Individuals with Disabilities Education Act.

Respite services are early intervention services offering breaks for family members from child care.

Retinopathy of prematurity (ROP), once known as retrolental fibroplasia, is a limitation of vision occurring during the neonatal period.

Seamless system is a term referring to a set of services that has no gaps or delays between Part C early intervention and Part B preschool services or other prekindergarten programs.

Section 504 is a civil rights provision in the federal Rehabilitation Act. It prohibits any program receiving or benefiting from federal financial assistance from discriminating on the basis of disability. Section 504 predated, but remains in effect concurrent with, the Americans with Disabilities Act.

Section 619 of Part B of the Individuals with Disabilities Education Act authorizes preschool special education and related services for children from three to five inclusive.

Sensorimotor stage is the Piagetian period in which young children perform goal-directed actions and acquire the idea of object permanence.

Service coordinators (formerly called case managers) facilitate service delivery to families and represent the family in negotiations with public and private service providers.

Shaping is a method of successive approximations in which only ever-more-accurate behaviors are reinforced.

Social or emotional development (sometimes called psychosocial or affective development) refers to young children's age-appropriate ability to understand their own feelings, and those of others, and to respond to both with behavior that is socially acceptable for children of that age. It also includes behavior children exhibit in play.

Social workers are trained human services professionals who help the family to qualify for, and receive, needed services for which the family and/or the infant or toddler is or are eligible. Social work services also are "related services" under Part B of the Individuals with Disabilities Education Act (IDEA).

Socioeconomic status (SES) refers to family income and other demographic characteristics. Disability is disproportionately common among low-SES families.

Special education is specially designed instruction to meet the unique needs of the child. The term is used in Part B of the Individuals with Disabilities Education Act (IDEA).

Speech is the oral expression of meaning, usually—but not always—with symbols (words).

Speech recognition is computer comprehension of spoken words or sounds. Speaker-dependent speech recognition systems can understand one person's voice, while speaker-independent systems can comprehend the speech of many different individuals.

Speech synthesis is computer-generated speech.

Spina bifida is a condition in which the spinal cord does not close completely during fetal development.

Spinal cord injury (SCI) occurs when the spinal cord is stretched, bruised, or even severed. It is one of many conditions categorized in the Individuals with Disabilities Education Act (IDEA) as orthopedic impairments.

Stay-put provision is an important due-process right under Part B of the Individuals with Disabilities Education Act (IDEA). While a dispute is pending, the child with a disability is to continue receiving a free, appropriate public education and is to remain in the current placement.

Stuttering is dysfluent speech or disrupted oral communication.

Summative evaluation looks to outcomes, or results, to assess programs and activities, usually in comparison with other activities or programs. It is in contrast to formative evaluation, which focuses more on process than product.

Supplemental Security Income (SSI) is a federal-state guaranteed minimum income program for individuals who are poor and have disabilities. Most SSI beneficiaries also receive Medicaid.

Supports are links to neighbors, friends, and community resources upon which the family may rely in times of need. Supports may empower the family so it functions more effectively on behalf of the infant or toddler.

Syntax is a rule system for language governing the order of words or parts of sentences.

Teaming is an approach in which individuals from different professions come together on multidisciplinary teams. Family members are integral parts of such teams.

Telecommunications is the moving, storing, and manipulating of information by electronic means. It includes voice telephony as well as data telephony.

Telemedicine links medical specialists in one location with a patient in another, usually via fiber-optic cable, which can transmit high-quality video as well as voice and data.

Therapists and other services personnel include speech and language pathologists, occupational therapists, and other professionals delivering related services to preschool-age children or early intervention services to infants and toddlers with disabilities.

Teratogens are harmful substances, including alcohol and controlled substances, that can cause disabilities or other health impairments.

Traditionally underserved children with disabilities come from rural or inner-city families, and/or are members of ethnic or racial minority groups. Native American tribes and tribal organizations are among "traditionally underserved" groups. The 1991 Individuals with Disabilities Education Act (IDEA) amendments call for greater emphasis on serving children and families from such groups.

Transdisciplinary play-based assessment (TPBA; Linder, 1993) is a qualitative approach to testing in which young children interact with play materials, professionals, and other children.

Transition is movement from one stage or program to another. An important transition in Early Childhood Special Education is that from early intervention programs to preschool programs.

Traumatic brain injury (TBI) was added to the Individuals with Disabilities Education Act as a recognized disability in 1990. Automobile, motorcycle, sports, and gun-related accidents resulting in sharp blows to (closed head injuries) or penetration of (open head injuries) the head cause TBIs.

Trust versus mistrust is the Eriksonian stage in which infants learn to trust their caregivers, particularly parents.

Video telephone service allows both parties to see each other while they talk. Video telephone service usually requires fiber-optic cables, which can carry voice, data, and video at the same time. Also required is a video camera and video receiver or monitor at both ends of the conversation.

Virtual reality refers to something that does not exist, but appears as if it did; an artificial reality.

Voice telephony is the traditional use of telephones to transmit voice-based information over telephone lines.

Vulnerable child syndrome (VCS) is an attempt to describe the condition of children exposed prenatally to cocaine, heroin, and other controlled substances, formerly called "crack babies."

Z

zone of proximal development (Lev Vygotsky) is the edge to which children's development has brought them, that is, what they can learn, if helped. Teachers should not attempt to introduce more cognitively challenging material, however, until children progress to higher levels of development.

Index

F

G

M

P

S